An American Liaison

An American Liaison

Leamington Spa
and the Hawthornes
1855–1864

Bryan Homer

Madison • Teaneck
Fairleigh Dickinson University Press
London: Associated University Presses

PS
1884
.H66
1998
oct.1999

Associated University Presses
440 Forsgate Drive
Cranbury, NJ 08512

Associated University Presses
16 Barter Street
London WC1A 2AH, England

Associated University Presses
P.O. Box 338, Port Credit
Mississauga, Ontario
Canada L5G 4L8

Library of Congress Cataloging-in-Publication Data

Homer, Bryan, 1934–
    An American Liaison : Leamington Spa and the Hawthornes, 1855–1864
/ Bryan Homer.
        p.   cm.
    Includes bibliographical references (p.   ) and index.
    ISBN 0-8386-3755-8 (alk. paper)
    1. Hawthorne, Nathaniel, 1804–1864—Homes and haunts—England—
Leamington.   2. Americans—Travel—England—Leamington—
History—19th century.   3. Leamington (England)—Social life and
customs.   4. Novelists, American—19th century—Biography.
5. Consuls—United States—Biography.   6. Leamington (England)—
Biography.   I. Title.
PS1884.H66   1998
813'.3—dc21
[B]   97-28773
                                                             CIP

PRINTED IN THE UNITED STATES OF AMERICA

For Elizabeth and Michael

Contents

Acknowledgments

I must record my thanks to the following institutions and individuals. First of all, the staff of my local library in Leamington where one always receives expert advice and where unending patience and good humor is brought to bear on whatever problem needs to be solved. And then, in England and Scotland, in no particular order, the Library of the Arts Department of the University of Warwick (where, fortunately, there can be found all the volumes that have been published so far of *The Centenary Edition of the Works of Nathaniel Hawthorne*); the Liverpool Records Office; Trinity College, Cambridge; the County Records Office and the Warwick County Museum, Warwickshire; the Whitby Literary and Philosophical Society of Whitby, North Yorkshire; the National Library of Scotland, Edinburgh; the Johnson Birthplace Museum in Lichfield, Staffordshire; the Uttoxeter Heritage Centre and *The Uttoxeter Advertiser,* Staffordshire; Glyn Roberts; the John Murray Company and Baring Brothers & Co., London; James O'Donald Mays; John H. Drew; the Land Registry, Gloucester; Denton, Hall, Burgin, and Warren, Solicitors, London; the Central Library, Edinburgh; The Spiritualist Association of Great Britain, London; The Spiritualists National Union, Stansted Mountfichet, Essex; the Incorporated Society for Psychical Research, London; the Records and Research Unit of the Shropshire County Council, Shrewsbury; the Records Office of the Shakespeare Birthplace Trust, Stratford-upon-Avon; the Local Studies Section of the Central Library, Coventry; Marion Richardson; the County Records Office, Northallerton, North Yorkshire; *Punch* magazine; Denise F. Weston; Dr. C. A. Wood; the National Railway Museum, York; the *Malton Gazette & Herald;* Mrs. E. Bush; nearly all the Wrigleys, Copperthwaites, and Copperwheats of northern England; the Department of Archaeology and Ethnography of the Birmingham Museums and Art Gallery; Bill Gibbons; the Arts, Languages, Literature Department of the City of Birmingham Public Library; Kathleen Allen; the University of Reading Library; the British Homoeopathic Association, London; the Royal Leycester Hospital, Warwick; Mr. and Mrs. Don Locke; Mr. and Mrs. Brian Pooley; Joan Borrowscale; the Bodleian Library, Oxford; Jean Field; Joseph G. Rosa; the (now demolished) Warneford Hospital, Leamington Spa; the Oxford University Press; and the Reader Services Department of the British Library, London.

As most of my research has had to be conducted through the mail I am particularly grateful to the many individuals and institutions abroad with whom I have corresponded. They are (again in no particular order) the Bibliotheque of the Ville de Havre, France; the Massachusetts Historical Society, Boston; the Historical Society of Pennsylvania; the Huntington Library in San Marino; the Houghton Library at Harvard University; the St. Lawrence University in Canton, N.Y.; the Harvard University Press in Cambridge; the Yale University Library; the Library of the Boston Athenæum; Prof. Rita K. Gollin; Barbara L. Bacheler; the Serial and Government Publications Division and the Manuscript Division of the Library of Congress, Washington, D.C.; the Bibliographical Society of America in New York; the Special Collections Department, Bowdoin College, Brunswick, ME; Raymona E. Hull; the Bancroft Library of the University of California, Berkeley, CA; the Peabody and Essex Museum, Salem; the Alderman Library of the University of Virginia at Charlottesville; the Concord Free Public Library; Houghton Mifflin Company, Boston; the Folger Shakespeare Library, Washington, D.C.; the Society for the Preservation of New England Antiquities, Boston; the Beinecke Rare Book and Manuscript Library, Yale University; the Pierpont Morgan Library, New York; Prof. Thomas Woodson; Prof. Bill Ellis; the Henry W. and Albert A. Berg Collection of the New York Public Library; the National Archives, Waltham; the Northern Illinois University Press, DeKalb; the Nathaniel Hawthorne Society in Brunswick; the University of Chicago Press; the Boston Public Library; Edwin Haviland Miller; the Photograph Library of the Metropolitan Museum of Art, New York; the Antioch College, Yellow Springs, OH; the Rosenberg Library, Galveston, TX; the Boston College, Chestnut Hill, MA; the Stanford University Libraries, CA; the Princeton University Libraries; the Milton S. Eisenhower Library, Johns Hopkins University, Baltimore, MD; the Middlebury College; Columbia University Libraries, New York; the Cleveland Public Library; the Duke University, Durham, NC; the Lilly Library, Indiana University, Bloomington; the Wellesley College, MA; the Dartmouth College Library, Hanover, NH; Haverford College, PA; Washington University, St Louis; the Newberry Library, Chicago; the University of Chicago Library; Washington State University, Pullman; Southeast Missouri State University, Cape Girardeau; the University of California, Los Angeles; the University of Texas at Austin; the State Historical Society of Wisconsin, Madison; St. John's Seminary, Camarillo, CA; Knox College, Galesburg, IL; Skidmore College, Saratoga Springs; the University of Rochester, NY; Brown University Library, Providence; Randolph-Macon Woman's College, Lynchburg, VA; the University of Michigan, Ann Arbor; the University of Southern California, Los Angeles; the Civil Reference Branch of the National Archives and Records Administration, Washington, D.C.; the Chapel Hill Historical Society, N.C.; Greenwood Press, Westport; the Public Library in The Colony, TX; the Kansas State Historical Society, Topeka; and the Spenser Research Library and Spencer Museum of Art at the University of Kansas, Lawrence.

My thanks are due to the editors for permission to reproduce letters and extracts from journals and diaries contained in certain volumes of *The Centenary Edition of the Works of Nathaniel Hawthorne* (it is regretted, however, that this present book was written and the publication process had commenced prior to the publication of Volumes 21 and 22 [*The English Notebooks*] of *The Centenary Edition*); to the Henry W. and Albert A. Berg Collection, the New York Public Library, Astor, Lenox and Tilden Foundations for permission to reproduce material in their possession; to the Massachusetts Historical Society, Boston for permission to reproduce extracts from the Mary Mann letters to be found in chapters 9 to 13; to the James Duncan Phillips Library of the Peabody & Essex Museum, Salem for permission to reproduce extracts from Sophia Hawthorne's Account Books and to quote from other documents in their possession; to the Ulysses Sumner Milburn Collection of Hawthorniana, Owen D. Young Library, St. Lawrence University, for permission to reproduce Hawthorne's consular appointment documents in the Prologue and Julian Hawthorne's lay in chapter 13; to Yale Collection of American Literature, Beinecke Rare Book and Manuscript Library, Yale University for permission to publish material from its Hawthorne collection, the letters of Ada Shepard and David Rice to be found in chapters 5 to 7; and to the Royal Leycester Hospital and Warwick County Museum, Warwick and the Records Office of the Shakespeare Birthplace Trust, Stratford-upon-Avon for permission to reproduce extracts from some of their Visitors Books.

Finally, I should like to thank the editorial staff of Associated University Presses for the support and assistance they have provided, to an absolute amateur, in the preparation of this book. If there are any faults and errors still contained in it, they are all mine.

Editorial Note

It will become apparent that in some instances I have been unable to make out with any real certainty some words and phrases in the letters, diaries, and journals that I have either reproduced in full or quoted from in part. Where the word or phrase is completely illegible, I have rendered it thus [. . . .?]; where an "educated" guess has been made as to the missing word or phrase, I have rendered it thus [*Leamington?*]; where the writer has inadvertently omitted a word or phrase and it is fairly obvious as to what it is, or should have been, I have rendered it thus [Leamington?].

Many of Hawthorne's journal entries were made one day, or even several days, after the actual events took place. In quoting from entries of this type, I have, where it has proved necessary, substituted [Today] for an entry that began, for example, "Last Saturday."

An American Liaison

Prologue: Life before Leamington

There is no doubt that Nathaniel Hawthorne's impressions of Leamington Spa were favorable at first, though toward the end of the family's third period of residence he came to believe that, due to their particular circumstances at the time (prior to their return to the United States) a home *anywhere* else would be preferable to their remaining in the spa; and true to his style and character, he intermingled his assertions of that affection for the town and surrounding countryside with other more barbed and controversial opinions regarding individuals and the society with which he came into contact. Perhaps, as will become apparent, his children did not altogether share his enthusiasm (if that is a word that should be used in connection with such a self-effacing man) and certainly his wife found in the end that the local climate was none too beneficial to her delicate health. However, following their first short stay in 1855 they did return on two further occasions through choice and, as a result, resided for the best part of a year in the town, out of the five and a half that were spent in England following Nathaniel's appointment as United States consul at Liverpool, and his subsequent resignation; and though the family lived in Rock Park and Southport for longer periods than Leamington, the latter could be considered a more important hometown than Southport, for instance, due to the events that occurred while they were there. The reasons as to why Leamington was chosen as the first alternative to life in Liverpool are not immediately apparent. Possibly, given their circumstances at the time, it was a case of eyes being closed and a pin being stuck in a map of England to decide on their destination, though it was understood that wherever the destination was to be it would only be a temporary resting place. Whatever the reason, in coming to Leamington the family would have been aware, or could have had the means of making themselves aware of, the town's fame as a spa. It would have offered them all the attractions that were conducive to the maintenance of that fame; the spa water itself; the comfortable hotel accommodation and rented property; the high-class shopping facilities; the recreational opportunities, both physical and intellectual; and the very important benefits arising from its central location in the land within great areas of pleasant countryside that in turn encompassed many places of outstanding historical interest, and all served by the most modern means of communication.

The fact that an internationally known author and his family were residents in the town appears to have created no local repercussions at all and it must be assumed, now, that the Hawthornes went about their business unrecognized and unacknowledged. How much this may have been due to a command from Nathaniel to the rest of the family that he wished to remain incognito would have to be a matter of conjecture, but there was no doubt that he would have wished to be able to come and go as quietly as possible and, indeed, on the occasion of the first visit to Leamington he only reluctantly admitted to the fact that he was an American consular official, without making any reference to his undoubtedly far greater claim to fame in another area of life. An examination of the local papers of the time will bring to light nothing to confirm that Leamington knew of the existence in its midst of the most famous American author of the day. Undoubtedly, the town had its fair share of American visitors as can be seen from a study of the Notices of Arrivals at the various hotels that were displayed each week in the newspapers, so that an American accent overheard on the Parade (the main street) would not have turned too many heads as being something extraordinary, but there is nothing to suggest that the family mixed with, or sought the company of, those other American visitors who may have been more likely to have known who this particular Hawthorne was and, by unguarded comments, made plain the identity of the author and his family. There are several entries in the journals kept by Nathaniel and his wife that indicate that they were rather unhappy with some of the characteristics displayed by their fellow countrymen while visiting the Old Country and would have liked to disassociate themselves from such behavior, underlining the fact that Nathaniel was not what most English people of the time considered to be a typical Yankee, in that he was not an extrovert. So the family kept to itself, a tight-knit little community of its own—father, mother, children, nursemaid, and, at one time, governess—mingling with that part of Leamington's society and trade only as was strictly necessary, thus reflecting in part Nathaniel's personal wish to lead a life of quiet reflective independence, essential to him as a precursor to literary composition, which in turn was a reflection of the attitudes that had been fostered in him as a result of his somewhat unusual childhood (as a result of and during which, according to one recent biographer, he "internalized an identity he was both required and forbidden to fulfill" and then in later life "recurrently sought to reproduce the incestuous self-enclosure of his boyhood home")[1], education, and early manhood in America.

By the time he came to England in July 1853, as the United States consul in Liverpool, accompanied by his wife Sophia, son Julian, and daughters Una and Rose, he had already published the majority of the works that had resulted in his being regarded at that time as the foremost writer of fiction in America, such as the stories contained in *Twice-Told Tales, Tanglewood Tales,* and *Mosses from an old Manse* and, more importantly, the novels *The Scarlet Letter, The House of the Seven Gables,* and *The Blithedale Romance.* The paucity of the financial rewards accumulated through his

DEPARTMENT OF STATE,

WASHINGTON, *april 17th 1853*

Nathaniel Hawthorn, Esq,

Appointed Consul of the United States for *the Port of Liverpool, England.*

SIR:

THE PRESIDENT, by and with the advice and consent of the Senate, having appointed you Consul of the United States for *the Port of Liverpool in England, to take effect from and after July 31st, 1853.* I transmit to you a printed copy of the General Instructions to Consuls, to the 1st and 2d Chapters of which your immediate attention is called; a form of the Consular bond; and other documents for the use of your Consulate, of which a list is subjoined. Among them will be found a circular of July 30th, 1840, which contains a copy of an act of the 20th of that month, not embodied in the Instructions, and with the provisions of which it is important you should be fully acquainted.

Your Commission will be sent to the Legation of the United States at *London* with instructions to apply to the *British* Government for the usual Exequatur, which, when obtained, will be forwarded to you with the Commission.

You will communicate to the department the name of the State or Country in which you were born: and if you have ever resided *in Liverpool.*

I am, Sir,
Your obedient servant,

W. L. Marcy.

DOCUMENTS TRANSMITTED.

General Instructions, Blank bond, List of Ministers, Consuls, &c., Forms of Returns and Statement of Fees. Ink lines, Circulars of writing and the two spells of employment that he had had in the Custom Houses at Boston and Salem had been partly the reason for his having approached his old college friend, Franklin Pierce, prior to the latter's presidential election campaign. Pierce rewarded him for providing a campaign biography of the ultimately successful candidate with the post of consul in England. It would have been invidious to suggest that Nathaniel was the wrong man for such a post. He was not unsophisticated, of course, and had experienced politics of a local nature. But the move across the Atlantic to what may almost be called a different civilization into a position of power and consequence as a representative of the United States government, must have given him cause to reflect on how he was to manage in such circumstances. From the English side of the ocean his arrival was not wholly unannounced or unexpected, though for different reasons. His work had received favorable notices in various newspapers and journals over the past few years, such as *The Athenæum*, the *Westminster Review*, and *The Times* and one of his publishers, James Fields, had already been to England where he had lost few opportunities to meet with many of the leading English literary figures, extolling Nathaniel's various virtues and advising all and sundry of his imminent arrival in the Old Country. But there was a reticence in his character that would appear not to have been the best foundation for the type of personality that would succeed in, or be happy with, the necessarily public life of a consul in a thriving, rambunctious, English port such as Liverpool. That is not to say that Nathaniel's personality was unsympathetic or unappealing; he just did not thrive in a crowd or make new acquaintances easily, both of which characteristics it would have been thought were essential for the successful undertaking of the type of duties incumbent on a consul.

However, whatever outsiders may have seen or felt when making his acquaintance he was, apparently, a god to his family. That, of course, is not always the attitude adopted by children to their fathers or, indeed, by wives to their husbands. It will become clear in succeeding chapters of this book how much he was adored by all the members of his household and it will be realized, eventually, that this was not without reason even though the household was a very tight-knit one in which emotions and display were kept under control, not always to the advantage of each member, as there were very different temperaments all conforming to the same mode as laid down by the head of the family. Rose and Julian wrote several books after their father's death in which they described his character and what he had meant to them both when they were children, when they had been uprooted, willy-nilly, from their American home and taken across that enormous stretch of water to a foreign land. Rose, in particular, wrote retrospectively (in 1897) of her father's personality at this time, portraying him in a haze of idealized memory, although much of her recollections (as she was only two years old in 1853) was, of necessity, a distillation of her future experiences.

To begin with, of course, Nathaniel was anxious to make a success of his consular activities but was not keen to do any socializing other than that occasioned by the nature of the job. And despite what he wrote in the voluminous journals that he kept at the time, in which he was frank and unsparing in the comments on his surroundings and acquaintances (which gave rise to some unpleasantness in the future with a few of the subjects of his honesty) he could, on occasion, be a charming, genial, and amusing companion to those outside the immediate family circle. Maybe he did, as he admitted in letters and journals, need some alcoholic stimulation to boost his morale enough to be able to get to his feet at a banquet and make a speech (though he came to be more adept at this, without the alcohol, as time went by). Due probably to a lonely and introspective youth he obviously did find it difficult to unwind socially, though he had not led a completely solitary life unenlightened by any opportunities for personal and intellectual meetings with that type of person with whom he could feel at ease. With those whom *he* called friends he appears to have shown all the qualities that those who were not so favored said that he lacked.

Apart from his family, the weather, and the Englishness of the English, there was little else of importance that occupied Nathaniel's mind at first than the amount of money he was able to earn. The consul's post did not command a fixed salary; his earning power depended on the number and amount of the fees that he was (legitimately) allowed to charge for all manner of political, commercial, and legal services that he supplied as the consul in the second of the two main ports of England, through which was conducted the majority of the maritime trade between England and America. Out of his earnings he had to pay all official and staff expenses, salaries, office rent, and, of course, meet all his personal and family's expenditure. The fees in Liverpool were very considerable, as his predecessor had found, and Nathaniel became obsessed with the rate of their flow according to the season, and continually harped upon his present accumulations and future expectations in letters back to America. He was far from being miserly but it was an important matter to him and to his family's future. He was very conscious that while his income was considerable it was critical that a certain economy in domestic expenses should be maintained. After all, he was going to be a consul for a limited period only, not for the rest of his life, and he was always thinking of Sophia's poor health; how it could be improved, hopefully, in the future by their residing in some more favorable climate that would suit her weak lungs and chest. Such thoughts and intentions could only be fulfilled and financed by this golden opportunity that he had at present.

He became greatly concerned on hearing of a bill that was to be presented to the Senate in Washington that protested the fee-earning capabilities of the United States consuls in general and proposed that their rewards be limited to a fixed salary. The House Committee on Foreign Affairs was also concerned at the apparent lack of application to their jobs displayed by certain consuls, who appeared to regard their position as a means of traveling for personal benefit, and at the government's expense, throughout the countries in which they represented the United States, leaving all consular activities in the hands of foreign (i.e., native to the particular country) vice-consuls and clerks. As far as Nathaniel was concerned, the proposal to pay fixed salaries was ill-considered, unless those in power were prepared to take proper advice as to what could be considered an adequate figure. With regard to Liverpool, what with one thing and another, business and social expenses were such that a (personal) salary of at least fifteen thousand dollars per annum would be necessary to maintain both his and the American government's proper standing.

He was probably justified in protesting the difficulties of maintaining his position on a fixed salary, unless that salary was to be set at a much higher level than was envisaged in the bill, but he did rather overdo his protestations both then and later, as he was frank in his private comments to his friends and publishers that he was in the job mainly for its monetary value rather than for any social kudos that it commanded and that he was, in the future, to take every possible permissible advantage of being away from his office, traveling round the country with his wife and children, leaving the consular activities to be controlled by his clerks. The bill (which, together with other consulates, fixed the salary of the Liverpool post at $7,500 per annum and insisted on the employment of Americans as clerks in consulates and made various provisions about the charging of fees) was eventually passed in Congress on 1 March 1855 and the effects of the deliberations that accompanied its passage toward the Statute Book had a marked influence on Nathaniel's regard for his office and his possible length of tenure. Yet he knew that he was, in most respects, onto a very good thing and that it would be just as well to carry on as best he could while the emoluments were so considerable. There was also the problem of income tax to worry about, as he was being asked to state the sources of his income to the Commissioners of Inland Revenue at Somerset House. But appeals to James Buchanan, the United States minister in London, who in turn passed them on to Lord Clarendon, eventually resulted in an assurance from the latter that "the Lords Commissioners of Her Majesty's Treasury have issued directions to the Board of Inland Revenue not to require returns from Consuls of Foreign States of the emoluments of their office."[2]

From now on many of his letters home to his political friends were full of expressions of his continuing disappointment at the likely outcome of the consular bill; and of the proposed tightening of regulations concerning the organization of the consulates. The reduction of the hitherto customary financial benefits would in no way compensate for the so-called glories of office and he was certain that a reduction in salaries would result in a lower standard of personnel being attracted to the service, from consuls themselves down through the ranks of employees. His thoughts became increasingly occupied with calculations as to when it would be most expedient, and profitable, for him to resign. Much would depend, of course, on when the new bill would take effect.

The bill, in fact, was to take effect from the following 1 July 1855. Nathaniel's worries were at least partly put to one side as he knew now that his resignation was inevitable and consequently he began to look forward to spending the next winter on the Continent with the family. But then the new bill's effect was delayed until 1 January 1856, so it was, in some respects, back to square one with regard to the most advantageous date for leaving office. The year 1856 would see a new presidential election; there would, no doubt, be delays about the naming and installation of his successor in Liverpool and, meanwhile, the status quo with regard to his emoluments would be maintained until, at least, the New Year. He felt that the future political situation was so uncertain that he wouldn't mind (or, at least, would be prepared to endure) another year in office while matters sorted themselves out, hopefully to his financial benefit. Perhaps it would be best to make no decision at all, as yet.

For two years after their arrival in England, the Hawthornes had remained in Liverpool and its environments living, for the most part, in a house on the Rock Park estate within Rock Ferry, a ferry's ride away from the city, across the river. They had left Rock Park to make only two short trips, to the Isle of Man and North Wales. Because of the anticipated expense and his desire to save every last penny from the permissible emoluments of his office there was little other socializing, traveling, or entertaining, except what was necessary as part of the consul's obligations as the representative of the United States government. The duties imposed as part of the consul's position within the city of Liverpool were taken seriously enough, however, for Sophia to complain on occasions of the few hours that her husband was apparently able to spend with his family. Much of his working day was spent in contact with Americans of all kinds, professionals and laborers, honest men and charlatans, rich and poor, and sailors of all degrees. On the whole, they were all given Nathaniel's undivided (though not always enthusiastic) attention. His attitude toward the country in which he had come to work, and its inhabitants, was ambivalent, to say the least, and his opinion of the climate and the city in which he worked was stark, though to be fair the climate was always seen from the viewpoint of its likely effect on Sophia and the children's health rather than on his own well-being; in fact, he came to like it. From the first he had decided views on the English and on the society in which he found himself, viewing the apparently bullheaded patriotism displayed by most Englishmen as somewhat anachronistic as he was convinced that English power and the Empire was heading for its comeuppance in the not-too-distant future. But, as he admitted not too long after taking office, he came to like individual Englishmen.

Nathaniel had little inclination or inspiration (or time) to contemplate writing for immediate publication, certainly not in the realms of fiction, although he did keep fully detailed journals and diaries concerned with his day-to-day experiences. He was certainly aware of and reading other authors' works and gave encouragement to, and sought assistance for, some writers who actively engaged his interest, such as Lewis Mansfield, William C. Bennett, and Delia Bacon. But his work as consul was time-consuming and despite his complaints of the drudgery involved in carrying out his duties he was a conscientious official. The drudgery, no doubt, was not likely to render him susceptible to any visitations from the literary Muse but he probably required no such visitor as a preliminary to the composition of his journals. However, he never lost sight of the fact that he was an author first, a consul second.

The spring and early summer of 1855 saw a growing conviction on Nathaniel's part that in view of the satisfactory level of his savings to date, together with the probability of additional emoluments accruing during the few months left before the new bill regulating his income came into effect in the New Year, now was the time to use some of the perks of his position to enable the family and himself to see a lot more of the country in which they had been living for the last two years and to go on a few "rambles," perhaps to the Lake District and Scotland and anywhere else that took their fancy, just so long as Nathaniel was close to a means of communicating with the consulate in the event of any emergency.

"Rambling" about the country meant that a certain amount of reorganization on the domestic front had to take place before Rock Park could be left in good order. They sublet their house during the remainder of the summer as the lease did not expire until August, and most of their belongings had to be placed in storage so as to leave only essential items that could be taken with them on their travels. The number of servants in the household would have to be reduced. It had already been found necessary to get rid of the two Herne sisters who had come with the family from America, and their cook was also given notice. That left but one servant, Fanny Wrigley, who was to accompany the family on its travels. She had been engaged as a nursemaid for Rose as a result of Ellen Herne's dismissal in 1854, and although her only nursing experience had been as a result of looking after a sick adult relation, it was not long before she became greatly loved by them all and she assumed an important role in the maintenance of stability in the family life. This could not always have been an easy task in view of Sophia's frequent ill health and emotional intensity, together with the children's sometimes willful behavior that could be attributed to the somewhat claustrophobic atmosphere and their strictly monitored activities, both of the intellect and body.

No doubt much discussion took place as to which direction their travels should take them, presumably an initial direct evacuation to London and its attractions being rejected from the point of view of expense. The family can be imagined as gathered round the parlor table in the evenings after the children's lessons had been completed, when Nathaniel had returned from the consulate and tea had been taken. Although the holiday was to be as much educational as recreational, with the help of a *Guide to England* that had been purchased earlier in the year, everyone chose a different town or city—one for the country, another for the seaside. Finally, and maybe only because it was in the center of the land and by taking it as a starting point for the great adventure one could then branch out from it in any direction,[3] it was decided to make for Leamington Spa. And so, on Monday, 18 June, with the house and furniture situation sorted out, the servant problem solved, and various accounts settled, with the bags having been packed and forwarded to the railway station, the Hawthorne family and Fanny Wrigley boarded the train and settled down to while away the next few hours on the journey to Leamington.

1

Leamington, that "handsome" town: June 1855

The train was boarded at Birkenhead at 12:30,[1] and for this rather special occasion Nathaniel had ensured that they would travel first class, at a cost of £4.3s.4d., much to Sophia's satisfaction (though it may have had its hidden hazards, as she was to explain later in a letter to her sister, Mary). As it was a six-hour journey and the weather was far from good it must have been something of a strain to keep the children from becoming bored and fractious but apparently, for at least the first part of the journey, they had the carriage to themselves. If it was of the type that was subdivided into four compartments but with a central connection through glass doors to each of the other compartments, there must have been a lot of space to move around in. That, no doubt, allowed the children to change from side to side to watch the passing scenery; but even that possibility could not be a guaranteed feature of the journey. Nathaniel's journal recorded that

We left Liverpool and Rock Ferry, [today], at 12½, by the rail, for this place; a very dim and rainy day, so that we had no pleasant prospect of the country; neither would the scenery along the Great Western railway have been in any case very striking; though sunshine would have made the abundant verdure and foliage warm and genial. But a railway naturally finds its way through all the common-places of a country; it is certainly a most unsatisfactory way of travelling, the only object being to arrive. However, we had a whole carriage to ourselves and the children enjoyed the earlier part of the ride very much. We skirted Shrewsbury; and I think I saw the old tower of a church near the station, perhaps the same that struck Falstaff's 'long hour.'[2] As we left the town, I saw the Wrekin, a round, pointed hill, of regular shape;—and remembered the old toast, "To all friends round the Wrekin."[3] As we approached Birmingham, the country began to look some-what Brummagemish, with its manufacturing chimnies [sic], and pennons of flame quivering out of their tops; its forges; and great heaps of mineral refuse; its smokeiness [sic]; and other ugly symptoms. Birmingham itself we saw little or nothing of, except the mean and new brick lodging-houses, &c, on the outskirts of the town. Passing through Warwick, we had a glimpse of the castle,—an ivied wall and two turrets rising out of the embosoming foliage; one's very idea of an old gray castle. We reached Leamington at a little past six and drove to the Clarendon Hotel, a very spacious and stately house, by far the most splendid hotel I have seen in England, though not equal in splendor or convenience to many in America; but then, in the latter, the accommodation is for the public in a mass, whereas here it is for individuals of the public. The landlady [Mrs. Hughes], a courteous old lady in black, showed my wife our rooms; and we established ourselves in an immensely large and lofty drawing-room, with red-curtains, and ponderous furniture, perhaps a very little out of date. The waiter brought us the book of arrivals, containing the names of all visitors for, I think, three to five years back; and there were not more entries than, in a popular American house, there might have been in a week. During two years, I estimated that there had been about three hundred and fifty; and, while we were there, I saw nobody but ourselves to support this great house. Among the names we saw princes, earls, countesses, baronets, and dignitaries of that sort; and when they learned from nurse that I was a man of office, and held the title of Honorable in my own country, the people of the house greatly regretted that I had entered myself as plain Mister in the book [possibly Fanny was not too popular for having let the cat out of the bag in this manner]. We found this hotel very comfortable, and might doubtless have made it luxurious, had we chosen to go to perhaps five times the expense of similar luxuries in America; but we merely had comfortable things, and so came off at no very extravagant rate [£2.19s.6d. plus tips, 3s.6d.]— and with great honor, at all events, in the eyes of the waiters, to whom (as Americans are usually foolish enough to do) we gave more than Englishmen would, in like circumstances.[4]

The Clarendon Hotel was closed down in 1983 and following several years of neglect is now known as George House, having been extensively refurbished inside and out as self-contained office accommodation. Unfortunately, it has proved impossible to locate the whereabouts of the hotel's old visitors' books. But it is something of a mystery that Nathaniel said that the family was alone in the hotel at that time. By referring to the Arrivals and Departures column in *The Royal Leamington Spa Courier* of Saturday, 16 June, it is apparent that sixteen persons had checked in during that week and that, in addition, two families were still there from the week before. Moreover, the edition of the following Saturday, 23 June, confirms that a further twenty-seven persons checked in (in addition to "Hon. Nathaniel Hawthorne, U.S. Consul at Liverpool, Mrs Hawthorne and family"). The papers do not specify on which days the various individuals arrived and departed, but out of all these people it appears very strange that Nathaniel saw not a single one while he was at the Clarendon. Even more extraordinary is that among the other guests listed as having arrived the same week as the Hawthornes were a "Dr.C.Mifflin, Mrs, and Misses . . . . Boston (USA)." Dr. Mifflin was the father of the George Mifflin (about eleven years old at the time but apparently left at home on this trip), who subsequently became the founder of the Houghton Mifflin publishing company in Boston that would eventually publish several books by members of the Hawthorne family. Probably the Mifflins arrived after the Hawthornes had left the hotel, but what an amazing coincidence it would have been if the two families *had* met and become acquainted, even though they were not to know of the future connection.

The unsettled weather that the travelers had experienced on their journey was a feature of that summer in the Midlands, although *The Leamington Advertiser* of 21 June wrote of ". . . a succession of fine growing weather during the past ten days. . . ." Probably the Hawthornes, snug in the Clarendon Hotel, did not take much notice of another downpour of rain that evening,[5] though it prevented Nathaniel from taking a walk around the town. The rain, however, did put something of a damper on the meeting of the local Oddfellows Society (one of the several friendly societies in the town that lent money to needy residents). A procession had taken place earlier in the day through the streets of the town to celebrate the anniversary of the Battle of Waterloo, everyone dressed in their regalia, with banners and a band. In the evening, it had been intended that the celebrations would continue on the nearby Parr & Wisden's cricket ground (the present Victoria Park) but, due to the rain, everyone had to crush into the large marquee that had been erected, allowing the festivities to continue unabated.[6] While all this was going on, some more sober-minded of the citizens of Leamington had ignored the rain and met at the Town Hall for a public meeting of the ratepayers of the town, and at 8:30 in the evening Mr. Richard Russell (plasterer) was called upon, as chairman, to open the proceedings. Two motions were proposed, seconded, and passed without much opposition; one, "That in the opinion of this meeting, the local rates of this town have been unnecessarily high & exorbitant: that for many years, previously to the present year, there has been great extravagance and reckless expenditure in the conduct and management of the town affairs, to the great cost of the ratepayers and the injury of the town; and that, with a view to prevent such extravagance for the future, and ensure the good management of the town, it is expedient and desirable to form a Ratepayers Protection Committee," and the second "That the Committee be requested to watch the proceedings of the Local Board of Health, to expose and make public, by advertisement, handbill, public meeting or otherwise, any unjust or improper outlay of the funds of the town; and generally, to take such proceedings to economize and reduce the yearly expenses as such Committee in their discretion shall think best."[7]

There is extant a fragment of Sophia's journal, on a loose page, that begins:

Leamington, Warwickshire. We all, Mr. Hawthorne, children & nurse arrived at this fair town [this evening] at six. We had had a dreary drive in the Railroad carriages, with a busy rain, which blurred the windows, & the lovely scenery after passing Chester, we could scarcely appreciate. The sumptuous English First Class carriages are almost as comfortable as a bed—stuffed so thickly & softly—each seat so large with a rest for the head on each side & for the elbows as well. We had one quite to ourselves, though

And that is all there is;[8] but another member of the family was also putting on record her impressions of the day. Rather commendably for a child of nine in view of the excitement of the day and the strange surroundings in the Clarendon Hotel, Una replied to a letter received that morning from her cousin, Rebecca,[9] presumably having been part of the mail on board the steamer *America* that had arrived the day before at Liverpool from Boston; as there is no reason to doubt Una's word, it appears that prior to their departure for Leamington the consulate in Liverpool must have been advised not only of the family's destination but also that they intended to stay at the Clarendon:

June 18 Leamington /55

My dear cousin Rebecca, Today I received your letter,[10] of which I was very glad. Also one from my cousin Ellen.[11] It is a long time since we have heard from each other, but I hope you are well, which I suppose you are, as you seem to be studying very hard. You see, my dear Rebecca, we are no longer in Rock Park. We came away from Cheshire this morning at half past twelve & arrived here about half past six.

We are now in the Clarendon Hotel, Leamington. The scenery is lovely, especially in Wales. We came through Birmingham, or "Brummagum" as a great many people call it here. I assure you it is no very interesting place. I do not think there can be any streets much more than a yard wide in the whole city. I suppose it is not quite literally so, but the roofs of the houses seemed to go somewhat so ⌐⌐ These are the roofs of two houses. Leamington is near London, Warwick, Kenilworth, Oxford & many other grand places, besides being very beautiful itself. So we are told by a gentleman & lady who have been very kind to us, & directed us to all the pleasant & interesting places about the middle of England. Their names are Mr & Mrs Steele.[12] We are so very sorry that it should have been such a rainy day, for, though the scenery did look very lovely under the sad gloomy sky & rain, it would have been so much lovelier if it had been set off by a bright sun & clear blue sky. And Papa would have liked to take a walk this evening very much. Tomorrow will be the 19th & these wise men say the weather will be fair & lovely till the 10th September. So we shall have a lovely summer, at least, for our travels. We have a vixonella of a chambermaid. She is not very prepossessing in her looks, either, to make a small atonement for her disagreeable tone & manner. Well my dear Rebbeca [sic], my paper has come to an end before I thought of it, so goodbye & believe me to be, your affectionate cousin Una.[13]

The most important thing on the following day was to be the search for suitable lodgings to enable them to dispense with the formality and expense involved in staying at a prestigious hotel. Which one of the party undertook to find the lodgings is not clear. Perhaps Nathaniel would not have considered it quite right that he should have been the one to trudge around to the various agencies that catered to such requirements, though he may well have done his bit by inquiring of the "courteous" Mrs. Hughes as to whether she had any recommendations or advice, and Mr. and Mrs. Steele might have made some suggestions as to where accommodation could be found.

On at least one other occasion, in similar circumstances, Sophia took part in the hunt for lodgings in a strange town, but whether on her own or not, it would appear more likely that the task was normally undertaken by Fanny making the necessary inquiries and inspecting whatever was on offer; if she did, it would not be the only occasion on which such a task was to be her responsibility.[14] In any case, it was not long before lodgings were found. Having settled the Clarendon's bill of £2.19s.6d. and tipped the staff, a cab was hired for 2s.6d. (which appears to be rather excessive in view of the short distance to be traveled, but no doubt their luggage bumped up the cost) and they all moved off to their new quarters.

> During the afternoon, we found lodgings, and established ourselves in them before dark. Leamington seems to be made chiefly of lodging-houses, and to be built with a view to a continually shifting population. It is a very beautiful town, with regular streets of stone or stuccoed houses, very broad pavements, and much shade of noble trees, in many parts of the town; parks and gardens, too, of delicious verdure; and throughout all an aspect of freshness and clean-ness, which I despaired of ever seeing in England. The town seems to be almost entirely new. The principal street has elegant shops; and the scene is very lively, with throngs of people more gaily dressed than one is accustomed to see in this country; soldiers, too, lounging at the corners, and officers, who appear less shy of showing themselves in their regimentals than it is the fashion to be elsewhere. This English custom of lodgings (which we had some experience of, at Rhyl, last year) has its advantages, but is rather uncomfortable for strangers, who, on first settling themselves down, find that they must undertake all the responsibilities of house-keeping at an instant's warning, and cannot get even a cup of tea till they have made arrangements with the grocer. Soon, however, there comes a sense of being at home, and by our exclusive selves, which never could be attained at hotels or boarding houses. Our house is well situated and respectably furnished, with the dinginess, however, which I suppose is inseparable from lodging-houses—as if others had used these things and would use them after we are gone—a well-enough adaptation, but lack of peculiar appropriateness; and I think one puts off real enjoyment from a sense of not being really fitted.[15]

The lodgings that had been found were at No. 13 Lansdowne Crescent (the present No. 43; the result of a subsequent renumbering exercise by the post office).[16] Prior to the arrival of the Hawthornes there had been no lack of tenants occupying the house during the earlier part of the year. *The Leamington Advertiser* had noted the arrival and departure of a Mr. and Mrs. Fox, Miss Hawkes, Miss Saxon, Mr. Pierce, Mr. Pearson, and a Mr. and Mrs. Blanchard, and for the rest of the year, after the Hawthornes had left, there were several more individuals quoted as having been in occupation.

"Dinginess" is the very last word that would come to mind when describing the interior of the present-day No. 43. The owners, Mr. and Mrs. Pooley, rescued it from a state of some decrepitude nearly a decade ago and it is now one of the few houses left in the crescent that is occupied by a single family, the others being subdivided into apartments. No major reconstruc-

Lansdown Crescent Leamington.

Lansdowne Crescent in the 1850s. Courtesy of the Leamington Spa Library, Warwickshire.

tion has been undertaken, the essential differences between the house now and when the Hawthornes were there being those that have resulted from the installation of the usual modern conveniences. Despite its large size it is not easy to determine how the accommodation would have been distributed between the various members of the family and Mrs. Price, the owner (who remained in occupation throughout their tenancy, as Nathaniel confirmed later in a letter to William Ticknor, the senior partner of his publishers in Boston, Ticknor and Fields). There are three large rooms in the basement or lower ground floor, one of which was obviously the kitchen; one of the other two has a large fireplace in it and there are walk-in areas for larders and wine cellars. At the rear of the house there remains the original coach house, the only one left standing in the crescent.

The ground floor consists of two large rooms, the front one possibly having been the dining room. The first floor contains two more large rooms, one of which was probably the drawing room or "parlor," as the Hawthornes would have called it, and the other may have been used by them as the schoolroom. Both the second and third floors contain two further rooms apiece, plus one other smaller room that could have been a bathroom. It is not known who had which bedrooms and who may have shared; nor is it apparent as to where Mrs. Price was to be found (though it seems unlikely that she would have relegated herself to the two rooms in the attic on the third floor, as apart from the inconvenience, there would have been ample room on the lower ground floor to accommodate her; maybe it depended on what type of lady she was and whether she considered it dignified or not to live in the basement). There may also have been at least one live-in servant, as Fanny was not considered to be either a servant or a cook. The permutations are numerous. The house remains a magnificent one.

It seems likely that there would have been little time during the rest of that day for the family to do much else than to settle down in their new surroundings, unloading their baggage and putting away their belongings and settling with Mrs. Price the organization of their domestic routines. Perhaps in the evening, though, they all took a short stroll to inspect the immediate neighborhood, maybe walking up to the Parade or down to the Royal Pump Rooms and Baths. No one took the opportunity of writing any letters so, possibly, it was an early night for them all before beginning on the morrow the exploration of Leamington and its surroundings. Rather disappointingly, however, all that was recorded about Wednesday's events can be found in the two lines of Nathaniel's journal where he merely recorded that

> Julian and I took walks [this] forenoon and afternoon—very pleasant walks; but as I mean to take many more such, I defer a description of rural scenery for the present.[17]

During most of the day, therefore, Sophia, Una, Rose, and Fanny were left behind to fend for themselves. As the weather was, in the words of *The Leamington Advertiser,* "delightfully propritious," [*sic*] it seems likely that they also went out, and it is not beyond the bounds of possibility that having walked into the town they would have been sufficiently attracted by the sound of the band of Her Majesty's Second Life Guards to investigate the reasons for the large crowds that were wending their way to the Jephson Gardens at the bottom of the Parade. In which case, they would have found that it was the opening day of the Leamington and Midland Counties Annual Grand Archery Meeting, "the second anniversary of this promising society of toxopholites," at which both ladies and gentlemen were competing. Despite the propitious weather, there was an annoying wind in the morning that had a marked effect on the standard of shooting, but during the afternoon the wind dropped and an all-round improvement in marksmanship was displayed. Two thousand people were present, and if the children were able to see anything in the crush it must have been an exciting occasion, a fairly typical example of the sort of entertainment on offer to the public during the Spa's summer program.[18]

Next day, Thursday, was again sunny and warm, and during the morning Nathaniel, Sophia, and Una set out on an expedition to the northeast of the town, toward Lillington:

In the forenoon of [today], wife, Una and I took a walk through what looked like a park, but seemed to be a sort of semi-public tract on the outskirts of the town— hill and glade, with a fair gravel path through it, and most stately and beautiful trees overshadowing it. Here and there benches were set beneath the trees. These old, vigorous, well-nurtured trees, are fine beyond description; and in this leafy month of June, they certainly surpass my recollections of American trees—so tall, with such an aspect of age-long life. But I suppose what we know of English trees, of the care bestowed on them, the value at which they are estimated, their being traditional, and connected with the fortunes of old families—these moral considerations inevitably enter into physical admiration of them. They are individuals—which few American trees have the happiness to be. The English elm is more beautiful in shape and growth than I had imagined; but I think our own elm is still more so. Julian compared an English oak, which we saw on our journey, to a cauliflower; and its shape, its regular, compact rotundity, makes it very like one;—there is a certain John-Bullism about it. Its leaf, too, is much smaller than our oak; and with similar advantages of age and cultivation, the latter would be far the noblest and most majestic form of a tree. But in verdure, in the rich aspect of the country, nothing surely can equal England; and I never enjoyed weather anywhere so delightful as such a day as [today]; so warm and genial, and yet not oppressive—the sun a very little too warm, while walking beneath it, but only enough too warm to assure us that it was warm enough. And, after all, there was an unconquered freshness in the atmosphere, which each little motion of the air made evident to us. I suppose there is still latent in us Americans (even of two centuries date, and more, like myself) an adaptation to the English climate, which makes it like native soil and air to us.

Beyond the park-like tract, we crossed a stile, and still followed the path, which led us through the midst of several fields and pastures. Men were whetting their scythes and mowing in adjacent fields. I delight in these English by-paths, which let a wayfarer into the heart of matters, without burdening him with the feeling of intrusiveness. Very likely, many, and most, of such paths are of more ancient date than the high roads; inasmuch as people travelled on foot before they had carriages or carts. In America, a farmer would plough across any such path, without scruple; here, the footsteps of centuries are sure to be respected.

Soon, as we went along this path, we descried some brick farm-houses, looking rather venerable; and they proved to be ranged along a public road, leading from Leamington to some town to me unknown. These houses stood close together in one row; for it is to be noted that we seldom see scattered farm-houses here, as in New England;—they cluster themselves together in little hamlets and villages. These edifices were all of a ripe age, with roofs of tiles, and some of thatch; and, in two or three of them, the windows opened on hinges. Several of the houses were good large dwellings evidently inhabited by respectable people, well to do in the world; but others in the same range were the veriest old huts I have seen in England;—the thatch mossy, and in one case covered with a great variety of queer vegetation—tufts of grass, house-leeks, and other plants, all differing in their shade of green. The windows were latticed (there was one little bit of a window right up in the eaves, half hidden by the thatch); the doors were time-worn; and this cottage, if I remember right, was built with its framework appearing through the stone and plaster, and painted black. I have seen several of these old houses hereabouts. The oaken frame seems to be more durable than the brick, stone or plaster, which fills up the spaces; for, in some instances, these materials had evidently been renewed, while the frame-work still looked as solid as ever. As with an old man's back, however, so an old cottage betrays its decrepitude by the crookedness of its ridge-pole. Perhaps these huts may have descended from father to son, and remained in one hereditary line, longer than the castles and manor-houses of the nobles who hold the title-deeds of the estates over which they are strewn. These thatched cottages seem like something made by nature, or put together by instinct, like birds' nests, more than houses built by man. They have a great charm for the observer; and artists, no doubt, like them better than the best edifices that could be built by rule and square; and yet they are as homely, and really ugly (if it were not for what decay and moss, and house-leeks, do for them in the way of beautification) as any pig-sty. No new stone and thatched cottages seem to be built, now-a-days; and, for the first hundred years, they would be eye-sores.

Beyond the first row of cottages, and on the opposite side of the road, there was another row—a block (as we should call it in America) of a dozen or more old brick cottages, all adjoining, with their thatched roofs forming one contiguity. The American idea of a cottage is, that it should be insulated; and I should not take it to indicate proper self-respect, and a due atmosphere of cleanly reserve, to have families growing in a mass, in this fashion. What an intimate community they must be, passing lives and generations, so near together. It is impossible, however, to think what a strangely rural and verdant scene was formed by this row of contiguous huts; for, in front of the whole was a hawthorne hedge, and betwixt the precincts of each was a dividing line of hedge; and belonging to each was a little square of garden, chock full—not of esculent vegetables—but of flowers and green shrubs, flowers not of the conservatory, but of homely yellow and other bright colors, fit for cottage garden-plots. The sunshine fell warmly and brightly into these small enclosures, and into the old doors and small windows of the cottages; and the women and children were seen, looking very comfortable, and enjoying themselves. There was a great buzz, too, in the air which we at first took to be the buzz of gnats, or musquitoes [sic], and which was very proper to the bright sunshine; but soon there came an old, witch-like woman out of one of the garden gates, holding forth a shovel, on which she clanged and clattered with a key; and then we discovered that a hive of bees had swarmed, and that the air was full of them, whizzing by our ears like bullets; and then we thought it best to retreat.

Not far from these two congregations of houses and cottages, a green lane parted from the main-road, and we saw the square gray tower of a church, and wended thitherward to inspect it. It proved to be the very picture and ideal of a country-church and church-yard. A low, massive turreted tower, of gray stone, and evidently of old date, as also were portions of the wall of the church, though it seemed to have been repaired no long time since. There was a stone platform, much worn and grass-grown, on which perhaps the font had stood (as at Bebbington church) in past times. A path, well-trodden, led across the church-yard; and we went in, and looked at the graves and monuments. Most of them were headstones, mossy, but none very old, so far as was discoverable by the dates; some of them, so far from being old, had glaring inscriptions in bright gold letters. Besides the headstones, there were a few monuments of granite or free stone, laid massively over the graves; one was to a former vicar, who died about twenty-five years ago. I suppose the ground must have been dug over and over, innumerable times, and that the soil is made up of what was once human clay. This church is but of humble size, and the eaves are so low that I think I could have touched them with my cane. I looked into the windows, and saw the dim and quiet interior, the nave being separated from the sides of the church by pointed Saxon arches, resting on very sturdy pillars. There was a small organ; and the pews looked very neat; and the woodwork seemed not to be of antiquity. On the opposite wall of the church, between two windows, was a mural tablet of white marble, with an inscription in black letters—the only one I could see within, though doubtless many dead people lay beneath. There were no painted windows, nor other gorgeousness; and probably it is the worshipping-place of no more distinguished congregation than the farmers and peasantry who live in the houses and huts which we had been looking at. Had the lord of the manor been one of the parishioners, there would probably have been an eminent pew in the church.

We rested ourselves on a flat tombstone, which somebody had been kind enough to place at just the height from the ground to make it a convenient seat. We observed that one of the head-stones stood very close to the church; so close that the droppings of the eaves must have fallen on it;—the pious inmate of that grave had doubtless wished to creep under the church-wall. After a while, we arose and went our way; and I had a feeling as if I had seen this old church before, and dimly remembered; so well did it correspond with my idea, from much reading about them, of what English rural churches are. Or perhaps the image of them, impressed into the minds of my long-ago forefathers, was so deep that I have inherited it; and it answers to the reality. Part of our way home lay through a delightful shadowy lane; but we soon found ourselves getting into the brick work and stuccoed lines of houses, and macadamized roads of Leamington.[19]

This walk to Lillington became a favorite of the family's, particularly of Nathaniel's. There is little that remains from the time of this first visit, although the route that the Hawthornes took retains within its length a considerable amount of pleasantly semirural surroundings. To follow the Hawthornes' trail as closely as possible it would be necessary to turn left out of (the present) No. 43 Lansdowne Crescent and to take the second road on the left, Upper Holly Walk. At the end of the Walk the road bends to the left and a footpath leads straight up to the top of Campion Hills, from where, looking out over Leamington, Warwick Castle can be seen in the middle distance. The footpath skirts what could be the remains or descendants of a clump of trees and undergrowth that used to be known variously as Newbold Beeches or Lovers Grove. It leads into Black Lane, which, in turn, leads into Buckle Road. Crossing over immediately into Wellington Road it is here that the eyes should be modestly averted from the surrounding modern housing estate in order that the atmosphere of a Victorian walk can be maintained as far as possible! Wellington Road leads into Valley Road, on the other side of which are two paths that border an infants' school and its playing fields. Both of these footpaths lead into Cubbington Road. A left turn along Cubbington Road quickly brings the traveler to Vicarage Road and St. Mary Magdelene church is a short way up this road, on the left. After their inspection of the church and graveyard, it must be that the Hawthornes' return journey took them down Church Lane, which is still partly "a delightful shadowy lane," into Rugby Road, along which they would have turned left to walk back into Leamington and that would have led them almost directly to Lansdowne Crescent.

On this occasion, Julian and Rose had been left behind. Perhaps Julian had been told of the Archery Competition and decided that he would rather go there, probably in the charge of Fanny. If so, they would have found plenty happening on this the second and final day of the Meeting. The gentlemen were adding spice to the competition by entering into a sweepstake for cash prizes at the various distances; the marquees were doing good business, the weather was still fine, and the Life Guards band was still oompahing away, with pieces by Auber, Meyerbeer, Schubert, and Ettling as part of the program. The band had performed, in addition, at a Promenade Concert the previous evening at the new Public Hall in Windsor Street.[20]

Having returned to the lodgings, Nathaniel sat down to write to Ticknor to bring him up-to-date with their present circumstances:

Leamington, June 21st 1855

Dear Ticknor,
We left Rock Ferry for this place on Monday, and arrived same evening in good order. It is a beautiful place, and unlike all other English towns (so far as I have seen them) looks perfectly clean. We have taken an entire house (except what is occupied by the mistress of it) at 13, Lansdowne Crescent, and shall be most happy to receive a visit from you, any time within a month. I doubt whether Sophia will go back to Liverpool again, except for a visit, now and then. According to my calculation, we shall be able to live more cheaply at watering-places and country-towns, or even in London, in respectable lodgings, than we have heretofore done in Liverpool, or than we could at Mrs. Blodgett's boarding-house [where the family stayed, in Liverpool, on first arriving in England and where Nathaniel stayed thereafter if he was on his own]. Our whole expenditure here, with these ample accommodations, will not exceed seven guineas a week. We are beginning to get an insight into English economical customs. They know how to be comfortable and make a good appearance, on a great deal less than Americans spend for a poorer result.
I shall go back to the Consulate whenever business may require my presence, but mean to spend the greater part of the time with my family.
Mr. Wilding [one of the clerks at the consulate, who looked after Nathaniel's consular and personal finances] will send you, by this steamer, bills on the Department for $1399.92.[21] I deposited £125 to your credit with the Barings, on Friday last [Nathaniel's profits, which he could consider to be his salary, were deposited at the local (Liverpool) branch of Baring Brothers, credited to Ticknor, and eventually would percolate through to the latter's bank account in Boston from where it would be debited to Nathaniel].
I send a letter for Mary Ahern [one of the sacked Herne sisters], which I wish you would direct to her at Eastport. I got her a place as stewardess on board the ship John Knox, which sailed for that place, last week; and I believe she has engaged with the captain to continue in office during the year.
Massachusetts must be a very uncomfortable place, just now, with your liquor laws and other nonsense.[22] I wish we could annex this island to the Union, and that I could have an estate here in Warwickshire. We mean to go to Stratford on Avon tomorrow; and there are a great many other desirable places within easy reach.

Truly Yours
Nathl Hawthorne[23]

June

			£	s	d
	Gold pen 5/			5	
	Nankeen			6	
	Teunel's bill £3. 3. 0	3	3	
	Mrs Husson's bill music	9	13	6
18	Cabman			2	
	4 Tickets for Leamington	4	3	4
	Leamington				
	Cabman			2	
19	Bill at the Clarendon Hotel				
	for 24 hours	2	19	6
	To servants			3	6
	Cab to Lansdowne Crescent			2	6
	Grocer — Food — 1st week Sundries			13	6
20	Ham			7	1
	Beef			7	5
	Wine			3	6
	Ale			1	8
	Bread			2	6
	Horseradish				1½
	Potatoes				5½
		1	16	3

It is impossible to be certain whether Nathaniel's assertion to Ticknor that he would be spending less than seven guineas a week in Leamington proved to be justified, though it would appear to have been unlikely. Sophia's Accounts Book,[24] in which she noted expenditures on food, clothing, and other small amounts that were spent on a daily basis, does not specify any charge made for their lodgings. Ignoring that unknown sum (and allowing for a slight uncertainty in deciphering a few figures in the book) it is apparent that during their stay in Leamington they spent, at least, £12.4s.7d. on food and drink and £7.15s.0d. on what she classed as "varieties"; thus a total of £19.19s.7d. over a period of three weeks does represent an expenditure of less than seven guineas a week, but there is the problematical and unknown figure of rent to be added to that which would certainly have brought the final figure in excess of £22.1s.0d. The question of payment for a cook's services ought to be considered as well, as there are no references to Fanny ever being involved in serious cooking for the family (though she shopped for food). There is no mention of payment in the Accounts Book for an item of this nature, so one may presume that Mrs. Price's cook catered for the whole household. Perhaps her services were included in the rent, but there is no entry in the Book relating to a fee or tip to a servant or cook in the household, at the end of their stay in Lansdowne Crescent. Maybe modern-day nutritionists might look askance at what the family's meals consisted of, but the food that was consumed appears to have been fairly normal, and although sugar was bought regularly, the children were not allowed the luxury of sweets or candy at anytime. The Accounts Book also gives insight into what was happening on an almost daily basis with regard to events that were not considered to be of sufficient importance to be mentioned in journals, letters, or diaries. For instance, even though they knew that they would not be in Leamington for long, at some time between 20 and 27 June a piano was moved into the house, and although the Accounts Book only details a tip to the porter, it could be assumed that it was hired from one of several places in town, possibly either from Mander's Warehouse or Knight's Music Warehouse on the Upper Parade, or Ward's Musical Repository in Regent Street. Perhaps Mrs. Price was not a cultured lady, and the piano, presumably, was mainly for Una's benefit, but there is no record of any lessons being taken to keep up the good work instilled by the Hussons, from whom she had received lessons while in Liverpool. They spent 1s.6d. on a guide during the same period, and as the top-of-the-range *Beck's Leamington Guide, with an Historical and Descriptive Account of the Neighbourhood* cost 2s.6d., it was probably the less expensive but equally useful *Beck's Tourist Guide* that covered all the area around Leamington in which the family would have been interested. Sometime between 29 June and 3 July Una and Julian were taken to the baths, for one shilling. Whether these were of the medicinal variety that could be obtained at the Victoria Baths in Victoria Terrace, Gardiner's Baths in Bath Street, and at the Royal Pump

Food

21	Soles 1½ anchovies &c		5	3½
	Coffee			
22	Cheese &c		3	10
	Coffee – mutton chop			
	Capers – Leg of mutton			
	orange – bread		7	7
23	Butter, oil, Eggs, raisins		8	10½
	Lemon Cinnamon		3	10½
	Soles		1	2
	Peas & potatoes		1	5½
	Lamb &c		6	8
	Bread			1
25	Eggs & cabbages			9
	~~Fanny paid for me~~		~~1 2~~	
26	Milk		4	7½
	Vegetables?			11
	Bread			6
	Chips		2	8½
	Laundress		4	2½
		3	0	8

Rooms at the bottom of the Parade (in the charge of Mr. Wincote where "the attention shewn . . . to invalids and visitors who require the water or baths, is generally acknowledged to be most polite, every comfort being provided for, and every want anticipated") or the swimming baths at Old-ham's in Mill Street, an open-air, nonsaline establishment where the water was "kept constantly pure by the action of the mill wheel, while small rooms are fitted up with the necessary conveniences," one cannot be certain; how-ever, rather ominously, 1s.0d. at both the Victoria Baths and the Royal Pump Rooms would only purchase a "cold or shower bath," but then the whole family was used to daily cold-water ablutions at home, in any case. The Accounts Book confirms that the family read *The Morning Post* while in Leamington and on a couple of occasions bought the *Illustrated News*, pre-sumably the *Illustrated London News* that cost sixpence at that time. In addition, there are eighteen entries that relate to the purchase of items of clothing and materials for embroidery and for the repair of clothing; so often do they feature within a relatively short span of time that Fanny, and presumably Sophia also, would appear to have been employed in this task almost on a daily basis. And finally, and not surprisingly for such a family, there are eight entries relating to the purchase of stationery and stamps.

Unfortunately, the visit to Stratford on Friday was canceled, a disappoint-ment for Julian in particular, as it was his birthday. Nathaniel explained why in his journal:

> Nothing of note happened [today]. We had purposed to go to Stratford on Avon, to celebrate Julian's birthday, who is nine years old; but he seemed not very well, and there were other incommodities; so we put off the expedition. In the forenoon I took a little walk with Una and Rosebud, but saw only the useful [usual?] verdure and fertility, and a respectable old farm-house (large and handsome enough, how-ever, to have been a gentleman's residence) of brick, with several gables, and with lattice-windows—broad windows, hinged on either side, and closing in the middle. The immediate vicinity of the house was laid out in a lawn and flower-beds, and with gravel walks, and beautiful old trees, all with great neatness and taste; but a few hundred yards off were the barn-yard and farm-offices. I should like to see the tenant of precisely such a farm-house as this. In New England, it would be thought a very handsome residence for a Senator, a Judge, or any dignitary of State.[25]

It was bad luck for Julian, being sick on his birthday; perhaps, after all, it explains why he did not go on the walk to Lillington the day before, as he may already have been exhibiting symptoms of some illness. However, a short walk during the morning was in order for Una and for the four-year-old Rosebud (the family's nickname for Rose). Possibly, if they had known about it, they might have considered it worthwhile going into Warwick to watch the embarkation of some of the local militia to Aldershot, en route to the Crimea, though Nathaniel's interest in the war was rather lackluster despite the necessity of his having to reflect in public, as a consul, his country's official attitude toward the belligerents, with particular reference to the consequent relations between America and England. As *The Leamington Advertiser* of 28 June reported, it was this day that "nearly two hundred more of the Second Regiment of the Warwickshire Militia which has been quartered in this town [Warwick] for a length of time past, was despatched per Great Western Railway to the Aldershot Camp. A few, comprising the staff, now only remain, and are expected to leave in a few days. The men are reported to be in full health, and perfectly satisfied with their camp site." *The Royal Leamington Spa Courier* of 30 June confirmed that "The Second Regiment now encamped at Aldershot, is, we are glad to hear, inferior to none assembled there for military duty; presenting in all respects, a far cleaner appearance, and being better officered. The soldiers were inspected by Lord Panmure, who visited the camp yesterday, and among other promotions which have just taken place, we may mention those of Serjeant Major Newbold as Quartermaster, and Quartermaster Serjeant Brookes as Serjeant Major."

But the restless Nathaniel went out again that evening:

> About six o'clock I took a walk alone, on a road which I know to lead to Warwick, though I think not the most direct road. The hedges here are very luxuriant, and all the better, I think, for not being trimmed so scrupulously as I have seen them elsewhere. It was almost, or quite, a sultry evening; or else I have forgot what sultriness is. At any rate, it made me feel listless and languid. I sat down on a hospitable bench, a mile or so from the town, and smoked a cigar. A lady passed me on horseback, with her groom, with cockade in hat, riding at some distance behind; then two horsemen, looking like respectable farmers; an open phaeton, and various sorts of wagons and carts. Women and girls carrying baskets to or from the town, mostly, I thought, laundresses, with clothes for the gentry; a servant in livery; yeomen, in velveteen breeches, stout, shortish figures, in good flesh; and foot-travellers, with long staffs, one of whom observed to me—"Very warm, Sir !"—being the only words which I exchanged with anybody. In the course of my walk, I passed the Leam (pronounced Lemon, and Leamington Lemonington) by a bridge. It is a sluggish and dirty stream, about twenty-five to thirty yards across, but a pleasant object (unless you consider its muddiness too closely) on account of the verdure of its banks, fringed with grass right into the water, and the beautiful trees which see themselves in the placid current—though I could not perceive that there was any current. What one misses most in the scenery here is that which makes so great a charm in New England—the little sheets of water which there open their eyes out of the face of the country—and the little brooks and streamlets, every mile or two. I do not remember having seen a single brook anywhere in England. If it were not for cultivation and trees, and old houses and churches, the country about Leamington would be very uninteresting; being flat and tame in its natural features.[26]

That seems to be a somewhat sweeping remark for one who had only arrived in the locality four days previously, and the pronunciation peculiarities that he mentions do not appear to have withstood the test of time, but it is certainly true that the Leam is not, in its progress through the town, comparable in the rapidity of its flow with a mountain stream. However, from the description in the journal it seems that his evening walk had taken him across the Parade and down Adelaide Road, as the latter crosses the river Leam and joins the "old" Warwick Road in due course. Although Nathaniel had noted the extreme sluggishness of the Leam when crossing the bridge, he apparently did not notice or was not concerned about the situation with regard to the cleanliness of the surroundings there, which in the eyes of at least one citizen of the town was an outrage:

Nuisance near Adelaide Bridge.- *To the Editor*

Dear Sir:
Would you kindly inform me what right your Local Government have to call themselves a Local Board of Health, when they appear to encourage the most abominable nuisances in several parts of the town? One I'll quote—The Adelaide Bridge, deposit for putrid and other offensive matter, a nuisance to the whole neighbourhood. This hot weather does not improve it; consequently it is unbearable. Pray interfere for us.

Yours truly, A Sufferer.[27]

By the next morning, Julian appears to have recovered his spirits though Sophia's health, which had suffered an almost immediate setback on arriving in Leamington, was still not good. She had begun to cough rather badly, having caught a cold, she thought, while they were traveling down from Liverpool or from the damp evening air, and her general well-being was at a low level, sufficiently so that it prevented her from taking part in most of the family's perambulations for the first ten days or so of their stay in the town. It cannot have been much fun for her to rest in Lansdowne Crescent while everyone else was exploring the surrounding countryside, for she was a dedicated sightseer. However, having had to leave her behind again with Fanny and Rose, the rest of them set off, southward this time, down the Parade, under the railway bridge, up Clemens Street, and along the road leading out to Whitnash:

Una, Julian, and I, took a walk out of town, [today's] forenoon; the road presenting the same features of hedge and stately trees, and broad green fields, elsewhere to be seen in this region. About a mile or more from Leamington, we came to a little rural village more picturesque and Old-English in its way, than anything we have seen yet. It seemed to be quite shut in by trees; and it was a cluster of a few old-fashioned cottages round a small ancient church. Not one of the dwellings appeared less than two or three centuries old, all being of the thatched, wooden-framed, and stone, brick, and plaster order, though the one nearest the church was quite a fair-sized and comfortable house, with several ends and gables. This, I suppose, may have been the vicarage: and it was most convenient to the scene of the clergyman's labors;—indeed, not more than a score of yards from the church-door, though with a small, narrow lane betwixt it and the church-yard wall. The church has the square, gray, battlemented tower, that seems to be the general form hereabouts; and it was much moss-grown, and time-gnawn, and the arched window over the low portal was set with small panes of glass, cracked, dim, irregular, and evidently of old date. The frame of this window, and of the one over it towards the summit of the tower was of stone; and there were loop-holes up and down the sides of the tower, very narrow and small. No part of the church looked as if it had been repaired, for a very long time back; but masons were now at work in the churchyard, and in front of the tower, sawing a slab of stone, digging, building up bricks; and had we come a month or two later, no doubt we should have found the little edifice much sprucer, and not half so well worth looking at. They had dug an immense pit or vault on one side of the church, ten foot deep, at least;—yes, much more than ten—for I could see the depth of earth that was discolored by human decay, and the pit went far deeper than this. Probably they mean to enlarge the church. The grave stones have been much disturbed and scattered about, by these proceedings; they were mostly head-stones, some of them looking very old, but none that were legible were much over a hundred years old. The church-yard was very small, and surrounded by a gray stone fence, that looked as old as the church itself. On the outside of this fence, in front of the tower, was an elm of great circumference; and the children soon found out that it was hollow, and had opening large enough to admit them; so they both got in, and peeped forth at me with great delight. Examining it more closely, I found that there would have been room enough for me, too;—the whole trunk of the tree being a cavity, open to the sky at considerable height overhead. Besides the door into which the children had clambered, there was another opening that served for a window; and though its wooden heart was quite decayed and gone, the foliage of the tree was just as luxuriant as if it had been sound; and its great roots caught hold of the earth like gigantic claws, and, by their knots and knuckles, had doubtless afforded seats to the inhabitants, in summer evenings, and other idle times, from time immemorial.[28] The little, rustic square of the hamlet lay in front and around the church, with all the cottage-doors opening into it—all visible and familiar to one another; and I never had such an impression of smugness, homeliness, neighborliness—of a place where everybody had known everybody, and forefathers and foremothers had grown up together, and spent whole successions of lives, and died, and been buried under the same sods, so closely and conveniently at hand—the same family names, the same family features, repeated from generation to generation—as in this small village nook. And under that gray church-portal, no doubt, young people had sat at midnight on mid-summer eve, to see who among their neighbors—whose apparitions—would pass into the church, because they were to die that year. And, long ago, mass had been said there; and the holy water had stood at the door. It is rather wearisome, to an American, to think of a place where no change comes for centuries, and where a peasant does but step into his father's shoes, and lead just his father's life, going in and out over the old threshold, and finally being buried close by his father's grave, time without end; and yet it is rather pleasant to know that such things are.

I saw no public house in the village; there was a little shop, kept by an old woman, with papers of pins, cheap crockery, and other small matters, displayed in the window, where also I saw a wood engraving of the church (St. Margaret's, Whitnash) on a sheet of note-paper, to be sold towards paying the expenses of rebuilding the chancel. I bought six pence worth. Just out of the heart of the village, there was a tailor's sign over a cottage door. Probably there is no family of note or estate having its pew and place of worship in this church. The shadowiness and seclusion among the trees—and yet admitting sunshine into its little heart—is essential to the idea of this village. On our way home, we took a by-path that led to Leamington through the fields, and met a gentleman, evidently clerical, who probably was the village-pastor. He seemed a staid, starched man, very conscious of being a priest.[29]

If it *was* the vicar that Nathaniel and the children met, then the gentleman in question was the Reverend James Reynolds Young who, in 1851, had called upon the services of the architect, Gilbert Scott, to inspect and report on the condition of the church's chancel. Mr. Scott had recommended that a complete reconstruction was necessary and it was on 28 May, only a few weeks previous to the Hawthornes' first sight of the church, that the work of pulling down the old chancel had commenced, Holy Communion having been celebrated in it for the last time the day before. *The Royal Leamington Spa Courier* covered the occasion and confirmed in its edition of 2 June much of what Nathaniel had felt regarding the antiquity and simplicity of the area and its inhabitants:

> The Parish Church.
> The Church of this little village was, on Sunday last, the scene of the celebration of a service which will long be remembered by those who were privileged to share in it. Whitnash is a picturesque village of 300 inhabitants, one mile from Leamington, and the Rev. J. R. Young is the first resident Rector for 300 years. The state of things ecclesiastical may be imagined. Churchwarden improvements had been made from time to time; as a specimen we may mention the vestry, which occupied a *fourth of the chancel,* formed by a *canvass screen, painted to imitate stone;* it was aptly described in the transition style, something between a meat safe and a handbox. Towering above, under a semicircular hole, which did duty for a chancel arch, in a wall of lath and plaster, stood the pulpit, which was entered through the desk. The Rector has effected many improvements. The Hon. and Rev. S. W. Lawley has given a handsome font, in lieu of the little basin formerly used. Lord Leigh has given new oak for the roof. A stained glass window, altar table of oak, and other special donations, have been given by friends. In addition to the usual morning and afternoon service there was a third service at eight o'clock. A touching and impressive sermon was preached by the Rector to his people on their meeting for solemn worship for the last time in the old chancel, and the holy communion was administered to 50 communicants. The choir is composed of village labourers, who sang the Sanctus in its proper place in the communion office, and very sweetly and solemnly it sounded on Whit Sunday night. The chancel was brightly lighted, and decorated with evergreens, with a cross in the centre. All present appeared to be deeply impressed with the solemnity of the service in which they were engaged. The chancel restoration will fall heavy on the Rector, and there are none in the village to assist except farmers and labourers, still it is hoped the rest of the church will some day be restored.[30]

Sunday, 24 June, appears to have been a complete day of rest in all respects as there is no mention of any activities undertaken by the family. The Hawthornes were Unitarians so they might have had a little difficulty in deciding which church to attend in Leamington, if they were so minded. Disregarding the parish church of All Saints and the Roman Catholic chapel of St. Peter's, they could have tried any one out of the Episcopal Chapel at the top of the Parade, the other Episcopal Chapel at the far end of Regent Street on the road to Warwick, the Wesleyan Chapel in Portland Street, the Independent Chapel in Spencer Street, or the Congregational Chapel in Brandon Parade, Holly Walk. Plenty of choice, but without knowledge of the standard of the sermons given in the different places of worship, it is probable that the Hawthornes stayed at home. One wonders what they all did throughout the day; whatever it was, it was not considered important enough to mention in diaries or journals as Nathaniel's next entry, for example, was not made until the following Tuesday and made no mention of the Sabbath at all.

On Monday, however, it was considered time to visit Warwick (though still without the ailing Sophia):

[Today] forenoon, Una, Julian and I walked to Warwick, which is not above two miles from Leamington. We had hardly left the latter place, before two turrets of the castle, with trees rising high towards their summit, appeared in view; and likewise the tall tower of Saint Mary's Church. As we approached the town, we began to see antique houses: and near the beginning of the main street, we passed a venerable school-house (St. John's School, I think it was called) a stone edifice, with a wide enclosure before it, surrounded by a high, antique fence.[31] The front of the building had four gables in a row; and there was a large open porch, with seats under it. In the rear, the edifice seemed to be spacious, and adapted for domestic accommodation of the masters and scholars. It was striking to see a venerable house devoted to the youthful—to think how this old gray front had witnessed the sport of generations that had long ago grown decrepit and vanished. There was ivy on the wall of the playground and also here and there on the edifice itself. But I find it is getting to be quite a common-place—this description of old, ivied and lichen-stained walls. It is entirely American; the English (unless antiquaries) care nothing about a thing merely on account of its being old, and perhaps would rather see a house just erected, than one built a thousand years ago. And when one sees how much antiquity there is left, everywhere about England, and reflects how it may stand in the way of improvement, it is no great wonder that they should laugh at our estimate of it. An old thing is no better than a new thing, unless it be a symbol of something, or have some value in itself.

There are a good many modern houses in Warwick, and some of them handsome residences. It seems to be the fashion, now-a-days, to imitate the Elizabethan or some other old style of architecture; and the effect is good—only nobody seems to be building a house in real earnest, to live and die in, but rather as a sort of plaything. We are likely to leave no fashions for another age to copy, when we shall have become an antiquity. Getting further into the heart of the town, the old houses become more numerous;[32] and I think Chester itself can hardly show such quaint architectural shapes as these;—such bowed, decrepit ridge-poles—such patched walls, such a multiplicity of peaked gables, such curious windows, some opening on the roofs, and set in their own little gables almost all opening lattice-wise, and furnished with twenty panes of glass, where one would suffice in a modern window. The style of visible oaken frame-work, showing the whole skeleton of the house (as if a man's bones should be arranged on the outside, with his flesh showing through the interstices) was prevalent. Some houses of this order were in perfect repair, and very spacious, and even stately, and probably presented quite adequate specimens of the aspect of the town, when this style was modern.

About the centre of the town, we saw an arched gate way, with a church of [*sic*] it, standing across the street; and this, I think, was the most ancient-looking and picturesque portion of Warwick—all the adjacent houses being mediaeval, and evidently the abodes of old gentility; also, in near vicinity, there were public edifices of long ago.[33] As we approached, we saw soldiers marching up the main-street, and turning a corner;[34] and soon afterwards, when we found our way to the market-place, it was quite filled by a regiment, which was going through the drill. I suspect they were not regular soldiers, but a regiment of the Warwickshire Militia, commanded, I suppose, by the earl. They were young men of healthy aspect, and looked very well in a body, but individually had little of the soldier's mien—slouching into yeomanlike carriage and manners, as soon as dismissed. Their uniform was a red short-jacket and blue pantaloons. I saw an officer dressed in blue, and wearing embroidered on his collar the Warwick cognizance—the bear and ragged staff. The regiment being dismissed from drill, we afterwards saw squads of soldiers everywhere about the streets, and sentinels posted here and there, perhaps before officers' quarters; and I saw one sergeant, with a great key in his hand (which might be a key of Warwick Castle) apparently setting a guard. Thus, centuries after feudal times have past, we find warriors still clustering under the old castle-walls, and under the command of the feudal lord. In the days of the Kingmaker, no doubt he often mustered his troops in the same market-place where we found this regiment.

Not far from the market-place stands the great church of St. Mary's—a huge church indeed, and almost worthy to be a cathedral. It is said not to be in any good and pure style of architecture, though designed by Sir Christopher Wren; but I thought it very striking, with its great, elaborate windows, its immense length, its tall towers, and a gray antiquity over the whole. While we stood gazing up at the tower, the clock struck twelve, with a very deep voice; and immediately some chimes began to play, and kept up their music for five minutes. This was very pleasant, and seemed not unworthy of the huge church; although I have seen old-fashioned parlor-clocks that did just the same thing. We rambled round the town, finding old churches and other old matters everywhere, and wondering that the little children should look new, like other children, seeing they had come into existence under such old circumstances. We did, however, see one fresh, ruddy-cheeked, smiling urchin, who might have been taken for the child of a by-gone century; he was dressed in a collarless, wide skirted coat, and salmon colored breeches, and was probably a scholar of a charity-school in town.

The irregularity of old towns and villages is one of their most striking peculiarities. There is nothing square about them, and no street seems to have reference to any other street; and this absence of plan—this evident fact that the town has made itself, growing according to its necessities, from age to age—produces an effect worth all that science could do. There is a constant unexpectedness; and even after one is familiar with the twists and turns, I should think it never could grow tame. Now as regards modern Leamington (though certainly a handsome town, and with many edifices which you perceive to be beautiful, when you force your attention to them) its streets soon get wearisome; and to have seen one, and only once, is as good as seeing all a thousand times. We left Warwick in the omnibus at one; not intending this as anything more than an exploratory visit, and meaning to return with Mamma, and see the castle, and the interiors of churches, and many other things now left unnoticed. In about half an hour, we were at our lodging house.[35]

Probably by this time the children had had enough of walking and sightseeing for one day and were happy to stay at home and tell Sophia, Rose, and

Fanny all that they had seen, but Nathaniel was made of sterner stuff and went out again, this time taking a southeasterly course along the Southam (London) road:

> In the afternoon, I took a walk by myself to the village of Radford; a village of the customary thatched roof, timber-framed cottages, very bowery and green-grassy. Most of these cottages stood alone, with its own little precincts about it; and this was much more agreeable to look at than the plan of several homesteads under one long roof. The doors of many of the houses were open, affording views of the stone or brick-floored kitchen, with its homely furniture. A man was repairing the thatch of one of the cottages with new straw, and scraping away the dust and dirt of ages from the part of the roof where the old thatch had been. Passing through this village, I turned aside into a path that led across fields, expecting that it would bring me into the same road by which I had left Leamington. But, instead of this, the path led me through various gates, and over stiles, and along cart-tracks, and once across a broad ploughed field, where it threatened to become quite trackless (but still remained a path) until suddenly it came out directly behind the little old church of Whitnash, whither the children and I wandered the other day. Stopping to look at the tower, I saw that, at each extremity of the arched mullion (if that be the proper phrase) over the great window, above the portal, there was a sculptured stone-face, very perfectly preserved. It shows how a general impression overcomes minor details, that—whereas, at my former visit, I saw nothing but old dwellings, and recorded that there were no others—I now found that there were several new brick cottages and outhouses in the village, directly in front of the church—and very ugly ones too, though they seemed to be built after the plan of old cottages, and perhaps were merely renewals of them. But their cold, meagre, and indeed ugly aspect (uglier than almost anything in an American village) showed how necessary is the mural ivy and moss of antiquity to make these dwellings pleasant to the eye.[36]

It appears that the walk to Radford (Semele) did not greatly excite Nathaniel. The village lies a mile or so outside the boundaries of Leamington and the walk to it remains pleasant enough as, on one side of the road at least, there has been little real encroachment by suburbia since the 1850s. He could hardly have failed to notice the Warwick and Napton Canal and the (now disused and much overgrown) cutting of the Rugby and Leamington branch of the L & N.W. Railway, both of which the road crossed, or the very adjacent part-Jacobean Radford Hall or St. Nicholas's church that stood back across some open fields. Perhaps if he had read his guidebook he might have noted that the church still retained a small window of twelfth-century origin and some fourteenth-century remains in the porch; but then again, he might already have been tired of noting such things. Otherwise, little remains today in the village that Nathaniel would recognize, though the path which, inadvertently, he took across the fields on the way back to Leamington is still in existence, due to its being a public footpath.

The next day, Tuesday, was another blank in the sightseeing calendar as no mention can be found of any worthwhile expedition having been made from Lansdowne Crescent. Both Una and Sophia were to mention subse-

	Varieties		£ s	d
20	2 brushes Rose & Julian	...	4	6
	Ink			3
	Postage stamps		3 .	4
	Leads for Una's Pencil			6
	Shoes 5/			
	To Porters for fetching Piano		2	
	Belt for Una		2	
	Toothbrush for Julian		1	
	Bugles			6
	Reels of cotton 2			4
	Envelopes, note paper			
	wafers		1	6
	Fanny paid for me			10
	Guide		1	6
	Illustrated news			6
	Note paper			6
	Cab from Warwick		1	6
27	Phaeton to Stratford		17	6
	Books & pictures bought in			
	Shakspere's birth room		4	8
	Fee to the portress		1	

quently in letters to America that while they were in Leamington the weather was very good indeed, but perhaps it was considered that a little local perambulation would be sufficient for the time being; certainly it does appear that weather conditions and an apparent improvement in Sophia's health were such that it was considered safe for her to brave the elements as there is an entry in the Accounts Book for 26 June to the effect that a wheelchair was hired "for an hour's excursion" so it is more than likely that she was well wrapped up and pulled up and down the Parade for a bit of fresh air and excitement. Apart from the delights of window-shopping or the visiting of a bookshop or two (perhaps for Nathaniel to surreptitiously check on his popularity with Leamington's reading public), there was not all that much going on in the town that day that could have been classed as entertainment. They could have attended the second day of the auction of the entire contents of Stanhope Villa, Wellington Street, where "costly and valuable household furniture and other effects" were up for sale; or looked in at the auction of some of the stock of the late Mr. John Stafford, wine merchant, at the rear of No. 8 Victoria Terrace where the public might sample and bid for any of the 300 dozen of 1847 and 1851 port, "fruity, full of colour, and dry" or the seventy dozen of pale sherry, "very superior, First Class." But it is unlikely that either of these events would have attracted their interest. Possibly slightly more calculated to have gained their attention would have been a visit to the first day of the four-day chess festival being held by the Northern and Midland Counties Chess Association in the Public Hall, Windsor Street, at which the president, Lord Lyttelton, welcomed the "throng of distinguished players and visitors," those who could "appreciate the higher sources of pleasure and amusement with which the cultivated mind ever finds fellowship and communion." This first day was one on which the local club was reported to have "gained fresh laurels" in its performance against the Birmingham and Edgbaston club, though the phrase might not readily be taken as confirmation that Leamington had won! But with their mother in a wheelchair, none of these events is likely to have attracted the family's undivided attention. Nor would they have been interested in rounding off the day by paying a visit to the Theatre Royal in Clemens Street where a performance of Balfe's operetta, *Bohemian Girl,* was to be given that evening by the English Opera Company.

Whether or not the family purposely took a day off on 26 June, the morrow turned out to be something special. As Julian's birthday treat of the previous week, that of a visit to Stratford-upon-Avon, had had to be postponed due to his illness, it was decided that the trip would be put off no longer. The morning's weather was promising and after arrangements for hiring a phaeton had been made (costing 17s.6d.) the family set out, Sophia apparently being well enough to accompany them this time but Rose was left behind (once again) with Fanny.

Leamington

—	Luncheon at the Red Horse	6	
—	Fee to the waiter		6
—	Toys for baby		6
—	Gloves for Julian		9½
—	Fee to Beadle of the Holy Trinity — (Shakspere's burial place)	3	
—	Fee to old man		6
—	Bounty to driver for ale		6
	For a glass of very bad warm water at Warwick		4
26	An hour's excursion in Bath chair	1	
27	Note paper & envelopes	1	1
29	Excursion to Coventry	2	
	Illustrated news		
	Morning Post		
	Luncheon		
	Toys		4
	Cloth	9	
	Shoes 2 pairs	9	
	Bath for Mrs	1	
	" " Julian	1	

This day promising to be a very fair one, we devoted it to our pilgrimage to Stratford-on-Avon; and Mamma, Una, Julian, and I, set out in a phaeton, at about ½ past 9. It was really a bright morning, warm, genial and delightful; so that we saw English scenery under almost an American sun, and the combination made something very like perfection. Our road lay through Warwick; and I observed on the wall of an old chapel in the High-street, some fox-glove flowers growing, as also grass and little shrubs, all at the height of perhaps twenty feet above the ground. Adjacent to this chapel (which stands almost across the street, with an archway for foot passengers beneath it, and causing the carriage track to swerve aside in passing it) there is an ancient edifice, in excellent repair, and with coats of arms and the cognizance of the Bear and Ragged Staff painted on its front. This turns out to be Leicester's Hospital, an institution for the support of twelve poor brethren; and I think we saw the better part of a dozen old faces, idly contemplating us from the windows or about the doors of the old house. I must try to get a better knowledge of this institution.

The road from Warwick to Stratford is most beautiful; not that it owes any remarkable features to Nature; for the country thereabouts is a succession of the gentlest swells and subsidences, here and there affording wide and far glimpses of champagne [champaign?] scenery; and near Stratford it becomes quite level. Altogether, throwing in a few higher hills, and opening the eye of the scene, here and there, by a sheet of water, like Waldenpond, it would look a good deal like the country near Concord—so far as its natural features are concerned. But the charm of the English scene is its old and high cultivation, its richness of verdure, its stately trees, with their trunks clustered about by creeping shrubs;—a great deal of which man has done, and in which he could be partly rivalled in America; but much, too, is due to the moisture of the climate, and the gentle sunshine. At any rate, the effect is beyond all description, and seen, as I have just said, under an American sun (that is to say, once or twice a year) nothing more could be asked by mortals, in the way of rural beauty. All along the way, there were cottages of old date, many so old that Shakespeare might have passed them in his walks, or entered their low doors; a few modern villas, too; and perhaps mansions of gentility or nobility hidden among the trees—for such houses seldom show themselves from the road.

There is nothing remarkable in the approach to Stratford. The spire of Shakespeare's church shows itself among the trees, at a little distance from the town. Then come shabby old houses, intermixed with more modern ones, mostly mean-looking; and the streets being quite level, the effect on the whole is tame and quite unpicturesque. I think I might ride into such a town, even in America, and not be much struck by many peculiarities. Here and there, however, there are very queer dwellings, that seem to have been growing queerer and odder during the three or four centuries of their existence; and there appear to be more old people, tottering about and leaning on sticks—old people in breeches, and retaining all the traditional costume of the last century—than could be found anywhere on our side of the water. Old places seem to produce old people; or perhaps the secret is, that old age has a natural tendency to hide itself, when it is brought into contact with new edifices, and new things, but comes freely out, and feels itself in sympathy, and is not ashamed to face the eye of man, in a decaying town. There is a sense of propriety in this.

We stopt at the Red Lion, a hotel of no great pretensions and immediately set out on our rambles about town. After wandering through two or three streets, we found Shakespeare's birth-place, which is almost a worse house than anybody could dream it to be; but it did not surprise me, because I had seen a full-sized facsimile of it in the Zoological gardens at Liverpool. It is exceedingly small—at least, the portion of it which had anything to do with Shakespeare. The old, worn, butcher's counter, on which the meat used to be laid, is still at the window. The upper half of the door was open; and on my rapping at it, a girl dressed in black soon made her appearance and opened it. She was a ladylike girl, not a menial, but I suppose the daughter of the old lady who shows the house. This first room has a pavement of gray slabs of stone, which, no doubt, were rudely squared when the house was new, but they are all cracked and broken, now, in a curious way. One does not see how any ordinary usage, for whatever length of time, should have cracked them thus; it is as if the devil had been stamping on them, long ago, with an iron hoof, and the tread of other persons had ever since been reducing them to an even surface again. The room is white-washed, and very clean, but woefully shabby and dingy, coarsely built, and such as is not very easy to idealize. In the rear of this room is the kitchen, a still smaller room, of the same dingy character; it has a great, rough fire-place, with an immense passage way for the smoke, and room for a large family under the blackened opening of the chimney. I stood under it, without stooping; and doubtless Shakespeare may have stood on the same spot, both as a child and man. A great fire might of course make the kitchen cheerful; but it gives a depressing idea of the humble, mean, sombre character of the life that could have been led in such a dwelling as this—with no conveniences, all higgledy-piggledy, no retirement, the whole family, old and young, brought into too close contact to be comfortable together. To be sure, they say the house used to be much larger than now, in Shakespeare's time; but what we see of it is consistent in itself, and does not look as if it ever could have been a portion of a large respectable house.

Thence we proceeded upstairs to the room in which Shakespeare is supposed to have been born, and which is over the front lower room, or butcher's shop. It has one broad window, with old irregular panes of glass; the floor is of very rudely hewn planks; the naked beams and rafters at the sides and over head bear all the marks of the builder's axe; and the room, besides, is very small—a circumstance more difficult to reconcile one'self [sic] to, as regards places that we have heard and thought much about, than any other part of a mistaken ideal. I could easily touch the ceiling, and could have done so had it been a good deal higher; indeed, the ceiling was entirely written over with names in pencil, by persons, I suppose, of all varieties of stature; so was every inch of the wall, into the obscurest nooks and corners; so was every pane of glass—and Walter Scott's name was said to be on one of the panes; but so many people had sought to immortalize themselves in close vicinity to him, that I really could not trace out his signature. I did not write my own name.

This room, and the whole house, so far as I saw it, was white-washed and very clean; and it had not the aged, musty smell, with which Chester makes one familiar, and which I suspect is natural to old houses, and must render them unwholesome. The woman who showed us upstairs had the manners and aspect of a gentlewoman, and talked intelligently about Shakespeare. Arranged on a table and in chairs, there were various prints, views of houses and scenes connected with Shakespeare's memory, editions of his works, and local publications relative to him—all for sale, and from which, no doubt, this old gentlewoman realizes a good deal of profit. We bought several shillings' worth, partly as thinking it the civilest method of requiting her for the trouble of shewing the house. On taking our leave, I most ungenerously imposed on Sophia the duty of offering an additional fee to the lady like girl who first admitted us; but there seemed to be no scruple, on her part, as to accepting it. I felt no emotion whatever in Shakespeare's house—not the slightest—nor any quickening of the imagination. It is agreeable enough to reflect that I have seen it; and I think I can form, now, a more sensible and vivid idea of him as a flesh-and-blood man; but I am not quite sure that this latter effect is altogether desirable.[37]

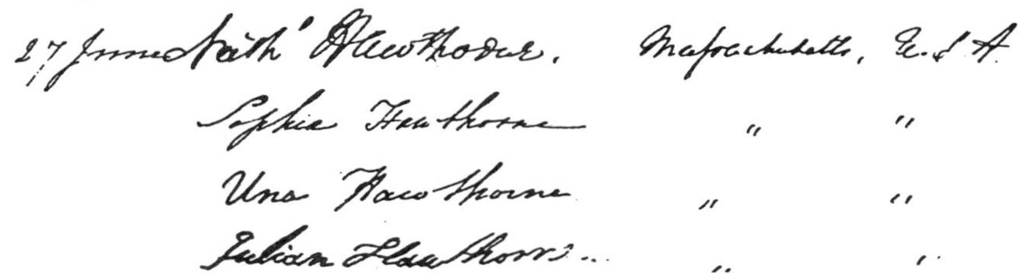

[handwritten signatures:]

27 June Faith Hawthorne,   Massachusetts, U.S.A.

Sophia Hawthorne   "   "

Una Hawthorne   "   "

Julian Hawthorne   "   "

From Shakespeare's house (after doing a little shopping and buying some toys for Rosebud) we inquired out the church—the Church of the Holy Trinity—where he lies buried. The aspect of the edifice, as we approached it, was venerable and beautiful, with a great green shadow of trees about it, and the Gothic architecture and vast arched windows obscurely seen above and among the boughs. An old man in small clothes was waiting at the gate of the church-yard; he inquired whether we wished to go in, and preceded us to the church-porch and rapped— all which we could have done quite as well ourselves; but, it seems, the old men of the vicinity haunt about the churchyard, to pick up a half-elemosyanary [sic] sixpence from the visitors. We were admitted into the church by a respectable-looking man in black, who was already exhibiting the Shakespeare monuments to two or three visitors; and other parties came in while we were there. The poet and his family seem to have the best burial-places that the church affords—or, at least, as good as any. They lie in a row, right across the breadth of the chancel, the foot of each gravestone being close to the elevated floor about the altar. Nearest to the side wall, beneath Shakespeare's bust, is the slab of stone bearing an inscrip-tion to his wife; then his own, with the old anathematizing stanza upon it; then, I think, the stone of Thomas Nash, who married his granddaughter; then that of Dr. Hall, the husband of his daughter Susannah; then Susannah's own. Shake-speare's grave stone is the commonest looking slab of all, just such a flag-stone as a side-walk of the street might be paved with. Unlike the other monuments of the family, it has no name whatever upon it; and I do not see on what authority it is absolutely determined to be his. To be sure, being in a range with his wife and children, it might naturally be guessed that it was his; but then he had another daughter, and a son, who would need a grave somewhere. Perhaps, however, as his name was on the bust, above, and as his wife, when he was buried, had not yet taken her place between him and the church-wall, his name was thought unnecessary. Fifteen or twenty feet behind this row of grave-stones is the great east-window of the Church, now brilliant with stained glass, of recent manufacture; and one side of this window, under an arch of marble, lies a full length marble figure of Shakespeare's friend John a Combe, dressed in what I take to be a robe of municipal dignity, and with his hands devoutly clasped—a sturdy English figure of a man, with coarse features. There are other mural monuments and altar-tombs in the chancel; but methinks one who cared about a monument would rather not have it overshadowed by Shakespeare's.

Now, as for the bust of Shakespeare, it is affixed to the northern wall of the church, the base of it being about a man's height (or more) above the floor of the chancel. The bust is quite unlike any portrait, or any other bust of Shakespeare, that I have ever seen, and compels me to root up all old ideas of his aspect, and adopt an entirely different one. For my part, I am loth to give up the beautiful, lofty-browed, noble picture of him which I have hitherto had in my mind; for this bust does not represent a beautiful face or a noble head. And yet it clutches hold of one's sense of reality, and you feel that this was the man. I don't know what the phrenologists say to this bust; its forehead is but moderately developed, and retreats somewhat; the upper part of the skull seems rather contracted; the eyes are rather prominent. The upper lip is so long that it must have been almost a deformity; the showman of the church said that Sir Walter Scott's upper lip was longer, but I doubt it. On the whole, Shakespeare must have had a singular, rather than a striking face; and it is wonderful how, with this bust before its eyes, the world has insisted on forming an erroneous idea of his appearance, permitting painters and sculptors to foist their idealized nonsense upon mankind, instead of the genuine Shakespeare. But as for myself, I am henceforth to see in my mind's eye a red-faced personage, with a moderately capacious brow, an intelligent eye, a nose curved very slightly outward, a long, queer upper lip, with the mouth a little unclosed beneath it, and cheeks very much developed in the lower part of the face. Sophia (when the sexton and other visitors were in a distant part of the church) seized the opportunity to clamber upon a nameless, oblong, cubic tomb, supposed to be that of a collegiate dignitary of the fourteenth century; she thus gained a near profile view of the bust.[38] Afterwards we saw two identical casts from it, and made the observations above recorded. As to the length of the upperlip, it is possible that the sculptor exaggerated it, in consideration that it was to be viewed from below, and thus would be foreshortened to the proper proportions.

In a side-chapel of the church, we saw a monument of a certain Clopton Esquire, and his wife, with their figures at full length upon it—he in armor, and she in stately robes. The material seemed to be some kind of marble, but so highly polished that it looked like china, and was in excellent preservation;—excellently well manufactured, too. There was another monument, or two, to members of the same family, I believe, after it had been ennobled. The race is now extinct; and the sexton told us that interments have ceased to take place in any part of the church. This may be well; but it adds greatly to the impressiveness of a church to see it adorned with these mortuary memorials. We had now done one of the things that an American proposes to himself as necessarily and chiefly to be done, on coming to England. Leaving the church, we walked about the church-yard, and at last sat down on the border of it, over the river, while the children and mamma ate each an orange. The Avon is a narrow and exceedingly sluggish river, with flags along its banks, and here and there some beautiful forget-me-nots growing among the flags, but quite out of reach from the banks. I do not know an American river so tame; in fact we have no river of just that size, or smallness;—if not bigger, it would be rather less, either a river or a brook. It is very lazy, and by no means pellucid; and it loiters past Stratford Church as if it had been considering which way to flow, ever since Shakespeare used to paddle in it. Most of the grave-stones in the church-yard are modern.

From the church we went back to the hotel,[39] and there got a luncheon of cold lamb, cold ham, and Stratford ale, which does not seem to me a very good brew-age. We then took leave of Stratford, directing the driver to pass by the grammar-school where Shakespeare was supposed (for his whole biography has nothing more tangible than suppositions, and more or less probabilities) to have been educated. Our road back to Leamington was different from that which we came, and took us past Charlecote Hall, the description of which (being very tired of this present writing) I must leave till another opportunity [the description of the journey home was not recorded until two days later].

I should have done better to have continued my narrative, and described Charlecote forthwith; for the hues of a recollection fade as quickly as the colors of a
dead dolphin. As we passed Charlecote Park, we saw the most stately elms, singly,
in clumps, and in groves, scattered all about, in the sunniest, sleepiest, shadiest
fashion—trees, all of which were civilized, all known to man, and befriended by
him, for ages past; not portions of wild nature, like our trees. There is an indescribable difference between this tamed, but by no means effete (on the contrary more
luxuriant) Nature of England, and the shaggy and barbarous Nature of America.
By and by, among the trees, we saw a large herd of deer, mostly reclining, some
standing in picturesque attitudes—some running fleetly about, with here and there
a little faun at its mother's heels. I never saw anything so like a picture; so
perfectly fulfilling one's idea as this scene of an old English park. I thought so
before I saw the deer, and they came in as all that was wanted to make it perfect—
the want, too, not being felt till it was supplied. And these deer are in the same
relation to their wild, natural state, that the trees are; they are not domesticated,
not tamed, but yet how unlike forest-deer. They have held a certain intercourse
with man for immemorial years;—very likely, the deer that Shakespeare killed
was one of the progenitors of this very herd, and that deer was himself a humanized
deer, like these. They are, perhaps, a good deal wilder than sheep; but still they
do not snuff the air on the approach of human beings, nor feel alarmed at their
pretty near proximity; although they toss their heads and take to their heels, in a
kind of mimic terror, or something like feminine skittishness, with a dim remembrance or tradition, as it were, of their having come of a wild race. But they have
been fed and protected by man, ever since England had its institutions; and, I
suppose, now, they could hardly get through a winter without human help. One
rather despises them for this, but loves them too; and I think it was this partially
domesticated state of the Charlecote deer that may have suggested to Shakespeare
the tender and pitiful description of a wounded deer, in As You Like It.[40]

Arriving at the gate of the park, near the house, we alighted and went in; for
the Lucies [the owners] seem to be a kindly race of people, and do not throw any
unreasonable obstacles in the way of curious tourists. The house, however, cannot
be seen within, during the absence of the family (as was the case now) but we
seemed to be at liberty to view on all attainable sides; and so we did. Before the
front entrance, at the distance of some hundreds of yards, and almost hidden from
passers-by by many trees between, is an old brick archway and porter's lodge,
very venerable; and there appears to have been a wall and a moat in connection
with this—the moat being still visible, a shallow, grassy scoop along at the base
of an embankment of the lawn. Within this gateway, fifty yards off, perhaps, stands
the house, forming, on this side, three sides of a square, surrounding a green
ornamented space. Peaked gables, three in a row, one on each of three sides; and
there are several towers of quaint shape at different parts and angles of the house.
All is in perfect repair, and there seem to have been large recent additions, which
do not shock one by any incongruity. Over the gate way is the Lucy coat-of-arms,
emblazoned in its proper colors. The impression is not of gray antiquity, but of
stable and time-honored gentility, still as vital as ever. The mansion, I believe, was
built in the early days of Elizabeth; and probably looked very much the same as
now, when Shakespeare was brought before Sir Thomas Lucy for deer-stealing.[41]
All about the house, and the park, however, there is a perfection of comfort and
domestic taste, and an amplitude of convenience, which it must have taken ages,
and the thoughts of many successive generations, intent upon adding all possible
household charm to the house which they loved, to produce. It is only so that real
homes can be produced; one man's life is not enough for it; especially when he

feels that he is probably making his house warm and delightful for a miscellaneous race of successors none of whom are likely to be of his blood. Looking at this estate, it seemed very possible for those who inherit it, and the many in England similar to it, to lead noble and beautiful lives, quietly doing good and lovely things, and deeds of simple greatness, should circumstances require such. Why should not the ideal of humanity grow up, like ideal trees, amid such soil and culture. I do not know anything about the private character of the Lucies; but I feel inclined to think well of them, from merely looking at their abode. Yet most of the aristocracy of England have as good or better.

Between the gateway and the church (only at a short distance, standing on the border of the Park) is an avenue of ancient elms, with a shadowy path only partially traced among the grass, running beneath. The church is new; the old one, if I mistake not, having recently been taken down. Much has escaped me that should have gone into the above sketch of Charlecote Park, but the memory of it, and of the perfect day in which I saw it, is as beautiful as a dream. It seems to me there should have been a colony of rooks in the tree-tops of the churchward avenue.[42]

The weather continued fine for several days after this but it seems that the Stratford trip had temporarily blunted their appetite for further sightseeing as there is no record of anything having happened on Thursday. Perhaps a day at home was preferred (maybe Sophia needed a rest after the exertions of the previous day), quietly reading the papers; *The Leamington Advertiser* was published on Thursdays. There was not much taking place in town that was new; the chess congress was still going strong; in fact too strongly, for some of the matches that had been scheduled to be played and completed that day were still in progress by nightfall and the contestants involved had to miss the dinner that was held in the evening at the Regent Hotel, with Lord Lyttelton as chairman. The English Opera Company was still at the Theatre Royal, performing that evening Donizetti's *Fra Diavolo;* the management of the theater would have been glad to have seen the Hawthornes there as the week's performances were reported as having been given to "fashionable, but not very numerous, audiences."[43] Apparently there were no special festivities in the town to celebrate the fact that it was the seventeenth anniversary of Queen Victoria's coronation.

It may have been that day that Nathaniel received, via Liverpool, a letter from William Allingham, the Irish poet and customs official, who had visited him at the consulate in February of the previous year:

Ballyshanno, Ireland
25th June 55

Dear Sir,
I hope you will kindly receive the little volume of poems by me which I have told Mr. Routledge to send.

It would be a particular favour if you let me know to what papers & men in America it were best to send copies. Very slender are the compositions & I am in good truth ashamed of appearing to make much of them: but they have some good qualities, & are the best I could do, hitherto.

You will perhaps remember that when I called at your office I was on my way to London to write in newspapers etc, having resigned a situation in the Customs. I soon ascertained my total unfitness for that new manner of life, & being fortunate enough to obtain a reappointment to my former office, have been living in Ireland, very quietly, during the past year.

I have just received through the post Thoreau's 'Walden' & am hoping for that addition to life which a really new book gives. I like his Concord & Merrimack, though he seems to attitudinize just a little.

Do you know of Arthur Clough once of Oriel, Oxford, a little while of Massachusetts, & now of the Board of Education?[44] A friend of Emerson's he is, & a very excellent man, of most rare pattern.

I think of being in Liverpool next month, & hope for leave to call upon you.

I am, my dear Sir,
with much respect,
Sincerely yours,
W. Allingham

To N. Hawthorne Esq
P.S. A copy of my volume was addressed to Mr. Bright also, to whom pray present my compliments should the opportunity occur.[45]

The volume of poems referred to by Allingham was *Day and Night Songs;* his poetry, it could be said, was not of the highest quality but he had a certain reputation and his life was spent contentedly enough between not very onerous customs duties, writing, and fulfilling a surprisingly active social life that brought him into contact with many of the literary lions of those days. He became especially friendly with Tennyson, who on several occasions complimented him on his verse, but in the end all that he may be remembered by are the lines from *The Fairies:*

> Up the airy mountain
> Down the rushy glen
> We daren't go a-hunting
> For fear of little men.

Unfortunately, the book had not arrived as yet, but Nathaniel replied to the letter next morning:

Leamington June 29th 1855

My dear Sir,
Having spent a week or two at this place, your letter did not immediately come to hand. Mr. Routledge has not yet sent the volume of poems; but I thank you most sincerely for them, and shall read them, I am quite certain, with very great pleasure. I cannot, at this moment, particularize such American papers or personages as it would be desirable to send copies to; but if you will entrust me with a few (directed to me at the Consulate, Liverpool) I will send them to a friend [Ticknor] who will distribute them in the best manner for the author's fame. It would be well to write "With the author's compliments" on the fly-leaf; but this is not essential.

I (like yourself) have become weary of official duties, and intend to resign at no very distant period; but, in my case, there would be little hope of a re-appointment however much I might desire it. But it is a very irksome office; and I am heartily tired of it. During the few months that I may remain in this country, I shall spend much of the time away from Liverpool, but should I be there when you come, it will delight me to see you.

Very sincerely,
& Respectfully,
Nath¹ Hawthorne[46]

It is very surprising to find Nathaniel admitting to an almost total stranger that he was ready to give up his job as in several subsequent letters to close friends he was always careful to stress the confidential nature of his mentioning his intention to resign; though possibly the fact that both he and Allingham were government employees tended to make him feel that they were two of a kind with regard to dissatisfaction with their work. He would have been horrified to learn, if it had been possible to do so, that another eighteen months were to elapse before he actually tendered his letter of resignation and that he would not be able to quit the consulate for a further nine months after that!

However, having gotten the letter out of the way, it was considered time for the next excursion. On this occasion it was to be Sophia, Una, and Rose who were left behind.

[Today] I took rail at 10.55, with Julian, for Coventry; a bright and very warm day; oppressively so, indeed; though I think there is never, in this English climate, the pervading warmth of an American day. The sunshine may be intensely hot, but an overshadowing cloud, or the shade of a tree or building, at once affords relief; and if the slightest breeze stirs, you feel the latent freshness of the air.

Coventry is some nine or ten miles from Leamington. The approach to it, from the railway, presents nothing very striking—a few church-towers and one or two tall steeples; and the houses that first present themselves are of modern and unnoticeable aspect. Getting into the interior of the town, however, you find the streets very crooked, and some of them very narrow. I saw one place where it seemed possible to shake hands from one jutting-storied old house to another. There are whole streets of the same kind of houses (one story impending over another) that used to be familiar to me in Salem, and in some streets of Boston. In fact, the whole aspect of the town, its irregularity and continual indirectness, reminded me very much of Boston, as I used to see it in rare visits thither, when a child. These Coventry houses, however, many of them, are much larger than any of similar style that I have seen elsewhere, and spread into greater bulk as they ascend, by means of one other jutting story. Probably the New Englanders continued to follow this tradition of architecture after it had been abandoned in the mother-country. The old house built by Philip English, in Salem, dated not much earlier or later than 1692; and it was in this style, many gabled, and impending. Here, the edifices of such architecture seem to be Elizabethan, and earlier. A woman in Stratford told us that the rooms, very low on the ground floor, grow loftier from story to story, to the attic. The fashion of windows in Coventry is such as I have not hitherto seen. In the highest story, a window, of the ordinary height, extends along the whole breadth of the house—ten, fifteen, perhaps twenty feet—just like any other window of a common-place house, except for this inordinate width. One does not easily see what the inhabitants want of so much window-light; but the fashion is very general, and in modern houses, or houses that have been modernized, this style of window is retained. Thus young couples, who grow up amidst old people, contract quaint and old fashioned manners and aspects.

I imagine that these ancient towns—such as Chester, and Stratford, and War-wick and Coventry—contain even a great deal more antiquity than meets the eye. You see many modern fronts; but if you peep or penetrate inside, you see an antique arrangement, old rafters, intricate passages, ancient staircases, which have put on merely a new outside, and are likely still to prove good for the usual date of a new house. They put such an immense and stalwart ponderosity into their old frame-work, that I suppose a house of Elizabeth's time if renewed has at least an equal prospect of durability with a house new in every part. All the hotels in Coventry, so far as I noticed them, are old houses with new fronts; and they have an arch-way for the admission of vehicles &c into the courtyard, and doors, admitting into the rooms of the hotel, on each side of the arch. You see maids and waiters darting across the arched passage, from door to door, and it requires (in my case, at least) a guide to show you the way to bar or coffee-room. I have never been up-stairs, in any of them, but can conceive of infinite bewilderment of zig-zag passages, between staircase and chamber.

It was fair-day, in Coventry, and this gave what no doubt is an unusual bustle to the old streets. In fact, I have not seen such crowded and busy streets in any English town; various kinds of merchandise being for sale in the open air, and auctioneers disposing of miscellaneous wares, pretty much as they do at musters and other gatherings in the United States. The oratory of the American auctioneer, however, greatly surpasses that of the Englishman in vivacity and fun. But this movement and throng of the street, together with the white glow of the sun on the pavements, make the scene, in my recollection, assume more of an American aspect than any other that I have witnessed in sluggish England;—a strange effect, in so antique and quaint a town as Coventry.

We rambled about, without any definite object, but found our way, I believe, to most of the objects that are worth seeing. Saint Michael's Church seemed to me most magnificent—all that I could conceive of, in the matter of a church; so old, yet so enduring, so huge, so rich, with such intricate minuteness in its finish, that, look as long as you will at it, you can always discover something new directly before your eyes. I admire this in Gothic architecture—that you cannot master it all at once—that it is not a naked outline, but as deep and rich as human nature itself, always revealing new little ideas, and new large ones. It is as if the builder had built himself up in it, and his age, and as if the edifice had life. Grecian edifices are very uninteresting to me, being so cold and crystalline. I think this is the only church I have seen, where there are any statues still left standing in the niches of the steeple. We did not go inside of the church. The steeple of Saint Michael's is three hundred & three feet high; and no doubt the clouds often envelope the tip of the spire. Trinity, another church with a tall spire, stands near St Michael's, but did not attract me so much; though perhaps I might have equally admired it, had I seen it alone, or earliest. We certainly know nothing of church edifices in America; and of all English things that I have seen, methinks they are what disappoint me least. I feel, too, that there is something much more wonderful in them than I have yet had time to make myself know and experience.

In the course of the forenoon, poking about everywhere in quest of Gothic architecture, we found our way, I hardly know how, into St Mary's Hall. The door

Julian and Una Hawthorne. A daguerreotype of ca. 1853. Boston Athenaeum.

was wide open; it seemed to be a public affair; there was a notice on the wall, desiring visitors to give nothing to attendants for showing the hall; and so we walked in. I observe in the guide-book that we should have obtained an order for admission from some member of the Town Council; but we had none such, and found no need of it. An old woman, and afterwards an old man, both of whom seemed to be at home on the premises, told us that we might enter, and troubled neither themselves nor us any further.

St Mary's Hall is now the property of the corporation of Coventry, and seems to be the place where the Mayor and Council hold their meetings. It seems to have been built (early in Henry 6th's time) by one of the old guilds, or fraternities of merchants and tradesmen; and was the place where they held their annual feasts, and all their gatherings for pleasure and business;—being provided with kitchens and offices, and all conveniences for the exercise of public hospitality. The old woman shut the kitchen-door, when she saw me approaching; so that I did not see the great fire-place and huge cooking utensils which are said to be there. Whether these are ever used now-a-days—and whether the Mayor gives such hospitable banquets as the Mayor of Liverpool, I do not know.

I have forgotten all particulars about the exterior of the edifice, except that it looked exceeding venerable, and that I peeped into the basement (now used as a coal-cellar) and admired the massive stone arches, intersecting each other in all sorts of ways, on which the building rests. We passed up a black staircase, with an oaken balustrade, and entered the Great Hall, which is more than sixty feet long, and about half as wide, and, I should think, much more than half as high, from the floor to the angle of the roof. It has the original oaken roof, in shape like the roof of a barn, with all the beams and rafters visible; but carved, as the roof of barn never was nor will be, in beautiful style, with Gothic angels, and present-ing, no doubt, the old artist's idea of the sky. The whole space of the hall is unimpeded by a single column, and the roof supports itself with its proper strength. There were rows of benches (which I wished were away) on the floor of the room; and one side (on an elevated dais, if I mistake not) was an ancient Chair of State, looking very much like one of those old black settles which I have seen in America, and which are placed before the fire-place with the high back to the door, to keep off the wind. It was not so large as those to be sure, but would afford rather scanty accommodations for three persons; and is very straight, angular, and rigid in its make. Julian and I sat down in it, and did not know, till I read it in the Guide-Book, that English Kings and Queens (now heaps of dust for ages past) had sat there before us. I presume it was the old principle to manufacture chairs of state so that they should be as irksome and uncomfortable, physically, as they appear to be morally.

The great hall had an aged darkness diffused over its wood-work, and would have looked somewhat bare and lacking in adornment, but for a very large and magnificent arched-window at the northern end, full of old painted glass. It is in nine compartments, and represents the figures and coat-armories of many English monarchs. This window is very rich, and would be glorious no doubt, with the sun shining through it. There are also windows of modern stained glass, which I did not much notice. Another ornament (or what must once have been so) is a piece of ancient tapestry, ten feet high, beneath the great painted window, and extending across the whole breadth of the hall. In it are wrought King Henry the Sixth and his nobles, performing religious exercises, and above are saints, angels, and apostles, and Heaven itself; and the Deity was once there in person, but was long since taken out, and a figure of Justice sewed into the beatific vacuity. Julian says that the figures of Henry and his court are engraved in Markham's history of England. The whole is now so faded that the design is not readily discernible; the whole, in the sombre light of the hall, appearing almost of one neutral tint; but when the whole hall was covered with such rare tapestry, and all was glowing in its pristine freshness of color, and when the carving of the vaulted roof had not been so obscured by the darkening of the wood, it must have been such a chamber of state and festivity as modern times cannot show. There are full length pictures of English kings, from Charles II, downwards, hung up in the hall. At the southern end is a gallery for minstrels, and beneath it hang several suits of armor, with spears, pikes, and other such weapons; the armor has no brightness, being painted black, and probably was not intended for knights or persons of rank, but for men-at-arms in the pay and service of the city. We went to the Red lion, and had a luncheon of cold lamb and cold pigeon-pie. This is the best way of dining at English hotels—to call the meal a luncheon, in which case you will get as good or better a variety than if it were a dinner, and at less than half the cost. Having lunched, we again wandered about town, and entered a quadrangle of gabled houses, with a church, and its church-yard on one side. This proved to be St John's Church, and a part of the houses were the locality of Bond's Hospital, for the reception of ten poor men, and the remainder was devoted to the Bablake School. Into this latter I peered, with a real American intrusiveness, which I never found in myself before, but which I must now assume, or miss a great many things which I am anxious to see. Running along the front of the house, under the jut of the impending story, there was a cloistered walk, with windows opening on the quadrangle. An arched oaken door, with long iron hinges, admitted us into a school-room about twenty feet square, paved with brick tiles, blue and red. Adjoining this there is a larger school-room which we did not enter, but peeped at, through one of the inner windows, from the cloistered walk. In the room which we entered, there were seven scholars' desks, and an immense arched fireplace, with seats on each side, under the chimney, on a stone slab resting on a brick pedestal. The opening of the fireplace was at least twelve feet in width. On one side of the room were pegs for fifty-two boys' hats and clothes, and there was a boy's coat, of peculiar cut, hanging on a peg, with the number "50" in brass upon it. The coat looked ragged and shabby. An old school-book was lying on one of the desks, much tattered, and without a title; but it seemed to treat wholly of Saints' days and festivals of the Church. A flight of stairs, with a heavy balustrade of carved oak, ascended to a gallery, about eight or nine feet from the floor, which runs two sides of the room, looking down upon it. The room is without a ceiling, and rises into a peaked gable, about twenty feet high. There is a large clock on one side of the room, which is lighted by two windows, each about ten feet wide, one in the gallery, and the other beneath it. There were two benches, or settles with backs (on the plan of the Chair of State, only smaller and plainer) one on each side of the fireplace. An old woman in black passed through the room while I was making my observations, and looked at me, but said nothing. This school was founded in 1563 by Thomas Wheatley, Mayor of Coventry; the revenue is about £900, and admits children of the working classes at eleven years old, clothes and provides for them, and finally apprentices them for seven years. We saw some of the boys playing in the quadrangle, dressed in long blue coats or gowns, with cloth caps on their heads. I know not how the atmosphere of antiquity, and massive continuance from age to age, which was the charm to me in this scene of a charity school-room, can be thrown over it in the description. After noting down these matters, I peeped into the quiet precincts of Bond's Hospital, which, no doubt, was more than equally interesting; but the old men were lounging about, or lolling at length, looking very quiet and drowsy, and I had not the heart or the face to intrude among them. There is something altogether strange to an American in these charitable institutions—in the preservation of antique modes and customs which is effected by them; insomuch that, doubtless without at all intending it, the founders have succeeded in preserving a kind of model of their own long past age, down into the midst of ours, and how much later nobody can tell.

We were now rather tired and sated [especially Julian, one would imagine] (for old things, and old houses, and all sorts of antiquity, pall upon the taste, after a little while) and went to the railroad, intending to go home. We got into the wrong train, however, and were carried by express, with hurricane speed, to Brandon, where we alighted, and waited a good while for the return train to Coventry.

There, too, we had more than an hour to wait, and therefore wandered wearily up into the city again and took another look at its bustling old streets, in which there seems to be a good emblem of what England itself really is—with a great deal of antiquity in it, and what is new chiefly a modification of the old. The new things are based and supported on the sturdy old things, and often limited and impeded by them; but this antiquity is so massive that there seems to be no means of getting rid of it, without tearing the whole structure of society to pieces. We reached home between eight and nine;[47] and so ends this book [i.e., he had come to the end of one of the notebooks in which he wrote his journal].[48]

One imagines that the rest of the family were somewhat concerned at the lateness of the hour at which the two wanderers returned and that Julian, in particular, must have been very tired. But it didn't cool Nathaniel's enthusiasm one bit, for the next morning he was off again, this time on his own, tramping along the road to Warwick. He had run out of a supply of notebooks when he came to write up the day's happenings but eventually found some spare pieces of paper in the emergency:

Here are some fly-leaves, however; so I may as well write down (what would else probably be lost) my observations during a visit to Warwick [today]. I set out early in the forenoon, and walked thither, and passing Leicester's Hospital, at the end of the High-street, made bold to inspect it more closely. A small old stone church stands right above the street, compelling the latter to swerve aside in order to pass it; and there is also an arched passage-way (only for pedestrians, I think) through the foundations of the church. This foundation is very lofty; not less—probably more—than twenty feet; and weeds and foxgloves grow in the interstices of the stones, and wave above the street, the dust of which gives them soil to live in. This old gray church is the chapel of the brotherhood, and devoted to their religious services. The Hospital is adjacent to it, and consists of some old gabled edifices, in admirable repair, and ornamented with coats of arms, and devices, and with all the oaken beams of the frame-work nicely painted out—standing on one side of the street, on the same level with the chapel and surrounding a quadrangle. There were two or three of the brotherhood sitting sleepily on benches, and looking down on the street and whatever passed there—at me, among other objects. They said nothing, as I passed them, and after a moment's hesitation, entered an archway through the side of the front edifice, giving admission to the quadrangle within. An old woman happened to be crossing it, and I asked her whether it was permitted me to enter. She was a plain, neat old woman, who seemed to be in some position of care and superintendance [sic]. She told me very readily and civilly "Oh yes, Sir, you can come in"—and said I was free to look about me—hinting a hope, however, that I would not open the private doors of the brotherhood, as some visitors were in the habit of doing. Under her guidance, I looked into a very spacious, raftered, barn-like hall, in which was an inscription, stating that King James I had here been feasted, in old days. It looks now not very fit for the exercise of princely hospitality, with its naked walls, and, if I remember right, red brick floor; but I presume it may have looked splendidly with its old adornments. It is now used as a wash-room, and for such miscellaneous purposes as occur in a large establishment.
The old lady now left me to myself, and I returned to the quadrangle. It was very quiet, very handsome, and must be a comfortable place for the old people to lounge in, when inclement winds make it inexpedient to be elsewhere. Opposite

the arched entrance, the building rises into three ornamented gables; and along this front, a little above the level of the eye, were the following inscriptions— "Honor all men" "Love the Brotherhood"—"Fear God"—"Honor the King"— and over a door, at the side "He that ruleth over men must be just"—all in black letter. There are shrubs against the wall on one side; and on another is a cloistered walk, beneath a covered gallery, up to which leads a balustraded staircase. Three stags' heads and antlers are fastened up against the house, in the cloistered walk. (One inscription—very necessary to be observed among these idle old people— I forgot to set down—"Be kindly affectioned one to another".) Everywhere on the walls—over the windows and doors, and on every other place where the slightest reason for it, or no reason at all—were coats of arms, cognizances, and crests—especially the Bear and Ragged Staff was repeated over and over, and over again [it having been the emblem adopted by the 5th Earl of Warwick, Richard de Beauchamp, in the fifteenth century and used as a badge or crest by the successive families on whom the earldom devolved]. All these were emblazoned in their proper colors; and there was likewise a large image of a porcupine, on a heraldic wreath, and apparently the crest of a family. Certainly, the founder, or founders of this old charity seemed disposed to take all credit for their beneficence. The founder, originally, was Queen Elizabeth's Earl of Leicester; the hospital was intended for twelve poor men, native or inhabitants of Warwickshire or Gloucestershire, and must not possess more than £5 per annum of their own. They are to wear blue cloth gowns, with the bear and staff embroidered on them.

In the portion of the edifice opposite the entrance, is the residence of the master, a clergyman; and looking in at the window (as the old woman said I might) I saw a low, but exceedingly comfortable looking parlor, very handsomely furnished— a really luxurious place. It had an immense arched fire-place, with all its ancient breadth (extending almost across the room) but so fitted up in modern style that the coal-grate looked very diminutive in the midst. On the cloistered side of the quadrangle, through a curtained window, I saw a great blaze of what was doubtless the kitchen fire, and heard the bubbling and squeaking of something that was being cooked.

As I was about to depart, another old woman, very plainly dressed, but fat, comfortable, and with a cheerful twinkle in her eye, entered through the arch, and looked curiously at me. She asked me whether I wished to see the Hospital, and said that the porter was dead, and was to be buried that day; so that the whole could not conveniently be shown me. She offered, however, to show me the apartment occupied by herself and her husband; so we went up the antique staircase, and she led me into a small room, in the corner of the edifice, where sat an old man in a long blue garment, who arose and saluted me very civilly. They both seemed glad to have somebody to talk to; but, ever and anon, the old man nudged his wife—"Don't you be so talkative!" quoth he; and, indeed, he could hardly find space for a word. The old lady told me that they had their lodging and some other advantages free—I forget exactly what—but they appear to be placed, in some degree, on their individual responsibility. They carry on their household matters at their own pleasure, but can have their dinners cooked at the general kitchen, if they like; so that the immense old-fashioned cooking-establishment is probably used for frying, or stewing, or boiling, the humble and scanty messes which these poor people choose to provide for themselves. I must inquire further into this. The old woman told me that her husband had spent his life in the marines. She seemed far more alive, and doubtless enjoyed life a great deal more than he— partly, no doubt, because she has something to do, her little household matters to attend to, while he sits and mopes, and so has got all eaten up with rust;—not that he seemed miserable either. I mean to go to this Hospital again, and carry my wife. Afterwards, I went into a museum, chiefly of Natural History, but also

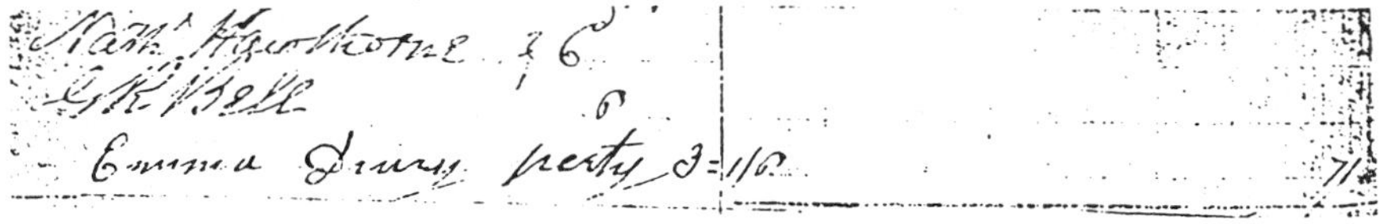

[handwritten manuscript facsimile]

containing some old coins and other antiquities. I saw an iron arrow-head, all rusty, which had been dug up in the church-yard of Radford Semele. Probably it had been buried in the body of some man slain in battle, and the rust on it was of his blood. It was fair-day in the town. I sat down to smoke a cigar and drink a glass of ale in an inn, looking on the market-place; and while so occupied, five or six butchers came in, all in white aprons, and each with a steel hanging at his girdle. They appeared to have been dining (it being between 12 & 1) and now took each a glass of gin and a pipe—occasionally looking through the window at their stalls (which were close to the inn) and numbering and naming what joints and other cuts they saw there.

On my way homeward, I took the road by the gate of Warwick Castle, and across the bridge of the Leam, whence is the magnificent view ot it.[49]

Nathaniel made a slight mistake in his rivers here, as it is the Avon that flows past the castle and over which that particular bridge stands, from whence many, many views of the castle have been drawn, painted, and photographed over the years. The Leam actually joins the Avon on the other side of Warwick, near to the Emscote Road, along which he had walked with Julian and Una the previous Monday, on their first trip into the town.

2

"Perfectly clean" Leamington: July 1855

The remainder of that weekend was spent sufficiently quietly not to warrant much mention of the family's activities in any journal or letter. Just a short walk was taken on Saturday evening by Nathaniel, Una, and Julian in the neighborhood of the crescent, possibly down toward Southam Road, crossing on the way the meadows that flank the river Leam at that point. During the day, Nathaniel had received at least two letters from the consulate, one from Wilding and the other an invitation to dine in London during the following week (on his birthday, as it happened, though the latter event never held much sway over his affections and he rarely mentioned it as being of any significance at all). So part of Sunday was spent in writing letters:

> Mr. Hawthorne begs to acknowledge the honor which Mr. Peabody does him, by his kind invitation to dinner on Wednesday July 4th. Mr. H. regrets that the present feeble health of Mrs. Hawthorne compels him to spend any leisure from official duty in attendance on her, and renders it impracticable for him to be in London on that day.
> Leamington, July 1st.'55
> Geo. Peabody, Esq[1]

Quite why Nathaniel should drag in Sophia's ill health as the reason for not attending the dinner is not clear. It was a rather lame excuse as he knew that he would be in Liverpool on 4 July and pleading official business as the reason for the rejection of the invitation might have seemed more appropriate. It would have been one of those occasions most likely to have driven him into his shell, for he was probably aware of the nature of these entertainments. George Peabody was a well-known American merchant banker and philanthropist who had lived in London since 1837, and probably due to his personal background of having made a fortune after being born in poverty, he had come to express his gratitude for his success and his belief in the American way of life by giving an annual dinner, to which he invited as many influential people as possible. The dinners were the last thing in haute cuisine and, one assumes, not many people turned down an invitation to attend, though not everyone thought highly of Peabody's personal attributes as can be gathered from the journal kept by Benjamin Moran, one of the secretaries at the United States Embassy in London. Moran had a sizable

Leamington

	Food June 2d week		
27	Bread eggs	1	6
25	Sugar /5 Oatmeal /4 Butter 1/6		
	Coffee 2/6 Macaroni 1/ Cocoa 8/		
	Tapioca /8	7	3
29	Oatmeal /4 Sugar 4½ Rice /5	1	10½
28	Raisins /3 Citron 7½ — Eggs /6		
	Sugar 2/½ butter 6½	1	6½
29	Cooked beef 5 lbs 13 oz	5	9½
	Laundress 4 — 5½	4	5
30	Pork	2	2
	Vegetables & apple	1	4
	Lobster ½ & bread	3	3½
	July		
2	Rhubarb & vegetables	1	2½
	Grocer	2	10
	Bread	1	
	Laundress	4	5
	Bread — dough		3
	Sugar 4½ — Butter 13	2	10
3d	Oranges 1/6 Potatoes /4 Cabbage /2	2	
		2 3	1
	Mutton	1	5
	Bread	1	
	Milk 4. 8. 0	2 3	6

chip on his shoulder and wrote many harsh words about fellow Americans whom he saw in London, but his opinion of Peabody is entertaining, at least:

> George Peabody, the puffing American note shaver, has returned to London from a tour of self-glorification in the U. States. This is the fellow who gives <u>private</u> dinners on the Fourth of July at public taverns to which he invites every one in a good suit of clothes who will applaud him, and then publishes the proceedings, toasts and all, in the <u>public journals</u>. It is worth noting that he pays his clerks less and works them harder than any other person in London in the same business, and never gave a man a dinner that wanted it. His parties are advertisements, and his course far from benevolent. He never gave away a cent that he didn't know what its return would be. He has no social position in London and cannot get into good Society. He generally <u>bags</u> the <u>new</u> American Minister for his own purposes and shows him up around town, if he can, as his puppet to a set of fourth rate English aristocrats and American tuft-hunters who eat his dinners and laugh at him for his pains.[2]

Nathaniel was not the only one who wrote letters on that Sunday. Una wrote two in fact, both to her aunt, Elizabeth (Peabody), Sophia's unmarried elder sister. Both letters are extant and it would appear that the first, maybe the one she wrote on her own, was considered not good enough to send to the formidably intelligent "Aunt Lizzy" and, possibly with a little help and instruction from either Sophia or Nathaniel, the second was composed in a more literate and entertaining manner. The first letter read:

July 1st Sunday Leamington

Dear Aunt Lizzy
We are in Warwickshire in Leamington now, near Warwick, Coventry, Stratford & London. Last Wednesday we went to Stratford, early in the morning & came back after having had a delightful day, at five o'clock. The scenery is very pleasant going there, & you go through Warwick town which has a great many old houses in it. Stratford does not look a very pretty or interesting place. But the house where Shakespeare was born is of course, very interesting. We went into his chamber where he was born & the kitchen, & another room which was, I suppose the sitting room. Those are the only rooms which are to be shown in the house. The room where he was born has a picture engraving of him, which was taken from a very old & authentic painting. It is very beautifully done, & the engraver has made all the cracks & imperfections on the face, which the picture had. The room is also filled with engravings & pictures to be sold. We bought some things. Then we went to see the Church where he was buried, a very beautiful Church dedicated to the Holy Trinity. The tombstone is very plain, & has this inscription. "Good friend, for jesus sake forbear, to dig the dust enclosed here, Blest be the man who spares my bones, & curst be he who stirs these stones."
Above the grave is a bust of Shakespeare, I do not think him very handsome. All his family, or some of them at least, are buried in a line with him. The Church is very beautiful indeed both inside & out, & has a beautiful avenue of trees arching over & making a most lovely walk to go out of the gate. On one side of the churchyard the river Avon runs peacefully along, & we sat down on some stumps of old trees & ate our oranges & biscuits there.

	July - Leamington	£	s	ds
	3d week Food			
4	Bread		1	...
	Veal		2	2
	Vegetables			9½
	Grocer		2	
5	Mutton		2	6
	Vegetables		1	
6	Mutton			8
	Vegetables			10
	Bread		1	1½
4	Strawberries for children		2	4
	Powdered sugar			6
7	Lamb or mutton		4	11
	Vegetables		2	1
	Salmon		2	4
	Bread		1	9

Then we went to see the Grammar school where Shakespeare was educated. It is almost all renewed, & is a long rather low building. We have seen the town of Warwick but not yet the Castle, yes, we have <u>seen</u> the Castle but not been inside. We saw it as we were coming home from Stratford & had a full view of the towers & the front. It stands right on the bank of the Avon. It has no trees of course on that side though it had on all the other sides. There are the most beautiful majestic trees I ever saw in Warwickshire. Especially elm trees. Goodbye dear aunt Lizzy

Your affectionate
niece Una
13 Lansdowne Crescent[3]

And the second letter went like this:

July 1st Sunday Leamington

My dear Aunt Lizzy
Here we are in the middle of England, in Warwickshire. Leamington, the town in which we are now, is a very pleasant one & only a few miles from Warwick, Coventry & London. We came here a week or two ago, from Rock Ferry. And Mary went to America a few days before us. Papa has been with us all the time, & we have seen Warwick & Stratford on the 27. A most lovely day, & not a cloud crossed the blue sky all day. We started at half past nine in the morning & came back at five. We saw Shakespeare's birth-place, & The Church of the Holy Trinity, where he was buried, & last we saw the Grammar school where he was educated. All but the roof has been made over, so it looked almost like a new house, except the curious small panes of the casement windows.

To-morrow Papa is going to his office for a few days. [deletion] Mamma has not been well at all since we have been in Leamington. Her cough has been very bad & made her very weak & tired. The rest of us are quite well. We have not been inside of Warwick Castle yet but we saw it as we were coming home from Stratford, & it looked very grand & beautiful, rising from amidst the trees, we saw its full front, because it is right on the banks of the river Avon, with no trees on that side. I shall like to go inside very much. I write a journal & have put down every thing we have done. Papa writes a journal too, & Mamma began hers, but was not well enough to continue it. Julian does not write anything [oh wretched Julian!].

Last evening Papa & Julian & I went to take a walk. We got some wild flowers, & in or near the swamps in England, there are very large forget-me-nots. Here is one of them, which I will draw. I think it is quite as large as that. Then here is one of the smaller ones. Is it not very small? Both are very badly drawn but I only wanted to give you an idea of their size. One grows in damp places, & the other in corn & hedges & dry places. Mamma likes them both very much. Then yesterday I got a very, pretty little white flower that grows in the water. I never saw anything like it in America. Goodby. Perhaps you have not time to write to me, so I will not ask you to.

From your affectionate niece
Una Hawthorne
13 Lansdowne Crescent[4]

It must have been as a result of having to get out the writing materials for the letter to Aunt Lizzy that Una found the one that she had written to her cousin Rebecca on 18 June, still unposted. So a postscript was added to it, across what had already been written on the first page:

P.S. July 1st. I thought Papa had sent this letter long ago, dear Rebecca, & I am surprised & sorry to see it still here, but Papa is going to Liverpool tomorrow so he will carry it with him. Your affectionate cousin Una.

Nathaniel's return to the consulate was not being undertaken by him as a matter of pressing urgency as it was his intention to return by a somewhat circuitous route, via Lichfield and Uttoxeter, and it would be the best part

		Varieties June July	£	s	ds
		Soap			4
		Elastic			2
July.		Socks		4	
		Blank book			6
	3	Muslin frock for Una		16	6
		" dress for myself		12	
		Blank books for Una & Julian 1/10		1	10
		Vase		1	
		Ribbed stuff for baby		2	9
		Embroidery for baby		14	
		6 yds diaper 1/6		9	
	6	Phaeton		2	6
		Muslin		3	
		Gloves		1	2
	4	Boots		3	6
	7	Ribbon		1	5½
		Needles			2
		Lace edging			8

of two days before he arrived back in Liverpool.[5] Monday morning was spent quietly; he brought his journal up-to-date (the entry relating to the visit to Warwick on the previous Saturday morning) and ended it with the words: "Today, I shall set out on my return to Liverpool, leaving my family here." The remainder of the day's events were not recorded until 4 July, however,

I left Leamington [today] shortly after 12—having been accompanied to the Railway station by Una & Julian, whom I sent away before the train started [he must have caught the 12:10 from the Avenue station]. While I was waiting for the train, a rather gentlemanly, well-to-do, English-looking man sat down by me and began to talk of the Crimea, of human affairs in general, of God and his Providence, of the coming troubles of the world, and of spiritualism—in a strange, free way for an Englishman, or, indeed, for any countryman whatever. It was easy to see that he was an enthusiast of some hue or other. He being bound for Birmingham, and I (in the first instance) for Rugby, we soon had to part; but he asked my name, and told me his own—which I did not much attend to, and immediately forgot.

My ride to Rugby, and thence to Lichfield presented nothing to be noted;—the same, rich, verdant country, and old trees, which I had grown accustomed to, in a fortnight past. I reached Lichfield (which, I find, is Saxon for the "Field of Dead Bodies" referring to two sons of a King of Mercia, who, being converted by Saint Chad, were martyred for their Christian faith)—I reached this scene of the old martyrdom, at, I think, not far from four o'clock, and put up at the Red Lion Hotel. In these old towns, all the hotels and inns are named after some animal or object, a Lion being as common as any—likewise deer, Bulls of all colors, Bull's Heads, &c, &c. It is the more modern fashion only to show the names of the Lion, the Bull, or what not; but in these old towns of Warwickshire and the Midland counties, you often see the thing or animal represented as the sign. Two or three centuries ago, when these signs were adopted, they would have been intelligible to very few persons in any other form. The Red Lion of Lichfield is a very good, old-fashioned, quiet house. The entrance from the street is by an archway, through which vehicles drive into the inn-yard; and in the two sides of the arch are the doors of the hotel. The interior arrangement is somewhat intricate. To finish off with the hotel, I may add that I got a very good supper, and a good breakfast, dinner, and sherry, the next day—no, I forget, I did not get exactly a dinner on either day, but something like it [today]. The waiter was feminine, and greatly preferable to the male. The cream and butter of this part of England are greatly preferable to those articles in Lancashire, where, indeed, they are much inferior to what we have in America. At this house, I had the great, dull, dingy, coffee-room (which did not look at all like a coffee-room) all to myself, and no books but the London Directory, and two Worcestershire, Staffordshire, and Midland Counties Directories, until I bought a guide-book of Lichfield. There seemed to be no other guests [again?]; at least, if so, they were in their private parlors. After all, I have made a mistake about the name of the house; it was not the Red Lion, but the Swan, and had a picture of the Swan (black, if I remember right) hanging before it.

The streets of Lichfield are very crooked, and the town stands on an ascending surface. There are not so many old gabled houses as in Coventry, but still a great many of them;—and very few of the edifices, I suspect, are really and fundamentally new. They hide their age behind spruce fronts, but are old at heart. The people have an old-fashioned way with them, and stare at a stranger, as if the railway had not yet quite accustomed them to visitors and novelty. The old women, in one or two instances, dropt me a curtsey, as I passed them;—perhaps it was a mere obeisance to one whom, in their antique way, they acknowledged as their better;—perhaps they looked for sixpence at my hands. I gave them the benefit of the doubt, and kept my money.[6]

Next morning, Nathaniel was out and about in the town:

The Swan Hotel stands, I believe, in Bird-street. At my first sally forth, I turned a corner at a venture, and soon saw a church before me. At this point, the street widens so much (though not very much either) as to be called Saint Mary's Square; and adjacent to it stands the market-house. In this square, not quite in the middle of it, is a statue of Dr. Johnson, on a stone pedestal, some ten or twelve feet high; the statue is colossal (though perhaps not much bigger than the mountainous Doctor), and sits in a chair, with big books underneath it, looking down on the spectator with a broad, heavy benignant countenance, very like those of Johnson's portraits. The figure is immensely broad and massive—a ponderosity of stone, not fully humanized, nor finely spiritualized, but yet I liked it well enough, though it looked more like a great boulder than a man. On the pedestal were three bas-reliefs;—the first, Johnson sitting on an old man's shoulders, a mere baby, and resting his chin on the bald head which he embraces with his arms, and listening to Dr. Sacheverell preaching;[7] the second, Johnson carried on the shoulders of two boys to school, another boy supporting him from behind;[8] the third, Johnson doing penance at Uttoxeter, the wind and rain beating hard against him, very sad and woe-begone, while some market-people and children gaze in his face, and behind are two old people with clasped hands, praying for him. I think these last must be the spirits of his father and mother; though in queer proximity, there are dead and living ducks.[9] I never heard of this statue before; it seems to have no reputation as a work of art, and probably may deserve none;—nevertheless, I found it somewhat touching and effective. The statue faces towards the house in which Johnson was born, which stands not more than twenty to forty yards off, on the corner of a street which divides it from the church. It is a tall, three-story house, with a square front, and a roof rising steep and high; on a view, the house appears to have been cut in two in the midst, there being no slope of the roof on that side. The house is plaistered [sic] and there was a high ladder placed against it, and painters at work on the front. In the basement corner apartment, what we should call a dry-goods store (and the English, I believe, a haberdasher's shop) is kept. There is a side, private entrance, on the cross-street between the house and the church, with much-worn stone steps, and an iron balustrade. I set my foot on the worn steps, and laid my hand on the wall of the house, because Johnson's hand and foot might have been in those same places. I forgot to say that the statue was sculptured by Lucas,[10] and erected in 1838, at the expense of the Reverend Chancellor of the Diocese, Law.

From Saint Mary's Square, one passes by a piece of water, centuries old, but which appears to be artificial, and to occupy the cavity whence the stone for the Cathedral was taken. It makes a very pretty and quiet object, with its green bank, and the trees hanging over it, and a walk beside it; and I saw some boys and little children fishing in it; the latter, I think, with pin-hooks. This pond (perhaps two hundred yards in diameter) is called the Minster Pool. Dam-street leads to it, and runs by the side of it, affording a partial view of the Cathedral; and it was in a house on one side of this street, that Lord Brooke was shot from the battlements of the Cathedral, which he was then assaulting, and which had been turned into a royalist fortress. There is said to be a stone, commemorating this fact, on the wall of the house in the porch of which he was shot; but I could see no such memorial.[11]

The Cathedral of Lichfield seemed to me very beautiful indeed. I have heretofore seen no cathedral save that of Chester, and one or two little ones, unworthy of the name, in Wales. No doubt, there may be much more magnificent cathedrals, in England and elsewhere, than this of Lichfield; but if there were no other, I should be pretty well satisfied with this; such beautiful shapes it takes, from all points of view, with its peaks and pinnacles, and its three towers and their lofty spires, one loftier than its fellows; so rich it is with external ornament, of carved stone-work, and statues in a great many niches, though many more are vacant, which I suppose were once filled. I had no idea before (nor, possibly, have I now) what intricate and multitudinous adornment was bestowed on the front of a Gothic church. Above the chief entrance, there is a row of statues of saints, angels, martyrs, or kings, running along the whole front, to the number, no doubt, of more than a score, sculptured in red stone. Then there are such strange, delightful recesses in the great figure of the Cathedral; it is so difficult to melt it all into one idea, and comprehend it in that way; and yet it is all so consonant in its intricacy— it seems to me a Gothic Cathedral may be the greatest work man has yet achieved—a great stone poem. I hated to leave gazing at it, because I felt that I did not a hundredth part take it in and comprehend it; and yet I wanted to leave off, because I knew I never should adequately comprehend its beauty and grandeur. Perhaps you must live with the Cathedral in order to know it; but yet the clerical people connected with it do not seem oppressed with reverence for the edifice.

In the interior of the Cathedral, there is a long and lofty nave, and a transept of the same height and considerable length; and side aisles, and chapels, and dim, holy nooks, which I cannot describe, and did not know the purpose of. The nave, I thought, had not the naked, simple, aged majesty of that of Chester; the great pillars, made up of many smaller pillars in a cluster, seem to take away from the sense of a vast space; the great interior is too much broken into compartments, and goes up into a lofty narrowness. I should be more impressed by one great aisle, than by all these intersecting arches, with the rows of pillars, in long vistas up and down, supporting them. Still, it was good to be there; and I think it a noble fashion, this of erecting monuments in churches;—no matter if the people do not deserve a monument, still the sculptured marble is a good thing. There are a good many monuments in this Cathedral, though the greater part of them are of undistinguished people, clergymen connected with the establishment, or their relatives and families. I saw but two monuments to persons whom I remembered one to Gilbert Walmsley[12] and the other to Lady Mary Wortley Montague[13] erected by a lady in gratitude for having been benefitted [sic] by inoculation. But, then, the white marble sculpture on these old stone walls, in the shape of altars, obelisks, busts and sarcophagi has a beautiful effect, and speaks sadly and pleasantly of the dead people; and the white statues that stand or recline in the side chapels have a kind of real life, and you think of them as inhabitants of the spot. Indeed, few spots have older inhabitants. I saw one upper half of a stone lady, the half having doubtless been demolished by Cromwell's soldiers; and she is still praying with clasped hands, as she reclines her half of a slab. There is another very curious monument; it is a reclining skeleton in stone, apparently of great antiquity, and as faithfully represented as an empty anatomy could be in a solid material—very ghastly and Gothic; somewhat Egyptian, too, for it looked much like the mummy, with fleshless arms and shanks, which I saw, the other day, in the Museum at Warwick.

The Cathedral service seems to be performed here twice a day, at 10 o'clock and at four. When I first went into the room, the choristers, young and old, had just got through their duty, and came thronging forth from a side door upon the pavement of the Cathedral, dressed in white robes, and looking very fit to haunt and chaunt in that dim, holy edifice. All at once, one of the younger cherubs took off his white gown, and thus transformed himself into a youth of the day, in a modern frock coat and trousers. I do not know that I need to say any more of the Cathedral; except that the Canonical people seem to have made very creditable arrangements for the admittance of the public, and that visiters [sic] may enter (in service time) without being bothered with showmen, explaining everything that you do not care about knowing, or that you have learnt for yourself out of a guide-book, for a shilling.

The space about the Cathedral is called the Cathedral Close, and in it are the dwellings of the dignitaries of the Diocese, and perhaps some other respectable persons. The walk along the side of this Close, the principal front of the Cathedral, is quite an illustrous spot;—having been chosen by Farquhar as the locality of one of his principal scenes in the Beaux Stratagem, where Aimwell and Archer make acquaintance with the ladies of the Comedy. Here, too, was the favorite spot of Major André,[14] where he used to walk before he went to America to be hanged. Addison, also, must have once resided here, in his father's house, when the latter was the Dean of Lichfield. The house is still standing; and I take it to be a large edifice of brick, stately enough to be the residence of the second dignitary of the Diocese. The episcopal palace is a very noble-looking mansion of stone, built rather in the Italian style—not at all Gothic—and bears on its front the figures 1687. All this row of episcopal, canonical clerical dwellings, have an air of the greatest quiet, repose, and dignified comfort, looking as if no disturbance or vulgar intrusion could ever come there—with fine, ornamented lawns in front, and beautiful gardens about them, and everything that a saint—and a great many things that a sinner—might desire. And before them, on the outside of their iron fences, lined with rich old shrubbery, extends this beautiful and shadowy walk, over-arched by noble trees, so that it is as good in its way as the arch of the Cathedral nave. From the end of the walk you have a fine view of sites known and noted in the life of Dr. Johnson. Lichfield has several of those old charities—Hospitals for decayed men and women, schools &c—which form so singular and picturesque a feature in many of the antique English towns. One edifice for the former purpose, at the extremity of Saint John-street, has a very aged aspect, and is supposed to have been one of the earliest structures erected after the introduction of chimnies [sic]. A line of half a dozen chimnies [sic] stand like buttresses against its wall, and rise high over its angular roof. Saint Michael's church, in which old Michael Johnson lies buried, stands just without the town, on a rising ground. All these old, indirect streets, these old gabled houses, these churches, these hospitals, are contrasted with a great number of young soldiers, in red jackets, who lounge about, appear in the door-ways, and narrow passages that open between the houses, walk arm-in-arm smoking pipes, flirt with the girls, and always look as if they had had a little too much ale. Ever and anon, a bugle sounds at some street-corner. These soldiers seem to be new recruits of a militia regiment, and are mostly very youthful—mere boys, hardly grown. I talked with one of them; and he said he enlisted because he had "got a little of the drink" in him, but did not now regret it. He told me that his regiment was at Corfu, but he did not know the name of his commanding officer. Probably this poor, ruddy, thick-skulled English lad will volunteer into the regular army, go to the Crimea, and go to nourish the grass and weeds of that foreign soil. One likes the looks of these peasant boys of old England—stupid, but kindly and homely, and with a suitable comeliness of aspect, and exceedingly wholesome. At about 11, I left Lichfield for Uttoxeter, on a purely sentimental pilgrimage, to see the spot where Johnson performed his penance. Boswell, I think, speaks of the town (pronounced Yute-oxeter) as being about nine miles from Lichfield; but the map would indicate a greater distance, and by rail, passing from one line to another, it was as much as eighteen. Johnson's father could hardly have performed the journey thither, transacted business during the day, and returned at night. I have always had an idea of his trudging thither on foot; but very likely he went in a cart or other vehicle, with his stock of books.

On arriving at the rail-way station, the first thing I saw, in a convenient vicinity, was the tower and tall gray spire of a church. It is but a very short walk from the station up into the town. It was my impression that the market-place of Uttoxeter lay round the church; and if I remember the incident aright, Johnson mentions that his father's bookstall had stood in the market-place, close by the church. But this is not the case. The church has a street, of ordinary width, passing around it; while the market-place, though near at hand, is not really contiguous to the church, nor would there probably be much of the bustle of the market about this edifice, now-a-days. Still a minute's walk would bring a person from the centre of the market-place to the door of the church; and Michael Johnson may very well have had his stall in the angle of the tower and body of it;—not now, indeed, because there is an iron railing round it. The tower and spire of the church look old; but the walls have evidently been renewed since Johnson's time. The market-place is rather spacious, and is surrounded by houses and shops, some old, with red-tiled roofs, others with a pretence of newness, but probably as old as the rest. Unless it were by the church, I could not fix on any one spot more than another, likely to have been the spot where Johnson stood to do his penance.[15] How strange and stupid, that there should be no local memorial of this incident—as beautiful and touching an incident as can be cited out of any human life—no inscription of it on the wall of the church, no statue of the venerable and illustrious penitent in the market-place, to throw a wholesome awe over its earthly business. Such a statue ought almost to have grown up out of the pavement, (and thus have shown me the spot) of its own accord, in the place that was watered by his remorseful tears, and by the rain that dripped from him.[16]

Uttoxeter-market is still held, Wednesday being market-day. The town has no manufactures, nor any business, except, I suppose, as a mart of agricultural produce. It seems to contain some thousands (say two, three, or four) of inhabitants, and consists of indirect streets, paved (side walks and all) with little, round, uncomfortable stones, and bordered with gabled houses, almost entirely of red-brick, and with red brick-roofs. Here and there stands a loftier mansion; but the whole impression of the place is, that the inhabitants are in very moderate circumstances, but comfortable, and that the town undergoes small alteration from cycle to cycle, and may now look much as it did in Johnson's time. The people seemed very idle, in the warm afternoon, and clustered together, about the streets, in idle groups, and stared at me, as they would not, if strangers were more plentiful. I question if an American ever saw Uttoxeter before. What especially struck me was the abundance of inns—scores of them—at every step or two, the sign of the Red Lion, White Hart, Bull's Head, Mitre, Cross Keys—nobody knows which; probably for the accommodation of the agricultural people on market-day; for if all the inhabitants drank at these inns from morning to night, it would do little towards supporting them.

I got some dinner at one of these rustic inns—bacon and greens and a chop, and a gooseberry pudding, altogether enough for six yeomen, besides ale—all for a shilling and sixpence. There was a man in the public room who seemed to be an artisan from Manchester, and we had some talk together—a shrewd, humorous man, of good information, and making up his own ideas about matters;—loyal, too, I thought and not caring about changes in church or state. Afterwards I drank a glass of ale at an old inn, called the Nag's Head, standing on the side of the market-place, in a very attainable position, and as likely as any inn could be to have entertained old Michael Johnson, on the days when he went to sell his books. He might have eaten his bacon and greens, and smoked his pipe, in the very room where I sat—a low, ancient room, with a red brick-floor, and a white-washed, cieling [sic], with the bare-rough beams running across—but all extremely neat, and adorned with prints of prize oxen, and other pretty engravings, and with figures of earthen-ware.[17]

I spent I know not how many hours in Uttoxeter, and, to say the truth, was heartily tired of it; my penance being a great deal longer than Dr. Johnson's. It is a pity I did not take the opportunity to repent of my own sins; but I forgot all about them till it was too late. No train passed the town, by which I could get away, till five o'clock. As I sat waiting for its appearance, I asked a boy who sat near me—(a school-boy, of some twelve or thirteen years, he seemed to me; and I should take him for a clergyman's son)—I asked him whether he had ever heard the story of Dr. Johnson's standing an hour by that church, whose spire rose before us. He said "no." I asked if no such story was known or talked about in Uttoxeter. He answered, "No, not that he ever heard of!" Just think of the absurd little town, knowing nothing about the incident which sanctifies it to the heart of a stranger from three thousand miles over the sea!—just think of the fathers and mothers of the town, never telling the children this sad and lovely story, which might have such a blessed influence on their young days, and spare them so many a pang hereafter!

From Uttoxeter I rode in the first class to Crewe; thence in the second-class through Warrington to Liverpool, arriving at ½ past 9 P.M. It is foolish ever to travel in the first-class carriages, except with ladies in charge. Nothing is to be seen or learnt there; nobody to be seen but civil and silent gentlemen, sitting on their cushioned dignities. In the second class, it is very different [in what particular way, one wonders?].[18]

The next day, Wednesday, 4 July, was Nathaniel's birthday, but as usual there would be no celebration and in any case he was both away from the family and back at work, a situation which, in the circumstances, was not likely to fill him with delight or prompt any ceremonies. While he was in Liverpool for this short period, he stayed at the Rock Ferry Hotel. It appears to have been a sufficiently busy (or uneventful) day to have prevented anything being recorded in the journal; presumably he was, at least, attending to the business that had necessitated his return to the consulate. On Thursday, however, there was more time available, despite unwelcome visitors, both to write letters and to see Bright:

[Today],[19] the door of the Consulate opened, and in came the very sociable personage who had accosted me at the Railway Station, in Leamington. He was on his way towards Edinburgh, to deliver a lecture, or a course of lectures, and had called, he said, to talk with me about Spiritualism, being desirous of having the judgement of a sincere mind on the subject. In his own mind, I should suppose, he is past the stage of doubt and inquiry; for he told me that, in every action of his life, he is governed by the counsels received from the spiritual world, through a medium. I did not inquire whether the medium had suggested his visit to me. The medium is a small boy. My remarks to him were quite of a sceptical character, in regard to the faith to which he has surrendered himself. It seems he has lived in America, in times past, and had a son born there. He gave me a pamphlet written by himself, on the cure of consumption and other diseases by antiseptic remedies. The author's name is Dr. Washington Evans.[20] I hope he will not bore me any more, though he seems to be a very sincere and good man; but these enthusiasts, who adopt such extravagant ideas, appear to me to lack imagination, instead of being misled by it, as they are generally supposed to be.[21]

Probably through boredom, and in hope, Nathaniel wrote to Bright:

Liverpool July 5th 1855

Dear Mr. Bright,
I have come back (only for a day or two) to this black and miserable hole.

Truly yours,
Nath[l] Hawthorne

P.S. I don't mean to apply the above two disparaging adjectives merely to my Consulate, but to all Liverpool and its environs—except Sandheys[22] and Norris Green.[23]

and

US Consulate
Liverpool July 5th 55

My dear Sir,
I have been absent from town, and have only just read your note. It gives me much pleasure to comply with your request.

Respectfully yours
Nath[l] Hawthorne

Mr. James T. Lamb, Paisley[24]

Presumably, Mr. Lamb was merely asking for an autograph. Next day, Nathaniel fired off a letter to Ticknor full of his exasperation with the job, his concern over Sophia's health, and the latest ideas as to how long it would be before he would resign. He was sufficiently frank in his comments to warrant marking the letter Private:

(Private)
Liverpool, July 6th 1855

Dear Ticknor,
I got back from Leamington on Tuesday night, and shall return thither tomorrow.
    The Attorney General's construction of the bill, allowing me the notarial fees,

would be more for my pecuniary benefit than the first construction put upon the bill, supposing I were to continue in office two years longer. I think the notarial fees would do rather more than pay the expences. Perhaps I might clear $8000 per annum—out of which, with my recent economical reforms, I would not spend much more than $3000.

But I am most anxious to get rid of the office, and would gladly relinquish $5000 for my liberty from next December. The truth is, I dare not keep Mrs. Hawthorne in England another winter, on account of the effect of the climate on her health. I have written to Bridge to consult the President as to the feasibility of my getting leave of absence for two or three months, in order to settle her on the continent. If this can be done, I will hold on for the present—if not, I shall have to resign, to take effect the first of December, at furthest.

Do not let the above be known.

I thank you for the books sent by the last steamer. I have been so busy since my return that I have had no time to read them, except a little of Christie Johnson—which I like greatly.[25]

In much haste,
truly yours,
Nathl Hawthorne

P.S. I send a package for Elizabeth Peabody. Please to forward it at my expense.[26]

The new consular bill's introduction had been postponed once more and was not due to come into effect until 1 January 1856, and Nathaniel had already written to Ticknor about the possible results that could ensue for him, financially speaking, depending on how he resolved the tricky problem of when to resign. But whatever the financial benefits would or would not be, he was ready, almost, to sacrifice everything for an improvement in Sophia's health and for his own peace of mind.

In any event, by the next day it would appear that the business that had brought him back to Liverpool had been settled and he arranged his time-table so that he could leave and return to Leamington in the early afternoon. He did go into the consulate in the morning, for

At the Consulate [today], a queer, stupid, good-natured, fat-faced individual came in, dressed in a sky-blue, coarse, cut-away coat, and mixed pantaloons, which (both coat and trowsers) seemed rather too small for his goodly size. He turned out to be the Yankee who came to England, a few weeks ago, to see the Queen, on the strength of having sent her his own and his wife's daguerreotype, and having received a note of thanks from her secretary. Having been swindled by a fellow-passenger, he has loafed about here ever since his arrival, unable to get home—and, indeed, unwilling, until he shall have gone to London to see the Queen; and, to support himself, he has parted with all the clothes he brought with him, and thrusts himself into the narrow limits of this sky-blue coat and mixed pantaloons. It is certainly a very odd-looking court dress; and he hinted, with a melancholy, stupid smile, that he did not look quite fit to see the Queen now. Of course, he wanted my assistance; but it is marvellous, the pertinacity with which he clings to his idea of going to court, and, though starving, will not think of endeavoring to get home, till that has been effected. I laid his absurdity before

No. 43 (formerly No. 13) Lansdowne Crescent. Photo by the author.

him, in the plainest terms. "My dear man!" quoth he, with good-natured, simple stubborness, "if you could but enter into my feelings, and see the business from beginning to end, as I see it!" And this he repeated over and over again. He wished me, if I would not help him myself, to give him the names of some American merchants, to whom he might apply for means to get to London; but I refused to interfere with his affairs in any way, unless he promised to go back immediately to the United States, in case I could get him a passage. Besides his desire to see the Queen, he has likewise (like so many of his countrymen) a fantasy that he is one of the legal heirs of a great English inheritance. No doubt, this dream about the Queen and his English estate has haunted his poor, foolish mind for years and years; and he deems it the strangest and mournfullest perversity of fate, and awfullest cruelty in me, that now—when he has reached England, and has wealth and royal honors almost within his grasp—he must turn back, a poor, penniless, be-fooled simpleton, merely because I will not lend him thirty shillings to get to London. I had never such a perception of a complete booby before, in my life; it made me feel kindly towards him, and yet impatient that such a fool should exist. Finally (as he had not a penny in his pocket, and no means of getting anything to eat) I gave him a couple of shillings, and told him not to let me see him again, till he had made up his mind to get back to America—when I would beg a passage for him if I could. He thanked me, and went away, half-crying, and yet with something like a dull, good-natured smile on his face; still fixed in his inveterate purpose of getting to London to see the Queen![27]

I left Liverpool at ½ past 1 [today] by the London and North-western railway, for Leamington.[28]

What had the family being doing in Nathaniel's absence? What with Sophia's continuing poor health and the probability that she did not set foot outside the front door of No. 13 too often, it may well have devolved on Fanny to chaperon the children around the town on short walks and shopping expeditions. There is no record of any of them doing anything out of the ordinary during the few days that Papa was in Liverpool; no visit to the second Grand Horticultural Exhibition at Kenilworth Castle, for instance, which seems to have been the major public event in the neighborhood during that week, at which the attendance amounted "at least about to five thousand," and as the weather that day "was in every degree favourable" it "would be almost impossible to describe the animation of the scene," although *The Royal Leamington Spa Courier* did so at great length. Perhaps they were too reliant on Nathaniel to provide the impetus to get them out of the house to explore new areas, and with their mother incapacitated it meant that the children would have to wait for his return before excitement and exploration would be renewed. If they had been aware of it they may have been moved to attend the Laying of the Foundation Stone of the New Chancel of Whitnash Church, where they had been on 23 June with their father and witnessed the upheavals that were going on around the church. As the *Courier* reported:

In a previous number we alluded to the state of things in this parish, with reference to Church accommodation, and gave a brief account of the last service in the old chancel. It has been determined by the respected Rector (the Rev. J. R. Young) to rebuild the chancel and vestry, from designs by the eminent architect (Mr. Scott) at his own expense. The interesting ceremony of laying the foundation-stone was performed on Tuesday evening last. The villagers and a few neighbours, among whom were Lady Mackenzie, Mr. M. Wise (Shrublands), Mrs. Waller, Rev. W. Staunton, &c.,&c., assembled at the Church, for divine service, at half-past six, the officiating Ministers being the Rev. J. R. Young, Rector, and the Rev. T. R. J. Laugharne, Curate. The service concluded, the congregation proceeded to the spot where the stone was to be laid. After a short address from the Rector, an appropriate chant was performed by the villagers composing the choir. Prayers were then offered up, and the stone was laid by Master Young, eldest son of the Rector, and godson of Lord Leigh. The Sanctus was then sung, and the Minister concluded the ceremony by pronouncing a blessing upon those present. Several other stones were afterwards laid by the parishioners and others. The builder selected for executing the works is Mr. William Ballard, of Leamington.

But there was some movement on 6 July, the day before Nathaniel's antici-pated return, as there is an entry in the Accounts Book relating to hiring a phaeton for 2s.6d. There is no clue, elsewhere, as to who used it or where they went, but it could not have been far, as can be seen by comparing the cost of this phaeton with that hired for the journey to and from Stratford, 17s.6d. Maybe it was for a short trip to Warwick; there is an earlier entry in the Accounts Book referring to the cost of a "cab from Warwick" that possibly was the "omnibus" that Nathaniel and Julian had caught on the way home on 25 June. But where the phaeton went to on 6 July is not known.

Next day, in anticipation of her father's return, Una wrote to Ticknor:

July 7 Leamington

Dear Mr.Ticknor,
This is a day of great rejoicing to us, because our dear Papa is coming home to us from dusty, grimy Liverpool, to neat, clean Leamington. He went away last Monday. We have had a very dreary week without him. Mamma's cough is very bad, & to add to it, she has a very bad head-ache to-day. Next Monday or Tuesday Papa is going further north than Liverpool on some Consular business, & he is going to take Mamma & Julian with him, he can't take us all so Rose, Nurse & I are going to stay in this pleasant place. Mamma says they will only be gone one night.
    Rose is sitting beside me writing. We take a walk every day & she pretends to write a journal like the rest of us. She can print her name very well for such a little girl. There are a great many wild roses in the hedges, & we bring home a bunch of them every day. Though I believe that three quarters of the pleasure, at least, has to consist in gathering & arranging the flowers, as we have hardly any places to put them in when we bring them home [possibly that is why the Accounts Book registers the purchase of a "vase" on 3 July].
    I like the town of Leamington very much. It is very clean, & you would think it was almost in a different world from Liverpool, it is so quiet, & so very clean. In these days when it does not rain there are watering carts that come round very often & damp the streets so that the town need not be dusty, & streets are so flat that there are no puddles of water ever. There is a pretty walk of trees, called

Regents grove, & you can go down in town through the trees when it is hot & you had rather not be in the sun [the trees, or their descendants, are still there]. Do come here & we will rest you & refresh you & take you [on?] some lovely walks. Only we shall go away soon. Yours affectionately, Una.[29]

It is not clear how the news became known that Nathaniel, Sophia, and Julian were to be going north on their own (and then returning to Leamington), as there appears to be no communication from Nathaniel to the family advising them as to the necessity for this northern trip, and it must, in fact, have been a fairly late change of plan, as according to a subsequent letter of Sophia's, they had all been intending to go to London directly after leaving Leamington. In any case, as will be seen, they *all* went north together (and did not return to Leamington); but what the particular "Consular business"[30] in the north that necessitated their leaving Leamington was, was never made clear or even mentioned in any of the journals or letters of the following days. Nathaniel arrived back in Leamington "between 8 & 9, P.M." Probably the children were allowed to stay up late that evening to welcome their father home and the next day was spent quietly enough not to warrant any reference being made to it. On Monday, 9 July, having packed their bags and settled all accounts, Nathaniel shepherded them down to the railway station where, he recorded later, they "started at about 12½ for the English lakes, taking the whole family. We should not have taken this journey, just now; but I had an official engagement, which it was convenient to combine with a pleasure excursion."

And so the family's first visit to Leamington came to an end. It may perhaps be thought strange that there is little evidence of the Hawthornes having paid much attention to the town itself in between their trips around the surrounding countryside. However, it must be remembered that Leamington hardly existed at all even as recently as 1800 and that the town's growth had been due solely to the discovery of the beneficial effects of the mineral spring in its midst by Messrs. Satchwell and Abbotts in the 1770s and the subsequent commercialization of that discovery after 1800. Nearly all the significant buildings in the town, apart from the parish church, were the products of that growth and there is little likelihood, therefore, that the Hawthornes, or any other visitor for that matter, found Leamington to be of historical interest; its main purpose, apart from offering a cup of saline water to the fashionably sick, was to provide a base from which visitors went further afield to see and marvel at what the surrounding countryside could provide, which was principally scenic beauty (that incorporated first-class hunting facilities) and buildings that were of great value and interest either because they were ruins or were painstakingly preserved, and that were physical manifestations of the history of the country over the past millennium. On the whole, if there was no history or scenic and architectural beauty related to an object, then the Hawthornes were not particularly interested in it and certainly were not keen to describe it in their journals and letters. And they were not interested in taking advantage of the various attractions that the spa had to offer in the way of entertaining its visitors. One disadvantage, no doubt, to participating in those attractions was the expense, as, of course, the good citizens of the town (or those whose livelihood depended on the tourist trade) wished to part the visitors from as much of their cash as possible. And to a family that was, in theory, trying to save money as best it could, it was necessary to keep a low profile.

There are two more letters of a later date that need to be quoted that are of interest and relevance to this part of the story. One of them was written by Sophia to her younger sister Mary (Mann) that is typical of both her style and of the enormous length that many of her letters ran to, though neither of these characteristics need impair their interest to readers of succeeding generations:

July 11th 1855
Newby Bridge at the
foot of Lake Windermere
[Westmoreland-*deleted*] Lancashire

My dear Mary,
I received your letter of May 31st[31] in Leamington, Warwickshire, where we all were for three weeks. Yesterday we arrived here at nearly 10 at night after two days—or rather a day & a half travel. Mr. Hawthorne had official business here which brought us just now. Otherwise we were to go from Leamington to London. I am sorry to say that in all the time since we left Rock Ferry I have been too ill to write a letter home. My cough was excessively aggravated after arriving at the Royal Spa, whether from a damp carriage or from a breath of evening air. I was much fatigued by it, so that I could not even think, but it became a little better before I left. My cough seems to be entirely in my throat & not at all in my lungs. I am going to answer your letter of May 31st & one before it, & then I will tell you about us. That great budget of letters I made up when you got but a wee note, was not so many letters but so large letters to few. One was to dear Aunt Rawlins,[32] which I have been contemplating for a year. I know you would rather she had it, than to receive one yourself. Another was to Nat[33] which I had long delayed & was anxious to write because he writes so satisfactorily & at length to me. I feared he would feel neglected. And he is the last person in the world I would have think I neglected him. Another was to Ellen in reply for a very sweetly toned & confiding letter from her, which touched my heart. Human beings expand under the sun of love & I do not refer to the love now, but only to my expression of tender interest in her.[34] Mr. Hawthorne, in obtaining a passage to America for Mary Aherne, not only did this but thro' his clerk obtained for her the situation of stewardess—in a fine ship, with an uncommon Captain, for wages of £2 a month! £24 a year. Mary was so surprised & enchanted that she was deprived of expression. The Captain had an interview with her & liked her so much, he wanted her to engage for a year & she did. He was to have a lady-passenger to Eastport (his home) & he was to fetch his wife. So Mary is in clover & will not be available on land at present. I gave her a nice recommendation to present when she wished to live in a family again. But the Captain thought he might like to take her into his family & she was willing, & so I suppose we may bid her farewell for an indefinite time. We made her a handsome gift of a large workbox, sumptuously furnished & she was very

happy & pleased. Julian gratified his taste in giving her a marvellous cushion, emery bag & jewel-case all in one, carved out of alabaster in the shape of a sarcophagus, with a crimson velvet cushion on the top. It was not exactly appropriate as she would have no marble toilette slab upon which to place it, but it delighted her beyond measure—so much more pleasing to the royal soul is beauty than use. One is a farm-yard & the other a lordly Park. I hope your American girl will be a Phoenix. Do you mean to keep Catherine[35] in your house to be confined, you darling little Donna Quixotina? What will you do in Heaven, where there will be no sickness nor sorrow? Your occupation will be gone, & yet perhaps not. You will probably be one of God's ministers to troubled man, & never rest in doing—though you cannot be tired any more [Sophia then left the letter and, what with climbing mountains and visiting Morecambe Bay, Ulverston, and Furness Abbey, didn't have a chance to return to it for another two days, by which time they were at the Low-wood Hotel on the shores of Lake Windermere]. 13th. I am afraid I shall quite miss Rebecca Pennell[36] for we are moving all over the Lake country—I am very sorry for I should like to see her very much. We left Rock Ferry a day or two after your date of her marriage & shall have no home for a very long time—No, I did not say that I thought the "fire" left out of that engraving of Mr. Mann. I think the engraving very coarse, giving the idea of a sensual person & I probably said it had no fineness, was not fine. The lower part of the face outbalances the upper—Whereas in the original man & Mann the brow wholly puts in subjection the less noble portions. I see him in it & I am the more provoked, because it is not he after all. The sweetness is left out too. There is <u>fire</u> enough however—fire & force to drive the earth out of its orbit—but not <u>my</u> beloved brother somehow. The Sun is awfully bold at design when he has life to deal with.

In one of Georgie's letters [Mary's second son] he speaks of playing innumerable times with one hand. Did you know that this is the worst possible habit? Mrs. Husson, who has the most thorough & magnificent classical education in music, beginning at seven years old, & devoting her life to it, never would allow Una to play one bar without using both hands. One thing that makes her so peerless a teacher is that she never allows even the commencement of a single bad habit in any particular. The position of person & arms & fingers must be right <u>at first</u>, & I see the admirable effect upon Una. It is a very lazy & easy way to thrum—with one hand, and I should much mistrust any teacher who could permit it. I wish I had your skill in teaching & your experience. But it is very bad for regular study to be travelling & we do not care to drive them seriously yet. They are getting a general culture which is apparent at every turn, & the freedom of Julian's intellect causes a wonderful beauty & depth of observation—& so with Una as well. Julian has a way of improvising upon matters & things in general which is astonishing. The profoundness & brilliancy of his remarks, of his half chanted exordiums surprise me. In driving to & from Furness Abbey yesterday, he suddenly broke out, & the flow & rhythm, the wisdom & poetry amazed me. He has Spenser's tendency to simile. Everything that we saw & that happened he wove into his web without hesitation & educing all kinds of wit & sense from each event & each object at the same time. I cannot do justice to his expressions but once he said something like this. "Behold that lovely & lofty mountain. I see that its summit & its sides are covered with trees & flowers & richest green—while within I am aware that there are stones & dirt & all uncleanness—Alas! this reminds me of the wonderful tree at Whitnash (a village in Warwickshire) which while it threw out on every side branches with foliage & made a goodly show, I saw its trunk was all hollowness & decay, for I myself stood within it & looked up its empty shaft. This all tells me that man may be of a fair countenance with gracious ways

Sophia Hawthorne. Photograph taken in 1855. Courtesy, Peabody & Essex Museum, Salem, Mass. Essex Institute Collection.

while within he may hold bad passions or be but a hollow bubble." The best of this are his words, but I cannot recollect the literation entirely. A dirty forlorn old man passed the carriage & he exclaimed, "And I see a man pass by & I perceive that a man may be & is precisely like us, & yet wholly unlike—for we can say that that man resembles Papa, & yet we know that in reality he must be [un?]like him!" Was not that a profound insight? He was very desirous yesterday to have his drawing-book so that he might sketch the Abbey when we should arrive & I told him I would buy him one at Ullsverstone [sic] on our way. But our coachman drove directly past the stationers & he was so disappointed. This incident came into his poem afterwards & one expression was so singular I must tell you. "And the mother said My son, grieve not, thou shalt have thy book at Ullsverstone [sic]. But behold at Ullverstone [sic] she tarried not, but the chariot & horses rushed furiously by. And then was her son cast down, but the mother would have comforted him & lo! had it been possible, she would have snatched the skin from her body & given that to her son, whereupon to draw, such is the love of a mother!" But I cannot fill up my letter with any more of it. Mr. Hawthorne went to Coventry while we were at Warwickshire, & took Julian, & he said that after a collation he sat down on a couch & suddenly became inspired & for twenty minutes he delivered an oration upon Nature, Arts & Science, [at this point, having reached the end of her fourth page, it seems that Sophia had temporarily run out of paper as the following sentences are continued up the left-hand margin of the fourth and first pages] with all appropriate gestures & intonations, his face lighting up at any brilliant sally, & then grave by turns.[37] His wonderful power of language and its elegance comes from his familiarity with all the best writers, Shakspere, Cervantes, Spenser, & Tasso & Bunyan—he has never heard nor read anything commonplace. His father's books help him also to English undefiled[38] [now some more paper had come to hand].

Thank you for every item you tell me about your children & husband—I am rejoiced the latter is so well—Yes, I have received the Cuban letters & the Dedham journal from E[39]—but I cannot think where my little books of poetry are. Dear mother had them once. (Before I write any more, will you please not to cross your letters. It is no matter on our account how many sheets there are, only on my account the more the better).[40] Now I have taken up your May 9th letter. Thank dear Horace for the slippery elm.[41] I received it exactly as I was booted & spurred for our travels & took the box in my hand & ate to his memory all the way. I do wear flannel doubled over my chest. Yes indeed—Rock Ferry was very damp & this is why we have left it & the fogs are very bad there. Leamington is in the very heart of England & therefore we went there. But as it happened, my cough was far worse there. It is better in this mountain district. We did think we should go to Lisbon in the spring; but now we rather incline to remain the other two years at our post, as this Bill has been so modified it becomes possible to live upon the income of the office & lay by somewhat besides. And we have not half explored England, & cannot this season, though we are going to keep moving around till black November drives us under roofs. Leamington is close by Stratford on Avon, Kenilworth, Warwick & Coventry. I had but one well day in three weeks, & on that day—oh, Mary, Mary, we went to Stratford on Avon! It was a day so divinely beautiful, so still, so glowing warm, & so bright with clear sunshine, that Syria could not surpass it—At the same time an angel of a breeze kept fanning us, as if it were a wing dipped in that fine perfume called "Bouquet of a thousand Flowers" iced—for it is a peculiarity of England that the air—the wind, is always cool, though the sun may be fire. And it is fire this wonderful summer— a really hot summer like ours, without the mosquitos or simoons & there has not been such a summer for very many years here, & it is said it will not rain till 10th September, instead of everyday. Yet we were very fortunate last summer. Our three weeks at the Isle of Man was unclouded weather—tho' to be sure the Isle of Man is not England. But our three weeks at Rhyll were also quite fair. The three weeks at Leamington were without rain, too, but that day I refer to was pre-eminent of all days in any land. In an open chariot we could see on all sides, & the superb road was like hard marble & the regal trees on each side made the whole ten miles like a triumphal entry into Shakspere's birthplace. The country was beautifully undulating & rich with flowers, grain & such lofty & grand trees as we do not see on our Eastern shores. Any single clump, or brotherhood, was enough to make the land illustrious. And the hedges were radiant with flowers, foxglove, sweet briar roses, broom, gorse, & many whose names I did not know, making such a tissue of purple, blue, rose, yellow & crimson as [*deletion*] inclined me to shout "Glory, glory! glory!" all the way along. And there was not one sign of neglect. Every field, every inch of road & hedge seemed to have been especially cared for by some loving hand. You never can see anything slovenly or neglected in England—& Warwickshire is celebrated for its trees. The Lords of Warwick have had a voice in every bit of the land & they have tenderly nursed the trees as they would have done immortal children. This makes them look so kingly, so proud of their own beauty. Every thing appears to be arranged in relation to them—Houses stand respectfully back from the royal presences. In the town of Leamington, a fair & beautiful town, you come constantly upon a noble company of trees from which stately blocks of houses curve inwards to give them room. They bow their lofty heads together, interlace their wide-blessing arms & stand with room enough all round, & with such a grandeur of air, as I can in no wise convey. Revenons Shakspere. I have lately been reading a book about Shakspere, written some time ago with great ability; a book all about his family & residence & also with criticisms on his plays, very luminous, illustrated by the times. It was a book which dispelled entirely from my mind all doubt that Shakspere wrote Shakspere's plays.[42] So when I was at Leamington, I realised him as I never had before at all. He might well have been in many places I saw as it is only ten miles from Stratford. His reality & his sweetness & humanity were very vivid to me. But in approaching nearer & nearer to where he undoubtedly lived, I felt a wonderful awe creeping over me. I could not help the tears coming. "The throstle with the note so true, The wren with little quill"[43] were singing of him. "The cuckoo buds of yellow hue did paint the meadows with delight"[44] just where I was looking, perhaps the very identical meadows, & "Hark, hark the lark at Heaven's gate"[45] at that moment, rising from his nest, urging his way up & up—raining down melody—all nature announced him & sang & bloomed him & the "Sovereign Eye"[46] of day was not once overshadowed "with envious clouds."[47] My memory teemed with his inimitable descriptions of natural objects, & the lovely visions of Imogen & Ophelia, kept passing. Ophelia with her wreath—hanging it on the willow & falling into the melodious brook beneath. It was to me so consummate to be going with my husband, Shakspere's true lover—to his house and tomb. Mr. Hawthorne's soul was alight in his face & a great solemn light shone on his brow.[48] The divine Day was reflected on it & in eyes twice as large as usual. Una was lovely in pale blue, seriously reposeful beneath a broad brimmed hat & blue ribands, and Julian's great brown eyes gleamed with joy. Finally we saw the beautiful spire of the church of the Holy Trinity—Shakspere's funeral monument & soon we drove into the homely little town & alighted at the Red Lion Inn. We did not go into the Inn, but immediately went in quest of the house. The reflection of the sun from the stone & brick of the town made it very hot. By aid of a man's directions we found the house. "The immortal Shakspere was born here" said an old double sign over the window.

One broad window below, arranged with a wooden lid that shuts down & lifts up—as butchers' windows are planned—was on one side of the door. A descendant of his sister kept a butcher's shop there! I stepped over the threshold with reverence & found myself in a very small apartment paved with great flag stones, very smooth & miraculously clean, but making anything but a nice floor. They were in all sorts of angles & entirely uneven, as if they had been hammered upon where they joined together, so that the edges were jammed down. In this room we were received by a ladylike young person, in mourning, who took us into an inner room, where was a huge fireplace & stone seats within upon which the young poet must often have sat. The floor is of broad stones. At one end is an old desk upon which is an open book where visitors must write their names & there I found dear Sarah Shaw's, her husband's & daughter's,[49] written about a fortnight before! For I knew that they had passed through Leamington (allowing two days

Mr & Mrs Fran^d Geo Shaw, Boston U.S.A
Miss Shaw
Miss Russell

for Liverpool on purpose to see me) & did not know I was there! Then an elderly widow lady[50] came & took us up stairs, stone stairs, or they would not be there now. And we went into the birth-chamber. This was much the largest of the three rooms. Here was a wonderfully fine colored engraving of the famous Chandos portrait, large as life—a very handsome face, and quite different from any I have ever seen.[51]

The other letter that rounded off the family's connection with Leamington Spa on this, the first visit, was written by Una to Ticknor while the family was still in the Lake District:

July 18 Low-wood Hotel
Wednesday. Lake Windermere

Dear Mr. Ticknor
I wrote a letter to you a great while ago [7 July], & then it was put in my dear little portfolio you gave me, & forgotten till yesterday.[52] I found it, & now I am going to send it, & write you an apology.

Since Saturday I have been very unwell, & had to stay in bed, but today I am almost well. I am perfectly delighted with "The Queen of the Lakes" as this lake is called. These are such beautiful mountains & hills & such lovely walks & drives. We are at Low-wood Hotel now, but we staid nearly a week at the Swan Hotel, Newby Bridge, on the river Leven, which I like better than Low-wood. The lodging house we went to we found was not a good one & the people we found very mean. They took butter and things, but the worst of it is this. We were in a great hurry when we were coming away & Nurse [Fanny] left a very precious brooch of hers which no other can replace, in her room on her toilet table, & a nice cloak of hers in the closet, & Mamma left a great bottle of Arnica[53] on the mantle piece, & when we got here we found it out, & wrote to the woman & asked her to send them to us, & the mean woman denied anything was left there. Is it not a pity? I should like to have you write to me very much, dear Mr. Ticknor, & I hope you write if you have time, but I hope none of the letters will go to Leamington as some of this steamer's letters have, because Mrs Price won't send them to us.[54]

I am going back to Newby Bridge today, if it is fair, & Papa and Mamma & Julian, are going to travel round the lakes which I am not well enough to do now, & Nurse & Rose are going with me. I call New Bridge home, because the Hotel really is more like a home than any hotel I have ever been to. And the Landlord, Mr White, is very good indeed from top to bottom. I think it is a nice hotel. Goodbye, I am sure everyone sends you love though I have not asked them.

Your affectionate friend
Una[55]

3

An Intermission (1)

Two years and two months would elapse before the Hawthornes returned to Leamington, a period in which the family journeyed from one end of the country to the other as a result of their "rambles," in which Sophia, Una, Rose, and Fanny spent some months in Portugal, and Nathaniel was finally able to tender his resignation, although at the end of the period he was still officially in residence at the consulate. Despite the many upheavals that they had to undergo as a result of their desire to see as much as they could of England and the separation that was caused by the Portuguese holiday that was undertaken for Sophia's health, it was, in several ways, a more beneficial period than had been the first two years of their stay in this country. The children were growing rapidly, and inevitably their exposure to much of the heritage of the land contained in the places, buildings, museums, and exhibitions that they visited gave them the trappings of a sophistication that was not the norm for most children of their age. Nathaniel's way of life was no longer totally dominated by the drudgery of the consul's job and the gloom of Liverpool's environment although, of course, the more time he spent away from the consulate the more he came to regard the periods when his duties demanded his presence there as intolerable. So he had little compunction in taking time off, with or without the family. Visits were made to the Lake District during July 1855; to London during September and October (Sophia, Una, Rose, and Fanny then left for Lisbon); to Glasgow in May 1856; to Southampton in June (the family having returned from Madeira); to London again in July and August; to Southport in August and September (where the family subsequently stayed until the following July 1857 (during which time visits were made to Chester, York, Lincoln, Boston, Nottingham, and Scotland); and finally they moved to Manchester in July, to attend the exhibition there. Of course, Nathaniel commuted to the office whenever it was necessary for him to do so. But a computation of the number of weekdays on which he was at the consulate during this period (although Saturdays were usually workdays, as well) up until the day that his successor took over reveals that out of a possible 590 he was absent ("rambling") for approximately 125. It is difficult to be absolutely accurate on this matter as his letters and journals do not record every day's events, but the approximate figure gives an idea of his eventual unconcern as to the necessity of his attending the office on a daily basis in the second half of his period in office.

It was stated in one of the sections of the new consular law that no consul "shall absent himself from the country to which he is accredited, or from his consular district, for a longer period than ten days without having previously obtained leave from the President of the United States, and that during his absence for any period longer than that time, either with or without leave, his salary shall not be allowed him."[1] Nathaniel was prepared to flout this rule on occasion, even stating that, in an emergency, he would be prepared to go to Portugal with or without official approval. In fact, there was no need for him to leave England for Sophia's benefit, so this rule remained unbroken in that respect, but it was somewhat naive of him to expect to be able to leave Liverpool, for whatever reason, without his absence being noted officially and, in the event of his being away from the office for more than ten days, escape from official censure, loss of salary, and any other possible recriminations. Usually in his absence he was very careful to make known his whereabouts to Pearce (the vice-consul) and Wilding at the consulate in the event of any urgent business that would require his being summoned back to Liverpool at short notice.

There are a number of entries in the journals that Nathaniel continued to keep, recording in great detail and at length his and the family's visits to all manner of places throughout the land, which show that he was in a condition that could almost be described as happiness or, at least, contentment; particularly when he was in London, tramping around the streets of the City, and now that he was finding it somewhat easier and more pleasurable to expand his social horizons by meeting with that class and type of person with whom he felt personal and intellectual affinities. For instance, the acquaintances he made during one short period in London included Richard Monckton Milnes, Robert and Elizabeth Browning, Jenny Lind, the Marquis of Lansdowne, the Bishop of Coventry and Lichfield, and the mother and sister of Florence Nightingale, among others. Of course, being a committed family man, there were other periods when he was in some distress, increasingly so during the months when Sophia and the girls were in Portugal, a prolonged absence that represented the only time that he and his wife had been parted for so long and at such a distance since they had first been married. But happy or not, it was during these two years that plans for the future were constantly in Nathaniel's mind and the necessity of fixing upon the all-important date for the tendering of his resignation, allied with his ideas as to how the ensuing years were to be spent, and where, was constantly referred to in letters to political and personal friends, Ticknor in particular being favored on many occasions with his agonizing as to when it would be best for him to resign, taking into account the amount of money he may or may not have lost if his resignation was not submitted at the most advantageous time. However, the decision had to be made and on 13 February 1857 he addressed a letter to the president of the United States: "Sir, I beg permission to resign my office as Consul of the United States at this Port, from and after the date of August thirty-first, 1857."[2]

It must have been as a great load lifted from his shoulders. Now plans could be laid for the future with more confidence and with a greater tolerance for the idea of continuing with the irritations of office in the knowledge that in the not too distant future (a matter of months only) he would be free to go where he pleased and do whatever he liked. As he explained to Ticknor, the plan was that the family would leave for the Continent, probably in September, passing through Paris and Marseilles en route for Rome, staying there during the winter of 1857–58 and remaining in Italy, mainly, for at least another year, before returning home to America. In fact, Nathaniel admitted that if it was left to him they would never return home but the children, in particular, were longing to get back to all things American. The one fly in the ointment that appeared during the months after tendering his resignation was the fact that no one in the State Department notified him as to who his successor at Liverpool would be and when he would take over.

During these two years, between the first and second periods of residence in Leamington, Nathaniel (as did other members of the family, to a lesser degree) wrote voluminous accounts of their wanderings and of his work at the consulate but produced nothing for immediate publication in the realms of the short story or a longer work of fiction. However, he did have two short pieces published. One, an article that appeared during 1857 that was based on the journal entry that he had made as a result of the visit to Uttoxeter on 3 July 1855 when returning from Leamington to Liverpool; the other being a preface to Delia Bacon's book that contained her theory as to the true authorship of the plays of Shakespeare, in which she maintained the impossibility of a man of (the Stratfordian) Shakespeare's limited (if any) education and experience having had the ability, experience, and opportunity to produce works of such genius, stating, with appropriate evidence, that the plays were the product of known intellectuals such as Francis Bacon (principally), Walter Raleigh, and other Elizabethan men of letters. He was asked to contribute to magazines and Ticknor was anxious to know as to when he would be likely to produce something substantial but he usually pleaded that pressure of consular business militated against his being able to concentrate on literary endeavors, though he did acknowledge that he was maintaining journals that contained what he considered to be pretty hot stuff (perhaps too hot for public consumption, especially by the English public).

Money, of course, continued to be a subject close to his heart and was frequently referred to in correspondence, particularly with Ticknor. During these two years, though he was adamant that the new consular law curtailed his income at the same time as his expenses remained as high as ever, he was able to bank sufficient sums of money that even with his changed circumstances were considerably more than he had a right to expect. His initial expectations as to the financial value of the consul's post were, perhaps, a little too high and he may have been dazzled by a glimpse of a mountain of gold that turned out, in the end, to have been a mirage or, at least, only a hill, and despite his observations that he needed to achieve economy in personal affairs, he did not make too significant an effort to cut back in an endeavor to save for the rainy days that may or may not have appeared to cloud the horizon. The other subject of concern to him, and Sophia, was the education of the children and the manner in which it was to be continued. Till now, their education had been guided solely by Nathaniel and Sophia, with Sophia taking the more active role in the daily discipline of maintaining a schoolroom atmosphere at home, for the children had never attended a school and consequently had not been exposed to the rough-and-tumble of such an institution. It was that same rough-and-tumble that would have been considered one of the reasons that persuaded Nathaniel and Sophia to keep Una and Julian at home for their lessons. As a result, the children were influenced totally by their parents' predilections, particularly in the realms of literature. From their earliest years they had been subjected to an idealization, particularly by Sophia, that was buttressed by an expectation of the highest possible achievements and the assumption of their having talents that eventually and perhaps inevitably were not to be realized. Parental love was there, in abundance, and the children loved their parents in return (perhaps adoration was more near the mark with regard to their father), but such expectations would have been too much for most children, whatever their circumstances. Of course, at this time they were all following a nomadic existence and it would have been difficult, if not impossible, for the children to have attended a school in the normal manner for any length of time. They were talented children of talented parents (perhaps Rose was the least talented of them all) but the fact that they led lives closeted in the home, away from much of the rough-and-tumble associated with school life, may have been responsible for some of the indiscipline that reigned at times (as it must also have been responsible for the sophistication of the children at this early stage of their lives), and for the intensity of emotion that was evidently part of their characters. Una, for example, was at times a fractious and difficult child, with a moody temperament that may well have been unwittingly fostered by Sophia's insistence on complete control of her daughter's upbringing; she felt that too great a responsibility in this direction for Nathaniel would be a time-consuming distraction from the long periods of contemplation that he needed for his own work, though he did take a share in superintending the daily lessons. No other children were allowed to play with Una. Even at the age of three, she was being read to from Milton's poetry, and though deaths in a family in those days were more likely to be occurrences that were viewed at closer range by all members of a household than is the case nowadays, at the age of five she was allowed to stay in the room in which her grandmother was dying, fanning the flies away from her face. Even Nathaniel had to confide to his notebook that "there is something that almost frightens me about the child—I know not whether elfish or angelic, but, at all events, supernatural. She steps so boldly into the midst of everything, shrinks from nothing," and "seems at times to have but little delicacy, and anon shows that she possesses the finest essence of it; now so hard, now so tender; now so perfectly unreasonable, soon again so wise. In short, I now and then catch an aspect of her, in which I cannot believe her to be my own human child, but a spirit strangely mingled with good and evil, haunting the house where I dwell."

To a certain extent, however, the move to England did represent a liberation for the children. The new life was to be as strange to them as to their parents though, of course, it would have been considered necessary for certain essential features of their education to be maintained, whatever the circumstances. They were still not allowed to go to school, lessons being held at home under Sophia's supervision, and there was to be no letting up in the general moral tone of the authors that they were allowed to read or of those works from which they were read to in the evenings. They were not allowed to wander around and explore the neighborhood on their own. But allowing for their different temperaments, there was little open expression of resentment of such a closely monitored existence, and that can only be explained by the love of their parents for them and for each other.

But there *was* a widening of horizons. Una was taken to dancing and music lessons in Liverpool, and at one time spent the winter months there, up until Christmas 1854, away from the family, boarding with the Hussons, where she received instruction in French, music, and dancing. Otherwise, lessons in chronology, Latin, geographic science, painting, and drawing were supervised by Sophia; walks were taken and emotions heightened each day on the arrival home from the consulate of their beloved father. After tea and before bedtime for the children games were played and stories read from such authors as Cervantes and Scott, although Julian also read adventure stories such as *Westward Ho!* and *A Boy's Adventures in the Wilds of Australia.*

In October 1855, Sophia, Una, Rose, and Fanny were dispatched to Lisbon to stay with the O'Sullivans, John Louis O'Sullivan being the United States minister in Portugal. It was hoped that Sophia would benefit from the more sympathetic climate out there, and while her health did improve and her cough largely disappeared, it was a period that brought increasing unhappiness due to the separation of husband and wife, and both of them regretted that, for some months, until the following June, they were each missing the opportunity of watching the growth of all their children at an important stage of their development. Sophia did what she could to maintain the daily lessons for Una and Rose but Nathaniel was conscious that his elder daughter, now nearly twelve years old, though safely guarded by Sophia and Fanny, was in an environment and culture where he could have no real influence on her behavior. Back in Liverpool, however, Julian had a fine time, although Sophia, correctly in some respects, guessed that he was being allowed to run wild by his father who was more than content to allow the ladies running the boardinghouse where they were lodging to minister to Julian's every wish.

However, much to everyone's pleasure, the family was reunited during June of 1856. Following the reunion, and while Nathaniel went back and forth to the consulate, the family was quartered first in the Southampton district and then near London, where they stayed at Francis Bennoch's house in Blackheath, Bennoch being one of the few Englishmen with whom Nathaniel felt really at ease. It was there that steps were taken for the employment of a governess, no doubt because of Sophia's anxieties about the need for a more disciplined approach to the education of the children, but also to prepare them, to some extent, for the forthcoming removal to the Continent after Nathaniel's resignation from the consulate had been finalized.

On Bennoch's return in mid-September, a removal to Southport was undertaken; the sea air would be beneficial for Sophia's health and its proximity to Liverpool meant that Nathaniel would have little difficulty in commuting to the consulate. Bennoch had been acquainted with the need for a governess, someone who would be prepared, if approved of, to accompany the family to the Continent. A recommendation had been made by Mrs. Anna Maria Hall, the wife of S. C. Hall, a publisher and editor, and in due course, on 18 October a Miss Browne joined the family in Southport. She was apparently a lady of good breeding, having had three years of experience of living in France and, so it was understood, suitably qualified to teach French, music, dancing, and drawing, as well as arithmetic, geometry, geography, and English composition (though the latter qualification would, in theory, appear to have been a superfluous one in that household). At first, all went well but it was not long before opinions changed as to Miss Browne's capabilities. Poor Miss Browne must have been made aware at the time of her appointment that she was to be the first person outside the family to assist in the education of the children, but she could not have been aware, at the same time, of the impossibly high standards that would have been required by any governess to satisfy Nathaniel and, particularly, Sophia. Personal charm may well have enabled her to fit in with family life but lack of a suitable intellectual standard (Sophia's standard) would damn her in the eyes of the latter, and if she *had* displayed precocious intellectual abilities (for a female) she would have been damned in Nathaniel's eyes. Whatever Miss Browne's shortcomings (and they were such that Sophia had decided she would not be suitable for their purposes on the Continent as early as 23 October)[3] she was, perforce, considered to be capable enough in some respects for her to be entrusted with the care of Una and Rose while Sophia, Nathaniel, and Julian departed for trips to the north and east of England and to Scotland as, much to everyone's dismay, Fanny had had to leave the household on 6 October for family reasons. With little regard for the consequent increase in expenses (but as an indication of Fanny's importance to the household) Sophia had almost immediately engaged a further two servants to assist her, one of them being their former cook at Rock Park. However, Fanny was reengaged during the following July (1857). During October, despite continuing uncertainties connected with the consular situation, Nathaniel felt it worth their while to move lodgings once more, partly because Southport was a boring place (for him) and partly because it did not appear, in the event, to be doing Sophia all that amount of good. And, more to the point, there was the opportunity for all of them to spend some considerable time at the huge Manchester Arts Exhibition.

At the same time as all this was taking place, moving lodgings, sacking Miss Browne, and welcoming back Fanny, steps had to be taken to engage a new governess. Sophia's brother-in-law, Horace Mann, president of Antioch College in Yellow Springs, Ohio, had recommended Ann Adeline (Ada) Shepard as a suitable candidate. Ada had what appeared to be impeccable credentials. She came from a family interested in transcendentalism and abolitionism; was a friend of the Mann family; her subjects were French, German, and Italian; and she had graduated in the recently inaugurated Antioch College's First Class in July of that year. President Mann was so appreciative of her abilities that he was prepared to offer her a Professorship of Modern Languages but suggested that she first expand her linguistic horizons by accompanying the Hawthornes on their Continental trip as the children's new governess. This appeared to be a sufficiently satisfactory plan (particularly as there seemed to be little time available to the Hawthornes in which they could verify the suitability of other ladies for the job) that Ada was engaged and it was arranged that she should leave for France and await the family's arrival in Paris, which it was anticipated would be in late September.

The move to the Manchester lodgings had been made on 21 July and for the next six weeks, while Nathaniel continued to commute to the consulate, little else was done except spend time at the exhibition. On 8 August, Ada set sail for France on board the *Ariel* and on arrival in Paris took lodgings at the Protestant College in the Rue Balzac, where she enrolled for French lessons from the director, M. Fezandie, and became a dedicated sightseer. Ada was in the Sophia mold as far as letter-writing was concerned, and it wasn't long before a steady stream of letters began to wend their way back across the Atlantic to friends, relations, and her fiancé, Clay Badger. Clay had graduated with Ada from Antioch College and was now studying at Harvard Divinity School in preparation for a return to Antioch as a Professor of Logic and Belles Lettres. She wrote to Sophia to inform her of her arrival and received a reply giving her the latest position with regard to the family's likely departure for the Continent; meanwhile she was to carry on with the French lessons and sightseeing.

The Hawthornes (particularly Nathaniel) became rather tired of the Manchester Exhibition and an unending diet of culture, but more importantly it was not surprising that they had found that Manchester was not the place for someone with a weak chest. To preserve Sophia's health it was deemed necessary to move once more, even for a period that it was anticipated would be of only a few weeks' duration. But where to go? Nathaniel did not want to be too far from the consulate or have too difficult a journey to make when he had to return to Liverpool on business; it could not have taken them too long to decide on a return to familiar territory in Leamington Spa where they knew that Sophia's chest would benefit from a pollution-free atmosphere. On Monday, 7 September, Fanny was loaded into a cab and dispatched by train to Leamington to look for suitable accommodation but apparently she did not find it too easy a task as the Accounts Book lists a cab fare to and from Warwick that must have meant that she made an unsuccessful trip there in her search. Perhaps one of the first things that she did on arrival was to go back to No. 13 Lansdowne Crescent to check with Mrs. Price as to whether the house was free at the time or just to ask her if she knew of anywhere that was available. According to *The Leamington Spa Advertiser*, however, it appears that No. 13 was already occupied by a Miss York;[4] perhaps it was Mrs. Price who recommended to Fanny the possibility of a vacancy just round the corner in Lansdowne Circus (maybe she knew the owner, Mrs. Edith Maloney).[5] Whatever means Fanny did employ in finding lodgings, she ultimately succeeded by taking Mrs. Maloney's house in Lansdowne Circus and she was able to retire for the night to her hotel (bed and breakfast 4s.0d.) secure in the knowledge of a job well done, making a mental reservation at the same time to remember to leave a message at the railway station next morning so that the Hawthornes would be made welcome with the good news.

4

"Genteel" Leamington: September 1857

We had got quite weary of our small, mean, uncomfortable, and unbeautiful lodgings at Chorlton Road, with poor and scanty furniture within doors, and no better prospect from the parlor-windows than a mud-puddle, larger than most English lakes, on a vacant building-lot opposite our house. The Exhibition, too, was fast becoming a bore; for you must really love a picture, in order to tolerate the sight of it many times. Moreover, the smoke and sooty air of that abominable Manchester affected my wife's throat disadvantageously; so [this] morning, we struck our tent and set forth again, regretting to leave nothing except the kind disposition of Mrs. Honey, our housekeeper. I do not remember ever meeting with any other lodging-house keeper who did not grow hateful and fearful on short acquaintance; but I attribute this not so much to the people themselves, as primarily to the unfair and ungenerous conduct of their guests, who feel so sure of being cheated that they always behave as if in an enemy's country—and therefore they find it one. The rain poured down upon us as we drove away in two cabs, laden with mountainous luggage, to the London Road station; and the whole day was grim with cloud and moist with showers [just as it had been on the first journey to Leamington two years previously]. We went by way of Birmingham, and staid three hours at the great, dreary Station there, waiting for the train to Leamington, whither Fanny had been sent forward [yesterday], to secure lodgings for us. England is a monotonous country to travel through by railway; its beauties and picturesque points are not panoramic, but require leisure and close inspection in order to be appreciated; besides, the day was so dreary that there was little temptation to look out. We all were tired and dull by the time we reached the Leamington Station, where a note from Fanny gave us the address of our lodgings. Lansdowne Circus is a nice little circle of pretty, moderate-sized, two-storey houses, all on precisely the same plan, so that on coming out of any one door, and taking a turn, one can hardly tell which house is his own. There is a green space of grass and shrubbery in the centre of the Circus, and a little grass plot, with flowers, shrubbery, and well-kept hedges, before every house; and it is really delightful, after that ugly and grimy suburb of Manchester. Indeed, there could not possibly be a greater contrast than between Leamington and Manchester; the latter built only for dirty uses, and scarcely intended as a habitation for man; the former so cleanly, so set out with shade-trees, so regular in its streets, so neatly paved, its houses so prettily contrived, and nicely stuccoed, that it does not look like a portion of the work-a-day world. 'Genteel' is the word for it; a town where people of moderate income may live an idle and handsome life, whether for a few weeks or a term of years. The tasteful shop-fronts on the principal streets; the Bath-chairs; the public gardens, the servants whom one meets, and doubts whether they are groom, footman, or butler, or a mixture of the three; the ladies sweeping down through the avenues; the nursery maids and children; all make a picture of somewhat unreal finery; and

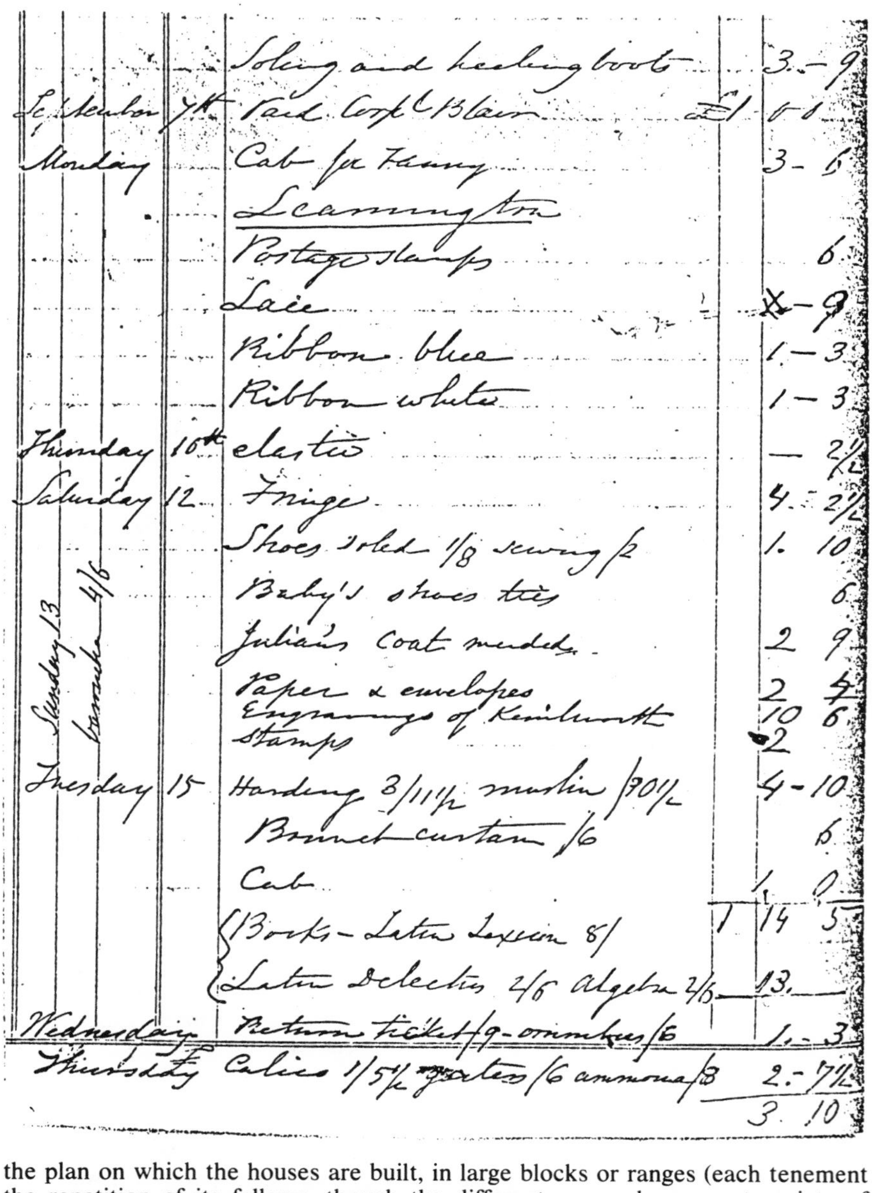

		Soling and heeling boots		3	9
September	7th	Paid Corpl Blair	£1	0	0
Monday		Cab for Fanny		3	6
		Leamington			
		Postage stamps			6
		Lace			9
		Ribbon blue		1	3
		Ribbon white		1	3
Thursday	10th	elastic		—	2½
Saturday	12	Fringe		4	2½
		Shoes soled 1/8 sewing /2		1	10
Sunday 13 Warwick 4/6		Baby's shoes ties			6
		Julian's Coat mended		2	9
		Paper & envelopes		2	4
		Engravings of Kenilworth		10	6
		Stamps		2	
Tuesday	15	Harding 3/11½ muslin /10½		4	10
		Bonnet curtain /6			6
		Cab		1	0
		Books – Latin Lexicon 8/	1	14	5
		Latin Selections 2/6 Algebra 2/6		13	—
Wednesday		Return ticket /9 – omnibus /6		1	3
Thursday		Calico 1/5½ gaiters /6 ammonia /8		2	7½
				3	10

the plan on which the houses are built, in large blocks or ranges (each tenement the repetition of its fellows, though the different ranges have great variety of style) betokens a town where the occupant does not build for himself, but where speculators build to let. The names of the streets and ranges of houses are characteristic; Lansdowne Crescent, Lansdowne Circus, Clarendon-street, Regent-street, the Upper Parade, and a hundred other grand titles of Terraces and Villas. To say the truth, unless I could have a fine English country-house, I do not know a spot where I would rather reside than in this new village of midmost Old England.[1]

Immediately, it became apparent to the family that Fanny had made an excellent choice in taking the house at No. 10 Lansdowne Circus, and once they were settled in they came to appreciate the peace and tranquillity around the little circle of houses, a calm that is retained to this day as the Circus remains, to a great extent, cut off from the noise and bustle of the nearby main road that leads in and out of the town. As with Lansdowne Crescent, where the family had stayed two years previously, Lansdowne Circus was another of the designs of William Thomas, an architect who subsequently moved his practice to Toronto, Canada, where he became very successful. Perhaps Mrs. Maloney was not totally dependent on her income as a lodging-house keeper as prior to the arrival of the Hawthornes there had been only two lots of tenants listed that year in the local newspapers as "visitors," a Mr. and Mrs. R. Marriot who had stayed from January to March, and Mr., Mrs., and Miss Watts who had been there in May and June. The rest of the time, and for the remainder of the year after the Hawthornes left, no occupants were listed in the papers at all, not even Mrs. Maloney herself. Presumably Nathaniel was happy with the rent of £2.12s.0d. per week which, unless Sophia's Accounts Book is at fault, appears to have been paid in arrears. What with the weather, their arrival late in the day, the "mountainous luggage" that had to be sorted out, and the organization of who slept in which room, there was no time for any walks to be taken, though it was likely that Nathaniel would have refused to be caged indoors after a day spent in a railway carriage, and in any case he must have walked down to the telegraph office opposite the Pump Rooms to notify his staff of his address (as next day some mail arrived in Leamington that would have originally been received at the consulate).

No. 10 Lansdowne Circus has been renovated and maintained by the present owners, Mr. and Mrs. Locke, to such effect that the Hawthornes would be very familiar with its appearance if they were able to see it now, despite the additions and alterations that have been necessary to bring its amenities into line with those of the twentieth century. The basement, or lower ground floor, has one large room that would have been the kitchen and several other small rooms or areas that would have served as scullery or larders. On the ground floor are two large rooms that would have been used as the parlor and the schoolroom. Upstairs on the first floor there are three rooms, and on the second floor four more rooms (not so large as those on the first floor). There would, therefore, appear to have been ample room for everyone to be accommodated comfortably though it is not known how the various bedrooms were shared. Una, for instance, was now thirteen years old and could well be expected to have had her own room; possibly Rose slept in the same room as Fanny, who was still regarded as a nurse. The usual imponderable question, however, as in the case of Lansdowne Crescent, was whether there were any live-in servants (as part of Mrs. Maloney's household, but used by tenants; on the occasion of the 1851 Census, for example, the house was occupied by Mrs. Maloney, her daughter, two

Leamington

	£ s d
Extra luggage for Fanny	6 - 0
Fare to Leamington	14 . 6
Fare to & fro Warwick	0 . 8
Hotel bed & breakfast	4 . 0
Carriage to get lodgings & luggage etc.	3 . 6
	1. 8. 8
Tuesday 8 Meat 3/6 potatoes apples 1/3	
Bread /7 beer /2½	5 - 6½
Wednesday 9 Beef 5/8 scotch ale 4/6 eggs /6	
tomatoes 1/ horseradish /1 man /6	12 . 3
Thursday 10 Salmon 4/ tomatoes /9 veal 1/	
apples /4 lemon parsley /2	
potatoes scarlet beans /8 wine 5/	11 . 11
Friday 11th Groceries from the 8th	1 . 3 . 7½
Potatoes, apples 1/ lamb 3/3	4 " 3
Saturday 12 Tomatoes /8 peas /9 biscuits /6	1 " 11
Veal 5/½ eggs /6 butter /8	6 " 2½
Monday 14th Loaf of cake 1/ French beans carrots /6	1 - 6
Tuesday 15 Apples. potatoes 2/10	2 - 10
Meat 3/10 sausages /8	4 - 6
Rent	2 - 12 - 0
	£ 6 6 6½
Wednesday 16 Bread 3/11½ and milk 3/5	7 - 4½
Thursday 17 Meat 9/2½ Groceries 9/7½	18 - 10
	7 6 . ½

tenants, and two servants). There is no reference made in any subsequent letters or journals as to the distribution of the rooms among the family but they could not have been too pushed for space as later on they were able to accommodate another adult who arrived completely unexpectedly and who, in the circumstances, would probably have been offered a bedroom of her own.[2]

Sophia's Accounts Book reveals something of the daily routine that the household's organization required and that had to be followed from the time of their arrival. As to who cooked the food for the family, which was purchased almost every day from various sources, there is no mention; no record of any wages for a cook or of tips for a servant whose wages may have been included in the rent. No real attempt was made to establish any buying on credit with the local merchants, settling bills on a weekly basis, for instance. There are one or two entries for purchases made over a three- or four-day period but there appears to have been no real plan. However, before anything of significance occurred, worthy of note, some mail had arrived via the consulate, one letter being from Fields, a rather uncommon occurrence:

Leamington, Sep[t] 9th 1857

Dear Fields,

I received your note only this morning,[3] at this cleanest and prettiest of English towns, where we are going to spend a week or two before taking our departure for Paris. We are acquainted with Leamington already, having resided here two summers ago; and the country roundabout is unadulterated England, rich in old castles, manor-houses, churches, and thatched cottages, and as green as Paradise itself. I only wish I had a house here, and that you would come and be my guest in it; but I am a poor, wayside vagabond, and only find shelter for a night or so, and then trudge onward again. My wife and children and myself are familiar with all kinds of lodgement and modes of living; but we have forgotten what home is— at least, the children have, poor things; and I doubt whether they will ever feel inclined to live long in one place. The worst of it is, I have outgrown my house in Concord, and feel no inclination to return to it.

We spent seven weeks in Manchester, and went most diligently to the Arts Exhibition; and I really begin to be sensible of the rudiments of a taste in pictures.

I hear nothing about my successor in the Consulate, and have not been favored with a word on the subject from Washington, since sending my resignation. However, some-body may turn up any day with a new commission; but meanwhile I am going to take Mrs. Hawthorne to France, and shall divide my own time pretty equally between Paris and Liverpool, (taking London in the transit) until released from durance. My official life may be made tolerably pleasant on such terms. If we reach Rome in December, it will be time enough.

What an idle fellow Ticknor is to run off to the White Mountains, leaving you to toil and sweat under the entire weight of business! I suppose you never leave the old 'Corner' from year's end to year's end.[4]

I made up a huge package the other day, consisting of seven closely-written volumes of Journal, kept by me since my arrival in England, and filled with sketches of places, and men and manners, many of which would doubtless be very delightful to the public. I think I shall seal them up, with directions in my will to have them opened and published a century hence: and your firm shall have the refusal of them then.

Remember me to everybody, for I love all my friends at least as well as ever.

Nath[l] Hawthorne[5]

Despite the moments of jocularity, the letter reflected Nathaniel's deep-seated weariness with their way of life. Two years before, not long after having come to England, he had already confided to his journal his unhappiness at the nomadic form of existence he and the family had endured to that time and the potential for a personal form of insecurity it could cause, particularly to the children. And he also wondered whether even the Wayside in Concord would bring them the peace and fulfillment that once it had appeared to promise:

> I sat, last evening, as twilight came on, and thought rather sadly how many times we have changed our home, since we were married. In the first place, our three years at the Old Manse; then a brief residence at Salem, then at Boston, then two or three years at Salem again; then at Lenox, then at West Newton, and then again at Concord, where we imagined that we were fixed for life, but spent only a year. Then this farther flight to England, where we expect to spend four years, and afterwards another year in Italy—during which time we shall have no real home.[6]

Sophia had also received some letters from America, more than one of them from Elizabeth:

Lansdowne Circus, Leamington
Warwickshire
September 9th 1857

My dear Elizabeth
Do not suppose that we are among horses, mountebanks and clowns by my date. On the contrary, we are in a charming little paradise of gardens, with a Park in the centre, towards which all these gardens converge. It is such a Paradise as the English only know how to make out of any given flat bit of land. Fancy a circle of houses at the end of a street, in this way. They are white stucco houses with balconies leading out of the drawing rooms, in which to sit and enjoy the gardens, made up of many green lawns, bright rainbow flowers and dark green shrubbery and trees. The park is full of lovely trees and evergreens, with lawns, and grand walks. We are in profound quiet. Nothing but a bird's note ever breaks our stillness. The air is full of mignonette roses and wall flowers. It is autumn, but the grass and foliage are like those of early spring or summer. Since you have never been so unfortunate as to be in Manchester and its suburbs, you can scarcely imagine our relief and enjoyment at being in this delicious retreat. I found that the foul air of the manufactories made me cough more, and the moment Mr. Hawthorne perceived it, he decided to come away. Nothing but the Palace of Art would ever have made us think of being one

hour in such a nasty old ugly place. We thought we had pretty well studied the pictures and could afford to leave them now. I had spent nearly a month in looking at them from morning to night—and I was ready to cease, though I could never be weary at looking at some of the Masterpieces, to the end of my days. I should think the Good Shepherd could convert the jew, Baron Lionel Rothschild, to Christianity—for it is his. No words can possibly do justice to that, or to the Madonna in Glory. Rembrandt is superbly represented in portraits, history and landscapes. There is a painting of Eli teaching Samuel of an altogether wonderful beauty. Samuel's face is unique in feature & expression. He stands at a table before an open book, with his eyes upon it. A turban fastened with a superb jewel is wound round his head, and he wears a purple robe, over which a gold chain hangs round his neck. He looks like a Prince of Heaven; but his sacred, intent, simple and devout expression transcends the rest. He looks dedicated and immutably holy. Old Eli is a marvel of art. The hand with which he is pointing to the page, is so perfect an old man's hand in every vein and fold of wrinkled skin, that it is difficult by close scrutiny, to believe it is not a living hand. There is Dutch nicety in it, and Samuel's face is finished like a miniature, though large as life.

David before Nebachadnessar is also gorgeous in splendor and admirable in expression. A bird of Paradise plume in the turban of the King rises into the dusky air like soft, gold light. It is not a painting of it, but a real bird of Paradise plume— And so is the mirror upon the wall, made of pearl instead of glass. It must be an ornament as one cannot see one's face in pearl—but it is vast, and it is pearl. The Magi who sit to listen to David are real old stiffnecked Jews in concentrated essence and figure—And as to the gold robes of the King and the velvet and jewels, there they all are, stiff, rich and glowing, and the King is terrible and grand. A poor old woman who sat by me on the couch, as I was looking at it, and to whom I explained it, said at last "Well, I think I'd as soon buy that one as any."

But I am not going to talk of the Exhibition just now—only a gentleman told Mr. Hawthorne that there was in England five times as many great pictures as are there collected!

We received the letters from America to-day. Yours are very rich in interest as usual and I have put them before me to answer, before I say anything else. It is not the last letter you can write me, however, by the Consular bag, for we are still Consul indefinitely, and Mr. Hawthorne is now content to remain so till our visit to Paris be over. Your recent letters, which I have not particularly answered, are not attainable just now, so I will confine myself to this very last of August 23rd, Roxbury.[7] In the first place you had better keep my letters of travels about England and Scotland at least till some other turn of destiny. You shall always have all the journals and letters descriptive of what I see, whenever I can get them to you, as I consider it a duty to be eyes and ears for you as much as possible. All James Clarke[8] said is very interesting about Architecture, and I will observe it comparatively.

I have had two letters from Miss Shepard[9] [and Ada was confirming to Clay, at the same time, that she had just received one from Sophia].[10] The first announced her arrival and showed she had not received my note which I sent to America, and it was a little formal. But I wrote to her at once and her second note was very sweet and satisfactory.

The reason why we are not now in London, is because Mr. Hawthorne would be so far from us, and he must still take care of his business, and it would be no pleasure at all to be there without him. So we are at Leamington for the sake of its pure air, and because we wish to spend a day at Kenilworth and another at Warwick Castle, both close by. And we are going to Coventry also to walk down

Lady Godiva's street, and see the image of Peeping Tom. Mr. Hawthorne can always be absent ten days—according to law—After this absence, he will return to Liverpool to arrange about going to France with us on the twentieth of September. He can have ten days in each quarter, and so he will have twenty days together then. After that he will come back to Liverpool and arrange about his affairs. It is but two days from Liverpool—or one day, if he travels fast. We shall take apartments in Paris in an agreeable place, and the children and I shall catch the French accent and tournure, and all the graces we can seize. Ada Shepard will therefore have a fine chance for French finish.

Julian took in Old Trafford some fencing lessons of a drill sergeant there which he enjoyed to the utmost, and he was a splendid scholar. The soldier was perfectly gentlemanly and a classical scholar, and had a fine physique, and was as gentle as the brave always are. Julian loved him enthusiastically—and he loved Julian. He said he was the strongest young gentleman he had ever known, and understood the technics marvellously for one so young. He was very proud of him indeed & engaged him as a correspondent.[11]

For some reason, Sophia put the letter aside at this point, uncompleted. Next day, Thursday, dawned fine and clear and as she must have been feeling particularly well in the morning, Mr. and Mrs. Hawthorne took the air, with their son, and strolled with the other fashionables into the town:

In the forenoon [today], my wife and I, with Julian, walked down through the Upper and Lower Parade (but first through Warwick-street—I like to repeat these grand names) to the Jephson Gardens, which are open to the public at the price of three-pence. The English, principally by aid of their moist climate, and not too fervid sun, excel in converting flat surfaces into beautiful scenery,[12] through the skilful arrangement of trees and shrubbery. They do it in the little patches under the windows of a suburban villa, and on a larger scale in a tract of many acres. This garden is named in honor of a Doctor Jephson, who first found out the virtues (if any there really be) of the well which has given Leamington its renown,[13] and converted it from an old rural village into a smart watering-place. A short distance within the garden-gates, there is a circular temple of Grecian architecture, beneath the dome of which stands a marble statue of the Doctor, very well executed, representing him with a face of fussy activity and benevolence; just the man to build up the fortunes of his native village, or perhaps to ruin all its inhabitants by his speculations. He has now been dead many years;[14] but I believe the prosperity of Leamington is a growth of the present century.

The Garden is a beautiful pleasure ground, shadowed well with trees of a fine growth, but with spaces large enough for a breadth of sunshine, and with bright flower-beds, set like gems in the green sward; old trunks of trees, too, here and there, are formed into rustic chairs, and some of them are made into flower-pots. There is an archery-ground, with targets; and, all the time we were there, three young ladies were practising archery, and sometimes hitting the mark. The Leam, a very lazy stream, after drowsing across the principal street of the town beneath a handsome bridge, skirts along the margin of the Garden, without seeming to flow at all. Its water is by no means transparent, but has a greenish, goose-puddly hue; and yet is not unpleasant to sight; and certainly the river is the perfection of the gently picturesque, sleeping along beneath a margin of willows that droop into it, and other trees that incline lovingly over it; on the garden-side, a shadowy, secluded grove, with winding paths among its boskiness, and on the opposite side the church, with its church-yard full of tombstones and shrubbery. Two anglers were fishing from the church-yard bank [impossible to do that now; the town's main post-office occupies the site]. With a book and a cigar (but I rather think the garden-deities forbid smoking) I cannot conceive of a more delightful place for a summer day than this grove on the margin of the Leam. Besides the river, there is another object of water-scenery in the shape of a small artificial lake, with a little green island in the midst. This piece of water is the haunt of swans. I forget whether I mentioned the swans in the Botanical Gardens of Old Trafford [in Manchester]; how beautiful and stately was their aspect and their movement in the water, and how infirm, disjointed, and decrepit was their gait, when they inadvisedly chose to emerge, and walk upon dry land. In the latter case, they looked like a breed of uncommonly misshapen and ill contrived geese; and I record the matter here for the sake of the moral—that we should never pass judgement on the merits of any person or thing, unless we see it in the circumstances for which it is intended or adapted.

This is the pleasantest public garden I ever was in; not that it is superior to all others in its adornments and arrangements, but because it is so quiet, and, like other Leamington characteristics, so genteel. I think the better of this glossy gentility, from observing what a pleasant surface it puts upon matters here. We now emerged from this bosky seclusion and still water-side into the lively street, and walked up the Parade, looking at the shop-windows, where were displayed a great variety of pretty objects and knickknacks, indicating much idle time and some superfluous means among the visitors of Leamington [was it then that Sophia said to Nathaniel "Just a moment, dear, I must go in here for a moment" and popped in and bought the piece of elastic that is itemized in her Accounts Book?]. They are the most brilliant ranges of shops that I have seen out of London; though I suppose that the most valuable part of the stock is displayed in the windows.[15]

The Jephson Gardens were, and still are, one of the central attractions of the town, the main entrance being situated across the road from the Pump Rooms. The area was once private property but as the *Guide Book* said:

Through the liberality of E. Willes, Esq., the gardens are appropriated to the use of the public . . . and . . . form one of the most frequented promenades for visitors and residents. Within a very recent period, considerable improvements have been effected; the gardens have been enlarged and beautified; the name changed to its present designation, in commemoration of the provincial abilities and private virtues of Dr. Jephson. . . . At the principal entrance to the gardens are two small but handsome lodges, of an ornamental construction. . . . The one on the right hand has a handsome clock . . . which indicates Greenwich time; and the other was converted into an Electric Telegraph Office in the year 1853. . . . At a short distance up the broad walk, on the left, stands a circular eight-columned temple, in the Corinthian order, which contains a finely executed statue of Dr. Jephson. . . . The statue, which was placed there in 1849, is . . . generally considered to be an excellent likeness of the Doctor . . . . The large number of fashionables who are attracted hither for the purpose of promenading and healthful recreations, is the best proof of the estimation in which the gardens are held. They are under the management of trustees, composed of some of the principal inhabitants of the Spa, Lord Somerville officiating as chairman; and the terms of admission are regulated by a scale. . . . During the summer months, a succession of public fetes are held in these gardens, which have hitherto been carried on with the most complete success, and have been the means of attracting thousands of visitors to the town.

Lansdowne Circus. Photograph taken in the 1860s. Courtesy of the Warwickshire County Record Office, Warwick.

That other principal landmark of the town, the Royal Pump Rooms and Baths, had been erected in 1813 "at a cost of nearly £25,000." The edifice,

extending 106 feet in length . . . is surrounded on each side by a spacious colonnade, formed by duplicated pillars of the Doric order, and built of native stone . . . . and forms one of the most complete structures of the kind in the kingdom. At each extremity of the central building are two entrances into the pump room, formed by folding doors. This room is of large extent and noble proportions; the ornamental parts of the ceiling, the cornices, and all the interior embellishments being chaste and elegant. Some well-executed casts from the antique . . . are not among the least interesting of its internal decorations. . . . At the west side of the room there is an orchestra erected, and at the south end is the pump, with a basin in the centre, standing on an ornamental pedestal of Derbyshire marble, inclosed by a mahogany balustrade. . . . The hours for taking the waters and promenading are from seven till ten in the morning. . . . There are two divisions of baths, entirely separate. . . . In number there are twenty baths, of every description, viz., hot, cold, tepid and shower; hot and cold douches for topical applications, and a bath chair, which is an excellent contrivance for the safe and easy conveyance of the bather from the undressing chair into the bath. . . . Mr. Wincote has for many years conducted this establishment. . . . The process of heating the bath generally takes place while in the act of undressing; so that the bather has the opportunity of having whatever temperature his disease may require or his inclination dictate.

Later in the day, Nathaniel and Julian were off again:

[This] afternoon, Julian and I went along the Holly Walk, and ascended what I believe is called the Newbold Hill to the "Lover's Grove"; a range of tall old oaks and elms, from beneath which we can see Warwick Castle, and a wide extent of generally level, but beautiful landscape. So far, the walk was familiar to us when we were in Leamington before. Thence we took a field-path, which led us along hedge-rows, chiefly of hawthorn, but intermixed with blackberry bushes, on which the berries hung abundantly, mostly red, but with here and there a black one, which we plucked and ate. After a walk of a mile or so, our track ended in a farm-establishment, which, house and outbuildings, were entirely new [probably Glebe Farm], and of red brick. At a short distance, in a hollow, lay an old brick-village; and after enquiring at a house, and being barked at by a chained dog, we found our way thither, and entered its narrow, crooked, and ugly street. The village was Cubington [sic], formerly Combeington—so named from Combe, a hollow. It is a very ancient place, though wholly destitute of ivied beauty or any kind of antique grace; its houses being all of brick, which, in many cases, has been patched into the old timber-frames that still look as stable as they were in Elizabeth's time. Of all English villages, I think this is the meanest and ugliest; and, small though it was, it had two ale-houses. A little apart from this wretched street, we found the church, with its low, square, battlemented tower, perhaps of Norman antiquity; and, playing and laughing at the church-gate, there were some village-girls, of whom I enquired the way back to Leamington, and heard myself laughed at as I followed their instructions. We returned by the high-road, which led us through Lillington, a prettier little village than Cubington [sic]; one range of thatched cottages was very pretty indeed, with their little gardens before every door, sepa-rated by trimly luxuriant hedges, with fruit-trees, and beehives, and glimpses of brick floors, or stone ones, through the open doors; and women and children peering out at the passing wayfarers. These cottages were a range of comfortable little nests, where, I suppose, the inmates may have had a longer hereditary tenure than the owners of many a castle or manor-house. The church of Lillington is reached by a shady lane, and is not visible from the high road. Since I was here last, it has been almost entirely renewed, but, I believe, on its ancient plan; and the gray, square tower remains unchanged. I observed a stained window (of recent date) in the Chancel; and it is as fine and picturesque a little church as I have seen.[16] All over England, there seems to be a great zeal for the preservation and reverential re-edification of old churches. When I first came from America, I valued nothing but the genuine old article, the very old stones that the Saxons or Normans first laid one upon another; but I have passed through that phase of the love of antiquity, and now prize the antique idea more than the ancient material. Therefore I love to see an old church lovingly rebuilt.

We had a short walk hence into the stately avenues of Leamington.[17] In my remarks about the town's prettiness and gentility, I have hardly done justice to some almost palatial ranges of edifices, and separate residences, which look quite equal to any in London. Among the range of thatched cottages, mentioned above, I must mention one, the garden of which was adorned in a way indicating taste and fancy in the occupant; for instance, a bee-hive curiously made of oyster-shells, a stump of a tree with flowers growing out of it.[18]

Perhaps it was while she was resting in the afternoon after the exertions of the morning walk that Sophia completed her letter to Elizabeth:

Sept. 10th. Dear Elizabeth, We have been walking in Jephson's gardens this morn-ing, where the archery grounds are. The river Leam flows on one side with noble trees bending over, [*deletion*], and stately bosquets [*sic*] on the banks. Broad, paved walks, rich shrubbery, lawns, a little lake with a white swan and grey swans, a temple (after Tivoli, containing a marble statue of the good founder of the gardens, Dr. Jephson) rising in the midst, grand trees, borders and circles of flowers, compose the gardens. Seats of all kinds invite to sit, and there are covered bowers for a shelter from showers and sun and a maze for the curious. It is perfectly elegant and beautiful. Three ladies were shooting at targets this morning. Leamington is the fairest town we have seen in England and the stateliest, for its size, and the trees—the trees of Warwickshire! The whole town was once perhaps the Chase of Warwick Castle—close by—Rooks still caw on one group of old trees in front of a crescent of princely houses. It is very clean and bright here also, very different from the smoky western towns. It is a Royal Spa and a Grecian temple is raised over the medicinal waters and baths. Goodbye dear Lizzie, now— I have all my arrangements to make for Paris in these few days, besides that I wish to be always ready when my husband says "Come with me". Heaven bless you,

Your affectionate sister,
Sophy[19]

The next day was a washout, literally, as it poured with rain ceaselessly, and although the family stayed indoors the Accounts Book confirms that someone had to sneak out and make a few purchases of food and settle a small grocery bill. English weather conditions were bad but in Paris it was a much better day where Ada was continuing to record for Clay's benefit her adventures, several of which concerned her effect on her fellow boarders (the male ones) at M. Fezandie's establishment; but while she was meeting a number of acquaintances she was not making any real *friends*: "There is one quite interesting young gentleman who sits near me at table, with whom I am beginning to form a little acquaintance. He is a Frenchman and appears to be out of health, but he is very cultivated evidently, and is rather hand-some. On the whole I think I fancy him more than anyone here, except M. Fezandie. But there are no companions for me here, and I shall be very glad to greet Mrs. Hawthorne when she comes. From her letters I feel sure that I shall be very happy with her."[20]

The following morning didn't appear to promise too much in the way of good weather either, but at least one member of the Leamington party felt sufficiently confident of local conditions to warrant their undertaking a trip to the hitherto unvisited Kenilworth. Nathaniel's description of the trip was duly recorded in his journal:

The weather was very uncertain through the last week; and [this] morning, too, was misty and sunless; notwithstanding which, Mamma, Una, Julian and I,[21] took the rail for Kenilworth at a quarter to eleven. The distance from Leamington is less than five miles; and at the Kenilworth Station we found a little bit of an omnibus, into which we packed ourselves, together with two ladies, one of whom, at least, was an American. I begin to agree partly with the English, that we are not a people of elegant manners; at all events, there is sometimes a bare, hard, meagre sort of deportment, especially in our women, that has not its parallel elsewhere. But perhaps what sets off this kind of behaviour, and brings it into alto-relievo, is the fact of such uncultivated persons travelling abroad, and going to see sights that would not be interesting except to people of some education and refinement.

We saw but little of the village of Kenilworth, passing through it sidelong fashion in the omnibus; but I learn from the Guide Book that it has between three and four thousand inhabitants, and is of immemorial antiquity. We saw a few old, gabled and timber-framed houses; but generally the town was of modern aspect, although less so in the immediate vicinity of the Castle-gate, across the road from which, there was an inn, with bowling-greens,[22] and a little bunch of houses and shops. A little apart from the high road, there is a gate-house, ancient, but in excellent repair, towered, turretted [sic], and battlemented, and looking like a castle in itself. Until Cromwell's time, the entrance to the castle used to be beneath an arch that passed through this structure; but, the gate-house being granted to one of the Parliament officers, he converted it into a residence, and apparently added on a couple of gables, which now look quite as venerable as the rest of the edifice. Admission within the outer precincts of the castle is now obtained through a little wicket, close beside the gate-house; at which sat one or two old men, who touched their hats to us in humble willingness to accept a fee. One of them had guide-books for sale; and finding that we were not to be bothered by a cicerone, we bought one of his books.

The ruins are perhaps two hundred yards (or more, or less) from the gate-house and the road, and the space between is a pasture for sheep, which also browse in the inner court, and shelter themselves in the dungeons and state-apartments of the castle. Goats would be fitter occupants, because they could climb to the tops of the crumbling towers, and nibble the weeds and shrubbery that grow there. The first part of the castle which we reached is called Caesar's Tower, being the oldest portion of the ruins, and still very stalwart and massive, and built, (as all the rest is) of red free-stone. Caesar's Tower being on the right, Leicester's buildings (erected by Queen Elizabeth's favorite) is on the left; and between these two formerly stood stood [sic] other portions of the castle, which have now as entirely disappeared as if they had never existed; and through the wide gap thus opened appears the grassy inner court, surrounded on three sides by half-fallen towers and shattered walls. Some of these were erected by John of Gaunt; and in this portion of the ruins is the banquetting-hall [sic]—or rather was—for it has now neither floor nor roof, but only the broken stonework of some tall, arched windows, and the beautiful, old, ivied arch of the entrance-way, now inaccessible from the ground. The ivy is very abundant about the ruins, and hangs its green curtains quite from top to bottom of some of the windows. There are likewise very large and aged trees within the castle, there being no roof nor pavement anywhere, except in here and there a dungeon-like nook; so that the trees, having soil and air enough, and being sheltered from unfriendly blasts, can grow as if in a nursery. Hawthorn, however, next to ivy, is the great ornament and comforter of these desolate ruins. I never saw so much and such thriving hawthorn anywhere else; in the court, high up on crumbly heights, on the sod that carpets roofless rooms; everywhere, indeed, and now rejoicing in plentiful crops of red berries. The ivy is even more wonderfully luxuriant; its trunks being, in some places, two or three feet across, and forming real buttresses against the walls, which are actually supported and vastly strengthened by this parasite, that clung to them at first only for its own convenience, and now holds them up lest it should be ruined by their fall. Thus an abuse has strangely grown into a use; and I think we may sometimes see the same fact, morally, in English matters. There is something very curious in the close firm grip which the ivy fixes upon the wall, closer and closer for centuries. Neither is it at all nice as to what it clutches, in its necessity for support. I saw, in the outer court of the castle, an old hawthorn tree to which (no doubt a hundred years ago, at least) a plant of ivy had married itself, and the ivy-trunk and the hawthorn-trunk were now absolutely incorporated, and, in their close embrace, you could not tell which was which.

At one end of the banquetting-hall [sic], there are two large bay-windows, one of which looks into the inner-court, and the other affords a view of the surrounding country. The former is called, I think, Queen Elizabeth's dressing-room. Beyond the banquetting-hall [sic], is what the guide-book calls the Strong Tower, up to the top of which we climbed, principally by the aid of ruins that have tumbled down from it. A lady sat half way down the crumbly descent, within the castle, on a camp-stool, and before an easel, sketching this tower, on the summit of which we sat. She told my wife that it was Amy Robsart's Tower; and within it, open to the day, and quite accessible, we saw a room that we were free to imagine had been occupied by her. I do not find that these associations of real scenes with fictitious events greatly heighten the charm of them.

By this time, the sun had come out brightly, and with such warmth that we were glad to sit down in the shadow of the ruins. Several sight-seers were now rambling about, and among them some schoolboys, who kept scrambling up to points whither no animal, except a goat, would have ventured. Their shouts and the sunshine made the old castle cheerful; and what with the ivy and the hawthorn, and the other old trees, it was very beautiful and picturesque. But a castle does not make nearly so interesting and impressive a ruin as an abbey; because the latter was built for beauty, and on a plan in which deep thought and feeling were involved; and having once been a grand and beautiful work, it continues grand and beautiful through all the successive stages of its decay. But a castle is rudely piled together for strength and other material conveniences; and having served these ends, it has nothing left to fall back upon, but crumbles into shapeless masses, which are often as little picturesque as a pile of bricks. Without the ivy and the shrubbery, this huge Kenilworth would not be a pleasant object, except for one or two window frames, with broken tracery, in the baquetting [sic] hall. Moreover (it is a small thing to say, but true nevertheless) the sheep are a nuisance and a nastiness, and commit great abominations; and, whether by their fault, or whatever else, the more secluded recesses are not pleasant to creep into.

We staid from a little past eleven o'clock till two, and identified the various parts of the castle, as well as we could by the Guide Book. The ruins are very extensive, though less so than I should have imagined, considering that seven acres were included within the castle-wall. But a large part of the structure has been taken away to build houses in Kenilworth village and elsewhere, and much, too, to make roads with, and a good deal lies under the green turf in the court-yards, inner and outer. As we returned to the gate, my wife and Una went into the gate-house to see an old chimney-piece and other antiquities; and Julian and I, emerging through the gate, went a little way round the outer wall, and saw the remains of the moat, and Lunn's tower, a rent and shattered structure of John of Gaunt. The omnibus now drove up, and one of the old men at the gate came hobbling up to open the door, and was rewarded with a sixpence; and we drove down to the King's Head,[23] and got some luncheon. It consisted of a prime round of corn-beef, and some ale; real English cheer. We then walked out, and bought ten-and-sixpence worth of prints of the castle, and enquired our way to the church, and to the ruins of the priory. The latter, so far as we could discover them, are very few and uninteresting; and the church, though it has a venerable exterior, and an aged spire, has been so modernized within, and in so plain a fashion, as to have lost what beauty it may once have had. There were a few brasses and mural monuments, one of which was a marble group of a dying woman and her family, by Westmacott. The sexton was a cheerful little man, but knew very little about his church, and nothing of the remains of the Priory. There is nothing else particularly to be told of this day, which was spent very pleasantly amid this beautiful, green English scenery, these fine old Warwickshire trees, these broad, gently swelling fields.[24]

It must be said that in the case of Kenilworth Castle, though much of the shrubbery and ivy have been removed since the Hawthornes inspected the ruins, it undoubtedly retains a massive and overwhelming presence that recalls to the visitor the centuries that have washed over it and the reality of its associations with people and events that are to be found in the history books.[25] Nothing could be further from the atmosphere generated by the nearby Warwick Castle, where the fact that it was a family residence till very recent times, and the continual restoration of the fabric, combine to detract from it its equally historic associations. Perhaps it is something to do with the feeling that although Kenilworth is a ruined castle its atmosphere readily conjures up in the mind's eye its history and associations, whereas Warwick, in its presentation, is still alive and because of the physical presence of objects from bygone ages there is not the compulsion to create mentally for oneself the associations with the past. There is much in this quotation from Nathaniel's journal regarding their visit to Kenilworth to confirm the feeling that despite his knowledge and appreciation of English history he was not duly impressed, after prolonged exposure to its visible remains, by its tangible appearance, and displayed an American impatience with its maintenance, in that he was prepared to revere the *idea* of the centuries-old history, but saw no good reason for its physical upkeep as something intrinsically good in itself, particularly with regard to people continuing to live in dwellings that should have been demolished ages ago as unfit for human habitation, but that were maintained simply because they *were* old. It is probable that he would have given the orders to raze a village like Whitnash to the ground, given the authority to do so (but sparing the church), for by rebuilding it it could be brought into the nineteenth century as a fit place for its inhabitants, even though the latter would probably have been outraged at the desecration.

It couldn't have been long after they returned from Kenilworth that Sophia sat down and wrote the following massive letter to Elizabeth that, in comparison with Nathaniel's journal entry on the same subject, gives the impression that her descriptive talents were the equal of, if not better than, his:

Saturday Eve.
Leamington Sept.12th

My dear Elizabeth.
We intended yesterday to go to Kenilworth to spend the day, but it rained from morning to night, and we were all shut into our pleasant fold like so many lambs.

This morning, early, there was shadow and mist and I was the only one who hoped for a bright day, but I knew [these?] [autumn?] days often begin with mist, and become resplendent at noon, and so it proved on this occasion. It was nearly the last of my husband's leisure ten days, for tomorrow, being Sunday, we could go to no show-place, and I was most anxious to make sure of Kenilworth as soon as possible. There was not blue sky enough to encourage Mr. Hawthorne for the half past nine train, but at quarter to eleven we set forth in very good sunshine and delicious air. By a short turn out of our Circus we come into a street called Regent's grove, on account of a lovely promenade between noble trees for a very long distance, almost to the railroad station, and Una and I walked that way, leaving Mr. Hawthorne and Julian to follow, because we wished to saunter. They overtook us, having gone down the Parade, which is the principal street of Leamington—containing hotels and shops—and it crosses at right angles Warwick St, which reaches for several miles until it arrives at Warwick Castle itself.

In fifteen minutes after entering the carriage we were at Kenilworth station, and we should have been there sooner, if we had not been delayed at the Warwick depot.[26] We found a nice little omnibus in waiting for any one bound to the Castle, and we got into it, followed by two women. One of them was a thin, American-looking, vulgar person, who proved to be an American from her conversation, and she talked on in a way Englishwomen never do, revealing all her intentions and experiences. The other was evidently English, and reserved accordingly. It was very curious to see one of our careworn, inquisitive, business looking countrywomen, of the grade of a shopkeeper who sells gingerbread horses and small wares, vis à vis in a coach driving to Kenilworth. Not apparently because it would delight her imagination to see the castle for historical and poetical reasons, but because it was a place to be seen, and a part of her business in hand. She may have been a ship-master's wife—and she told her companion that next Saturday at the time she was then speaking, she expected to be on the sea, making her way home.

The country was very beautiful indeed through which we passed, with its magnificent trees, sunniest green meadows and lawns, all as fresh as Young Creation. The very rain we deplored yesterday had been painting the face of the earth with these freshest lines of green, and wherever, on the darker-hued trees, a yellow leaf betrayed the approaching autumn, it did not seem to be a sign of decay, but only an additional splendor, as if the richness had turned to veritable gold for fuller expression. The bright greens of England seem to be lined with gold, and in the autumn the leaves merely turn their golden linings. The approach to the domain is through roads bordered with trees, winding along, and also through a narrow river which we should call a brook, glympses of the castle towers appearing at every turn. When we alighted we found ourselves at a wicket, at each post of which sat two endlessly old men, and an old woman. The old woman had a basket of apples and pears, and Una bought some, and then the gate was opened to us without any questions or any offer of guidance, except a description book. But the grass was very wet and I had no india rubbers, and Mr. Hawthorne went off with Una to buy me some, being resolved to make them, I believe, if he could not find any in the only shop not explored—for we had already tried one shoe-store nearer the station. He returned with the only pair in Kenilworth that would fit, and the only pair the shopman had left in his box. Julian and I had gone in and sat down in the great Gateway or Barbican, now made into a dwelling by some one of Cromwell's officers. It is a lofty square keep, with a tower at each corner and we sat in a vestibule upon some sculptured pieces of alabaster disposed upon the stone floor. An arched doorway, shut and locked, had an inscription upon it to the effect that for sixpence each, persons should be allowed to see an alabaster chimney piece and a carved wooden one, severally brought from the castle at the time Cromwell destroyed it. But we did not wait for this at first, and after thankfully putting on my rubbers, we went through another little iron gate into the great outer Base Court. In the palmy days of the Castle, that high strong building we had sat under was the Grand Entrance—and a carriage drive passed along where we sat, beneath vast arches. It is in such perfect repair and preservation that it looks as if it might stand a thousand years or more still—and behind it, a modern house is placed on in a very discordant manner, as if it had fled to the Doujon Keep for protection.

The great outer Base Court is a soft green pasture now for sheep, and a flock was peacefully grazing all about it. On the left as we entered were once the Stables, the ruins of which are at present built into the outhouses and barns of the farmer who occupies the Gatehouse. A hedge separates these structures from the lawn, and opposite, on an eminence, stands the lordly ruins which history and poetry have made so interesting. As we ascended the gently rising ground, and entered the Inner Court, on our right was the famous Caesar's Tower, built before the Conquest, still looking of mighty strength & power of resistance—and except for Cromwell, it still would be almost entire. The stone is so sharp in outline and surface that in many parts it seems just cut, and even the mullions of the windows remain whole. It is a greyer red than the rest, and ruder in design and ornament. It was in Caesar's Tower that the clock hung which during Elizabeth's visit was made by the Lord of Leicester to point always to the the Banqueting hour, two o'clk—as if there were no other hour to be recognised but that of revel. When you remember that the magnificent Earl spent six thousand pounds a day, while the Queen's first visit lasted, that [deletion] ten [deletion] oxen were roasted every morning, forty hogsheads of beer drunk daily, and sixteen hogsheads of wine, it would seem as if there could be nothing but revel and wassail. On the left, opposite Caesar's, stand the far more beautiful ruins of the portion that Robert Dudley built himself at the time he received the castle as a gift from Elizabeth, when his repairs and additions cost a half million sterling! These Leicester buildings are upheld, embowered and superbly adorned with enormous vines and trees of ivy. The strong branches clasp the towers and sides with arms of iron. They support on forks of thick sturdy sprays whole windows and turrets—and spread out like huge forest timber cut [word blotted] in halves—all over [word blotted] crumbling flanks [word blotted] most resolute force arranges itself in the very only effectual way to prevent the beloved from falling. It really seems to have a human heart and friendship for the ruins. The trunks look four centuries old—as they probably are, and while the first leaves seem never to die, new tender sprouts are yearly coming out & adorn the old bark—beauty and youth veiling ugliness and age in successive layers—and after climbing up the sides in this diffusive embrace, it reaches the crumbling battlements, and to conceal the gnawing teeth of time there it rises into perfect trees, full and round where it is not lovelier to trail over and hang in festoons and wreaths and tassels. Ivy and Time contend for the mastery and have a drawn battle of it. Constant decay, constant fresh growth. Enormous hawthorne trees, large as our largest horsechestnuts also abound around the castle, and they are now made rich and brilliant with scarlet haws. I shall enclose you a bit of hawthorne from Queen Elizabeth's dressing room and also a leaf of ivy from the same place. I do not send it as a precious relic to be loved, for I am sure you cannot love that imperious, vain, vindictive Princess—but only as something historically and poetically valuable, as coming from that spot.

Entering the Inner Court, with Caesar's Tower on the right and Leicester's on the left, directly in front is John of Gaunt's Great Hall or Banqueting room, forming one side of the original Quadrangle, which was shut in by the Earl of Leicester's Lobby and Henry the Eigth's [sic] Lodgings, now utterly gone. Nearest to Caesar's Tower, beneath one extremity of Henry the Eigtht's [sic] Lodgings, was the entrance to this Inner Court, and opposite to it was the arched door of the Great Hall reached by a lofty flight of steps, for there was another room under it, where the subordinate officers and retainers dined. But now there is no floor to be seen either below or above and when we stepped into "time-honored Lancaster's" once magnificent structure, we stood upon the grassy ground; and where once a gorgeous roof arched over the hall, carved elaborately in pendants, thus, —now is ambient air, through which we gaze up into the sky. And instead of the rich silk hangings that graced the walls when Elizabeth entered, now waved the long wreaths of ivy—and instead of gold borders was sunshine, and for music and revel, SILENCE—profound, not even a breeze breaking it—for we had again one of those brooding, still days which we have so often been fortunate enough to have among ruined castles and Abbeys. One great bay window, large enough for a little room, was Elizabeth's boudoir, where she arranged her toilette during those seventeen days. A great deal of the fine carving remains on the stone mullions and canopies of this enormous window. Base stone seats are still left around it, upon which, when softly cushioned with velvet embroidered with gold, Elizabeth sat and saw a fair prospect. For then a lake, two miles in extent, stretched from the couch walls to the woods and plains beyond, where deer abounded. For the Park and Chase extended twenty miles! and superb forests closed them in. Cromwell's officers drained the lake and cut down acres of trees, and portioned out the land between themselves. Opposite the Queen's window is another Bay window, looking into the Inner quadrangle. Six tall arched windows besides lighted the Hall, three on each side. Some of them are broken away and ivy covers the rents and fissures. One I sketched for you, and will put it in by and by. At one end, where the Dais was placed, on which Elizabeth shone like a mine with jewels, the outer wall has quite fallen, and beyond on a crag sat a lady artist with her easel, painting a portion of the ruin. We passed her to climb up on the summit of the Strong Tower, which makes one corner of the Inner Court on the side of Caesar's Fortress. From it we had an enchanting view of the lovely plain, once the lake, and the country beyond, where was the Chase and the woods. I made a sketch of part of the ruins as I sat on that height. When we came down, I asked the artiste to let me look at her painting, and she consented, and said it was Tresilian's Room, where poor Amy Robsart fled. So we found we had been sitting over it. We now went into it and looked out of its narrow windows with deepest interest. Very small space had the lovely Amy to retreat from the rough Michael Lambourne. We saw from the window the site of the Pleasance where she ran from his abominable presence. So this was Mervyn's Tower, also called the Strong Tower. Here is a plan of the Quadrangle.

It is not so perfectly square as my lines but it is all right with respect to each part. We entered exactly the opposite way from Queen Elizabeth as I will show you on the other page.[27]

From the Gallery Tower to Mortimer's was the Tilt Yard. To the right of Mer-

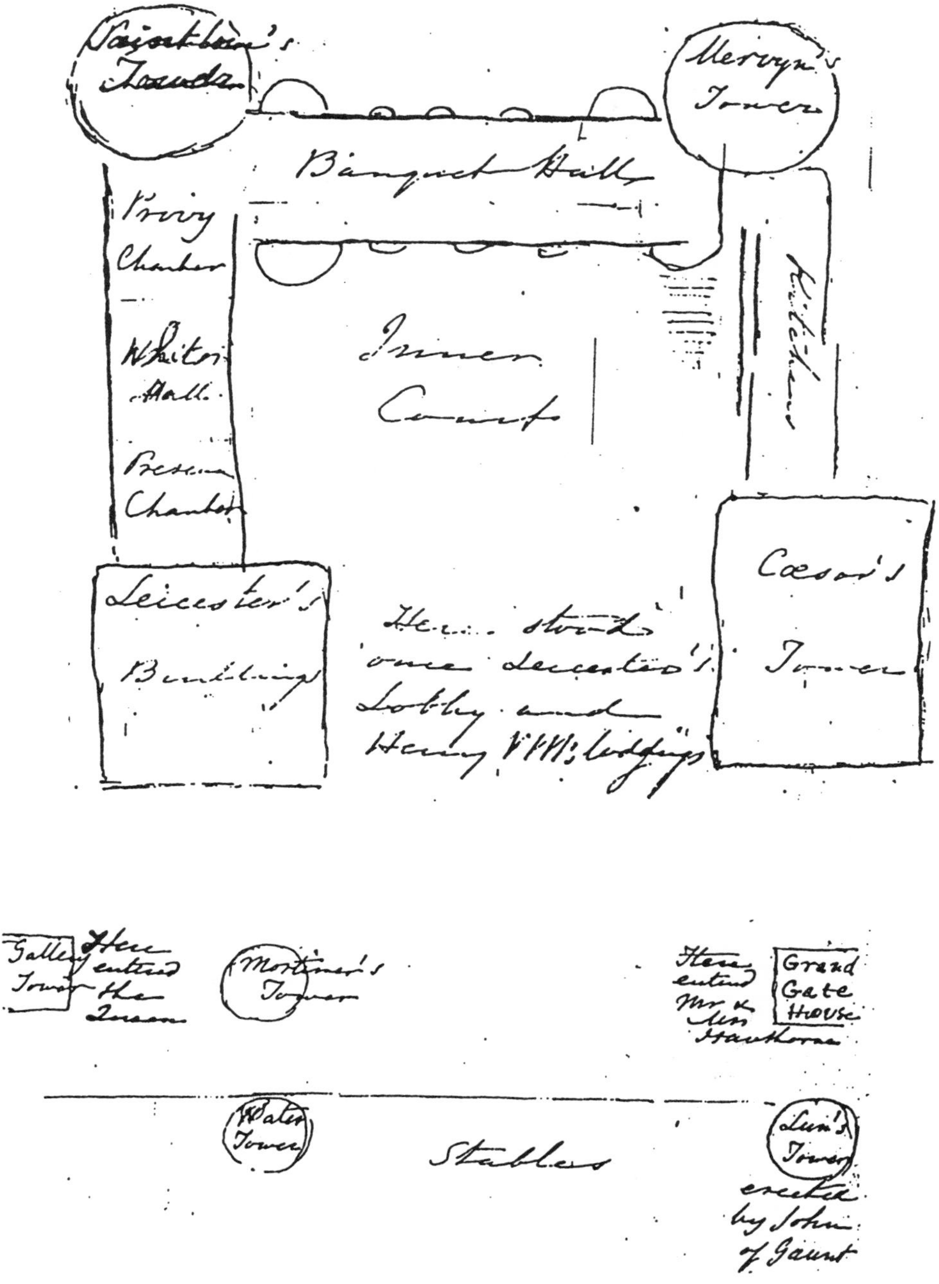

Saintlow's Tower

Mervyn's Tower

Banquet Hall

Privy Chamber

White Hall

Presence Chamber

Inner Court

Kitchen

Leicester's Building

Caesar's Tower

Here stood once Leicester's Lobby and Henry VIII's lodgings

Gallery Tower — Here entered the Queen

Mortimer's Tower

Here entered Mr & Mrs Hawthorne

Grand Gate House

Water Tower

Stables

Lun's Tower erected by John of Gaunt

vyn's Tower (as you look at it on the page) was the Pleasance. Outside the kitchens was the Garden. Enclosing these was a wall, including seven acres. Beyond the wall were two miles of lake—and then the Chase and Parks. When we left Tresilian's room, we found Una sketching Caesar's Tower, and Mr. Hawthorne and I went into my Lord of Leicester's buildings. Not a floor is left throughout above or below, but looking up from the ground we could see in each story brackets which once supported the floors. On one window-sill a sizeable tree was growing, and overwhelming ivy hung every where. It is about three hundred years since these broken towers and halls were in their greatest magnificence and they would have withstood time well, if Cromwell had not forcibly destroyed them, and afterwards they were left for many years without a Keeper, and every vagabond worked his will upon them. Now they are the property of the present Earl of Clarendon and are carefully guarded by the Keeper who lives in the Gatehouse.

It would seem as if Kenilworth Castle ought to be demolished if the scene of wicked actions may share in the retribution for sin. Walter Scott has thrown an interest over Leicester but he was so thoroughly unprincipled, so weak, heartless and unscrupulous in his ambition—a murderer even to gain his ends—(as I find here in the very theatre of his deeds) that one would expect the ground to be cursed where he trod. I have seen several contemporary portraits of him, and he is handsome and of noble figure; yet not so handsome as his brother, who has come down to this time with the title of the good Ambrose Dudley, Earl of Warwick.

And yet one cannot help mourning over the wreck and ruins of such lordly palaces as monuments of artistic beauty and skill of man [Nathaniel had not agreed with her on this point]. What an extraordinary vision or rather sternest reality is that of the Iron Cromwell passing over England like a vast ploughshare, and without tolerance, mercy or misgiving, overturning abbeys, castles and palaces like clods, so that often the place that knew them knows them no more. He was the Minister of Retribution for enormous wrong, and he ploughed the land and spared not—at best, letting the air of heaven into secret halls of crime and superstition. For he razed roofs, if he did no more, and God's rain and sunshine and winds purified the inmost recesses of luxury and guilt and idolatry. It is said that he was reluctant to destroy Conway Castle, on account of its exceeding beauty and it remains more perfect than any other. Even some floors are left—that of Queen Eleanor's bower—and others, and the battlements are almost entire. It was one of Edward First's fairest creations, wondrous builder of castles, as he was. But Cromwell stabled his horses in sublime cathedrals and beautiful churches. I suppose that this was to air the aisles and naves and choirs from the steps and breath of corrupt priests, and to drive out the odor of prayers offered to the Virgin and the saints. Alas for it! How not only the innocent human being must suffer from the guilty, but even innocent Beauty, Sublimity and Grandeur also must suffer. And it is a comfort to think that even as God is not dead, but lives today as in the remotest Eternity, so also Genius and Creativeness still live and there are other forms for it in the future that will doubtless transcend all former expressions. Nothing but music, however, can ever equal or surpass Architecture in variety of utterance. Music is poetry to the ear, architecture to the eye, and poetry is music and architecture to the soul, for it can reproduce both. Music, however, seems to be freer from all shackles than any other art and I remember that in one of my essays for Margaret Fuller I made it out to my own satisfaction to be the apex of expression. The old Glasgow verger had not got so far as to see that it needed the "Kist of Whistles" to make his beloved Cathedral soar & glow with life and praise to its utmost capacity.[28] But I cannot say that it does not sing even without a sound in its "immortal curves" (as Ruskin calls those curves that return in no conceivable time or space). Cathedrals sing and they also pray with pointed arches for folded hands. So I mused and sat on the broken stones of Robert Dudley's once splendid Towers, and sketched the lofty windows of the Banquet Hall. But the sketch is mislaid and I cannot copy it into my note for you. You will, however, see some fine and accurate engravings of the whole, when I return to America, for I bought five in the village of Kenilworth which were taken from photographs, and exactly render the scene. Julian liked these ruins better than any he had seen, he said, and he climbed up on the dismantled turrets of Leicester's buildings, and settled himself among the ivy like some rare bird with wonderful eyes. His hair had grown very long and clustered round his head in a hyacinthine fashion, and I think my lord would have been glad to call him his own princely boy. All the princeliness that lies in clustering locks, Julian has lost today, however, for a hairdresser has cropped him like a puritan.[29]

Mr. Hawthorne and I walked round the inner circle of the walls that remain, and were filled with amazement at the huge hawthorne trees, which alone are standing of all the shrubbery. It seems to have been a favorite tree of the Earl and now, with ivy, it makes all the foliage. Descending into the base court, we walked to the corner where the Water Tower stood—and then Una and I knocked at the Gate House door beneath the arch, to gain admission to the room where the famous chimney piece is put up. An old woman opened to us, an animated mummy of a woman, and we followed her into the apartment filled with the carved panelling and cornices of some of the state rooms of the Castle, picked up after Cromwell had scattered it. A fireplace of alabaster, surmounted with wood-sculpture, must have been magnificent—for it is now very handsome. It is carved in escutcheons and bears with ragged staves (which is the device of the Earls of Leicester & Warwick) and the ciphers R L and also E R, for Queen Elizabeth. I daresay it was prepared for the very visit of the Queen so brilliantly described by Sir Walter—as this chimney piece was taken from the Presence Hall. It was formerly gilded, as traces of the gold still remain. Here is a wretched sketch of Leicester's building at one corner of the Quadrangle with Caesar's Tower far off on the other, as viewed from the Gallery Tower end of the Base Court.

We explored Caesar's Tower on the side of the Kitchens but did not have a very satisfactory examination. Inside is a vast hall and there are small rooms all round it. We had ordered the carriage to come for us at two, and we then left the outermost wicket. A deep moat extends on that side, till it meets the lake—or what was the lake. The old men still sat at the posts, lying in wait for sixpences and when the carriage approached, one of them hobbled to the door and opened it for us very superfluously, but I put into his withered hand a silver token just as if he had performed a needful duty, and off we drove to a hotel for lunch. Kenilworth is one long street, made safe at each end by a church—one eight hundred years old [St. Nicholas's] and the other modern [St. John's]. It is considered a very pure town, and healthy, and the hotels are fitted up conveniently for families to board. After lunch, we walked out to see the ruins of the Priory of Black Canons, and the ancient church. But first we went to a nice print shop and bought the five engravings I spoke of just now.[30] Then we proceeded to the Abbey grounds. We entered by a turn-stile into an extensive lawn, with a gravel path quite across it. Two shapeless masses of ruins were all that remained of the walls of the building. But a beautiful arched gateway still stands, and a chapter house, dug up from the earth about twenty years ago stands in a line with the gateway, but is so demoralised with a modern gable roof and very shapely mendings, so as to be a secure shelter for cattle, that we were repelled from it entirely, notwithstanding the mullioned windows and one or two other signs of venerable beauty. For four hundred and thirty years the Black Canons exercised power over the county, from the time of Henry First. Several magnificent trees stand upon the lawn, and the fish ponds of the monks, overhung with elms and willows, skirt one side. Through another turn stile we entered the grave yard of the Church, which has a finely carved Saxon door and a beautiful bell tower and steeple, mossy and ivy wreathed. A very intelligent, bright eyed beadle came and unlocked the door for us. The Lord of Kenilworth had roofed the Chancel aforetimes and mounted on its roof his Bear and Ragged Staff. The beadle did not know where his Lordship sat in the church and I rather think that he did not sit there at all, for though full of deeds of ostentatious charity he could not have loved to pray. From the Porch and cemetery the beautiful Towers of his Castle rose from out the rich, deep foliage, finishing a picture of wonderful beauty on every side. At five o'clock we left in the train after a day of rare enjoyment.

There is a portrait of the Earl of Leicester in the Manchester Exhibition in his white velvet suit in which Scott describes him as arraying himself on the evening of his arrival with Elizabeth to the Castle. No one could deny that he is handsome and with an air of grace and state; but yet his forehead, which, Sir Walter says, had "only the lordly fault of being too high"—is not intellectual though so high; and this is its fault, and not that it is lofty. But the truth is, that there is an abundance of clear expanse without those mysterious lines and curves in which genius and mental power lurk, and I daresay you may recall to your memory the moony and washy splendor of Billy Stearn's forehead as a case in point.[31] I suspect the facial angle is too acute, and if there were a bust of Leicester, we should feel it so. When an inventory was made of his library, the only books he possessed consisted of an old Bible, the Acts and Monuments, ancient and torn, some Psalters and Service book! One would fancy he must have been some pious christian but since he was far from it, the inventory seems to proclaim him quite unlettered, though Scott has made him appear an elegant and cultivated wit. When we went to Cumnor Place, we found that Anthony Foster was a very respectable gentleman and Knight, and instead of dying of starvation on a chest of gold, involuntarily sealed up in his own miser hole, that he departed in the odor of sanctity, and was buried in the very chancel of the old, old church—that now stands entire, with a fine inscription on his marble sarcophagus. I saw it myself and read it. What could dear Sir Walter mean by so blackening with mire and soot that pious man? I wish

I knew whether he had a secret knowledge of him that was concealed from the
world, for it would seem impossible that Sir Walter Scott should injure the memory
of the meanest human being.[32]

Sometime I must try to give you a history of my visit to Oxford, including
Cumnor Place, Blenheim Palace, Godstow Abbey and Stanton Harcourt.[33]

I think I have come to the end of my long gossip about Kenilworth, and it is to
me inexpressibly flat and inadequate, but I hope it will be entertaining to you who
have not seen it. You will see it in my fine engravings, however, in time to come—
and yet you will miss the Od[34] that still abides upon the very spot, and communi-
cates to the visitor such a mysterious sense of character and reality. And we have
such a tiny speck of knowledge of all spiritual laws and results, that we can in no
wise measure the influences that the former presence of persons remarkable for
either good or evil, may exert upon the present hour in the same locality. Exe-
unt omnes.[35]

It must have taken Sophia all evening to complete a letter of this length
and it is evident from the handwriting of the manuscript that toward the end
she was beginning to tire; the inclusion of the stage direction squeezed in
at the very end of the thirty-sixth page, rather than her normal signature,
gives the impression that she did not want to start another page just to say
"your affectionate sister"; perhaps, at the same time, she turned to Nathaniel and said "Thank God that's finished!"

Sunday, 13 September, was a blank day in the records of the family's
movements, no mention being made of any worthwhile trip; however, some
or all of the family did go *somewhere* and the journey could not have been
a short one as there is a note in the Accounts Book to the effect that 4s.6d.
was spent on hiring a barouche. No mention is made of such a carriage in
The Royal Leamington Spa Courier's guide to charges for various types of
vehicles, and even allowing for a mistake in terminology on Sophia's part
when making the entry, it is very difficult, if not impossible, to compute
from the sum spent how far and for how long the journey lasted.

But the following day's expedition was documented; it was a renewal of
the acquaintance with Warwick:

[During] a warm and bright afternoon, Julian and I took a walk together to Warwick; a walk which I think I remember taking more than once, when we were at
Leamington two years ago. It appeared to me that the suburbs of Warwick now
stretch further towards Leamington than they did then; there being still some
pretty reaches of sylvan road, with bordering hedges and overshadowing trees,
and here and there a bench for the wayfarer; but then begin the vulgar brick
dwellings for the poorer classes, or the stuccoed Elizabethan imitation for those
a step or two above them. Neither, in the town itself, did I find such an air
of antiquity as I thought I remembered there; though the old archway at the
commencement of Jury Street looks as ancient as ever. But the hospital close by
it has certainly undergone some transmogrification, the nature of which I cannot
quite make out.

We turned aside, before entering the heart of the town, and went to the stone
bridge over the Avon, whence such a fine view of the Castle is to be obtained. I
suppose I have described it already; and therefore I have no heart to attempt

describing it again; but I am certain that there is nothing more beautiful in the world, in such a quiet, sunny, summer afternoon, as those gray turrets, and towers, and high-windowed walls, softened with abundant foliage intermixed, and looking down upon the sleepy river, along which, between the bridge and the castle, the willows droop into the water. Many spectators have stood on the bridge and admired it, as is evidenced by their initials cut in to the soft freestone of the balustrade; and it was pretty to observe how the green moss had filled up some of these letters, as if it were taking pains to make them legible. I have observed the same thing on tombstones; and indeed the moist air of England is always producing one beautiful effect or another.

I staid a good while on the bridge, and Julian mounted astride of the balustrade, and jogged up and down like a postillion, thereby exciting a smile from some ladies who drove by in a barouche. We afterwards returned towards the town, and turning down a narrow lane, bordered with some old cottages and one or two ale-houses, we found that it led straight to the castle-walls, and terminated beneath them. It seemed to be the stable-entrance; and as two gentlemen and a groom were just riding away, I felt ashamed to stand there staring at the walls which I had no leave to look upon; so I turned back with Julian, and went into the town.[36] The precincts of the castle seem to be very extensive, and its high and massive outer wall shoulders up almost to the principal street. We rambled about, without any definite aim, and passed under the pillars that support the spire of Saint Mary's church, and thence into the market-place, where we found an omnibus just on the point of starting for Leamington. So we got on, and came home. I have never yet seen—what those who have seen it call the finest old spectacle in England—the interior of Warwick Castle; it being shown only on Saturdays. I do not blame the Earl; for I would hardly take his magnificent Castle as a gift, burthened with the condition that the public should be free to enter it.[37]

Tuesday, 15 September was rent day (£2.12s.0d.), duly noted in the Accounts Book and preparations were made for Nathaniel's return to the consulate. He had not quite reached the end of his permissible ten consecutive days of absence but there is some confusion as to the actual reason for the return to Liverpool at this point. In several letters over the next few days the plan that had been referred to in Sophia's letter of 9 September was, apparently, still being put into operation (that Nathaniel would be taking the family to Paris before the end of the month and after a final return to the consulate he would rejoin them in Paris for good). But in a letter of 29 September he was to state that the reason for his having left Leamington had been the receipt of a telegraph from Liverpool requesting his immediate return, due to the illness of Wilding, his right-hand man in the office. This apparent discrepancy was never referred to by any of the parties concerned; coincidentally, he had seen in an American newspaper, *The Washington Union*, that President Buchanan had announced the appointment of his successor as consul though, tantalizingly enough, there appeared to be no date fixed for the handing over to the new incumbent. Beverley Tucker, a businessman, congressional lobbyist, and editor of the *Washington Sentinel* since 1853, was a swashbuckling character whose life before coming to Liverpool had been one of questionable success and afterward took on a more sinister aspect as he became an agent in the Confederate army and at one time was accused of being involved in the assassination plot to kill President Lincoln. With events now seeming to take on a new significance and urgency, Nathaniel took the opportunity to write to the American Legation in London to start the ball rolling with regard to obtaining passports for the trip to the Continent:

Leamington, Sept 15ᵗʰ '57

Dear Sir,
I am about to accompany Mrs. Hawthorne and my family to Paris, where I shall leave them until my successor in the Consulate arrives. As I do not propose to pass through London, I shall feel much obliged if you will send me the necessary passports, directing them to me at Liverpool.
    The following is my own description—age (I am sorry to say) fifty-one;—height, five feet, ten and a half inches;—hair dark, and somewhat bald;—face, oval;—nose straight;—chin, round. As regards any other particulars, I can put them in myself.
    Mrs. Hawthorne is forty two years of age, five feet high, an oval face, light hair, ordinary nose &c &c &c—her name is Sophia Amelia Hawthorne.
    We have three children—the eldest a girl of thirteen, the next a boy of eleven, and the youngest a girl of six. These, I presume, will need no separate passports. Mrs. Hawthorne will be accompanied by a nursery governess, an English woman, who may likewise, I think, be included in her own passport.
    After spending some weeks in France, we intend going to Italy, where we shall spend the winter.
    If you will be kind enough to obtain the necessary signatures from the French Legation, I will send you whatever amount may be paid on them.
    I return to Liverpool today, and shall probably set out for Paris early next week.

                                                Very truly
                                                & respectfully
                                                Nathˡ Hawthorne

P.S. I learn by the newspapers the appointment of Mr. Beverley Tucker to the Liverpool Consulate. Have you received instructions to obtain his Exequatur?
B. Moran, Esq
American Legation[38]

Quite why Nathaniel felt it necessary to lie about his age, which in fact was fifty-three, and Sophia's, which was forty-eight, is a mystery, particularly as he was lying to his employer, who is most likely to have had such facts in his records, even in those days when statistics were not so all-important as they are considered to be now. And there is more confusion in his mentioning a "nursery governess, an English woman"; Miss Browne had already left their employ and Ada, an American, was to be the children's governess on the Continent. The only other English dependent that they had was Fanny, and she was not going to the Continent, nor was she a governess. However, the letter was received by Moran the next day; he noted in his journal that "Hawthorne writes me he is going to Paris; & seems anxious to get home," though what led him to deduce from the letter that Nathaniel was homesick is not clear.

Nathaniel left for the railway station that morning no doubt much happier in his own mind as to the possibility of the attainment of his freedom being measured in a matter of days rather than weeks.

> Today] I took the train for Rugby, and thence to Liverpool; a dull, monotonous, swift rush. It is wonderful how little one sees, from the railway, in traversing England in whatever direction; not a feature keeps its hold on the memory.[39]

It was probably after he had left for Liverpool that some items of shopping were bought, the usual pieces of haberdashery, food, and three additions to the schoolroom's library in the shape of a Latin lexicon and delectus and a textbook on algebra. Not everyone would have been in good spirits, what with Nathaniel's enforced absence in Liverpool, but in Paris emotions were reaching fever pitch; Ada was becoming extremely apprehensive as she had not heard from Clay for some time, nor from any of her family. For all the excitement that she found in the unfamiliar sights and sounds of Paris, she acknowledged that she would be "heartily glad when the Hawthornes come, and I think they will certainly be here some time next week. My position as the only young lady among so many young gentlemen is not the pleasantest one imaginable on all occasions."[40]

However, all was well and she didn't have to wait long for the precious letter from Clay as, after a day on which nothing is known about anything that might have happened among the Hawthornes in Leamington (although the Accounts Book reveals that a "return ticket" costing 9d. was bought, perhaps for an omnibus trip to Warwick), she returned from a visit to the "jardin des Plantes" and found a letter that had taken three weeks instead of the more usual two to reach her. Moreover, there was one from home, as well.

Meanwhile, in Liverpool Nathaniel had received what appears to have been the first communication in which he learned (unofficially) something about his successor at the consulate:

Liverpool, Sept 17th '57

Dear Bridge,
I have received your letter,[41] and the not unwelcome intelligence that there is another Liverpool consul now in existence. It is a pity you did not tell me how soon he will be here; for that is a point which must have a good deal of influence on my own movements. I am going to set out for Paris in a day or two, with my wife and children [which is somewhat at variance, as has been seen, with his later affirmation that he was at this time detained at the consulate due to the illness, and absence, of Wilding] and shall leave them there while I return here to await my successor. Poor fellow! Being such as you describe him, he will soon find the

resources of the consulate too narrow for him. As for the Liverpool tradespeople, they will trust the new consul a little while on the fair reputation which I leave behind me; but they are shrewd men, and I do not apprehend their being "done" to any great extent.

I thank you most sincerely for that paragraph in the Union.[42] It is just what I should have liked to have said; for I was somewhat apprehensive that my resignation might have been misconstrued, in consequence of a published letter of Gen. Cass to Lord Napier, in which he intimated that any Consul found delinquent in certain matters should be compelled to retire. Cass is not only an "old fogy", as you truly style him, but an old fool; and I think I have made him sensible of it in a despatch which I sent him about two months ago. But for your paragraph, I should have thought it necessary to enlighten the public on the true state of the case as regards the treatment of seamen in our merchant vessels, and I do not know but I may do it yet; in which case I shall prove that General Cass made a most deplorable mistake in the above-mentioned letter to Lord Napier. I shall send the Despatch to Ticknor, at any rate, for publication if necessary.[43]

I expect great pleasure and improvement during my stay on the Continent, and shall come home at last somewhat reluctantly. Your pledge in my behalf of a book shall be honored in due time, if God pleases; but I doubt much whether I do anything more than observe and journalize, while I remain on abroad. It would be a crowning pleasure to Mrs. Hawthorne and me, if Mrs. Bridge and you could join us in Italy. It is within the bounds of possibility that we may yet meet there.

Mrs. H. and the children are now a hundred miles off, at Leamington, in the center of England; or she would cordially join me in regards & remembrances to yourself and wife.

Your friend,
Nathl Hawthorne.[44]

Both of the other letters that Nathaniel wrote that day were in connection with his continuing involvement with Delia Bacon, whose book had been published earlier in the year, mainly through his endeavors, but whose health had broken down while she was living in Stratford-upon-Avon. He had received a letter from Dr. David Rice[45] advising him of her situation, friendless, witless, and almost penniless. Nathaniel had mixed feelings about being caught up again in a professional relationship with Delia, seemingly having ended it after having provided a preface to her book, seeing to it that the book (with Bennoch's help) found a publisher, paying for the production costs himself, and finally had made some inquiries at the Liverpool docks that ended in his having found a ship on which she could make her passage home to America. But her illness did touch a nerve and he was to do what he could on her behalf while he remained in the country.

Stratford on Avon
16 Septr 1857
To N. Hawthorne Esq

Dear Sir,
I much regret to have to inform you that all probability of Miss Bacon being able

to sail on 20th inst. and even to be fit to be sent home under any circumstance at an early period, has vanished.

I attribute this decidedly unfavourable change very much, if not entirely, to the circumstance of her brother Dr. Bacon[46] having most improvidently written letters of business to her, and in his last having made a remittance of a money draft payable only to her order. In the unsettled state of her mind, the possession of this document, which reached her before I was aware of its arrival, it not having been transmitted under cover to you or me or indeed any one else, completely upset her, and led her to again abuse the people in whose house she is lodged and taken care of, to charge them with robbery and indeed to go over the whole category of crimes and misdemeanours both against them & myself and every body who has waited upon, or interested themselves about her. This communication reached her on 29th or 30th August, but she did not open it for some days, her usual custom. In the interval M[rs]. Flower[47] had seen Miss Bacon, and she was inclined to return to America and we had found a young female, daughter of the man at whose house she lodges who was willing to have accompanied her to Liverpool or to America even, if wished, at a very moderate cost, indeed M[rs]. Flower would have accompanied her as far as Liverpool and seen her on board under your arrangements. I was about to write to you to this effect, when the unfortunate change of circumstances occurred.

She has been much worse than ever she was, mentally, though her general health has been good. She has continued in bed, ¾ dressed night & day, has never left her room nor changed her linen for nearly three weeks, and obstinately resisted every persuasion to do so. Matters became so bad, that on Monday evening last, I authorized the woman of the house and her daughter, with the aid of the special nurse (whose service had only been occasionally required since 27th July) to forcibly compel her to have her bed made and change her linen, and at the same time to take possession of her brother's letter & its contents, if they discovered the same. I was obliged to threaten Miss Bacon that if she did not submit, I would call in other authority to deal with her, for the people of the house could no longer allow her to remain in such a filthy state, and with the uncertainty of being repaid for the expense & trouble of boarding and lodging and attendance. I remained near at hand in the house, and subsequently informed her that I had possession of her brother's letter & money order. Will you kindly advise me how to act? On Monday I received a letter from D[r]. Bacon, in which he says he fears he has done wrong, but unfortunately all the mischief has been done. I should be anxious to do whatever is my duty, in this distressing case, and have communicated, both with M[r]. & M[rs]. Flower, but we really feel overwhelmed with the difficulties which surround us. The Flowers are expecting some American friends from Newhaven [sic], and intend to ask them to see Miss Bacon.

Yours respectfully,
D. Rice[48]

Nathaniel replied:

U. S. Consulate
Liverpool, Sept 17th '57

My dear Sir,
I am much pained by your bad accounts of Miss Bacon's condition, and am at a loss what to advise in the matter. For my own part, I have entire faith in your

discretion and kindness, and feel myself under great obligations for the care you have already bestowed on my poor countrywoman. I shall enclose your note to D^r.Bacon, because it will give him a full and adequate idea of his sister's situation, and show him the necessity of taking some decisive steps in the matter.

Meanwhile, if you should judge it advisable to remove her to an asylum, I feel confident that D^r.Bacon would approve of the step, under the circumstances.

I am on the point of setting out for Paris, but shall return to this place in a fortnight or three weeks.

> Very Sincerely
> & Respectfully
> Nathl Hawthorne[49]

And to Leonard Bacon, he sent the following:

Liverpool, Sept 17th 1857

My dear Sir,

I greatly regret the necessity of sending you the enclosed very unfavorable account of your sister's condition.

I had succeeded in procuring a passage for her to America, under very good auspices, but this change renders it impossible to take advantage of it.

I was at a loss what to advise Mr. Rice to do; but have written to say that I felt confident that you would approve of her being sent to an asylum, if he should judge that step expedient.

Mr. and Mrs. Flower, of Stratford, are people of the highest respectability, and I am glad to see that they take an interest in Miss Bacon. From what I know of Mr. Rice, I am persuaded that he is a person of benevolence and integrity, and entirely to be trusted.

I am not quite certain as to the date of my finally leaving England; but it will probably be in four or five weeks time.

> Very respectfully
> Nathl Hawthorne[50]

Back in Leamington, nothing much appears to have happened that day, apart from the purchase of yet more haberdashery and the settling of some small grocery and meat bills. Even Ada, in Paris, found little to add to her current letter to Clay, content to bide her time before she heard from the Hawthornes as to their imminent arrival: ". . . . I take up my Corinne now,[51] which I am going to finish before Mrs. Hawthorne comes. . . ."[52]

Friday, 18 September, was a quiet day on all fronts. Ada was too busy or else nothing of any consequence happened, to warrant her adding to the letter to Clay. The daily shopping for food took place in Leamington and if the Accounts Book can be read correctly it appears that Julian ("J"?) had another haircut, and purchased a comb. Up in Liverpool, Nathaniel would have had his hands full due to the enforced absence of Wilding, and probably he was finding that he had to do various chores that normally would not have come his way. He wrote one letter, presumably to an autograph hunter.

U. S. Consulate
Liverpool, Sept 18th '57

Dear Sir,
I am happy to comply with the request contained in your letter of July 9th, and am

Very truly yours
Nath[l] Hawthorne

Ed. Brown Houghton, Esq
Boston.[53]

Apart from work at the consulate, Nathaniel may have met Bright over
the weekend of 19–20 September and discussed with him what was to be
done with the journals that he had been keeping since his arrival in England.
On several occasions in the past, when alluding to them in letters to Ticknor
and others, he had revealed their existence but had always stressed that he
thought them too candid for publication. Bright was an enthusiastic collector
of manuscripts and may have expressed his interest to Nathaniel, not only
in their intrinsic value in the event of an eventual publication but also as a
memento of their friendship that had evolved out of Nathaniel's appointment
to the consulate. If they did meet at this time and discussed the matter it
would not appear that anything was definitely settled with regard to his
parting with the journals.

In Paris, on Saturday, Ada was engaged in more sightseeing and had
received letters from Clay, Mary Mann, and Sophia: "Mrs. Hawthorne's
letter was most kind, indeed, like the other two I have received from her. I
am sure I shall love her."[54] In Leamington it appears that money was no
longer considered as being too much of a problem, as it is noticeable that
for the remainder of the family's stay in the town the number of entries in
the Accounts Book increases daily and there was a constant outflow of cash
on food, clothing, trips (and rent, of course). Perhaps now that the end of
his official tour was definitely in sight, Nathaniel had intimated that expenditure need no longer be strictly curtailed. He had already admitted in several
letters that he expected to live beyond his means when on the Continent
and that time was fast approaching, so perhaps Sophia now felt little need
to maintain such close control of her household budget. Besides, certain
preparations had to be made to ensure that everything was in order for the
departure, particularly with regard to their clothing, as expenditure on that
item definitely increased.

From an entry made in the Accounts Book, and a reference made to it
by Ada in a subsequent letter of hers to Clay, it is apparent that a visit
was made to Warwick Castle; Sophia, certainly went but whether she was
accompanied by the rest of the family is unknown. It seems unlikely, however, that she would have gone on her own. St. Mary's church and Guy's

Cliffe house were also visited and tips were lavished on cabdrivers and various attendants at each of the venues.

By Monday, Nathaniel had made up his mind as to what to do with the six volumes of his journals, and contrary to what he had written to Fields on 9 September, had decided to give them to Bright:

Liverpool, Sep^{tr} 21st '57

Dear Mr. Bright
Here are these journals. If unreclaimed by myself, or by my heirs or assigns, I consent to your breaking the seals in the year 1900—not a day sooner. By that time, probably, England will be a minor Republic, under the protection of the United States. If my countrymen of that day partake in the least of my feelings, they will treat you generously.

> Your friend
> Nathl Hawthorne.[55]

There is no report of any movements in Leamington during that week except that someone went to Kenilworth on Saturday, 26 September. Apart from the rent of £2.12s.0d. on 22 September the Accounts Book details several purchases of articles of clothing and materials so presumably there was a lot of sewing and mending being done in preparation for the Continental trip that didn't leave much time for sightseeing. Perhaps the weather was not too good, as an umbrella was bought on Wednesday. There is a slightly mysterious entry in the book for Monday, when a loan was made to Una and Julian, although Una's name is not mentioned. What did they do with the money? There was also the "lotion" that was bought on Thursday; was this for Sophia, as an application to the flannel that she normally wrapped round her chest as a protection against harmful changes in temperature? Maybe it was that lotion of Professor Holloway's manufacture, regularly advertised in the local newspapers, sold at his establishments in London and New York and at "all respectable Druggists and Dealers in Medicines throughout the civilized world" and that could be efficacious in the cure of "Bad Legs, Bad Breasts, Burns, Bunions, Bites of Moschetoes and Sand Flies, Coco-bay, Chiego-foot, Chilblains, Chapped hands, Corns (soft), Cancers, Contracted and Stiff Joints, Elephantiasis, Fistulas, Gout, Glandular Swellings, Lumbago, Piles, Rheumatism, Scalds, Sore Nipples, Sore Throats, Skin Diseases, Scurvy, Sore Heads, Tumours, Ulcers, Wounds and Yaws"? Perhaps not; anyway, it cost a minimum of 1s.1½d. per pot.

One event that might have caught Sophia's eye and prompted her to venture out was a talk at the local Temperance Hall:

TEETOTALISM AND THE MAINE LAW.—On Monday evening last Mr. James Teare, one of the earliest and oldest "advocates", addressed a numerous company in the Temperance Hall, Warwick Street, on the above topic, in strong terms—denouncing the aiders and abetters of the liquor traffic as the manufacturers of drunkards and criminals by wholesale. The infliction was borne with evident goodwill by many present, who, though they did not admire the style of the lecturer's "oratory", yet professed adherence to the same principles.[56]

It sounded like a riotous meeting with plenty of heckling so perhaps Sophia might not have been too happy to have attended but Nathaniel, if he

			£	s	d
	Leamington	Sept.	oris 1.	6	½
Friday	18	Potatoes 1/ eggs /6 butter 1/5	2.	11	
		Fruit & vegetables 1/1½	1.	1	½
Saturday	19	Meat 6/11½ tomatoes, berries 1/8			
		Pears & potatoes 1/3	9.	10	½
		Marmalade 1/ macaroni 1/ sugar 1/4	3.	2	
Monday	21	loan 1/ Julian /6	1.	6	
Tuesday	22	Milk 3/9 bread 3/3 potatoes fruit 1/	8. - 3.		
		Berries - veg. macaroni herbs /6		6.	
		Rent	2	12	
		Beef 6/ sundries	6. - 3		
			5	5	9½
Wednesday	23	Beans, tomatoes /8 lemon 1/½	3		
		Candles & cheese 3/3½	3 - 3½		
Thursday	24	Meat and wine &c	10.	11	½
Friday	25	Beef	4	3	
Saturday	25	Biscuits 1/ eggs /6	1	..	6
		Rice &c	4	11	½
		Laundress 3 weeks	1.	2	.9
		Sugar 3/4 Beef 6/8	9.	10	
		Butter /8 apples /6	1.	2	
Monday	27	Milk Rent	2	13	
			5	11	7
Wednesday	29	Rent & for	2	12	6
		Beefsteak 2/	2.		
Thursday	30	Grocer from 29 to Oct 3rd	17.	10	½
			19.	1..	

had been in Leamington, may well have considered going as, for different reasons, he had put on record his disapproval of the Maine Laws. But Maine Laws apart, Sophia's mind was cast back to America as some mail had arrived from back home:

Leamington, Warwickshire
Sept.1857[57]

My dear Mary, I was glad to get your note yesterday[58] and am sorry you and your husband have been obliged to leave that delicious retreat so soon yet I am thankful that you have had such an interval of rest in your careful life.[59] We are still in England, but think now we shall be in Paris the first day of next week on the 29th Sept[60] I am exceedingly aggrieved that Miss Shepard should have been put to such straits for her passage money, when we arranged that it should be all easy and pleasant. We have had several interchanges of letters since she arrived. She met a gentleman at Havre whom she knew and who escorted her safely to M. Fezandie's door in Paris, dear little wandering bird of passage that she is. I long to have her in safe and loving keeping, but she says she wishes to be at M. Fezandie's for some time. Her letters are very satisfactory [*There is at least one sheet missing at this point*] an inference of yours, not an assertion of mine. As to Judge Taney, I know nothing. I never heard of him till the Scott Case,[61]and because I suggested that he might have decided according to his conscience, you think I advocate him and his decision. This must be because you have got into a suspicious mood toward me on these exciting subjects. I insist that human beings may not be wholly bad, because they have erroneous views. And I am still more impressed with your unjust way of looking at people by my own experience. For if you can think that your own sister, whose life and character you have known intimately since childhood, whose abhorrence of oppression and cruelty and every shadow of wrong has been vital—could for one instant advocate the most awful institution that ever disgraced the earth, because I happen to be in a certain position!!!! that I could forget all my inmost principles for expediency or for a preference for any man living—why then I cannot be surprised that you think half the world fiends with very small reason for thinking so. If you should take the trouble to look over my letters, you will find I never defended any one for upholding slavery—but at the worst, merely have questioned whether such or such a person were not honest in his opinion, instead of being consciously a villain. You are more angry with me for hinting at a charitable construction of a man's acts and thoughts, than if I had taken a flail of destruction and gone through the land, striking dead every slaveholder and member of the democratic party. Yet why should I have a right to assume the place of the Almighty and take vengeance even in feeling upon thousands of human beings, whose inner minds I know nothing about, and whose difficulties I cannot appreciate? Both you and Elizabeth, but especially Elizabeth, have sneered at me all along for my efforts to judge justly—as if it were disgusting weakness and venality. But I know my own mind and heart so far as to know the smallest error in which my own husband were involved so disinterested is my condign judgement of wrong. You don't know him at all if you suppose he is in the least influenced by office or by men. He is as free as an eagle from every personal tie or bias. It amuses me to have you speak so confidently of his motives for judging and also of his opinions. Because you only infer them, and do not know them. And you will in future see the transparent purity of his nature and mode of action, and feel ashamed that you ever expressed any contrary idea. But I do not wish to shame you. I only wish you knew better.

You always speak as if he were an ignorant baby and very weak. But as William Channing [a poet, of sorts, and a friend of Sophia and Nathaniel's since before their marriage] says "He has the awful power of insight" and he has also the strength of ten thousand Samsons upon any given point. You think this is all partiality and doting. But it is the severest truth and who knows him so well as I? Am I a fool and blind in his regard though I can blink in others? Of course, there is no convincing you on this point. But yet I know that we live most independently of each other's intellects—that we debate points of general interest—like two strangers—that we decide upon the inherent merit of a thing, and not with reference to each other—that he never tries to govern my ideas upon any point whatever and that our identity consists only in complete union of heart and equal horror of wrong. I have seen him in countless trials for fifteen years & more and with all my idealism I cannot find that he tarnishes my ideal by any one of his actions or ideas. I am one of the happy wives who is not obliged to feel above her husband in moral rectitude and reach. Were it otherwise, my peace and rest would ebb at once. This makes me have what even an accomplished courtier could not help calling "the _happiest_ face he ever looked on". I have always known what I was saying, my dear Mary, and perhaps your husband would have understood me better than you did. But you were so kind to withhold my letters from him when you thought they could disgrace me. But as _inferences_ always depend upon the mind of the person who draws them, I think he might not have drawn from my words the same that you did. And now I will say no more of slavery, since there is this obstacle to material understanding. I never have yet written a careless sentence about it—I have always pondered with suspended pen over every expression. I can do no more—and as that has failed, it is a waste of time and thought.

Meanwhile, I believe, as Mary Motley told me the other day,[62] that the fierce excitement of politics and parties fill the very air in America, and there can be no calmness in any thing there. And to this I attribute your error about me and I am just as confident of your love finally as if nothing had occurred—also my love for you is perennial—

Your ever affectionate Sophia[63]

Ada had received a visit from an old friend, Emma Fisher and her husband, who were intending to stay in Paris for a week, by which time, she reported confidently to Clay, "the Hawthornes will be here."[64] In Liverpool Nathaniel was indulging in one of his less frequent occupations, that of writing letters of introduction to friends in the United States on behalf of persons whom he had met in England, sometimes of the very briefest acquaintance.

Liverpool, Septr. 24th '57

My dear Mr.Duyckinck,[65]
Allow me the pleasure of introducing Doctor Charles Mackay,[66] to whose name it would be impertinent to add anything explanatory or laudatory. I could not put him into better hands than your own, with a view to his seeing whatever would interest a poet, scholar, and man of the world, in your metropolis.

Truly Yours
Nathl Hawthorne.

Evert A. Duyckinck, Esq.[67]

Liverpool, Septr 24th '57

My dear Emerson,
I have not often (if indeed ever) sent anybody to you with a letter of introduction; so that you would pardon me even for introducing a common man; and I know you will thank me for being the medium of making Dr. Mackay known to you. Will you be kind enough to show him Thoreau, and Ellery Channing, and any other queer and notable people who may, by this time, have taken up their abode in Concord?
    I have resigned my Consulate, but instead of drawing homeward, am going farther than ever from my old cottage and sand-hill. In fact, I have continually seen so many of my countrymen (more than ever before in my life) that I feel as if I were now only on the point of first coming abroad.

                                        Truly Yours
                                            Nathl Hawthorne.

R. W. Emerson[68]

Liverpool, Sept 24th '57

My dear General,
I never had greater pleasure in introducing any person to you, than the honored and laurelled bearer of this letter. It is Dr. Charles Mackay, some of whose lyrics even you (though little given to poetry) must be familiar with; for they have had more potency than many state-papers. He comes to see our country, with the best disposition and ability to comprehend and do us justice; and I am glad to make such an Englishman (or rather, Scotchman) as Dr. Mackay known to such an American as yourself.

                                        Truly your friend
                                        Nathl Hawthorne

P.S. I am just taking flight, having been detained longer than I expected or wished. Are we to see you on this side next summer? But I will write you further on this point, after settling myself on the Continent.
Genl Pierce.[69]

All was still quiet on the Leamington front (did Sophia or the children notice an advertisement in *The Leamington Advertiser* on 24 September that "The Original and Celebrated American General Tom Thumb" was coming to the town during the next week, to appear at the Royal Music Hall?) but someone, according to the Accounts Book, paid a visit to Kenilworth on Saturday. However, Nathaniel, in the light of the latest information, was making further preparations for the departure to the Continent and had written to the American Legation in London: "Had a letter this morning from Hawthorne, our Liverpool Consul, who is anxious for the arrival of his successor. He wants a passport for his wife whose appearance he described as having no 'very striking points, though, as a whole' says he

'the face is exceedingly pleasant in my eyes.' A delicate dash of husbandly affection, that."[70]

Liverpool, Sept[r] 26th '57

Dear Ticknor,
I thought I should have been in Paris by this time; but I was telegraphed back from Leamington on account of the severe illness of Mr. Wilding, who is prostrated with a nervous fever, attended with delirium. This has thrown a load of business upon me, making it impossible for me to leave at present. The worst effect of it is (so far as I am concerned) that it will cause an embarassing delay in the adjustment of my accounts, and the arrangements of my financial concerns. I can see my own way through, however.
    I had a letter from the new Consul per last Steamer.[71] He is to leave New York tomorrow; and nobody will pray for his safe passage and speedy arrival more sincerely than I shall. You may be sure I shall send him no money nor back him up with any responsibility; indeed, he will immediately find himself in possession of funds (not his own, to be sure) that will put him beyond the necessity of fleecing anybody but Uncle Sam. To that I have no objection, provided his own conscience will permit him.
    I think I have nothing more to say. Good bye.

                                        Your friend,
                                        N H.[72]

He wrote also a stalling letter to the fifth auditor, Department of State, concerning the difficulty of presenting the consulate's accounts in the prevailing circumstances:

Consulate of the United States
Liverpool
September [26?] 1857

Sir
I regret that the preparation of my Quarterly accounts has been delayed by the protracted illness of the clerk who had them in charge.
    They will be proceeded with as speedily as the difficulties of the case will permit, it having been necessary to instruct another person in the Method of this peculiar class of accounts under the disadvantage of receiving no assistance or explanation from his predecessor.
    I hope and expect to forward them at a very early date.

                                    I have the honor to
                                    be Your Obt servt
                                    Nath[l] Hawthorne
                                    Consul.[73]

On Sunday, 27 September, Ada certainly went to church and was in a particularly happy frame of mind, looking forward to the Hawthornes joining her: "Before my next letter leaves Paris, I shall probably be with the Haw-

thornes. . . ." and although she had received no confirmation was so confident on the Monday that "I expect them every day now, and should not be
at all surprised if they came this afternoon."[74] Nathaniel probably hadn't
gone to church as he was on his own, and it could perhaps be stretching the
imagination too far in wondering whether Sophia and the family (weather
permitting) made the short journey up the Tachbrook Road to the Arboretum
to partake in the last of a series of open-air services being held there:

> OPEN AIR SERVICES.—The open air services, which have for some time been
> successfully conducted on Sunday afternoons, in the Arboretum, by the Rev.
> James Key, and his ministerial brethren, were brought to a close on Sunday after-
> noon last for the present season. The attendance was not quite so numerous as
> on many former occasions, but sufficiently so to encourage the belief that they
> may be resumed next summer with considerable promise of usefulness.[75]

At this point it would appear appropriate (as much here as anywhere else)
to reproduce a letter that Una wrote to her father; it is included as being
part of the family's Leamington connections despite its possessing a number
of debatable points that *could* mean that it was not written at this particular time:

> My dearest though naughty father,
> Who was so tired of us he would stay ever in Liverpool, to be out of our way on
> Sunday. It was a disagreeable Sunday at any rate, but without you, almost unbear-
> able, but you see though we did not beat or submit to it we are on the other side.
> Nurse and I went to Church in the morning and Nurse and Baby went in the
> afternoon. Julian did not go. In the afternoon, Mamma lay down and Julian and
> I and Rose and Nurse amused ourselves two and two.
>   I never knew such weather in England as these few days have been. Warmth,
> but making us feel full of aches, and so sleepy and tired that we can scarcely keep
> our eyes open. That is the way we women have felt since you have been away,
> though the two children seem to feel as "jumpy" as ever. We feel as if we had not
> strength to keep our different parts togethr to keep them together, and yet no strength to let them fall
> apart. Do you feel so, and are you having as bad weather in Liverpool?
>   We had for dinner yesterday veal cutlets, beans, potatoes, and cauliflower, and
> for desert, roast apples. I sit at the head of the table where you used to sit and
> Mamma tells me every time that I act you to perfection, and I do also in everything
> so exactly like you that she does not feel your absence in the least, is indeed
> rather glad of it as she is more at freedom, and can talk and go out without her
> respirator, and do just as she likes, and she never takes her oil, today however
> she has put on your ring to remind her of it.
>   I am very glad there are so many ships in harbour, I hope you will come home
> laden with gold, and as you will be so rich I want you to get me a beautiful
> watch inlaid with diamonds and rubies, and Mamma a complete set of the finest
> diamonds. Do not spend more than a hundred thousand on the set or more than
> a 1000 on my watch. And as for Julian he would like an equarium [*sic*], and
> complete fishing tackle with two guineas pocket money. For Rose a large peck
> measure of all the fruits in season and a splendid doll all dressed.
>   We shall die of disappointment if these things are not bought, and then you can
> leave your Consulate next month, and get a new wife who has a great fortune,

and there are plenty of beggar children in London from whom you can select three, and that will save your wife the trouble of having them born.

Goodbye sweetest father.
Your own loving daughter
Una[76]

For the remainder of the month there is no mention of anything happening on the home front in Leamington and there are hardly any entries in the Accounts Book for these few days. Monday was noted as being rent day (£2.13s.0d. this time) which is somewhat confusing as it was less than a week since it had last been paid; perhaps the confusion is to do with the fact that the dates entered in the book are incorrect, in that the previous Friday and Saturday were both dated as 25 September and the resultant errors were not put right until Friday, 2 October. It would appear that for the rest of their stay at Lansdowne Circus, as the days that they spent waiting for Nathaniel's return from Liverpool dragged into weeks, it came to be recognized that it was more sensible that the daily purchases of food should be obtained mainly on credit, with a fairly frequent settling of the various bills at the butcher, grocer, and dairy. There wasn't anything of great interest going on in the town that could be classed as entertainment and to which the children could have been taken to relieve the boredom; the only public event was at the Town Hall on Monday when a "PUBLIC MEETING of the Inhabitants of Leamington" was held "at the Hour of Eleven of the Clock in the forenoon, for the purpose of taking into consideration . . . the Fund, opened under the sanction of the Lord Mayor of London, for the relief of our fellow countrymen who have become victims of the unheard-of atrocities of the rebel army, and of the rabble abettors of its cruelty to helpless women and children, and our unarmed fellow subjects in the East." But perhaps Sophia would not have felt herself to be sufficiently and person-ally involved enough in that subject to warrant any of the family attending. However, it was during this week, before the end of the month, that she wrote to Ada, perhaps at the instruction of Nathaniel but certainly with the latest news from him concerning his situation at Liverpool in mind, telling her that there would be a further delay in their departure for Paris and that she left her to decide as to whether she remained in Paris (at their expense) to await their arrival there or made her own arrangements to come over and join them in Leamington.

5

Leamington, that "cheerfullest of English Towns": October 1857

Paris, Oct. 1st 1857

Dearest Clay!

I <u>am going to England alone</u>; Are you astonished? Listen, and I will tell you why. I received a letter, a few moments ago, from Mrs. Hawthorne,[1] saying that they would probably be detained there a month longer, owing to the alarming illness of Mr. Hawthorne's chief secretary, which left all the important business attending the transfer of the consulship to the new consul in the hands of Mr. Hawthorne.

They wish the children to commence studying as soon as possible, and propose that I should go to them if I have the courage, or continue to stay here at their expense, if I have not. Well, I <u>have</u> the courage I believe, and I immediately decided to go to them. They are in Leamington, Warwickshire, in the very centre of England.

I shall write to Mrs. Hawthorne immediately,[2] informing her of my determination. I came to tell you first, "as a soldier says his prayers before going to battle", to use a simile which you employed once in writing to me under similar conditions.

Do you know what was the strongest, selfish argument that urged me to stay here? Not the benefit I should receive from studying French longer; but the painful thought that your letters would be greatly delayed in reaching me.

Ah, my beloved! my beloved! How the thought of thee links itself with every great and every trifling circumstance connected with my life!

But I must write my reply. . . .

There must have been constant communication between Nathaniel and the family while he was away in Liverpool for so long at this time but it appears that only one of the letters that sped back and forth is extant (perhaps there were telegraphed messages as well), and it confirms that Sophia *did* see that advertisement in *The Leamington Advertiser*:

Liverpool
October 2d 1857

My dear little Pessima,

I am very glad that Mamma is going to take you to see "Tom Thump"; and I think it is much better to call him Thump than Thumb, and I always mean to call him so from this time forward. Its a very nice name, is Tom T H U M P. I hope you will call him Tom Thump to his face, when you see him, and thump him well if he finds fault with it. Do you still thump Mamma, and Fanny, and Una and Julian,

139

Ada Shepard. Yale Collection of American Literature, Beinecke Rare Book and Manuscript Library.

as you did when I saw you last? If you do, I shall call you little Rose Thump, and the people will think you are Tom Thump's wife. And now I shall stop thumping on this subject.[3]

Your friend little Frank Hallett is at Mrs. Blodget's [in Liverpool].[4] Do you remember how you used to play with him at Southport, and how he sometimes beat you? He seems to be a better little boy than he was then, but still he is not so good as he might be. This morning, he had some very nice breakfast in his plate, but he would not eat it because his mamma refused to give him something that was not good for him; and so, all breakfast-time, this foolish little boy refused to take a mouthful, though I could see that he was very hungry, and would have eaten it all up, if he could have got it into his mouth without anybody seeing. Was not he a silly child? Little Pessima never behaved so—Oh, no!

There are two or three very nice little girls at Mrs. Blodget's; and also a nice large dog, who is very kind and gentle, and never bites anybody; and also a tabby cat, who very often comes to me and mews for something to eat. So you see we have a very pleasant family; but, for all that, I would rather be at home.

I sent somebody over to see how Mr. Wilding does, this morning; and he has just come back and says that Mr. Wilding is a great deal better. He has kept his bed for a long time, but yesterday he sat up a little while, and he is sitting up to-day. He has sent me a great bundle of papers that I wanted, and I shall go to see him next week, when, I hope, he will be able to tell me some things that I wish to know.

I want you to ask Mamma if she does not think that my old frock-coat could be made into a sack or jacket for Julian. It is a very good and strong cloth, and is not nearly worn out, and I think it would be a great pity to leave it here, when it costs so much to buy clothes for that great boy. I should like to have it made up for him before we leave Leamington.

And now I have written you such a long letter that my head is quite tired out; and so I shall leave off and amuse myself with looking at some pages of figures.

Be a good little girl, and do not tease Mamma, nor trouble Fanny, nor quarrel with Una and Julian; and when I come home, I shall call you little Pessima[5] (because, I am very sure you will deserve that name) and shall kiss you more than once.

Your affectionate father[6]

It was obvious that Nathaniel was having some trouble in sorting out his final accounts and that their presentation to the State Department, culled from the "pages of figures," would take more than a little hard work on his part. Alas, it was to be another two years before the matter was finally settled, even after Wilding had returned to the office.

Over in Paris, Ada was making preparations for her departure:

Friday Oct. 2nd

For the last time in the little chamber that has been my home for almost six weeks, I come to write to thee, my beloved! "Perhaps for the last time on earth", says a little whispering fear; but we will hope that wind and wave and steam will prove as propitious as they have ever done to me, to _us_, dearest, and that I shall address you from Mrs. Hawthorne's temporary home in Leamington, on Sunday.

I go, at five this afternoon, to Dieppe, and sail from thence to Brighton at half-past seven, tomorrow morning; thence by railroad to London, and thence to Leamington, which I shall reach some time tomorrow night. The Hawthornes will be surprised to see me so soon, as they thought I would wait until they wrote again, making arrangements for my meeting the United States Consul who is in London, and who would put me in the cars for Leamington. But of course that is not necessary, and I should only be losing so many days by waiting; not absolutely _losing_ them of course; but I should not feel quite content, having once decided.

So, having gained all the necessary information from Mr. Lane,[7] I shall go this afternoon. . . .

He went with me to make all my arrangements at the United States Legation and the Prefecture of the Police, yesterday (passports have to be examined and stamped at both these places when an American desires to leave Paris for England) and now all is ready for my departure except that I have my trunk to pack.

I go by Dieppe because I wish to take a different route from that by which I came, in order to see more of the country.

By Dover and Calais there is too little travelling by sea for me, and by Boulogne and the Thames the time is not quite so favorable; so all things considered, I chose Dieppe and Brighton. And I fancy that when you have finished reading this little letter, you will take your map and trace out the course which your Ada has followed to take her to the place (and safety) where she will probably then be in peace, thinking or dreaming of thee, her only love, her guardian, her <u>companion</u> wherever she may be. . . .

I await the hour when the next distribution of letters takes place, with trembling anxiety, almost. It seems as though there <u>must</u> be one from you before I go; but I shall leave directions to have it sent to me immediately, if it does not come now. Continue to direct as heretofore until you hear to the contrary, dear. We shall be in Paris by the first of November, I suppose, and M. Fezandie will send on my letters which come before then.

If I were superstitious enough to believe in a dream which I had last night, I should not go as I am going to-day; but I put aside the little cloud that must always arise, under such circumstances, since my life is not all my own, and I hope, I trust that all will be well. You will probably receive a letter from England, telling you of my safe arrival, almost as soon as this reaches you.

But, my beloved, my light, my strength, my soul! should this short journey be less safe than the long one of two months ago; should no other letters greet thee, <u>know</u> that the last thought of thy Ada was of <u>thee,</u> the last prayer; God guard and guide my Clay!

I did not mean to end my letter thus mournfully, dear Clay. I am afraid you will imagine me lacking in courage and in trust after reading it. Do not think so! I was only desirous of considering all possible chances. We can never feel <u>sure</u> of safely arriving at our destination, when starting on a journey, you know. <u>Dear</u> Clay! do not feel anxious for a moment. But I need not entreat you thus. You are wiser than I, and do not give yourself alarm unnecessarily. . . .

Dearest, good-bye until I may write from England.[8]

The Accounts Book has no entry regarding the purchase of tickets for the Tom Thumb show but perhaps it was on Saturday that they went to see him even though on that day (and during the following week) there was yet more shopping done for clothing and allied materials. There must have been a major overhaul of the family's wardrobe undertaken in time for the anticipated departure for the Continent. Perhaps they were all able to get into the show free of charge and Nathaniel might have been able to make his influence felt, as an American official, with the management of the theater to effect a meeting between the children and the little man himself; Julian did record later that he had had "the distinction of meeting them [Tom Thumb and his "associate" Miss Warren] on their English tour"[9] but for a hint of what the show was like it is necessary to consult, once more, the local press:

GENERAL TOM THUMB.—This famous little man paid a visit to our town on Thursday, Friday, and Saturday last, exhibiting his unique talents and personage in the Music Hall. The Hall was thronged in the mornings with the beauty and fashion of the town. In the evening portion of his entertainment the little general had a crowded hall of admirers of the popular stamp [can it be inferred that the morning performances were "family" entertainment and the evenings more "adult"?]. All classes were astonished and delighted with the miniature man's

				£	s	d
		October				
Saturday 3d	Gloves Rose					8½
	Satin Ribbon blue					11½
	Stamps					4
	Nail			19		
	Pearls & twist				4	4
	Brown ribbon elastic				1	10
	Braid blue				2	-
	Red cotton 1/ thread					
Tuesday 6th	Stamps				1	
	Trimming 2/6 bookboard 1/2				3	8
	Silk & pearls 4/4				4	4
	Pearls 1/ whalebone /6				1	6
	lining /4 toy /6 buttons 6/½				1	4½
Saturday	Silk 3/11 velvet 2/8				6	7
	Shoes for Rose 3/10				3	10
	Woolen dress				19	
	Stamps & bill to Gillett				5	00
	Red riding hood					
	Miss Shepard's Expenses	£22			4	6
	Coventry fares 4/6 lunch 3/ fee/6				10	
	Scarf and ribbon				3	6
19th	Shoes for S H				6	
Wednesday 21st	Velvet 3/1 Combs /2 papers /2				3	5
	Oct					
23d	Braid and buttons				1	9
	Cod liver oil 3/ /3				3	
29th	Pins				1	
	Purse twist				7	
	Whalebone				1	7½
	Spool Cotton				1	
	Shoes baby				4	

appearance and performances. His "make-up" is very good whilst his appreciation of character and position are really excellent and though there was, at times, a tendency to extravagance, he was kept in check by the conductor in so admirable a manner that it was scarcely perceptible to the general observer. In the Poses Plastiques or Grecian Statues the little general's perfect formation may be seen to advantage particularly in the representation of "Romulus defending the Sabine Women", "Discobulus throwing the Discus or Quoit", "Ajax defying the Lightning", "Samson bearing off the Gates of Gaza", and, "Cain Slaying his Brother Abel".[10]

TOM THUMB.—This diminutive specimen of humanity, who was exhibited in Leamington thirteen years since, commenced his entertaining series of performances at the Music Hall, on Thursday, when he appeared in public three times. He continued his exertions yesterday, and will conclude his visit to-day. It is scarcely necessary to record that his "Levees", especially those held in the evening, have been crowded, and, in every respect, attended with the success which has marked his re-appearance in the English provinces. The nature of the exhibition is so perfectly familiar to our readers as to preclude the necessity of an extended notice. The General, who has attained his twentieth year, is hearty in his mirth; sings with taste; dances with gracefulness, and goes through his varied performances with vivacity and rapidity. His "character songs" are great favourites with his audiences; those of "Bobbing aroun'," and "My own Mary Anne," were especially so on Thursday evening. His repeated change of costume, in which the man-child appears to much advantage, pleasingly diversifies the entertainment, than which none will prove more attractive, during the present season, to the public of this town and neighbourhood, or more remunerative to the speculators concerned. The General, it is announced, is about to retire "for *ever* to private life;" so that we may regard his present as a "farewell" tour through this country.[11]

If it *was* Saturday when the family went to see the general it was while they were enjoying the show in Bath Street and while Nathaniel, presumably, was slaving away at the consulate and gazing despairingly at the mound of papers from which he had to prepare his last presentation of accounts to the State Department, that Ada was undergoing all manner of excitements, including the possibility of another unwanted romance. As she had intimated to Clay, she had not waited for any further instructions from Sophia so it must have come as a complete bombshell to the family when she arrived at Lansdowne Circus early on Sunday afternoon. What an upheaval there must have been—meeting the children, Sophia, and Fanny, unpacking her enormous trunk, sorting out her accommodation,[12] describing her journey, discussing at least in part with Sophia (if there was time that day) what her schoolroom duties would entail, and then, at the end of the day, catching her breath and writing to her beloved Clay:

Leamington, England, Oct 4th 1857
Sunday night.

Yes, my dearest, my best earthly friend! Sunday night! Our blessed night again has come to me, and, though it is against my rules to write by lamplight, in these days, I surely cannot sleep until I have written thee at least a few words of greeting on my first Sunday night in England. Wind and wave and steam <u>were</u> propitious, darling, and I arrived here safely this morning instead of last night. Tomorrow I will write you the details of my journey, but now I must only say that I am very, very happy;—that I most cordially love and extravagantly admire Mrs. Hawthorne, Una and Julian, and that I feel very certain of being happy with them the whole year. They seem to me thoroughly charming in every way. Mrs. H. has all the good qualities of Mrs. Mann without those which we do not so much admire [? !], and with a thousand additional graces. She is as wise and kind as Miss Peabody, without her neglect of necessary forms [? !]. "In short", as Mr. Micawber would say, she is very, very lovely. Una is the most remarkably developed child, to all appearances, that I ever saw, remarkably developed physically, mentally and morally [it is rather nice to think that Una had found a very sympathetic female companion, not too much older than herself, with whom she could share her emotions at this important time of her life]. Julian is a very Hercules in miniature. I believe I <u>never</u> saw so fine a physique in a boy as he has. And he has splendid great eyes, and beautiful chestnut locks, though his features are not handsome. Little Rose is a sweet creature, but less remarkable, evidently, than the other two [poor Rose, she appears always to have been dismissed thus]. Ah! how I shall love these beautiful children!

Mr. H. I have not yet seen, as he is in Liverpool.

But let me talk no more of them, to-night, dearest! There are days enough to come for that, and this is Sunday night, sacred to <u>us</u> and hence to <u>love</u>. I can write nothing that will convey the thoughts that swell my heart and crowd my brain to-night, dear, <u>dear</u>, Clay, and so I shall throw aside my pen, and hasten to my comfortable bed where alone, and yet not alone, since girt about by this angelic love of thine, I shall revel in waking dreams of thee till sleep comes to bring me, as I hope, visions of thy dear, <u>dear</u> face and form!

Good night, my beloved![13]

There can be no doubt that Ada and the children immediately became very fond of one another and that her role as governess was made that much easier due to her comparative youthfulness and her ability, therefore, to appreciate fun as a necessary accompaniment to the task of learning; in a comparison with the late unlamented Miss Browne she would have won hands down and one must assume that her intellectual accomplishments were far and away greater than those of that unfortunate lady. Julian wrote of her influence on them:

It was in Leamington that we were joined by Ada Shepard. She was a graduate of Antioch, a men-and-women's college in Ohio, renowned in its day, when all manner of improvements in the human race were anticipated from educating the sexes together. Miss Shepard had got a very thorough education there, so that she knew as much as a professor, including what would be of especial service to us, a knowledge of most of the modern European languages. What seemed, no doubt, of even more importance to her was her betrothal to her classmate, Henry Clay Badger; they were to be married on her return to America. Meanwhile, as a matter of mutual convenience (which rapidly became mutual pleasure), she was to act as governess of us children and accompany our travels. Ada (as my father and mother presently called her) was then about twenty-two years old; she had

injured her constitution—never robust—by addiction to learning, and had incidentally imbibed from the atmosphere of Antioch all the women's-rights fads and
other advanced opinions of the day. These, however, affected mainly the region
of her intellect; in her nature she was a simple, affectionate, straightforward
American maiden, with the little weaknesses and foibles appertaining to that estate; and it was curious to observe the frequent conflicts between these spontane-
ous characteristics and her determination to live up to her acquired views. But
she was fresh-hearted and happy then, full of interest in the wonders and beauties
of the Old World; she wrote, weekly, long, criss-crossed letters, in a running hand,
home to "Clay", the king of men; and periodically received, with an illuminated
countenance, thick letters with an American foreign postage-stamp on them,
which she would shut herself in her chamber to devour in secret. She was a
little over the medium height, with a blue-eyed face, not beautiful, but gentle and
expressive, and wearing her flaxen hair in long curls on each side of her pale
cheeks. She entered upon her duties as governess with energy and good-will, and
we soon found that an American governess was a very different thing from an
English one. Her special aim at present was to bring us forward in the French and
Italian languages. We had already, in Manchester, made some acquaintance with
the books of the celebrated Ollendorff;[14] and my father, who knew Latin well, had
taught me something of Latin grammar, which aided me in my Italian studies. I
liked Latin, particularly as he taught it to me, and it probably amused him, though
it must also often have tried his patience to teach me. I had a certain aptitude for
the spirit of the language, but was much too prone to leap at conclusions in my
translations. I did not like to look out words in the lexicon, and the results were
sometimes queer. Thus, there was a sentence in some Latin author describing the
manner in which the Scythians were wont to perform their journeys; relays of
fresh horses would be provided at fixed intervals, and thus they were enabled to
traverse immense distances at full speed. The words used were, I think, as follows:
"Itaque conficiunt iter continuo cursu." When I translated these, "So they came
to the end of their journey with continual cursing" I was astonished to see my
father burst into inextinguishable laughter, falling back in his chair and throwing
up his feet in the ebullience of his mirth. I heard a good deal of that "continual
cursing" for some years after, and I believe the incident prompted me to pay
stricter attention to the dictionary than I might otherwise had done.

However, what with Ollendorff and Miss Shepard, we regarded ourselves, by
the time we were ready to set out for the Continent, as being in fair condition to
ask about trains and to order dinner. My mother, indeed, had from her youth
spoken French and Spanish fluently, but not Italian; my father, though he read
these languages easily enough, never attained any proficiency in talking them.[15]

But despite everyone's best intentions (and possibly with some apprehension on the part of the children as to how the new governess would approach
her task) there was not too much regard paid to learning on the first day of
the term under Ada's tuition:

Monday morning.

I come to tell thee that I am going to Kenilworth Castle, in about ten minutes,
dearest! How I wish you were going with me. Una, Julian and I are going together,
and we go to-day because the weather is so remarkably fine that we cannot afford
to lose it. We shall stay until five o'clock so there will be time only for one lesson
to-day, the Chronology lesson, which they are both industriously preparing at this

moment. Dear children! they are so eager to learn that it is the greatest pleasure to teach them.

But the anticipation of this visit to the renowned Kenilworth is so delightful that I can hardly write of anything else. It is but a few miles from here, and we shall go by railroad.

I must go and prepare for the visit, so good-bye till to-night, dearest![16]

Presumably the children were more than happy to miss lessons and probably took great delight in showing Ada the sights, assuming a superior air in being able to demonstrate their familiarity with all things English. In view of the weather being so fine, possibly Sophia and Fanny took things easy, maybe continuing with their sewing and mending (in the garden or in the center of the Circus?) and keeping Rose happy. No shopping was done, according to the Accounts Book. And in the evening, after the excitement of the day's events had died away and things were quiet again, there was a great deal of information that had to be recorded for Clay's benefit:

Evening.

Ah! my beloved Clay! It has taken me almost all the evening to read this dear, dear letter which I found awaiting my return from Kenilworth Castle, this afternoon[17] But I must not write of the various themes suggested by it. I must try to get the pain which your surprising news with regard to Mr. Bennett and Miss Blaisdell[18] caused.

(Do not let me forget, however, to ask you what you mean by calling this "a double seduction"? How double?).

I must write my account of my journey and of my enchanting visit to-day, before other ideas drive them from my mind, or deprive them of their distinctness.

I left Paris at five o'clock, on Friday afternoon, alone, instead of with Mr. Lane; for the news which he that day received compelled him to stay in Paris. He came to bring me the letter which decided him thus, with a most rueful expression of countenance, for he seemed to have quite depended on going with me. "I thought" said he "that we should have commenced our journey together if we might not end it thus." And his tone was so earnest, so peculiar that I began to tremble and to fear a scene; yet I remembered the seven children, and thought it could hardly be that he meant to try to take me by storm. But he began (you see that I am going to tell you my adventures of all sorts, very fully) to ask me about you, and to question if I were in earnest in intimating that in America there was some-one who might some day be dearer than all else besides. (What a question, darling! "who might some day"!) "Is there positively no hope for me", said he, in just the tone in which Mr. London[19] asked it a year ago. "I shall always hate Mr. Badger", exclaimed he vehemently, but immediately repented of that, and was very gentle in his manner, and really seemed to suffer so much that, in pity for his disappointment (which, however, will not last long, of course) I forgot to be amused at the idea of his fancying that I could ever think of such a thing as loving one whom I should regard as a father more than a companion. He is certainly more than twice as old as I, and I have, all the time, looked up to him in the most confiding way, believing that he had the kindest, fatherly regard for me,—all the time until, one day when we were walking together, and I saw that indefinable something in his manner which induced me to lead him to the knowledge that I belonged to some one else.

I am very sorry for this closing scene between us. It will always cause a shade of sadness to linger with the memory of one whom I had delighted to regard as a good, kind friend.

He begged me to write him just a few lines, on my arrival at Mrs. Hawthorne's, to assure him of my safety and happiness, and to enclose my address in Dorchester [her hometown] and in Yellow Springs.

He says he shall certainly come to America to find me before long, and he feels quite hopeful that either you or I, during this year of separation, shall learn to be content without the other. Are you sorry I have written you all about him, dear Clay, or do you want to know, as I want to tell you, all that occurs to me?

I wrote him a little note, yesterday, telling him of my safe arrival, and before tomorrow night, he will be on his way to Lisbon, whence he is to go to South America, so that I shall not be troubled by any farther pursuit. Is it not strange? And it is very vexatious, too, that he should have fancied, because I was interested in him intellectually, and liked to talk and walk with him, that I must necessarily be in love with him!

But I will not dwell on this disagreeable topic. I was going to tell you of my journey. I reached Dieppe at about half-past ten in the evening, and spent the night at rather a poor hotel, although it was recommended as the best or one of the best in town. In the morning, after obtaining a permit to embark (Is it not strange that the extreme vigilance of the emperor should exact this in addition to one's passport? Besides this we have to get a permit to land afterwards) I left belle France in a little cockle-shell of a steamer, and in the course of five or six hours of very rough sailing, landed at Newhaven, the little sea-port town where Louis Philippe landed when he fled from Paris in eighteen hundred and thirty.

I was sick during the whole passage, and rejoiced, for the first time since I commenced my travels, that you were not with me, dearest. Ah! I know now what sea-sickness is; I did not before. I shall not soon forget the misery of those five or six hours. The sea was so rough that every few moments the water would come dashing over the deck, and we who were so miserably sick that we could not go below from fear of suffering still more, were obliged to submit to salt water baths in this unceremonious manner.

I think every one on board was more or less sea-sick. But there came an end, and we joyfully stepped on the soil of "merrie England", and after an hour or two's detention at the custom-house, we sped away towards London, which we reached at about six o'clock, P.M.

But very little was to be seen, during this ride, except lovely green pastures separated from each other by hedges of a dark, richer hue, and occasionally, browsing leisurely and contentedly, flocks of milk-white sheep.

But we entered the mighty city of London, the heart of this mighty, little island, and I felt plainly the throbbing of the busy life that centers here. I did not realize until I rode through London, on my way to the North-western Railroad Station, whence I was to start for Leamington, how quiet a city is Paris. London is Paris intensified, Paris aroused. But what an immense city is London! I do not wonder that Dr. Quincey calls it a *world*.

I rode, rode, rode, until it seemed as if I had been far enough to make the whole circuit of Paris, itself so large a city. Finally the cabman stopped, and I alighted with my immense trunk, (It makes me ache still to think how you carried it in your arms at Honeoye Falls) and found, to my dismay, that I could not reach Leamington that night as I learned from Mr. Lane and Mr. Jones (one of my travelling companions of whom I must tell you) that I should be able to do without doubt.[20] I had to go on to Rugby, and, spending the night there, came to Leamington on Sunday morning.[21]

I believe that the Rugby school is the one from which Dickens is supposed to have drawn his pictures of Squear's [*sic*] school in Nicholas Nickleby, but I am not quite sure.[22] I stood by the window on Sunday morning (I can hardly believe that it was only yesterday) and read the sign of the shops across the way,—— and——, booksellers to Rugby School, and various others which I have forgotten now, but the rain poured down so pitilessly that I could not walk out to see the famous school.

Fancy the interesting situation in which I arrived at the George's Inn, in Rugby, on Saturday night. It was nearly eleven o'clock and the rain was drizzling down in the most disagreeable style, and I was all alone, of course, except my big trunk and my carpet-bag. But I quite enjoyed the novelty of the thing and did not <u>feel</u> half as forlorn as I <u>looked.</u>

But ah! my eyes tell me to stop. It is something new for me to write in the evening these days.

So good-night, my dearest. I shall sleep with your letter pressed to my heart.

God guard thy slumbers, dearest! It is again cloudy so that I cannot see our Lyra,[23] but I will think how beautiful she was on Friday night, as I watched her from the window of my room in the Hotel de l'Europe, at Dieppe, a long, long time before closing my eyes, for my last sleep in France for some time, at least.[24]

The next day (it was rent day again, £2.15s.8d. this time!), after the morning lessons had been completed, Ada ended this particular letter to Clay:

Tuesday morn. Oct. 6th.

Good morning, dear Clay! I feel almost as if I could <u>say</u> that to you, at this moment, so <u>near</u> me do you seem, as I take my seat before the old desk and resume my letter.

Poor Miss Blaisdell and Mr. Bennett! I pity them, indeed, dear Clay. <u>This</u> Miss Blaisdell was not my pupil. It was her sister.

But I must tell you about Mr. Jones, my travelling companion from Paris to London. He happened to sit opposite me when I entered the car, at Paris, and we soon fell into conversation, he imagining that I was English, like himself, until after a while, I undeceived him. He was an enthusiastic admirer of Mr. Mann and we talked much of him and of Antioch College, in which he took the most lively interest. He heartily agreed with me in my ideas of education, and we had quite a delightful conversation on various books.

When we entered the cars at Newhaven, he wrote on a card, which he handed to me: "You are fond of literature. I wish to be allowed to send you a number of my humble productions. Will you please write your address below?" So I discovered, what his conversation had led me to suppose, that he was an author.

I shall expect the books in a few days, and am quite curious to see what they are. He was very kind to me all the way. Is it not providential that I always am sure to find some one to assist me, wherever I go, even although I need no care taken of me? I believe I have been nowhere since I left home but that some kind person has taken upon himself the responsibility of securing my safety and comfort.[25]

But all this time I am saying nothing of my visit to Kenilworth, that most beautiful and interesting ruin.

I can give you no idea of the luxuriance of the ivy which constitutes its chief beauty, and which, too, forms a remarkable support for what remains of what Scott describes in his "Kenilworth" as so magnificent a structure. I had no idea of the immense size and power of these ivy trunks. They are frequently as large as the trunks of quite a mighty tree, and they wind around and hold up the stones in the most wonderful manner. And oh! the richness and beauty of this glorious ivy! I never saw anything in vegetation to compare with it.

The castle is of red sand-stone, and has lost most of the red hue, from its extreme age (it was built in the time of Henry I.), so that the rich brown which it has assumed forms the most beautiful contrast with the shining green of the ivy that clings to its sides and overtops its ragged stones.

I could almost thank the soldiers of the ruthless Cromwell for tearing down as much as they did of this magnificent structure, for I could hardly believe that with all its pristine splendor, it could be as fair a sight as now, enveloped in its mantling ivy just at this season in full blossom. The blossom is a lighter green than the leaves, and the "harmony of analogy"[26] is here exhibited in the most striking manner. All around in the old "plaisance" of the castle, grow immense <u>trees</u> of Hawthorne. I never saw it except in hedges before; but here it grows as large as common apple trees at home, and the crimson berries contrast most beautifully with the dark green leaves. And the ivy trunks which spring up at the foot of the Hawthorne trees are almost as large as those of the Hawthornes, and send out their lovely branches to cling around the trees and mingle their foliage with the brilliant Hawthorne berries.

The largest tower of the castle is called "Caesar's Tower" and was built by Geoffrey de Clinton, Lord Chamberlain and Treasurer of England in the reign of Henry I. Only portions of the walls remain; the staircases and floors have entirely crumbled away since Cromwell's soldiers commenced their despoilation of the mighty structure.

One of the most interesting spots is the tower where Amy Robsart was murdered, according to Scott. It is Leicester's building, the most beautiful part of the castle. We ate the luncheon which we carried, in the famous banquet-hall where Leicester entertained Queen Elizabeth.

We stayed a long, long time, and as the day was beautiful, we had the most enchanting visit possible.

Julian was not with us, and Una and I sat, for an hour or two, in the window of Queen Elizabeth's dressing-room, and heard the wind sigh through the branches above us.

But there comes the dear child, all ready for our walk, and I must take this letter, or it will be too late for tomorrow's steamer.

Excuse the abruptness of its close. I will commence another tonight.

Adieu, dear, <u>dear</u>, Clay!

Your Ada.[27]

Tuesday, 6 October was something of a red-letter day for Nathaniel, one for which he had been waiting for months. It was the day on which the *Baltic* docked in Liverpool bearing not only letters from the Department of State but also his successor, Beverley Tucker.[28] Perhaps he even took time off from the office to get down to the docks to greet his long-awaited deliverer and to make some arrangements for his accommodation. At long last, in two letters, the Department had officially brought to his notice the fact that they had received his own letter of resignation and, rather belatedly, thanked him for his services and advised him of his successor's name. The first letter went thus:

Department of State, Washington, Sept. 24th, 1857
Nathaniel Hawthorne, Esq., U.S. Consul, Liverpool.

Sir,—I have to acknowledge the receipt of your despatches to No. 95, inclusive, with their respective enclosures. In transmitting the enclosed communication, in which you are requested to deliver the Archives of the Consulate at Liverpool to Mr. Beverley Tucker, the gentleman appointed by the President to be your successor, it gives the Department pleasure, on your voluntary retirement, to express its acknowledgement for the valuable information and suggestions relative to our commercial interests, which you have, from time to time, communicated, and to assure you of its satisfaction with the manner in which you have discharged the laborious and responsible duties of the office.

I am, Sir, your obedient servant,
Lewis Cass.[29]

In other words, thank-you and good-bye! The second letter was rather longer and while it expressed some further appreciation of Nathaniel's activities as consul was somewhat in the nature of a parting shot that had been fired in the knowledge that there was little to be feared from any return of fire:

Department of State, Washington, Sept. 24th, 1857.
Nathaniel Hawthorne Esq., Consul, Liverpool.

Sir—Your Despatch, No. 90, of the 17th of June last, upon the maltreatment of seamen on board vessels of the United States, was duly received. The note to Lord Napier, which accompanied it, was correctly published in the English journals, but without the previous knowledge or consent of this Department. You seem to suppose that some of its expressions may have been intended to charge you with delinquency in your official duties towards seamen. No such intention, however, was entertained; and now that you are about to retire from your position, I am happy to bear witness to the prudent and efficient manner in which you have discharged your duties. I owe it to myself, however, to add that I perceive nothing in the letter to Lord Napier which justifies the construction that you have placed on it. On the contrary, while it admits that some delinquency, on the part of our Consuls, in executing the laws of the United States concerning seamen, is not absolutely impossible, it expressly disclaims all knowledge of such delinquency; and where offenders have escaped punishment, it attributes the escape to causes over which our Consuls could exercise no control. What you say with regard to the evils that afflict our commercial marine, it is not now necessary to consider; but you quite misapprehend my views if you suppose that I am insensible to the magnitude of these evils, or could have ever intended to deny their existence. I concur with your opinion, however, that they are not so much chargeable to defective laws as to the want of that very class of persons whom the laws were made to protect. While, therefore, our statutes may be, and probably are, as well adapted to their objects as those of any country, it is none the less true that our merchant service suffers constantly from the want of American seamen. How this want can be supplied, is a question to which, in my note to Lord Napier, it was not my purpose to reply. I am, Sir,

Your obedient servant,
Lewis Cass[30]

After the initial excitement created by Ada's arrival had died down, a stricter schoolroom routine was established and Sophia must have been delighted with the way in which Ada and the children had apparently immediately settled down together. No doubt Ada was a pretty efficient teacher but she realized that she had entered into a household where the pupils were already well advanced in some respects, and that at least two of them were eager for knowledge. She was immediately aware of the contribution that Nathaniel and Sophia had made to the precocity of the children's learning and was already beginning to regard with great devotion the parents of these seemingly extraordinary children. It is thanks to her letters to Clay that a real picture of the family's life at this time can be visualized.

Leamington, England, Oct.7th, 1857

Dearest Clay!

I could not commence the letter which I told you I should, last night, after des-
patching yours, because my eyes would not allow it, after I had been reading a
while in Kenilworth, which I did to refresh my memory with regard to certain
points in the history of the castle whose ruins I saw with such delight on Monday.
I find I was mistaken in telling you that in Mervyn's tower, or the Strong Tower,
Amy Robsart was murdered. Her death took place in Cumnor Place, and it was
here that she fled for refuge and here that Tresillian discovered her in his apartment. It was so long ago that I read it that I had forgotten the details until I looked
in the book last evening. Una and I read aloud by turns. It is surprising to see
how appreciative she is of almost everything in which either her mother or I take
any interest. I never saw such a child in my life. Although she is only thirteen,
she reads with the greatest delight books which scarcely any girl of sixteen would
think of reading and understands and appreciates them as fully as most persons
of twenty. Dear Clay! I shall draw the most useful lessons for <u>us</u> from the manner
in which Mr. and Mrs. Hawthorne have educated these beautiful children. I never
knew children in so promising a state of development. Una and Julian will certainly
do something wonderful in the world.

Last evening, after I had ceased reading, Mrs. H read to me from a little journal
which this boy of eleven wrote while he was in Scotland, this summer, and I was
convulsed with laughter very frequently at the infinity of funny things with which
it was spiced. He has a great deal of genius.

But I meant to have told you, before, that, in going to Kenilworth, we crossed
the Avon, the veritable Avon, on which is Shakespeare's Stratford, not far from
here. I shall certainly make a pilgrimage there, if it is possible, before I leave
England. The Avon is so very small as to make it seem almost ridiculous to call
it a river. It is no wider than our glen stream at Yellow Springs, where I saw it,
and but little wider anywhere, Mrs. H. says. But how delightful it will be to go to
Shakespeare's home! And next Saturday, if it is pleasant, Una and I are going to
Warwick Castle. I think it is extremely fortunate that we happen to be in this
portion of England, one of the very most interesting of all.

I shall never forget the quiet rapture of last Monday among the ruins of Kenilworth, with that pure, beautiful Una as my companion, and with thoughts of thee
intensifying the pleasure that the lovely associations could not but cause. We sat
perfectly quiet for a long, long time, and enjoyed the spirit of the ruin most thoroughly. And I thought, all the time: "How blissful it will be to come here with
him in the days that are to be."

Yes, dear Clay, this year <u>will</u> be very, <u>very</u>, long to me, and I can hardly feel
that I have a <u>right</u> to enjoy anything since only <u>half</u> my being is here. I can only
now think how much we shall enjoy everything that is grand or beautiful.

The town of Leamington is remarkably pretty, with the very loveliest and grandest elms I ever beheld. I thought we had beautiful elms in New England; but the
trees in Leamington (and throughout Warwickshire it is the same) surpass all that
I have ever seen.

It has been quite rainy to-day, and between two showers, Una and I went to
walk in "<u>Lovers' Grove</u>", which is very beautiful.

I wish you could be made to realize the beauty of these English hedges of
Hawthorne, Ivy and Holly, with, frequently, thickly covered blackberry-bushes.
Is it not <u>late</u> for blackberries? We found great quantities of them, at Kenilworth,
the other day, and every day we see them in our walks when we go towards the
country, instead of in the town.

You will wish to know, by this time, how my days are employed since I have commenced my work of teaching.

Before breakfast, which is at half-past eight, both Julian and Una attend to Chronology for an hour; then for two hours after breakfast they have Arithmetic and French; dinner at one, and from two to four, Geography and Italian; tea at six, after that anything we please. I shall write and read some each evening, but not after ten o'clock as I am going to continue my good habits of retiring early.

We walk just before dinner and just after the afternoon's study. I enjoy it all extremely, and, after I have fairly launched them both in all their studies, I shall find considerable time for pursuing my own studies, I hope. This week I am doing scarcely anything. I have commenced hearing Una read one of Racine's plays, Andromaque, in addition to her regular lessons. She knows a great deal of French, I find, and can translate quite well, for which I am very thankful as it will be much more interesting to teach her.[31]

Perhaps it was as a result of receiving the letters from the secretary of state and the indignation that their rather brusque tone may have aroused in him, that a letter that Nathaniel wrote to his sister-in-law at this time was succinct and bordering on rudeness:

Liverpool, October 8th, '57

Dear E.

I read your manuscript abolition pamphlet, supposing it to be a new production, and only discovered afterwards that it was the one I had sent back. Upon my word, it is not very good; not worthy of being sent three times across the ocean; not so good as I supposed you would always write, on a subject in which your mind and heart were interested. However, since you make a point of it, I will give it to Sophia, and will tell her all about its rejection and return. Can [excision] . . . . ting always on one spot, and that the wrong one. You agitate her nerves, without in the least affecting her mind.

As you have suggested dropping your correspondence with Sophia, I hope you will take in good part some remarks which I have often thought of making on the subject. I entirely differ from you in the idea that such correspondence is essential to her peace of mind; not but what she loves you deeply and sincerely, and truly enjoys all modes of healthy intercourse with you. But it is a solemn truth, that I never in my life knew her to receive a letter from you, without turning pale and [excision]

And the very fact of my speaking so implies all the love and respect which, because I speak so, you are ready to disbelieve. As for Miss ——, I have long ago taken her measure, though she has failed to take mine. What you tell me about the letter is very curious, and it goes to confirm my previous idea of such revelations. A seeress of this kind will not afford you any miraculous insight into a person's character and mind; she will merely discover, through the medium of the letter, what another person, of just the same natural scope and penetration as the seeress, would discover normally by personal intercourse and observation of the person described. Thus her revelations (like all our conceptions of other person's characters) have some truth and much error.

I do not know what Sophia may have said about my conduct in the Consulate. I only know that I have done no good; none whatever. Vengeance and beneficence are things that God claims for himself. His instruments have no consciousness of His purpose; if they imagine they have, it is a pretty sure token that they are **not**

His instruments. The good of others, like our own happiness, is not to be attained by direct effort, but incidentally. All history and observation confirm this. I am really too humble to think of doing good! Now, I presume you think the abolition of flogging was a vast boon to seamen. I see, on the contrary, with perfect directness, that many murders and an immense mass of unpunishable cruelty—a thousand blows, at least, for every one that the cat-of-nine-tails would have inflicted— have resulted from that very thing. There is a moral in this fact which I leave you to deduce. God's ways are in nothing more mysterious than in this matter of trying to do good.

This is the last letter I shall write you from the Consulate. My successor is in town, and will take the office upon him next Monday. Thank Heaven; for I am weary, and, if it were not for Sophia and the children, would like to lie down on one spot for about a hundred years.

We shall be in England, however, some weeks longer. Good-bye.[32]

Back in Leamington, Ada was making a short addition to Clay's letter as well as writing others:

Thursday morning.

I snatch a few moments to tell thee, dearest, how calmly happy I am, this beautiful morning. Yet I know, even now, dearest, I know too well the longing and yearning moods of which you speak. This will be a year of unrest to me, try as hard as I may to be simply content and earnestly industrious; but the longings were never so strong as now. Dear, _dear_ Clay! we can sympathize here more fully than ever before.

But I close my little letter abruptly now, as I am just going to send a letter to Horace, and I mean to enclose this.

Your own loving,
Ada.

P.S. A letter came from Mr. Lane to-day, in which he tells me that his departure is delayed, and he begs me to write to him once more; but I shall not. I do not like the tone of his letter after what I have told him.[33]

And another letter went off, to one of her sisters:

Leamington, England,
October 8th, 1857

Dear Kate,

It seems such a long time since I have written to you that I almost forget when I stopped in my account of myself. Did I tell you of my delightful visits with Emma?[34] She stayed in Paris about ten days, and we called to see each other several times and I dined at her hotel once. She is now in England, but has not the least idea that I am here, for it was not until after she had left Paris that I received the letter which decided me to come. She will sail from Liverpool a week from to-day.

I wrote Otis[35] a hasty note just before I left Paris, telling him why I was coming to England, and I intended to write as soon as I arrived here, that you might not be anxious, but I have really found no time this week until now, when I could write a sufficiently long letter to send to America, except one that I sent to Clay on Tuesday. I have now been here four days, and consider myself quite established. Mrs. Hawthorne is the loveliest woman I ever knew, I believe, without exception. I admire her extremely and already love her very much. The children are all thoroughly charming.

Una is certainly the most remarkable girl I ever knew. Although only thirteen years old, I should think, from her conversation, that she was at least seventeen or eighteen, and her appreciation of books is really wonderful. She looks seventeen too, and she is just as amiable and interesting as she is wise.

Julian is a splendid boy with great black eyes, almost the handsomest I have ever seen, and with beautiful, curly brown hair, but without beauty of feature. I have not yet seen Mr. Hawthorne, for he is still detained in Liverpool.

Rose is but six years old, but she is a very sweet little child, although not so remarkable as the other two.

I must tell you about my journey from Paris to Leamington.

I started Friday, at five P.M. from Paris and reached Dieppe at about ten; thence I sailed, on Saturday morning, in a very small steamer, and over a rough sea;— so rough that I was miserably sick all the way, and could well understand how people can almost desire to be thrown overboard when they are seasick. I did not really know what sea-sickness was until then.

But I arrived safely at Newhaven, at two in the afternoon, and came directly to London, expecting to take the car directly to Leamington that night. But I found that I could only go as far as Rugby, and so stayed there (at Rugby) over night, and came on to Leamington Sunday morning.

But it is time for Julian to take the letter in which I am to enclose this to the office. So I abruptly close this little letter, and promise to send another very soon.

With exceeding great love and with a thousand apologies for the indolence which induces me to send so small a letter.

Your sister
Ada.

Your letter enclosing Mr. G's reached me yesterday, from Paris.[36]

So the end was almost in sight for Nathaniel, with just a few days left before Tucker could officially move into his chair of office and he could wash his hands of the whole business (apart from settling his accounts). One final letter to Ticknor was penned while he was still United States consul:

Liverpool, October 9th 1857

Dear Ticknor,

Here I am, writing you one more scribble from the old place. Mr. Tucker arrived by the Baltic, but could not take the office immediately, his Exequatur not being out. He will come in on Monday, and then I shall draw freer breath than for many a day past. Mr. Wilding being ill, and Mr. Pearce so nervous that he can hardly speak or stand, I have had a heavy burthen on my shoulders; but a man never knows what he can do till he is put to it. Mr. Wilding's illness has most seriously inconvenienced me by the delay of my accounts; for they are of a peculiar class, and it has been necessary to instruct another person how to make them up without aid or advice from him;[37] and he held all the clues in his hands. However, this difficulty is in a fair way to be surmounted; and I shall soon know how I stand with the Treasury Department.

Wilding has run a narrow chance for his life, which was at one time despaired of. He is now on the recovery; and Mr. Tucker has promised to give him the place of Vice Consul, which will be vacated by Mr. Pearce, who retires with me.

The new Consul will be very popular with the shipmasters and American residents; a bluff, jolly, good natured gentleman, fond of society, and an excellent companion—wholly unlike me in every possible respect. He is not nearly so bad as you think him, but still there is a likeness in the picture you draw; and if I were to lend him even a ten-pound note, I should be very doubtful of ever seeing it again. The clerks will run no risk of him, as Mr. Wilding will be Cashier, and will pay himself and the others regularly. I shall give Wilding some slight hint of his character. We have met in a most agreeable way, and seem to like one another vastly.

I have long heard rumors from the knowing ones here of the terrible crisis that was coming in the finances of the United States. Very likely, some of my investments may suffer, for the trouble seems to come down like an avalanche. If there were any ready cash to be had, I should think it would be a first-rate time to buy a place to live in; but I leave everything to your judgement, being sure that you have done, and will do, all for the best.[38]

Mrs. Hawthorne and the children are still at Leamington, and our new American governess has joined them there. She seems to prove entirely satisfactory.

I shall enclose you a bill of lading of another large box of books, and miscellaneous articles, which I hope will meet with the same favor from the Collector as those which have already been sent; and for which I beg you to convey to him my best thanks. You may assure him on my part that these articles are all for our own use, and none of them dutiable to the best of my belief. The books are not new; some of them were brought from America; others have been presented to me here; and all have been used. There is a writing desk in the box, and private papers &c &c &c.[39]

We shall make no long stay in Paris, but go almost immediately to Italy, via Marseilles; unless, indeed, Italy should be in a combustion before we can get there. There are many signs of an outbreak.[40]

I shall continue to write to you frequently by mail; and you must do the same by me.

Your friend
N. Hawthorne.

P.S. Old Cass has sent me a despatch, referring to mine, and bearing testimony to the "prudence and efficiency" of my official conduct.[41]

Saturday's weather, in Leamington at least, was fine and clear and an excursion to Warwick was planned by Ada and Una. Unfortunately, Sophia was not feeling too well and was confined to her room, but even so more shopping for clothes was undertaken by someone and bills at the butcher, grocer, and dairy settled. According to the Accounts Book, it appears that it was this Saturday that Ada's expenses were reimbursed; £22.4s.6d. seems quite a large sum though it covered, no doubt, such items as her passage from America as well as all hotel bills, M. Fezandie's lessons and travel costs from France. She made no reference to having received the money (from Sophia?) in any of her letters to Clay.

Nathaniel wrote to London:

Liverpool, October 10th 1857.

My dear Sir,
I have not had time, since I last wrote to you, to pay a visit to London. I shall continue in England some time longer, (during which my address will be at 10, Lansdowne Circus, Leamington) and I still hope to fulfil my engagement with regard to the photograph.—It would have been for my interest to sit sooner; for every day seems to have added a grey hair or two to my head, and a deeper line to my face.

Very truly
& Respectfully,
Nath[l] Hawthorne

Mr. Herbert Fry[42]

During that evening, Ada started on another letter to Clay with the news of the visit to Warwick:

Leamington, Oct. 10th, 1857
Saturday evening.
Dearest Clay!
Just returned from a visit to Warwick Castle and its surroundings. I come to write to thee a few moments, before the tea summons comes. Your letter commenced on the twentieth reached me this morning,[43] just before I started with Una to go to Warwick. My soul blesses thee for the dear, dear missive, my Beloved! I have read it but once, as I started for Warwick as soon as I had finished reading it, and have been there all day; tomorrow I shall have leisure to enjoy it fully.

We walked to the castle, which is about three miles from here, and enjoyed the excursion very, very much. The day was most beautiful and our walk was through one of the loveliest streets imaginable. These English roads bordered by lofty trees and winding so gracefully as they often do, are extremely beautiful after having been accustomed for several weeks to the straight streets of Paris.

The clouds were of a peculiarly soft and graceful texture, this morning, and the sky was of the blue that we love best. I never saw nature more lovely, and never longed more for thy dear presence which is always needed to make any enjoyment complete.

This castle is very beautiful and extremely interesting to me, of course, as it is the first one I have seen, of this kind. I enjoyed the view of the outside, as we approached it, more than our hurried visit to the few apartments which are shown to strangers; for, although these are magnificent, and contain some masterpieces by Vandyke, and Rubens among others,—we had scarcely a moment for each picture; for our guide hurried us through at a tremendous rate, much to our chagrin. It is always so here, Mrs. H. says, and we have to content ourselves with seeing what we can in the very short time allowed.

It is the most amusing thing to hear these guides repeat their long strings of information in a parrot-like tone,—evidently saying precisely the same words that they have used for thousands of times and with not the slightest interest in what they are saying.

The two principal towers of the castle are Caesar's tower, supposed to have been commenced at the conquest and still in a wonderful state of preservation, though moss-grown and very ancient-looking, and Guy's tower, built in the fourteenth century. We ascended the latter and enjoyed therefrom a fine view of the castle-grounds, the park consisting of twelve hundred acres, I think the gardener said, and the old town of Warwick, supposed to have been commenced in the year 1 A.D. says the guide-book. The Avon (our guide called it the <u>Havon</u>) winds through the town and washes, in its course,the foundation stones of the castle, passing directly by its base. It is here three times as wide as where we saw it in going to Kenilworth, and is very lovely. The whole view from this tower is most beautiful. I broke off a piece of the stone (sandstone I think) of one of the battlements at the summit of the tower, to take home to Julian, who is remarkably fond of such relics.

The walls of this tower are ten feet in thickness, and its basal diameter is thirty feet, its height is one hundred and thirty feet, and it stands on a high rock so that it overtops Caesar's tower, although the latter is nearly a hundred and fifty feet high.

Entering by the "Great Arched Gateway" we passed into the inner court, and found ourselves in full view of the main body of the castle, and, ringing a bell, we summoned the housekeeper, who conducted us through the Great Hall, where are exhibited various suits of Armor of many of the Earls of Warwick, their trophies, such as antlers of rein-deers, &c. the helmet which Cromwell wore, the leathern doublet in which Lord Brooke was killed at Lichfield, in 1645, and numerous other relics of great interest. This hall is immense, and one can easily fancy, while admiring its vast proportions, its Italian marble floor, its Gothic ceiling of massive oak, and the numerous trophies with which its walls are hung, how a merry company of knights might have been entertained there with all the hospitality of those times, in the Middle Ages or, afterwards, in the days of the Charleses and Jameses.

The red-drawing room, the cedar-drawing room (whose walls are of beautifully carved cedar, and indescribably rich) and the boudoir of the Countess of Warwick all contain pictures, cabinets, statues and furniture of the most exquisite finish. All these and the grand dining hall we passed through very hurriedly, and we visited, also, the chapel which is adorned with windows of stained glass.

But our visit to the garden was most pleasing, I believe. Here are numerous Cedars of Lebanon, two hundred years old, forming what they call "Cedar Grove". Have you ever seen any of these magnificent trees, dear Clay? They are grander and more majestic than any that I ever saw, and formed such a surrounding for this stately old castle that I was perfectly enchanted. Nothing can surpass the velvety beauty of the turf all over these grounds. We know nothing of the beauty of green grass in America, I find, since I have seen a few of the English lawns. There is a green-house (containing but a few flowers, however, compared with many which I have seen in America) erected for the purpose of affording a receptacle for an immense marble vase, which will hold one hundred and sixty gallons, and which is of exquisite Roman sculpture, having been excavated near Tivoli, by Sir William Hamilton and purchased by one of the former Earls of Warwick.

There are but few flowers on the grounds; for the present Earl, finding that the numerous splendid trees everywhere bestowed here shaded them too much, caused the demolition of the beds, and replaced them with shrubs. I like better that there should be only these lovely tints of green around the time-worn old castle. It is more in harmony with the scene than bright, variegated tints would be. It is very curious to see the grass growing from the walls, a hundred feet, perhaps, from the ground. Every where we see evidences of extreme antiquity, yet all is in a fine state of preservation. I was sorry not to have a sight of the Earl, himself. Mrs. Hawthorne happened to see him in the garden, when she was there.[44]

But I forgot to speak of the entrance to the castle. The lodge is but a small structure, but it contains many relics of Guy of Warwick "who stood eight feet three inches in his shoes" said the old woman in charge of the lodge. She shows his brass porridge-pot (still used in the occasion of the heir of Warwick coming of age, always, for punch drunk at the feasting) his armor, his flesh-fork, his sword, his lady's slippers, &c,&c.

The entrance to the castle is cut through the solid rock for a hundred yards, and the beautiful English ivy, which covers everything here, overhangs the stone sides of the avenue, while shrubs and trees of various kinds grow above.

But I must not lengthen this tedious description. We visited also St. Mary's church, and saw the tombs of Leicester, Elizabeth's favorite, and his brother Ambrose, Earl of Warwick, as well as of Richard, Earl of Beauchamp, the founder of the "Ladye Chapelle" in which are all these tombs. Leicester's tomb is very beautiful, and it was most interesting to see it so soon after beholding the proud castle where he passed the days of his splendor, the lordly Kenilworth.

St. Mary's church is one of the most beautiful Gothic structures in England and I enjoyed studying it in its details; but I will not weary you by my tedious description of it.

We visited the "collegiate hospital" which Leicester founded in 1571, for a "Master and twelve Brethren". He endowed it with lands whose revenue supports the institution at present. The "Brethren" are disabled soldiers who are allowed to live here with their wives, if married, but without their families. They have each a parlor and bedroom, neatly furnished, a plot of ground, and a pension of eighty pounds a year; but they are subjected to numerous restrictions. For instance, if not married when they enter the hospital, they cannot marry without the consent of the master, who is appointed by Lord de Lisle, the heir of the Leicester estates and titles. They cannot keep a dog or a hawk and cannot earn money in any way; cannot leave the building without their livery, &c, &c,. Certain towns have the right to send brothers to the hospital, in turn, when vacancies occur by death.

I was sorry that all the brethren were out, so that we could not have the pleasure of seeing them. But the building is very ancient, and we examined it quite minutely. We entered the rooms of an old Waterloo soldier, one of the brethren, and were quite pleased with the air of comfort that prevailed there.

In the Great Hall is an inscription "Here King James the first was right hospitably entertained", &c, giving the date and stating that the master addressed him in Latin. The massive oaken chair in which he sat was shown to us.

Throughout the building the armorial crest of Leicester and his initials, R.L. with his motto "Droit et Loyal" are repeated at every turn. His crest is a <u>Bear</u> hugging a ragged staff. In one of the rooms is a piece of tapestry consisting of a white "bear and ragged staff" on a blue ground, which is said to be the work of the unfortunate Amy Robsart. When Una and I wrote our names in the visitors

Oct 10th, Ada Shepard, Dorchester, Mass
Oct 10th Miss Hawthorne. Boston Mass.

book, in this room, the guide, seeing that we were Americans, told us that this tapestry was placed in its rich oaken frame by the generosity of an American who visited the hospital, some time ago, and left money for the purpose.

But I am sure you are tired of reading all this, and I will stop short, here.

What is all this to us now? We will visit all these places together, in the years that are to come, dear Clay, and <u>then</u> will come the right enjoyment for me; <u>then</u> can I feel that I have a <u>right</u> to give myself to their influence completely. <u>Now</u> I feel as if only <u>half</u> my being were here. I remember at this moment, a line near the beginning of Corinne: "Voyager est un des plus tristes plaisirs de la vie." When I read it in Paris, soon after my arrival there, I wrote, as a note, in the margin; "Oui, si l'on est seul", as I thought what delight it would be to travel with <u>thee,</u> my beloved. Ah! together will we travel, not merely through America or through Europe, but through the pathway of life! What more blessed companionship than that of a soul earnest and faithful like thine, ever dear and blessed Clay?[45]

Sunday was the usual day of rest, and although church may have been attended, nothing that was done either in Liverpool or Leamington was recorded. The weather was not too good that day so there appeared little else possible to do except continue the letter to Clay!

Sunday morning, Oct 11th.

While the musical church-bells are pealing through the town, and the little birds in the plaisance before the house sing on undaunted by the gloomy clouds that make the day so dark, I come to make my glad heart more glad by communing with my beloved one. Before I arose this morning I reread the blessed letter that came to me yesterday, and my heart rose in prayer to our Father that he would make me worthy of so great and noble a love as thine, dear Clay,—that he would make me worthy to be the companion of so noble a being as thou art. But, dear and life-giving as are the fond words on which I dwelt so rapturously, they smote me with a terrible pain, too; for I could not but feel that you see me better and higher than I am, dear Clay. Oh! tell me that you know I am weak and faulty;— so weak and so faulty that years of earnest striving can only make me <u>approach</u> the standard of strength and excellence to which thy bride should have attained, my own dear Clay! I cannot <u>bear</u> this too high praise of thine, now when I seem to myself so unworthy, so little. Never before, dear Clay, did I realize as fully as now, how far short I fall of the womanly excellence that should make me worthy of the affection of such a lover as thou, Clay Badger. Do not again reproach me by intimating that I may be able to bring more than thou wilt, to our life, at the end of this year of separation. It seems to me that I am doing scarcely anything. I never was more dissatisfied with myself than now. I seem to accomplish scarcely anything. This week which I have spent in England has been almost a nonentity to me as far as work is concerned. I <u>will</u> be more industrious henceforth. Still I forsee that my time will necessarily be but small for uninterrupted study. As Una and Julian are in quite different states of progression in almost all studies I have to give twice as much time as if they could go on together, of course. Mrs. Hawthorne has been exceedingly kind to me. She could not be more so were I her sister, and my relation with her will be delightful, I am sure. The children, too, are the most interesting pupils imaginable; but of course it is something of a trial to spend so much of my day with them when I long to be studying language, of which I find myself so lamentably ignorant, the more I examine myself. M. Fezandie thought that I accomplished a great deal in the six weeks which I spent with him; but it seems very little compared with what I wished and wish to do. I say all this to you, not because I wish to trouble you, but because you ask me to tell you all my vexations as well as my pleasures, and because I do not wish you to have a false estimate of what I am doing. When we are settled for the winter, in

Rome, I shall probably find more leisure but now everything seems unsettled. I do not know how much longer we shall be in England. Mr. Hawthorne has not yet come from Liverpool. He sends a letter every day, and Una or Mrs. Hawthorne write to him each day also.[46] I believe that here is an instance of a true marriage, dear Clay, and I rejoice in it. Mrs. H. has been too unwell to leave her room, for two or three days, and I quite long to see her down stairs again. Ah! how precious is health, dearest! Fear not that I shall not care for mine while I am away from thee. I am too firmly impressed with the duty I owe to thee, in this regard, not to employ every means in my power to strengthen and invigorate myself before coming back to thee. I am resting quite enough now, dearest. I retire at ten and do not rise till six, at present.

I am sure that you are accomplishing a great deal intellectually and I fear that I shall bring but very little to add to our united stock of wisdom compared with what you will be prepared to add in a year's time. Yet I shall try earnestly to do what I may, believe me, dear Clay!

I am anxious to hear more of the progress of affairs at Yellow Springs, and wonder why Mary R.[47] does not write. I have not heard a word from her since I left home, and have sent her two letters.

You ask if I have an extensive correspondence. No, I have written to scarcely any one excepting the folks at home, and do not intend to write at all frequently to most people while I am away. It takes too much time which is so precious to me now. I can never tell thee, dearest Clay, how refreshing to my spirit are thy dear letters, and how deep is my regret at not being able to send more worthy replies to them.

I could almost believe that the memory of those days of sweet communion with thee, the months we passed together at Antioch, the weeks at home, were all a dream, and that I am only the Ada Shepard of old, unblessed by the love of so noble a being as thou, were it not that I can read these dear words of thine,— away from thee and from all else belonging to my former existence,—that I can read these dear, living, glowing words and assure myself that it is not all a dream too sweet to be true.

O my beloved Clay! My dearest, only friend! My daily and nightly prayer is that I may be rendered worthy of thee. May God help us in our strivings, dearest! May He lead us towards Himself as, with joined hearts and hands, we journey on in life![48]

It does appear that Ada was a little below par, possibly due to the added work that must have put on her shoulders by Sophia's indisposition as, besides schoolwork, no doubt the children then looked to her to keep them happy and amused throughout the rest of the day. There must also have been an almost palpable atmosphere of heightened excitement due to the imminent return of Nathaniel within the next few days. But her natural good spirits would see her through, even though Monday began with another yearning communion with her beloved.

Monday morning, 12th.

Before I begin the work of a new week I must come and greet thee in my silent way, dearest being, so constantly in my thoughts.

I blessed God, in my morning prayer, that two out of the twelve months have passed. I look forward to the close of this year as an exile from his native land longs for the repeal of his sentence. Not that I do not feel still, dearest Clay, that this separation is best for us. I am more and more sure of <u>that</u>; but the yearnings for thy presence are <u>very</u> strong, and sometimes it seems almost as though I could hardly endure to be thus alone for a whole year. But in my highest moods I feel so sure of thy continued presence with me, feel so sustained and guarded by this pure and noble love of thine that there is no room for regret that I may not <u>see</u> thy beloved form and hear that voice that makes such music for my soul.

Ah Clay! Dear, <u>dear</u> Clay!

I am going to try to be very strong and brave this week,—to work steadily and contentedly on in my little sphere, to work while the day lasts and retire to rest when the night comes, that I may grow healthier day by day as well as wiser. And every day and every hour I shall be sustained and encouraged by the thought of the true, noble heart that beats in unison with mine, far, far away beyond the sea.

Dearly beloved, receive my earnest blessing for all that thou art to me![49]

Up in Liverpool it was supposed to be the first day of the new régime under Tucker but Nathaniel was both overseeing the smooth transfer of power and, no doubt, struggling with the final presentation of his accounts. It appears that the exequatur had still not arrived by the time the consulate opened for business that day, as Nathaniel (most unusually, but certainly due to the continuing absence of Wilding) took a deposition from one of three aggrieved passengers of the recently docked American ship *Great Western* and, in so doing, reference was made to Tucker as being a "Commercial Agent of the United States" rather than as United States consul.[50] However, whatever the continuing irritations involved in the delay in obtaining the exequatur and thus being able *finally* to hand everything over to Tucker, at some time during the day he did find time to try to say good-bye to the Heywoods (or perhaps just Mrs. Heywood?) at Norris Green:[51]

Liverpool, October 12th '57

Dear Mrs. Heywood,

I was really grieved not to find you at home to-day; it being so long since I have seen you, and my departure so close at hand. However, I shall return to Liverpool for a short time, two or three weeks hence;[52] and then I will make another attempt to see you.

I left at Norris Green an American Edition of one of my books, which I meant to put into your hands, with a very pretty speech (if I could think of one) expressive of my gratitude for the hospitality and many kindnesses of yourself and Mr. Heywood. However much I might have said, it would all have been true, and more; for there are few places in the world of which I shall have such delightful recollections as of Norris Green.

Believe me, dear Mrs. Heywood, most sincerely yours,

Nath[l] Hawthorne[53]

The next day Ada was awake bright and early, as usual, and immediately rushed to her writing desk:

Tuesday, October 13th

I awoke this morning, an hour ago, from so vivid a dream of thee that it cost me an absolute <u>pang</u> of <u>agony</u> to come to the consciousness that I was so many miles, so many <u>months</u> from thee. My second thought was: "To-day is the semi-anniversary of our sacred thirteenth of April." A year and a half old are we to-day, darling. Dost remember, dearest, our evening spent in Miss Wilmarth's hospitable little parlor, a year ago?[54] Ah! where shall we spend it a year from to-night? God grant that it may be <u>together</u>, wherever it may be! I hardly see how we could brave another year of separation like this. Yet those words argue weakness, do they not, dear Clay? I would I could blot them out, or that I could entirely overcome the spirit that prompted them, resting content always with the blissful consciousness that thou art <u>mine</u> (Mine! dear <u>Clay</u>)! and willing to wait until, in God's own good time, we may do our daily work together.

Do you feel now, dearest Clay, as though it were probable that we should both be at Antioch next year? I hardly dare to hope for it at all. It seems to me now as if our last summer's visions were all too bright. But I do not concern myself much about what is to come next year, for myself, at least. I care far more where <u>you</u> may be, what <u>you</u> may be doing, than what <u>I</u> shall do. I can find some work that I shall be glad to do, I doubt not; but thou, my beloved, must be placed in a position suited to thee. Let us hope, let us pray that God will befriend us, poor, helpless children "crying in the night."

Just half a year, darling, since we met in Mr. Smith's parlor,[55] and burned the old letters! Have we been true to the high resolves we made then?

At least we have <u>grown</u>, and we will watch and strive and pray yet another half-year, that, at our second birth-day, our self-examination may result nobly and proudly for us, both.

Dear Clay, I leave thee (no; leave the pen only with which I commune with thee; thou art still with me) to attend to my little round of duties.

Although it is nearly seven o'clock, the day has but just fully dawned. At six, when I rise, it is scarcely beginning to grow light, and all the time it seems as dark here as when the twilight begins at home. This damp, foggy old England! There have been scarcely any bright days since I came, excepting when Una and I went to Kenilworth and Warwick. But I write no more now, dearest. It is <u>hard</u> to cease, when writing to thee![56]

But having put Clay's letter on one side, it wasn't long before she turned to start one to her friend, Lucy Noble.

Leamington, England
October 13th 1857

Dear Lucy
I thank you for the little letter that I received from you, a short time ago,[57] and will try to write one to you this morning, if I can find time before I am summoned to breakfast.

I began to tell Beckie in my letter to her,[58] about my visit to Warwick Castle, and told her I would conclude the account in your letter. So if you would like to read the whole, I refer you to her note.

We first entered the "Great Hall", as it is called, an immense apartment with oaken walls and wainscoted ceiling, and with floor of red and white Italian marble of the most beautiful polish. Here are displayed numerous warlike trophies, coats of mail of the old Earls of Warwick, their swords, and helmets, the veritable helmet worn by Cromwell, the doublet in which Lord Brooke was slain at Lichfield, etc, etc,. Beckie would have especially delighted in this room, I think. There was such a variety of interesting objects of which I fancy she would have made a list, questioning the guide as often as she had an opportunity.

But that would not have been very often, for he hurried us through the rooms, so that we hadn't a tenth part of the time we needed to get a good idea of the contents, to say nothing of leisure to admire the numerous pictures and works of art which adorned the drawing-rooms. There are the red drawing-room, whose walls are of the color indicated by the name; the cedar drawing-room, the most tasteful of all I think, with walls and ceiling of richly carved cedar which sheds its fragrance through the apartment; the state bed-room hung with green velvet and satin wherein is a bed with counterpane of embroidered white satin on which once slept Queen Anne; the boudoir of the Countess of Warwick, the loveliest and most tasteful little room imaginable for a Countess's sitting-room, and in all these state rooms, which I have only mentioned only [sic] without wearying you by an attempt at describing them, are numerous master-pieces by celebrated artists and sculptors with furniture of the most exquisite finish, whole tables and cabinets composed of mosaics of precious stones, and rare articles of the most enormous value. We entered the chapel which is a beautiful little structure adorned by windows of stained glass. Some of the most interesting of the pictures were the family portraits. There were two or three portraits of the famous Dudley, Earl of Leicester, minister of Kenilworth, and brother to Ambrose, Earl of Warwick. Then there were pictures by Vandyke, Rubens, Tenier, and various other portraits of the greatest genius. But since I cannot begin to give you an idea of them, I must not weary you by an enumeration of those which I saw. I did not have time to examine a tenth part of them, so rapidly were we hurried through. Mrs. H. says that we always are thus hurried at Warwick, and at many of the places in England which are occupied by their masters and thrown open occasionally to the public.

The earl of Warwick allows visitors to enter the castle on Saturday, each week. Of course his own rooms are not shown; only these state apartments. The castle park is twelve hundred acres in extent, and is adorned with a large cedar grove, composed almost entirely of Cedars of Lebanon of two hundred years growth, as I think I mentioned in Beckie's letter. There are so many trees in the grounds that the present Earl caused the demolition of the large flower-beds that formerly occupied one part of them, and replaced them by shrubs which would not be much injured by the shade. There is a green-house of rather inconsiderable size and without a great variety of flowers, but built especially for the reception of an immense marble vase which can hold one hundred and sixty gallons, and which was dug up by Sir William Hamilton, at Tivoli near Rome. It is all cut from a single block of marble, and is an exceedingly beautiful monument of the old Roman art. We walked down to the bank of the Avon, which washes the base of the castle. It is a beautiful little river. Our guide called it the "Havon", with the accustomed misplacement of the H which characterizes the uneducated English. We visited St. Mary's church and I wish I could describe it to you; especially the "Ladye Chapelle" wherein is the tomb of Leicester and his third Countess as well as that of Ambrose of Warwick, and Beauchamp, the founder of the Chapel, which is within the church.

Then we visited the collegiate hospital founded by Leicester in 1571, for indigent old soldiers. Twelve of them called "brethren of the hospital" with a master, live here, supported by the revenues of the lands with which the hospital is endowed.

I shall have a great deal to tell you about what I have seen and learned in my travels when I come home. I hope you will all have patience to bear with my letters until then, imperfect as my want of sufficient time and descriptive power must make them. I intend to write to Charlie soon and send the letter home to be enclosed to him. It is very long since I have written to him, although he owes me several letters, I am sure.[59] Still I shall not mind that, of course. Mr. Hawthorne will be here to-day, I hope. I have told you in some of my letters home, since I have been here, how very much I like Mrs. H. and the children, have I not? Mrs. H. is very, very kind, and lovely. Her smile is almost angelic. But I must not write more now. With the warmest love for you all.

                                                                        Ada.[60]

Presumably the days passed with the usual lessons and short walks. It was rent day once more (£2.15s.8d. this week!). Sophia's health may have improved each day in direct ratio to the decreasing number of hours that they had to endure before Nathaniel returned, but the time of his arrival was still a matter of conjecture, even though so close. Ada took up Clay's letter again:

Evening.

And so I come, dear Clay! to finish the little letter which I intend to dispatch tomorrow. And on this evening, sacred to thee and to love, I do no work. It is holy time, and, after writing a little while, I mean to go to my comfortable little bed, where, resting but not sleeping for some time I am sure (for I am weary but not sleepy this evening) I shall live over the scene of that first Sunday evening when "commenced the Sabbath of my life".

I have reread, this evening, before commencing to write, thy last, dear letter, and again my soul blesses thee for its cheering words.

I would that I might send thee a worthy reply, but I feel very incapable of doing anything well now. A sort of torpor seems to overpower my intellectual faculties, since I have been in England. I hope it is only due to the influence of this murky air and cloudy sky, and that the sunny skies of Italy will disperse the clouds.

I realize more and more how our last year's life tended to fatigue us thoroughly, and see that it will take a long time to rest me completely. But I am full determined to rest sufficiently, this year, whatever it costs me. That is what you most desire, as I well know, and for what do I live but to endeavor to work the will of God faithfully and to make myself worthy of thy dear companionship?

Of news, dear Clay, I have not a single item, I believe, since my last letter. Mr. Hawthorne has not yet returned, but is expected tomorrow, and then I hope we shall know more definitely what will be our movements. I long to be fairly settled, for the winter, in Rome.

And now, dearest, when I feel that I must not linger more over this tedious letter, but must speed it on its way to thee, receive my heartfelt blessing, dear, noble being! Know, feel always that to thee my heart turns whenever weariness overpowers my frame, whenever loneliness clouds my spirit, whenever discouragement threatens to invade my mind. In thee, in thy dear love, is always rest, companionship and brave cheer for thy Ada in all troubles.

God bless thee and guard thee forever, dearest Clay!

Forever, forever I am thine!

P.S. Never fear, beloved one! that you will say too much to me about your increasing health and strength. I thank you from my deepest heart for the joy such an assurance gives me. I, too, rejoice daily in returning physical strength. I do believe you will never see so jaded and worn-out an Ada as when we graduated. I mean that you shall not.

Dearest Clay! do not ever write a word to me when you do not feel inclined and write just as long letters as the spirit prompts, please, without regard to the length of mine. I have to make mine very long when I try to tell you about my visits to places of interest, you know.

My travelling companion from Paris, Mr. Jones, sent me the book he promised. It proves to be a collection of so-called poems which are supremely ridiculous.[61]

Once again the weather changed, this time for the better, and it immediately had a beneficial effect on Ada's lethargy; perhaps it also made the waiting for Nathaniel that much easier, for he was definitely expected to return that day. It wasn't until evening, however, that he finally arrived:

Leamington, England
Oct.14th 1857

Dear Clay!

I cannot sleep to-night until I have written of the joy that fills my soul at the contemplation of this beautiful union. Mr. and Mrs. Hawthorne are perfectly united, I believe, and it gives an added depth and tenderness, if that were possible, to my love for thee, to see the perfect affection that renders them so happy.

Mr. H came this evening, and I was quite surprised to see so handsome a man as he is. He has the most beautiful brow and eyes, and his voice is extremely musical. I do not wonder that Mrs. Hawthorne loved him, any more than that her angelic loveliness attracted his poet-heart. Ah! what rare delight it is to see two rightly married!

And shall there not be one more perfect union before we die, dearest, if God so wills it?

I can write to thee with a clearer conscience this evening than sometimes; for I have been less stupid than usual to-day. I had begun to be almost discouraged about myself, and to think that I was the most incorrigibly indolent being since I came to England; but to-day, when the sun came out and the air lost its accustomed dampness, and became bracing and clear, I found that it was the weather had exerted its depressing influence upon me, and rejoiced in the buoyancy and life which the sunlight gave me.

Blessed be the sunshine, whether in the sky or heart!

This day has been absolutely perfect. How I longed for thy companionship as I walked this forenoon and at sunset! Dear Clay! Dear Clay! What a delight it will be to walk with thee every day as I may sometime hope to do!

But it is after ten, and I must not allow my unusually vigorous state of mind to cause me to neglect my rule to retire punctually at my time.

Good night, my beloved, my treasure, my only love![62]

With Nathaniel at home once more and the consulate now a thing of the past (although there were still the accounts to be finalized), the daily routine could now be established that would suit all the members of the household. Nathaniel was content to do almost nothing except go for walks, often by himself, and to maintain his influence over the household by his calming presence. No doubt Sophia was able to relax and recover from her recent poor spell of health and the children could settle down with Ada and look forward to the next red-letter day when they would leave for Paris and the Continent. Ada continued to be the only regular commentator on the family's doings:

Thursday eve, Oct. 15th

Another month half gone! How fast the days speed, even when away from thee, dearest! I rejoice that it is so, for I look forward to the end of the year with rapture. But I must not write that again. It forms the chief burden of my letters each week, I believe.

We had another sunshiny day to-day, and I have rejoiced in its glad influences from early morning till now, with scarcely a cloud upon my spirit for an instant. I shall have much to say to thee, when I may talk with thee, dearest! of the way in which Mrs. Hawthorne has brought up her children. I never have known children thus reared, and it is very beautiful to me to observe them, to be with them constantly. No secondary motives have ever been appealed to in their education. They are taught to do things simply because they are right.

In almost all respects they have been treated just as I always hoped and believed it would be possible for me to treat children committed to my charge,—just as I always intended to treat the child whom I had planned to adopt, before the Ides of April, eighteen hundred and fifty-six, when my plans were so unfortunately overthrown.

They have the best physical development of any children that I have ever seen, their mode of life has always been so simple and regular. Although Una is thirteen years old, she never tasted candy in her life until a short time ago, since they have been in England; they never eat cakes or pies, and all their food is as simple and wholesome as possible.

I am very glad, for my own sake as well as theirs, that we live so simply as regards diet; for, at M. Fezandie's, although I liked the time of the meals very much, I disliked the manner extremely. All the food was very rich, and it was impossible to make a simple meal. How delightful it will be to arrange a mode of life for ourselves, by and by, dear Clay! Think what a little heaven our home (!) will be! A heaven afar off, now, it is true, but so much the more intensely enjoyed when reached.
Dear Clay! Dear Clay!

Friday, Oct. 16th

I snatch a few moments, while the children are studying their Chronology, to write to him ever so near, so dear to me. I rejoice in the hope of a new letter from thee in a few days, for it will be a week tomorrow since the last one came.

Yesterday I received half a dozen little ones from home.[63] Kate said that Otis had received one from you a little while before. They speak of you with great admiration and love, dear Clay. Kate says that our good minister, Mr. Hall (whose call on us was so delightful to us, you remember, on the evening of the music on the hill) was exceedingly pleased with you, with us, if I may presume to tell you this "without a shadow of vanity". I had not talked with him so long before for a great many years, for I wandered away from his church long ago, and went to Mr.

No. 10 Lansdowne Circus. Photo by the author.

Parker's, as you know. But we will go and hear Mr. Hall together, the next time we are in Dorchester; shall we not?

Kate says that you won the most golden opinions from all our friends who saw you. But why do I tell you of these things? Of course you must know that it would be so, my dear, noble, Clay! <u>Das versteht sich</u> [that goes without saying] as clearly as any axiom, I am sure.

I suppose you have heard that Lucy[64] has gone to Eagleswood, New Jersey, to teach, and Lucy Noble writes me that she thinks of returning to her father, in New Orleans, this fall. If she goes the family will be quite reduced in size.

What a terrible disaster occurred on the sea, near Havanna! [sic] I have not read about it yet, for M. Fezandie did not send my tribune, but I shall when I go to Paris and find it there.[65] Do not trouble yourself to send any more papers, dearest. Mr. Hawthorne will doubtless always have American papers which I can read, when I can take the time.

Mr. Hawthorne has at last finished his duties as consul, and his successor, Mr. Tucker, has been installed in his office. But we shall be delayed here until the secretary who has been so ill shall have recovered sufficiently to assist in the final adjustments of numerous official documents.[66]

Probably aware that time was going to drag somewhat, and casting around for something to do, it had occurred to Nathaniel to get in touch with Bennoch and to ask him to come up and stay for a while; he could show him around the local sights at the same time as bringing to his notice the benefits of an American governess as opposed to the English variety. Quite where he was to be put up in No. 10 is a little difficult to imagine as now there could have been little, if any, spare accommodation in the house. However, he could always be booked in at a local hotel:

10, Lansdowne Circus
Leamington, Oct^r.16th '57.

Dear Bennoch,
I have got rid of the Consulate, and we are spending a few weeks here while my accounts with the U.S.Government are being made up—previous to which we cannot leave England. It is not to be thought of that we should go away without seeing you; so I wish you would take your carpet-bag and come and pay us a little bit of a visit. We have a very nice young lady here whom we have imported from America to fill the immense vacancy left by Miss Browne. I should like to give you the opportunity of comparing an American governess with that admirable specimen of an English one.
    Do come.

Truly Yours
Nathl Hawthorne.

P.S. Mrs. Hawthorne sends her best regards to both Mrs. Bennoch and yourself.[67]

The weather next day, Saturday, was calm and clear so Nathaniel and Sophia decided on a trip to Coventry, catching the 10:45 train from the Avenue Station; there is no indication as to what the rest of the household did in their absence.

[Today], my wife and I took the rail for Coventry, about a half-hour's ride distant. I had been there before, more than two years ago, and my wife about a month since.[68] No doubt I described it on my first visit; and it is not remarkable enough to be worth two descriptions; a large town of crooked and irregular streets and lanes, not looking nearly so ancient as it is, because of new brick and stuccoed fronts which have been plastered over its antiquity, although still there are interspersed the peak gables of old fashioned, timber built houses; or an archway of worn stone, which, if you peep through it shows like an avenue from the present into the past; for, just in the rear of the new-fangled aspect, lurks the old arrangement of court-yards, and rustiness, and griminess, and many things that would not be suspected from the exterior.
    We went into St. Mary's Hall, the old edifice where the municipal meetings and police Courts are held; formerly the hall of one of the guilds, where their feasts used to be held. In the basement, there is a great, gloomy kitchen, and a cellar, with pillars and arches like the crypt of a cathedral. Above, there is a fine old medieval apartment, some sixty feet long, and broad and lofty in proportion, lighted by six high windows of stained glass on each side, and a large arched

one at the end; the latter being of genuine ancient glass, representing old kingly personages, and heraldic blazonries; but notwithstanding all the colored light that comes through these windows, the hall, panelled with black oak, is sombre and dark. At the end opposite the great arched window (which is mullioned with stone) is an oaken gallery for minstrels, extending across the hall, and on the balustrade hang old suits of armor belonging to the city. Under the gallery are arched doors, leading to dusky rooms which are used for committees and other municipal purposes. I have spoken of the hall as being oak-panelled; but I now remember that it is partly covered with tapestry of Henry VIs time, representing historical persons; very elaborately wrought, and no doubt very rich and magnificent in its day, though now so faded and darkened as to be hardly distinguishable. Coats of arms were formerly painted all round the hall, but have been obliterated by the garments of people brushing against them. I have not seen anything in England more curious than this hall; and I must not forget its oaken roof, vaulted quite across, without any support of pillars, and carved with figures of angels, and, I suppose, many devices which are lost amid the duskiness that broods up aloft there like an over-hanging cloud. The floor of the hall is now covered with rows of benches. In a recess on one side, near the entrance of what is called the Mayoress's parlor, there stood an ancient chair of state, big enough for two. Kings and queens, the guide-book says, have sat there in former times; and my wife and I sat down as their successors. There are full length portraits of George III and George IV hanging in this hall, and some other portraits which I did not particularly examine. In the Lady Mayoress's parlor, I remember, I saw many pictures at my former visit; but there seemed to be a court in session there to-day; so we did not inspect it.

Right across the narrow street stands St. Michael's church, with its tall tower and spire, more than three hundred feet high. The body of the church has been almost entirely recased with stone, since I was here before; but the tower still retains its antiquity, and is decorated with statues that look down from their lofty niches, seemingly in good preservation. The tower and spire are most stately and beautiful; the whole church very noble. We went in, and found that the vulgar plaster of Cromwell's time has been scraped from the pillars and arches, leaving them all as fresh and beautiful as if just made. There are a few monuments in the church; but it seems to be paved along the aisles with flat tombstones.

We looked also into Trinity Church, which stands close by St. Michael's, separated, I think, only by the church-yard. We also visited Saint John's church, which is very venerable as regards its exterior, the stone being worn and smoothed—if not roughened—by centuries of storm and fitful weather. This antique wear and tear, however, has almost ceased to be a charm to my mind, comparatively to what it was when I first began to see old buildings. Within, the church is spoilt by wooden galleries built across the beautiful pointed arches.

We saw nothing else particularly worthy of remark, except Ford's Hospital, in Grey Friars' street. It has an Elizabethan front of timber and plaster, fronting on the street with two or three peaked gables in a row, beneath which is a low arched entrance, giving admittance into a small paved quadrangle, open to the sky above, but surrounded by the walls, lozenge-paned windows, and gables of the Hospital. The quadrangle is but a few paces in width, and perhaps twenty in length; and through a half-closed doorway, at the farther end, there was a glimpse into a garden. Just within the entrance, through an open door, we saw the neat and comfortable apartment of the Matron of the Hospital; and along the quadrangle, on each side, there were three or four doors, through which we caught glimpses of little rooms, each containing a fireplace, a bed, a chair or two, and a little homely, domestic scene, with one old woman in the midst of it; one old woman in each room. They are destitute widows, who have their lodging and home here—a little room for every one to sleep, cook, and be at home in—and three and sixpence a week to feed and clothe themselves with; a cloak being the only garment bestowed on them. When one of the sisterhood dies, each old woman has to pay two-pence towards the funeral; and so they slowly starve and wither out of life, and claim each their two-penny contribution in turn. I am afraid they have a very dismal time. There is an old man's Hospital, in another part of the town, on a similar plan. A collection of sombre and lifelike tales might be written on the idea of giving the experience of these Hospitallers, male and female; and they might be supposed to be written down by the Matron of one—who might have acquired literary taste and practice as a Governess—and the Master of the other, a retired school-usher.

It [was] market-day in Coventry, and in the Market-place, and far adown the street leading from it, there were booths and stalls, and crockery ware spread out on the ground, and apples, pears, vegetables, toys, books, (among which I saw my Twice-told Tales, with an awful portrait of myself as frontispiece) and various country-produce, offered for sale by men, women and girls. The scene looked lively, but had not really much vivacity in it. We lunched at the King's Head on cold beef, roast and boiled, together with half a pint of port, all of which came to six shillings and six pence;[69] and after some rather aimless wanderings about the streets, found our way to the Station, and took the rail homewards at a quarter to five.[70]

Sophia wrote up the visit in her journal and once again made the day appear to have been much more interesting than Nathaniel's account of it; of course, he had seen it all before, but not since some two years previously, and he said that Sophia had been there only a month ago, but it appeared that he had lost a great deal of his former enthusiasm for traipsing around sites of historic interest, particularly those that he was visiting for the second or third time. That was not the case in all instances, however; he never lost his interest and delight in wandering around London, even just walking the streets there, never mind going into the famous buildings. Was he *made* to go to Coventry on this occasion by Sophia, who probably just wanted a day out on their own without the children? He obviously didn't care much for "aimless" wandering.

[This] morning my husband and I went together to Coventry by the rail road. The weather promised to be pretty fair, though the sun did not shine outright—but it was mild and pleasant. We took the quarter to eleven train, stopping a few moments at the Milverton Warwick station and at Kenilworth. At Milverton a burly Englishman with his bags and rugs dared to intrude into our private carriage and sat down between us, and thus interrupt our electric currents, for how could they penetrate his beef and ale! He had that singular air of being a gentleman and of not being a gentleman that so many well-dressed Englishmen have. Something of coarseness—of lack of cultivation in the face and expression, with handsome features, good figure, and an easy manner, good broadcloth and kid gloves. He might have been a fox-hunting squire, with very little perception of high art and with great skill in leaping fences, possessed of a fine stud, keen hounds, and a beautiful Hall, but with a small library and no gallery of statues. The country still looked deliciously green but the trees were many of them of russett gold, with here and there some American glory among the vines. I think we were not half an hour on the way, as it is but ten miles to Coventry. We walked up into the old town along a broad, green road to Hertford St, at the top of which, from the second story of a corner house leans Peeping Tom, gazing after the fair phantom of the Lady Godiva, whom no-one else can see. His position is such that his glance commands four streets. His jerkin is slashed with gold and adorned with gold buttons and his two curious eyes are staring their last, for Earl Leofric put them out for their audacity in disobeying his commands.

We turned into the High St from the Market Place, upon which Hertford St opens, and first visited Ford's Hospital for old widows, down Grey Friar's Lane. It is an ancient edifice of timber and plaster with three gables in front, and a quadrangle in the centre—long and narrow. There is a good deal of carving on the timber—and it all has the appearance of black and white mosaic. The entrance is through an archway, on each side of which is a room, one the nurse's and the other a committee-room. On both sides the quadrangle are small dismal rooms, and opposite the entrance-arch is another which leads to a lawn beyond, where the poor, forlorn old women walk. The house is two stories high, and steep old staircases lead up to the chambers, which are far brighter and pleasanter than the lower apartments. There is a row of narrow closets, which the nurse said were supposed to have been nuns' cells once, but now they were used for coal. The Charity was founded in 1529 by William Ford, a merchant of Coventry, and affords 3/6 per week to twenty or thirty women, and coal for four months. They are obliged to fund themselves in every thing for food and raiment—and coal for the other eight months out of this small allowance and when I told the nurse I thought it must be slow starvation, she said 'it was'. Their uniform is a blue cloth cloak, in which they are obliged always to appear out of doors. When one of them dies, each of the rest must pay sixpence[71] towards the funeral. Sometimes they are so forlorn that they go away and return to their former abodes, however wretched they may be. When they are ill, they have very scant attendance, and probably often die alone without any tender care or final aid. The Charity now is 500L rich and if ten women only were admitted it might do some good and cause comfort. I think it is questionable, as it is now. It was when I went to Coventry a month ago with Una and Julian that I went over it and talked with the nurse.[72] Yesterday my husband and I merely walked in to the Quadrangle and out again without speaking to any one.

From this Hospital we went to St. Michael's Church, through a narrow street, across which two persons could shake hands from the projecting windows of the second stories. It is a marvel why houses are so crowded in these ancient towns when there are such broad spaces all around. St. Michael's towers grandly up at the top of this narrow street. Opposite its side is St. Mary's Hall, and we first went into this. It is a most picturesque, old, time-worn, reddish stone building, belonging to St. Katherine's Gild, or Guild, built in Henry the 6th's time. The entrance is under a solid gateway, sculptured overhead, with a groined roof, meeting in a boss in which is carved God the Father & the Virgin Mary. At the springing of the arches opposite is the Annunciation on one side, and animals on the other, and faces of angels—large as life—are cut at the crossings of the groins. Then we came into a small quadrangle. On the right side, broad stone steps led into the cellars, which look like a Crypt, with columns and arched stone roof. On the side opposite the entrance is a door leading into the kitchens, where are mighty boilers for the dinners of the fraternity. An endlessly old man was there, as always there is in these old edifices—as if contemporaneous with them. On the left side of the

Quadrangle a door led into a lobby, at either end of which was a staircase and at the foot of one staircase a statue (of King Henry sixth, I suppose). This staircase leads to the Great Hall, and the other to what is called the Mayoress's Parlor. We went up to the Great Hall; more than sixty feet long and thirty broad. It is lofty and its oaken roof arches over without the support of columns. There are seraphim sculptured on the roof with musical instruments. At the upper end is a vast window—filled with old painted-glass, which must have been magnificent when in its prime. Even now the ruby and blue tints are brilliant. There are several kings upon this window and escutcheons and heraldic devices, and it forms a noble arch. Beneath the lights is hung a piece of gobelin tapestry—very faded now. It is in six oblongs. In one, Henry Sixth is kneeling at a table in prayer. His crown is upon the table by the holy book, on which his hands are folded. Behind him stands Cardinal Beaufort and other lords. On the right is Queen Margaret—also kneeling with folded hands surrounded by her ladies, the Duchess of Buckingham first. Above this group are female saints. The whole has a most grim aspect, but when the colors were fresh, it must have been splendid, and the figures and faces are very good. Full length portraits of Georges Third and Fourth hang on each wall at the sides. It is the handsomest George the Third I have seen, and the Fourth is just like himself, all flaunt and bows and chains and robes and supincumbent [sic]—full blown cheeks and an air of coxcombry—king of coxcombs—most disagreeable and repelling. The floor of the hall is covered with seats, but at this upper end are wooden tables. There were once merry wassails here. A small circular recess opens on the left hand of the Hall, immediately before the upper portion. It has a window filling the whole space lighted with colored glass with ribbon scrolls—and a desk stands within the recess and near it a carved oaken chair. Six windows, three on each side, filled with painted glass,[73] but modern, light the Hall. Escutcheons and heraldic devices filled all this space between the floor and the window sills aforetimes, but now are quite rubbed off by the constant crowding-by of the worshipful fraternity. At the lower end is the minstrels' gallery, before which hang some of the city armors. Beneath are doors leading into the private rooms of the Council, provided with tables covered with baize and high uncomfortable wooden carved seats round the walls and a few grim pictures hang thereon. Two screens covered with gobelin tapestry stand near these doors in the Great Hall and full length portraits of kings and queens hang on each side, and a large classical picture covers the back part of the minstrel-gallery but I could not make out the subject. Near the entrance of the Mayoress's Parlor is a very curious elaborately carved chair, large enough for two persons and we sat down in it. In this many kings and queens had sat. There was a trial going on in the Parlor, so that we did not go in then, but when I was in Coventry with Una and Julian I went in and found it full of tables and desks and adorned with paintings of Royal Persons and of the Lady Godiva, veiled in her golden hair, riding down High St to save her people from oppression. It is a kind of couch-room rather than a lady's boudoir.

We next went into St. Michael's, across the narrow St. Within was space enough. It is a grand, majestic old church, eight hundred years old and more. The interior has lately been cleaned and scraped. From Cromwell's time, the beautiful pale red stone had been whitewashed and plastered. Now it looks just built. The pillars are slender and light, supporting lovely and lofty arches and the clerestories are half-filled with old painted glass. In the chancel, over the altar, is a superb window of modern painted glass in memory of Queen Adelaide, and at the sides are two other large windows of ancient [glass?], looking more like kaleidoscopes than anything else, at first glance. They seem to be made up of little bits patched together; but upon close examination, kings and saints and angels appear. In the Lady Chapel is another window of modern glass, painted in memory of a young hero who fell in the Crimea, Thomas Grosvenor Hood. His father before him fell in the Peninsular War—and the woman who was following us, and babbling incessantly of every object, remarked that "so it was the father died in battle, but the son went just the same to be killed also." St Michael's is by far the grandest parish Church I have seen in England—approaching nearest to cathedral grandeur. We walked round it outside. The Eastern end is newly cased in the beautiful pale red stone of the original—just a covering, close-fitting. All the battlements and slender pinnacles come out anew also, delicate and sharp. But the noble lofty tower as yet remains defaced and crumbled though entire in the mass. It rises three hundred feet, terminating in a fine spire—sharp as a needle at its apex and so perfect in proportion and symmetry and grace that Sir Christopher Wren pronounced it a masterpiece of art. The little tabernacles around the middle part are filled with [Roman?] Saints in white stone. Once in a while the great bell boomed in an inward majestic and deeply musical tone, like a noble heart beating, giving a wonderful life to the mighty [form?]. One of the finest organs of the kingdom is in the nave, but we did not hear it, as it was past the hour of service.

We went to Trinity afterwards. It is very near and too near the glorious old St. Michael's—because tho' a fine church, it can bear no comparison with the former. It is very much smaller, but beautiful inside, and it has one eminent beauty. In the choir the clerestory lights are made of rich golden-tinted glass, and though there was not a ray of sunshine, but a grey, threatening sky, a flood of yellow radiance poured into that upper region and lay upon the ceiling like veritable sunbeams, so that a perennial sun shines over that altar as if from the new Jerusalem, and never will set. I think that where there can be no saints and angels for light to stream legitimately through, this golden glass would always be significant and lovely in the Chancel. And the clerestories would be better always so, because at that height it is not possible to see figures. There is a curious old stone pulpit, considered a gem, but quite put out of countenance by a brass gilt balustrade mingled with blue that leads up to it. The ceiling is bright azure with gold stars and coats of arms, painted oak, I believe. Una and I attended the service here a month ago, but at this hour the Church was empty, excepting one little girl, who kept watch and ward in a pew near the entrance, and said nothing to us. A stone font in gothic pomp of colors, stood at the western end.

Coventry manufactures ribbons, and we went into a shop and bought some of a cerise tint, and a scarlet satin scarf, bright as an autumn maple leaf.[74] It began to sprinkle when we left the shop, so we immediately took refuge in the King's Head Hotel, which has the first rank in the town. There we lunched & I had a nap on the couch while it rained merrily. In an hour or so it cleared, however, and though it was very wet on the pavements, we went out again and this time visited St. John's Church. It is cruciform and picturesque and fine outside, but spoiled within by galleries—though a few noble arches are left unharmed at the western end. We hardly stayed there a moment, but walked through the whole market to see the people and customs. Each person has his wares and vegetables in a small compass close upon the side-walk—sometimes on the ground, and sometimes in booths—but not encroaching upon the domain of foot passengers. Just room enough was left in the middle of the street for carriages to pass. One woman sat down in the middle of an expanse of crockery, with her hands clasped round her knees, waiting for purchasers. Three times a week, the good people of Coventry have these markets.

Returning through the ranks and files of sellers, we walked down High St. I wanted to go to the Cemetery, but my husband thought it would be too far. So we went into a Palace Yard, said to be Earl Leofric's, out of which the Lady Godiva rode. It is a quadrangle surrounded by strange old gables, with diamond framed windows. It seems now a timber yard. On the present site of St. Michael's and Trinity Earl Leofric endowed the rich monastery of Benedictine monks. There was then a Cathedral also and the group of buildings was exceedingly magnificent. From the Palace Yard we walked still farther along the High St and at last turned, as we thought, towards the rail station. But we walked in vain, being guided astray, till we came to a beautiful green meadow and a view of noble trees, and then some boors told us all wrong, and we painfully retraced our steps. I was very tired indeed. We went through strange little lanes, with thick green hedges on each side and after a weary evening tramp, arrived at an opening from which steps led right upon the station. I sat down in the waiting room with much gratitude, and my husband bought the Illustrated Times and a Daily Telegraph that I might read about India.[75] Here we waited until 10 of five when we came home.[76]

Many years after this outing to Coventry took place, Julian recalled in one of his biographies of his father that he had been with his parents in Coventry:

I recollect a visit we made to Coventry about this time, because of a little incident that happened there, not much in itself, but which impressed at least one of those present in a manner not to be forgotten. Hawthorne, his wife, and son arrived in Coventry after dark, and took a cab, the driver of which was ordered to drive us to a hotel. Off we rattled accordingly, and presently pulled up at a place the outward aspect of which was not inviting. The cabby got down to open the cab door; but Hawthorne told him to bid the landlord step out to us. The landlord came out in his shirt-sleeves, and, putting his head into our window, filled the vehicle with the aroma of inferior brandy. Hawthorne felt indignant, but asked the man, courteously, whether he could furnish us with a private sitting-room. "I don't know, sir," he replied; "I'll see what we can do for you!" "Driver, this won't do," said Hawthorne; "take us somewhere else." We rattled along once more, and at length again halted, and the driver came to the window. We were in a shabby and ill-lighted part of the town, and alongside of an iron railing, with a gate through it. "If you'll come with me, sir," said the cabby, "I'll show you a place—"But here Hawthorne interrupted him. "Why should I go with you?" he demanded, in a tone that made the unfortunate jehu start as if he had been kicked; and then, in a voice as terrible as the blast of a trumpet, "Why don't you drive us to the best hotel in town, as I told you to?" As he spoke, there was an expression in his eyes—a sudden flame of wrath—which, together with the voice, not only sobered the half-tipsy cabby and sent him flying back to his box as if he had been blown thither by an explosion, but so appalled the other two auditors that they scarcely recovered their breath until they were safely ensconced in a good suite of rooms in "the best hotel in town." Mrs. Hawthorne afterwards said, "That was the first time I ever heard papa raise his voice to a human being." But in the days before his marriage, when overseeing the perverse and conscienceless coal-shippers on the Boston wharves, Hawthorne had made his voice heard and his indignation felt as forcibly as now.[77]

Whatever it was that the children and Ada did while Nathaniel and Sophia were in Coventry it was sufficiently absorbing and time-consuming for Ada not to be able to add to her letter to Clay that evening, nor did she shed any light on what the day's events had been when she went to the writing desk next morning:

Sunday Morning, Oct. 18th

I awoke from dreams of Antioch to see a foggy English sky and hear a drizzling English rain against my window. The day promises to be unpleasant, but I look forward to spending it in quiet delight, writing to you and the dear ones at home and reading a little, perhaps.[78] I still adhere to my resolution not to study on Sunday. If I had any of Mr. Parker's sermons, I should read one of them each Sunday, as you do. There are no churches here except Episcopalian and Methodist ones,[79] and I have not the courage to endure either of those at present, so I do not think of going to church any more than if it were not Sunday. I speak of my studies; but it seems almost foolish to call the pleasant pastime of reading French drama study. That is what I am doing now, for I have not the books, and wait until we go to Italy to procure them, wherewith to continue my study of Italian, excepting the Ollendorff which Una and Julian use. So while we linger in England I intend to make myself acquainted with Racine and Corneille. Now I read Racine, and I admire him very much, and rejoice in the thought that we will enjoy his plays together sometime.

In "Athalie" which I was reading last evening, he introduces the chorus, after the manner of the Greek tragedians. I give Una little stories to translate into French sometimes now, when I can find simple ones in some of Rose's books, and this practice benefits me as well as her, of course.

Mr. Hawthorne is reading aloud a book of Charles Reade, "Never too late to mend"[80] to which I usually listen. He reads well and it is quite a delight to me to listen for an hour or two, after having finished my day's work.

And a quiet delight is with me all the time while I sit with these happy people, so comfortably established before the cheerful fire, while the children sleep peacefully over their heads, as I think how we shall read the new books together in those bright days that are to come.

Do you know that one chief reason of my admiration for Mr. Hawthorne is that he resembles you in many things?

And Mrs. Hawthorne is just the kind of person whom you ought to love; that is to say I ought to be like Mrs. Hawthorne, and I shall try to grow like her in some respects.

Mr. Hawthorne does not seem to me to work at all now. I suppose he is resting from his labors which have been very arduous lately. He takes long walks alone each day, and sometimes short ones with Mrs. H. who is not able to walk far. Ah! this curse of ill health! I must grow strong in body this year, whatever else I do.

Emma Guild [Fisher] talked to me very seriously about my duties to you in this respect, dear Clay! and warned me, from her own painful experience, not to neglect taking the utmost care of my health, if I would avoid the most painful consequences hereafter. She thinks that she inflicted lasting injury upon herself by a too exclusive devotion to brain-work the last few years before her marriage.

Dear Emma! she must be on her way home now.

But now I am going to cease writing, and read your last letter before going down to breakfast. Tomorrow I may have another from thee, dearest!

Sunday evening.

I come to write my good-night to thee, darling, and to tell thee how I have spent the day. It has been dark and cloudy and smoky and foggy and rainy all day, so that not one of us has been out; and I concluded, after breakfast, to allow myself the unusual indulgence of reading a novel. So I possessed myself of Mr. Hawthorne's "House of Seven Gables", which I read long ago, when it first came out, and read it all day with the greatest interest, in the very presence of the author.

It seemed very strange to look up occasionally from my book and meet his eye as he sat ensconced in an easy chair in a meditating mood apparently, his eyes resting occasionally upon his lovely children as they pursued each some favorite pastime,—Julian drawing shells for which he has the greatest passion, Una reading Scott's poems and little Rose flitting about among her toys, while Mrs. Hawthorne, the beautiful mother of the interesting group, reclined on the sofa with the London papers in her hand. It was an almost perfect picture of domestic bliss. Not that any individual of this family is absolutely perfect, of course (although I hardly see how any one could approach perfection more nearly than Mrs. H.) but their relations to each other are so delightful that it does my very heart good to be among them.

This evening Mr. H has been reading to us again, and again I have been listening admiringly and observing the resemblances between you and him. Tell me, dear Clay, if you have ever read many or any of his writings. I should like to know your opinion of the "House of the Seven Gables" I have enjoyed it extremely today, and have learned a great deal of him from it. He has the same intense love of nature and of solitude that you have, my dearest Clay! and the same demand for perfection in whatever comes into relation with him. I notice, too, in his manner the same shyness that is natural to you.

I even think that you will look like him when you are of his age, and my busy fancy wandered to the days,—so far off,—when <u>we</u> should sit in <u>our</u> quiet little parlor and read together as they do now; all this I pictured to myself as the low, pleasant tones of the good man's voice made music for my ears.

Charles Reade was less entertaining than my own waking dreams.

Ah <u>dear</u> Clay! Do not those blessed days look afar off to thee? And dost thou, too, delight in their anticipation as does thy absent Ada?

I go to bed happy in the thought that another letter <u>must</u> come very soon. And let me tell you, while I think of it, not to send any more letters to Paris, but to direct your next to me in the care of Packenham and Hooker, bankers, Rome, Italy. I do not know what their address is, but I presume it will be sufficient to put their names. I send to you to direct in their care because they are correspondents of [Monne?] & Co., on whom I have a letter of credit, and will keep my letters for me if any arrive before I reach Rome. I should have found out their address when in Paris, had I thought of the necessity of sending you this direction before leaving England. Mr. Hawthorne does not know what his address will be there, at present.

But I must not write longer although I feel as if it would be a pleasure to sit here all night and hear the soft rain patter on the windows, forming a musical accompaniment to my happy thoughts of thee, my darling. <u>Sunday night</u>, dearest Clay! as I seek my pillow I shall breathe a prayer that God may grant me the power to give thee as much joy as thy blessed love imparts to me, my beloved. For I feel this glorious, mighty love of thine stretching out its wide wing to me across the broad sea, and gathering me to thy great, pulsing heart as closely as when, in Mrs. Dean's[81] or Miss Wilmarth's parlor, I could lean my head upon thy breast and rest within thy enfolding embrace as the blissful Sunday nights throbbed out their tide of new, rich life for us. So high, so pure is my love, my trust, to-night, that the distance between us is as nothing. I am almost content to write my simple good-night as I should be could I seal it on thy lips with a kiss of love that should tell thee more than could any poor word I might speak,—were there, indeed, aught to tell.

Ah, Clay! dear Clay! My angel of light who hast revealed to me such treasures of unknown, unimagined bliss! God bless thee and give thee such joy as is mine through thee![82]

And so the quiet, almost dull, routine set in, with Nathaniel passing the time by walking and reading (very little went into his journal nowadays), Sophia taking the air when the weather and her health allowed it, the children attending to their lessons and walking in the locality with Ada. Not much happened, very few letters were written, except by Ada:

Monday afternoon.

A rainy morning has been succeeded by a sunshiny afternoon, and I am only waiting for Una to finish her French lessons before commencing our usual sunset walk. I tried not to feel disappointed when the postman passed without leaving a letter, this morning, and I was not, by any means, wretched, as I once was in Paris when my hopes were deferred for a week. I believe I shall never feel again as I did then. All alone in the great, busy city, I was morbidly anxious about thee, and depended on thy weekly letters for my very life almost; but I am stronger now, and have learned to trust more firmly in the goodness of our Father. Ah! I cannot believe that harm will come to thee, my dearly beloved Clay! Yet I long for thy next letter, and rejoice as the day wears on, at the thought that the hour of the postman's visit tomorrow draws nearer and nearer, and that then I may hope again. And I pray often that there may never be another year in our life when I must be exiled from thy presence, or, at least separated from thee by an ocean. Were I in Dorchester and you in Honeoye, I could be comparatively content, for the telegraph could summon me to your side with the utmost speed, were you suddenly smitten with illness or other misfortune; but I dread to imagine what would be my state of mind should I hear that you were suffering while so vast a barrier is between me and thee.

O thou dear, dear being![83]

Perhaps it was when the sun came out that afternoon that Sophia ventured into the town and bought a pair of shoes for herself, costing 6s.0d. Apart from anything else, Ada thought it was time to start another letter to her sister:

Leamington, England, Oct 19th, '57

Dear Kate,
I received your letter of September thirtieth last Friday,[84] and was, as I always am, perfectly delighted to get it. You are very kind to send such long letters, telling me everything so fully. Clay sends me long ones each week, too, and his with yours at home are about all that I have. I wonder very much that Mary Richardson does not write to me. I have written to her twice, but have received not a word in reply. I suppose she must be in Yellow Springs; is she not? I sent her one letter there besides the one I enclosed in Horace's letter, some time ago.

I am obliged to you for copying Miss Allen's[85] letter, and sorry you should take so much trouble. I asked about it because, from various reasons, I thought it rather strange that she should write to me. Perhaps I shall send a note to her in reply, with this letter. If so, will you ask Horace to please send it to her. I think I will write to Horace myself, this time, however.[86] I shall expect to write to him oftener than he does to me owing to his "pet aversion" (as Miss Wilmarth used to say) to writing letters.

I am anxious to know more of the terrible steamer accident to which you allude. I could not help thinking a great deal of Charlie for a long time after I read it, and feeling that it was <u>possible</u> he was on his way home, at that time, after all, and how the Popes[87] must feel, all uncertain as it is about Henry.[88]

Ada broke off at this point and did not return to the letter for some days but in the meantime, next morning, carried on with the unfinished one to Clay:

Tuesday morning.

I almost <u>tremble</u> with anticipation of the joy that <u>may</u> come to me in an hour or two. Yet I must not depend upon it, and so let me write and think of other things, if possible.

Una and I set out on our usual walk just before sunset, yesterday afternoon, and we met Mr. Hawthorne returning from a solitary ramble, but he turned back with us and walked through "Lovers' Grove", a very beautiful little grove of elms and walnut-trees, not far from here, whence, as it is on high ground, we have a fine view of the surrounding country. On a clear day we can see the towers of Warwick Castle in the distance. Last evening a beautiful bluish mist was over everything but the sunset clouds were gorgeous with purple and gold, and we stood and watched them as their glories changed with the rapidity of kaleidoscopic changes almost.

Then we walked across some fields in little by-paths known to Mr. H. although new to us, and came to a lovely little English village called Linnington [sic]. It is just such a little cluster of houses as we sometimes read about in English stories of rural life. The neat little thatched cottages, ancient and moss-grown, with their pretty garden plots in front, so neatly tended and so tastefully arranged, the beautifully trimmed hedges, and everything in the scene seemed as familiar as it is possible for written description to make things which we have never seen.

And then we came to a beautiful little stone church with an ancient Norman tower, moss-grown like the roofs of the cottages. We entered it and found the interior exceedingly pretty, with Gothic arches and a window of colored glass whose effect was very fine.

A little grave-yard surrounded the church, as is almost always the case with these English churches, and they were digging a new grave, beside which were several children playing merrily. It was painful to behold them. Near the church was the neat little vicarage, a building of stone and of humble pretensions, but very pretty and nice looking, and we met a slender, spiritual looking man, as we left the village, who must have been the vicar, I think.

Mr. Hawthorne says this village must be about two hundred years old. The cottages look as though they might have been handed down from father to son for as long a time as that, so fixed and unchangeable an air had they.

They are built of brick with thatched roofs, which look like an outgrowth of the house, and not as if they had been placed there by any human agency.

Little rows of these cottages join each other like the blocks of buildings in our large cities, and this constitutes a great difference in the aspect of English and American villages. Then the stacks of hay which we see all around, near the houses, here, are purely an English feature, and are extremely picturesque.

But what pleases me most about these little English cottages is that each family has its pretty little garden, kept with a nicety and a taste of which American laborers know nothing.

Scarlet geraniums, bright little nasturtiums, and sweet little monthly roses still in blossom adorn each patch of ground and give an indescribably attractive air to the poorest house.[89]

Then everywhere we see here the most magnificent fuschias. Do you know this flower which droops so gracefully and which has so much meaning, as it seems to me? It is cultivated in green-houses and in flower-pots in America, but here it seems to be indigenous, and grows before every house, in great perfection.

The leaves are falling rapidly now. Every day we find the paths more and more strewn. Yet the trees look scarcely less green than before they began to shed their leaves, and the grass is just as bright and fresh in color as ever.

We shall see no brilliant Autumn leaves, this year, as the English climate does not admit of the sudden frosts, which paint our American forests so beautifully. I wonder how the trees around your home are tinged now, dearest Clay. But I suppose they must have lost nearly all their leaves now, for to-day is the twentieth of October.[90]

As usual, Ada was up with the lark, this time in eager anticipation of the postman's arrival bearing a present from America. But it was not to be; the postman didn't come and her emotions took their usual course in such a situation—downward—as she pondered all the possibly disastrous things that could have happened to Clay and that had prevented him from writing to her. Nathaniel at last sat down and made an entry in his journal but which day he did it is not clear; he reported on his return to Leamington on Wednesday of the previous week and described the visit that he and Sophia had made to Coventry on Saturday. He must have been pretty bored.

I returned hither from Liverpool on Wednesday evening of last week and have spent the time here idly, since then, reposing myself after the four years of unnatural restraint in the Consulate. Being already pretty much acquainted with the neighborhood of Leamington, I have little or nothing new to record about this prettiest, cheerfullest, cleanest of English towns, with its beautiful elms, its lazy river, its villas, its brilliant shops—its whole smartness and gentility in the midst of green, sylvan scenery and hedgerows, and in the neighborhood of old thatched and mossgrown villages clustering each about the little, square battlemented tower of a church; villages such as Leamington itself was before Dr. Jephson transformed it into a fashionable watering-place, fifty years ago.[91] Our immediate abode is a small, neat house, in a circle of just such houses, so exactly alike that it it [sic] is difficult to find one's own peculiar domicile; each with its little ornamented plot of grass and flowers, with a bit of iron fence in front, and an intersecting hedge between its grass plot and that of its neighbor; and in the center of the Circus a little paddock of shrubbery and trees, box, yew, and much other variety of foliage, now tinged autumnally. I have seldom seen, and never before lived in, such a quiet, cozy, comfortable, social seclusion and snuggery. Nothing disturbs us; it being an eddy quite aside from the stream of life. Once or twice a day, perhaps, a cab or private carriage drives round the Circus and stops at one or other of the doors; twice a day comes the red-coated postman, delivering letters from door to door; in the evening, he rings a handbell as he goes his round, a signal that he is ready to take letters for the post; in other respects, we are quite apart from the stir of the world. Our neighbors (as I learn from the list of visitors and residents in a weekly newspaper) are half-pay officers with their families, and other such quiet and respectable people, who have no great figure to make or particular business to do in life. I do not wonder at their coming here to live; there cannot be a better place for people of moderate means, who have done with hope and effort, and only want to be comfortable.[92]

Still no letter had come from Clay by Thursday, so Ada had to complete hers in order that she could catch the post:

Thursday eve, Oct 22nd.

Ah, beloved! no letter has come yet to gladden my longing heart. Yet I hope as fondly as ever that tomorrow will not pass without bringing this joy.

O thou dear Clay! My heart turns to thee with almost a painful yearning, tonight, for it is cold and dreary without, and as the wind whistles around the house, I sit by the cheery fire (the English coal-fires are very beautiful) and picture to myself the evenings that are to come when we may sit together by a comfortable fire and defy the raging of the storm without, happy in our peaceful home.

Ah! Clay! dear Clay! Dare we hope that thus it may be? Sitting and dreaming waking dreams by the fire this evening I have felt the joys to come if Heaven is propitious. This haven of peace and joy looks so far off, our home is so distant, that I am almost despondent at the thought of what may occur to prevent its ever being reached.

Dear Clay! do not reproach me for my weakness. I hope to be stronger tomorrow. Certainly I shall be when your next dear letter comes.

Ah! can you realize what your letters are to me, my beloved? Can you know what immeasurable bliss there is for me in the thought that you are mine, dearest.

So far away from all the associations of my former life; leading, for the present, a monotonous life of quiet, humble usefulness as I hope; but with no excitements, no distractions of any kind, excepting the blessed excitement of receiving the dear missives from thee, I live in thy love more than ever, my darling; I depend on thy letters for my daily food.

And I reproach myself constantly for sending thee such feeble testimonies of the living and growing love for thee which animates my heart, my own dear Clay! I have delayed sending this letter, because it is so miserable, but it must go tomorrow in order that Saturday's steamer shall bear it across the ocean. Believe, my own dear Clay! that it is but a feeble and unworthy expression of the love that grows within me more and more, day by day. Judge not my heart by my feeble utterance, my beloved.

I shall close my letter now, all unworthy as it is; and sit by the fire a while, ere I retire to happy dreams of thee, as I hope.

May all good spirits attend thee in thy slumbers, to-night, my beloved! My prayers will ascend to the Father's throne, that He will grant to thee the joy and peace that thy love sheds in the heart of thy

Ada.[93]

	Oct				
Friday	23d	Finnan haddock		1	
		Ferns – potatoes		2	3
		Ducks 4/6 – muttons			
		Vegetables – fresh potatoes		6	
		Sherry		4	0
	27th	Potatoes Apples & Cauliflowers		2	4
		Baker		12	6
		Milk		4	3
		Butcher	1	3	9½
	27th	Fish	2		6
	29th	Meat	3		11
	30	Meat	5		8½
		Fish	5		9
		Baker		5	10
		Grocer		15	8
	28	Pork		4	4½
	20	Laundress		7	6
		Vegetables		0	10

But of course all was well on the morrow as the postman *did* come, and he brought not only a letter from Clay but also several more from family and friends. But there appears to be no record of any letters written by the Hawthornes, or of their having received any, during the whole of that week; further, there is no record of their having *done* anything during the week. The children would have been fully occupied with their daily routine of lessons, walks with Una, and so on. But Nathaniel and Sophia (who may have been unwell but, again, there is no report on that) appear to have done nothing out of the ordinary. Perhaps the weather was bad; it certainly was changeable, as was noted in Ada's letters. Perhaps there was just *nothing* to do and *perhaps* they liked doing nothing. It must be admitted that the public entertainment that was offered in the town was not of startling interest, even if public entertainment had been to their liking (there is not much evidence to support that supposition either). On Monday, 19 September, Miss Amy Dolby and Miss Dolby, backed by The Vocal Union and supported by Monsieur Sainton on the violin, gave a performance of "Favourite English Glees and Madrigals" at the Royal Music Hall and on Tuesday, at the Temperance Hall, there was a "Tea Party and Concert" organized by the Committee and Members of the Leamington Philharmonic Society. On Friday there was a lecture in the Public Hall in Windsor Street on "The History and Position of the British in India," (of great topicality), given by the Reverend Arthur O'Neill from Birmingham. None of these happenings were of great moment and apparently they did not inspire any of the Hawthornes to wend their way either to Bath Street or Windsor Street, or so it appears from the lack of evidence to the contrary. Perhaps, as Ada said in her letter and Nathaniel in his journal, the last four years in the consulate really had fatigued him so much that he was content to spend some time just watching the world go by.

Leamington, Oct. 23rd '57

Dearest Clay!
I bless you for the cheering letter that greeted my longing eyes this morning![94] It was mailed at Honeoye Falls on the thirtieth of September, yet did not reach me until to-day.

How long an interval has to elapse between the writing and the reading of our letters now! Yet we need no letters to assure each other of our mutual affection! We are equally certain of that now, I believe, and could we be as sure that all circumstances surrounding each were propitious, there need be no anxious longings for these outward modes of communication.

Do you know, dear Clay! that I felt a deeper joy than usual in reading this letter, from the very reason that you might have supposed would be a cause of pain.

I felt your mood of painful unrest and dissatisfied self-questioning more keenly than any other mood of yours, at any time in our life, perhaps. Dear Clay! Dear Clay! we may sympathize in this pain as completely in the joy of loving each other. I may tell you, dear Clay, to whom it is my privilege to pour out all my soul, that I have known some of the saddest hours that I ever experienced since I came to England, and that from the very cause which you mention as the origin of your pain,—a thorough self-examination and the result of it. From this examination I find that I am culpably weak and indolent; that I care a thousand times more than I ought for the opinion of the world (especially that part of the world that is dear to me,—my own special friends—) that I am daunted too often by slight difficulties in my path, which ought rather to stimulate me;—that in short, I am quite a wretched specimen of humanity instead of the noble, simple earnest being whom you ought to love, and in whose love you ought to find happiness, my dear, dear, Clay. Oh! I will become more worthy of thy love in this year of separation, my darling. Thou shalt clasp a nobler, truer being than the Ada of last summer, when the sea renders me to thee, my beloved.

Taking up a French translation of Thomas à Kempis's "Imitation of Jesus Christ", one of Mrs. Hawthorne's favorite books, I read, this evening, those words which I thought extremely appropriate for you and me now, dear Clay: "Il en a beaucoup qui se trompent malheureusement, et qui sout presque tout à fait stèriles en bons fruit, <u>parce qu'ils s'etudient plus a savoir beaucoup qu'a bien vivre</u>. Certainement en jour du jugement il ne nous sera pas demandé ce que nous aurons <u>lu</u>, mais ce que nous aurons <u>fait</u>; il ne sera pas question de savoir si nous avons <u>dit</u> de belles choses, mais si nous en avons <u>fait</u> de bonnes at de saintes." [There are many who sadly deceive themselves, and who are almost sterile of good fruit, <u>because they study more for knowledge rather than living</u>. It is certain that on the day of judgement we will be asked not what we read but what we <u>did</u>; it will not be a question of knowing if we have said fine things but if we have <u>done</u> good and holy things.]

How often we forget this, and how hard, how almost impossible is it, with the utmost vigilance to hold ourselves strictly and sternly true to the standard, which we have set up for ourselves! Do you know, dear Clay, that since I have been reflecting so much upon my real character as it is apparent to me upon a candid consideration (have I not divided [*sic*] that word wrongly, professor?) I am more and more astonished at the good opinion which I cannot help seeing that my friends have of me?

I am ready to weep over a few lines which M. Fezandie wrote on the envelope of a letter from Uncle Ayres which he enclosed to me,[95] just at the thought of how far my real character falls short of the excellence which he ascribes to it; and the confidence which all my friends at home have in me, the undeserving praise which your dear letters contain, <u>dearest</u> Clay, all give me pangs of veritable anguish.

O my lover, my beloved! see me as I am! Recognize my faults, my culpable weaknesses! Rend the veil with which thy fond affection has covered my many imperfections, and see what a weak being I am. See how I cling to thee for sympathy and assistance! See how little I have and am of myself! Pray for me, darling, that I may grow worthier of thy love, worthier to be a child of God!

Do not imagine, from what I have said to thee of my pain of late, that there is anything in my surroundings that induces this. On the contrary, I am most agreeably situated in this charming family. Mr. and Mrs. H. are as courteously kind as if I were a dear friend and never once have manifested the slightest <u>condescension</u> of manner, which you know would be exceedingly offensive to me. Una and Julian progress remarkably well in their studies and are the most agreeable pupils possible; and little Rose shows me especial favor. Her mother says that she evidently likes my "sphere". She is an extremely fastidious child, and does not usually admit people to her heart without a long acquaintance, but she seemed much attached to me at once. Indeed they all seem to take it for granted that I am all that they hoped me to be. Mrs Mann must have embellished me greatly in her descriptions of me. I hope there will be no sudden coming down in their good opinions when they <u>find me out</u> more extensively than they have been able to at present.

Ah! it is one of the greatest of all pains to <u>know</u> that you are miserably unworthy of all the love and esteem of those whose good opinion you most desire to merit.

Ah dear, <u>dear</u> Clay! Will your Ada <u>ever</u> be noble and strong and wise and pure?

A letter came from Joseph to-day,[96] telling me of Yellow Springs affairs. Dear boy! How I love him! It is strange that I have not received a word from Mary Richardson yet. Nor did she even send a message by Joseph. It is very strange. I long to hear from her.

Letters came from home to-day, too,[97] so that I was abundantly rewarded for my long waiting in patience.

I think I shall send you what M. Fezandie wrote, not out of vanity, I hope (though I know that I am very vain, and am laboring to exterminate this glaring fault); but partly in answer to what you asked me once about the opinion I had won from him, and partly to show you "what manner of man he is". I had written him a note with reference to sending on my letters to which he alludes at first.[98]

But it is growing late, and I must not write more. Good night dearly-beloved Clay! I shall remember thee in my prayers to-night, as usual.

Good-night, my own dear, dear Clay![99]

Saturday was another quiet day. Perhaps the weather was poor again; whatever did happen it was not worth a mention, even in the letters that Ada wrote that evening, the one to Kate that she completed and the continuation of the self-analysis that she was inflicting on Clay:

Saturday evening, Oct 24th.

So almost a week has elapsed since I wrote these few lines, and not a word have I added! And meanwhile another dear little packet of letters has come from home, accompanied by one from Uncle Ayres and one from Joseph, in addition to Clay's usual letter. I feel myself greatly blessed, and feel all unable to respond worthily to so many excellent epistles. Indeed, I never was so ashamed of any letters as I am of these that I have sent home since I have been in Europe. How can you have the heart to show them or read them to any-one? I should think the words would choke you in righteous retribution for the misery you inflict upon your auditors. Pray spare yourself and me further mortifications of this kind. It is to be expected that people will ask you to let them read or hear the letters. People usually intend to write something worth reading when they are travelling in foreign lands; I should try to do so, were I at liberty to dispose of my time as would be most agreeable,—roving around sight-seeing, and devoting my intervals of rest to writing descriptions of what I saw; but, as it is, I go to see but little, and take only little odds and ends of time to write. Added to this I am in the most stupid state of mind conceivable since I have been in England, and I am sure I "cannot edify" now, at all events. The letters that I receive are so much better than mine that I put mine in the office with pangs of self-reproach every time; yet I cannot very well help it. I must not take much time to write, and I must write to Clay during a portion of that time. So please be contented with my miserable scrawls, and please don't publish my remissness any more than is necessary, that is to say don't read the wretched things except to the family. Say "no" if people ask you to read them to them. I am really ashamed of them.

How glad the Popes must have been to see Henry! It seems really providential that he was prevented from embarking in that ill-fated steamer. Have you seen him? Where is Harris now?[100] Give my love to them all when you see them. I hope I shall be able to see them all when I am at home again.

How strange it must seem at home without Lucy! I can hardly imagine how you all get along without her, she was so constantly in the house always when not at school, and seemed so much of a permanency there. But after all we can become accustomed to such changes more readily than we imagine before we try. Although I have been with the Hawthornes but three weeks, I feel as much at home here as though I had always lived with them.

They are a most charming family, and I love them all more and more. I believe I have not written anything about Mr. H. yet, because he was not here when I last wrote. He has been here for a week and a half now, and thus this beautiful little domestic circle is complete. Of course I do not feel much acquainted with him,—he is so reserved, so really shy in his manner that I do not expect that; but

I admire him very much. He has one of the most beautiful faces that I ever saw, and is evidently a noble as well as a gifted man. I do not wonder that Mrs. Hawthorne loved him, and I only admire him the more for his loving her. It seems to be a <u>perfect</u> union, and I rejoice in it, and in its beautiful fruits every day. The children are certainly very remarkable,—Una and Julian especially. They are much beyond all children whom I have ever known in general intelligence, and in special cultivation in some few things, although in others they have had but little training. They are quite deficient in Mathematics, for example, but advanced in languages. Una is very well acquainted with French, and she progresses rapidly in Italian. She is remarkably fond of study, but Julian, like most boys, thinks it is a painful instead of a pleasant duty. He is remarkably fond of shells, and spends his leisure moments in drawing them from engravings in various books of conchology which he buys with his own pocket money. He has no playmates except little Rose, and so he devotes himself to his beloved shells constantly.

But I must not finish my little letter without answering your question about the venerable bonnet. I have not purchased a new one yet but I suppose I shall have to when I go back to Paris, on my way to Rome. I cannot boast much of the fine appearance of this, since it was wet with salt water when I last crossed the channel. But my veil covers it at present. I shall do very well until I go to Paris again.

Always your affectionate sister
Ada.

P.S. Please give much love to Abby.[101] I will write to her and to her mother as soon as possible. Her letter was most welcome. I send these little engravings to the children, thinking they may be pleased to see representations of the places I have seen. They came off of [sic] note-paper. These note-paper views are very common in England, and some of them are extremely good. The one of Kenilworth is not the most beautiful view that might be taken, by any means, nor is it very good; but it will give you a slight idea of it. The water which you see in the picture of Warwick Castle, is the Avon river.[102]

And then she continued her letter to Clay:

Saturday evening, Oct. 24th

As I commence writing, there occurs to me a little hymn which in my childish days I used to repeat, the first line of which was: "How pleasant is Saturday night when I've tried all the week to be good"; and I remember with what reproaches of conscience I used always to say it, remembering the numerous sins of the week. So I reproach myself to-night, as the dear old hymn recurs to my memory.

Will there <u>ever</u> be a time when I can feel that I have tried with all the earnestness and faithfulness of which I am capable, to be good and true? My greatest fault now seems a lack of energy and vigor. I think it may be partly due to the weather, for we seldom have sunshine here now. The days are cloudy and often rainy, and the streets muddy, and the air damp. I have no doubt that, coming from the clear, dry atmosphere of Paris into this foggy England, at this season when fogs are so numerous, my physical condition is somewhat affected by the change, and that helps to throw my mind into its present almost torpid state. But it is not all that. It is partly my own fault, I am sure; and, being thoroughly <u>awake</u> to-night, for the first time for three weeks, I believe, I am forming good resolutions to "mend my ways", and fall to work more vigorously.

As yet I have accomplished nothing in the three weeks I have spent in Leamington, but reading about three hundred pages of French as easy as English. Monday I shall commence reading Italian besides my French. I leave the German for the present, because I wish to devote this winter to the study of French and Italian, hoping to find facilities for perfecting (I mean for improving) my pronunciation of both these languages in Rome. Then in the Spring I hope we shall go to Germany, and that I can there pursue German with advantage.

Una progresses very rapidly in both French and Italian. I shall have to study the latter now, whether I wish it or not, in order to be able to give her all the assistance she needs.

I long to be in Rome, for here I have no more facilities for studying than if I were at home;—less, indeed, for books are so enormously high here that I do not wish to buy them, even if I could find what I wish, which would be almost impossible here.

Yet do not imagine me always in the complaining and distressed state of mind in which this letter seems thus far to be written, my dearest Clay! I write the utmost of my troubles to thee because I know thou wishest to know all that concerns me, and because I am sure thou must know that every picture has its shades as well as its lights. I wish you to have a complete knowledge of my daily life, and so I write you what I should never think of hinting to anyone but the "dimidium meae animae" [other half of my soul], just as I want you to tell me all the cares, all the sufferings, little and great, that afflict you in my absence, my dearest one.

There is no suffering for me so great as the pain of feeling that you might conceal from me some care and trouble that had invaded your peace of mind, fearful that I could not endure it bravely did I know it. Tell me all always, dear Clay! I can bear any calamity that I can imagine, so that I am sure of thy love and sympathy.

I can bear to know that thou art suffering, if I may be sure that thy love for me is so great as to give me my share of that suffering, dear Clay!

I have reread thy letter of yesterday, this evening, my beloved, and bless thee anew for its cheering words of sympathy and love. There is no need, as thou hast said, dearest, of our repeating the old formulae again and again, as in the early days of our love. "I love thee" is so wrought into every fibre of my frame; is so completely the warp and woof of my every emotion; the incentive to so many of my daily acts; the crowning joy of my life, that it would seem but mockery to write the words to thee now. And I feel as sure of thy love for me as if thou wert by my side at this moment, and I could read in thy dear, beautiful eyes the same blessed assurances that have so often thrilled me through with the strange, deep joy that only one loved as thou lovest can know.

Ah Clay! my beloved! When I am myself (as I am tonight, thank God!) I feel how little to those who love as we do, are such barriers as oceans, mountains or continents. Thou art mine, dear Clay! The storm may howl without, the thick clouds may hide from me our Lyra; thy presence is with me; the consciousness of thy love fills me with a high, serene content. I am happy, dear Clay, and thank God for thy priceless love.[103]

Sunday proved to be another dark and gloomy day that hid any activities by the family from view but, of course, Ada went on writing:

Sunday morning.

Another dark, cloudy Sunday, dear Clay! Yet I begin it cheerfully and hopefully, allowing myself the privilege of writing to thee, for a few moments, ere I answer the letters from home and from Uncle Ayres. It is just three weeks this morning since, in that pouring rain, I made my entrance into Leamington, and was warmly received by the dear friends who now make my stay among them so pleasant. I feel almost as much at home here now as though I had always lived in this family, and I love them all more and more every day. I would that thou, too, dearest Clay! couldst see this realization of our imaginings of what bliss might attend a rightly arranged marriage; what a beautiful home two spirits united by pure and true affection and striving to assist each other in the path towards the highest life, can make for themselves and their offspring; what lovely characters these children of such a union develop. This is certainly the most perfect union I ever beheld, and I thank God that I have been permitted thus to stand on the borders of this paradise.

Not that there are never discords in this harmony. The little Rose has a very strong will and so has master Julian, and these two often come into collision, whereupon arises a great hue and cry from both; but Mr. and Mrs. Hawthorne are never arbitrary in their government, and allow them to settle their own difficulties, as far as it is possible. I suppose these little disagreements among children are never quite avoidable. Certainly if perfect harmony between the parents could prevent them entirely, Mr. and Mrs. H. could have been able to do so.

I wish I had something of interest to write to you, dear Clay; for I can hardly yet believe that you can enjoy a letter all about myself as I do (or should could I receive them) those speaking only of you. I can never weary of reading the most minute details of your life and surroundings, and feel it is my highest privilege to be admitted into the sanctum of your thoughts and emotions; but I cannot, I dare not, believe that what I can say of myself is so welcomed by you as your dear words are by me. I know that your love, your priceless love, is mine. I am sure of your constant, all-sustaining affection and of your perfect sympathy; yet I am so painfully conscious of my many imperfections that I dare not yet believe my love can be to you all that yours is to me.

O my beloved! my beloved! Do you know how great is this love of mine? Do you know what you are to me?

But the words that should attempt to express this all-conquering love would be vainly written, indeed. I must not write on this theme.

And I must not now write any more to thee, hard as it is to turn from thy letter to those of others.

Ah! what is all the world to me compared with thy satisfying love?[104]

It is a great pity that Clay's letters do not appear to be extant as it would be fascinating to learn whether his were couched in the same vein as Ada's, whether they also contained endless repetitions of his love for her in the same style as hers (that does become *slightly* wearing, but only because of seeing just the one side of the relationship) or whether he answered her repeated requests for an assurance of his love for her in a more brusque manner, perhaps telling her not to be so fearful of possibilities that could never have a chance of proving to be realities, and concentrating on boosting her morale in a situation that they had, after all, brought upon themselves due to Ada's decision to join the Hawthornes in Europe.

However, Ada's was essentially a cheerful character backed by common sense, and her resilience was such that her spirits were never dampened for too long by immediate events.

Sunday evening.

Again our sacred Sunday night has come, my beloved, and again I am permitted to commune with thee so near and dear to my soul.

The day has been a quietly happy one for me. All the morning I wrote letters, and, after dinner we went to walk with the children in the public garden. This is quite a pleasant place or resort open to the public on Sunday afternoons, but visited only by subscribers on other days. There is here a very beautiful lawn, on one part of which are placed targets where ladies practise shooting with bows and arrows. Then there are very beautiful trees all through the garden (the horse-chestnut being the predominating species) with but few flowers and shrubs. The Leam river flows through the garden, and in one part of it (the garden I mean) is quite a pretty pond. The Leam is an exceedingly sluggish river and always looks muddy. But its banks are very pretty. The trees are fast shedding their foliage now, and we walked over the dry, fallen leaves with pitiless tread. I thought of thee, dearest, and wondered if thou went wandering on the banks of the Honoeye listening to the sound of its musical fall, and thinking perchance of the Sunday morning that shines so like a star in the distance when we walked there together to view its beauty and hear its voice. And I prayed that thy soul might be filled with as serene a bliss as was with me.

Dear Clay! My own dearly loved one!

This evening I have been reading "In Memoriam" and it carried me back to that blessed spring when I read it each night with thoughts of thee. And I read the verses so dear to me:

"O days and hours" &c; you know them, dear Clay.[105]

Mr. and Mrs. Hawthorne have been telling me stories of Una's babyhood, which have made me even more interested in her than before. She is certainly a very remarkable child. I remember that Mrs. Dean told me how beautifully Mr. Hawthorne watched over Mrs. H. before the birth of Una, taking care that only lovely and graceful objects should surround her, and only pleasant thoughts should fill her mind. Into this pure atmosphere she was born, and in it she has always been nurtured, and we need not wonder that she is of angel-like purity herself. Dear child! I was almost afraid of her at first,—afraid, I mean, that I should not know how to meet her wants, and that her fastidious and delicate taste would not be satisfied in me; but I know now that she loves me very much, and am sure that she feels far more confident than I deserve of my ability to teach her.

She is very affectionate, and has never been taught to conceal her emotions, or, rather, has always lived in such an atmosphere of love that she naturally expresses her affections for those around her in the most charming way, although she is very timid and shrinking like her father. She is far more like him than either of the others. "Sweet Miss Shepard! I love you very much," she exclaims sometimes suddenly, and embraces me warmly, blushing scarlet and running from the room, perhaps, a moment after, as if astonished and almost frightened at what she had said.

I feel more flattered by her good opinion of me than by almost any testimonial I could receive,—her perceptions are so keen and pure. I cannot tell you, dear Clay! how the presence of this child affects me. I feel almost as if in the company of an angel, so unlike common people is she. She seems to read people's very hearts. Her comments upon the faces of those whom we meet in our daily walks are extremely wise, often, and show uncommon insight into character. Fanny, Mrs. Hawthorne's housekeeper, remarked this evening, that "one need never think of hiding anything from Una, for she could read one's deepest secrets."

How I wish you could know this beautiful spirit! She has already taught me more than I can teach her.

But ten o'clock approaches, and I must not forget my promise to sleep sufficiently all the time I am away from thee. Dear Clay! mayst thou rest as happily tonight as will thy Ada![106]

But it was no good; Nathaniel was becoming bored (again). With the presentation of his accounts still not completed and with no certain date in mind as to when they would be, he was beginning to feel, naturally enough, that Leamington did not hold any further attraction in their present circumstances and that they might just as well move to somewhere where they could be sure of any number of pleasing distractions while they awaited the final day of release from all consular associations. Such a place was London. For some reason, perhaps due to his growing difficulties that were part of the widespread economic and commercial failure that was prevalent at that time, Bennoch had not answered Nathaniel's letter of 16 October and so he wrote again:

10, Lansdowne Circus,
Leamington, Octr 26th '57

Dear Bennoch,
Your face has not yet shone upon us.

I am getting tired of Leamington; and we think it a pity to waste so much time here when it might be better spent elsewhere. It may be three or four weeks yet, before I can leave England. We therefore meditate coming to London or the vicinity; and I should be glad to know if lodgings are attainable at Sydenham, for instance. We have here five bedrooms, a parlor, and dining-room, all for not quite three pounds. We might possibly exist with four bedrooms, but scarcely be comfortable.

Supposing Sydenham to be out of the question, could you recommend us to good lodgings in London?

As long as I tread the same soil with you, you must expect to be bored and pestered with my continual demands for advice and assistance. If I knew anybody else half so available, or a hundredth part so kind, I would not always come to you.

With best regards to Mrs. Bennoch.

Your friend
Nathl Hawthorne.[107]

Whether he wrote this letter early or late in the day it was rather ironic that having said he was tired of Leamington he then recorded in his journal that he had broken new ground by making a visit to Hatton, on his own once more:

[Today], the day promising better than most days now, I took the rail at half past ten for Hatton, about seven miles off; being moved to go thither, chiefly because it had been the residence of the learned Dr. Parr,[108] and because his church is still remaining there. On reaching the Hatton station, however, I could see no signs of a neighboring village, and wandered hither and thither, a long time, in quest of it, through narrow country-lanes, bordered with untrimmed hedges. Blackberries grew plentifully in them, but were tasteless; their flavor, I suppose, having been washed out of them, besides that it is too late in the year for them to ripen sweetly. There were one or two farm-houses in the first long lane through which I went, and one of them a very old, timber-framed structure, with old apple-trees about it, and the noise of a threshing-machine audible in its barn; but I could see nobody about. I walked on till I came where the lane ran into a somewhat broader road, with a broken guide-post at the corner, one finger pointing to Warwick, distant four miles, and another to some illegible town, which was not Hatton; so I retraced my steps, and tried the same lane in the opposite direction. It was still narrow, hedge-bordered, muddy, and had here and there a little grass in the midst of it; but by and by it again ran into a broader road, which looked as if it might lead somewhere or other. Behind me came a man driving a pony, harnessed into a little cart laden with boxes and packages; and he stopt at a farm house and took another package from the good woman there. When he came up with me, I inquired whither the road led; and he named some place which I could not make out, as he pronounced it; but he said it was about two miles off, and that the distance might be shortened by taking a cross-road;—so I determined to go thither, whatever the place might be.

The pony-driver seemed to be a common-carrier, and stopt at every house to gather up his freight; thereby keeping in my rear. Soon, I came to a cross-road at the beginning of which was a cross-barred gate, which was wide open, however, and seemed to be permanently so. Just at the entrance, was a little old picturesque cottage, thatched, mossy, and sheltered, I think, under a shadowy bank. The door was open, and a comely young girl stood at it, but withdrew inward as I approached; and when I put my head within the door, she was standing close to the wall beside it. A tall, thin, respectable old woman was ironing, in the kitchen, parlor, and (for aught I know) bedchamber of the cottage, which looked neat and comfortable enough, though gloomy except for the fire. She told me that the cross-road led to 'atton; so, after all, I found myself within reach of the town I had come to see, though I had now given up the hope of finding it. It was about a mile off, the old lady said. The cross-road seemed well-travelled, and led through a fertile and pleasant tract of country, with large farm-houses scattered along the way. The common-carrier came at a distance behind me, and stopt at the first farm-house so long that I saw no more of him. The day had been overcast till now; but now the sun came out, and made me feel uncomfortably warm in my Talma; whereupon I took it off and carried it on my arm, but yet the wind was chill, and the sunshine fitful, insomuch that I soon put it on again. Anon, I came to the long-sought village of Hatton, if village it might anywise be called, where there was no public-house, no shop, no contiguity of houses (as in most English villages, however small) nor, as I at first thought, any church. The houses, however, had an ancient aspect of rural comfort and abundance; it seemed to be a community of well-to-do farmers, and I have never seen so few traces of poverty in any English scene. I remember only one building that seemed new, and in that one I thought I heard the voice of a Schoolmaster. Yes; there was one other new building, and I think it was a new church or chapel; but of the old church I had as yet seen nothing.

At last I espied it quite beyond and out of the straggling village of farm houses, and on a road that crossed at right angles and led to Warwick. It had a low, grey, battlemented, square tower; and as I approached it, the tower spoke, and told me it was twelve o'clock. It was a remarkably deep-toned bell, and wonderfully impressive, considering how small it was. The church stands among its graves, a little removed from the wayside, and quite apart from any houses; a good deal shadowed by trees, and not wholly destitute of ivy. The body of the edifice, however, has been neatly covered with plaster of a yellowish tint, so as quite to destroy the aspect of antiquity except upon the tower, which wears the dark gray hue of many centuries. The chancel-window is painted with a representation of Christ upon the Cross; and all the other windows were full of painted or stained glass— but none of it ancient, nor (if it be fair to judge from without of what ought to be seen from within) of any great merit. I trod over the graves, and peeped in at two or three of the windows, and saw the little, snug interior of the church, fitted up with comfortable pews, where the farmers and their families repose, Sabbath after Sabbath. Those who slept under Dr. Parr's preaching now mostly sleep, I suppose, in the churchyard roundabout: but it struck me as an example of a man much misplaced—this enormous scholar, great in Greek, and making a learned tongue even of the vernacular, set here to tell of salvation to a rustic audience, to whom I do not see how he could speak one available word.

There are seldom any interesting tombstones in an English churchyard; the climate rendering them illegible while they are still comparatively new. Any New-England graveyard, in one of our elder towns, will gratify the curious in such matters with more ancient inscriptions. I saw none here worth noticing, except it be one to the memory of a Mr. Edwards, a chirurgeon of the last century, who seems to have owned the estate of Guy's Cliffe, and burthened it with charitable bequests to the poor of this parish. While I was looking at this tomb—a massive one, close beneath the church-tower—a man crossed the churchyard by a path leading through it to the village; and I inquired of him whether I could be admitted into the church. He pointed out the clerk's residence—a small brick-house, at some distance—but as I had already got a notion of the character of the interior by peeping through the windows, I did not think it worth while to summon him.[109]

From the church of Hatton to Warwick is about three miles; and within half-a-mile, I was glad to find myself approaching a way side inn,[110] which I entered and called for a glass of ale and a cigar; the ale, a dark-brown liquid, harsh, and a little pricked, and almost as potent as the Arch Deacon, wherewith we made acquaintance at Oxford;[111] the cigar, not much less potent in its way. A good many boors were quaffing ale and smoking pipes in the tap-room; so I took my refreshments in another brick-paved room, which probably served for a parlor; but a yeoman or two soon came in and took out a private store of bread and cheese;—so, fearing to incommode them with my cigar-smoke, I resumed my walk.

Guy's Cliffe, I believe, lies somewhere between Hatton and Warwick, but I knew not exactly where the entrance to this estate might be, and, in fact, felt no very great interest in seeing the spot. After walking a mile or so, the tall tower of St. Mary's appeared at a distance; and I reached Warwick a little after one o'clock, and went to a hostelrie called the "Rose and Crown", a little removed from the market-place.[112] It seemed to be market-day in Warwick; for the tap-room was quite crowded with farmers, clowns, gentlemen's servants, and people akin to horses and cattle; and in the parlor there were two farmers drinking ale, and brandy-and water pot, and talking over their affairs. I called for some luncheon; and a rosy-cheeked damsel brought me some bread and cheese, and a tankard of just such nut-brown ale as I had drunk at the wayside inn. It needs a life-time to make this beverage agreeable, but I drank it without any great repugnance. Indeed,

*   *   *

Here lies the body of
Mr William Edwards Chirurgeon
A Native of this Parish
Eminent in his Profession
Kind and Generous to the Poor
In His Practice
of Great & Prosperous Industry
He Departed this Life
A Loss to his Country
The 5th Day of April AD 1722
Aged 64
In Memory of whom
This Monument is Erected by
Mary his Mournful Relict

Mr William Edwards here buried Did by his Will and
Testament Charge his Estate of Guy's Cliff with Twenty Pounds
per.ann for ever for a Free School in this Parish
He likewise gave certain messuage with Land and other
Appurtenances in Kenilworth now let by lease at twenty
Two Pounds per.ann for the benefit of a Free School to be settled
at Kenilworth aforesaid Having provided likewise for the
Building of a School House there
He likewise gave certain lands of the yearly Value of
about Sixteen pounds for the Cloathing Six Poor Men and Six
Poor Widows every Christmas, one year in Kenilworth
and another Year in Hatton, Shrewley and Beausale & so
on alternately for ever. The Overplus of the said income to be
laid out in Bibles to be distributed to the Poor Persons

*   *   *

after serving an apprenticeship to one kind of English ale, you find that you have a new variety to get acquainted with, wherever about England you happen to go; and, so far as I have experienced, they are mostly disagreeable at first.
I walked from Warwick, and reached home between three and four o'clock.[113]

No one else appears to have ventured as far either that day or the next as the weather seems to have been rather threatening most of the time and it was not warm enough to make walking far a very attractive proposition. However, there were bright spells and these had to be taken advantage of if the remainder of the stay in Leamington was to be pleasurable. Nathaniel recorded in his journal on the Tuesday that

We have had wretched weather almost ever since my last return to Leamington; cloudy, chill, always threatening rain, and sometimes actually raining; with now and then a sunny and balmy hour or two. My excursions, therefore, have been few and brief, and to places hereabouts which I have already seen and described.

The autumn has advanced progressively, and is now fairly established, (as well it may be, being now more than half way towards winter) though still there is much green foliage, in spite of many brown trees, and an immensity of withered leaves, too damp to rustle, strewing the paths—whence, however, they are continually swept up and carried off in wheelbarrows, either for neatness, or for the agricultural worth as manure of even a withered leaf. The pastures look just as green as ever; a deep, bright verdure, that seems almost sunshine in itself, however sombre the sky may be. The little plots of grass and flowers, in front of our circle of houses, might still do credit to an American mid-summer; for I have seen beautiful roses here, within a day or two, and dahlias, asters, and such autumnal blossoms are plentiful; and I have no doubt that the old year's flowers will bloom till those of the new year appear. Really, the English winter is not nearly so terrible as ours.[114]

Both Monday and Tuesday were sufficiently busy (though in what respect is not known, apart from the routine of lessons) for Ada not to add anything to her current letter to Clay. Wednesday turned out to be a day of especially good weather, and the family split up into two parties and went their separate ways, though Julian and Rose (once again) appear not to have been involved:

[Today] was one of the most beautiful of all days, and gilded almost throughout with the precious English sunshine; the most delightful sunshine ever made, both for its positive fine qualities, and because we seldom get it without too great an admixture of water. However, my wife and I made no use of this day, except to walk to an "Arboretum and Pinetum" on the outskirts of the town. Una and Miss Shepard made an excursion to Guy's Cliffe.[115]

This is the first time that the Arboretum has been mentioned in any of the family's records relating to either of their periods of residence in the town. Situated a short way up the Tachbrook Road (on the site of what was until recently The Royal Midland Counties Home but that is now being altered into yet another bland housing estate), it offered what would have been a rather pleasant alternative to the Jephson Gardens, not that much further away from Lansdowne Crescent or Circus that it would have constituted too long a walk. It had been laid out a few years previously, and bearing in mind the Hawthornes' constant appreciation of the trees that formed such an important part of the beauties of the region, it would have appeared that its attractions were such that they would have visited it on several occasions (even though it was not a potentially exciting place to visit); as the *Guide Book* stated:

The grounds comprise about eleven acres and a-half of land and, taking into consideration that the whole of it has been tastefully laid out within the last four years, it is remarkable that they should have obtained so much order, beauty and popularity within so short a period. . . . It is the object of the spirited proprietor . . . to promote the introduction into Great Britain of a variety of exotic trees not hitherto much known or cultivated in England. . . . Several thousands of the Araucaria Imbricata or Chili Pine, and also of the Cedrus Deodara or Himmalayan [sic] Cedar . . . have been successfully raised from seed at this extensive nursery. . . . There is a suite of greenhouses about 140ft. by 18ft. wide. . . . In a very few years, we venture to predict that the Arboretum at Leamington will scarcely be surpassed by any establishment in the kingdom. . . .

Sometime during that day, apparently in answer to a reply from Bennoch to his last letter to him, Nathaniel wrote again to his friend:

10 Lansdowne Circus
Leamington, Octr 28th

Dear Bennoch,
If we took the lodgings next week, we should want them certainly for a fortnight, and not improbably three or four weeks.
I mean to go to the Continent; but, to tell you the truth, I shall hardly think it advisable to set out until I know whether the financial hurricane is to have any disastrous effect on me. I have no reason to apprehend anything; but, at such a time, nobody can feel safe.

Your friend,
Nath[l] Hawthorne.[116]

In the circumstances, it was possibly not in the best of taste to mention money difficulties to Bennoch in view of the latter's imminent bankruptcy. Meanwhile, Ada was in great spirits because she had had another letter from Clay and school lessons had again been passed over for the day, this time in favor of the visit to Guy's Cliffe house:

Wednesday evening, Oct 28th

Dear Clay, I bless thee anew for the joy that thy letters give me. I have just finished reading one which came to-day,[117] and which I found awaiting my return from an excursion which I have been making with Una to-day. It was accompanied by one from Mary[118] enclosing also notes from Rebecca Rice[119] and Maria Speer.[120] They tell me of Yellow Springs, the dear, dear place to which my heart so often makes pilgrimages. I have often thought that my affection for places is less marked than that of most persons; for I could be happy anywhere with those whom I love; but certainly I feel the tenderest love for that place where the brightest days of my life were passed,—where commenced the happy days that are to last forever as I fondly hope;—where I first knew thee, my soul's beloved! Ah! There can never be dearer associations connected with any place, it seems to me.
Do not ask me if your letters are satisfactory, dearest being. They are my meat and drink. I read them again and again with kisses and smiles and tears. They are very, very dear to me, my beloved, and I would that I could give thee a thousandth part of the joy thou givest me.
But I must tell you where we went to-day. When we visited Warwick Castle we regretted that we had not time to go about two miles beyond it, to visit the residence of the famous old Guy of Warwick, now the country seat of the Honorable C. B. Percy, and called Guy's Cliff (though very inappropriately, as there is no appearance of a cliff anywhere near it), praised as a spot of great beauty by the author of our guide-book. The weather being remarkably fine to-day, we concluded that it would be a good idea to give up books for the day and commune with

Nature instead; so we prepared for a long walk and chose the road towards Guy's Cliff as the direction of our ramble. We passed over a high bridge on our road, from which we had a delightful view of the Castle and St. Mary's church, at some distance, for the nearest road to Guy's Cliff did not take us by the castle.

I never felt more inclined to give myself up to the full enjoyment of a holiday, and consequently never enjoyed an excursion of this kind more, although, as I shall tell you, we failed in executing several projects with which we started. The day was perfectly lovely,—almost "as rare as a day in June".[121] The sky was of that exquisite hue which we love so much, and the fleecy clouds that sailed across it but added to its enchanting beauty. The air was as mild and balmy as if it were May or early June instead of October, and, as the grass in every field was greener and fresher than in the earliest spring-time at home, and many of the trees had not begun to change their colors at all, we could hardly believe that it was so late in the fall as the almanac says. The elm trees preserve their rich green longer than any of the others excepting the evergreens here, and they are of rare size and beauty. I <u>wish</u> you could see them, dear Clay!

When the trees turn at all they become yellow or brown at once here. There are no brilliant shades of crimson and scarlet as in our American forests.

But the beauty of the various tints of green in the trees, the hedges and the grass, and their harmony in the landscape all around this fertile region is inconceivable.

Having arrived at Guy's Cliff,[122] we entered the gate at the entrance of its large grounds, and confidently informed the keeper of the lodge that we wished to visit the mansion, (as our guide-book had said that we could enter it) but she coolly replied that that was impossible, since the family were at home, and never admitted the public when they were at the mansion; so that we were obliged to relinquish the very purpose for which we had taken so long a walk. However, we had set out with a determination to pass the day pleasantly, so we passed on to see what we could discover which we might visit, and as we went, had various tantalising views of the old stone mansion with its adornments of luxuriant ivy.[123]

One of these views was from the road directly in front of the house, whence we looked through a long avenue of noble old cedars inter-spersed with elms and oaks, all of them, perfectly <u>magnificent</u> trees! Then we saw it from the old mill, beyond the house, where we went to rest on some seats by the river (the Avon). This was a beautiful spot. The Avon, here quite broad and <u>river-like</u> was as clear as crystal and reflected the oaks and willows that grow upon its margin, and rippled in the sunlight, and dashed over the dam that the miller had built across its bed, with as merry and happy a sound as if Nature herself had formed the cascade, while the grand old house beyond with its background of noble trees, and the little rustic bridge across the stream, and the picturesque mill (which looked as if it might have stood there for centuries) made as perfect a picture as one could well imagine. We sat on some rustic seats under the trees (they were old and moss-grown like everything in England) and ate the luncheon we had taken with us, and soon there came tripping along over the bridge a band of young girls (apparently a school) taking their morning walk. We meet some school or other almost every day. Poor scholars! They have to go marching along, in prim procession, talking in subdued tones and watched over by lynx-eyed governesses or governors (as they invariably term their male teachers in England: that is, the head teachers).

We asked the pleasant-faced miller with beautiful blue eyes and fresh pink complexion (under the flour) whom we saw standing at the door of the mill, to allow us to enter, and he kindly took us all round, and explained the machinery &c, &c., telling us of the improvements that had been made since the time of his grand-father, also a miller (one sees here, constantly, how almost invariably the same occupation descends through families, generation after generation). He weighed us and I found that I had gained a great deal since I was at home. Do you know that I actually weigh <u>one</u> <u>hundred</u> and <u>thirty</u> <u>four</u> <u>pounds</u>? Did you think I was so <u>substantial</u> a person?

We both took a great fancy to the miller, but we tore ourselves away from his lovely abode,[124] and passed through "Guy's Toll-gate" and walked along the beautiful winding road, bordered by hedges of holly, hawthorne and ivy, and shaded by elms and chestnut-trees, until we came to the wood wherein stands a stone monument erected to mark the spot where Piers Gaveston, the favorite of Edward II, was beheaded in 1312. It consists of a solid stone cross mounted upon a pedestal which stands upon four stone columns, of three feet in height perhaps, and which are themselves mounted upon a square pedestal standing upon a tier of stone steps (there are four of them, I think). This description must be extremely lucid, and is especially beautiful since I commenced at the summit instead of the base of the monument. Upon the monument is this inscription.

* * *

In the Hollow of this rock
Was beheaded
On the 1st day of July, 1312
By persons lawless as himself
Piers Gaveston, Earl of Cornwall
The minion of a hateful King
In Life and Death
A memorable Instance of Misrule[125]

* * *

I am glad that you are reading English history while I am visiting some of the places connected with its stirring scenes;—it seems to bring our pursuits nearer together. I wish I had the time to read the history now while here; but I must not think of it. I read Italian as well as French each day now.

But, to return from my digression, we admired the view from the eminence whereon the monument stands, for a long, long time, and then (can you imagine how we could thus descend from the stirring associations connected with the spot to so sublimary an occupation?) spent a half-hour perhaps, in picking up chestnuts under the trees in the grove around the monument. These chestnuts were much larger but less sweet than our American chestnuts.

As we returned from the wood towards the town of Warwick, we met a procession of old ladies dressed in uniform with white caps and blue dresses, marching, two by two. We felt great curiosity to know who they were, and made various inquiries afterwards, but found out nothing. We made one or two abortive attempts to enter some interesting places, one of which proved to be a private boarding school, but were refused admittance by the <u>lionesses</u>, as Una called them, in the porters' lodges. However we returned home feeling that the day had been delightfully spent, and not in the least fatigued by our unusually long walk.

Next, we must go to Stratford-on-Avon. Ah! how I wish that I could have thee for a companion in these expeditions, dear Clay!

Mrs. Hawthorne told us last night that they were deliberating a removal to Sydenham for a short time before leaving England. I wish we could go there, for then I could see the Crystal Palace and London.

But have I not wearied you completely, dear Clay?

Will this letter <u>ever</u> have an end, I fancy you saying, as you disconsolately finish the fifth sheet, and that that is not all. I will not write longer to-night however, for I must commence a letter to Mary before I go to bed.[126]

Good-night, dearly beloved![127]

Perhaps because they had decided that their stay in Leamington was shortly to come to end and particularly because the next day's weather was a continuation of the sunshine and clear skies of Wednesday, Sophia and Nathaniel must have granted another day's holiday from lessons, as they all set off for different destinations (minus Rose, again; poor little Rose, left behind with Fanny once more—what *did* they do?):

[Today] was likewise a promising day, at the outset; the wind being from the eastward, and therefore indicative of fine weather. Miss Shepard and Una, therefore, set out for Stratford-on-Avon, at 10 o'clock, by stage-coach, and my wife for Warwick by the same conveyance;[128] while Julian and I went on foot to the latter place. I like very well to visit Warwick, and, I suppose I have described its aspect, over and over again, in the journal of our former stay in this neighborhood. The first interesting object that presents itself, on entering the town, is Saint John's Schoolhouse; a gray stone edifice, mossy and antique, with four gables in a row along its front, alternately plain and ornamented, and wide, projecting windows;— in the centre, a venerable portal, and before it a large grassy lawn, shut in by a solid stone-wall, moss-grown, like the edifice itself, and with a gateway of open iron-work, through which I peeped at the ancient school. It being, I presume, vacation-time, there was a notice on a board, in the centre of the lawn, of apart-ments to let. It seems to me that grown men must retain very delightful recollec-tions of an old schoolhouse and play-place like this.

Thence we pursued our way into the interior of the old town, which certainly gives the impression of being ancient and venerable; though, when you come to analyze the streets, you find that the modern brick fronts bear a very large propor-tion to the old projecting, storied, gabled, timber-and-plaster built houses of past times. Soon, the east-gate appears in sight, an open archway striding half across the street, and bearing on its shoulders a gray, Gothic-looking edifice with a spire or cupola. Passing beneath or beside this archway, you find yourself in the High-street, which goes on with a gentle ascent, between shops with modern plate-glass, and ancient houses that have been re-glassed and varnished, towards another gateway, which bestrides the street at a distance of perhaps a quarter of a mile. Here, likewise, is an open archway, burrowing through the natural rock, and over the arch a Gothic chapel, with its battlemented tower, rising to a height of nearly a hundred feet; and the street divides itself, passing both beneath the archway and on one side of it, and re-uniting beyond. On the right, as you approach from the east-gate is Leicester's Hospital, with its venerable Elizabethan front of timber and plaster, in perfect repair; and being on a level with the top of the arch and foundation of the chapel, it looks down stately upon the street.

From this point, Julian and I went through some crooked cross-streets to the market-place; and soon, while we were standing under the pillars of the market-house, mamma appeared, and likewise the stage-coach, behind which, on the outside, sat Una and Miss Shepard, smiling at us very joyously. Here we divided ourselves according to our various objects; Una and Miss Shepard rumbling off in the coach towards Stratford; Julian ascending to the second-floor of the market-house, where there is a Museum of Natural History; and Mamma and I turning back to Leicester's Hospital, which we had come to Warwick specially to see.

Entering beneath the carved oaken portal, we were met by a man who seemed to be the steward or upper servant of the establishment. We should have preferred to be escorted by one of the twelve old soldiers, who compose the brotherhood of the Hospital, and, if I remember rightly, I did meet with some such guidance on the occasion of my former visit. However, this man performed his part very well, and discoursed like a book (a guide-book) about the history and antiquity of the edifice, which, he said, had been a sort of religious establishment before Lord Leicester converted it into a Hospital, in 1571. All round the quadrangle, which the four sides of edifice enclose, there are rep[et]itions, large and small, of the Leicester cognizance, the Bear and Ragged Staff, and escutcheons of the arms of the families with which he was connected. I presume there is nothing else so perfect in England, in this style and date of architecture, as this interior quadrangle of Leicester's Hospital; and it probably gives an accurate idea of the appearance of a great family residence—a Hall or Manor-House—in Elizabeth's time. On one side is a corridor, on the ground-floor, giving admittance to the Kitchen and other offices, and above it an open gallery, looking down into the quadrangle. On the opposite side is what was formerly the Great Hall, where James the First was once feasted by one of the Earls of Warwick, as is still commemorated by an inscription at one end of the room. It is a large, barnlike apartment, with a vaulted roof, carved in oak, and a brick-floor; on one side there is a fire-place and conveniences for brewing ale, and on the other several wooden partitions, where the brethren keep their respective allotments of coal. Nevertheless, the Hall may have been very magnificent, when hung with rich tapestry, and gleaming with wax torches, and glittering with plate and brilliantly attired guests. Then, I think, we went up the old staircase that leads to the apartments of the twelve brethren and, in this part of the edifice, our guide showed us portions of the timber-framework, which are supposed to be eight or nine hundred years old. He likewise led us into the comfortable little parlor of one of the brethren; it had a bedroom adjoining, and really seemed an abode where a warworn veteran, satiated with adventure, might spend the remnant of life as happily as anywhere else; especially as it is permitted to the married men to have the society of their wives, and as much freedom as is consistent with good order. These twelve brethren are selected from among men of good character, who have been in military service, and, by preference, natives of Warwickshire or Gloucestershire; their private resources must not exceed five pounds a year; and I suppose this regulation excludes all commissioned officers, whose half-pay would of course exceed that sum. The brethren receive from the Hospital an annuity of eighty pounds each, besides their apartments, a garment of fine blue cloth, with a silver badge, an annual quantity of ale, and a right at the kitchen fire; so that, considering the class from which they are taken, few old men find themselves in such rich clover as the brethren of Leicester's Hospital. Really, bad as Leicester was, I cannot help having some hopes of his eternal salvation because he imagined such kind things for these poor people.

The little parlor, which was shown to us, had a portrait of its occupant hanging on the wall; and on a table were two swords crossed. One of them, perhaps, had been the weapon which he carried in his warfare; and the other, which I drew half out of the scabbard, had an inscription on the blade, purporting that it had been taken from the field of Waterloo. We saw none of the brethren; and I rather think, being made so comfortable and comparatively wealthy, they do not like to think themselves objects of charity, and are shy of being seen about the premises in their quaint, old-fashioned tunics. For, indeed, they become gentlemen of income, and invested with political rights; having (if I correctly understood the guide) three votes a-piece, in virtue of their brotherhood. On the other hand, they are subject to a supervision which the Master of the Hospital might make very annoying, were he so inclined, as relates to personal freedom and conduct; but, as they have all their lives been under military restraint, these matters will not so much trouble them, if fairly administered; and the guide bore testimony to their being as contented and happy as old people can well be. I wish I had an opportunity to look a little into their moral and intellectual state for myself.

We next went into the Chapel, which is the Gothic edifice surmounting the gateway that stretches half across the street. Here the brethren have to attend prayers every-day, but go to the Church of Saint Mary's for public worship on Sundays. The interior of the chapel is very plain, with a picture of no merit for an altar-piece, and a single old pane of painted glass, representing the Earl of Leicester, with very much the aspect of his portrait, as I saw it at the Manchester Exhibition. We ascended the tower of the chapel, and looked down between its battlements into the street, a hundred feet below us, and at the base of the archway, with weeds growing far upward on its sides; and, also, far around us, at the rich and lovely English landscape, with many a church-spire and noble country-seat, and objects of historic interest. Edge Hill, where Cromwell defeated Charles the First, was in sight, far off on the horizon, and, much nearer, the house where Cromwell lodged, the night before the battle. Right under our eyes, and half surrounding the town, was the Earl of Warwick's delightful park, a wide extent of lawns, interspersed with great contiguities of forest-shade. The guide pointed out some of the Cedars of Lebanon, for which the Warwick estate is famous. The roofs of the town, beneath and around us, were partly slate-covered, (and these were the modern houses) and partly covered with old red-tiles, denoting the more ancient edifices. There was a great fire, a hundred and sixty years ago, which destroyed a large portion of the town, and doubtless many structures of great antiquity; for it is said to have been founded by Shakespeare's King Cymbeline, in the year One of the Christian era; and Imogen and Posthumus may have strayed hand-in-hand through the country-lanes about Warwick.

The day, though it began so brightly, had long been overcast, and the clouds now spat down a few spiteful drops upon us, besides that the east-wind was very chill; so we descended the winding tower stair, and went next into the garden, one side of which is shut in by almost the only remaining portion of the old city-wall. The garden has a grassy and ornamental part, with gravel-walks, in the centre of one of which is a beautiful stone vase, of Egyptian origin, having formerly stood on the top of a Nilometer, or pillar for measuring the rise and fall of the river Nile. On the pedestal is a Latin inscription by Dr. Parr.[129] There is likewise a vegetable garden, the lion's share of which belongs to the Master of the Hospital, and twelve little adjacent patches to the individual brethren. In the farther part of the garden is an arbor for their pleasure and convenience; and no doubt they find a good deal of occupation and amusement here. The Master's residence (forming one whole side of the quadrangle) fronts on the garden, looking at once homely and stately, and just as it may have looked two or three hundred years ago; except that then the garden may have been rather more quaint, with old-fashioned eccentricities of the gardener's art, than it is now. The Master's name is Harris, and he is a descendant of the Earl of Leicester's family, a gentleman of independent fortune, and a clergyman of the established church, as the laws of the Hospital require him to be. I do not know what his official emoluments may be; but doubtless, the brethren being so well-to-do, the Master's place must be especially comfortable and jolly. It is pleasant to think of the good life which a suitable man, in this position, must lead, linked to old customs, welded in with an ancient system, never dreaming of change, and bringing all the mellowness and richness of the past down into the midst of these railway-times, which never make him or his community move one whit quicker than of yore. I wish I could know him.

From the garden we went into the kitchen, which is a fine old room, with an immense fire-place, beneath an arched oaken mantel which really seemed almost as spacious as the city gateway. The fire was burning hospitably, and diffused a genial warmth through the room. Over the hearth were crossed two ancient halberds, and some muskets hung against another part of the wall. A long table, with wooden benches on each side, stood permanently for the convenience of the brethren, who smoke their pipes and drink their ale here, in the evenings; the kitchen being prepared for their reception after a certain hour. In the daytime, each brother brings or sends what mess he will to be prepared by the Cook. There was a great, antique copper flagon for ale; also an ancient oaken cabinet; also, I think it was here that I saw, and sat down in, the oaken elbow-chair which was occupied by King James at the Earl of Warwick's banquet. Hanging up in the kitchen, too, is a piece of needle-work representing the Bear and Ragged Staff, reputed to have been wrought by Amy Robsart, and which has lately been set in a carved oaken-frame, through the munificence of a countryman of my own. The guide showed us his name in the visitor's book; a Mr. Conner of the Navy. These items seem to make up the sum of what we saw in the Hospital; but the sketch is capable of being elaborated and colored into a very effective picture of a patch of old times surviving sturdily into the new.

Philip. S.P Conner, } *United States*
April 30th 1857

* *This is the gentleman by whose generosity the Bear & Ragged Staff attributed to Amy Robs., was framed*

From the Hospital we went along the High-street to an old curiosity shop, the entrance to which is near the East-gate, and is not to be found without careful search, being only denoted by the name of 'Redfern' painted not very conspicuously in the toplight of the door. Immediately on entering, we found ourselves among a confusion of old rubbish and valuables, ancient armor, historic portraits (one of Charles Ist, for instance, by Dobson, which Mr. Redfern purchased at the recent sale at Alton Towers) old cabinets, clocks, china, looking-glasses, and every imaginable object that has gone out of date. The collection must have been got together at an immense cost. Some of the articles were bought at Rogers's sale;[130] and no doubt, whenever a virtuoso's treasures are scattered abroad, some of them find their way hither. It is impossible to give any idea of the variety of articles, which were so thickly strewn about that we could hardly move without overturning some great thing or sweeping away some small one, and occupied the whole house, in three stories. The person who waited upon us was exceedingly civil, and gave us his whole attention after some ladies (who were there when we came) had made their purchases and departed. Then we asked the prices of a great many things; for we wanted to buy something by way of paying an admission-fee; but it was hardly possible to find any article however trifling, that came within our prudential views. However, we finally fixed on a little spoon of George II's time, silver-gilt and curiously wrought, which was formerly the property of Lady Blessington, and for which we paid ten shillings [not noted in the Accounts Book]. I should like much (if my circumstances were in accordance) to spend a hundred pounds there.

From Redfern's we went back to the Market Place, expecting partly to find Julian at the Museum; but the keeper said that he had gone away about half an hour before, it being now a little past one. We went into the Museum, which contains the collections in Natural History &c. of a county society. It is very well arranged, and is rich in specimens of ornithology, among which was an albatross, huge beyond imagination. I do not think that Coleridge could have known the size of this fowl, when he caused it to be hung round the neck of his Ancient Mariner. There were a great many humming-birds from various parts of the world; and some of their breasts actually gleamed and shone as with the brightest lustre of sunset. Also, many strange fishes, and a huge pike, taken from the river Avon, and so long that I wonder how he could turn himself about in such a little river as it is, near Warwick. A great curiosity was a bunch of skeleton leaves and flowers, prepared by a young lady, and preserving all the most delicate fibres of the plant, looking like inconceivably fine lace-work, white as snow; while the substance was quite taken away. In another room, there were minerals, shells, and a splendid collection of fossils, among which were remains of ante-diluvian creatures, several feet long. In still another room, we saw some historical curiosities, the most interesting of which were two locks of reddish brown hair, one from the head and the other from the beard of Edward IV. They were fastened to a manuscript letter, which authenticates the hair as having been taken from King Edward's tomb, in 1789. Near these relics was a seal of the great Earl of Warwick, the mighty King Maker; also, a sword from Bosworth-field, smaller and shorter than those now in use; for, indeed, swords seem to have increased in length, weight, and formidable aspect, now that the weapon has almost ceased to be used in actual warfare. The short Roman sword was probably more murderous than any weapon of the same species, except the Bowie knife. Here, too, were Parliamentary cannon-balls, and many other things that have passed out of my memory.

At three o'clock, my wife took the omnibus back to Leamington, and I returned by the old road, passing the castle-gate, and over the bridge across the Avon, whence I had a fine view of the castle, through the scanty autumnal foliage of its embosoming trees. I particularly remember nothing else worth recording; unless it be, that our guide showed us one of the gowns or cloaks worn by the brethren of Leicester's Hospital. The cloth was very fine, a dark blue, the skirts long, and on one sleeve was the brightly burnished silver badge of the Bear and Ragged Staff, of solid metal, and as much as four inches long. Only two of these badges (I think he said) have been lost since the foundation of the Hospital; and this was one of the original set. The Earl of Leicester certainly showed a strong desire to glorify himself and his family by causing his heraldic cognizance and his badge to be repeated so abundantly on the front of the building, all about the interior quadrangle, over the kitchen fire place, on the brethren's sleeves, and wherever else it could be painted, carved, or sewn. But I suppose this may not indicate his individual vanity, but belonged to the manners and feelings of the age; and the whole was perhaps arranged for him artistically, as a pageant would have been. In our own day, Mr. William Brown suffered himself to be feasted and profusely eulogized in public (by myself as enormously as by anybody) for a charity more splendid certainly than that of the Earl of Leicester; but I do not know that the ancient benefactor showed more vanity than the modern one, in their several ways, and according to the fashion of their times. Both wanted to do a good thing, and were willing to have the credit of it.[131]

That was by far the longest entry in his journal that Nathaniel had made for some time, but however much the visit to Warwick had inspired him on this occasion, Sophia was equally committed to putting on record her own impressions of their sightseeing excursion:

[This] morning the weather promised very fair and my husband and I thought we would go to Warwick. I also thought Una and Miss Shepard had better take the fine day for Stratford on Avon, which I did not like to have Miss Shepard lose. Una had been there already two years ago with us. So then we arranged to have Julian go to Warwick also but instead of walking about with us, he was to visit the Museum of Natural History, which he had long wished to do very much. Meanwhile little Bud was to be taken by Fanny to the Jephson Gardens, [so that's what Rose and Fanny did!] that we might all be jolly together. We left the house at half past nine. Papa and Julian walked by the new road, or rather by the Stratford road. Una, Miss Shepard and I took the stage coach. As we waited for this coach, which started at ten, three gentlemen came into the little office to take seats for Shakespeare's town. One of them who was large-browed, dark eyed and anxious-looking, I fancied to be Miss Bacon's brother going to enquire about her.[132] They all looked as if they were also going to see the illustrious house and tomb. I alone took an inside seat. Una and Miss Shepard had a delightful place, and looked like two embodied [joys?], York and Lancaster roses, one glowing with a pink, and the other with a white light. Presently, on the road we overtook two old ladies (or old crones, rather, for they were not 'ladies') who got into the inside with me. One sat down opposite me, and looked mild and good-humored, and like some American person I had seen. The other's face I did not then observe. I found Mr. Hawthorne and Julian under the porches of the Museum, a large, square, stone building, whose superincumbent structure is upheld by this open gallery of square columns. Julian disappeared through the door with a happy hope in his face, and Papa and Mamma went out to seek Lions. We first went to the Earl of Leicester's Hospital for twelve worthy men. It is at the western gate of the original old town of Warwick, in High St, and the Chapel is built directly over the gate, which is thirty or forty feet in depth. The street to the building, now the hospital, rises gradually from the level of the town until the foundation of it becomes the plane above the arch of the gateway. It is a fine old timber and plaster edifice, looking like arabesque work on a white ground. A vestibule, with carved oaken pilasters and pediments and pendants first attracted our notice, but this was not the principal entrance, and seemed the access to a back yard through a narrow corridor with doors into apartments on each side. We passed on and were soon joined by a man, probably the porter, who asked us if we wished to be guided over the establishment. He first drew us out to examine the arched entrance to the Quadrangle. It is surmounted with a stone carving of the heraldic badge of the Earl, the Bear and Ragged Staff. 1571 is also carved, in red stone, over the arch. It is the date of the Earl of Leicester's purchase of the property for the purpose of devoting it to his charity. Originally it was a hall for the Guilds of the town. The whole front bulges very much as if it were pushing out to fall; but the porter said it had been lately pronounced secure for two centuries longer by a scientific architect.

Here is a picture of the side of the quadrangle which fronts the High St, with the Gateway West and the Chapel over it.[133] It looks here like a narrow house which will assuredly topple over, instead of a broad quadrangular building. After saying his lesson very well in regard to the entrance, the porter led us within the court, which is exceedingly picturesque and fine, and bright with color. For besides the contrast of the dark brown oak beams with the white plaster in regular patterns, the coats of arms of all those noble families which are connected with Robert Dudley, hang round the four sides of the hospital, illuminated with blue, red and yellow, each of them about twelve inches large. Opposite the deep arched entrance, along the whole of that side are the apartments of the Master, who must always be a clergyman. The present Master is the Rev. Mr. Harris, a descendant of the Earl of Leicester. A line of gables extends from one end to the other, and at every point was a bear, erased, grasping his ragged staff in every variety of attitude, the architect sporting with the device in the most lawless manner—Besides these many bears was a larger bas relief, or rather alto relievo, of the heraldic form of Bruin, and also a fierce looking Porcupine, in bright colors, and large as life—the cognizance of the Lords de Lisle. In the engraving beneath is this gabled side, occupied by the Reverend gentleman and on the right hand is a cloistered gallery, half of it belonging to the Master's portion and the other half free to the brethren. Along this gallery, the Master has a sheltered way to go to the old men when they are ill, and need ghostly comfort. This struck me as quite in keeping with the luxurious style of the English Churchmen. They will give the ghostly comfort, but the mace-bearers must precede them, crimson cushioned chairs must stand ready to receive their well rounded persons and carpets must be spread beneath their feet. How different from the way in which the Lord Jesus ministered to the wretched and suffering! How much grander they are than the son of God! The porter told us about every one of the escutcheons, whose they were, but I do not remember the names. But I know that Artgall, who was the first Earl of Warwick, first took the cognizance of the Bear, because the word Arth means bear. Then the second Earl, Moroidus, had an encounter with a giant, who had for a weapon a huge rough club, and Earl Moroidus being conqueror, added this ragged staff to the Bear, in memory of his victory. The Neville crest is a pied Bull. This Arthgall is the Sir Artegal of Spenser, who personifies justice in him. When we had sufficiently examined the Quadrangle (which was in perfect order, like a drawing-room) we were led into a door in the left hand corner, and found ourselves in a very large hall which reached along that whole side of the building. It was originally the great dining hall of the Guilds, and afterwards the brethren dined there for a while and once James First was entertained at the table with Sir Falke Greville, Earl of Warwick, in 1617. The roof is unceiled and supported by open rafters, upon some of which fine carving still remains. The grand Banqueting Room is now quite spoiled by being put to use; for along the side that looks upon the inner Court a row of coal bins have been built for the old brethren's convenience. The Earl of Leicester should have provided against this. The Hospital was first designed for his own retainers in their decrepitude—now, as they are of course all dead very long ago, needy soldiers are preferred—even quite young they can be admitted, if any accident has befallen their limbs and they are worth less than 5L a year. They have eighty pounds a year from this charity, which is worth 2000L, this being now the income of the lands and apanage belonging to it. They are also provided with a cloak of fine dark blue cloth, made like a minister's gown about the neck, and adorned with a pure silver badge of the Bear and Ragged Staff. These badges are now the same that were put on two hundred and eighty six years ago, excepting one, which is replaced in the stead of the one that had been stolen. The brethren keep their silver bright—and the cloaks beautifully brushed.

From the dining room of aforetimes we returned into the Court and went up a flight of stairs outside the building in the left corner. We were then on the landing of the covered gallery, but the porter took us inside a suite of rooms on the right again, which gave upon the High St. It was a specimen of the brethren's

accommodations—a parlor and bedroom. It had a carpet and good furniture, and
pictures on the walls, and a portrait of the occupant, who may have been a peninsular soldier, for there was a sword on his table with an inscription upon it, about
the peninsular war. A large engraving, in colors, of Warwick Castle hung over the
table. The bedroom looked very nice, with a white marseille quilt on the bed—
and in a little mid-room was a washing apparatus—all in perfect order. The old
gentlemen are allowed to have their wives with them under regulations by the
Master—and they dine in their own rooms. This is a charity that I enjoy, for it is
not slow starvation, like that of Ford's Hospital at Coventry—It seems real comfort, peace and rest from life's toil. We then went into a high vaulted apartment,
formerly a grand hall; but now two thirds of its width is filled up with suites of
rooms for the brethren on the right, commanding the High St. from their windows.
Upon the open groinings of the roof are still some sculptures in the spandrils; and
one very fine boss is left. It is an angel holding an escutcheon—the color still
distinguishable. On every part we saw iron clamps and supports and stays to keep
the beams and rafters from falling—though the wood is still very sound, and it is
only one particular kind of timber which is at all worm eaten.

The last place we were shown was the kitchen—oh most delectable place! with
a superb fire burning in the immense grate, and a [true?] kitchen, with pleasant
odor of a roast, before it, and delightful settles on each side. There is an inner and
outer division of this room. The inner contains the glorious fire, the cosie and
sociable settles of dark oak with their high backs half way to the ceiling. An ever
open entrance between the settles is surmounted on each side by Bruin, hugging
his Staff, carved in oak, and three feet high. Opposite the fire-place, at the end of
this snug Paradise of comfort is a window. The settles are all round both sides
and at the end, excepting where there are some shelves. Upon these shelves are
copper flagons, shining like gold, and one of them is enormous. I do not recollect
how many gallons it holds, but the brethren have it full of ale four times in the
year, one day being the 1st July, the day this Hospital was founded. They are
allowed two pounds worth of ale in addition to their income. As the day was chilly,
the fire was delicious. In the middle of this oblong was a table beneath a gas pipe,
and every evening it is alight and there the jolly old men sit and talk, and warm
themselves, and read if they incline, or doze, if they are sleepy. In Fra Angelico's
Judgement Day which I saw at the Exhibition at Old Trafford, the damned were
thrust into hot cauldrons by devils, armed with forks, who seemed to take huge
delight in poking them down and stirring them up. On each cauldron was inscribed
the class of crime for which these souls were in torment. I think for all the comfort
these elderly gentlemen get from the Earl of Leicester's fire, so much heat is
abstracted from the cauldron in which Fra Angelico would plunge his sinful spirits.
But however he may suffer, I am sure the Lord awards him balm for this good
charity, though history assures us the Earl's Charities were all false shows, and
not a desire to do good. I trust History is mistaken. In the kitchen's other half
we were shown one of the brethren's gowns, and a bit of embroidery by Amy
Robsart—the Bear and Ragged Staff worked in raised stitch, now faded nearly
white. It is about seven inches high, and is framed ponderously in a carved oaken
frame—the carvings originally having been a part of Kenilworth Castle. Last April
an American gentleman found this precious embroidery hanging up exposed, and
left money to pay for its being properly and securely framed in some wood of the
Castle. So it is done, and a plate glass guards it from all harm. The name of the
gentleman was Conner. Beneath this framed relic stands a carved old chair in

which foolish King James sat at the banquet given him by Sir Falke Greville. In that chair I sat me down, for even as a cat may look at a Queen, so any humble body may sit on a king's throne, when it happens to be a chair accessible. Over the chimney piece are the initials R L as well as the motto "Droit et Loyal". This motto and these initials are also over the arched entrance of the Quadrangle. The unfortunate Robert seems neither to have been 'Droit' nor 'Loyal', however.

We then went into the garden. From its high terrace there is a fine view over the country, and the gravel walk along which we passed is directly above the only portion of the old walls of the town that are left standing. Each of the brethren has a small lot of land in the garden to cultivate, and there is a bowling-green for them, and a circular tower—like a summerhouse—where they can sit and smoke their pipes and muse over the past. In the centre of the garden, directly opposite the summer house, stands upon a stone pedestal a wonderfully beautiful Egyptian vase of grey stone, fluted in waving lines, something in this way, but as I did not sketch it upon the spot, I miss all the exquisite art of the lines and the handles and every detail. This merely shows the form and the plan. It is a very precious relic and once stood where the famous Warwick Vase now stands in the gardens of Warwick Castle, and was presented to the Hospital by the father of the present Earl. It is no doubt three or four thousand years old. It stood in Egypt upon a nilometer, to measure the rise of the Nile. Standing by the vase we were in front of the Master's house which is very picturesque on this outer side. Here the porter told us that the brethren were allowed to play bowls and billiards, but not cards; that by asking the Master, they could leave the Hospital for a visit, not longer than a month, unless the permission were renewed, so that virtually they are quite free in their movements, though nominally they are subject to the master's will. They are however obliged to wear the blue cloak and badge when-ever they walk out, and if they commit any kind of misdemeanor, they are fined more or less, and the money thus deducted from their pay is divided among the rest of the number. I do not like this; for it causes the brothers to fatten upon the sins of each other. I think it would be far better to make the money gained a fund for repairing the hospital or for helping some of the town's poor. After seeing the garden we went into the church over the Gate, appropriated to the twelve men. There is a fine Eastern window to this private chapel of St. James, which was given to the Church in the time of Henry Ist by Roger de Newburg, Earl of Warwick. In the times of Richard II, Thomas de Beauchamp gave it to the Guild of St. George, when the present hospital was a Guildhall. It is a small chapel and has lately been ceiled with plaster for warmth—and a columnar stove is put up in the centre. Six seats on each side accommodate the brethren and each has a prayer book made of the finest paper with fair large type so that the dimmest eye can read. AND IT CAME TO PASS. A very poor picture hangs over the altar in the Chancel. One large square pew is devoted to the visitors. Once in three years, the Bishop comes to see that the service is conducted in an orthodox manner, and the Master is in proper train. "The Bishop cannot come oftener," said the porter. Every morning and evening, services are performed here, but on Sundays the old men are obliged to go to St. Mary's, and if they fail in attendance at either place, they are fined.

We mounted to the summit of the Tower, erected by Thomas de Beauchamp,

Earl of Warwick. It is about ninety feet high, and from the battlements there is a superb view. To the west on the horizon is Edge Hill, the scene of the battle between Charles Ist and the Parliamentary Forces—and elsewhere a lovely plain, and the straggling ends of the town, which lies beyond the walls. On the South stretch the magnificent domains of Warwick Castle. The Avon winds about the grounds and trees that can never be described rise in utmost majesty and sweeping state from the sunny lawns and swelling uplands. Caesar's Tower lifts its large head above the embosoming foliage. It is in this picture the tower nearest to the left. The other is Guy's Tower from which the flag is flying. It is the famous Avon that flows beneath this bridge. On the East lay the city—and on the North a rich country, where the porter pointed out several lordly seats—one, Lord Dormer's. We also saw a mighty reservoir in the town, just erected, for the filtering of the waters of the renowned Avon, to supply the people of Warwick. Fancy the good people of Warwick drinking of England's Castaly![134] But what if the Avon had no Swan after all?[135] What a pity it would be!

Now we had seen all, and we had written our names in the book in the outside half of the kitchen,[136] (where there was a handsome old carved cabinet which I

Nath' Hawthorne , United States
Mrs Hawthorne   "   "

did not mention) and we had been accompanied through-out by the two old crones who drove with me in the stage from Leamington. One of them was a hideous looking woman who scowled hate on all sides. My lord gave the porter a florin for his pains, & he advised us to visit the Curiosity shop of Mr. Redfern, near the East Gate. Thither we went therefore. We found an inextricable labyrinth of every imaginable relic and bijouterie, inestimable old Dresden and Sèvres china, ancient goldsmith's work in silver and gold, buhl cabinets and tables, ormulu and inlaid cabinets of very great value, filagree and enamel work, oriental agates, jasper handled knives and forks, even India jade ornaments, and carvings in ivory and wood, tortoise shell and pearl caskets, viniagrettes [sic] of fine Sèvres and enamel, snuff boxes of gold, silver, pearl, agate, tortoise shell & Sèvres—oil paintings—statues and statuettes, busts, and I might say specimens of every thing else in ornamental art. I puzzled myself into a maze, trying to decide with my husband what we should buy. There were six rooms full, but finally we purchased a silver gilt spoon, once belonging to the Countess of Blessingotn. The ball of the spoon is carved in a fine style in a leaf shape, and the tip of the handle is an open ornament. It was of the time of George II. We hesitated between this and an oriental agate salver, which was very beautiful. But I thought we had better take something wholly English, with an English story to it, since we will find oriental agate otherwheres. Several articles were from the poet Rogers' sale, and I would have preferred one of them; but they were four or five pounds apiece, & we thought that too much to spend about it. The spoon cost quite enough. The ingenious Mr. Redfern did not appear.

From the Curiosity Shop we went to find Julian, but he had been gone half an hour, and then we lunched—and finally we thought we would go and look at the Museum, till we were ready to go home. It was quite worth a visit. In the largest room we found every bird in the world from an Albatross and Emu to a humming bird, innumerable fishes and sea growths, corals and seaweeds—and a skeleton group of leaves and plants, beneath a glass shade, which was of miraculous perfection and beauty. It was not only wholly transparent, being reduced to mere fibre, but of snowy whiteness, like the spirits of the leaves and seed vessels, ascended, and clothed, like the shining ones, in raiments of light. There was a poppy plant with a very large seed vessel like this in size and a spike of the seed vessels of the beech nut, some holly leaves and a bunch of leaves of a network so fine that it was nearly as delicate a web as that of India muslin. There seemed not to be a break nor a blemish in any part of the whole group. It has a sculpturesque beauty, and the emotion it excites is wonder at the divine skill. It is plain that the Almighty's hand alone could have produced such a work. As plants and flowers they are nothing, the passion of Color being absent, and life extinct. They are dead and pure of all tendency to decay, a fairy frame-work, upon which the Creator wove the pattern of beauty not with hands, but with the shuttle of Thought, which alone is fine enough to embroider such tapestry. There was a gorgeous peacock in this room with his proud sapphire neck and emerald head crowned with upright jewelled feathers, and the amplitude of glorious tail spread abroad like pure gold with its thousand blue eyes and green lids—a very pomp of color. A bird of Paradise was also there, but very uncomfortably squeezed up in too narrow limits, so that the pale amber light of its plumed tail was quite lost. The emu looked like our dear friend Henry Bright. In a small side room we found Mexican antiquities and Egyptian—and American bank notes of lang syne—Edward the Fourth's hair, taken from his tomb at Windsor, and Richard Neville's seal, both very interesting to me, because I have just been reading the Last of the Barons.[137] There was also some point lace once worn by Queen Elizabeth, and now dark brown in hue. A cannon ball from Edge Hill we saw too and a great many Roman antiquities dug up here and there about England. Very many things were contributed by the Earls of Warwick. In another large room we saw a choice collection of shells, among them the rare and lovely glassy Carinaria, and fine Paper Nautili. Here also were a great many fossils of Saurians and Icthyosauri, embedded in lime stone—multitudes of Ammonites, and fishes and shells and plants and woods—most interesting—also specimens of all the metals and precious stones. I must not omit to mention a sheet of Brazilian butterflies as splendid as rainbows and flowers. One room was devoted to skeleton specimens, and here was an Egyptian mummy. Once the mummy was a beautiful woman, but alack! what must we come to, when against God's decree man insists upon holding back the body from dust? It is beyond words horrible—this mummy—more so than any I have seen. The mouth especially, with its grinning teeth, made me shudder. In the sculptured face, the mouth is very delicate and small, and the nose is straight and fine. But why should I write about a mummy? I wondered whether it were some Queen—it must have been some person of high rank, because of the signs and care in the embalming and if the noble lady now have [sic] "garments of light on", I think it is a pity to preserve here below the blackened, swathed, frightful wrecks of her mortal form. There was a foot and a hand in the case, the hand of exceeding beauty of form, and with the most delicately tapering fingers I ever saw, the nails quite whole. It seemed a miracle to be looking at the actual finger nails of a human being who lived three thousand years ago.[138] We spent two hours in the rooms but saw not a hundredth part of the show.[139] Yet it might be seen in a day very well—while the British Museum would take a good part of one's life. Next week we shall be in its neighborhood, and shall probably visit it again.[140] So then we put our names in the book, where Julian had already written his autograph very nicely, and made our way out. There was a comfortable fire in one large room and a great many long seats. I suppose there is some kind of meeting there of the committee once in a while.

I think Warwick is an exceedingly interesting old town, with very many timber and plaster houses and strange, straggling streets. I observe that where there is a lordly castle in England, the town at its feet looks rather poor and drained, as if there were a sort of capillary attraction in castles and palaces, drawing all the life and moisture out of the neighborhood. Linlithgow is a striking example of this.[141] My husband would not visit either St. Mary's Church or the grand castle, as I had been to both before with Una and Julian, and so I returned, the solitary passenger, in the omnibus, and my lord walked home.[142] It rained slightly two or three times in the course of the day, which made me rather anxious about Una and Miss Shepard at Stratford, and when I left the omnibus, it poured hard for a while. But they arrived safely and dry at about 6 o'clock, after a day of vast and rare enjoyment, seeing the birth-place, the Church, and Anne Hathaways's cottage. Warwick contrasts entirely with Leamington, which is all new, looking like the new parts of London, fair and stately and palatial—giving evidence of modern prosperity and convenience, and where the noble trees alone hold on to the Past.[143]

That evening must have been spent in a babble of conversation, as each of the parties explained what they had seen on their separate trips; hopefully, even little Rose had something to tell about the goings-on in the Jephson Gardens (if all the entries in the Accounts Book under the date of 29 October *do* relate to that day then at least she would have had a new pair of shoes to show everyone). And, of course, Ada would have been itching to get it all down on paper for Clay's benefit:

Thursday evening, Oct. 29th

I have been in the room where the immortal Shakespeare was born, dear Clay! To-day I have visited Stratford-upon-Avon. The weather promising to be fine, this morning, Mrs. Hawthorne insisted on our giving up lessons again to-day, and improving the opportunity to go to Stratford. So Una and I started, at ten o'clock, upon the top of the stage-coach that we might enjoy the beauty of the country during our ride of ten miles. Ladies ride upon the top of these country coaches frequently in England, and we found it most delightful, for the country through which we passed is perfectly enchanting. I never saw anything to compare with the beauty of the landscape during this drive of ten miles. We passed through the old town of Warwick which now seems quite familiar to me since I have seen it three times, and saw again the curious little houses with moss-grown roofs and quaintly patched walls, all joined together in the most remarkable manner.

It is very curious to see, in these English towns, houses of different sizes and shapes all strung along in a row and joined together like our large blocks of houses in Boston or New York. Some high, some low, some of brick, some of stone, some with gables and some without, some with thatched and some with shingled roofs, there they all stand huddled together, and forming a strange looking medley.

It was just so in Stratford, and this seems to have been the custom of building anciently here. Leamington is a comparatively new town, and looks far more like our large towns. But oh! that lovely drive this morning! How I wish I could describe what the ablest writer would find indescribable, the matchless beauty of the scenes through which the lumbering old coach drew us at a snail's pace. We did not quarrel with its want of rapidity, however, for we wanted to enjoy the prospect as much as possible.

Such lovely lines of hedges, such graceful slopes of emerald fields, such larches, elms, oaks and cedars!

I never realized how beautiful creations are <u>trees</u> until I saw these in Warwickshire. They seem so wondrously full of life that they are not content with putting forth their luxuriant verdure above where they branch out, but they send forth shoots all down the trunk, to the very roots, and these leave out vigorously and richly, and no one has the heart to lop them off. And where there are no such shoots appearing from the trunks of the trees, a rich growth of ivy takes their place, so that we seldom see a bare trunk here.

What bliss it will be to enjoy all these beauties with thee, some day, my own, my precious Clay! I always think of that, wherever I go and whatever I see that gives me delight.

Dear, <u>dear</u> Clay!

The road itself was not the least beautiful object on our route, winding along so gracefully and bordered by neatly trimmed hedges interspersed with noble trees it was delightful to behold. We passed but few houses; now and then a solitary farm-house substantially built and well flanked by outhouses and haystacks, all looking as if the very genius of comfort presided there; or, again, a little cottage with moss-grown roof; and once a windmill on a hill opposite which stood a little inn—"Windmill Inn".[144]

We entered the old town of Stratford at about half past eleven, and immediately inquired the way to Shakespeare's birthplace. We found it with but little difficulty, and were admitted by the old lady who shows the room in which the illustrious man was born. There is little else to see, in the house, indeed nothing, now, for they are repairing it as it was in a ruinous condition in some parts.

In Shakespeare's time it was separate from the other houses on this street, but afterwards there were built on each side and joined to it other houses. Lately these have been pulled down, and they are now restoring it to its original condition.[145]

It is very small and quaint. The little sitting-room below the chamber in which he was born and this chamber were the only rooms left untouched by the workmen who were engaged on it.

These both had rough, stone floors, and contained but a few pieces of old-fashioned, oaken furniture. In the birth-room was an old portrait of Shakespeare, said to be very correct as a likeness. It was very fine-looking at any rate, and much more pleasing than the bust which is on the monument in the church. There were busts of him here for sale, and various views of interesting spots in the town. I did not like the idea of thus making a sales-room of the very place where the great man was born.

The walls, the ceiling, the windows were completely covered with names of visitors.

We saw "Walter Scott", scratched upon the window with a diamond by his own hand.[146] Byron's name was quite effaced, and so were most of those which one cares to see, while numerous Smiths and Joneses were very conspicuous.

We saw H. B. Stowe's name on the wall down-stairs.

But we left the little house and passed through the town so unimportant in itself, so famous through its one great son. I never felt so impressed with the sense of what an influence one man can have over everything connected with the place of his nativity as while I walked the streets of Stratford, and saw constantly memorials of Shakespeare on every hand. I know not how many Shakespeare Inns there were. The very china in the shops had pictures of his birth-place, his tomb, his Anne Hathaway's cottage &c. Every little book-stall contained innumerable reminders of him. His portraits, his busts appeared at every turn. The town is no longer Stratford. It is Shakespeare's birthplace,—Shakespeare's home,—Shakespeare's burial-place. We passed by the little grammar-school in which he was educated, and before which were playing a group of sturdy urchins with their square Oxford caps. Almost all the boy's schools have some uniform to distinguish them, or the scholars wear these square, flat caps. I thought before that they were peculiar to colleges, but chubby little boys appear in them here. I wondered if among them all was another genius that should bless his native town like this grand old Shakespeare. But no. Avon has had her share of glory. She will never give birth to another Shakespeare, I am sure.

These little boys have very common faces,—round, healthy, <u>English</u> faces!

We visited the beautiful old church (so old that its roof is all moss-grown and its walls have been obliged to be rebuilt in various parts), wherein is Shakespeare's tomb, as well as those of his family. This church was built in the twelfth century. It stands upon the bank of the Avon which is quite wide and very beautiful in this part of its course.

We sat for some time under the old trees on the border of the stream, and listened to the cawing of numerous rooks overhead,—the only sound that disturbed the sacred stillness of this spot.

We passed around among the graves and read the curious inscriptions upon the stones, and, after patient waiting, the sexton appeared and admitted us into the church. It is very beautiful inside, with windows of stained glass and with exquisite carvings in various parts. Some of the tombs are exceedingly tasteful. Shakespeare's monument is in the chancel, and consists of his bust surmounted by a death's head. On the pedestal on which the bust stands is a Latin inscription: "Indicio Pylium genio Socratem arte Maronen Terra tegit, populus moeret, Olympus habet." There is an inscription in English under this, but I have forgotten what it is.[147] On the tomb, which is below the monument, is the well-known inscription, which I have copied just as it is:

"Good friend, for Jesus' sake forbeare
To digg ye dust enclosed heare;
Blest be ye man yt spares these stones
And curst be he yt moves my bones."

The sexton was very garrulous, like most such persons, and entertained us for some time. There were two other Americans there, at the same time, and, finding from our signature in the visitors' book, that we were also Americans, they talked with us for some time. They were a nice, elderly couple from New York, who are on their return from a tour on the continent.[148] But the most interesting part of our visit remains yet to be told. We walked a mile over lovely fields through which were nice little winding paths, to the cottage "where Shakespeare wooed and won his wife, Anne Hathaway." We sat in the very chimney-place where the young *c/29 1857 Mrs Hawthorne   Mass. U.S.A.*

"   Ada Shepard.   Dorchester, Mass.

"   Mr & Mrs S. G. W. Benj   New York. U.S.

lovers must have sat during the cold, winter evenings, and we looked up through the old chimney at the same blue sky that over-arched them, when they sought their Lyra and vowed to each other a love as unchanging as the light of the constant star.

Very beautiful it must have been on pleasant evenings to sit thus by the fireside, and look up at the sky through the chimney, but what could they do when the rain beat down upon the fire? Unromantic as it was to think of such an exigency, my practicality was sufficiently aroused to lead me to remark to the old woman who showed us over the cottage, that it must be inconvenient to have the chimney so open. "Oh, yes!" she said, "the rain and snow beat down into the room without any hindrance."

She showed us Anne Hathaway's bedstead (which is of curiously carved oak), as well as other pieces of old furniture.

I was more moved at the thought that I stood on the spot where the young poet and the beautiful maiden had passed the sacred hours of their early love, than I was when conscious that my eye rested upon the spot where he first opened his eyes upon the world or upon the ground where rested his remains. Is not love a more sacred mystery than either birth or death? The germ buried in the earth springs into life. But what is this life worth if the plant does not bud and blossom and bear fruit ere it dies? How does the death of the plant affect us if the life has been of no use? So what is the birth or death of man to us compared with his love, the crowning fact of his life?

Dear Clay! The little thatched cottage was very sacred to me. I would not think of the stories that are told of Shakespeare's domestic unhappiness. I only thought of the blooming maiden and the ardent lover, as they uttered their vows of love in this humble room wherein I stood. I am glad to have been there. We walked back to Stratford by the same path, I suppose, over which Shakespeare used to go with light heart and rapid step, to greet the loved one in the lowly cottage. "How beautiful this walk must have seemed to him!" exclaimed I and Una smiled quietly, as if she knew why I could say that with so much earnestness. I found, on the way home, that she did know about us. Mrs. Mann wrote to Mrs. H. about you at the same time when she first wrote of me, I believe. I have never yet said anything to Mrs. Hawthorne about it.

But the clock has just struck ten, and I have come to the end of my seventh sheet. I pity you, dearest Clay! with this long tedious letter before you. I promise to try never to write so long a one again.

And I am going to seal this up immediately to prevent my taking an eighth sheet tomorrow, which I might do if I were not thus wise.

Long as this letter is, it has left all unsaid what can never be said,—the boundless love and bliss of thy

Ada.[149]

Friday was another quiet day; Nathaniel and Sophia were completing their journal entries about the visit to Warwick the day before, so that must have kept them occupied for a good deal of the day, but Una and Ada went for a walk to the Arboretum, probably as a result of Nathaniel's recommendation as to the worth of including it in one of their daily afternoon walks, and then further on up the Tachbrook Road to look at the mill. One letter, at least, was received that morning:

Leamington Oct 30th 1857

My dearest Aunt Lizzie,
This morning I received your most welcome letter.[150] I am <u>very</u> glad to hear from you but I am sorry to find you were driven to writing by not hearing from me. When we were in Manchester, I wrote you a very long letter. Did you not receive that? If not, I cannot imagine where it is. I have very little time for anything but studying now. The newspaper report was true [?] and we have an American lady here to teach us. She is a very lovely person and exceedingly learned. She has been through the course of study that men go through at Mr. Mann's college in Ohio, and has a diploma proclaiming her <u>Bachelor of Arts</u>. Is it not funny for a lady to be <u>Bachelor</u> of Arts? I am now studying Bem's system of chronology,[151] and am reading Heroditus. I find it very interesting. Also French, Italian, Geography and Arithmetic. When we get to Italy I am going to study Latin and Greek. I like Italian very much indeed, better than French. I think I know a great deal of French now, and have read some of Racine's and Corneille's plays, and am reading Madame de Sévigné's letters. I like Corneille's Horace very much, but I do not like what I have read of Racine nearly as well. While I have been in Leamington I have been obliged to neglect music entirely, as we had no convenience for a piano, but I suppose I shall have masters again in Italy. Miss Shepard does not teach music. We have been staying here in Leamington ever since we left Manchester and next week we are going to London to stay till we leave England, which we shall probably do in two or three weeks. Papa could not go sooner, because he has some business to attend to in Liverpool. After that we shall go to Paris, and stay perhaps a week, and then straight to Rome. But you will hear from me several times before that, for I shall write from London and Paris. I do not think it is likely that we shall come home next summer, but Papa seems entirely uncertain about that, so I cannot definitely answer your question on that score. As to me, dear Auntie, I have <u>grown up</u> now, as far as that goes. I mean in height, for I am five feet four inches. But I suppose you mean by grown up, matured in mind and heart and that, I suppose, I am not tho' I feel a good deal older than thirteen, and everybody thinks I am fifteen or sixteen.
Aunt Dike[152] is very kind to enquire about mother's health. She is much better since she has been in Leamington; the dry, mild air of this midst of England suits her much better than the north. You know it is her cough that has troubled her for so long, and I think it is much improved of late, and we hope everything from sunny Italy. She is under the doctor's care,[153] and his medicine does her a great deal of good. Mother very easily catches cold, but I believe she was always susceptible on that point, and then her cough is worse for a little while, but I think she will be made quite well in Italy. And then our sweet Miss Shepard sets her mind perfectly at ease about us and all our studies and our own invaluable Fanny is such a tender nurse & friend that she has nothing to weigh upon her mind, that I know of,[154] and you cannot imagine what a difference there has been in her since

father left his office. It has been so miserable for us all, and mother especially, to have him so often away, and now to feel we have him always, is an infinite relief & comfort. I do not know at all whether we shall go to Egypt. Papa's plans are not at all settled so far in the future. But I think we shall perhaps travel in Spain and we all want to go to Germany and Switzerland, and so perhaps there will not be time for Egypt.

I am very glad you went to the Exhibition at Boston, and enjoyed it so much. I should think it was very necessary to your health to have once in a while an entire change from Salem and all its surroundings. Why do you never, by any chance, say a word about your own health, dear Auntie? I hope you are well, but I should like very much to know exactly about it. Do tell me when you write again. I found that it was a stupendous undertaking to learn the Lady of the Lake by heart, even more so than I had anticipated and so I contented myself with learning the finest scenes and passages. I can repeat the whole last scene which I think is one of the most exquisite I ever read, either in poetry or prose. How lovely that passage is where it says

> "As wreath of snow on mountain breast
> Slides from the rock that gave it rest;
> Poor Ellen glided from her stay,
> And at the Monarch's feet she lay."

I wish I was with you at Monserrat[155] with all my heart and I would repeat poetry to you and we would take lovely walks together, for I am a very good walker and Miss Shepard and I have lovely walks together in this lovely neighborhood. But that great pleasure is, I hope, in store for me when I return to my beloved home, and all the beloved people there. Since Miss Shepard came I have been with her to Kenilworth, Warwick, Guy's Cliff, and Stratford-on-Avon. I have been to all the places before but I went to show them to her, and enjoyed them myself a great deal more the second time. At Kenilworth are the ruins of the famous castle owned by Dudley, Earl of Leicester, where Queen Elizabeth was entertained by him, filled with such interesting associations of her and poor Amy Robsart. At Warwick is the splendid old castle, some parts of which were built at the time of the Conquest, and it is still inhabited by the Earls of Warwick. The grounds are very beautiful indeed. There is also a hospital there, founded by the Earl of Leicester for twelve old indigent soldiers and a master. They must be worth less than five pounds a year before they are admitted into the hospital. Just think how poor they must be! When they are once inside they are most liberally provided for. St Mary's church at Warwick is very beautiful, and some parts are very old, but most of it has been burnt down several times. Guy's Cliff is very near Warwick, and a most lovely place it is. You know it was one of the habitations of Guy the great Earl of Warwick, who also lived at the castle in Warwick; and we saw his great porridge-pot and other things belonging to him. In the great Hall of the castle, also, is Cromwell's helmet, the Hilt of the Pretender's sword, the coat in which Lord Brooke was slain at the siege of Lichfield in the reign of Charles Ist, &,&. The house at Guy's Cliff is now inhabited by an honorable family of the name of Percy, and is not shown to visitors, but we had beautiful views of it from different points. The Avon runs by it, and there is a water mill on it, and we asked one of the millers who was standing at the door, if he would let us see his mill, and he kindly showed us through the whole machinery, and weighed us. I weigh 122 pounds. Is not that a great deal?

Gaveston's monument (the wicked favorite of Edward II) is in a little grove near by, and we went to see it. It is nothing very elaborate, for it was hastily erected there by the barons who beheaded him on that spot, but it is very pretty, and I made a little sketch of it which I would send you if it did not cost so much to send packages now Papa is no longer Consul. I want to say that now we have no despatch bag you will have to write on paper at least as thin as this, and if you send any letters for us to the Ticknors, he will always know our address if anybody does. Will you please to tell this to cousin Richard? Please to give him also my love and say I should like to hear from him very much, and from Rebecca, for it is a very long time since I heard from either.

Yesterday we went to Stratford. After visiting the church and Shakespeare's birth-place or rather house, we walked to Anne Hathaway's cottage. It was a lovely walk over the fields, and we thought how often Shakespeare must have hurried along these very paths to see his ladylove. The reason I give you such short descriptions of all these places is that I have written detailed accounts in my journal which you will see when I get home.[156] Goodnight now. I will finish this tomorrow. Oct 30.[sic] Here it is the last day of October and tomorrow black November will begin. It looks as black this morning as if it had already begun.

Yesterday Miss Shepard and I took a long walk. We went on the Tachbrook road, which is a very beautiful one. There is a sort of nursery there kept by a Mr. Hitchman. It is a nursery for young pines and firs of all sorts, and some of them are very curious. At last we came to a windmill that looked very old and there was a pretty little rustic cottage by it over which grapevines were trained and a nice garden. We thought it would be very pleasant to go into the mill as we had never been in a windmill before, and so we asked the miller.[157] He was evidently much pleased and flattered at our interest and showed us all over it. He said these mills were fast going out of vogue now that water mills were so common and the wind very uncertain so that sometimes nothing could be done. We are going to sketch the house and mill some day, it is so picturesque and pretty.

Perhaps you would like to hear the order of my day. Now that the mornings are so dark, I get up at half past six. At half past seven I have Arithmetic for an hour, and then we have break-fast. From half past nine to eleven we have chronology. Then we walk from eleven till one. Then dinner, and we study from two till five. Then some gymnastic exercises for about quarter of an hour, and Miss Shepard and I read French till six. Then tea, and after tea I generally read French or write my journal. Now I am reading Charles Reade's book "Never too late to mend." It is so very interesting, do get it if you can. Goodbye.

Most affectionately your niece
Una Hawthorne[158]

Sophia wrote a rather unnecessary postscript to the letter (she was obviously concerned that Elizabeth should not be given the chance of denigrating Una's efforts for any reason), crushed into the small space left at the bottom of the last page:

Dear Elizabeth, Una has written this in great haste and carelessness. She can write a nice hand when she takes pains. With all our love to you and Mrs. Dike, yours truly Sophia.

Saturday, 31 October, saw the arrival of a letter from Bennoch giving the address of suitable lodgings in Bloomsbury, at No. 24 Great Russell St., the owner's name being a Mrs. Sievers; Nathaniel sent him a suitable reply of acceptance and thanks.[159] It seems that they then planned to remove to London on the following Wednesday, so much of the next few days must have been taken up with packing all their belongings and making the necessary arrangements with the owner of No. 10 to bring their tenancy to a conclusion. The Accounts Book's entries since the middle of September give the impression of being more and more perfunctory, especially under the heading of "sundries," but the food bills continued to be entered. No entry for the payment of rent had been made since 13 September.

Una must have finished off her letter to Aunt Lizzie in the morning before she walked into Warwick again, this time accompanied by Ada and Fanny (and perhaps Rose as well?), Julian having left earlier; they all went to visit the museum, Mr. Redfern's Curiosity Shop, and Lord Leycester's Hospital,

Una Hawthorne   Oct 31 1857 Mass. & L. A
Ada Shepard, Oct. 31st 1857, Dorchester, Mass
L A Wrigley   Oct. 31st 1857 Yorkshire

although Julian's interest, as ever, was in inspecting and copying the fossils and shells in the museum's collection so he didn't accompany the girls to the hospital. What with one thing and another, Ada hadn't written a line to Clay for two whole days, so Sunday was spent in bringing him up-to-date on the latest expeditions.

6

"This goodly town of Leamington": November 1857

Leamington, Nov. 1st, 1857
Sunday morning.

Dearest Clay,
I have just read your last letter as a pleasant commencement to my Sabbath. How I wish I could be with you, during the long winter evenings of which you speak, when you fear not being able to read with your dear eyes. If I could be eyes for you, how perfectly delightful it would be! My eyes are stronger than they have been before for a long time, thanks to the great care I have exercised over them since I left home.

It is now decided that we shall leave Leamington on Wednesday, and go to London to stay until Mr. Hawthorne can leave England for Paris. I am very glad we are going to be in London for a week or two.

Leamington is a delightful place, and I have enjoyed visiting its surroundings, so full of historical associations, very, very much; but I have visited nearly everything in the immediate vicinity that is of great interest, and am extremely glad to go to London where there is so much to be seen.

Una and I took another walk to Warwick, yesterday, and visited the museum there, and also one old curiosity shop containing relics of great interest. The man to whom it belongs is an Antiquary who goes around collecting whatever "remains of departed greatness" he can find at auctions and sales of any kind. He must be extremely rich, for he had many articles of the greatest value. He had innumerable specimens of Dresden china and Sevres porcelaine [sic] of exquisite delicacy. I asked the price of one diminutive cup, and found that it was four pounds! Boxes and cabinets beautifully inlaid and of rare workmanship were there in great numbers, and he had curious clocks which chimed most musically at each hour. Busts and portraits of royal and noble personages, paintings of battles, &c, &c, and a thousand rare and curious things, filled the shop. One might have spent a half-day in examining them all.

After leaving the curiosity shop,[1] we went to the museum, where we found Julian, who had been there all day, copying shells. He has the greatest passion for shells, as I believe I have told you; and buys all the books he can find which treat of them, spending all his leisure in copying the engravings they contain. He has a great deal of skill in drawing, and yesterday he succeeded admirably, bringing home two large sheets covered with copies of those that interested him most. The museum at Warwick is small, but contains a great many interesting things. There are numerous specimens of fossils from all the fossiliferous strata, and also of minerals of all kinds—I mean of many kinds, of course—and these were far more interesting to me than the gorgeously plumed birds of various species with which

218

Clay Badger. Yale Collection of American Literature, Beinecke Rare Book and Manuscript Library.

one room was filled, or the animals which were exhibited in another. How I wish we could have had a good cabinet when we studied Geology! We might then have learned something. And now I shall be able to visit the British Museum, since I am going to London! What a privilege it is! Yesterday, at the Warwick museum, I saw some of the hair of Edward IV, among other relics. It seemed like coming quite near to the monarch, to see a part of his person, thus.

After we had been through the museum, we went to Leicester's Hospital, about which I think I have written you something before. We visited it three weeks before, but, as we had time to go again, yesterday, and it is always more interesting to go to such a place the second time than the first, we made a second visit yesterday. The porter there is the very prince of porters. I liked him better than any whom we have seen,—he gave us so much information on all points on which we questioned him. I wish you could see the splendid fire in the old kitchen in the hospital. I never saw anything so beautiful of its kind.

An English girl there said; "I don't think you have anything like that in Yankeeland." Here the old soldiers meet together whenever they like to come from their rooms and talk over their experiences, I suppose, as they drink their ale.

I have forgotten whether I told you much about this hospital when I visited it before; but I will run the risk of "repeating myself", and say something about it now, for it is a very interesting institution, I think.

The name hospital might mislead you as to its character, for the English apply the term not only to institutions for the care and healing of the sick, but to various kinds of charitable institutions. This hospital was founded by Dudley, Earl of Leicester, in 1571, for the support of twelve indigent men, who were at first chosen from among his old retainers; but, when they became extinct, Lord de l'Isle, who inherited the Leicester estates, had twelve men chosen from certain towns in Gloucestershire and Warwickshire. They are all soldiers and to be entitled to a home in the hospital, they have to be worth less than five pounds a year, to give up all occupation, to promise not to marry (if unmarried when they enter the brotherhood) without the consent of the master who is appointed by Lord de l'Isle, with a salary of four hundred pounds a year. They cannot keep hawks or hounds; they cannot leave the premises of the hospital without their livery, which consists of a gown very much like our ministers' robes at home, and a badge consisting of a "bear and ragged staff" (the Leicester crest which is repeated an infinity of times all over this building) upon a long strip of broadcloth hanging over the shoulder.

In return for obedience to these rules and also to the one which compels them to attend divine service twice a day in a chapel belonging to the institution, they have a pension of eighty pounds a year, a nice little suite of apartments, consisting of a bedroom and parlor which they furnish themselves, with the exception of the bed and bedding. We visited several of the rooms. They are full of the objects which you would imagine would most interest an old soldier,—now and then a statue of Napoleon (one of the brethren is a Waterloo soldier), pictures of battles, portraits of the duke of Wellington, &c, &c. They look as comfortable as possible. The brethren are allowed to have their wives with them, or, if widowers, one daughter; but never any more of their families.

Each brother has a little garden of his own, and the master has, also, a nice garden. There is a beautiful little thatched summer-house where they can go and sit in warm weather, and play at chess or checkers, if they like. Cards are prohibited entirely.

This building is one of the most curious and interesting objects that I have seen. It is rich in old carvings, and is built in very great part, of massive oak. But I cannot give you much of an idea of it, so I will not try to describe it. I sat down in the chair in which King James the First sat on a certain occasion when he was "right hospitably entertained at this house by Sir Fulke Greville."

We ascended the tower of the chapel, from which we had a fine view of this lovely, lovely country. The porter pointed out the old mansion at which Cromwell slept on the night before the battle of Edge Hill, and we could see the old battleground in the distance.[2] At a little distance on the right of the tower lies the racecourse where are held public races twice in the year. On the other side is the Earl of Warwick's park extending for twelve hundred acres, a scene of rare beauty.

One thing I must not forget to mention. In the centre of the garden of the hospital is an Egyptian vase of beautiful proportions and of immense value as an old relic. It stood on the banks of the Nile and was used as a Nilometer. I should think that, including the height of the pedestal, it was eight or nine feet high.

If you have read Scott's "Kenilworth" you will know how much I was interested in a piece of tapestry shown at this hospital said to have been wrought by the fair Amy Robsart, and framed in massive oak, richly carved, taken from the castle of Kenilworth.

But I am afraid this long description has wearied you, dearest Clay! and I <u>will not</u> write any more of this.

The day before yesterday, we took a delightful walk, and visited an old windmill, which we entered and to the top of which we ascended, by the permission of the kind old miller. I take the greatest delight in coming in contact with the <u>people</u> everywhere I go. When we went to Shottery, to see Anne Hathaway's cottage, the other day, we walked across the fields in company with a poor woman with three little children, one in her arms and the other two trudging by her side, and I accosted her and had a long talk with her, during which she told me much of the history of her family. You would be amused to hear these English people talk English;—such expressions as they use are really remarkable! And the h's! I never shall cease wondering at the strangeness of their custom of pronouncing words spelled with h. The porter at the hospital talked about the battle of "Hedge-ill" yesterday! They preserve the old, old forms of English words, such as the Anglo-Saxon plural in en. All the common people here talk about "housen" instead of houses, &c, &c.

To-day I must finish my letter to Mary Richardson, and write to various people. Do you know, I scarcely ever feel inclined to write to any one excepting you, lately? It is almost a penance to me to have to write to other people. Yet I am always very much rejoiced to have letters from any of my friends, and I love Mary very much more, now that I am away from her, than I did when I was with her. I haven't written a word to Mrs. Mann since I have been in Europe. I certainly must write to her to-day. To insure my writing to other people I forbid myself to write more to you than this page, at least before evening.

We are having astonishingly clear weather, lately. I think Leamington is deter-mined to exert her powers of attraction to the utmost, to see if we may not be induced to prolong our stay, but we shall go on Wednesday, I doubt not, and I am glad. We shall be so much nearer Rome, at least.

Is it not nice that I have had this opportunity to visit England? It will be unfortu-nate, rather than otherwise, however, if I am detained here very long, for I shall have but little time to study languages, at the best, and cannot afford to lose much. However, I have no doubt that it will all be right.

I am very, very happy, dear Clay! and rejoice in the thought that thou, too, art quietly content,—<u>working</u> <u>and</u> <u>waiting</u>![3]

What Ada *didn't* mention in her letter, apart from the fact that Fanny, at least, was with them in Warwick, was that there appears to have been some kind of accident at the museum while they were all there (and from the ensuing silence on the subject it seems that neither Nathaniel nor Sophia was told of it). Perhaps Julian had been leaning too heavily on a showcase while he was sketching a specimen. Or, if Rose *did* go with them (in Fanny's charge), there was a little horseplay among the children that resulted in an unfortunate breakage of glass. Whatever happened, the museum's Visitors Book reveals that an immediate payment of 5s.0d. had to be made to cover the damage!

Whether or not the letters to Mary Richardson and Mrs. Mann were even started that day is not known but Ada did write one other letter, at least:

Leamington, England
Nov. 1st, 1857

Dear Lucy,
It certainly is your turn for a letter this time, for it seems an age since I have written to you. My letters home must all be the most stupid things imaginable, for it is distressing to have to write the same accounts over the second time, as I always do to you at home. First I have to write a minute account of all my <u>doings</u> and <u>seeings</u> to Clay, of course, and then writing the same things over I am so tired of them that I can give them no interest.

But I have so often enlarged upon the reasons for expecting only uninteresting letters from me that I will not dwell more upon that subject now, especially as so many other topics rush upon my mind when I commence to write.

I must first tell you that it is decided that we shall go to London next Wednesday. Will not that be delightful? There are so many places in and about London of the most thrilling interest; this great city so seems the very centre of the life of the world, that I am delighted at the thought of spending a week or two there and seeing what I may of it.

Don't you remember how strenuously you used to insist upon my coming first to Liverpool, in order that I might rush across England before fixing myself in Paris for a while? And how almost angry I used to get with you, as we lay talking in Kate's bed, because I couldn't convince you how entirely incompatible it was with my plans to visit England?

Well, it is very queer that, after all, I should have come here. I must say that I enjoy staying here and seeing a little of this famous island before establishing myself for the winter on the continent. Of course, I can only <u>read</u> French and Italian here. I can have no assistance in the pronunciation while here; but I trust to doing a great deal during the winter.

Leamington is one of the most delightful places to visit in England says Mrs. Hawthorne. I can well believe her for there are some of the loveliest walks around here that I have ever seen and, from the hill which is near, we have a fine view of the whole town and its surroundings, and a more fertile and beautiful region I cannot well imagine.

Then there are places all round which are of the greatest historic interest. Of Kenilworth and Warwick Castles I believe I have already written something. About ten miles from here is Coventry, which is interesting as the scene of the legend of Godiva, which Tennyson has rendered into verse. You have read his poem "Godiva"; have you not? If not, please read it and remember that Coventry was the town wherein the strange feat was accomplished by the noble lady.

I have not been to Coventry, but I went, with Una, the other day, to a far more interesting place, Shakespeare's home, Stratford-upon-Avon.

We started in the morning, on the top of the Leamington coach, and had the most lovely ride that you can imagine for eight, no, ten miles, over a gracefully winding road bordered by lofty elms, larches, willows and oaks; mostly destitute of houses, but, now and then, bringing us in view of a solitary inn with a quaint old sign, or a pretty little thatched cottage with moss-grown roof, or, again, an old substantial-looking farm-house, with ample gardens and extensive barns, well flanked with picturesque hay-stacks, giving an indescribable air of comfort to the whole. Now appeared, on the right, an old wind-mill with flying sails, while, on the left, a turn in the road brought the Avon in view. On the hillsides browsed flocks of beautiful, white sheep, while dignified herds of cows grazed in the low pastures near the river-side, and over all shone the most unclouded sky. I say shone the sky, for verily it seemed to shine all over, that day. I cannot begin to tell you how I enjoyed that ride to Stratford. And when we returned, in the afternoon, it was still more glorious, for, as sunset approached, a richer glow was shed over all objects, and the scene was transcendently [sic] beautiful. We visited the house where Shakespeare was born, entered the birth-chamber; and saw the grammar school-house where, in his boyish days, he was taught his earliest lessons; visited his tomb in the old church on the bank of the Avon; walked to Shottery to visit the cottage of his Anne Hathaway, going over the fields, by the very path which he trod, with so happy a heart, doubtless, when he visited his beloved; and enjoyed the whole day immensely. How much I shall have to tell you about all these things, when I come home! Ah! if I poured a perfect deluge of talk upon you all when I came home from Yellow Springs this summer, I think you will have to expect seven deluges in succession when I once "get your ears" again.

Una and I start out for long walks each day when it is pleasant, and we often have quite curious adventures. We went, the other day, to Guy's Cliff at Warwick. But I have no room to write about this, and besides, my bed-time has sounded from the clock in the entry. So good-night. Much love to all my friends who are with you. I long to hear from Lottie.[4]

Your sister Ada

P.S. I enclose a little note-paper view of the house in which Shakespeare was born. It is quite a faithful representation of it. You see from this picture [See chapter 5, footnote 133] the old custom which prevailed in these English towns of joining the houses together through a whole street although they were often of the most diverse style. It characterizes Warwick as well as Stratford,—and all the old villages and towns that I have seen. Leamington is too modern a town for that. It is queer enough to see strings of houses joined together some with and some without gables, some with thatched roofs and some with tiles, some high and some low, some of brick, and some of stone. The two that are in the picture joined to Shakespeare's house happen to be of the same height as his. They have been pulled down lately.[5]

The new week dawned with a rising excitement in everyone's heart with the prospect of the removal to London and with but a short time thereafter before they actually set foot on the Continent but, unfortunately, the weather broke in the Leamington area and the last few days that had been so sunny and clear were succeeded by a period of lowering gray skies, mists, and rain, so much so that it was almost impossible to venture out for any reason beyond that of obtaining necessary supplies of one kind or another. The idea of continuing to take pleasurable walks in the neighborhood was abandoned in favor of keeping close to the fireside. The only thing to be done was to continue school lessons in the usual manner and wait for the days to pass until the time came for departure on Wednesday. The prospect of the next few days must have held little but frustration for them all and it may have been difficult to maintain the normal atmosphere within the household of a purposeful calm and steadiness. Nobody appears to have put pen to paper, except Ada, of course:

Monday, Nov. 2nd

Dear Clay
Your letter mailed at Honeoye Falls on the thirteenth of October, reached me this morning.[6]
   Ah! thou dear, dear Clay! I cannot tell thee how it delighted me. I had not expected it until after I had reached London and written to M. Fezandie to send it on, for I asked him not to send any here after the last of October. He mailed this the very last day, I suppose. Dearest Clay! I never read a letter from thee with such joy. This love grows stronger and more absorbing every day. And there is much in this letter to cheer me, aside from its loving words which always are balm to my soul.
   I am glad to know that you feel so hopeful with regard to our going to Antioch. I have been feeling almost as if it were improbable,—I know not why. But, although I do not, by any means, acknowledge that we are at all dependent on Antioch, I should be very sorry to think that we should never make it our home again. I long to make that place the scene of my activity for some years. And the thought that we may both work there together, with Mr. Mann, dear Mr. Mann, is very delightful. I hope most earnestly that our plans will succeed. What is Mrs. Jay teaching?[7] I did not know that she was there. Mary does not mention it in her letter.
   It rejoices me to know that you are so happy, dearest Clay! I, too, am very, very happy now.
   Dearest Clay! Never so dear, never so dear as at this moment! My Clay! My own beloved one![8]

Unfortunately, there came a setback to their plans on Tuesday, as Nathaniel received a letter from Mrs. Sievers in Great Russell Street to say that she was unable to be ready in time for them to leave on Wednesday and that preparations for their arrival in London would be delayed, but only for a short time. It was annoying, nevertheless, and meant that a certain amount of unpacking had to be done to tide them over the next couple of days.

Tuesday evening, Nov. 3rd

A letter which Mr. Hawthorne received this morning will detain us here until Thursday, and perhaps longer; so I am not now, as I thought I should be, on the very eve of departure from this goodly town of Leamington.

Yesterday and today have been perfectly gloomy and dark and rainy and cloudy and smoky—perfect English days. Yet I have been very quietly happy, although confined at home all day, and deprived of my usual pleasant walk. We shall probably have enough of this weather while in London, and I might as well accustom myself to it.

I go on reading French plays. I have almost finished Racine, and, after tomorrow, shall devote myself to the two Corneilles until I have finished all their dramas which I have not yet read. I shall take up Molière when I go to Paris and can obtain the book, which I have not now. Meanwhile I shall hear Una read some of Madame de Sevigné's epistles so famous as specimens of letter-writing. I have never read them.

In Italian I am reading the only book I can command at present, a collection of extracts from an Italian history by Fra Giucciardini, which is not at all inspiring. As soon as I can find something better (I probably can in London) I shall seize upon it. I must read Dante, Tasso and Petrarch this winter, if possible.

I enjoy Racine, but can never be enthusiastic over a French play, I think. It all seems so artificial, so heartless (by it I mean the very spirit of the French drama) compared with Schiller and our Shakespeare that I take but little delight in it comparatively. I like Corneille far better than Racine, but have not yet read so many of his plays. His "Horace" is splendid and has all the old Roman fire in it. I speak of Pierre Corneille. I have his plays and also those of Thomas Corneille, but have as yet read none of the latter.

It is raining steadily without, and I sit alone by the comfortable fire, in the school-room, whither I usually betake myself after the children go to bed, leaving Mr. and Mrs. Hawthorne to enjoy their evening by themselves, and where I can be alone either to read or to write. It is almost the only time I have, to be really alone, through the whole day; for, even when Una and Julian are not reciting or we are not walking, little Rose scarcely gives me a moment's peace, rushing up to me with violent demonstrations of affection, and begging me to tell her a story or play at ball, or devote myself to her in some way. So that I feel quite as I imagine a mother must feel when her children are snugly deposited in their beds, when I know that they are securely reposing for the night, and I can have a few hours of quiet. But I enjoy this life very much, indeed,—far more than I thought I should when I first came here. The children all seem to love me very much, and I feel it a great privilege to be with these pure, beautiful beings. I never saw children who seemed to have led so perfectly natural a life as they. Mrs. Hawthorne told me, this evening, how constantly she and Mr. H. had devoted themselves to them ever since they were born. They never left them to other persons, even long enough to go out to tea, during their whole childhood, until they came to England, where Mr. Hawthorne's position compels them to attend rather more to the claims of society. Their friends opposed this course of conduct very much, Mrs. H. said, but she was convinced that it was the mother's duty to devote herself to her children first of all, and she lived up to this idea completely, as she does to every idea that seems to her true. She is a noble mother, a true woman, dear Clay! and she has her reward. I never saw such affection for their parents as these children all manifest. I wish you could see this realization of our ideas of a happy family, dearest Clay!

I go now to my happy rest. Good-night, my beloved! I go rejoicing in the thought that thy soul turns towards me to-night as mine yearns toward thee.

Wednesday night, Nov. 4th

I come to bid you good-night for the last time in Leamington, I hope, dear Clay! I hope we shall all go to London to-morrow, but we shall not know till the morning's mail comes. I have just finished letters to Mary Richardson and Joseph which I shall send tomorrow.[9] This I shall keep until I get to London and add some there.

To-day has been rainy, rainy, rainy. We have not been out for four days! I believe that no storm however hard shall keep me in doors another day.

But it is late, dearest! Good-night, and God bless you, my loved one![10]

But Thursday's news damped their ardor somewhat, as another letter came from Mrs. Sievers informing them that there had been a further misunderstanding over the dates, and now the lodgings would not be ready until the following week. Nothing could have been more annoying and frustrating but there was no time, and certainly at this stage of the proceedings, no inclination to try and obtain alternative accommodation, so teeth had to be gritted and another round of unpacking undertaken to enable them to drag through one more week of tedium before the attractions of London could be sampled. The disappointment appears to have been so acute that it even prevented Ada from adding to her letter to Clay that day, but Nathaniel wrote off to Ticknor:

10 Lansdowne Circus,
Leamington, Novr 5th 1857

Dear Ticknor,
Yours of October 21st, (I think) enclosing the letter of credit, was received a day or two ago.[11] I have not yet needed the credit, and am in hopes not to have to use it for some time to come; but the continued illness of Mr. Wilding has thus far prevented me from understanding precisely how the balance stands between myself and the Treasury Department. I had a narrow escape from being involved in a serious embarrassment by the stoppage of the Liverpool Burrough [sic] Bank; having drawn out funds to a large amount (owing to a rumor that had reached me) only a short time previously.[12] What a bother it is to have any money to take care of!

We are going to London early next week; and I suppose we shall have to remain there at least a fortnight, and perhaps more, before it will be possible for me to leave England. I expected to have been in Rome before this date, but should be well enough contented to be in London, if this wet autumnal weather were not so unfavorable to Mrs. Hawthorne's health. She continues pretty well, however, and I hope will not suffer seriously from the delay.

I understand that Mr. Alcott (of whom I bought the Wayside) has bought a piece of land adjacent to mine, and two old houses on it. I remember the situation as a very pretty one; and I do not doubt that those two old houses might be converted into a domicile that would just suit me. If he should swamp himself by his expenditures on this place, I should be very glad to take it off his hands; and it seems to me highly probable (judging from the character of the man) that he will ultimately be glad to have me do so. The matter may be ripe by the time we get back to America; but I should feel much more inclined to come home if I had the prospect of a more convenient home to come to. You would oblige me by having an eye to this.[13]

As regards the announcement of a book, I am not quite ready for it. If I could be perfectly quiet for a few months, I have no doubt that something would result, but I shall have so much to see, while I remain in Europe, that I think I must confine myself to keeping a Journal. Unless I return home next summer, however, I shall make a serious effort to produce something.[14]

I heard from Bennoch a few days ago, but have not seen him this long while. The commercial men seem to be in almost as much trouble here as on your side of the water. Good bye.

Your friend
Nath[l] Hawthorne.

You had better direct to me at the Consulate until further notice.[15]

Perhaps it was the bad news from London that prevented Ada from adding to her letter to Clay for two whole days:

Friday, Nov. 6th

Again I resume my letter in Leamington, though I thought to have been in London before this time. Mr. Hawthorne had a letter from the woman in whose house he had engaged lodgings, saying that she would be ready to receive us on next Tuesday, she having mistaken with regard to the time which Mr. Hawthorne mentioned as the date of our departure from Leamington, and cannot have the house ready until next week. So we are forced to unpack again, and submit to the necessity that keeps us here a week longer than we had expected to stay.

The weather has been most disagreeable all this week. I can easily imagine how people are forced to live by gas-light all day in some of the streets of London and Liverpool, during this season. It grows dark even here at about four o'clock in some of these days, that is so dark that I will not allow the children to study without candles.

In England they use candles altogether, except where they have gas. I dislike them exceedingly.

But in a little while I shall have to take this letter to the office, that it may go in tomorrow's steamer, from Liverpool, and it seems as though I had written scarcely anything. I have not begun to answer yours, but I never can do that, you know.

I must write one thing before I go on with my letter. Since I have been in England I believe I have several times (I <u>know</u> I have once) left the post-mistress to put the stamps on my letters. It was careless, and perhaps she neglected to do it. I beg your pardon, if so, and will take care to attend to it in future myself. I have omitted to write "per steamer" on them, too. I observe that Mr. Hawthorne always does it; so perhaps it is necessary, and my other letters have gone by sailing vessels and been consequently delayed. I will be sure to write it in future.

You ask my forgiveness for a very heinous sin truly, dear Clay! I <u>do</u> remember the little incident now, but I assure you that it was long ago forgotten, and never caused me anything but a momentary pang of regret that you were unwilling for me to read it. I never regarded it in the light in which you seem to, for a moment. <u>Dear</u> Clay! Do you think I can ever <u>forgive you</u> anything?

I thank you my dearest one! for telling me about your intentions with regard to Harvard,—for recognizing my "<u>right to know</u>" anything that so concerns you as this does. If you decide to do this, dearest, promise me not to feel anxious—over-anxious—about the result. I think, with you, that you ought not to rely on winning the prize, from the reasons which you mention.

As to your voice, my dear, dear Clay! what do you mean by talking of trying to change it? You know that I always admired it especially, and so does everybody else, I thought. What possesses you to wish to acquire a different tone from that which you always have had? Do you think that your voice is different from what it was when I first knew you, and are you trying to recover it? Or do you wish to cultivate an altogether new tone? I don't quite understand which of these two things you wish to do, and I really can't advise you, for I have perceived no change in it, and I love it better than any voice I ever heard in the world, my dear, dear Clay!

I am glad that you write me so much of Antioch. I am very, very much interested in all that concerns her future, as you well know.

Sometimes I almost long to rend the veil that conceals the future to know where you and I are to work in these coming years; but we must learn to be always patient, always hopeful. I am so almost always now. I am sure we shall find some good work to do. What matter it where? Yesterday was the anniversary of the Gun-powder plot, and last evening the Leamington people fired crackers and sent up rockets and made bon-fires, as they do all over England on this night. Fanny, Mrs. Hawthorne's house-keeper, says that they always observe it in this way, but not with as much ceremony as formerly.

Yesterday and to-day Una and I ventured forth into the smoke and dampness of Leamington; but we were glad to retreat soon, and had a game of ball in the house for exercise. Julian took some lessons in fencing and other exercise of a corporal, in Southport, and he drills us for a little while each day; we go through with similar exercises to those which we sometimes practised at Yellow Springs;— Una, Rose, Fanny and I, usually among great shoutings on the part of Julian and Rose. I never saw such an exuberance of spirits as these two children manifest. Una is naturally more inclined to sadness; but they are all very happy and I do not wonder that they are.

It is already beginning to grow dark, and I must write but a few moments longer, for this letter must go very soon.

Dear Clay, I wish I could ever write a letter that seemed to me an adequate expression of my love for you,—an adequate expression of myself,—I might say, for my whole being seems absorbed in this love for you, my dear, dear, Clay!

In two days more it will be precisely three months since the Ariel bore me away from thee.

Ah! when will I be with thee again?

I cannot tell in what month I shall be likely to return. It will depend greatly upon whether I return to Antioch or not. If I do, I shall hope to be at home in August. The Hawthornes will probably stay in Europe a year or two longer; but I must go home at the end of this year. I cannot think of staying away from thee more than one year, my dearest!

My own dear Clay! each day nearer and dearer than before, receive my poor greeting, believe ever in my constant and unwavering love, and in my deep, pure happiness in the consciousness of thy affection.

Thine own
Ada.[16]

The weather remained cold, damp, and miserable; there seemed nothing better to do than sit near the fires and read, learn, talk, and wait; but that was not to say that everyone was downhearted!

Leamington, Nov. 7th 1857

What a cheerful glow is in my heart, dearest Clay! as I draw my chair up to the table by the fire, and open my desk to commence a new letter to thee! More bright and warm is the glow in my heart kindled by thy dear love than is the blaze of this beautiful fire before me. Yet this fire is itself most lovely. I wish you could enjoy it, too. Next to the English ivy, which I so covet for our America, I most admire the English fires. They do not seem to use our ugly stoves at all, but everywhere there are grates in which they burn a kind of soft coal such as we never see in America, which blazes up so cheerfully and beautifully that it rejoices one's heart to behold it.

No fires are so beautiful except the old-fashioned wood-fires, such as we used to see at Judge Mill's[17] and Mr. Howell's.[18] I wonder if we shall ever go to see those good Howells again. I often think of them with quiet pleasure. Do you remember, dearest Clay! how very happy we were that afternoon in our Senior vacation when we rode to Selma to tell the Howells I could not go to see them that week? I think we never enjoyed a ride together so much as that.

Dear Clay! Dear Clay!

Mrs. Hawthorne and I lingered at the tea-table after the rest left it, to-night, and she talked to me a long, long time about Mr. Hawthorne. I never saw such perfect idealization of a husband as she manifests. It is a perfect delight to me to hear her talk of him, but I almost wonder that she can praise him so much to a third person. If I should attempt to utter all the praises of you with which my fond heart swells, I should feel almost as if I were talking of myself, so perfectly one do our natures now seem to be.

I am glad to know that Mr. H. likes me, as Mrs. H's conversation, this evening, proved. He is so excessively fastidious, so wonderfully shrinking and shy, and seems to have such a faculty for rendering himself utterly impervious to those around him when he chooses, that I hardly hoped at all that I should please him.

I never saw so exceedingly sensitive a person as he, at the same time that he is in perfect health. He seems to really suffer from contact with those who offend his taste in any way.[19]

In some respects he is altogether different from what I had imagined him. I had thought that he would be altogether wrapped up in his intellectual pursuits, with no interest in trifling matters; but, on the contrary, Mrs. Hawthorne says that he is a most excellent counsellor in all household matters. He seems interested in everything that is going on around us, and is wise and sensible on all subjects. I like especially his ideas of education, but more than anything else about him, I admire his perfect devotion to his lovely wife. This is, indeed, a beautiful union.

He is evidently desirous of writing a new book, and intends to do so if he can fix upon a subject. I shall be very glad if he does. Tell me, dear Clay! if you read any of his writings, what you think of his style. It seems to me very beautiful.

Una reads to me an hour, each evening, now, in Madame de Sevigné's correspondence (in French I mean, of course) and I am charmed with the grace and freedom of style of this remarkable woman. But she is eminently French in character, and you know that I can never thoroughly admire the French, always excepting M. Fezandie. What do you think (by the way) of the lines I sent you of M. Fezandie, in my last letter?

We have had another foggy day, although there has been no rain to-day. We ventured forth for a short walk, but it was exceedingly damp and chilly without. A whole week of this miserable weather! November comes in character, this year.

But I thank thee, dear Clay! that thy love has power to render me happiness quite independent of weather or other surroundings. I am sure of thy affection, at all times, and to this love I turn under all circumstances. Under its wing I take refuge when the storm comes, and I am safe and happy.

Good-night, dearly beloved! I feel thy presence, and bless thee for thy sustaining love. I am very happy, very happy through thee![20]

Sunday morning was slightly different from the past few days in that although it was still cold, wet, and miserable, it was not actually raining. But whatever the weather, Ada was in full flow again and continued the letter to Clay before any plans were made as to what should be done during the day:

Sunday morning, Nov. 8th.

Dear Clay! again I come to thee, on our sacred day, to vainly attempt an expression of the joy that pervades my being at the thought of thee.

Dost thou know that it is just three months to-day since I left thee in New York? Three times three months more must pass before I can hope to be blessed by thy dear presence again.

After I had finished writing, last evening, I went in to bid Mrs. Hawthorne good-night, and as Mr. H. had just gone up stairs, I sat down and talked with her a while, and told her the story of "Baskerville". Mrs. Mann had written to her of "it"—"the great it", as we used to say,—and she told me, after I had finished the story, that she had long been hoping I should feel moved to tell her of you. How I wish you could know Mrs. Hawthorne! She has not a beautiful face by any means,—not so pleasing a face as Mrs. Mann's except for the exceeding beauty and sweetness of her smile which I think is remarkable, such a world of love is expressed in it, such a depth of tenderness! She looks more like Miss Peabody than like Mrs. Mann and resembles her more in character, I think. I believe that she comes nearer to my ideal of a truly amiable, cultivated, womanly woman than any other person I ever knew. I have as yet observed no fault in her, and am almost convinced that she is utterly without fault. If she were only in good health she would be able to do much more good in the world than she now does, for she is very talented and accomplished; but she now makes a perfect heaven of her home, and sheds peace and joy around her as she moves. Ah! thus to be able to adorn and bless a home for thee, dear Clay! What hope so sweet, what ambition so powerful over my soul? I welcome the long years of toil that are to intervene between the present year and the realization of such anticipations of domestic bliss. Such hopes can sweeten labors and trials however severe.

Does the picture look as bright to thee as to me, dear Clay?

Ah, my beloved! These dreams will all be realized, some day. We shall not see our bright visions fade away beyond our grasp. It cannot be.

Somewhere and sometime we shall make for ourselves a happy home, dearest. Are you not sure of it?

We have another foggy day. And I imagine that you are having bright beautiful autumn weather; at least, I hope so, and that you can wander in the woods to-day, with your old, free, elastic step.

How glad I am to know that you have grown so much stronger since you have been resting at home! I, too, have gained much in health and strength since I left you.

I hope I shall never present myself to you in such a physical condition as I was in when I left Yellow Springs.

Whatever else I do I mean to take care of my health henceforth, remembering always that I belong to you and not to myself.

It is very tantalizing to think that there is probably a letter for me from you and perhaps from home, in Paris. As soon as we arrive in London I shall send for them.

Until then I can well content myself with this dear, dear letter that came last Monday.[21]

Although there wasn't too much of it in evidence, it was decided that some fresh air must be sought despite the unpleasant conditions, so Nathaniel, Una, Julian, and Ada wended their way along the familiar road to Whitnash village. Perhaps it was the effect of the weather combined with the irritating delays in their departure from Leamington that made this last visit to Whitnash a rather depressing experience for Nathaniel and that conjured in his mind the seemingly claustrophobic atmosphere of a centuries-old settlement such as this small village, with apparently little disturbing the course of the years beyond the essential events of birth and death:

All this month, we have had genuine, English November weather; much of it profusely rainy, and the rest overcast and foggy, making it a desperate matter to venture out for a walk. Since my last record—describing a visit to Warwick—I have taken only a few strolls up and down the Parade, or in the immediate neighborhood of the town. [This] afternoon, being merely damp, chill, and foggy, I made a little longer stretch of my tether, and walked to Whitnash Church, with Miss Shepard, Una, and Julian. This is one of the small, old churches of the vicinity, and stands in the midst of a village that retains as much of its primitive aspect as any one that I have seen; the dwellings being mostly the old, timber and plaister [sic] cottages and farm-houses, with thatched roofs; and though there are a few new brick buildings, the air of antiquity prevails. In front of the church tower is a small, rude and irregular space, in the midst of which grows a very ancient tree, with a huge, hollow trunk, and a still verdant head of foliage growing out of its mutilated decay. I should not wonder if this tree were many centuries old, and a contemporary of the of the [sic] gray, Norman tower before which it has flourished and decayed; perhaps even older than that. The old, rustic dwellings of the village stand about the church; and the churchyard with its graves is especially central and contiguous to the living village; so that the old familiar forms and faces have had but a little way to go in order to lie down in their last sleep; and there they rest, close to their own thresholds, with their children and successors all about them, chatting, laughing, and doing business within hearing of their gravestones. It makes death strangely familiar, and brings the centuries together in a lump. But methinks it must be weary, weary, weary, this rusty, unchangeable village-life, where men grow up, grow old, and die, in their fathers' dwellings, and are buried in their grandsires' very graves, the old skulls, and cross-bones being thrown out to make room for them, and shovelled in on the tops of their coffins. Such a village must, in former times, have been a stagnant pool, and may be little better even now, when the rush of the main current of life has probably created a little movement. We went a few paces into the churchyard, and heard the indistinct, dull drone of the parson within the church, but thought it not best to enter the church. Passing through the village, we paused to look at a venerable farm-house—spacious and dignified enough, indeed, to have been a manor-house—with projecting bay-windows, an old, square portal, a lawn, shadowy with great trees, and an aspect of ancient peace diffused all around. It was a timber and plaster house, the timber-frame marked out in black on the white plaster, and, if I mistake not, a thatched roof, though the house was two stories high and very extensive. These thatched roofs are very beautiful, when time has made them verdant; it makes the house seem to be a part of Nature, and, so far as man has anything to do with it, as simple as a nest.[22]

When they got home from their walk, it wasn't long before Ada was at her writing desk once more, writing for the last time in Leamington, to her sister:

Leamington, Nov. 8th, 1857

Dear Kate,
It is about four o'clock in the afternoon, yet it is already growing so dark that we shall have to ring for candles in a moment. I feel very sorry to see the days growing so short, especially since we use candles altogether here, and I dislike them exceedingly.
Una, Mr. Hawthorne, Julian and I have just returned from a long walk, which we bravely determined to take, in spite of the gloomy weather. For the whole week past, we have only been out two or three times, and then but for a few moments, so rainy and cloudy has it been all the time.
We had expected to go to London last Wednesday, but the woman at whose house Mr. H. had engaged lodgings unfortunately made a mistake about the time when we wished to go, and just as we were finishing our preparations for departure, Mr. H. received a letter saying that she could not take us into her house until next Tuesday. So we were forced to content ourselves in Leamington about a week longer. We shall probably go on Tuesday morning, if nothing else happens to delay.
It will be very nice to be in London for a while, if we can only have a little pleasant weather; but this is just the season for the famous London fogs to be in their perfection, I suppose. We went, this afternoon, to Whitnash, a quaint little village about a mile and a half distant. It has a very old church before which stands a venerable tree entirely hollow throughout its trunk, yet with quite a wealth of foliage still. Mr. Hawthorne thought that the tree must be five or six centuries old. The houses in the village were apparently very old. There was an old manor-house which we admired very much for its picturesqueness. It had a gabled roof and a beautiful little porch at one end, while at the other, was a bay-window with oaken panels. The garden was most tastefully laid out and neatly kept, and the luxuriant ivy which so glorifies every cottage and wall and hedge in England, was clambering up its sides, and soon will cover them, I doubt not. The house looked as if it were the home of some interesting family who took a good deal of comfort in a quiet way.[23]
But most of the houses in this little village were very humble and small. They had thatched roofs many of which were covered with bright green moss.
I suppose most of the trees in America have lost their foliage before this time, but there are many elms here which retain a goodly share of their leaves, with only here and there a tinge of yellow amidst the bright green.
It seems strange to see so many flowers still in perfection here. This afternoon we saw an abundance of the most beautiful chrysanthemums, crimson, pink, yellow, purple and white. I never saw any in such perfection as those which grow here. I suppose you may have chrysanthemums, at home now, but you certainly haven't roses, heliotropes, geraniums, fuschias, etc, out of doors, as they have

here. Laurustinus too, is quite abundant and the fuschias are perfectly splendid, and abound almost everywhere.

I wish you could look in upon us at the moment and see how comfortably we all are established around the table in the school-room. Let me see if I can describe the scene. First there is the fire, the most attractive object in the room, perhaps. You do not know how beautiful these English fires are. They eschew our ugly stoves, and have instead, grates piled with a nice kind of coal such as we never see in America, with a beautiful, cheerful blaze that warms one's very heart. On the mantelpiece stands a quaint old tea-pot and a sugar bowl with a single cup and saucer, valuable relics, doubtless, in the eyes of Mrs. Maloney, the proprietor of the lodging-house in which we are staying.

Above the mantel is an exceedingly ugly portrait of an exceedingly ugly man who holds a very dingy looking letter in his hand, said letter having a very red seal. Opposite this picture hangs one not less ugly purporting to be a likeness of the Duke of Wellington, but I am sure that the Duke (if some of the engravings I have seen of him are correct) would resent the imputation of such a forehead and such a nose as this picture presents to view, not to speak of the utterly lugubrious expression of the whole countenance.

Under this portrait stands a side-board, on which are ranged rows of school books. Then there is a little sofa, and a small stand in the room, and these, with the chairs and the large central table around which we sit completes the equipment of the room which at present serves us for a school-room.

Around this table sits an interesting group,—first little Rose, for a few moments quiet enough to sit still, (a rare occurrence with her, for usually she is dancing and flitting about the live-long day) who is pretending to write a letter although she is not yet sufficiently accomplished to be able to write. She prints beautifully. Next her is Fanny. But you do not know who Fanny is, and so I must stop to explain. When Rose was an infant Mrs. Hawthorne happened to find this Fanny at the time that she desired a nursery-maid for the little Rose, so she came as nurse and stayed a year or two in that capacity; and she proved herself so invaluable an assistant to the family in general, that Mrs. Hawthorne keeps her still, although in a different capacity now. She dresses Rose, sews, buys all the provisions and acts the part of housekeeper general, lady's maid, and I know not what else. She is quite a wonder—this Fanny. Her father was a very rich man, but lost his property by a series of misfortunes, and Fanny gave him the little competency which a relative had bequeathed to her, and determined to earn her own living. Having never been educated with reference to teaching, she thought she was not prepared to attempt that, and so sought a situation as nursery-maid. She is now perfectly devoted to Mrs. Hawthorne, and would be most happy to remain with her forever, I believe.

Next Rose then, sits this Fanny, a person of most unprepossessing exterior, of perhaps thirty years old; yet very gentle and lady-like in her manners and a great favorite with the children. She is not treated at all like a servant, except that she does not have her meals with us.[24]

On my right sits Una writing in her journal which she faithfully keeps and in which she records all the visits she makes, giving very good descriptions of what she sees, etc, and she allows me to read in it sometimes. You would think she was a young lady of seventeen rather than a child of thirteen, could you see her. She is perhaps, two or three inches shorter than I, with long, abundant hair of light auburn. I remember that when I saw her in West Newton, five years ago,[25] it was of bright red, as is Rose's now. Do not imagine that this colored hair which is usually so ugly, makes Rose's little face unattractive. On the contrary she is extremely pretty and interesting looking, and the red hair does not trouble me a bit. It will be modified in time, doubtless, as is Una's now. Una has a high, beautiful forehead and too small features to be called handsome; but there is such a pure, sweet expression in her whole face that I admire it very much. Her form is very fine and she is exceedingly graceful.

On my left sits Master Julian Hawthorne, perhaps the most interesting object in the group, although as yet quite an undeveloped character in most respects. He has a splendid head, with great, wide, white brow and flashing brown eyes, almost the most beautiful I ever saw. His hair too is of a beautiful chestnut. In his whole appearance he is as unlike his two sisters as can be imagined. Indeed, I never saw three children more unlike each other than these three, and that makes them the more interesting. Just now Julian is reading a translation of Tasso's "Jerusalem Delivered." He is eleven years old only. I think there are few boys of eleven who would care to read Tasso, [she could be right!] but he is perfectly absorbed in it at this moment, and evidently hasn't an idea of what is going on around him.

Mr. and Mrs. Hawthorne are in the parlor, sitting by the fire-light, I suppose. We retreated into this room with Fanny, that we might go on with our writing and reading before ten, as there are candles here.

But here comes the "respectable sewing woman" to set the table (for our school-room is also our dining room) and we must retreat from these quarters.[26]

That evening was spent quietly round the fire and the next day there wasn't much that could be done, as all their baggage was removed to the railway (and that due to an unfortunate accident wasn't actually delivered to them at their London lodgings until Wednesday); even though the weather continued cold and cheerless they all got out of the house for a little constitutional, but all that they really wanted to do, of course, was leave:

Monday morning Nov. 9th

Last evening I stayed in the parlor until after ten, hearing Mrs. Hawthorne read an entertaining new book, "Tom Browne's [sic] School Days"[27] instead of finishing my letters home, as I had intended; so I must finish them this morning.

Our trunks are to go this afternoon and I shall have to pack my writing desk before long, as it goes at the bottom, so I will finish writing as speedily as may be.

I had hoped we should have one more pleasant day in Leamington; but no. To-day is as foggy as ever. Una and I have been out to take a little walk, and Mrs. Hawthorne has been out in a "bath chair" as they call the little carriages which they have here for invalids to ride out in, men drawing them, just as we draw little children in small wagons. Mrs. Hawthorne's cough still troubles her so much that she cannot go out when it is so damp, unless she rides. Yet Leamington air is much better for her than London atmosphere, and I fear she will be injured by staying there. I hope we shall not stay long.

It is very tantalizing to think that quite probably there is a letter from home for me in Paris. I shall send to M. Fezandie to forward any that he may have to London, if we stay there long enough to make it an object.

I hope you are all well at home. It seems an age since I have heard from you. What does Charlie write? Do beg, beseech and implore him to come home next summer if not before. I can't bear to think of not seeing him when I come home.

Give much love to Grandfather and Grandmother when you see them. I shall write to them on Grandfather's birthday, next Thursday.

Give my love to Otis and Emily and a kiss to the beautiful little Horace. How I wish I could see him!

                                        Very affectionately your sister,
                                        Ada

P.S. I wish I knew when you are to have Thanksgiving this year. The time is quite near at hand, I suppose. We shall find out from the American papers, though, of course, and the Hawthornes will observe it with their customary turkey and plum-pudding. They always have since they have been away from home. But how much I shall think of you all! I hope you will enjoy it very, very much.[28]

Tuesday dawned as miserably as any other during the past fortnight, but that could be ignored, as they all made themselves ready to leave in time to catch the 10:05 train to London, no doubt imagining that they were seeing the last of Leamington.

We have been thinking and negotiating about taking lodgings in London, this some time past; and this morning we left Leamington at ten o'clock of a dreary day, with little mists almost amounting to rain; a very dismal day as the whole autumn has brought in its train. I rode in a second-class carriage with Julian, and Mamma, Miss Shepard, Una and Rosebud [and, presumably, Fanny] in a first-class one; and we reached London with no other mis-adventure than that of leaving the great bulk of our luggage behind us in Leamington; the van, which we hired to take it to the railway station, having broken down under its prodigious weight, in the middle of the street. It will probably make its appearance tomorrow. . . .[29]

Nathaniel was obviously in a difficult mood that day. No doubt the trouble with their luggage upset him, but why should he have gone in the second-class carriage with Julian? There seemed little point in making the small saving in cost that was involved especially, as Ada told Clay later, it meant their having had to spend four hours on "straight-backed, hard, board set-tees." And when they arrived at their new lodgings in Russell Street (despite finding them "without any great difficulty, they being in close vicinity to the British Museum") he was disappointed to find that "that is the greatest advantage we thus far find in them"; Ada told Clay that ". . . we found ourselves here in lodgings rather less comfortable than ours at Leamington, and less so than the Hawthornes had expected, from the account of the friend who engaged them for them." Almost immediately, Nathaniel "felt restless and uncomfortable, and soon strolled forth, without any definite object" and then lost his bearings on the way back to Russell Street!

So the family's second stay in Leamington Spa came to end, to a certain extent in a bit of a shambles, what with the poor weather over the past fortnight that had curtailed their activities; the continuing exasperation with regard to the uncompleted business of Nathaniel's accounts at the consulate and the consequent further delay that was bound to occur before he felt ready to leave for the Continent; the annoyance caused by the accident with the luggage; the disappointment concerning the unexpectedly lower standard of the lodgings in London; and not least, the continuing poor health of Sophia that everyone was relying on to improve when they exchanged the fogs of autumnal England for the, hopefully, clearer air of France and Italy. Not that it would have been considered to be a particularly happy event in itself, to be leaving Leamington, but every member of the family would have considered it to be an extraordinary (and unthinkable) idea if it had been suggested that there could be any set of circumstances that would have resulted in them returning to the spa sometime in the future!

7

An Intermission (2)

The Hawthornes left Leamington with the expectation that the immediate future would involve them in an exciting and rewarding period of their lives, being able to live among the almost inexhaustible antiquities and stimulating artistic treasures that were readily available for public inspection in towns and cities on the Continent that until then had only been familiar to them in books. Possibly each one of the party who left for London on 10 November had a different idea of what lay ahead and of what they hoped to gain from the Continental trip and of how long they were to be traveling before they finally left for America and home in Concord. Nathaniel, it could be suggested, did not know what he wanted to do; perhaps he would have preferred to have done nothing except sit and think and wait for the literary Muse to stir his imagination with the subject of a new book. Given his need for relaxation after the rigors of office, if he had been on his own, it is likely that he would have stayed in England where he had come to appreciate so many things about the English way of life that had overcome his initial desire to return immediately to his homeland. Sophia undoubtedly looked forward without any qualms to life in Europe, being quite prepared to put up with the difficulties that may have lain ahead in order that she and the family could take full advantage of this once-in-a-lifetime opportunity to explore what the Old World had to offer them. Una and Julian, perhaps, were simply excited by the sheer adventure of it all, seeing new lands, new people, new horizons. Little Rose, poor little Rose, was happy just to tag along. Ada had already tasted some of the delights of Paris, and while her appreciation of the worth of the Continental visit was circumscribed in some ways by the professional aspect of her post as governess to the children, she was, out of all of them, the one setting off with a definite goal in sight—that of sufficiently improving her knowledge of French and Italian (at least) before returning to America in less than a year's time to a job and marriage. Perhaps for all of them, the next two years turned out to be not what they had expected nor what they would have wanted, sowing the seeds of future disenchantment and despair.

Right from the start, after leaving Leamington, their plans to leave England were subjected to further delay. Nathaniel was not able to complete the forwarding of his final accounts to the secretary of state in Washington until the last day of the year. The time was spent in visiting the usual showplaces of London; meeting one or two acquaintances (Bennoch especially, battling against the misfortunes brought about by his firm's recent bankruptcy); and warding off illness in one form or another. Sophia was prostrated for some time due to the combined effects of the winter's atmosphere and London's fogs, the children and Fanny caught measles, and even Nathaniel felt groggy at times with a heavy cold.

However, on 5 January, they left London Bridge station for Paris (but without Fanny, whose father had been drowned in an accident just before Christmas and she had had to return to her stepmother's side in Yorkshire) and on 22 January had settled in an apartment ("2nd Piano") at No. 37 via Porta Pinciana in Rome, intending to remain there for the next four months. The weather remained bitterly cold and they were all, at one time or another, laid low with various ailments, Nathaniel taking it as a personal affront that his normal good health had succumbed to a continual cold and fever. But despite illness, every day was spent by at least one member of the party in walking round the seemingly innumerable cathedrals, churches, museums, and art galleries.

Only two months had passed before Nathaniel was reaching the end of his tether and it was decided that they would leave Rome, spend the summer in Florence, and return to the capital for the winter months. It was undoubtedly a low point (especially for him) and things, in some ways, could only get better (even in Rome), which they did as the weather became more summerlike. The continual visits to the art galleries, museums, and churches continued on a daily basis, presumably while the children were taking their lessons with Ada, although there is little, if any, reference to this in either journals or diaries. As Nathaniel admitted, Sophia was indefatigable in her pursuit of cultural interest, and while he dutifully followed her every step and, on occasions, pursued a lone path around the various attractions of the city, he admitted (to his journal) that he very soon became bored by the multitude of things to see, and that culture left him cold except in the case of a small number of paintings, sculptures, and buildings that he liked to look at by himself and to reflect on the reasons for his appreciation of them (usually they were not those artifacts that the rest of the world hailed as masterpieces of their genre).

Apart from sightseeing, most days found the Hawthornes in the company of some of the numerous other "foreigners" who were living in Rome, travelers and sightseers like themselves, or other writers, artists, and sculptors who had made their homes in the Eternal City for one reason or another. Many of them were fellow Americans, and compared with the confined social activities that the family had observed in England, their life now was a constant succession of visits to the homes and studios of acquaintances and artists, receiving visits from them in turn at their own lodgings and, in general, becoming part of, and enjoying, the social whirl that made up the expatriate community's life in the city.

Despite all these distractions, Nathaniel had started writing again, sketching the outlines of a romance that had been at the back of his mind ever since he had arrived in England. Despite his experiences at the consulate of Americans who had come to the Old Country with harebrained ideas as to the possibility of their being the beneficiaries of the estates of supposedly aristocratic forebears, he was very interested in tracing his own antecedents (the Hathornes of Bray, Berkshire), and had mapped out the basis of a plot involving the influences wielded through the succeeding (American) generations by the original (English) ancestors. What progress he had managed to make on the new manuscript[1] while in Rome was fatally interrupted by a couple of visits to the Capitol where, after looking at the pictures on display, he wandered into the sculpture gallery and immediately became interested in one particular statue, the faun of Praxiteles. He envisaged with increasing excitement that the faun could be made the subject of an interesting story: "It seems to me that a story, with all sorts of fun and pathos in it, might be contrived on the idea of their [the race of fauns] species having become intermingled with the human race . . . and the moral instincts and intellectual characteristics of the faun might be most picturesquely brought out, without detriment to the human interest of the story. Fancy this combination in the person of a young lady!"[2] Time passed and of all the party it was, perhaps, Nathaniel who alone was not enjoying himself or, rather, felt that he was wasting his time in a seemingly endless round of gawping at artistic treasures and unnecessary socializing. He continued to add to the Anglo-American manuscript but after May lost interest in it and concentrated on the new ideas concerning the faun.

Leaving Rome in the last week of May, the family took over the ground-floor apartment of a large house in Florence, Casa del Bello, and once again began a round of sightseeing, entertaining, and being entertained in turn by many of the local, foreign celebrities, among whom were Robert and Elizabeth Browning, the sculptor Hiram Powers, the poet Isabella Blagden, and the novelist Thomas Trollope and his mother. Life in Florence was pleasant and undemanding, and though the weather was good the atmosphere was found to be too oppressive in the town, so it was decided to move in August to another house, Villa Montauto, outside and above the town. No doubt as a result of the influence of this peace, tranquillity, and privacy, and the atmosphere of the strange old house in which they were staying, it wasn't long before Nathaniel was concentrating on expanding his ideas for the new romance, although, as he intimated to both Ticknor and Fields, he found the whole Italian atmosphere inimical to literary endeavor.

On 1 October the family departed for Siena and arrived back in Rome on 16 October. The summer had been pleasant enough and not unproductive for Nathaniel from the point of view of work, but whatever delights the city had to offer, their stay in Rome was to be marred by continual ill health; at one time it appeared that both Una and Ada were at death's door but they recovered, though it is probable that both Una and her father's constitutions remained scarred by the events of this winter till their deaths some years later. The sirocco was blowing at the time of their arrival and it affected them all with its hot and moist oppression. Nathaniel was able to continue with his projected romance but only in fits and starts, his concentration being sorely affected by illness and worry concerning the rest of the family. The one member who suffered least of all in the general malaise was Julian, and although she was ill herself, on occasions Sophia showed surprising reserves of stamina while nursing Una and Ada through their dreadful illness. The months passed, with Nathaniel scribbling fitfully at the romance, with the doctor frequently being called to look at one or other of the party who had collapsed with the Roman Fever (malaria), and, in the interim, with visits being made to the (now) familiar sights of the city; in the circumstances, there was also a surprising amount of social contact with fellow artists of one sort or another, all of whom gave unstinting help, where needed, to the family in its time of distress. There hardly seemed to be the time or enthusiasm to write letters, and it was not until February and March of the new year that Nathaniel thought fit to let Fields and Ticknor know of their harrowing experiences and to tell them that they would be returning to England in the summer. It was planned that they would then leave for America in July.

By late May all members of the party felt fit enough to travel. Setting out from Rome on 25 May, traveling by way of Civita Vecchia, Leghorn, Marseilles, Avignon, Valence, Lyons, Geneva, and Macon, they arrived in Paris on 16 June. Nathaniel wrote to Bennoch, asking him to arrange lodgings for them in London (specifying that they did not want to go back to Great Russell Street!) from either next Wednesday or Thursday as, in the meantime, they had to travel via Le Havre in order to say good-bye to Ada and to put her on a steamer back to America. Despite it undoubtedly being an emotional occasion, especially for the children, Nathaniel made no comment in his journal or diary about his feelings either for her or about her leaving the family, merely noting the details of the departure and the fact that he gave her the money for the passage to America. It seems likely that Nathaniel and (particularly) Sophia's previous appreciation of Ada's character had markedly deteriorated as a result of Ada having been subjected to a sexual attack by Dr. Franco, the physician who had attended both her and Una when they were desperately ill in Rome (and who Sophia had come to think the world of). Although the attack had not occurred as a result of encouragement on Ada's part (she described it in detail to Clay), it seems unlikely that she was able, or felt it necessary, to keep the matter a secret from Nathaniel and Sophia, and they may well have thought, uncharitably, the worse of her for being involved in such a sordid business, even though she was the innocent party. Staying overnight at Le Havre and Southampton on the way to London, the family arrived there on 24 June and were directed by Bennoch to No. 10 Golden Square where he had arranged that they should lodge preparatory to their return to America.

Perhaps it is unnecessary to reflect upon what the eighteen months in Europe had done for them. Certainly Nathaniel had spent a lot of money, but he had stressed in the past that he intended to live beyond his means on the Continent and to look to his pen to recompense him thereafter. He had found it not quite so cheap a place as he had anticipated but that hadn't resulted in any real control over expenditure.[3] Considerable expense must have been incurred, of course, over unforeseen medical bills. Nevertheless, money apart, and despite the various and inevitable discomforts attendant in traveling on the Continent, particularly with a large family and enormous amounts of luggage, and despite also the debilitating illnesses to which they had all fallen victim at one time or another, they had taken part in an experience that had benefited them in some ways and that, ultimately, proved to have made such a lasting impression that more than one member of the family returned to live and die in Europe. Una had written to her cousins the previous November that her "ideal of existence would be to live in Italy, in a house built and furnished after my own taste, often paying long visits to England, and sometimes to America, & pursue my studies and other occupations unmolested by mankind in general." Nathaniel, on the other hand, in the words of a recent biographer, as a result of the rigors of their experiences in Rome, "felt himself on the verge of death in multiple senses: the collapse of his customary defense against patricidal guilt and grief threatened a spiritual death brought on by the unburied corpse in himself that was still weirdly alive. Spiritual death was also threatened by his own sensuality, now no longer an expression of innocent boyishness but contaminated, like what he had projected into fallen women [in his books]. His own living death was all too similar to what Una suffered, comatose and delirious on the threshold separating youth from adulthood. . . . Sophia also recognized the analogy between Una's affliction and that of her husband, both rooted somehow in the poison of Rome. They both need a 'change of scene and diet and circumstances [she had written to Elizabeth]. . . . Mr. Hawthorne needs it almost as much as Una. He says he should die if he should . . . [remain in] Rome another winter. The malaria certainly disturbs him, though it is undeveloped.'"[4]

Almost immediately after their arrival in England, plans were changed. Sophia, for one, was in need of a complete rest, and possibly for that reason alone their departure for America was put back to 30 July. That, in turn, proved to be impossible as Wilding advised that there were no staterooms available on the steamer so a new departure date of 13 August was proposed. However, that fell through as well, as Fields was in London and he had managed (with his customary skill) to arrange a contract with Smith, Elder for the publication in England (thus securing the copyright) of Nathaniel's new (but far from complete) romance, for a sum of £600. The contract stipulated that the book had to be written in England and that it was to be published six days before the American edition came out. This meant that the return to America had to be postponed for an indefinite period as much work was necessary before the manuscript could be considered ready for publication.

So the berths for America were canceled, and after some sightseeing and socializing in London it was decided that somewhere quiet and without distractions was necessary in order that Nathaniel's full attention could be given to the task of completing the book. With the probability of their stay in England being prolonged for a period of some months, certainly over the coming winter, and with the necessity for assistance in the management of the household, everything was packed up once more and they all traveled north, where Sophia met with and reengaged Fanny. The next day they were off to look for some suitable lodgings, preferably in a place by the seaside to promote Sophia's health. Possibly on Fanny's recommendation they searched for lodgings in the Whitby and Lythe areas but found nothing satisfactory. Finally, on 22 July, they were able to settle at No. 120 High Street in Redcar on the Yorkshire coast as being their new home for the time being.

Nathaniel worked diligently at the manuscript every day, with varying degrees of success. He was not finding it as easy as he had first anticipated, although the circumstances in which he wrote were such that they afforded him few distractions: the children loved the seaside and the fresh air, he walked every day along the shoreline, but Sophia did not always appear to find the bracing atmosphere and climate too sympathetic. There was certainly little of cultural interest in the neighborhood to occupy her while Nathaniel ploughed his lonely furrow of writing and walking, and there was an almost total lack of visitors to see them in their seaside haven. So it was not too surprising that on receiving a letter from Fields, who at that time was on a tour of southern England and who wrote from Leamington asking what progress was being made with the book and suggesting that they meet,[5] Nathaniel's thoughts should once again turn toward Leamington as being a more suitable place in which he could finish off the manuscript and be assured of Sophia's well-being during the coming winter months.

By 10 September he was able to show Sophia what he considered to be the completed first half of the manuscript. There appear to be no letters extant that he addressed from Redcar during this period, though there was no lack of incoming mail. Even in these healthy surroundings not everyone in the family was free from illness, Nathaniel, Sophia, and Fanny being laid low at one time or another. One letter that arrived informed them that Horace Mann had died on 2 August and another that Ada had married her beloved Clay on 30 August. And then, with no warning as to the why and wherefore, on 5 October Nathaniel's diary recorded: "Fine morning. 10 before 9, Left Redcar (all of us) and came to Leamington, via Leeds."[6] Of course, it could not have been a decision taken without some discussion or a deal of preparation. In a letter to Bennoch he had asked for "advice about winter quarters," which would suggest that he had inquired about lodgings in London. A letter to her cousin Richard from Una stated that "We shall leave Redcar soon, but do not know where we shall establish ourselves next." So something must have persuaded them, amid the apparent indecision, to return to an area of which they had already had experience (though not during the winter months).[7] Whatever it was that precipitated the decision to move and that dictated the date of their removal from Redcar (they had been there just over ten weeks) it resulted in the now-familiar chore of repacking their belongings before the whole Hawthorne party took to the railroad once again and started on the seven-hour journey to Leamington Spa.

8

"An unfashionable part of" Leamington: October 1859

It was a case of being third time lucky with respect to the weather on this, the last visit to Leamington, as in contrast to those of 1855 and 1857 the rail journey from Redcar to the Spa was completed in fine and sunny conditions though Nathaniel, as he usually complained, probably found the seven hours on the train completely lacking in interest. Some communication must have taken place with Mrs. Maloney, the lady who had owned No. 10 Lansdowne Circus where the family had stayed in 1857, before they had left Redcar and possibly the information supplied by her had influenced the date of the departure from Redcar in the first place; whatever had taken place (and on this occasion there is no record to the effect that Fanny had been sent on the previous day to seek out a suitable lodging place) the good lady was there to meet them when they arrived at the Avenue Road station. As Nathaniel noted in his diary that evening, they "found Mrs Maloney at the station at Leamington, who came with us to our lodgings, No. 21, Bath-street."[1] It could hardly have been a coincidence that she was there at the station but the word "found" is rather a strange one in the circumstances.

Contrary to what can be read in one publication about the Hawthornes' life in England, Bath Street is still alive and fairly well, although as in the case of Lansdowne Crescent, there was a renumbering of houses late in the nineteenth century and the original No. 21 is the present No. 60, occupied by the Coventry Building Society. According to the *Warwickshire Directories* of 1850 and 1854, No. 21 Bath Street was (at least partly) occupied by Surcombe and Heard, confectioners, with an additional occupant in 1854 of the name of Frederick Hanon, a professor of music. The 1860 *Directory* lists no occupants. At some stage between 1854 and 1860, therefore, the confectioners left the premises and it appears to have become, at least in 1859, a lodging house as during that year *The Leamington Advertiser* details successively the names of a Mr., Mrs., and Miss Blunt; a Miss Wilson; a Mr. and Mrs. Whiting; a Mr. and Mrs. E. Noton; and a Mr. and Mrs. E. Sidgreaves as being occupants prior to the arrival of the Hawthornes. Moreover, in the 6 October edition of the *Advertiser*, Mrs. Maloney's name is listed as being the occupant, being joined by the Hawthornes' names in the

No. 60 (formerly No. 21) Bath Street. Photo by the author.

10 November edition (the same details appear in the 5 November edition of *The Royal Leamington Spa Courier*); in the 29 December and succeeding editions of the *Advertiser* the Hawthornes' names appear on their own, until their departure in March 1860. Thereafter, for the rest of that year there were a number of different occupants (but not Mrs. Maloney) and there were many weeks when the building would appear to have been unoccupied.

Although Mrs. Maloney's name appears in the local press as the occupant of No. 21 from 6 October, there is no reference in any of their correspondence, journals, or diaries to her having shared the accommodation with the Hawthornes while they were there. As was the case with No. 13 Lansdowne Crescent, there would have been fairly ample room for her to have done so, however, as the building is deceptively large despite its comparatively narrow frontage. The basement, which extends under the pavement of the street, has two large rooms with fireplaces (one certainly having been the kitchen) plus another rear area/room with a sink and accommodation for larders. The ground floor retains nothing of the original layout, having been altered several times over the years for commercial purposes, but it must have included, besides the entrance hall and stairwell, at least two rooms from the front to the rear of the building (one of them having been used by the Hawthornes as a dining room). On the first floor overlooking the street was a drawing room that extended the full width of the building, with side-opening casement windows that led onto a narrow strip of balcony that was guarded by wrought-iron railings (which are no longer in place); to the rear was a large bedroom (that was certainly occupied by Sophia and, presumably, Nathaniel). On the second floor, overlooking the street, was another big room, the same size as the drawing room beneath with a large tiled fireplace; to the rear was another good-size room. On a small landing at the rear of the building, between the second and third floors, was a very small room and on the third floor a further two rooms. There were, therefore, possibly five bedrooms at least to accommodate the family and Fanny and it can only be guessed at as to how they were allocated. It must be assumed that Sophia and Nathaniel shared one and that Una (who was now fifteen years old) had one on her own, as did Julian, presumably. Whatever the distribution, there would appear to have been ample room for them all and also for them to accommodate a weekend visitor at a later date, though the supposition that he stayed with them and not in a hotel cannot be proved in any way.

It cannot be confirmed either as to why they settled in these particular lodgings (as they took them sight unseen, it must be presumed that the price was right and that they were prepared to accept Mrs. Maloney's recommendation) or, more particularly, why they remained in them for so long, for as they found out immediately they arrived there the building was (and still is) situated within thirty yards of the railway bridge that took the lines across the junction of Bath, High, and Clemens Streets; so close is it, due to its alignment, that at the rear of the building the rooms on the first, second, and third floors are closer to the railway lines than those at the front and there must have been a fairly frequent rumble and roar of passing trains accompanied by devastating amounts of steam and soot. Such an atmosphere, even with the windows firmly closed, allied with the position of Bath Street being at the lowest part of the town (thus receiving any fogs and mists associated with the nearby river Leam), must have been very detrimental to Sophia's bronchial condition.

By the time they had got most things unpacked and distributed around the rooms of No. 21, deciding as to who should sleep where and, if there was time that day, making some arrangements with local traders, everyone would have been too tired to look around the town and to renew acquaintance with familiar sights. But next day it was business as usual, after Nathaniel had first written to Ticknor to bring him up-to-date with their present circumstances:

Leamington, Oct[r] 6th 59

Dear Ticknor,
I was very glad to receive your note of 20th Sept[r],[2] and a little ashamed of not having written for so long a time. But I am never a very good correspondent; but for nearly three months past, I have been constantly occupied with my book, which required more work to be done upon it than I supposed. I am now, I think, within a fortnight of finishing it. There will be three English volumes, or two of yours, each perhaps as big as the Seven Gables. Mrs. Hawthorne (the only person who has read it) speaks very much in its favour;[3] but I sometimes suspect that she has a partiality for the author. I have not yet decided upon the title.
Smith & Elder have signed an agreement to publish the book, and pay me £600 on the assignment of the copyright. It will, I suppose, certainly be ready for the press in the course of this month, (at furthest, by the end of it,) and these £600 will preclude the necessity of your remitting any money through the Barings. By-the-by, speaking of money matters, I should like to have some brief estimate of how much property I possess. If I find that I can prudently do it, I should be glad to spend some money before leaving England, in books and other matters.
I have heard nothing of Fields for some weeks past, but hope soon to hear of his return from the Continent. I do not intend to send the manuscript of the book to Smith & Elder till he comes back, as he has had the whole management of the business. No doubt, he will make arrangements about your having the sheets with a view to simultaneous publication.
We have been spending the summer, since the middle of July, at Redcar, a little watering-place on the shore of the German ocean. It was the most secluded spot I ever met with, and therefore very favorable to literary labor. We had not a single visitor or caller, while we were there. This suited Mrs. Hawthorne as well as myself; for she was quite worn out with her anxiety and watching, during Una's illness. Her health is now considerably improved; and Una herself is as plump and rosy as any English girl. We are all very well, considering what some of us have gone through.
You will see us, probably, by the end of June next. I must confess that I have outlived all feelings of home-sickness; but still there are some friends whom I shall be rejoiced to see again—and none more than yourself. I doubt whether I shall ever again be contented to live long in one place, after the constant changes of residence for nearly seven years past. I am much troubled about our house in Concord; it is not big enough for us, and is hardly worth repairing and enlarging.
I think we may probably spend the winter here in Leamington, as it is a very pleasant town, with many conveniences for transitory residents. You had better, however, continue to send your letters (when you write any, which I hope will be oftener than of late) through the Barings. I have only received one letter from you since we left Rome.
I write with a horrible pen, as you see, but, such as it is, it has served me to write my whole book with. Believe me

Most sincerely yours
Nath[l] Hawthorne[4]

6. Thursday. A fine day. Wrote a letter to Ticknor. At about 10 set out with Una, & walked to Warwick, by the old road, & home by the new. Got back at about 1.[5]

The walk with Una was probably taken after the children's morning lessons had been completed. No doubt they both stopped on the old bridge over the Avon outside Warwick and gazed at the Castle. It would be nice to presume that Una talked with her father about the new romance that was occupying so much of his time and that he, in turn, talked to her with a new appreciation of her interest in his work; during the recent months in Rome Una had fought strongly for her life in the face of her malarial illness and must have attained a maturity as a consequence, besides her intellectual gifts, that no doubt was recognized by her parents. She was now a young woman, no longer a child, and could well have provided stimulating opinions in any conversation about the romance and its development. Whatever the subject of their conversation on this occasion it is clear that they both considered her health to be good as they must have covered some five miles or so during the morning. Perhaps it was later in the day, after they had returned home, that Una completed a letter to her cousin Richard that had been started the previous month while in Redcar:

Redcar, Yorkshire
Sept [9th?] 1859

My dear Cousin Richard,
I quite despair of ever hearing from Aunt Lizzie in answer to the letters I perseveringly and dutifully write to her, in spite of her silence, & I have almost given up hoping to hear from you, for you have not answered a letter I wrote you a great while ago, but I am so desirous to hear how you all do in Salem that I will write once more, to beg you to write me at least a short letter.
    The last time I sent a letter to Aunt E. was by Gen. Pierce,[6] who was going to America and offered to take anything I wished to send. They sailed, I think, in the last part of July, so I should think she must have received it. This was from Whitby and I believe Papa had decided before I wrote it to stay all winter in England, because printing his book here will detain us till late in October, and after that it is not safe to cross the ocean. I am very impatient to get home, but there is no help for it. Another reason for our staying, which would be sufficient by itself, is that my mother's health is so very much broken by her long attention & anxiety about me, that we think the activity and excitement consequent upon going home after so many years abroad would be almost fatal to her and our physician says that she needs at least a year's perfect rest and quiet, and as we do not intend to leave England till June she will have nearly that.
    The history of our life since I last wrote is by no means complicated or particularly interesting. We found Whitby was a much more fashionable place than we wished to live in, and a still better reason for our departure was that we could not find suitable lodgings anywhere in or near it, so we left it on the twenty second of July, and as we heard that Redcar had a splendid beach and was a very healthy place, we concluded to try our fortunes here, and here you see we are established. The town consists of one street called High St, built on what was not long since sandbanks, and it is literally·and only a seaside place, with no other charms but

the blue German ocean and the broad hard sands, stretching uninterruptedly for ten miles, and as safe as is possible, there being no rocks. We find a great many pretty shells [*seawards?*] especially when the tide is low and a broad and long field of rock is uncovered, which is covered with all descriptions of sea plants and animals. It forms a crescent of a mile or two in extent and a formidable guard to the shore, which it would not be very safe to attack at most times, and boats are not infrequently wrecked on it.

We have a house about in the centre of High St on the side nearest the shore, so our drawing room which is at the back of the house commands a fine view of the sea, and my father's study and my bedroom the less delectable one of the street. My father writes from nine to three o'clock, and walks on the shore in the afternoon and sometimes after tea in the evening. There is a circulating library here, with some nice books in it, which I find great pleasure in reading. Within five miles of Redcar is the village and castle of Skelton, surrounded by the most lovely scenery, which Julian and I went to see mounted on donkies [*sic*] and it was quite refreshing to be among hills and woods once more after seeing no scenery for so long but sandbanks. In another direction is Kirkleatham which contains a very large hospital. Julian and I ride on horseback once a week which we enjoy very much. For amusements we have had two circuses and one cattle-show, which came off today, and I think must have been a fine one, for crowds of people have come from all parts to see it, and our usually quiet little town has been very lively all day. Unfortunately for the people's comfort there has been a tremendous wind all day, greatly to the inconvenience of ladies' crinolines and gentlemens' hats which have been flying about the streets continually, to the dismay of the disconsolate owners. But the visitors have shown a most praiseworthy perseverance & determination to improve their time, for in spite of the gale crowds are perambulating the shore, bathing and going out in pleasure boats which toss & tumble in a very unpleasurable manner.

I believe I have told you all our news and I hope you will write to me when you receive this. We shall leave Redcar soon but do not know where we shall establish ourselves next. You had better send letters either to the American Consulate, Liverpool or to the care of the Barings, London. Perhaps I shall add a postscript before sending this to tell you where we are going, but goodbye for the present,

Give my love to Aunt Lizzie
and believe me to be
Very sincerely your cousin
Una Hawthorne.

One month later, a postscript was added!

Leamington. October 6th. Dear cousin Richard, we arrived here last evening and shall probably remain all winter.[7]

Although the weather had deteriorated a little, Nathaniel continued his walks round the neighborhood and found time to send off a couple of letters.

Leamington
No. 21, Bath-street,
October 7th 1859

Dear Bennoch,
We came hither from Redcar, day before yesterday, and it is very agreeable to be so much nearer to you. If Fields has returned, tell him where we are. I shall

consider it not impossible that you may make a trip hitherward; and, at all events, I shall find it necessary to come to London, soon after my book is finished. It approaches the conclusion now—Heaven be praised.

Your friend
Nath[l] Hawthorne[8]

7. Friday. Wrote letters to G. S. Hillard[9] & to Bennoch. Walked a little about town. Rather dull weather.

It was not until the following Sunday that Nathaniel was able (or wanted?) to return once more to the manuscript:

8. Saturday. A dull overcast day. In the afternoon took a short walk.

9. Sunday. A dull morning. Notes from Bennoch & Fields.[10] Wrote till about 2. After dinner, walked with Julian in Jephson's Gardens, and afterwards on the outskirts of the town. Wrote a note to Fields.

21, Bath-street
Leamington, Oct[r] 10th, '59

Dear Fields,
The above is my present address, and probably will continue so for three months to come.
    As regards the Romance, it is almost finished, a great heap of manuscript being already accumulated, and only a few concluding chapters remaining behind. If hard pushed, I could have it ready for the press in a fortnight; but unless the publishers are in an hurry, I shall be somewhat longer about it. I have found far more work to do upon it than I anticipated.
    Mrs. Hawthorne has read it, and speaks of it very rapturously. If she liked the author less, I should feel much encouraged by her liking the Romance so much. I, likewise, (to confess the truth,) admire it exceedingly, at intervals, but am liable to cold fits, during which I think it the most infernal nonsense. This happens to be the case just at the present moment.
    You ask for the title. I have not yet fixed upon one. Here are some that have occurred to me; but neither of them exactly meets my idea. "Monte Beni; or the Faun. A Romance." "The Romance of a Faun." "The Faun of Monte Beni." "Monte Beni; a Romance." "Miriam; a Romance." "Hilda; a Romance." "Donatello; a Romance." "The Faun; a Romance." "Marble and Life/Man; a Romance." When you have read the work (which I especially wish you to do, before it goes to press) you will be able to select one of them, or imagine something better. There is an objection in my mind to an Italian name, though perhaps Monte Beni might do. Neither do I wish, if I can help it, to make the fantastic aspect of the book too prominent by putting the Faun into the title page.
    I presume you are going to stay on this side of the water till next spring or summer. We had better all go home together. I had a letter from poor old Ticknor, the other day, and answered it immediately. I long to see him, and shall be a little comforted in going home, by the prospect of it.
    Do not stay a great while in Paris.
    We are all very well, except that the Romance has worn me down a little. It is

not wholesome for me to write; but the bracing air of the German Ocean a little counteracted the bad effect, in the present instance.

With kindest regards to Mrs. Fields,

Your friend ever,
Nath¹ Hawthorne.[11]

10. Monday. A dull morning. Wrote till 3. After dinner, walked with Una. In the evening, Mr. Bennoch called. Spent the evening & took supper with us.[12]

There is nothing else that illuminates Bennoch's visit, or whether he stayed the night or put up in a local hotel. Julian kept a journal too (sporadically); his last entry had been made on 5 September. His handwriting was pretty atrocious but after a blank period of over a month the inspiration to take up the pen came upon him once more:

Leamington 11 of October 1859 Tuesday.

I suppose the first thing that I must do will be, to apologise for not having written during the last few remaining weeks of our stay at Redcar. But each day was very nearly the same so there would not have been much use in writing. But I will give a few prominent events.

In the first place I finished my boat. It was altogether much better than the [*former?*] one [which had been crushed], but it was not painted well at all. The masts and rigging were pretty well done, so the sails would furl and unfurl. It sailed very well too, and very fast indeed, but it leaned over to one side a little too much, perhaps. The topsail I found was not rightly arranged, and one of the flying jibs was not right. I took it to pieces for packing up, sometime before we left, so it is now only hull, not even the deck being on.

Una and I had several more rides on horseback and I had one ride alone. I liked my pony very much, so I was very sorry to leave it.

The weather was very nice the last few days and the woman said it would last a month she thought. But here it is not fine at all, and it is very damp. I think none of us feel as well as at the seaside.

There was a very curious penny show, which came to Redcar, to which Una and Fanny and Baby and I all went. It was pretty good considering the admission price. Then there was a cheap [. . . . ?] who went round and asked astoundingly cheap prices for his things.

When we left our house, the woman and her daughter Mary were both in tears.

We had a very tiresome ride to Leamington which took us all day, and as the days are very short we got there just before dark.

And now I will begin with Leamington. When we arrived here it was a fine day, and the first and last fine day we had, except now and then a few hours of sunshine. For the first few days I was not able to walk out, on account of a swelling on my foot, which made it impossible to walk on it, except on one side. But I had a poultice which cured it in two nights. I believe it was on Monday I first went out and I found everything the same as usual, except one or two new houses, which are building and have been built.

We have bought a battledore and shuttle cock. But the first shuttlecock was soon [*spoiled?*], so I got another, for which the woman asked threepence [*a pair?*], but gave it me for twopence. It is a very nice one indeed.

There are two most delightful little kittens here which we [*have?*] very often, one is gray with darker blotches and the other is white with [*yellowish?*] brownish blotches. The white one is not nearly so pretty as the other one.

I am getting on in my studies. I have finished the Fables of Æsop, and I shall now begin mythology. I am beginning Greek over again, because I do not remember what I had learnt.

I find nothing more to say so I shall leave off, and I am very tired so

[13]

The weather remained overcast and dull but Nathaniel and the family were now back again in their various routines. He wrote for the best part of the day, followed by walks around the locality, usually accompanied by Una or Julian, while the children attended to their lessons, superintended by Sophia with occasional assistance from Nathaniel.

11. Tuesday. Dull morning. Wrote till 3. Towards twilight, took a walk.

12. Wednesday. Rather pleasant morning. Wrote till 3. In the afternoon walked to the outskirts of Warwick, with Julian.

13. Thursday. Overcast morning. Wrote till 3, and again, after dinner, till about 5. A letter from Fields[14] now in Paris. After 5, took a walk along the Newbold road.[15]

It seems likely that in his letter (presumably in reply to Nathaniel's of 10 October) Fields took the opportunity of including his own suggestion as to a suitable title for the romance, "The Romance of Monte Beni," and also may well have intimated that it would be sensible for Nathaniel to include in the forthcoming publication a preface, not only because it had been a feature of some of his previous works but also because it had been some years since he had last come to the public's notice; he could jog their collective memory in this fashion. Such would appear to be the reasons why Nathaniel decided at this point, before he had completed the remainder of the book, to write a preface.

Julian was again sufficiently inspired to add to his journal:

September [*sic*] 13 Leamington Thursday, 1859

Yesterday I did my lessons as usual, except that I did only half and [*sic*] hour of Greek, instead of an hour and a half. That happened because Papa and I took a walk to Warwick or thereabouts. We met a great many people coming to Leamington. I suppose that there had been a fair or something of the sort. It was a very fine evening and a very fine moon.

I painted some ships, or rather [*drew?*] one in my book, and another on a rough piece of drawing paper. The paper was rough and thick and just the kind that artists use. The second was a good deal better than the first. Today I painted another which is pretty good. Today also I [. . . . ?] over the battledores with [..*paint?*]. These are better than the ones before. The last two or three days have been pretty fine, the sun shining a good deal.[16]

14. Friday. A rainy morning. Wrote till 3—the Preface of my book. It is not yet finished by 60 or 70 pages. About 5 °clock, walked with Julian along Tachbrook road, & to Whitnash village

15. Saturday. An overcast, but not unpleasant morning. Looked over manuscript of Romance till 3. After dinner, walked with Julian to Warwick by old road, & home by the other.[17]

PREFACE

It is now seven or eight years (so many, at all events, that I cannot precisely remember the epoch) since the Author of this Romance last appeared before the Public. It had grown to be a custom with him, to introduce each of his humble publications with a familiar kind of Preface, addressed nominally to the Public at large, but really to a character with whom he felt entitled to use far greater freedom. He meant it for that one congenial friend—more comprehensive of his purposes, more appreciative of his success, more indulgent of his short-comings, and, in all respects, closer and kinder than a brother—that all-sympathizing critic, in short, whom an author never actually meets, but to whom he implicitly makes his appeal, whenever he is conscious of having done his best.

The antique fashion of Prefaces recognized this genial personage as the 'Kind Reader,' the 'Gentle Reader,' the 'Beloved,' the 'Indulgent,' or, at coldest, the 'Honoured Reader,' to whom the prim old author was wont to make his preliminary explanations and apologies, with the certainty that they would be favourably received. I never personally encountered, nor corresponded through the Post, with this Representative Essence of all delightful and desirable qualities which a Reader can possess. But, fortunately for myself, I never therefore concluded him to be merely a mythic character. I had always a sturdy faith in his actual existence, and wrote for him, year after year, during which the great Eye of the Public (as well it might) almost utterly overlooked my small productions.

Unquestionably, this Gentle, Kind, Benevolent, Indulgent, and most Beloved and Honoured Reader, did once exist for me, and (in spite of the infinite chances against a letter's reaching its destination, without a definite address) duly received the scrolls which I flung upon whatever wind was blowing, in the faith that they would find him out. But, is he extant now? In these many years, since he last heard from me, may he not have deemed his earthly task accomplished, and have withdrawn to the Paradise of Gentle Readers, wherever it may be, to the enjoyments of which his kindly charity, on my behalf, must surely have entitled him? I have a sad foreboding that this may be the truth. The Gentle Reader, in the case of any individual author, is apt to be extremely short-lived; he seldom outlasts a literary fashion, and, except in very rare instances, closes his weary eyes before the writer has half done with him. If I find him at all, it will probably be under some mossy grave-stone, inscribed with a half-obliterated name, which I shall never recognize.

Therefore I have little heart or confidence (especially, writing, as I do, in a foreign land, and after a long, long absence from my own) to presume upon the existence of that friend of friends, that unseen brother of the soul, whose apprehensive sympathy has so often encouraged me to be egotistical in my Prefaces, careless though unkindly eyes should skim over what was never meant for them. I stand upon ceremony, now, and, after stating a few particulars about the work which is here offered to the Public, must make my most reverential bow, and retire behind the curtain.

This Romance was sketched out during a residence of considerable length in Italy, and has been re-written and prepared for the press, in England. The author proposed to himself merely to write a fanciful story, evolving a thoughtful moral, and did not purpose attempting a portraiture of Italian manners and character. He has lived too long abroad, not to be aware that a foreigner seldom acquires that knowledge of a country, at once flexible and profound, which may justify him in endeavouring to idealize its traits.

Italy, as the site of his Romance, was chiefly valuable to him as affording a sort of poetic or fairy precinct, where actualities would not be so terribly insisted upon, as they are, and must needs be, in America. No author, without a trial, can conceive of the difficulty of writing a Romance about a country where there is no shadow, no antiquity, no mystery, no picturesque and gloomy wrong, nor anything but a common-place prosperity, in broad and simple daylight, as is happily the case with my dear native land. It will be very long, I trust, before romance-writers may find congenial and easily handled themes either in the annals of our stalwart Republic, or in any characteristic and probable events of our individual lives. Romance and poetry, like ivy, lichens, and wall-flowers, need Ruin to make them grow.

In re-writing these volumes, the Author was somewhat surprised to see the extent to which he had introduced descriptions of various Italian objects, antique, pictorial, and statuesque. Yet these things fill the mind, everywhere in Italy, and especially in Rome, and cannot easily be kept from flowing out upon the page, when one writes freely, and with self-enjoyment. And, again, while reproducing the book, on the broad and dreary sands of Redcar, with the gray German Ocean tumbling in upon me, and the northern blast always howling in my ears, the complete change of scene made these Italian reminiscences shine out so vividly, that I could not find in my heart to cancel them.

An act of justice remains to be performed towards two men of genius, with whose productions the Author has allowed himself to use a quite unwarrantable freedom. Having imagined a sculptor, in this Romance, it was necessary to provide him with such works in marble as should be in keeping with the artistic ability which he was supposed to possess. With this view, the Author laid felonious hands upon a certain bust of Milton and a statue of a Pearl-Diver, which he found in the studio of Mr. Paul Aker,[18] and secretly conveyed them to the premises of his imaginary friend, in the Via Frezza. Not content even with these spoils, he committed a further robbery upon a magnificent statue of Cleopatra, the production of Mr. William W. Story,[19] an artist whom his country and the world will not long fail to appreciate. He had thoughts of appropriating, likewise, a certain door of bronze, by Mr. Randolph Rogers representing the history of Columbus in a series of admirable bas-reliefs,[20] but was deterred by an unwillingness to meddle with public property. Were he capable of stealing from a lady, he would certainly have made free with Miss Hosmer's noble statue of Zenobia.[21]

He now wishes to restore the above-mentioned beautiful pieces of sculpture to their proper owners, with many thanks, and the avowal of his sincere admiration. What he has said of them, in the Romance, does not partake of the fiction in which they are embedded, but expresses his genuine opinion, which, he has little doubt,

will be found in accordance with that of the Public. It is perhaps unnecessary to say, that, while stealing their designs, the Author has not taken a similar liberty with the personal characters of either of these gifted Sculptors; his own Man of Marble being entirely imaginary.
Leamington, October 15th, 1859[22]

Several more days followed of writing, revision, contemplation, and walking but probably as a result of a demand contained in a letter that had been received from Smith, Elder Nathaniel dispatched to them all those pages of the manuscript that he considered complete and ready for printing (including the preface), thus not being able to retain them in his possession before printing took place pending the return to England of Fields (as he had told Ticknor he would).

16. Sunday. A rainy morning. A letter from Smith & Elder, Publishers, London.[23] Also from Madame O'Sullivan at Lisbon.[24] Looked over manuscript &c.[25] After dinner, walked with Julian on Newbold road, through Jephson's Gardens.

17. Monday. Showery morning. Wrote till 3. After dinner walked with Julian through Lover's Grove to Lillington. Sent Messrs Smith Elder & Co. the manuscript of my Romance as far as page 429, by express; also, letter by post.[26]

18. Tuesday. A rainy morning. Letters from M[r].Wilding[27] & to Una & Mamma from Ellen Peabody.[28] Wrote till 3. After dinner, took a walk with Julian.

19. Wednesday. Overcast morning. Letter from Smith Elder & Co. acknowledging receipt of M.S.[29] Wrote till 3. After dinner, walked with Julian to Warwick-castle bridge.[30]

Next day came a letter from Hillard to whom Nathaniel had written from Redcar on 23 July, and hard on the heels of the letter came Hillard himself, almost literally on a flying visit as he was met at the station at 1 o'clock and (presumably because he was changing trains and had a short time to kill) spent one hour with the family before being seen off again at 2 o'clock.

20. Thursday. Pleasant morning, soon turning to clouds. Letters from G. S. Hillard,[31] & Mr. Miller.[32] Did not write today. At about 1, went to the railway station & met Hillard, who staid with us till after 2. Went to the railway to see him off. It rained in the afternoon, & I did not take a walk.[33]

Before Hillard had arrived, Sophia took the opportunity of replying to a letter that she had received from Elizabeth on 4 October, just before leaving Redcar:

Leamington Oct 20th
21 Bath St

My dearest Elizabeth,
Mr. Hillard has today announced a flying visit to us, and I shall send Una's journal

by him, if he will take it. I shall put inside "my consolations" which you said you wanted to see. Pray keep them snug for me. Do not send them to Salem. Elizabeth Hoar[34] saw them in Rome, and that, because she is a sacred person, you know, and was so near me then. I have no time now to write a letter as I would wish. We left Redcar on the fifth October and are now settled in Leamington till the end of December at least. We have taken apartments in an unfashionable part of this fashionable Royal Spa, but the rooms are pretty comfortable, excepting that we are close upon the railroad and have constant thunder, though no screams of the steam demon. Una is a blooming rose now, as round and solid as ever, and appears to be perfectly well, excepting that the sensibility to noise and confusion is still very great. She is taller and developed in form, and a lovely form it is. Her hair has its childish curl, as looks very graceful round her head in its hyacinthine rings. I can hardly believe the testimony of my eyes, when [word(s) obliterated] her, so flourishing a flower, and [word(s) obliterated] what she has suffered and how near to death she was, I am only a thanksgiving. Julian misses his Redcar sea baths, but is well and studies finely under his father's teaching, who hears his Latin every morning, before breakfast. I hear his Greek! He seems to have learnt nothing of Miss Shepard, but now he understands what he is about. Rose also is learning to read, write, draw, spell and cipher with great success under Mamma. She did read your primer[35] but somehow she always _hated_ to read with Miss Shepard, and nothing went on. Una is studying Latin, French, Italian and reading History.

[word(s) obliterated] had a letter from Fanny Channing[36] the other day. She says they have all been very busy for more than a month in preparing Frank's wardrobe for Oxford, where he went with his father last Thursday with three large trunks, that he had taken the very pleasant chambers once occupied by the Provost, that he was a splendid scholar and had passed his examinations successfully, and that they thought he would take high honours, that he had gone to Queen's College and knew several very fine young men. We are quite puzzled to conceive how Mr. Channing can afford to send Frank to Oxford in such style, or in any style, but perhaps Frank is sent by some rich relation in America. I hope he will not come out a Puseyite, or Roman Catholic. Fanny says in her letter that she does not know when they shall return to America or whether they ever shall. Mr. Channing has been attending a Social Science Congress in Bradford lately.

I had a letter from Ellen Howe acknowledging the check.[37] She says Aunt Mary had given her some bed linen and chamber furniture and her father had supplied her under clothes. She seemed full of good resolve and hoped you and Mary would not be disappointed in her. There certainly does not appear to be depth of character in her—but she [certainly?] now has the best intentions to fulfil all her duties.

Mr. Hawthorne has about finished his book. More than four hundred pages of MSS are now in the hands of the publisher. I have read as much as that, but do not yet know the dénouement. It is just as well that I do not say what I think of it. You will soon see it now. He is very well and in very good spirits, despite all his hard toil of so many months. As usual he thinks the book good for nothing, and based upon a very foolish idea which nobody will like or accept. But I am used to such opinions and understand why he feels oppressed with disgust of what has so long occupied him.

The true judgement of the work was his _first_ idea of it, when it seemed to him worth the doing. He has regularly despised each one of his books immediately upon finishing it. _My_ enthusiasm is too much his own music, as it were. It needs the reverberation of the impartial [word obliterated] to reassure him—that he has not been guilty of a bêtise.

Ellen tells me that Mary now sleeps quietly, for the first time since three months.[38] If she sleeps, I am encouraged for her. Your last letter came too late to prevent my reading "the enclosure" to which you refer. I hope my answer to that enclosure convinced you of your mistake, dear Elizabeth. There are good reasons, which I cannot give you, why I never can talk with you about either Mary's bygones or Nathaniel's[39] and I hope you will rest contented with never mentioning them any more. I assure you that my reasons are perfectly disinterested and that it is not because I wish to avoid personal pain. You must confide in me till we meet in spiritual forms, for I assure you my decision is irrevocable. I never will listen to any explanations or elucidations concerning the past, and in a future eternity you will agree that I am right. But meanwhile, remember, dear Elizabeth, that my reasons have no reference either to myself or my husband and that I love you [word(s) obliterated] and that your love is exceedingly precious to me—and that I can never forget any of your benefits and that I am grateful for your warm, generous, satisfactory love in which I confide as wholly as (I was about to say) in that of my Heavenly Father—so pure from all earthly alloy do I consider it. Is that enough? I want you to be content—are you content? I have no more time today.

Your affectionate sister
Sophia

I am better and quite solid again and even capable of color, though too easily tired as yet.[40]

Nathaniel took a short break from writing to entertain Bright, who had arrived on Friday. His arrival coincided with a brief flurry of winter weather but a visit was made to Rugby to meet Bright's young cousin Charles who was a student at the school. The absence of any mention of Sophia may have meant that she was not too well.

21. Friday. Clear and cool morning. Wrote till 3. Mr. Bright came, dined & spent the evening with us. I did not walk out. Very cool weather, & a slight fall of snow.

22. Saturday. Very cool morning; a frost last night. Did not write to-day. At 12¼, took the rail with Mr. Bright for Rugby. Saw the school &c. Afterwards, walked with Mr. B. to Bilton Hall (a residence of Addison). Saw the game of football in the school close; dined with Mr. and Charley Bright at the George Hotel. Took the rail for Leamington at about 9.[41]

23. Sunday. A cool morning. Letter from Mr. Macmillan, publisher.[42] Mr. Bright took Una to chapel at Warwick, in a cab, & walked back with her. He dined with us & spent the evening. After dinner, Mr. B., Una, Julian, Rosebud & I took the walk through Jephson's Gardens, & to Lovers' Grove &c. Mr. B. spent the evening with us.[43]

No doubt Nathaniel discussed the letter from Macmillan with Bright. It contained a degree of topicality insofar as Macmillan had published in 1857 the very successful *Tom Brown's School Days* by Thomas Hughes, a novel about Rugby school, but it would seem that in this instance the letter may well have contained an inquiry as to whether Nathaniel had anything that could be included in the forthcoming first number of *Macmillan's Magazine*, due to be published in November, or whether he would be interested in writing for succeeding issues. However, nothing appears to have arisen from the contents of the letter and there is no record of any reply having been written.

For the next fifteen days Nathaniel worked strenuously at the manuscript, sometimes returning to it again after the family had dined but, as he noted, not always with success or pleasure. No doubt he was not too concerned about seeking entertainment for himself after spending the day at his desk; a walk in the neighborhood would be sufficient for him to exercise both his body and mind. There is so little mention of Sophia during this period that it could be assumed that she was enduring another period of ill health, but that was not the case in fact, so her nonappearance in the records of the family's doings must be put down to the fact that she was simply supporting her husband during his hours of composition, ensuring his comfort during his periods away from the manuscript, overseeing the children's lessons, and generally keeping up morale.

24. Monday. Cool & bright morning. Wrote till 3. After dinner, walked with Julian to Whitnash.[44]

THREE ORATIONS will be delivered by Mr T. MASON JONES (late of Trinity College, Dublin), at the PUBLIC HALL, WINDSOR STREET, on TUESDAY, WEDNESDAY, and THURSDAY next, OCTOBER 25th, 26th, and 27th, 1859.

Subjects :—Tuesday Night—" R. B. SHERIDAN, the Dramatist, Orator, and Wit."—Chairman :. Dr. JEAFFRESON. Wednesday Night—" EDMUND BURKE, the Philosopher, Statesman, and Orator."—Chairman : Dr. THOMSON. Thursday Night—" JOHN WESLEY and Methodism."—Chairman : JOHN HITCHMAN, Esq.

Orations to commence at Eight o'clock. Admission :— Reserved Chairs, Single Ticket, 1s. 6d. (Course, 3s. 6d.) ; Front Seats, Single Ticket, 1s. (Course, 2s. 6d.) . To be had from Mr GLOVER, *Courier* Office, 1, Victoria Terrace ; Mr BECK, *Advertiser* Office, 8, Upper Parade ; Mr STONE (late Enoch), Bath Street ; Mr CURTIS, 10, Bath Street ; Mr BURGIS, 43, Regent Street ; and Mrs SLOW, at the Hall, where a Plan may be seen, and Chairs selected. Early Reservation of Chairs is desirable.

Probably as a result of having seen an advertisement in the local press it was decided that Una, at least, would benefit from, and enjoy being at, a series of lectures that was due to take place that week at the Public Hall in Windsor Street. Perhaps, indeed, she had asked if she could go on her own behalf. Quite why neither Nathaniel nor Sophia thought it possible that they could chaperon their daughter to the Hall must remain a mystery; it cannot have been through any feeling of intellectual snobbery or of particular dislike of the different subjects of each lecture. In any case, on such occasions a parent has to put aside personal feelings and take the rough with the smooth if the whole object of the exercise is the education and enjoyment of one of their offspring. In the end, it must be assumed that Nathaniel was too tired to contemplate further intellectual work during the evenings in question and that Sophia accordingly stayed at home to look after him and cool his fevered brow! So that left Fanny with the task of chaperoning Una.

25. Tuesday. Cool morning, between dim & sunny. Wrote drearily till 3. A heavy rain in the afternoon, so that I did not go out. Una & Fanny Wrigley went to a lecture in the evening [by Mr. Mason Jones on "R. B. Sheridan, the Dramatist, Orator, and Wit"][45]

26. Wednesday. A rainy morning. Letters from Mrs. Mann & E. P. Peabody.[46] Wrote till 3. After dinner took a walk. Una & Fanny went to Mr. Mason Jones's second lecture [on "Edmund Burke, the Philosopher, Statesman, and Orator"][47]

Since the Hawthornes had been in England, their house in Concord, the Wayside, had been occupied by Nathaniel Peabody and his family, free of charge. After Horace Mann's death, the Peabodys moved out and Mary and her three boys, Horace, George, and Benjamin ("Benjie"), had been allowed to stay there. She intended to make a certain amount of renovation and alterations to the house, mostly at her own expense, in gratitude for having had the good fortune to find a home after her husband's death as she had, of course, to leave the college in Yellow Springs where Horace had been president. Mary explained to Sophia her feelings with regard to her husband's continual pursuit of excellence in his work, a pursuit that in many people's opinion had resulted in his ignoring the welfare and happiness of his family, particularly during the last few years of his presidency of Antioch College. Not so, said Mary:

If he had fallen from his high estate of honor or worthiness I should doubtless have lost my faith, and that would have been misery indeed. For my happiness has always been in what he was in himself even more than in what he was to me, sweet & dear & indescribable as that has been. . . . When I look back upon all the years in which I have known him, I see him activated by no secondary motives & never flinching from the severest duty. . . . When my friends have imagined that I was laboring too hard in helping his labors, how little have they imagined the happiness it was to aid him in any thing, in ever so small a degree. . . . [For him] to be always drawn upon was very wearisome after exhausting labors, and during the last year I have kept every body at bay and subjected him to no company, but given him quiet & rest & the children to play with when he could relax at all . . . but I fear the peaceful enjoyment of his old age which I craved for him was one of those visions destined never to be realised even if he had lived much longer.[48]

. Thursday. Rather pleasant morning. Letter from Bennoch.[49] Wrote till nearly
3. After dinner, walked with Julian to Warwick Castle. Una & Fanny went to Mr.
Mason Jones' lecture [on "John Wesley and the Methodism"].[50]

October 27 1859
Leamington

My dear beloved Mary,
I received a double letter this morning[51] from you and E. the last date of which
on the envelope was 8th October. I do not at all understand why letters are twenty
days or nineteen days coming to me from you, when the voyage is ten or twelve
days. But I am beyond measure glad for the letters. My darling sister, how I wish
I could make you understand the depth and [. . . . *ness?*] of my sympathy. I will
never attempt to console you for that immense void which now must yawn before
you, in which you seek in vain for the eye, the smile, the presence that made
mortal life for you an immortal joy. I have not lost my husband and so I cannot
measure your calamity. The trial that I have passed through cannot be put side
by side with the trial that you have endured, it was all so different. I suffered
Una's death over and over. I wrestled with God's angels for her, many times
resigned her. I hung suspended in long torture of fear. The vast ocean of the
unknown seemed to absorb her in its ebb and then again with its flow she came
back—She remains—I have her still. I cannot quite recover my breath yet, but
my eye sees her, my ear hears her—she glows with a new, fresh, rosy life as if
she could never die, or fade—How then can I console you? How can I help you
endure? Alas—God alone can approach so vast, so sacred a sorrow. You speak
of a veil, dearest, between you and him. I wish I could communicate to you my
sense of the transparency of that veil between us and that other world. But my
husband is not behind the veil, and so I cannot assure you that it would be transparent to me in such event. No, I can do nothing for you, though I long to do so
much—I can only join with you in your eloquent songs over his memory, over the
rich inheritance he has left you in the nobleness and spotlessness of his character.
Wonderful is the providence of God that those whose value cannot be computed
for us here are those alone over whom we can rejoice when they vanish into the
upper sphere. How strangely the sorrow and the triumph change into one another
with the rapidity of light or of thought. In every tear must arch a rainbow. The
tears and the rainbow become one in the glorious sheen of such souls. "Ah, how
can I spare him!" plead our tears. "But he is so fit to be here," answer the rainbows. "Were he unworthy, would not your tears drown you in the blackness of
despair," urges the tender angels of those prisms of God, "for faces I could paint
no longer on the ever rolling globes of grief that fall from your eyes."
How true it is, that "the heart knoweth its own bitterness, and the stranger
intermeddled not with its joy!"[52] I have one abiding comfort when I think of you
in your inaccessible woe, and this is that your love was so unselfish, so without a
stain of earthliness. Therefore it must inevitably have its own divine consolations
wrapt up in itself, which will unfold more and more. I do not believe that among
the spirits in heaven he can find a purer, a more generous love. I am sure he
can keep it with him as a portion of his immortal bliss and content. For this I
thank God.
Bye and bye—not yet—but as surely as GOD is, will roll back upon your heart
in soft melodious thunders those full tides of disinterested love which without
measure you poured out upon his daily life. But now it is the ebb. All has gone
down to the horizon line, and desolate sands stretch wearily out. Your argosy is
stranded and leans sadly on its side—all sails drooping. Yes—yes—I think I feel

your very anguish. I seem to be the bereft one as I look through your eyes over the melancholy wastes. Yet for you, for such as you, I am confident of the Flow. Time will bring it—not the inexorable and merciless but the tender and gentle. It is the Heathen who paints Time with a cruel scythe, who ought rather to be drawn with Healing on his wings and in his hands exhaustless vases dropping balm— upon such as you—my darling—balm for the wound from one vase, and now the other—a divine Elixir of life for your fainting spirit, faint only from the sudden shock. "Crushed" I thought you might be on account of physical limitations, dear, because I knew you had the fortitude and courage of a martyr—and would stand, if your body could sustain your soul, as I knew you would try to live for your children, however you might yearn to follow your husband.[53]

The letter breaks off here, probably because Una and Fanny had returned from the lecture, full of the latest news, but on another different-size piece of notepaper Sophia wrote a further little note to her sister that also appears to have been written over a two-day period:

Oct 27 & 28

Dearest Mary,
The enclosed musings are those of an English poet. I fancy you the muser, and it seems to me that the lovely swan songs may match some of your moods. At any rate I hope so, for I long for some alleviation of your sharp anguish, and I wish to try all means to initiate a softening of the stroke. These melodies will perhaps only make your tears flow, but they may be sweet tears and not agony. I cannot help weeping myself when I send them as if I were you, and as if the words struck on your head through mine. It is sympathy I give you—not consolation.[54]

As Nathaniel ground out the daily stint at his writing desk, life at No. 21 continued in its familiar pattern, and though the weather (and circumstances) prevented any great deal of traveling around the neighborhood, it has to be assumed that the Hawthornes were becoming more aware of what Leamington itself had to offer in the way of distractions, in the form of public entertainment, particularly for the children as the lectures that Una attended were not the last occasions on which advantage was taken of performances of one kind or another.

28. Friday. Dim but rather pleasant morning. A letter from John Miller.[55] Wrote till 3. A letter from Mr. O'Sullivan, now in Paris.[56] It rained heavily in the afternoon; & I did not go out. A letter to Una from Miss Bracken, at Broadstairs.[57]

Sophia resumed her letter to Mary:

October 28th. Dearest Mary, I scrawled away last evening while awaiting the return of Una and Fanny from a lecture, or oration as they called it, about Burke.[58] They returned enthusiastic with delight. Una has been writing an immense account of this and another oration to Elizabeth.[59] You both know about Sheridan and Burke, but what will be valuable and interesting to you is the way in which she has comprehended what she heard, and gathered the pearls out of the oyster shells.

I will delay no longer to express my delight in the new room you are building for us. We are all very glad and I think you were quite inspired to project it. I feel now as if we might be able to breathe in the dear old house—and also to be contained in it till we add on more. I consider it a splendid present and I shall dedicate it to you. You are infinitely kind to superintend the additions we wish to make, but Mr. Hawthorne wishes to defer other alterations till our return for many reasons—He cannot tell just what he wants and he may conclude to do nothing— it all depends. When we return, we can profit by your opinion and take counsel together about building.

What is the small bedroom on the eastern wing used for now? It was the room in which my servants slept, Mary and Ellen Hearne. I am amazed to hear about the the annoyance you have had with suspectable intruders. We never had any trouble of the kind, but we were there only one year. Have you then painted over the floor and walls? I hope you will do whatever is effective for the suppression of [them?]. White of egg and quicksilver overcame that pest in the old Ripley beds of the Old Manse when we first went there.[60] I had the bedsteads all washed first with very strong and very hot soapsuds, and then with my own hands I bedaubed every part with a mixture of white of egg and quicksilver. The walls of old houses engender them. I am grieved enough that you should meet with any such trouble in my house.[61]

Once again the letter was put on one side, and despite the next few days being spent quietly and with no apparent distractions, Sophia did not complete it until another three days had passed.

29. Saturday. Rather pleasant morning. Wrote till nearly 3. After dinner, walked with Julian along the Newbold Road.

30. Sunday. Pleasant morning. Wrote till 2. In the afternoon, it rained heavily, & I did not go out.

31. Monday. A dim morning, boding rain. Wrote till 3. After dinner, walked with Julian along the Tachbrook road. Dreamed of seeing Genl Pierce.[62]

Whether this dream was a variation of the one that Nathaniel referred to in his journal some years previously, when he was still subconsciously worrying about his comparative lack of success in the commercial and political worlds when compared with his Bowdoin College contemporaries (despite his own real personal success in the artistic world), or whether something had subconsciously jogged his memory about his old friend (whom he had last seen in London in July but who was now back in America) cannot now be ascertained, but the incident has its interest as Nathaniel either did not now dream often enough to warrant his referring to them in his journals and diaries (as he had done in the past), or he felt that this particular dream was of such significance that he was impelled to record it (although he did not expand further on that possible significance). However, there was one member of the family who wasn't bothered by dreams:

October 31ˢᵗ.

Dearest Mary, I am growing better every day, I think. I really <u>look</u> pleasantly well. I have grown quite round and solid and wax rosy. I sleep very well and have a good appetite. I bathe in cold water in the morning in a cold room, and I walk almost every day. I am easily tired and still feel bruised when I wake. But the air of Leamington agrees with me very well, and the physicians say that Leamington is a very good place for a delicate person. It is central and we have had here none of the ice, snow & severest cold of even the southern shore and the eastern and northern shores. All the coasts of England are now strewn with wrecks. Such a storm as has scarcely ever been known has done all this, and the Royal Charter went to pieces and four hundred and seventy persons went down on the western shore by Anglesey on Wednesday morning. I hope you will have a mild winter— Has it been very cold during October? We had three days here of very cold weather, but not so cold as at London or Devonshire.

God bless you all. I am much relieved to hear that E. is well.[63] Mr. Hillard already has a note from me to her—and Una's journal. We shall send him these letters this week—as he goes in the Canada on the 5th November. Ever your own loving

Sophia.[64]

9

"Leamington is not so desirable a residence in winter": November 1859

November announced its arrival with a storm over the town, but for Julian it marked an event of some importance that partly dispelled the increasing boredom that he was experiencing with regard to their surroundings:

1st of November Friday 1859 Leamington.

It is a long time since I wrote, but even now I have not much to say. Life here is so very much the same, that it is very tiresome. We have had some severe storms this week, and last Wednesday there was a storm which wrecked the Royal Charter and 400 people perished and only some 30 were saved.[1]

I have got a Major who teaches me Calisthenic [sic] and Drill. He says I am the best pupil except 2 that he has ever had, and that by this he does not mean to say that they were better than me, but that they were only as quick. Indeed he does not know but I am better than they. I wonder who those wonderful two are. I am beginning the broadsword now.

Today was my first lesson. He has brought me two sabres, made of wood, of course, but he says that tomorrow he will bring his real sword, which he has used in battle, and he will put on his uniform.

The Major is a rather short man, with his eyes very near together and an aquiline nose, a bald head, &c.

Mr Bright has been here and gave us quite a long visit. He came from Malvern whither he wanted to take Papa, but Papa would not go. He staid over Sunday and went to church with Una to Warwick.

Papa and I have been to Warwick Castle. It is very beautiful reflected in the water of the river beneath it, and the large trees growing by the river look very beautifully [sic] too.

We have used up all the walks in the vicinity of Leamington and so we do not know where to go to, now, except to go over the places we have been before, and that is not a very pleasant thing to do. I am beginning to get tired of the vicinity altogether and so shall be very glad when we get out of it. I believe we are going to the Devonshire coast when we leave here.[2] I hope so at any rate.

I have been painting a good deal and have received some delightful additions to my apparatus consisting of a cake of paint, called Neutral Orange, which is necessary to put all over the paper in the first place, so as to give a tone to it. Then a large flat brush for the sky, and large washes of color. Lastly a large sheet of rough and tough drawing paper, which of all was the most necessary, of course.

I have painted two or three pictures of the Railway station, which is rather a nice subject, having some trees in the back ground &c. The last one that I did of it, everybody said was very nice, but I do not think it was at all. I have some thoughts of doing another one some time, on a larger piece of paper. But now I think I have exhausted almost all I have to say so with a goodwill I subscribe my name

Julian Hawthorne

3

    Julian had been able to draw upon his previous experience of fencing lessons that he had taken while the family had been in Manchester two years before, but the old major in Leamington was obviously a very romantic figure to the thirteen-year-old boy, and his fascination with the weapons and the major's participation in momentous events were recalled in later years in two of his own books of reminiscences:

Quite other was the old Peninsular Major, from whom I learned the swing and thrust of the sabre. In his hot youth he had followed Wellington to Spain; with him had endured the long pounding of Napoleon's guns, until the moment when "down we swept and charged and overthrew!" But to have been in the thick of Waterloo, and to have understood it—except by poring over published reports long afterward—were different things. Henry Kingsley, in one of his stories, tells what his hero saw of Balaclava: a stain on the back of the tunic of the man riding in front of him in the charge: how did it come there?—Oh, the Russian gunners!—right, left, point, and back to the lines; but the man with the stained tunic had disappeared.—My little Major was not much more explicit. "I was riding with the other chaps, you know: I saw a big fellow riding up at us with the point of his lance at my chest: I leaned over to the left and swung at him with my sabre: down he went!"—"Did you kill him?"—The Major gave a little laugh. "I hope not: but we rode over him."—And that was Waterloo as experienced by the Major. The day he told us of it he had brought with him the heavy cavalry sabre with which he had delivered that cut at the French lancer; and, holding it poised in his hand, he illustrated the incident with a shift of the shoulder, a turn of the blade—the merest drawing-room sketch of the little affair of life and death. He affected to treat it as a trifle, but his chuckle was forced, he was ill at ease, and after a moment he repeated: "I hope not!" Forty years before, that had been: but he was seeing it all again intensely, and that emotion of his made us see it. He was a small man, not over five foot eight, with a red, furrowed visage and little twinkling eyes: a soldier and a gentleman, who had done what he might in banishing the Corsican ogre; but, in his old age, must take in a pupil or two to make ends meet.[4]

    I was instructed in the use of the broadsword by an old Peninsular officer, Major Johnstone, who had fought at Waterloo, and had the bearing of such majors as Thackeray puts into Vanity Fair. I once asked him whether he had ever killed a man; it was on the day when he first allowed me to use a real broadsword in our lesson. "Well," replied the major, hesitatingly, "I was riding in a charge, and there came a fellow at me; but I let him have it, downright, at the same moment, and I caught him where the neck joins the shoulder, and he went down, and I went on, and what became of him I don't know; I hope nothing serious!" The major sighed and looked serious himself. "And was this the sword?" I demanded, balancing the heavy weapon in my hand. "No—No—it wasn't that one," said the major, hastily. "I've never used the other since! Now then, sir, if you please, on guard!"[5]

How often Julian took lessons from the major is not known, but they were not to last for very long, and this particular week was passed very quietly in the usual daily routine, the monotony not being broken until the following Saturday, when there was at least some mail to read.

1. Tuesday. A storm of wind & rain during the night; rainy & windy morning. Wrote till 3. After dinner, walked with Julian towards Warwick by the Emscote road.

2. Wednesday. A warm, showery morning. Wrote till 3. It rained in the afternoon; and I did not go out.

3. Thursday. Mild and pleasant morning. After breakfast, Mamma & Una walked to Whitnash. I wrote till 3. After dinner, took a walk with Julian.

4. [6] Friday. Dark & rainy morning. Wrote till 3. After dinner, took a walk with Julian along the Whitnash road.

5. Saturday. Rather dim morning. Letters from Mrs. Mann & E. P. P.[7] at Concord; and from Bennoch (London)[8] & G. S. Hillard, Liverpool[9] A rainy day. Towards dusk, I took a walk up & down the Parade. I wrote till 3.[10]

The letter from Mary, in contrast to her last, was a highly emotional, sometimes incoherent, and frequently indecipherable outburst concerning the circumstances of Horace's death at Antioch College, about which she was undoubtedly bitter and also harbored some guilty feelings. The last year had been a particularly difficult one for the college, both financially and administratively; such troubles had been assumed, in some quarters, to be due to Horace's incompetence. The final three weeks of his life had been occupied with the increasingly arduous preparations for the commencement which had included a very tiring dinner and speeches:

It was not during the very last weeks that I saw so little of him, but before the Commencement took place when he was so tired & busy & Benjie was so sick & then Georgie & I did not realise then as other people did who were with him more how feeble he looked . . . and this busy time lasted till nearly a week after the Commencement . . . over which he had presided. . . . (I have heard since that he there said words about [his?] exhausted powers which now seem prophetic). . . . A few days after he began to complain of pain in his limbs. . . . You can imagine it all but from that time I perceived that my fears for him were becoming realities & I devoted myself to him. . . . I am amazed that I did not see the truth & that he did not. . . . I lose the sense of days, & cannot tell how long it was . . . & at the very last he was surrounded with the alarmed & the anxious & in the whirlwind he was swept away & I had no chance to speak to him alone. . . . I have dwelt upon this sad & fearful scene. . . . I have dwelt upon it I say, till I find that I must turn away from it or I shall lose my self-poise.

But she was slowly coming to terms with the immediate pain and loss with the help of her boys, calmly rereading his letters to her, and finding some peace from looking after the garden at the Wayside, "I love to be out under the sky."[11]

Although there is no mention of it in Nathaniel's diary it must have been on 6 November that he received a letter from Samuel Lucas, who as well as being a writer for *The Times* was also editor of the illustrated periodical *Once a Week* that Bradbury & Evans had launched the previous July. The publishers were hoping to profit from the demise of Dickens's magazine *Household Words* but in this intention were confounded by his subsequent publication of the very successful *All The Year Round*.

"Once a Week" Office, No. 11 Bouverie St.,
Fleet St., London, Nov. 5, 1859.

Dear Sir,—Will you excuse the liberty which, as editor of "Once a Week", I take of addressing you without waiting for an introduction from any common friend, and will you permit me to trouble you, without preamble, on a matter of business?
    It would give me the greatest satisfaction if you are at liberty to entertain a proposal to write a tale for "Once a Week", and I am confident that Bradbury and Evans would meet your views in a pecuniary sense, should that desideratum be attainable. For myself I may claim better opportunities than most of appreciating the profound truthfulness of the descriptions in "The Scarlet Letter" and "The House of the Seven Gables;" for at one time I took a keen interest in cognate subjects, and must have gone over much of your ground to write, for example, papers like that in the Edinburgh Review, three or four years ago, on "The Fathers of New England." I mention these circumstances by way of excusing myself for breaking in upon you thus abruptly. . . .
    Hoping for your favourable consideration of my proposal, I remain,

Respectfully yours,
Samuel Lucas.[12]

Perhaps, in different circumstances, Nathaniel might have given some attention to Lucas's proposal, particularly if he had known that at the same time as they were approaching him, Bradbury & Evans were offering George Eliot £4,500 for the publication in *Once a Week* of her latest novel, the yet-to-be-completed *The Mill on the Floss*,[13] but as at that particular moment he was in the last throes of completing his manuscript, it would have been rejected without too much thought; the letter lay unanswered for some time.

6. Sunday. Beautiful morning. I wrote till 2 °clock, & again after dinner. It being a rainy day, I did not go out. Una & Julian walked to Warwick to chapel, in the forenoon & were caught in the rain, coming home.

LEAMINGTON
YOUNG MEN'S CHRISTIAN ASSOCIATION.

E. WHEELER, ESQ., C.E.

(Lecturer for the Society of Arts), will deliver

TWO LECTURES, in which there will be much to please the Eye as well as the Ear, at the PUBLIC HALL, WINDSOR STREET, on MONDAY and TUESDAY next, November 7th and 8th, commencing each Evening at Eight o'clock.—That on MONDAY Evening (Rev. Dr. BICKMORE in the Chair), will be upon "THE ELECTRIC TELEGRAPH," profusely illustrated by Diagrams, Voltaic Batteries, Electro-Magnetic Experiments, and by Electric Telegraphs in practical operation. That on TUESDAY evening (Rev. W. A. SALTER in the Chair), will be upon "OPTICS AND OPTICAL ILLUSIONS," familiarly explaining how we see, when we see, and what we see, with novel and remarkable experiments with the Kaleirope revolving 600 times per minute. Reserved Chairs (numbered), 1s. 6d.; Second Seats, 1s.; Third Seats, 6d.—Tickets may be had for the Four Lectures, forming the remainder of the First Course, including Mr Wheeler's—Reserved Chairs, 4s.; Second Seats, 3s. As many Seats are already reserved, it is very desirable that early application be made for Tickets, which may be had of Mr Beck, 8, Upper Parade; Mr J. Curtis, 10, Bath Street; Mr W. Southern, 63, Clarendon Street; or, of Mrs Blow, at the Hall.

---

7. Monday. A fine morning. Wrote till 3. After dinner, walked by myself to Whitnash, & returned by Tachbrook road. Una and Julian went, in the evening, to a lecture on the Electric Telegraph.[14]

The following day was a red-letter day as it was then that the romance was completed. Probably Nathaniel experienced a feeling of deflation rather than elation as the only record he made of the experience was the lugubrious entry in his diary:

8. Tuesday. A fine morning. Letters from Mrs. Mann, & E. P. Peabody.[15] Wrote till 5 minutes of 12, & finished the last page of my Romance. 508 manuscript pages. Towards twilight, took a short walk with Julian. Una, Julian, & Fanny Wrigley went to a lecture on optics in the evening.[16] Rain most of the day.[17]

No intimation of any celebration, relief, pride, or satisfaction! Not even a hint of freedom from the irksome labor involved in the completion of the manuscript that might have resulted in a desire to break out in some way (even to go to the lecture with the children!). Quite why Fanny went with them can only be surmised; perhaps after Una and Julian had been to the previous evening's lecture on their own, it was felt that they ought to have some adult with them for safety's sake, or maybe Julian had so enjoyed the previous evening's outing (particularly the practical demonstrations by the lecturer) that he promised Fanny that she would find it just as enjoyable and interesting as he did.

The letter from Mary, written the day after her last one (apparently in answer to a further—unrecovered—letter from Sophia) was another out-pouring of the emotions released by her husband's death, a mixture of bitter-ness, frustration, feelings of irreparable loss, but, finally, of happiness in and hope for the future:

> What I have suffered of pain in this world has had such compensation that after all & even in this hour I am more thankful to have lived than for any thing else . . . no one can suggest any thing to me that is comforting but what I know already, but I feel better for telling you even so much of my earthly suffering—all my happiness is very heavenly, & its power is upon me at times & you know & so do I that only that which is good is of infinite duration so I have all future time for happiness & bye & bye I shall lay down the present heartache & live only in the future happiness. . . . After sixteen years of closest intimacy I pronounce mine only so far earthy. The rest was glorified humanity. Am I not happy?[18]

Of course, Nathaniel's work in connection with the romance was not ended by the completion of the manuscript. There would be the essentially boring task of proofreading, final revisions and, no doubt, much contact with the publishers before the book was on sale in the shops. And, as yet, he was unaware as to what the official reaction would be to his suggestion regarding a suitable title for the romance if, in fact, he had made any suggestion when forwarding the first batch of manuscript. But all this apart, what were his intentions with regard to his plans for the foreseeable future? He certainly couldn't leave England before the book was published and had to ensure that the American edition came out immediately afterward. Did he have any real idea as to the time that that would involve? Book apart, there didn't appear to be anything to keep him and the family in Leamington any longer; Sophia was enjoying a period of relatively good health at the time, the chil-dren were becoming bored with their surroundings (at least Julian was); and in view of the fact that he had already intimated in letters that he would be staying in England until next summer, it seems surprising that he did not uproot the family once more and move to a more favorable (or, at least different) locality, perhaps London or its outskirts. When the daily history of the family's doings over the next few months are taken into account (and even though, in the event, their activities were controlled by illness in the family) it would appear that so little was done in the way of excitement of any kind that it can only be assumed that a cloud of debilitating boredom

---

IMMENSE ATTRACTION ! ! !

ROYAL MUSIC HALL, LEAMINGTON,
FOR SIX DAYS ONLY,
COMMENCING MONDAY, NOV. 7TH, 1859,

BATCHELDER'S MONSTRE PANORAMA
OF AFRICA AND INDIA,
EMBRACING

DR. LIVINGSTONE'S TRAVELS,
FOLLOWED BY A MAGNIFICENT

DIORAMA OF ST. PETER'S CHURCH AT ROME,
AND ACCOMPANIED BY

THE INFANT SAPPHO,
THE GREATEST NOVELTY OF THE DAY.

This Unrivalled EXHIBITION has been visited by upwards of 49,000 Persons during the past Three Months.

Doors open each Evening at half-past Seven; to commence at Eight o'Clock.

GRAND MORNING EXHIBITIONS on THURSDAY and SATURDAY, at half-past Two.

PIANIST, Mr J. BATCHELDER, jun., from the Crystal Palace, Sydenham.

---

and gloom hung over No. 21 Bath Street. Even the daily walks must have been conducted in a slight atmosphere of despondency; constantly going over and over the same stretches of pavement could not have been too inspiring.

But first, the final pages of the manuscript had to be mailed to the publishers with a covering note that surely must have included some suggestion as to the title that the author preferred, or rather the one that Fields had suggested should be used, *The Romance of Monte Beni.*

9. Wednesday. A fine morning. Sent off my parcel of the Romance to Smith Elder & Co by parcel express; also a note to them by mail.[19] Walked with Una to Radford Semele; started at 10 ½ & returned between 12 & 1. Julian breakfasted with Major Johnstone, & went with him to Whitnash. Towards dusk, walked with Julian along Warwick road.[20]

With the manuscript out of his hands, all that could be done now was to sit back and wait for the proofs to be sent to him.

10. Thursday. Cool & rather pleasant morning. In the forenoon, walked with Julian. In the afternoon, towards evening, took a short walk by myself. Mamma had a tooth out & many filled. She & Rosebud went to a panorama at 2 °clock. Julian to the same, at 8. P. M.[21]

PANORAMA AT THE MUSIC HALL.—Mr. Bachelder's highly interesting panorama of Africa and India has been well patronised during the week, and fully deserves the encouragement which it has received. Those persons who take an interest in the operations of the vast field of missionary labour in Africa, and especially in the untiring efforts and undaunted courage of Dr. Livingstone and others, should visit the Music Hall to-day, after which time the exhibitions will be removed to Warwick. Many of the scenes depicted upon canvases are cleverly painted, and the whole of these have been so judiciously selected as to gratify almost every variety of taste. The singing of Miss Bachelder, who possesses a very pleasing voice, has been much extolled as the performance of a clever child.[22]

11. Friday. A pleasant, cool morning. A letter from Smith Elder & Co dissenting from the title of my book.[23] Between 11 & 12, took a walk with Julian through Lover's Grove to Lillington &c. Home after 1. At nearly dusk, took a short walk with Julian.

12. Saturday. A fine, but cool morning. At 11, set out with Julian to walk to Warwick; market day; went into the Museum of Natural History &c. Got home at about 2. At dusk, took a walk by myself along the Whitnash road.

13. Sunday. Cool, pleasant morning. Letters from E. P. & Mrs. Mann.[24] Wrote a note to Smith Elder & Co suggesting various titles for the Romance.[25] A little before 5, walked with Julian along the Newbold road. Got back a little before 6.

14. Monday. Cool morning, with a slight November mist. Wrote in my Journal. Towards dusk, took a walk with Julian.[26]

Quite why Nathaniel suddenly started writing in his journal again after such a long interval (his last entry having been made on the previous 22 June) is not clear, although he was unlikely to have had any compulsion to do so during the intervening period while he was so busily engaged on the completion of the manuscript of the romance. Much of the entry has a lackluster air about it as though being hardly worth the effort of documenting such well-trodden areas of the locality. Whatever the compulsion to open the journal on this occasion, it quickly faded as he did not make another entry for a further three months.

21, Bath St, Leamington, Nov 14th '59. Julian and I walked to Lillington the other day, and went into the church-yard there. We found an almost illegible grave-stone, on which Julian, with some trouble, made out this epitaph

William Treen's gravestone. Photo by the author.

> "Poorly lived and poorly died,
> Poorly buried, and no one cried."[27]

It would be difficult to compress the story of a cold and luckless life and death
into fewer words. The grave-stone was on the shady and damp side of the church,
and within two or three feet of the foundation stones; and this brief space seemed
to be the entire length of the grave, so that the poor man seemed to be very poorly
buried indeed. If not a dwarf, he must have been doubled up to fit him into the
hole. His name, as well as I could make it out was TREEO—John Treeo, I think—
and he died in 1810, at the age of 74. The grave-stone was much over-grown with
moss and lichens and much corroded with the weather;—all these tokens of age
accrue on grave-stones here, in a tenth part of the time that would be required in
the drier climate of America. Ancient grave-stones are seldom or never met with
in English church-yards. A hundred years is a rare longevity for a grave-stone. I
suppose, when they become quite illegible, so as not to designate the occupant of
the grave, they are taken away.

This little church of Lillington was undergoing restoration when we were here,
two years ago, and now seems to be quite renewed, with the exception of its
square, gray, battlemented tower, which has still the aspect of unadulterated
antiquity.[28]

On Saturday, Julian and I walked to Warwick by the old road, passing over the
bridge of the Avon, within view of the Castle. No doubt, I have spoken of this
scene two or three times before; so I shall not attempt it again, although [it?] is
as fine an English piece of scenery as exists anywhere;—the quiet little river,
shadowed with drooping trees, and, in its vista the gray, battlemented towers and
long line of windows of the lordly castle, with a picturesquely varied outline;—
ancient though, a little softened by decay.

It was market-day in Warwick; and I saw little or nothing that was characteristic or striking enough to be worth describing. In the sort of colonnade, under the town-house, or whatever they call it, there were people selling small-wares, apples, vegetables, &c, and all through the market-place there was a little scattered trade of the same kind going forward; pigs, too, and sheep, alive and dead. All was very quiet and dull. We went into the Museum, and saw what we had seen before;— the most interesting object being some small portions of the auburn hair and beard of King Edward the IV.

The town of Warwick, I think, has been considerably modernised since I first saw it. At any rate, the whole of the central section of the principal street now looks modern, with its stuccoed or brick fronts of houses, and, in many cases, handsome shop-windows. Leicester's Hospital and its adjoining chapel, standing on an archway over the street, still looks venerably antique; and so does a gateway (I think it is one of the gates of the ancient wall) that half bestrides the street, with what looks like a church, or perhaps a town-hall, over it. Beyond these two points on either side (the hospital and the gateway) the street has a much older aspect, with many wood-framed, brick-and-plaster filled, old houses, gabled, and the second story projecting over the first. The bye-streets have many similar relics of antiquity. The wooden signs on them (oftener proclaiming beer and spirits for sale, than anything else) heighten the antique impression.[29]

15. Tuesday. Chill, foggy, overcast morning. After 4 °clock, took a moderately short walk with Julian.[30]

What he didn't mention in the diary was that now that he was free of the manuscript and with few other distractions he obviously thought that it was about time he replied to Samuel Lucas's letter:

21 Bath-st, Leamington
Nov[r] 15th 1859

Dear Sir,
Your kind note of 5th inst. has given me great pleasure; especially as I have read the article on the Fathers of New England, and recognize your qualifications to speak with authority on my attempts to depict their characters and times.

My mind, at this time, is not in a productive state; for I have worked it very hard and continuously during two or three months past, and I promise myself to be idle during the rest of my stay in England. I enjoy my residence here so much (even after four or five year's acquaintance with the country) that I wish to defer all literary toil and other business of life till my return home.

Your acquaintance with the New England history will have suggested to you, I think, that it affords very little variety of subject for the Romance-writer. Taking into view its limitations of accident, character, and colouring, and likewise the limitations of my own faculty, I doubt whether I could find the theme for another Puritan story.

Sincerely yours,
Nath[l] Hawthorne

Samuel Lucas, Esq.
London.[31]

16. Wednesday. Cool, pleasant morning. Letter to Una from O'Sullivan in Paris.[32] At about 12, set out with Mamma & walked to Whitnash, returning by Tachbourne [*sic*] Road. A letter from Fields in Paris.[33] About dusk, took a walk with Julian.[34]

This was the second letter that Nathaniel had received from Fields in a month, something of a record, even though it was occasioned by the latter's concern about the progress of the romance. In addition to inquiring about any news, Fields also let him know of the latest addition to the Ticknor and Fields "empire." This was one letter that had to be answered immediately (or almost immediately).

Leamington, Nov[r] 17th '59

Dear Fields,
I have no doubt you will spend the next two months more comfortably in England than anywhere else. The Italian spring commences in February—which is certainly an advantage, especially as from February to May is the most disagreeable portion of the English year. But it is always summer by a bright coal fire. We find nothing to complain of in the climate of Leamington. To be sure, we cannot always see our hand before us for fog;—but I like fog, and do not care about seeing my hand before me.
  We have thought of staying here till after Christmas, and then going somewhere else—perhaps to Bath—perhaps to Devonshire.[35] But all this is uncertain. Leamington is not so desirable a residence in winter as in summer; its great charm consisting in the many delightful walks and drives, and in its neighborhood to interesting places.
  I have quite finished the book (sometime ago) and sent it to Smith Elder & Co, who tell me it is in the printers' hands; but I have received no proof-sheets. They wrote to request another title, instead of the "Romance of Monte Beni"; and I sent them their choice of a dozen. I don't know what they have chosen; neither do I understand their objection to the above. Perhaps they don't like the book at all; but I shall not trouble myself about that, as long as they publish it and pay me my £600. For my part, I think it much my best Romance; but I can see some points where it is open to assault. If it could have appeared first in America, it would have been a safer thing.
  I had not heard of the purchase of the Atlantic Monthly; but my presaging spirit had foreseen the event.[36] I cannot but admire your wishing me to write for it, after all your friendly advice to the contrary. However, I will—that is, after I get home. I mean to spend the rest of my abode in England in blessed idleness; and as for my <u>Journal,</u> in the first place, I have not got it here—secondly, there is nothing in it that it will do to publish.[37]

Your friend
Nath[l] Hawthorne[38]

His statement to Fields as to the family's movements over the next few months certainly gives the impression that Nathaniel was quite happy to stay where he was, in front of the fire, and that essentially it was too much bother to start thinking about moving elsewhere and certainly too much bother in a practical sense to actually make a move. It must be assumed that as he was seemingly content to do nothing after "two or three months" work (!), the idea of the family's discontent (if there was any) was either not entertained by him or voiced by them. And, as has been mentioned, Sophia appeared to be in fairly good health (apart from her teeth) so there seemed little need to move again at present for that reason alone.

17. Thursday. An overcast morning. Wrote a note to Fields. After 4 °clock, walked by Tachborne [sic] road to Whitnash, with Julian.

18. Friday. Rather overcast morning. Letter from Bennoch.[39] Walked with Julian, at 11, to Warwick, & there met Mamma & Una, who had gone by omnibus. Did some shopping, & all walked home together, arriving before 2. After 4, took a moderate walk with Julian.[40]

No doubt Nathaniel was somewhat irritated to receive another letter from Lucas, as he probably felt that he had given him a fairly forthright refusal; however:

11 Bouverie St., Nov. 17, 1859

My dear Sir,—I am both gratified and obliged by your answer to my letter. More-over, it is quite as satisfactory as I could have expected, as it leaves me the hope that hereafter you may be induced to comply with our very earnest wishes. I agree with you that the Puritan chord is monotonous, and would indeed prefer any other theme. I know with what power you can touch other themes, for I have just read "The Blithedale Romance" [Nathaniel could have muttered here, "Just!!!"]. And perhaps, having lived so long in England as I am glad to hear you have [and he could have muttered here, "where's he been for the last six years?"], and enjoyed your sojourn, you may have acquired such an interest in some phases of English life that you may be prompted to weave these into a story. In this respect you seem to have an advantage possessed by none of your inventive compatriots whom I can recall, except Washington Irving; and I sincerely believe it is open to you, by striking into this track, to achieve as thoroughly an English and European reputation as he has. Highly honored as you are in England, in my opinion your name has not acquired here, as yet, nearly as much prestige as should fairly belong to it; and I do think your association with us would materially help towards this,—in the first place, because of our great and increasing circulation, and in the next, because I can put at your disposal for illustrative purposes the best artistic resources in this country. In this respect we are aiming at something unique. I may add that it will equally suit us if we could make arrangements with yourself for some time hence, say even towards the close of 1860. I shall be greatly pleased if you will give me a further warranty to discuss the matter with Bradbury and Evans, who are quite prepared to meet you on your own terms in a pecuniary sense.

Believe me yours sincerely,
Sam.Lucas[41]

19. Saturday. An overcast morning. Letter from S. Lucas, of 'Once a Week.' Walked out with wife, & went to the Bank, & drew a cheque for £60, on Baring Brothers. Wrote to advise them of it.[42] Towards dusk, took a walk with Julian.[43]

And so the days passed, during which Nathaniel was waiting for the first batch of proof sheets to arrive from Smith, Elder, and as far as can be ascertained, he did absolutely nothing at all except look at the weather and go for short walks, usually with Julian or Una. Of course, he must have been doing something to pass the time, probably reading a lot, but what he read is not known either. His inertia must have had some detrimental effect on the rest of the family; even though the weather was not too good now, there is no record of any outings by rail or carriage to anywhere in the surrounding areas to relieve the monotony. Presumably the children were continuing to receive their lessons (mainly under Sophia's supervision), though the number of times that Julian went out with his father on walks, at different times of the day, seems to indicate a rather more relaxed regime with regard to school lessons than had been the case in the past.

20. Sunday. A clear cool morning. Towards dusk, took a walk to the edge of Whitnash, with Julian.

21. Monday. Rather an overcast day. Nearly at dusk, took a walk with Julian.

22. Tuesday. A dim, but not cloudy morning. At about 1, went to the Bank, & rec[d] £60 for my cheque. Took a walk about town. At dusk, took a walk with Julian along the Warwick road.

23. Wednesday. A dark, damp morning. Towards dusk, took a walk by myself; Julian following [was Julian in a mood?].

24. Thursday. A very pleasant day. Mamma & Fanny went to Warwick. Between 4 & 5, Julian and I walked to Whitnash.

25. Friday. A dull & sombre morning. Towards dusk, took a short walk with Julian.

26. Saturday. Showery morning, with glimpses of sun. After 4, walked out with Una & Julian.

27. Sunday. A rather pleasant morning. Letters from Mrs. Badger (late Miss Shepard)[44] and E. E. Peabody, now Mrs. How.[45] After 4, took a walk with Julian.[46]

On Monday a fairly extraordinary letter was received from Fields, addressed to Sophia, so extraordinary that an answer was sent the same day:

Paris. Hotel de l'Empire
Rue Neuve S[t] Augustin

November 25, 1859

My dear Mrs. Hawthorne,
You will have seen by the paper that your husband's Publishers (T & F) are to issue 'The Atlantic Monthly' in future. Some time ago I advised the author of the 'Romance of Monte Beni' to refuse to contribute to any periodical for reasons sound and clear at that time. Now circumstances render those reasons void, and I have asked that Distinguished friend of ours to add his name and fame to help on the oceanic monthly. He will do it I know, albeit he says in a letter lately received from him that he has nothing at present to send in.

I am very anxious that not only the author of sundry great works which you and I and the public like so much should write for 'The Atlantic', but that his wife should also send some papers to its pages. I think she would be inclined to contribute if I could see her today and tell her how happy both the publishers can be made in the event of her forwarding to the house in Boston a communication for the early no⁵ of 1860.

I know how well pleased every body will be if you will comply with my request, dear Mrs. Hawthorne, and I rely on you to send me a favorable reply.

Mrs. Fields begs me to mention her kindest regards to yourself, Mr. Hawthorne & the children.

I cannot tell you how anxious I am to read the new Romance.

Very sincerely Yours
James T. Fields[47]

28. Monday. Cloudy & wet morning. A letter from Mr. Fields in Paris to my wife. My wife and I answered Fields' note. After 4, took a walk with Julian.[48]

Why did Fields send such a letter as this? He could have been aware of and appreciated Sophia's literary descriptive powers as contained in her letters and journals, some of which he may have had the chance of reading. But he must have known of Nathaniel's deep-seated objection to "scribbling females" (as well as Sophia's) although he would hardly have been likely to have used that phrase in relation to his (Nathaniel's) wife's efforts (even though, on more than one occasion, he had praised her literary abilities). He must also have realized that while it was worth his while making the suggestion to Sophia, he knew that unless he was able to do it person, and in private (". . . if I could see her today and tell her. . . .") he would certainly be turned down. But in making this initial request, perhaps he was preparing the ground for future possibilities? It can readily be imagined that when he had been shown the letter by Sophia (with whatever opinion she made on the contents) Nathaniel would have said, pointedly, "I don't think you would really want to do that, *would* you, dear?"

My dear Mr. Fields

I am very sorry indeed that you should ask me to do any thing for you which I cannot possibly do. I assure you most earnestly that nothing less urgent and terrible than the immediate danger of starvation for my husband and children would induce me to put myself into a magazine or a pair of book covers. You forget that Mr. Hawthorne is the Belleslettres portion of my being, and besides I have a repugnance to female authoresses in general. I have far more distaste for myself as a female authoress in particular. Though I shall be delighted to see you I am still glad that I have not to combat any of your arguments upon this subject viva voce; because I know you are eloquent, fascinating and of infinite good humour; and I should find it painful to oppose you. Yet I <u>should</u> oppose you with as steady and immovable pertinacity as the biggest created rock would resist the raging sea or the sweet lapsing tides. You have no idea how inexorable I am. Neither the honeyed words of Nestor, nor the artful insinuations of Ulysses, in short no one and nothing would prevail, except the one prospective horror aforementioned. But I wish all prosperity to the Atlantic Monthly, and I hope Mr. Hawthorne will help you, if it be best. Yet both Mr. Ticknor and yourself have formerly proved to him very clearly that it would be injurious to him to contribute to periodicals.

With our most cordial regard to Mrs. Fields, I am very sincerely yours,

Sophia Hawthorne.

Leamington, November 28th 1859
21 Bath St.[49]

Fields may well have smiled somewhat ruefully when he received that.

Leamington, Nov. 28th 1859

Dear Fields,
You are quite right in wanting Mrs. Hawthorne for contributress; and perhaps I may yet starve her into compliance. I have never read anything so good as some of her narrative and descriptive epistles to her friends; but I doubt whether she would find sufficient inspiration in writing directly for the public. I don't know how the Romance comes on; but I have a suspicion that they must have decided on deferring the publication till the Spring. This will suit me just as well, provided it comes out before June—and provided they pay me an instalment of the copy money within a month or two.

Are you coming over?

Your Friend
Nath[l] Hawthorne.[50]

Leamington, Nov[r] 29th 59

Dear Bennoch,
Plutarch came duly to hand, and gives great satisfaction. We should have thanked you at an earlier date, but have been daily in expectation of seeing you.

Smith & Elder told me, two or three weeks ago, that the Romance was in the printers' hands, and would go on rapidly; but I have since heard nothing from them, and begin to think that they intend to defer the publication till the spring. This will suit me equally well—that is, providing they pay me part of the £600 in the course of a month or two.

Unless called up by business, I shall not come to London at present. My experience of it, two years ago, had given me a distaste for London in latter autumn and early winter.[51]

Mrs. Hawthorne had a note from Fields, yesterday, requesting her to become a contributor to the Atlantic Monthly! I don't know whether I can tolerate a literary rival at bed and board; there would probably be a new chapter in the "Quarrel of Authors."[52] However, I make myself at ease on that score, as she positively refuses to be famous, and contents herself with being the best wife and mother in the world.

We rely upon seeing you in ten days, (according to your promise for the last two months,) and with our best regards to Mrs. Bennoch,

Your friend,
Nath¹ Hawthorne.[53]

29. Tuesday. A clear & cool morning. Note from Bennoch,[54] which I answered. At noon, went out shopping[55] with Mamma & Una. After dinner, walked to the first mile-stone on the Warwick road with Julian.

30. Wednesday. A moist morning. At about 1, took a walk with Una & Rosebud. After dinner, walked to Whitnash with Julian.[56]

10

"We have real winter weather" in Leamington: December 1859

The days were passing without incident; December was upon them, and still no proof sheets had arrived.

Leamington, Decr 1st '59

Dear Ticknor,
It is a good while since I heard from you; But I make no complaints, being myself so dilatory a correspondent.

I finished the Romance some weeks ago; and Smith and Elder wrote to me that it was in the printer's hands, and would pass speedily through the press. Since then, I have heard nothing about the matter, and I cannot account for the delay, except on the supposition that they mean to put off publication till the Spring. This, indeed, seems to me the most eligible course; because it would be quite impossible to make the necessary arrangements for the simultaneous publication on your side of the water, supposing the book to appear in this country at Christmas.

By Fields' advice, I gave the book the title of "The Romance of Monte Beni"; but as Smith & Elder thought it not a captivating name, I sent them several others to choose from. I do not know which they will select; but their choice need not govern yours, and, if you wish to announce the book, I should like to have you call it "Saint Hilda's Shrine." We can change the title afterwards, should it appear advisable.

The publication of the Romance being deferred, I cannot call upon Smith & Elder to pay over the £600, at present; so that you would oblige me by lodging £200, or thereabouts, with the Barings.

I had a letter from Fields, about a week ago. He is still in Paris, and seems to have given up the idea of spending the winter in Italy.

We hear from Bennoch occasionally, and are in hopes of seeing him here, in the course of a few days.

When we were at Marseilles, last June, I left three trunks in charge of our Consul there, to be transmitted to the United States, directed to your care. They contained clothing, books, and curiosities and works of art, which we collected in Rome. I gave directions to have them sent to Boston; but it is possible, if no vessel offered for that port, that they might go to New York. In either case, no doubt, you would be notified of their arrival. If they have been received, I wish you would let me know; and, if not, you would greatly oblige me by writing to our Consul at Marseilles on the subject. His name is Derbé, I think, or some

280

such name [actually, Derbes]; but you would find it in a blue-book or United States Register.

Please pay any bills that come to you, certified by Mrs. Horace Mann, for repairs on the house at Concord. I wish I had a better house, and I should enjoy far greater pleasure in the idea of coming home. As the case stands, I have hardly any other anticipation so pleasant as that of seeing you at the old 'Corner Store.'

We are all very well, and heartily hope that you are the same.

Your friend,
Nathl Hawthorne.[1]

1. Thursday. A moist day, with glimpses of sun. At mid-day, walked with Una by the Tachbrooke [sic] Road to Whitnash. Towards dusk, walked with Julian up & down the Parade. Wrote a letter to W. D. Ticknor, to-day.

2. Friday. A bright, cool morning. A letter to Una from Richd Manning.[2] At noon, took a short walk with Una. After dinner, walked with Julian to the first mile-stone on the Warwick road.[3]

Una took the opportunity to reply to her cousin at once:

Leamington Dec 2nd 1859

My dear cousin Richard,

I received your letter this morning, and was very glad of it indeed, it is such a very long time since I have heard from you. I wrote to Aunt Lizzie or to you once or twice last winter in the intervals of my illness, which letters you could not have received, as I told you in them what would always be our direction in Italy, and I sent a long letter to Aunt Lizzie from France, telling her all about our visits.

You are right in supposing that Papa and Julian and Rose are well now. In Rome Papa was very unwell a great deal of the time, but almost directly after we came to England he began to regain his usual health and strength, and now is perfectly well.

Julian's health has never wavered, and though Rose is not perfectly well, she has nothing at all serious to complain of.

I cannot tell you how deeply grieved we were to hear of your sad affliction in the state of your brother's health. We had not the least idea of it before, as you have never mentioned him in your letters, but I do not wonder you had not the heart to do it. I most earnestly hope he will recover, but I am glad you feel that trust in Providence which is the only comfort we can have in great afflictions. And what a dreadful illness poor Rebecca has had. I am truly glad she is recovering now, but I should think it would indeed be a long time before she regains her former health. I think you have had at least as sad a year as we have, indeed much sadder when I think of your brother Robert.[4]

What a nice account you give me of life in Salem, I have quite a picture of it in my mind now. Are you much acquainted with the Rev. J. M. Hoppin, of whom you speak? We saw him and his family when we were in London last July. They were staying at the same boarding house and though we had not known them before, became acquainted, as the same countrymen do in a foreign land. Mr. Hoppin presented Mamma with an address he had written on the completion of the Plummer Hall in Salem, in which he mentioned, or alluded to papa. The point of his allusion I could not comprehend. He said something about there being another Hawthorne without the <u>thorne</u>, but how there could be a Hawthorne without the thorne I do not see and I was not aware that Papa was at all a thorny person in any other way, or that anybody thought him so.[5] Papa finished his book two or three weeks ago, and sent it to his publishers, in London, but we do not know exactly when it will come out.

The scene of the story is laid in Italy. I have not read it yet, so you may imagine how anxious I am for it to come out.

If you were here you would hardly think it was the second day of winter, it is more like an American Indian summer day, for the sky is clear (for an English sky) and the sun shines (though in rather a watery & despairing manner) and though it is cold enough to have a fire and enjoy it, still we are by no means uncomfortable as I suppose you are. In the mornings there is generally a frost and it is very cold, but by about twelve o'clock the sun has become quite warm, and from then till two it is very pleasant. Then in the afternoon we often have rain, always damp & dark. But only too often it rains all day. I never knew a climate on which one could depend so little. Really, one never can tell what is going to happen from one hour to another.

I think Leamington is much the mildest and pleasantest of any of the middle or northern towns of England at the present time, in so many places there have been dreadful calamities from wind and rain, and on the coast there have been many terrible wrecks, while here though the weather has been bad enough, we have had nothing very remarkable.

I have even less to tell you about than you appear to have had, strange as it may seem to you, but our life here is very quiet & secluded, as we know no one nearer than London, and having been here before have seen all the sights.

I generally go to walk with Papa between twelve and two, either to the old town of Warwick with its beautiful castle, where the Earls of Warwick lived in the days of their power, and which has been inhabited, I suppose, by the king-making earl,—or to the little village of Radford, with its picturesque old buttressed church, and antiquated inn and thatched Elizabethan houses, or to Lillington with its old church and neat cottages with their pretty little gardens, that a short time ago were full of bright flowers, or some other pleasant country walk over fields and stiles, and between the trim hedges, green grass beneath, and the dear old cloudy sky of England above. Every inch of our English landscape, like every inch of our English person, seems to have <u>English</u> written all over it. The peculiar quiet sweet cultivated loveliness of an English scene can be found no-where else, a sort of in-born dignity and fitness seems to possess every tree and blade of grass, and say "I feel that I am in the place assigned to me and that no other place would suit. I am happy in my self and with the whole world."

For anyone who is weary of the bustling, noisy world & everlasting change & excitement, I think England would be the place to come to. In America everything is "go-ahead", and everybody has to go-ahead too, to a certain degree, I suppose, whether they will or no. Then in Italy it is too much the other way. One's moral sense is continually distracted by the idolatrous mummeries of the Catholic church, and one can never feel truly gay & joyous while seeing all around what was once a mighty and noble people, full of spirit & intellect and genius, crushed into the dust by religious tyranny, till every spark of mental life seems to be crushed out of them. Italy is beautiful and interesting but interesting only in the ruins of what once has been, in its grand buildings and splendid works of art,—it is a land of memories, and while there we seem to live with past generations. In the Roman Forum, in the Coliseum, in the Temple of Peace, and the Palace of the Caesars, everything carries us back to those long past ages of power & glory, when Rome was Queen of all the world. A shadow of melancholy seems to descend upon us when we enter the gates of the Eternal City, that envelopes us all the time we stay there—Those narrow streets, with their sepulchral gloom and lordly palaces, those palaces with their splendid architecture and gorgeous decorations, but so cold & dusty & desolate, those long dim galleries of pictures, those Roman people, with their graceful forms that have lost their spirit, and large dark eyes that have lost their fire—all speak of how great & glorious was the past, how melancholy and hopeless is the present and it cannot but be with sad feelings that we look upon it all. And I suppose everywhere on the Continent one does feel this death in life more or less, but in England it does not seem to be so. Wise people say that England is gradually going down, but it has not gone yet, most certainly, and "all-right" seems to be the word for it. It is still progressing enough to make one feel easy, and yet it has seen too much of life to rush on with that tumbling, helter-skelter haste & eagerness one sees in America generally, and one can either be grave or gay—in a continual round of amusements & excitements or in a quiet home-stead where you can have all the seclusion of a hermit, with all the conveniences of social life—supposing you have plenty of money in your pocket, which is a very necessary supposition, for I don't think anywhere in the world is money more absolutely necessary if you want to be comfortable than here. And reserved & peculiar as the English appear to be, if you once break the outer ice, where would you find warmer hearts, more cordial hospitality? We have had a most pleasant experience in every way in England, and we love it dearly. In itself, there is just enough of the past to temper and mellow the present, and just enough life in the present to lighten up the past, and in the most refined English people, their conservatism and national pride of birth and rank and country, gives them a sort of distinguishing isolated character, that is very pleasant to see for a change, when it is not too much exaggerated. And certainly they have a great deal to be proud of.

But what a long drawn length of tiresome talk I am inflicting you with, dear cousin Richard. I must stop, I think, or you will think you had better not encourage my correspondence.

I cannot help thinking of your brother all the time, it seems so very sad. But I cannot say it surprises me very much when a person who believes in a wrathful God and eternal damnation, and has a vivid imagination & power of thought, becomes deranged. It certainly is more than enough to make any one so.

It is only when we believe in a loving God & tender Father that we can be happy. And if we do believe in a loving God, how can we believe that his mercy and forgiveness can be less than ours. For we see much to excuse the greatest crimes in surrounding circumstances, & many temptations which every human being has to fight against here, and if we see it, how is it possible that God should not, who knows all our inward feelings & temptations, and who knows that the best of us are weak. Unless we are gods who know not sin, we must backslide sometimes, and though I do not believe that we can be with the first until we are perfect, still I believe that we all can and shall atone sometime for our worst sins and that we shall all see God and heaven at last. I am sure it cannot be otherwise.

But I will not make my letter any longer, and with love to Aunt Lizzie and Rebecca, who I hope will soon be quite well, and hoping to hear from you again before very long,

I am very sincerely
Your cousin Una Hawthorne[6]

Another four days were to pass before the the first batch of proof-sheets arrived.

> 3. Saturday. A cool & pretty clear morning. After 4 °clock, took a walk with Julian.

> 4. Sunday. A chill & snowy morning. Rainy pretty much all day. Between 3 & 4 took a walk about town with Julian.

> 5. Monday. A rainy day. A letter from Mrs. King, and daughter (of Redcar) to Mamma & Rosebud.[7] Towards dusk, took a walk with Julian.[8]

Next day, having received the first batch of proof sheets, Nathaniel was keen to make it clear that there would no be no delay at his end of the operation by ensuring that the sheets were read and returned as quickly as possible,[9] even though he knew now that there was no likelihood of the publishing process being finished in time for a pre-Christmas deadline.

21, Bath-st, Leamington,
Decr 6th 1859

Gentlemen,
I have received (and return by this post) some proof-sheets of the Romance, being the first which I have received.
    In reply to a letter of yours, disapproving of the title, I sent you a choice of several others; but I see that the printers adhere to the first one.[10]
    A friend of mine [Henry Bright] has requested to have the manuscripts of this work, after it has gone through the press; and I beg that it may be preserved for him.

Respectfully,
Nath¹ Hawthorne[11]

> 6. Tuesday. A clear morning. The first proof-sheets of my Romance arrived. Sent back the proof-sheets to Smith & Elder; likewise, a note to them. After 4, took a walk about town with Julian.[12]

The progress of the proofreading stage of the production of the romance was not made clear by subsequent references to it in Nathaniel's diary, but it becomes apparent that a steady daily flow of sheets back and forth between London and Leamington was maintained for a period of about a week after this initial batch had been received.

> 7. Wednesday. A clear morning. Recd & sent back a package of proof-sheets. After 4, took a walk towards Whitnash & back by the Tachbrooke [sic] road, with Julian. Una, Julian & Fanny, went to a lecture on Bunyan, with dissolving views, in the evening.[13]

> 8. Thursday. A pleasant morning, but dim. Recd letter &c from Smith Elder &

Co.[14] Rec[d] & returned some proofs. After 4, walked on the Warwick road with Julian.

9. Friday. A pleasant morning. At about 11, walked a mile on the Warwick road with Una. After 4, took a walk with Julian.

10. Saturday. A dim, but not cloudy morning. Letter to mamma from Miss Hosmer, inclosed in one from Sarah Clarke.[15] At noon, took a walk up & down the Parade with Una. Rec[d] & returned a proof sheet. After dinner, walked up & down the Parade by myself.[16]

Possibly Nathaniel took the walk by himself to let off steam in peace, having received a "single" proof sheet from the printer; at the rate of one a day, he might be in Leamington for another year!

11. Sunday. A dim morning. After 4 °clock walked to Whitnash with Julian.

12. Monday. A dark & rainy morning. A letter to Mamma from Miss Bracken in Paris.[17] Wrote to Smith Elder & Co, proposing the "Marble Faun" as a title.[18] After 4, walked up & down the Parade with Julian. A very black, foggy, and wet day.

13. Tuesday. Dark morning. Saw Major Johnstone give Julian his last lesson in the broadsword & gymnastics. At noon, took a walk up & down the Parade with Una. After four, took a walk with Julian on the Warwick road.

14. Wednesday. Clear & cool morning. A letter to Mamma from Bennoch.[19] After 4, took a walk with Julian.

15. Thursday. A cold, clear morning. Letter to Mamma from Mrs. Mann at Concord. After 4, took a walk with Julian.[20]

This latest letter from Mary was much more restrained than her last (and in slighter better handwriting), as she was beginning to relate to her husband's death in a more rational way and was learning how to combat her initial, seemingly irreparable, feeling of loss. She had been reading Elizabeth's letters to him, at the time when he had lost his first wife (and when Elizabeth had felt more than mere friendship for the bereaved Horace Mann); "They have brought him back very forcibly too—and after the happy change that came over him when he again let himself love and be loved, it seemed to be almost another person. . . . I love to think of him from every possible point of view & in every relation." There were moves afoot to erect a statue to Horace, which Mary was very dubious about, as she felt that nothing of stone or bronze could bring out his stature as a man; there was not even a good pictorial likeness of him, she felt, except for some India ink paintings that had been prepared from photographs.[21]

It seems that Una had her own peculiar system of dealing with her letters

The post office, Bath Street, directly opposite the Hawthornes at No. 21. Photograph ca. 1860. Courtesy of the Leamington Spa Library, Warwickshire.

after she had written them, a system that quite often resulted in their not being mailed at all, as in this latest instance she found that the letter that she had written to her cousin two weeks previously was still lying about the house (perhaps this explains why her letters to Richard and Aunt Lizzie, written in Italy and France, appear not to have been received in America). In this present case, it was all the more inexcusable, as No. 21 Bath Street was almost exactly opposite the main Leamington Post Office! So, as before, a postscript had to be added up, down and across the various margins:

Dec. 16th. Dear Cousin Richard. This letter was laid by and forgotten, and now it cannot go till next week, so I will add a little more.

When I wrote before I told you about our Indian Summer days, but now the scene has changed, and we have real winter weather. At least I suppose you would not call it so, but to us, who have been accustomed to Italian winters, it seems dreadful. The snow is about quarter of an inch thick and has remained on the ground several days, and the muddy old Leam is covered with ice thick enough for a miriad [sic] of eager boys and men to skate upon; which they are never tired of doing, and what is still more wonderful to me, ever so many people, in defiance of frost and cold, stand on the bridge by the hour together, gaping at the skaters with unabatable interest. I take a walk every day, as it is the only efficient way of getting warm, but it requires a good deal of resolution to go at first. I find I have not much to tell you, as I was interrupted and now I have forgotten what I was going to say, but my letter is long enough I think. Do you remember how we first began to correspond? I have been trying to think but I cannot, I was such a little girl when I commenced. Soon I shall have arrived at the mature age of sixteen. But I suppose you will think of me as a little girl of nine years old. I assure you I am very different now and I don't suppose you will know me. Goodbye again. I hope I shall hear from you as soon as you find time to write.[22]

16. Friday. Dull morning. Snow on the ground. After 4, walked out with Julian on the old Warwick road.[23]

The horrors of the Hawthorne family's morning ablutions in cold water (something the children had been accustomed to since their earliest childhood, and their parents for many years) are aptly demonstrated at this time by Nathaniel's entry in his diary for Saturday, as it appears that despite the wintry weather they were all still indulging in the daily ritual, although he does refer to "his" tub. If Sophia was still taking part it could be doubted whether it did her any good at all.

17. Saturday. Very cold morning; my bathing tub frozen over.[24] Proof-sheet from Smith & Elder; sent it back. At about 11, a telegraph from Bennoch; not coming here to-day. After dinner, walked to Whitnash with Julian.[25]

It was a disappointment to them all that Bennoch couldn't make the promised visit and a further disappointment, presumably, to Nathaniel in particular that only one proof sheet came from Smith, Elder. It seemed that the printer's progress was continuing to be laboriously (and perhaps purposely) slow.

18. Sunday. Cold morning. A note from Bennoch[26] After dinner, walked to Whitnash with Julian.

19. Monday. An exceedingly cold morning. After dinner, walked on the Warwick road with Julian.

20. Tuesday. Still very cold; everything frozen up. After 4, walked to the 1st milestone, Warwick road, &c, &c. by myself. The weather has moderated. The Doctor came to see Rosebud for some slight ailment.

21. Wednesday. Clear & rather mild morning. Letters from Ellen & Mary Peabody.[27] After dinner, took a walk with Julian. Much more moderate weather. Dr. Sutherland[28] came again to see Rosebud. She seems better.[29]

Leamington, Decr 22nd '59

Dear Ticknor,
I have received proof-sheets of the Romance as far as the commencement of the second volume. They were going on at the rate of 50 pages a day; and I was afraid

that they would get the book out, on this side of the water, before Christmas, without waiting for you to get it through the press and publish simultaneously. So I suggested that there was no occasion for haste, inasmuch as I should remain in England till next summer. The printing has gone on much more leisurely.

The exact middle of the work is at the 10th chapter (called "the Pedigree of Monte Beni") of the second volume; and you must commence your second volume with that chapter.

The publishers proposed to call the Romance "The Transformation; or the Romance of Monte Beni";—but this title did not suit me, and I rejected it.[30] I think I shall call it "The Marble Faun"; and unless I write you to the contrary, I wish you would prefix that title on the title-page.

It is a good while since I heard from Fields. Bennoch has been promising us a visit here, but probably will not now come till after Christmas.

We are all pretty well.

As the delay in publishing the Romance will prevent my receiving the £600 at present, I wish you to place funds to some moderate amount with the Barings. I don't know how my account stands with them.

I long to see you, and all my friends, and am at last beginning to be homesick.

Sincerely yours
Nath[l] Hawthorne

P.S. No letter from you this long while.[31]

Leamington, Dec[r] 22[d] '59

Dear Bennoch,
My wife thinks me very remiss in not writing to tell you how disappointed we were that your visit did not come off, as agreed upon. I assure her that the male sex does not make a conscience and a religion of writing notes, as women do, and that a man is neither bothered than otherwise by receiving epistles about nothing at all. However, she will not agree with me, and threatens to write herself, unless I do.

I have nothing to say, except that we were really very sorry not to see you, and shall begin to expect you again, immediately after Christmas.

The printers have advanced into the second volume of my Romance, and would probably have finished it, by this time, if I had not interposed to retard their progress. At the rate they were going on, they would have had it out, on this side of the water, long before Ticknor could have been ready for publication in the States; and so I should have hazarded my American copyright. Probably they will now make it a Spring publication.

I have heard nothing of Fields this very long while.

With our kindest Christmas wishes to Mrs. Bennoch and yourself.

Ever your friend
Nath[l] Hawthorne.[32]

22. Thursday. Tolerably mild & pleasant morning. Wrote a note to Ticknor. Also, a note to Bennoch. After dinner, walked out with Julian.

23. Friday. A foggy morning. After dinner, took a walk with Julian.

24. Saturday. A rather mild & pleasant morning. After dinner, walked with Julian. A barrel of oysters came from Bennoch. After dark, we distributed our Christmas presents.[33]

It must be relevant to introduce here the story that Julian remembered as having been written by his mother, possibly as some form of Christmas entertainment that could be read aloud to the assembled family; was this the sort of thing that Fields had in mind when he wrote to Sophia for a contribution to the *Atlantic Monthly?*:

They [reminiscences of her earliest years] were written in 1859, shortly before leaving England for America, [and must in theory, therefore, have been written in Leamington] and were designed, of course, solely to afford entertainment to her children. Only a beginning was made; after a few pages the narrative breaks off, and was never resumed. Enough is given, however, to justify a regret that there is no more; for, as the writer warmed to her work, it would evidently have increased in minuteness and suggestiveness. The full names of the *dramatis personæ* are not given, nor are they important to the matter in hand:[34]

When I was four or five years old, I was sent away, for the first time, from home and my mother, to visit my grandmamma. My mother was the tenderest and loveliest mother in the world, and I do not understand how I could have borne to be separated from her for a day. The journey I entirely forget, and also my arrival; but after I was there, I remember a scene in the sunny courtyard as plainly as if it were yesterday. I was playing with two tiny puppies, belonging to my aunt Alice, and I was endeavouring to take up one of them in my small, inadequate hands. It struggled vigorously and squealed, and was so hard and fat, I could not get a firm hold of it; so I dropped it on the pavement, which caused it to squeal louder than before. Hereupon, out rushed my aunt, and violently shook me by the arm, uttering severe words, that have entirely gone out of my mind. She was tall, stately, and handsome, and very terrible in her wrath. I felt like a criminal; and as it had never yet occurred to me that a grown person could do wrong, but that only children were naughty, I took the scolding, and the earthquake my aunt made of my little body, as a proper penalty for some fault which she saw, though I did not. I only intended to caress her unmanageable pet, not to hurt it; but innocence is unconscious, and not quick to defend itself. I was forbidden ever to touch the dogs again, and was sent into the house out of the bright sunshine. I can see now, as then, that bright sunshine, as it flooded the grass and shrubbery; the clear, fresh appearance of every object, as if lately washed and then arrayed in gold; the great trees, spreading forth innumerable branches, with leaves glistening and fluttering in the wind. I forget how I found my way to my grandmother's room upstairs; but I was soon looking out of her window into a street. I saw, sitting on a doorstep directly opposite, a beggar-girl; and when she caught sight of me, she clenched her fist and uttered a sentence which I never forgot, though I did not in the least comprehend it. 'I'll maul you!' said the beggar-girl, with a scowling, spiteful face. I gazed at her in terror, feeling scarcely safe, though within four walls and half-way to the sky—as it seemed to me. I was convinced that she would have me at last, and that no power could prevent it; but I did not appeal to grandmamma for aid, nor utter a word of my awful fate to any one. Children seldom communicate their deepest feelings or greatest troubles to those around them. What tragedies are often enacted in their poor little hearts, without even the mother's suspecting it! It may, perhaps, partly be caused by their small vocabulary; and, besides, they are seldom individually conscious, but take it for granted that their own experience is that of all other children. How can a child of three years old find language to express its inward emotions? A child's dim sense of almightiness in events that happen, overpowers its faculty of representation. My aunt Alice's anger was, to my mind, a very insignificant matter beside this peril; and as I fixed my eyes intently upon the girl, I recognized with dismay the fearful creature who had once met me when I had escaped out of the garden-gate at home, and was taking my first independent stroll. No nurse or servant was near me on that happy day. It was glorious. My steps were winged, and there seemed more space on every side than I heretofore supposed the world contained. The sense of freedom from all shackles was intoxicating. I had on no hat, no out-door dress, no gloves. What exquisite fun! I really think every child that is born ought to have the happiness of running away once in their lives at least. I went up a street that gradually ascended, till, at the summit, I believed I stood at the top of the earth. But, alas! at that acme of success my joy ended; for there I was suddenly confronted by this beggar-girl,—the first ragged, begrimed human being I had ever seen. She seized my wrist and said, 'Make me a curtsey!' All the blood in my veins tingled with indignation: 'No, I will not!' I said. How I got away, and home again, I cannot tell; but as I did not obey the insolent command, I constantly expected revenge in some form, and yet never told my mother anything about it. A short time after the grievous encounter, my hobgoblin passed along when I was standing at the door, and muttered threats, and frowned; and now here she was again, so far from where I first met her, evidently come for me, and I should fall into her hands and be mauled! What was that? Something, doubtless, unspeakably dreadful. The new, strange word cast an indefinite horror over the process to which I was to be subjected. Where could the creature have got the expression? I have never heard it since, I believe. Neither did I ever see the beggar-girl again in all my life.

Other memories of that visit to my grandmamma are neither rich nor sweet, but so indelibly engraven on my memory that I can discern them well. My aunt Alice had two sisters who were unkind and tyrannical to such a degree that she seemed quite angelic in comparison with them. My uncle George was my mamma's beloved brother, and radiant with benevolence and all the gracious amenities. I did not think, however, of taking refuge in him, or even of sneaking to him. He came into view, sometimes, like a gleam of sunshine, and passed away I knew not whither;—a kind of inaccessible blessing, or rather, an unavailable one to me. I perceive now that he was the only amiable individual in the house. The favorite pastime of my aunts Emily and Matilda was to torment me; and whenever they could take me captive, I was led off for cruel sport. The mischievous gleam of their dark eyes, and the wonderful rivulets of dark curls flowing over their crimson cheeks, are painted on my inner tablets in fixed colors. Sometimes they opened a great book (which I now fear was the Bible) and commanded me to read a lesson. If I miscalled the letters in trying to spell the words, they shouted in derision. My sensitiveness doubtless incited them to ingenious devices to mortify and frighten me. One day they asked me if I would like to see the most beautiful of gardens, blooming with the sweetest, gayest flowers; and when I gratefully and joyfully assented, trusting them without misgiving, they opened a door and gave me a sudden push, which sent me falling down several steps into utter darkness. Another time they took me into a courtyard full of turkeys, and drove the creatures, gobbling like so many fiends, towards me. I expected to be devoured at once, and my distress was immeasurable; and the enjoyment of the young ladies was complete. Their mocking laughter made me feel ashamed of being miserable. My loving mamma, in the unknown distance, seemed a Heaven to which I should return at last; but there was nothing like her here, except perhaps the visionary uncle George.

Grandmamma was a severe disciplinarian. I was always sent to bed at six o'clock, without liberty of appeal in any case; and this was right and proper enough. But I was put into an upper room, alone in the dark, and left out of reach of help, as I supposed, from any human being. It was my first trial of darkness and loneliness; for my blessed mother never inflicted needless misery on her children. Every night I lay in terror at street noises as long as I was awake. I am not aware of having derived any benefit from that Spartan severity, and I have always been careful that my children should have the light and society they desired in their tender age. At table, food was sometimes given me which I did not fancy; and I was sternly told that I must eat and drink whatever was placed before me, or go without any food at all. In consequence of this absurd decree, I hate even now some of those things that were forced upon me then. A sense of injustice turned my stomach. On one memorable occasion I utterly refused a saucer of chocolate prepared for me, and so stoutly set my will against it, that in all the rest of my life I have not been able to tolerate the taste of chocolate.

I was subjected to grandmamma's unenlightened religious zeal, and taken to church elaborately dressed in very tight frocks, and made to sit still; and after infinite weariness in the long church service, I was led into the sacristy, and, with other unfortunate babies, tortured with catechism, of which I understood not a word. I see myself sitting on a high bench, my feet dangling uncomfortably in the air, while I was put to the question; and I pity me very much. Grown people forget that the Lord has said, 'I will have mercy and not sacrifice.'

I remember one more circumstance of this unhappy visit. My aunt Alice had a large party,—an afternoon party,—and I was arrayed carefully for the occasion. Oh, shall I ever forget the torture of the little satin boots and of the pantalets, to which I was doomed, besides the utter general sense of discomfort and bondage! I was fetched into the saloon, where the bevy of fine ladies were sitting, in clouds of white muslin and bright silks,—to be passed round like a toy, as one of the entertainments, I suppose. But being in great bodily pain from my dress, as soon as I was released from their caresses, I escaped, and darted up the staircase, and fled into a room where I thought I should be undisturbed. There I untied the cruel strings that fastened the pantalets round my ankles, and somehow managed to pull them wholly off, though I could do nothing with the dainty little boots. However, glad to be released so far, I gayly returned to the drawing-room. Alas for it! My aunt Alice was immediately down upon me, like a broad-winged vulture on an innocent dove. I saw her white robe swirling about her as she swooped me up, and consigned me to a servant, to be put to bed in the middle of the afternoon. I dare say there was a bright scarlet line round my wretched little ankles, where the strings had cut into the tender flesh. I wonder I do not remember the relief of being freed from boots and frock; but that solace has passed into oblivion, and the memory of the pain alone survives.

The time at last arrived for me to go home. I can recall no joy at the announcement or at the preparations for the return, and probably I was told nothing about it. The idea of giving me pleasure seemed to enter none of their heads or hearts. But I found myself in a carriage, on a wide seat,—so wide that my two feet were in plain sight, horizontally stuck out before me, at the edge of the cushion. By my side sat a stately gentleman, who was very grave and silent; and I looked up at him with awe. It was my uncle Edward; and, with the enthusiastic delight in perfect form that was born in me, I gazed at the noble outline of his face, the finely chiselled profile, so haughty and so delicate. I adored him because he was handsome, though he did not speak to me or seem aware of my presence. When the carriage stopped at a hotel for refreshment and rest, I was lifted out by a servant as black as ebony, and deposited on a sofa in the parlor, where cake and wine were placed on the table. I was well content with the golden cake so politely offered me by my uncle, as if I were a grown-up lady; but when he put a glass of wine into my hand, I did not drink, and was inclined to rebel. His commanding eye was upon me, however, so that I tried to taste it; but, choking and shuddering being the only consequence of my efforts, he kindly smiled and took it away, saying, 'You do not like wine, then?' These were the only words spoken during the whole journey; and I had no more voice to answer him than if I had been dumb. I wonder where children's voices go to, when reverence and love fill their hearts? They are often scolded for not speaking, when it is physically and morally impossible for them to do so. I had worshipped my uncle for his beauty; and now this gentleman made me love him with all the ardor of my nature. A smile and a kind word cause little loss to the giver, but what riches they often are to the recipient! My uncle's smile was pleasanter to me than the sunshine; and the next thing I remember is being perfectly happy with my mother.[35]

Julian, who remembered his mother as a "blessing and an illumination wherever she went," might have been somewhat nonplussed by one modern interpretation of that Christmas tale:

Sophia's story is a parable of the cross-pressures inherent in the ideal of womanhood she sought to make her own. The beggar girl polices the genteel "feminine" order by reduplicating its commands with harsh clarity and by reminding the potential rebel of what lies outside. She is thus the object of the policing action she herself executes. The story invests the beggar girl with two opposed impulses, both of structural significance to the emerging gender arrangement as Sophia came to embody it: violence exploding in opposition to the standard of womanhood that was set before her as mandatory, and violence exerted to support the same standard.

The horror Sophia felt at the prospect of being "mauled" by this figure was generated by the psychosocial contradiction grinding away in her own personality. Her life was conditioned permanently by a psychic autoimmune reaction in which, spontaneously and with fierce dedication, she sought to rid herself of the very qualities of fierce spontaneity that were built into the reaction itself. A feedback loop of inner conflict was established that could be set in motion by a slight external irritation and would then, under its own self-driven dynamic, crescendo to a mind-splitting roar. The experience of being ripped apart, of being made into an "earthquake," of being "mauled," of being "destroyed": all these were imposed on her by the inherent contradictions of a social situation that both cultivated and repressed the direct exercise of her native force.[36]

Apart from listening to Sophia's ghoulish, Grimm-like memories of her childhood, there are two other descriptions of what this Christmas was like for the family; one of them will have to be taken out of context, but they afford a clear idea of how hard each individual worked to make the others happy. One is from Rose, the other from Sophia:

. . . In Leamington there seemed to be some opportunity for quiet pursuits. In the first place, there were great preparations for Christmas; which means, that my sister Una made a few little hand-worked presents in great secrecy, and there was a breathless spending of a few sixpences. If a good deal of money was used by my parents, it was never distributed with freedom, but for those luxuries which would gather the least rust; and not a little was exchanged for heavenly treasure itself, in charity that answered appeals too pathetic to disregard. And we children learned—though we did not learn to save money, because our parents could not— to go without the luxuries money oftenest brings; a lesson that comes to happy fruition in maturer life, if there is need of it. I say happy, because we look back with joy to the hours spent in toughening the sinews of endurance. I remember that long and Penelope-like were my own Christmas preparations; but what they evolved is a matter as lost to thought as a breeze on the desert, in spite of the clearness with which I remember the gifts from my sister and our genteel nurse, Fanny, who was with us again, and shone more sweetly than ever in Leamington. The handsomest objects we had were given us by Fanfan, or Fancy, as my mother called her.[37]

. . . On Christmas eve we endeavored to get up a merry symposium for the children. On a large round table in the drawing room I laid six covers of Xmas boxes for us five and Fanny. The name of each person was printed and put in each of the six chairs round the table. When all had seated themselves, I uncovered. Four wax lights kindled up the feast. Unfortunately many presents had been bestowed before the canonical hour, so our show was not so fine as it might have been, but it was perfect, because each person was satisfied with his own dish. Papa had a magnificently printed and bound edition of the Scarlet Letter, published in Paternoster Row. Its covers seem to be made out of the gorgeous robe which Hester embroidered for Pearl to wear to the Governor's house when she looked like an Eastern Bird. It is illustrated by Miss Dear. The first letter of the book happens to be A "A throng", and this capital A is a wreath of flowers and Pearl is playing with it. Papa had besides the crest of the Lord of Leicester in browne— a bear with a ragged staff, which device we see all about here in Warwickshire. A pen wiper of velvet, fastened in the middle with an ormulu swan (in reference to his swansongs), a pocket pencil with ivory tip and a pair of Russian slippers, completed his repast. Of course he was immediately absorbed in devouring the engravings of his book. Mamma had a hand screen, embroidered with a group of lovely roses and rosebuds on a black ground, with a deep maroon fringe and lining and gilt handle (Una's labor of love). Also a rich pearl paper folder damascened with color—and a garnet brooch with a carbuncle in the centre. Una had a ring made of an antique watch key of her grandfather Hawthorne, set with a topaz which Rosebud picked up in the Corso at Rome! so bright that it looks like crystallized Italian sunshine or a drop of Monte Beni "sunshine" imprisoned—of which you will read in the new Romance. Una had also a pearl and ormulu scent-stand on a marble block and a golden pen in an ivory holder. A superb papier maché mirror set with mother of pearl and enamel was upstairs, which was one of her gifts.[38] Julian also painted her a bullfinch from nature. But I think I will not go on as you may not care to hear all the items. It was pleasant to hear each one exclaim "oh I have just what I most wanted!" except Papa who however showed his content by his absorption. A friend of ours sent a cask of oysters for a merry feast and from the repast of presents we descended to a supper of oysters.[39]

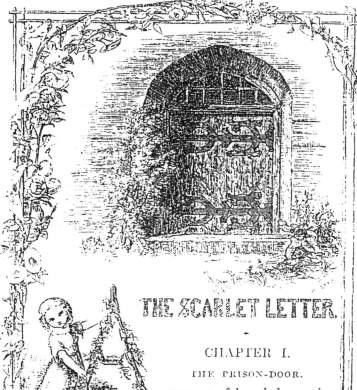

THE SCARLET LETTER.

CHAPTER I.

THE PRISON-DOOR.

THRONG of bearded men, in
sad-coloured garments, and
gray, steeple-crowned hats, intermixed with women, some wearing
hoods, and others bareheaded, was assembled in
front of a wooden edifice, the door of which was
heavily timbered with oak, and studded with iron
spikes.

The founders of a new colony, whatever Utopia
of human virtue and happiness they might originally

25. Sunday. A moist & sombre morning. A note from Bennoch.[40] Dined at 4 °clock. After dinner, took a walk with Julian. After our return, we all listened to a story by Julian, on the theme of "Sing a Song of Sixpence."[41]

26. Monday. A dark & moist morning. After dinner, took a walk with Julian. Very muddy.

27. Tuesday. A clear, mild, chilly morning. Letters from Mrs. Mann & E. P. Peabody.[42] After dinner, took a walk with Julian.[43]

Mary was continuing to dwell on the last days of her husband's illness and on the fact that after so much happiness together she had been prevented from being present at his death, even Benjie had seen his father then,

& he told me afterwards that when he went to look at Papa the last time he was oh so beautiful!. . . . It seems trivial in comparison with the whole, that my arms were not round him & that my voice was not in his ear—but these human hearts of ours do so crave the arms of love! and he was such a child in his craving for the words and sounds of affection—and to feel that he went away without a farewell from me!. . . . I wanted him to live & enjoy a tranquil evening to his days, rejoicing in his children & seeing the growth of his well-sown fields ripening before his eyes. How he fascinated me always! he was my first love—the realization of my ideal. . . . It has done me good to write to you. I am not so good as you think me, but you cannot exaggerate the depth & wholeness of my love for him. . . . My most fearful hour is the waking one, but sometimes I begin the day with the feeling that I can keep uppermost all that we enjoyed together, rather than what we have suffered—yes—let bygones be bygones—it helps one to forget to let all things slumber that cannot be rectified.[44]

28. Wednesday. A dark & moist morning. After dinner, walked out with Julian.

29. Thursday. A black & wet morning. After dinner, walked with Julian.[45]

Leamington, Dec[r] 30th '59

Dear Fields,
I have just received your note, and answer it at once, in hopes of anticipating your departure for Italy.
The printing of the book has advanced into the second volume; and they were going on at a rate of 50 pages a day, when I suggested to Smith & Elder that there was no occasion for such haste. It appeared to be their intention to bring out the work at Christmas; but in that case, the American edition must have been left altogether in the lurch. They have sent me no proofs for about a fortnight past; and I suppose they mean to publish in the Spring. I shall certainly tell them to forward the sheets to Ticknor, and I have already written to him to inform him of the probable length of the book. I had the idea that you had made some arrangements about forwarding the sheets. Was not this so?
Smith & Elder proposed the title to be "Transformation; or the Romance of Monte-Beni." This does not suit me at all; and I suggested "The Marble Faun; a Romance of Monte Beni." I have not heard what they think of this.
May will be too early to cross the Atlantic. Will not the latter part of June suit

you better? I shall not have been absent seven years till the 5th of July next, and I scorn to touch Yankee soil sooner than that. While I was at Liverpool, the 'Canada' used to be called the worst of the Cunard line.

I really envy you going to Italy, in spite of all the grief and trouble which there befel me and mine. You will go in the first place, I suppose, to Rome; though, to my mind, the pleasantest season there is from March to May.

We shall be delighted to have Mrs. Fields' company and your own on our return voyage. As regards going home, I alternate between a longing and a dread.

We are all well; and with our kindest regards to both of you,

> Ever your friend,
> Nath[l] Hawthorne.

If you receive this before leaving Paris, drop me a line.[46]

30. Friday. A pleasant morning, but then turning to cloud & rain. Rec[d] (and answered) a note from Fields in Paris.[47] Towards dusk, walked up and down the Parade with Julian.

31. Saturday. A black and wet morning. Towards dusk, walked out with Julian. I went to bed at 11, partly on account of a cold. The rest of the family sat up till midnight to welcome in the New Year.[48]

Perhaps that last entry of the year epitomizes one rather unsympathetic part of Nathaniel's character, insofar as he was up till 11 o'clock (although slightly unwell) but could not find it in himself to last another hour to see in the New Year with the family, even though his reason for not staying up was only "partly" on account of his illness (what was the other reason; perhaps he was depressed about his circumstances and the future?) and despite the fact that he must have been aware of their wish that he stay with them. As he did not carry on with his diary into the New Year his recovery from the illness is not documented; let's hope that his cold bath the next morning did the trick!

11

"Dr. Sutherland says Leamington is a bad locality for me": January-February 1860

Essentially, the story of the next three months could be told very simply; Nathaniel continued to receive proof sheets from the printers, read them, corrected them where necessary, and returned them to London. Finally, when all the arrangements were completed, the book was published in England on the last day of February and in America in the first week of March. Sophia was ill for a good deal of the time; no diaries were kept either by her or Nathaniel and he made only a few entries in his journal. Comparatively few letters were written or received. There is, therefore, not much that can throw light on the day-to-day events occurring at No. 21 Bath Street, and supposition has to take the place of facts when attempting to describe how these three months were spent by the family. The one thing that can be certain is that as the days passed the magic date of when they were to board ship for the return to America and their home came to be the beacon that illuminated their way through the intervening months and (particularly after the book had been published and Nathaniel's task completed) the increasingly irrelevant period of wasting and waiting.

Without there being in existence any regularly kept record of what was passing to and fro between him and the printers on a daily basis, it has to be assumed that at the beginning of the New Year proofreading was taking place in accordance with a fairly regular and satisfactory schedule, although it would appear that Nathaniel had a moment of apprehension (as he had intimated to Fields in his letter of 30 December) that Smith, Elder might not have been fulfilling their part of the arrangements that would enable the book to be published simultaneously in England and America.

21 Bath-street
Leamington, Jany 8th '60

Gentlemen,
I presume Mr. Fields made arrangements with you in respect to sending the proof-sheets of the Romance to his house in Boston, as they come from the press. In order to secure the American copyright, the work should be published there simultaneously with its appearance in England.

Nathaniel Hawthorne. Photograph taken in 1860. Courtesy of the Ulysses Sumner Collection of Hawthorniana. Owen D. Young Library, St. Lawrence University, Canton, NY.

Not doubting that this matter will receive your kind attention,

I remain
Respectfully yours,
Nath[l] Hawthorne.

Messrs. Smith Elder & Co
London.[1]

However, whatever had been the the arrangements and whoever had confirmed them to the printers, it subsequently appeared that the first batch of corrected proofs of the first volume of the book had been despatched to America on 6 January. But in the meantime, proof sheets were continuing to be forwarded to Leamington where they received the combined attention of both Nathaniel and Sophia.

It was probably about 12 January that Sophia received a (partly indecipherable) letter from Emelyn Story in Rome:[2]

Rome. Jan 9th 1860

My dear Mrs. Hawthorne,
Your kind words came to us a few days since[3] & my impulse was to answer at once, just to break the long silence which had thrust itself in between us.

It did our very hearts good to hear of dear Una grown strong & rosy & to think of her as free from aches and pain. It gave us impatient longings to hear of the new book by Mr. Hawthorne—we wanted you to tell us more about it & were half provoked with you for not talking more about it, as it is, we must bide our time, falling back upon the accounts of it which Mrs. Gaskell gave us in a late letter.—It made us sad to think of your prolonged weakness, but we feel that that that [sic] very weakness is the best argument for your sometime return to Rome, as last winter under what trial & anxiety were you able to bear up & be a support to all your dear ones! Then we looked in the glass you held up to us & rejoiced in the fair growth & promise of Julian & Rosebud & then I said God be praised that they have passed from under the shadow of the cloud.—As for us, we are passing the winter most quietly, no parties, no wearing visits to be made, but in that dear, sad, beautiful Rome all to ourselves. Had we the ordering of things & people how much rather had you been here this winter than the last—that was the most crowded busy noisy winter I ever spent in Rome as this is the reverse. We do truly enjoy it & try to to [sic] sip & taste our life of [. . . . .?] instead of drawing at a draught. We hang upon the skirts of these dear days & long to hold them fast.—But in Italy as every where else there is little hope of getting on the soft side of old Father Time he despises your coaxing & thinks the worse of you for your prettiest compliments.—Edith is hard at work, harder at work than she has ever before dreamed of being & is all the better & happier for it seemingly.— The Abbess who gives her, jointly with Penini Browning, lessons in Latin Mathematics &c is a most excellent teacher & as I have rarely ever found a woman sufficiently well grounded in learning to be a teacher of intelligent question asking youth I am well pleased with this winter's scheme. I ought perhaps to say a European woman for I know that America offers many exceptions to this only I cant get at the exceptions you know.

My boys are such dear pets & such robust little urchins that I should be glad to hear you say how well they look & thank God in my womanish heart. William is at work upon [two/the?] old Presidents—Italian—which now is up in the clay.— He would gladly [. . . . ?] the commission for Mr. Mann's statue & take great pride in striving to make a good & noble portrait statue of him, for he has great admiration for his character & would feel that Art owes its best work in keeping the memory of such green.—But since Mr. Sumner wrote & proposed it to William we have heard nothing more about it nor is it likely that the matter will be much pressed as William never under any circumstances makes such propositions & as Mr. Sumner will have his hands more than full with this [fierce?] Southern contest. I hope somebody [. . . . ?] [. . . . ?] very [clear?] as to American politics for to us it looks so stormy & mixed that there is more satisfaction & hope in hobnailed

Italian boots.—What it will all end in who can say but here at least, as it can be no worse than it is under the Popes, matters may mend—Mrs. Browning is full of faith in the Emperor & we wish we could share it completely with her but with our best endeavour can make little out of him other than a man of expedients & no principle.—There will be no Congress, that is clear, but with the forgone conclusions probably a Congress could have done little but confirm wrong so it is well. We are much absorbed in the Italian question, & if you have not already read Mrs. Tom Trollope's papers from Florence, in the Athenæum, I advise you to do so as they are very good & she is a very sympathetic woman. Mrs. Theodore Parker is near living with the Apthorps in Casa [. . . . ?]—just in front of us.— Miss E. Weston is [. . . . ?] & [poor?] [Lucia's?] gaining slowly. Mrs. Browning is well & busy writing. They are very near us in the Via del [. . . . ?]. Our best love to you all & pray write again.

Yours most sincerely, Emelyn Story.

We have just read Thackeray's 1st number of the "Cornhill Mag" which is, to my thinking, rather [. . . . ?], certainly not up to the mark I had set for it.

I sit before the fire in the little corner room which you & Una must remember. I met Dr. Franco the other [evening?]. He made affectionate inquiries for you all, particularly for Una & he seems much interested for your health & welfare. He was very pleasant & friendly.

Beg Una to write again, her letter to Edie was charming[4] I could write on over another sheet or two with good [will?] but the size of Edith's letters frighten me & make me keep within limits.

My only dissipation consists in riding on horseback & that I enjoy very much. I have been out with Mr. Browning for [. . . . ?] this afternoon.

The weather has been rainy & cold for the past month but there is no fever in Rome this winter, not one case within our knowledge. We seem to have entered upon Spring.[5]

There is no record of any reply to this letter having been made, just as there is no further record of any happenings within the family for the next two weeks. It is only later that it becomes apparent that there had been more illness in the family, and that Sophia in particular had been very ill and confined to her bed. What with Nathaniel's (presumably) daily slog through the proof sheets and the poor weather that they were experiencing, it would seem that the children must have had a very poor time of it. Perhaps lessons were given up altogether as both parents had reason not to be readily available to superintend them. The entertainments provided in the town were essentially indoor ones as it was winter, but there was no lack of advertisements in the local newspapers of stimulating lectures, concerts, recitals, and the like at the halls and assembly rooms, but whether the Hawthornes, or Fanny, went to any of them is not known. They must have done *something,* of course!

It is not until 25 January that the veil is lifted and a few details of what was happening becomes known. Two letters had been received that day, one from Mary. She had requested Mrs. George Combe, the widow of the Scottish phrenologist with whom Horace had conducted a lengthy correspondence over the years of their acquaintance, to forward her any letters of Horace's that would be of interest for her to see. There was some legal quibble over allowing such letters out of the country and Mary now wished Sophia to contact Mrs. Combe with a view to these letters being sent to her so that she could copy them for Mary's benefit: "Is it a thing you could do without fatigue & with pleasure to yourself, & with some assistance from Una perhaps? . . . Perhaps they could be copied under your eye by some indifferent person who would hardly remember them afterwards—in that case they must be compared with the originals after being copied & I suppose you could look at the originals while the copier read." Mary was thinking of writing about "my ascended one . . . I wish to make him understood . . . and I have much leisure for this work," and anticipating the arrival of the Hawthorne family back in Concord ("How early do you mean to come next summer?") and her consequent removal from the Wayside with her boys. She was able to assure Sophia that all the renovations to the house had been completed satisfactorily.[6]

Una replied to Mary's letter as Sophia, it is now apparent, was hors de combat.

Jan. 25th 1860. Wednesday.

My dearest Aunt Mary,
Mamma received your letter today, and as she is in bed, just beginning to recover from a severe attack of acute bronchitis, she wants me to write to you for her.

   This is the first attack of acute bronchitis she ever had, and fortunately there is a good homoeopathic doctor here who has brought her safely through it, though he was quite alarmed himself at first.

   Mamma says she will be delighted to execute your commission about the letters, and you must not think of it as a task to her at all, as it will give her the greatest pleasure.

   You seem to think Mamma has been almost annihilated by the dentist, but she only had one or two small holes filled, and a tooth out which did not hurt her at all, I believe, and that was all that was needed to put her beautiful mouth-full in order. She felt rather tired for a day or two afterwards, but has long since quite recovered.

   What I did in that way was most praiseworthy I think, for I had a perfectly sound double-tooth out, merely because it was too near some other ones,[7] and though the man tugged for two or three minutes, to my great agony, I did nothing but groan!

   Papa intends to leave England towards the end of June.

   Tell Horace I thank him for his letter very much[8] and that I should be most happy to tell him "what I am doing & all about it" as he asked me, if I had anything to tell, but unfortunately our life is so very monotonous here that I have not.

   He says he is studying Ancient Geography, but I think he cannot know much of modern if he thinks Leamington is near the sea, for it is very nearly in the centre of England. I have never studied Natural History, but I think I should like it very much, and perhaps Horace will teach me when I get home.

   We were perfectly astonished to hear of you with open windows and no fires in the middle of winter![9] I think America must be becoming tropical. Though we have not had much severe weather here, we have been glad enough of fires & hot bottles for a long time. Mamma wants me to ask you if you know what a comfort an earthen jug filled with boiling water is? With one in your arms & another at your feet, you may defy Jack Frost at any time, and in my illness I found the greatest relief from them. If you suffer from cold hands or feet I hope you will make the aquaintance [sic] of this warm-hearted friend.

I received your account of Ellen's marriage,[10] dear Aunt Mary, and was delighted with it. It was very kind of you to think of writing.

I believe I have told you all I can think of on Mamma's account and mine, and with love to the boys, whose aquaintance [sic] I am anxious to make,

I am most affectionately
Your niece, Una Hawthorne.[11]

The other letter that had been received was from Ticknor.

Leamington, Jany 26th 1860

Dear Ticknor,
Your letter arrived yesterday,[12] and was very welcome, after so long a silence.

The printers are now nearly at the end of the third volume of the Romance; but I presume the publishers will not think of bringing it out at present. I wrote to Smith & Elder, not long since, to remind them of the necessity of a simultaneous publication on both sides of the water. They replied[13] that they had already sent you the proof-sheets of the first volume, and would duly forward the remainder, and would also let you know the time of publication here.

I think I told you that your second volume should begin with the 10th chapter of the 2^d volume of the English edition, entitled "The Pedigree of Monte Beni." Each of the three volumes has about 290 pages.

I cannot think of a better title than "The Marble Faun"; and I hope you will call it so:—"The Marble Faun; or the Romance of Monte Beni." Smith & Elder do not seem to be decided, as yet, on this point; but I am well assured that the above title will suit the American public better than any which these English booksellers are likely to substitute for it; nor is there any reason, that I know of, why the book should not have two titles in two countries!

We are passing rather a dull winter here; for the cloudy, chill, and rainy weather leaves us little inclination to make excursions, and, besides, Mrs. Hawthorne's health is not so good, in this damp atmosphere, as it was in Rome. I shall really be glad to get home, although I do not doubt I shall be tortured with life-long wishes to cross the sea again. I fear I have lost the capacity of living contentedly in any one place.

I want to spend some money in books and other things before my return. How much can I afford? Anything? Very little, I fear; but I should be glad if you could give me some approximate idea of what my investments amount to. But do not put yourself to any trouble about it.

I heard from Fields, two or three weeks since, when he was on the point of starting for Italy. I suppose you will be taking your turn for a visit to Europe, as soon as he returns; and certainly you deserve some recreations after so much labour.

Bennoch sent his remembrances to us at Christmas, in the shape of a barrel of oysters; since which I have not seen or heard from him.

I will write again, when I hear anything definite about the publication of the Romance.

Affectionately yours,
Nath¹ Hawthorne.[14]

In a subsequent letter of Nathaniel's to Smith, Elder it is apparent that Ticknor had expressed some concern as to the current position with regard to the publication of the romance, as he informed Nathaniel that so far (on 10 January) he had not received any proof sheets from the English publishers. As (according to Nathaniel) some six hundred pages of proofs had already been produced by the printers (and read by him), it should have been the cause of some immediate concern that nothing had yet been sent to Ticknor, but it seems that the situation was not brought to Smith, Elder's attention until another week had passed.

Perhaps, in mentioning Bennoch's name in his letter to Ticknor, Nathaniel had had a twinge of conscience in remembering that he had not yet thanked Bennoch for his Christmas gift, although he had been awaiting the chance to do so in the event of a visit in person by his friend.

Leamington, Jany 27th '60

Dear Bennoch,
I can't go on any longer without some communication; the last thing that past between us having been your barrel of "natives", which we ate with great gusto on Christmas Eve. Almost ever since that epoch, Mrs. Hawthorne has been much indisposed and latterly confined to her bed, (as at present) with a sharp attack of her bronchial complaint. I shall thank God when we are safely at home in our own drier atmosphere. However, she is now very much better, and the Doctor speaks most encouragingly.

The book has dragged its slow length nearly through the press; and this morning's proof-sheet brings it to the 192 page of the third volume. It seems to me that there is a good deal of very nice writing in it; especially in the 2nd and 3rd volumes; but I somewhat doubt whether your dull English public will quite appreciate its excellencies. It depends upon the view a reader happens to take of it, whether it shall appear very clever or very absurd. If I were myself the reader, instead of the writer, I rather think I should condemn it.

It must be yet a considerable time before its publication, because I shall lose my American copyright unless it come out simultaneously there.

I had a letter, a day or two since, from Ticknor, on whom Fields has thrown an immense amount of extra labour by not coming home in the autumn, according to agreement.

We have been expecting to see you here; and if you come anywhere near us, you must not fail to let us have the sunshine of your presence, though Mrs. Hawthorne, I fear, will hardly be able to share it personally. Her illness has made the house very gloomy.

Your friend,
Nath¹ Hawthorne.[15]

More "gloomy," blank (or rather, unrecorded) days passed but it appears from Nathaniel's next letter to Smith, Elder that he had received a communication from them (in addition to the one mentioned in his last letter to Ticknor) in which they had informed him of their decision regarding the title, and much to his disgust they had decided upon one that he had probably included in his unrecovered letter to them of the previous 13 November, and that most likely had been one that he rattled off in a sequence of titles that he had considered as second-best, third-best, and so on, never imagining that they would actually treat some of them with any seriousness at all. Their letter also contained information as to their communications with Ticknor and the intended date of publication of the English edition, information that gave cause for some concern to Nathaniel.

Leamington, Feby 3rd, '60

Gentlemen,
I had quite forgotten that the title, "Transformation," was one of my suggestions; but I am very glad it was so, because, in condemning it, I shall criticize nobody but myself. It seems to me very flat and inexpressive, and ill-adapted to the character of the book, suggesting a narrative-pantomime rather than such a sombre affair as is here in question. Nevertheless, it may well be supposed that you know the taste of the British public better than I do; and I am quite willing to abide by your choice, so far as the English edition is concerned. In America, I shall call the book "The Marble Faun."
At the date of Ticknor's last letter to me (Jany 10th) he had not received any portion of the advance-sheets. Unless he shall have acknowledged to you the receipt of them, you would oblige me by sending him another copy of the first two volumes.

Very truly,
& Respectfully yours
Nathl Hawthorne

Messrs. Smith Elder & Co
London.[16]

At least the pace was quickening on one side of the Atlantic, so much so that another letter to Ticknor was considered advisable in the circumstances and the fact that Smith, Elder now had a definite date in mind for publication also enabled the Hawthornes to make more detailed plans for their departure for home.

Leamington, Feb^{ry} 3^d '60

Dear Ticknor,
Smith & Elder tell me that they shall send you the sheets of the 3^d volume by this steamer, and shall bring the book out on the 28th inst. Supposing the former volumes to have come seasonably to hand, this will doubtless allow you time to

get the work out simultaneously;—otherwise, the consequences may be rather awkward.

Smith & Elder are determined to take a title out of their own heads, though they affirm that it was originally suggested by me—"Transformation."[17] I beseech you not to be influenced by their bad example. Call it "The Marble Faun; a Romance of Monte Beni." If you are in any doubt about it, ask Whipple to read the book, and choose or make a title for it;[18]—but do not let it be "Transformation."

Give copies to Whipple, Hillard, Longfellow, and others whom you know to be friends of the author. Give one to Elizabeth Peabody; send one to my sister, care of John Dike, Esq, Salem;—also one to David Roberts, Esq, Counsellor at Law, Salem,[19] and to William B. Pike, Esq, Collector, Salem. I can think of no others at this moment. Of course, Gen[l] Pierce is to have one; Lowell, too.[20] In short, you know pretty well who are the persons whom I should like to please, and who would be gratified by a presentation copy.

In haste,
Your friend,
Nath[l] Hawthorne.

P.S. I saw Bennoch the other day, and am going to dine with him in Coventry tomorrow. I think I shall spend two or three months in the vicinity of London, between now and the latter part of June, when I purpose sailing.[21]

It appears that Nathaniel's letter to Bennoch of 27 January had produced an almost immediate response from him, as, whether coincidentally or not, he had come to Coventry thereafter and took the opportunity of journeying to Leamington without delay.

Leamington, Feb[y] 5th. 1860. Mr. and Mrs. Bennoch are staying, for a little while, at Mr. Bill's, a retired manufacturer, at Coventry; and Mr. Bill called upon us the other day, with Mr. Bennoch, and invited us to come and see the lions of Coventry; so, yesterday, Una and I went. It was not my first visit, by two or three, so that I have little or nothing new to record, unless it were to describe a ribbon-factory, into which Mr. Bill took us. But I have no comprehension of machinery, and have only a confused recollection of an edifice of four or five stories, on each floor of which were rows of huge machines, all busy with their iron hands and joints in turning out delicate ribbons. It was very curious (and unintelligible to me) to observe how they caused different coloured patterns to appear, and even flowers to blossom, on the plain surface of a ribbon. Some of the designs appeared to me pretty; and I was told that one manufacturer pays £500 annually to French artists (or artisans, for I do not [know?] whether they have a connection with higher art) merely for new patterns of ribbons.

The English find it impossible to supply themselves with tasteful productions of this sort merely from the resources of English fancy. If an Englishman possessed the artistic faculty to the degree requisite to produce such things, he would doubtless think himself a great artist, and scorn to devote himself to these humble purposes. Every Frenchman is probably more of an artist than one Englishman in a thousand.

We ascended to the very roof of the factory, and gazed thence over smoky Coventry, which is now a town of very considerable size (thirty or forty thousand inhabitants, I think) and rapidly on the increase. The three famous spires rise out of the midst, that of Saint Michael being the tallest, and very beautiful. Had the

Francis Bennoch and caddie. Taken from a negative supplied by Mr. R. W. Moore of Blackheath Golf Club, London.

day been clear, we should have had a wide view on all sides; for Warwickshire is well laid out for distant prospects, if you can only gain a little elevation to see them from.

Descending from the roof, we next went to see Trinity church, which has just come through an entire process of renovation, whereby much of its pristine beauty has doubtless been restored, but its venerable awfulness been greatly impaired. We went into three churches, and found that they had all been subjected to the same process. It would be nonsense to regret it, because the very existence of these old edifices was involved in their being renewed, but it certainly does deprive them of a great part of their charm, and puts one [in?] mind of wigs, padding, and all such devices for giving decrepitude the aspect of youth. In the pavement of the nave and aisles, there are worn tombstones, with defaced inscriptions, and discolored marbles affixed against the walls; monuments, where a mediæval man and wife sleep side by side on a marble slab, and other tombs so old that the inscriptions are quite gone. Over an arch, in one of the churches, there was a fresco, so old, dark, faded and blackened, that (Heaven be praised) I found it impossible to make out a single figure or the slightest hint of the design. On the whole, after seeing the churches of Italy, I was not greatly impressed with these attempts to renew the ancient beauty of old English churches; it would be better to preserve as sedulously as possible their aspect of decay, in which consists their principal charm.

We likewise went into St. Mary's Hall, which I am pretty sure I must have described two or three times already. This edifice, at all events, has been left to be as venerable as it may, except for the insertion of several windows of modern painted glass, adorned with (I believe) the arms of prominent members of the city corporation. These, however, do little or no harm; and the old Hall retains its proper aspect of old-time state and dignity, with the curiously arranged beams of its oaken roof, its stone walls, showing here and there an adornment of faded tapestry; its dais at one end (under a majestic window) and its gallery for musicians at the other; its two chairs of state, in which kings and queens have sat, alone, or side by side; its suits of armour, hanging beneath the gallery; its arched entrances, two of which give admission into little side apartments, as venerable in their small way, as the large one. The armour, by the by, belongs to the city, and, whatever may have been its original purpose, was formerly worn by marquesses in the procession and pageant of the Lady Godiva, which of late years has fallen into disuse.

City banquets used to be given in this hall; but I understood [from?] Mr. Bill that these are no longer in vogue. It is a pity. I should like very much to attend one. I do wish that I could bestow some one touch that would convey anything like the impression of this dim, time-blackened, old hall, picturesquely lighted by its ancient windows, one which has really old glass in it, and the others transmit very much the same kind of light.

On our way to Mr. Bill's house, we looked into the quadrangle of a charity school and old man's hospital, and afterwards stept into a large Roman Catholic church, erected within these few years past, and closely imitating the mediæval architecture and arrangement. It is strange what a plaything, a trifle, an unserious affair, this imitative spirit makes of a huge, ponderous edifice, which, if it had really been built five hundred years ago, would have been worthy of all respect. I think the time will soon come, when this sort of thing will be held in utmost scorn, until the lapse of time shall give it a sort of claim to respect. But, meantimes, we had better strike out any sort of architecture, so be it our own, however wretched, than thus tread back upon the past.

Mr. Bill now conducted us to his residence, which stands a little beyond the outskirts of the city, on the declivity of a hill, and in so windy a spot, that, so he assured me, the very plants are blown out of the ground. He pointed to two maimed trees, the tops of which were broken off by a gale, two or three years since; but the foliage still covers their shortened summits in summer, so that he has not thought it desirable to cut them down. His house itself is a very good and unpretending one, and Mr. Bill seems to live [in?] a most quiet and comfortable style, without coach-house or man-servant, though Bennoch says he has an income of £3000, besides retaining an interest in his former business. In America, a man of that property would take upon himself the state and dignity of a millionaire. It is a blessed thing, in England, that money gives a man no pretensions to rank, and does not (any moderate degree of it, I mean) bring the responsibilities of a great position.

We found three or four people to meet us at dinner; a Mr. Draper, a connection of Mr. Bill, and himself a manufacturer; and a Mr. Bray, a retired manufacturer, and now editor of a newspaper in Coventry. He is an author, too, having written a book called "The Philosophy of Necessity" and he is acquainted with Emerson, who spent two or three days at his house, when last in England. He was very kindly appreciative of my own productions, as was also his wife, next to whom I sat at dinner. She talked to me about the author of Adam Bede, whom she has known intimately all her life. Her intimations were somewhat mysterious; but I inferred from them that the lady in question had really been the mistress of Mr. Lewes, though it seems that they are now married. Miss Evans (the name of the Adam Bede lady) was the daughter of a steward, and gained her intimate knowledge of English rural life by the connection into which this origin brought her with the farmers. She was entirely self-educated, and has made herself an admirable scholar, classical, as well as in modern languages. Those who knew her had always recognized her wonderful endowments, and only watched to see in what way they would develope themselves. She is a person of the simplest manners and character, amicable and unpretending; and Mrs. Bray seemed to speak of her with great affection and respect, notwithstanding all that may have been amiss or awry in the conduct of her life. By the by, she is no longer young.[22]

The dinner was a very plain and very good one, a turbot, boiled fowls, and roast mutton, with no side-dishes, being, I verily believe, the very first table in England at which I have dined as a guest, without seeing something of the kind. We had a handsome desert, and sherry, port, and claret, all excellent of their kind, particularly the latter. Mr. Bill is an extremely sensible man, and it is remarkable how many sensible men there are in England; men who have read and thought, and can develope very good ideas, not exactly original, yet so much the product of their own minds that they can fairly call them their own. We had sat down to dinner at two or thereabouts (Mr. Bill's usual dinner-hour, I think he said, is one) and between three and four we took our leave, Bennoch attending Una and me to the Railway Station. As we passed through the principal street of Coventry, it presented somewhat the aspect of a Fair, being bordered with canvas-topt booths, and thronged with [people?] buying and selling vegetables, meat, fish, &c. Cooking ware was displayed on the pavement. This was merely the Saturday market, and Mr. Draper (who had accompanied us, part of the way) spoke of it as a nuisance. We bade farewell to Bennoch and started for Leamington at 4.20.[23]

So, not everything was gloom and doom and there were times when the tedium of life in Leamington was lightened by contact with friends and other interesting acquaintances. It would appear that by this time the proofreading stage of the production schedule of the romance had been completed as Nathaniel had confirmed to Ticknor in his letter of 3 February that Smith, Elder were in the process of sending him (Ticknor) the proof sheets for the third volume of the book (the English edition was to be published in three volumes), so that meant there would have been another reason for time to hang heavily on his hands, waiting for the day of publication that would free him from all further ties with England.

In view of Sophia's continuing illness he felt it necessary to forewarn Smith, Elder of the possibility of there being some difficulty in his being available for the completion of the various formalities.

21, Bath-st, Leamington
Feb[y] 7th, 1860.

Gentlemen,
If necessary, I will be in London on the 27th or 28th inst. Mrs. Hawthorne is at present much indisposed, and if the copyright could be entered without my actual presence, I should prefer it; and the transfer might be made at an early subsequent occasion—it not being quite convenient for me to leave home. But this state of things may be altered, in the two or three intervening weeks; and, at all events, I can certainly spare a day.

Very truly yours,
Nath[l] Hawthorne.[24]

Probably uppermost in Nathaniel's mind at this moment was the £600 that he would receive for the signing over of the copyright! However, it wasn't long before he received letters from both Ticknor and Fields, the former confirming that not everything was going as planned and that delays were being experienced in communications with the English publishers. There was not much that Nathaniel could do about that but his attitude in the circumstances was somewhat lackadaisical, displaying (maybe to Ticknor's eventual annoyance) a possibly unjustifiable assurance that everything would be satisfactory and that things would work themselves out to everyone's advantage.

Leamington, Feb[y] 10th '60

Dear Ticknor,
Yours of the 26th ult. is this morning received;[25] and I am surprised that the first volume of the Romance had not sooner reached you. Smith & Elder told me that they had sent it as early as the 6th January. I should have objected to their publishing so early as the 28th inst., but they did not give me notice of their design until after they had sent off the 3[d] volume, and made all their arrangements. I fear you will be pressed for time; but if you bring out your edition before the importation of any copies of the English one, it will save the copy right. This will give you a whole week, or more, in March. Moreover, if your first edition consists only of a single copy, it will guard the copyright as well as if it were ten thousand. If the whole work should not be ready, you could publish the first volume.
I am fully determined not to retain their absurd title of "Transformation." Let it be "The Marble Faun; a Romance of Monte Beni"; unless Whipple (if he will do me the kindness to set his wits upon the matter) should think of a better.
If you have an opportunity, by any person going to Rome, I wish you would send William W. Story a copy. If I could bring any public notice upon his sculptural productions (which are shamefully neglected) I should feel that I had done a good thing.
Fields means to come home in the same steamer with me; and it is my purpose

to sail in the latter part of June. I long to be at home; and yet I can hardly anticipate much pleasure in returning, when I consider the miserable confusion in which you are involved. I go for a dissolution of the Union; and, on that ground, I hope the Abolitionists will push matters to extremity.

I should be very glad to send you an article for the Atlantic Monthly, but I see little hope of being able to do it, at present. I have lost the habit of writing Magazine articles, and it would take me a long while, and very favourable circumstances, to get into a proper fix for such compositions. I have many proposals from Magazines on this side of the water [two at least!], but shall certainly decline them all, and listen to nobody but yourself. It is possible that some good idea may occur to me, and, if so, I will do my best to take advantage of it.

I have come to the conclusion that New England is the healthiest country in the world. Everybody here has one sort of sickness or another; throat-complaints, being the most prevalent. Mrs. Hawthorne has been confined to her bed for some weeks past, by a severer access of her old bronchial complaint. The Doctor speaks favourably of her case; but I shall be rejoiced when we leave England.

As soon as Mrs. H. is able to remove, I intend to take my family to Blackheath, or somewhere else in the neighborhood of London, there to remain till the time of sailing. All the advantages of residing in England are concentrated in London. Leave out that, and I would rather be in America—that is to say, if Presidential elections and all other political turmoil could be done away with—and if I could but be deprived of my political rights, and left to my individual freedom. The sweetest thing connected with a foreign residence is, that you have no rights and no duties, and can live your own life without interference of any kind. I shall never again be so free as I have been in England and Italy.

Truly yours,
Nathl Hawthorne.[26]

Leamington, Feb^r 11th 1860

Dear Fields,

I received your letter from Florence,[27] and conclude that you are now in Rome, and probably enjoying the Carnival—a tame description of which, by the by, I have introduced into my Romance. I thank you most heartily for your kind wishes in favour of the forth-coming work, and sincerely join my own prayers to yours in its behalf, but without much confidence of a good result. My own opinion is, that I am not really a popular writer, and that what popularity I have gained is chiefly accidental, and owing to other causes than my own kind or degree of merit. Possibly I may (or may not) deserve something better than popularity; but looking at all my productions, and especially this latter one, with a cold and critical eye, I can see that they do not make their appeal to the popular mind. It is odd enough, moreover, that my own individual taste is for quite another class of works than those which I myself am able to write. If I were to meet with such books as mine, by another writer, I don't believe I should be able to get through them. Have you ever read the novels of Anthony Trollope? They precisely suit my taste; solid and substantial, written on the strength of beef and through the inspiration of ale, and just as real as if some giant had hewn a great lump out of the earth and put it under a glass case, with all its inhabitants going about their daily business, and not suspecting that they were made a show of. And these books are just as English as a beefsteak. Have they ever been tried in America? It needs an English residence to make them thoroughly comprehensible, but still I should think that the human nature in them would give them success anywhere.[28]

To return to my own moonshiny Romance; its fate will soon be settled, for Smith & Elder mean to publish on the 28th of this month. Poor Ticknor will have a tight scratch to get his edition out contemporaneously; they having sent him the third volume a week ago. I think, however, there will be no danger of piracy in America. Perhaps nobody will think it worth stealing.

Give my best regards to William Story, and look well at his Cleopatra, for you will meet her again in one of the chapters which I wrote with most pleasure. If he does not find himself famous henceforth, the fault will be none of mine. I at least, have done my duty by him, whatever delinquency there may be on the part of other critics.

Smith & Elder (who seem to be pig-headed individuals) persist in calling the book "Transformation," which gives me the idea of Harlequin in a pantomime; but I have strictly enjoined upon Ticknor to call it "The Marble Faun; a Romance of Monte Beni."

Before you leave Rome, I want you to ask Mr. Hooker what was the additional amount to be paid upon Miss Lander's bust of me, besides what has already been paid. For reasons unnecessary to mention, I cannot personally communicate with the lady herself; but I should greatly regret to remain in her debt. The amount being ascertained, will you do me the further favour to pay it, either to Miss Lander or to Mr. Hooker. The bust, my friends tell me, is not worth sixpence; but she did her best with it.[29]

Your friends here, whenever I see any of them, speak of Mrs. Fields and yourself with great enthusiasm of regard; the gentlemen esteeming you the most fortunate husband in the world, and the ladies (I believe) equally envying her as a wife. If I were you, I would not leave a country where your merits are so adequately recognized. If you do go home, you need never expect that Ticknor will let you come back. He groans horribly under the weight of business, and avers that he has almost forgotten how to sleep, and works through the twenty-four hours without an interval of rest.

Mrs. Hawthorne, I regret to say, has been confined to her chamber and bed for the last two or three weeks. I shall heartily thank God, when we all see New England again.

Most Truly yours—
Nath¹ Hawthorne.[30]

Another week passed in an atmosphere of frustration and tedium that was not lightened by the cold, damp, foggy, depressing weather that curtailed their enthusiasm for almost everything, although a few short walks were taken to get out of the house and to break the monotony. Nathaniel was sufficiently frustrated to warrant venting his feelings in another of the now rare entries in his journal:

Leamington, Feb.ʸ 18th '60. I think I never felt how dreary and tedious winter can be, till the present English winter; though I have spent four or five in England before. But always, heretofore, it has been necessary for me to venture out and look the dark months in the face; whereas, this winter, I have chiefly moped by the fireside, and at most have ventured out for an hour or two in the day. It has been inconceivably depressing; such fog, such dark mornings, that sulked onward till nightfall, such damp and rain, such sullen and penetrating chills, such mud and mire; surely, the bright severity of a New England winter can never be so bad as this. I have not really emerged into life through the whole season.

This present month has been somewhat less dismal than the preceding ones; there have been some sunny and breezy days, when there was life in the air, affording something like enjoyment in a walk, especially when the ground was frozen under foot. It is agreeable to see the fields still green through a partial covering of snow; the trunks and branches of the leafless trees, moreover, have a verdant aspect, very unlike that of American trees in winter; for they are covered with a delicate green moss, which is not so observable in summer. Often too, there is a twine of green ivy up & down the trunk. The other day, as Julian and I were walking to Whitnash, an elm (which some people were felling) came down right across our path; and I was much struck by the verdant coating of moss over all its surface—the moss plants too minute to be seen individually, but making the whole tree green. It has a pleasant aspect, here, where it is the natural aspect of trees in general, but in America a mossy tree-trunk is not a pleasant object, because it is associated with damp, low, and unwholesome situations. The lack of foliage gives many new peeps and vistas hereabouts, which I never saw in summer. Warwick Castle shows itself more fully, and so do the broken and ivy-grown arches of the old bridge, that crosses the Avon just beneath it. The square, battlemented towers of the village churches, hereabouts, are visible from points where I have not hitherto seen them.[31]

Another five days passed without any record being preserved of the family's activities; presumably Nathaniel was content to leave matters in the hands of the two publishers and simply looked forward to the end of the month when he could, at least, end his part in the publication, but another letter was received from Ticknor that must have given him cause for concern that still not all was going well at the American end of the production line. And time was getting short now.

21-Bath street, Leamington,
Feb[r] 23rd, 1860.

Gentlemen,
I purpose being in London next Monday, and remaining till Tuesday.

You will oblige me by sending an early copy of the Romance to Mr. Francis Bennoch, 77, Wood-st, Cheapside, and also one to Mr. Henry F. Chorley, 13 (I believe) Eaton-Place West—with the author's regards.

I have just received a letter from Mr. Ticknor (date of Feb[y] 7th)[32] in which he tells me that he has had no sheets subsequent to those of the first volume. He seems very uneasy about the delay, and to anticipate difficulty in getting the work out seasonably; but your arrangements have proceeded so far that I suppose it is now impossible to alter them.

Respectfully & sincerely yours,
Nath[l] Hawthorne.

Messrs. Smith, Elder & Co
London.[33]

Perhaps now deeming the situation to be out of his control, Nathaniel does not appear to have replied to Ticknor's letter and must have considered a simple report to the English publishers of the situation with regard to the state of affairs in America to have absolved him from any possible charge of disinterest in the matter. Having taken up his pen, he took the opportunity of writing to Bennoch, whom he probably hoped to meet again at the end of the month.

21 Bath-street
Leamington, Feb^r 23rd '60

Dear Bennoch,
Mrs. Hawthorne wishes me to remind you that you promised to celebrate Una's birth-day (which occurs on the 3^d March) with an Ode. We shall not absolve you from the obligation, although we will not hold you strictly to an ode, if a ballad, a sonnet, or any other metrical form should suit your genius better. But verses of some sort must certainly be forthcoming.
Mrs. Hawthorne has improved very considerably since you were here. The Doctor wishes us to leave Leamington as soon as she can bear removal, but says that Blackheath or the vicinity of London would not be desirable for her.
I am coming to London, next Monday morning, to go through the necessary forms of transferring my copyright to Smith & Elder. I shall stay till Tuesday; and I wish you would do me the favour of recommending me to a Hotel, and securing a room (a bed-room only) in it. I am not at all acquainted with London Hotels; but my business being exclusively in the city, I should not wish to go further west than the Strand; nor do I care about splendid quarters.
I have asked Smith & Elder to send you a copy of the Romance, as soon as ready. Nevertheless, I wish my friends would not read it; as for my enemies, I do not trouble myself.
With our kind regards to Mrs. Bennoch and yourself,

Most truly Yours,
Nathl Hawthorne.[34]

Beneath the veneer of jocularity Nathaniel was probably genuinely concerned as to the worth of the romance and how those whose opinions and characters he valued would receive it. But nothing could be done about it now, it was out of his hands, and on the following Monday he traveled up to London to meet with Smith, Elder.
The same day, there was a bumper mail from America, with letters being received from Nathaniel Peabody, Elizabeth, and (possibly) Mary. Sophia was well enough now to be able to start answering one of them, revealing that since Una's letter of 25 January to Mary there had been much going on in the household that Nathaniel's letters had given no hint of at all, and that once again Una had been displaying evidence of her growing maturity of character and personality.

February 27th 1860 Monday.

My dear Elizabeth,
It is a little more than seven weeks now since I was taken ill. Six weeks I was a-

Elizabeth Peabody. Courtesy, Peabody & Essex Museum, Salem, Mass. Essex Institute Collection.

bed and the seventh week I began to sit up and creep into the drawing room (on the same floor as my bed room) and at the end of the seventh week I was dressed for the first time. This has therefore been my longest and only serious illness with danger attending that I have had since my marriage. Acute bronchitis is a terrible malady and it has become a widespread calamity in England this winter. Hundreds died every week of it in London, and all over the land it has laid hundreds low. It would have been almost a miracle, if with my tendencies, I had escaped. Dr. Sutherland says Leamington is a bad locality for me but yet he thought that if I had sent for him at once and not waited five days, that I should not have been alarmingly ill at all. Now he says the nervous tone of my system is low, and needs bracing, and he is bent upon sending me to some airy heights where dry winds may blow upon me. We have not decided upon the town, but it may be Malvern. It is an immense disappointment to me that we cannot spend the last months of our residence within daily reach of London, because I wanted Mr. Hawthorne to take a very full draught of London at leisure—before we embark for America. But I shall persuade him to go up to the grim, glorious old city by himself if possible. He has gone to-day to see about the English copyright of his Romance which, I suppose, will be published to-morrow. These stupid people have taken for it the ugly name of "Transformation", but we all wanted it "The Marble Faun; a Romance of Monte Beni". Monte Beni is our beloved Montauto.

You would be impressed to see how well I look after all that weary time of illness. I have a healthy look & not a pallid look. My old elasticity and strength of constitution are really serving me well. But I have to confess to a lack of energy of action and enterprise—My brain is reluctant to arrange and plan. Yet through all those weeks I had to still remain <u>head</u> for Fanny has none at all, and I can never shake off responsibility.—If a blunder can possibly be made, Fanny makes it—and her memory is null! Yet she is admirable <u>hands</u> and an unfailing devoted heart, so we forgive her the head. And there are some advantages in just this state of things, as you can see. While I was helpless on the bed Rose first, then Julian, then Una, were all made ill by a very strange eruptive disease, which puzzled the Doctor, and which we are sure was caught of a very dirty and diseased housemaid who went off to the hospital from here.[35] It was very light with Rose and she was in bed only two days. But it was quite a violent fever of short duration with Julian, and Una was excessively uncomfortable. Julian's head was so bad that I was very anxious, and you can easily fancy my agonies of desire to get at him, because Fanny has no judgement and Una no experience. But Una was devoted to him. No sooner had Una become quite well of her attack before Fanny was taken violently ill! Mr. Hawthorne said it would not have been poor Fanny, if she had not been taken ill when it was impossible to spare her. So suddenly all the house-keeping (very difficult here) and all the care of me was piled upon dear Una's shoulders, together with the nursing of Fanny and the dread responsibility of each & every. I was very much distressed for Una, for she has not recovered the robustness of the days before the Roman fever. She had to go up and down stairs so much, always irksome to her, and her conscientious discharge of all the duties was so exact that I was sure she would break off somehow, and as soon as Fanny's bad symptoms gave way, Una was pale and ill. I immediately, at the moment, sent to Dr. Sutherland, and his remedies arrested the malady. And then Rose and Julian were nurses. Has it not been a tragedy? Una was equal to all the emergencies (except physically) and "she is all my fancy painted her" at every point.[36] I have something to say about her—but now I can wait no longer before expressing my boundless satisfaction and joy at the relief of Nathaniel.[37] His troubles have weighed heavily upon me and have been my only shadow for years, and abiding grief for many reasons. I have been deeply disappointed at the small result of Mr. Hawthorne's four years' toil at the Consulate, but for no reason more than that I could not effectually help Nathaniel. I never felt content that you with your mite should keep helping him. Now I am rejoiced that Mary can, and how kind and thoughtful you are, you dear Elizabeth, making your small pittance do so much meanwhile. In a letter from Nathaniel[38] that came by the same mail as your darling little book of blessed news,[39] he says he has been told that Mary has fifty-eight thousand dollars [presumably as a result of an insurance policy on Horace's life]. I wish she had an hundred thousand, for there is no-one who would be a more just and generous steward than she with her open hand and kind heart.

I long to get home where we shall have no rent to pay, and where our own land will yield us increase, for rent and food are very dear in England. Your darling little book came as a restorer when I was ill. I was a perfect thanksgiving and could think of Nat with delight instead of with a sharp pang. I believed his health would utterly succumb to so much harassing anxiety, and that soon there would be no use in helping him. Oh blessed Elizabeth—Oh blessed Mary—Oh happy both to be able to relieve a fellow mortal in utmost need. It is the one enviable power possessed by man, the power to help another. It is the only thing I could covet, but even that I might not covet—and since Nat is relieved I should be wicked to lament that I did not do it myself. I do not for a moment. I never thought of anything but my joy that he is no longer crushed into the earth. I am very tired and must leave off now.[40]

Presumably, all went well with Nathaniel at Smith, Elder's and the necessary formalities were completed. The romance was published on Monday, 28 February, in three volumes, and cost £1.11s.6d. Whether the check for £600 for the copyright was actually handed to him straightaway in return for his signature cannot be ascertained, but within ten days he was able to confirm that the money had been received, so for the time being he did not lack for a few pennies with which to buy the "books and other things" that he had advised Ticknor he wanted. On the following Tuesday, before he returned to Leamington, he dropped a note to the publishers reminding them that they had not complied with his request that they send Bennoch a copy of the book.

London, Feb[y] 28th, 1860

Gentlemen,
Will you have the kindness to hand Mr.Bennoch a copy of the Romance for a friend of mine, and oblige.[41]

> Yours very sincerely
> Nath[l] Hawthorne.

Messrs. Smith, Elder & Co.
65, Cornhill.

If ready the bearer can take also the copy for Mr. Bennoch.[42]

Back in Leamington, Sophia took up her letter to Elizabeth and added two more pages:

We never received any charts from you at any time. If you sent any to Miss Browne, then they were lost.[43] Of course it is not worth while to send anything to us now, as we shall be at home in June.

Our twelfth cake was a superb little illuminated Book of Ruth which never can be eaten up and will be a joy forever to all our posterity after us and our contemporaries.

I want to tell you a little of the children, these dear, beautiful chalices of the love and truth of God. To Una has come since I wrote you "the turning tide" which changes the world for her. Suddenly there has passed from her heart and brow the occasional heaviness of dim struggle and I have never seen any thing so lovely and touching, so profound and so religious as her happiness and hope. It is exactly as if she had rounded some dark headland, and floated into a smooth golden sea, arched over with a dome of sapphire sky. She has, through the most sincere effort, climbed up the Hill of Difficulty and caught sight of the City of the great King, which never again will fade from her eyes. Her soul has been too heavy, but now it is light with myriad wings. I knew it would be so, but I did not know when. But now it is.[44]

Hopefully, Nathaniel traveled back from London in a fairly contented frame of mind, especially if he had in his pocket the £600 check from Smith, Elder for the copyright (though this cannot be verified). If he didn't carry the check, maybe he at least brought back some copies of the book for presentation to his family and friends. However, on Wednesday, Sophia wrote a letter to Mary in which, strangely enough, she made no mention at all of the book having been published or of any opinion regarding its contents or appearance.

29th February—Wednesday.

My dear Mary—Today I took a breath of fresh air for the first time for eight weeks nearly. I wrapped myself well and walked out on the balcony before our drawing room windows in a blaze of sun and on the second story and therefore raised out of the dampness of the ground. I believe I was never before so long shut up wholly. I must write to you by this week's mail, at least as far as business reaches, if my powers hold out no farther.

In the first place, of first interest are the letters. Your enclosed letter to Mr. Cox [Mrs. George Combe's nephew] came while I was very ill[45] and I could do nothing about it but when I was able to hold a pen I sat up in bed and wrote to Mr. Cox,[46] putting in a plea of my own for the possession of the letters, but at any rate for for the loan that I might copy. Fortunately, my physician, Dr. Stuart Sutherland, is an Edinburgh man, and knows Mr. Cox, and he sent my letter to him care of his brother who is a member of the household of the Duke of Buccleigh, and who knew very well Mr. Cox. Mr. Cox duly replied, and I will enclose you his note[47] to save the time and strength required to tell you its contents. I shall be rejoiced, as you must well know, to help you in this matter, and Una and I together can do a great deal of copying, and I trust, get all you want. You cannot think, or rather you can very well fancy my relief and satisfaction, in really doing something for you in this respect.

Then I wish to tell you that we shall go home in June. I do not now know whether to arrive in the middle or at the end. But Mr. Hawthorne will soon engage our passages and then I can tell you the very day we embark. You are very good to think of having carpets taken up and whitewashing done for us. As we certain shall not alter any of the ceilings, it would be a blessing to have them clean. B you must not trouble yourself too much nor get weary with overseeing nor ta too much of your time and quiet. I am very glad you have found a ready ma house and little farm that you like, and I suppose it is better to have it so far for the sake of a <u>certain</u> long walk very often, but I was sorry it was at the ve other end of Concord. However, that you are in Concord at all I am thankful and glad, and I can easily reach you for I am a good walker. I think we shall n want three servants, as Una said,[48] but probably we may need two—a cook a a maid—for Fanny as a regular thing will not be available as a maid. She wou not take such a place and is not able to do housework as she has a feeble constit tion. She will sew and transact all the business of housekeeping and be nur when we are ill and take care in general. I shall be glad to try your present co if you consider her honest and careful. I dread the misery of service in Americ the insolence and the changes—It will be a blessing if your Mary be good as s seems to be. I suppose she is Irish, alas! But perhaps you cannot get your c woman, and then you must retain this one. I should think we could share yo gardener if he have time for two gardens, and prove a capable man. It would nice to have the same man for both our uses. Dr. Sutherland says he thinks t return to my native air will do me more good than any thing else. Both the h summers and the bracing winter will do me good, he says. I look forward with perfect rapture to going home and to the dear little old Wayside. I conceived immense love for it during the one year we lived there, and it seems to me perfect Paradise of rest and peace and comfort. When we are once there, all the rich European memories will be richer and more glorious and I shall then rea enjoy my life here. The children are wild with enthusiasm about going home. Juli is Young America embodied. Nothing has ever diluted his fervid love, and fro every place he has turned longing eyes homeward. Una has had variations desire, but the result is a complete tendency to the Wayside. As to Rosebud, s wants to go so as to have room to run on the lawns and in woods, to feed chicke and bring up a Newfoundland dog and a cat—and above all to have a garden her own and cultivate flowers and beans. It is the promised land to Rosebud, a I hope her elm is big enough for her to sit under. How does it or has it grow How tall is it? It is on the lawn opposite the East parlor or East piazza—and wh we left, it was a pretty little vase-shaped tree.

Let me not omit to say that Mr. Hawthorne wishes you would open all lette directed to him that come to your hands and use your own judgement abo sending or speaking of them. Both these—one received yesterday, were reques for autographs! I was very jealous to get only from you by the last mail tho words on the outside of this valueless letter. I hope you were not ill, that you d not write me a letter with it. I trust you are well as usual. Are you very thin a pale? Give me a picture of yourself just as you are, dress and arrangement of ha and all. I am so impatient to see you.

Why cannot you send in a letter a photograph of the undeanlike likeness of M Mann which you tell me of? Elizabeth asks me to sketch his figure, but I know could not give any faithful idea of it for a sculptor. I am sorry Mr. Story is not make the statue. He is a great and appreciative admirer of Mr. Mann and wou do it con amore therefore as well as with consummate ability for he is really ve great as a sculptor and works from the highest rules of severe art as well as fro an inward fiery impulse. He has ideas and hands. I do not believe there is anoth man who could have embodied the grandeur, the massiveness, the sensuousne and the mystery of Egypt as he has done it in Cleopatra. And his Judith is n only as Mr. Hawthorne says, an ideal Patriotism, but it is fervid Syria roused to noble passion—delicate, beautiful—glowing and strong as fire when thoroughly roused. But I only know of Ball Hughes through Elizabeth's commendations, which are probably all just. I only hope he is the best person and I would do or say any thing I could to ensure the best. But there is a great prejudice against Mr. Story in Boston, which is a city of stupid notions as well as of some bright ones. Do tell me when the work is commenced and by whom. Mr. Hughes may be a fine sculptor, but it requires a comprehensive intellect and vivid power to make a proper statue of Mr. Mann and rapid combinations also. Mr. Story has a very rich and varied faculty for every form of art.

I am stronger than two days ago when I wrote the accompanying letter to Elizabeth.[49] I can now think of packing without dismay and despair.

I think I have not—I know I have not—answered a letter of yours dated Jan 10th, for on the 13th Jany I was taken ill. First you speak of the Dentist-business. I was brave enough to have extracted a wisdom tooth, which ought to have been taken out long ago. And I had four filled, one of them a difficult and painful affair. But Dr. Wilkinson made me take Gallic acid last summer in a crude form. I had to lay it on my tongue and let it dissolve away. He forgot to caution me about my teeth—and my nice strong teeth at last began to feel ajar and on edge and actually the front teeth to decay—though all out of sight, the faces appearing as sound as ever. I was alarmed at perceiving a roughness of one with my tongue, and much against my will, put myself in the torturer's hands. He not only found the one I indicated to be partly decayed—but three others! So that if I had delayed, I would have soon presented so wide a barn door that all pleasure in looking at me would have gone in, never to return.

But I am all right there now—for the present. My head and nerves in general were [. . . . ?] up for a good while after the many days handling—especially as I had pulled up my resolution to under-go the misery, when I had no power to do it. I really am not inclined to commend myself but I confess I quite admired myself to find myself in that fearful green chair of Mr. Hordern[50]—for it was a disinterested sacrifice to my family—and when you need it you will doubtless make such a one to your boys. I think boys are more particular about mamma's appearance than girls. Next you speak of the letters to Mr. Combe—then of the house. I am glad nothing has been done to the shed, because that we may alter. How I thank you for stocking the borders with flowers and for all your doings there, dear Mary. I shall enjoy my snuggery—for it is not comfortable to live in palaces—except in hot weather. One can never be cosy in a palace.

Goodbye now, ever your affectionate S.[51]

12

"That weary old Leamington": March 1860

Unbeknownst to Nathaniel, and before the English literary press had published any reviews of the romance, the *Boston Daily Evening Transcript* included a short criticism of the book on 1 March, courtesy of Ticknor and Fields, no doubt as a means of creating interest prior to publication in America:

HAWTHORNE'S NEW NOVEL. We have had the pleasure of glancing over the proof sheets of Hawthorne's new novel, entitled "The Marble Faun, or the Romance of Monte Beni," which will be issued next Wednesday by Ticknor and Fields. It is now eight years since Hawthorne has published anything and these years have been passed in Europe. "The Marble Faun" proves that this period has not been unfruitful, for in none of his previous works does he exhibit superior if equal power. Considered simply as the record of a tour in Italy, we doubt if this romance is excelled by any other book of travels, in vivid descriptions of scenery, in sharp delineations of manners and character, in refined criticism on the masterpieces of sculpture and painting.

But Hawthorne has contrived to make these pictures of Italy, admirable as they are in themselves, strictly subordinate to the weird interest of his story. In none of his other novels, do we find a more delicate perception of the most evanescent shades of individual character, a clearer insight into the spiritual laws which govern individual action, and a stronger grasp of the complicated relations of individual natures. There is hardly a page in the book which has not some original observation on art, or nature, or human life. As a work of thought, it is more daring, closer to the inmost facts of emotional experience, with a wider range of reflection and sentiment, than any of his previous works. The character of Danatello [*sic*], alone, is one of the subtlest conceptions of modern genius.

In regard to the plot, it may be said that it has the advantage of including a mystery, which both tempts and baffles curiosity, and which we are impatient to have the author solve for us after our powers of guessing have failed to penetrate it. If any objections be made to the romance, they will relate to the rather unsatisfactory manner in which this mystery is explained. Too much, perhaps, is left for the sagacity of the reader to make plain, and the closing chapters may disappoint the highly wrought expectations which the earlier ones excited. We are not sure at the end that the fate of two of the most interesting characters is thoroughly known to us. The author intends to sting our suggestive imagination into action, and make it do what he provokingly declines doing. The explanation of the mystery is by hints rather than by clear revelations.

The style of the romance is the perfection of quiet and strength. Its simplicity is the appropriate vesture of its powers. It is ever austerely plain and pure. The genius that thrills through the expression is a genius that practices the most rigid economy in words, while it is prodigal in thought; and vivid conception and intense sentiment make simple words, which a child can understand, do more of the efficient work of description than could be done by the rhetoric of Ruskin.

Apart from being a favorable piece that could have done nothing but good in ensuring satisfactory sales, it put its finger on what would prove to be an immediate source of concern to some critics on both sides of the Atlantic and consequently (though not necessarily) to the author, namely the denouement of the plot. Nathaniel had ensured that Smith, Elder would send a copy to Henry Chorley, partly as a gesture of friendship, but also in the knowledge that Chorley would review it in *The Athenæum,* which duly happened in the 3 March edition. It would be nice to assume that the country-wide distribution of copies of the magazine was capable enough for it to have been on sale in Leamington that same day; as it was also Una's birthday there could, therefore, have been much excitement for more than one member of the family in anticipation of different kinds of presents, some through the mail and others from the local shops.

Not with impunity can a novelist produce two such books—each, of its class, perfect—as 'The Scarlet Letter' and 'The House of Seven Gables.' He is expected to go on; and his third and fourth romances will be measured by their two predecessors, without reference to the fact that there may be slow growth and solitary perfection in works of genius. The yew and the locust-tree have different natural habits. Then, for one to whom all Europe is looking for a part of its pleasure, to stop the course of his labours is a piece of independence hard to forgive. Thirdly, there is hazard in an attempt to change the scale of creative exercise when an artist has shown himself perfect in the one originally adopted. The masters of cabinet-painting whom it would be wise to commission to cover a ceiling are not many. Raphael could produce the Pitti Ezekiel and the Cartoons, it is true; Rembrandt could paint the Temple scene in Jerusalem, which England possesses, as also the gigantic Duke of Gueldres in the Berlin Gallery; but Raphaels and Rembrandts are few.

It is only fit, fair, and friendly that the above three considerations should be allowed their full weight in adjudging the merit of Mr. Hawthorne's fourth and longest work of fiction, produced after the pause of many years. It would be idle to appeal to them were the production which calls them forth not a remarkable one—one of the most remarkable novels that 1860 is likely to give us, whether from English, French, or American sources. Such an Italian tale we have not had since Herr Andersen wrote his 'Improvisatore.'[1] How potent is the spell of the South, as filling the memories and quickening the imagination of the stranger! how powerless over her own strongest sons in literary works of Art and Fancy we have occasion to see almost as often as we take up an Italian novel. Mr. Hawthorne has drunk in the spirit of Italian beauty at every pore. The scene of this romance is principally at Rome, and the writer's intense yearning to reproduce and accumulate his recollections of that wonderful city appears to have again and again possessed itself of heart and pen, to the suspense, not damage, of his story. Who would object to wait for the progress of passion and the development of mystery on being beckoned aside into such a land of rich and melancholy enchantment as is disclosed in the following exquisite picture of the Borghese Gardens? . . .[2]

In other pages the Catacombs of St. Calixtus, the Tarpeian Rock, the Pantheon, no less poetically and richly frame scenes of a passion and wild interest in harmony with their beauty. Most of all do we enjoy Mr. Hawthorne's sympathy with the world's cathedral, St. Peter's, having rebelled for years against the bigotry with which sticklers for pointed arches or unlearned constructions have decried this gorgeous centre of Roman Catholic rite, as a place mundane, theatrical, and "out of style". For such censors Art, Nature, and Beauty have no existence, save by the complacent favour of their own vanity!

We have inadvertently touched on the great scenic power and beauty of this Italian Romance ere offering a word on its matter and argument. Whether the elevating influences of remorse on certain natures have ever been taken as the theme of a story as fearlessly as here, may be questioned. Casuists and moralists must discuss the truth of the data. To Mr. Hawthorne truth always seems to arrive through the medium of his imagination;—some far-off phantasy to suggest a train of thought and circumstance out of which philosophies are evolved and characters grow. His hero, the Count of Monte Beni, would never have lived had not the Faun of Praxiteles stirred the author's imagination; and this mythical creature so engaged the dreamer's mind, that he draws out of the past the fancy of an old family endowed with certain attributes of Sylvan gaiety and careless, semi-animal enjoyments such as belonged to the dances and sunshine of Arcady. Such is Donatello at the beginning of the tale; and with these qualities are mixed up unquestioning, simple love and fidelity, which can take a form of unreasoning animal fury in a moment of emergency. He is hurried into sudden murder for the sake of the woman he loves; and with that the Faun nature dies out, and the sad, conscience-stricken human being begins, in the writhings of pain, to think, to feel—lastly, to aspire. This, in a few words, is the meaning of 'Transformation'; and for the first moiety of the romance the story turns slowly, with windings clearly to be traced, yet powerfully, round its principal figure. The other characters Mr. Hawthorne must bear to be told are not new to a tale of his. Miriam, the mysterious, with her hideous tormentor, was indicated in the *Zenobia* of 'The Blithedale Romance,'—Hilda, then pure and innocent, is own cousin to *Phoebe* in 'The House of Seven Gables,'—Kenyon, the sculptor, though carefully wrought out, is a stone image, with little that appeals to our experience of men. These are all the characters; and when it is added that Miriam is a magnificent paintress with a mystery, that Hilda is a copyist of pictures from New England, and that Kenyon is her countryman, enough has been told to define the brain creatures who figure in the wild 'Romance of Monte Beni.'

Mr. Hawthorne must be reckoned with for the second moiety of his book. In spite of the delicious Italian pictures, noble speculations, and snatches of arresting incident, which it contains, we know of little in Romance more inconclusive and hazy than the manner in which the tale is brought to its close. Hints will not suffice to satisfy interest which has been excited to voracity. Every incident need not lead to a mathematical conclusion nor *coup de théâtre* (as in the comedies of M. Scribe),[3] but the utter uncertainty which hangs about every one and every thing concerned in the strong emotions and combinations of half of this romance, makes us part company with them, as though we were awaking from a dream,— not bidding tearful farewell at the scaffold's foot to the convict,—not saying "Go in peace" to the penitent who enters a religious house for the purposes of superstitious expiation,—not acquiring such late knowledge of the past as makes us lenient to crime, wrought by feeble human nature under the goad of long-drawn torture; and thus willing to forgive and accept the solution here proposed in so shadowy a fashion. Hilda and Kenyon marry, as it was to be seen they would do in the first page; but the secret of Miriam's agony and unrest, the manner of final extrication from it, for herself, and the gay Faun, who shed blood to defend her, then grew sad and human under the consciousness of the stain, are all left too vaporously involved in suggestion to satisfy any one whose blood has turned back at the admirable, clear and forcible last scenes of 'The Scarlet Letter.'[4]

As promised, Bennoch had written a poem to celebrate Una's birthday and forwarded it to Nathaniel through the mail to reach Leamington on 3 March.

> A verse!—My friend, 'tis hard to rhyme
> When cares the heart enfold,
> And Fancy feels the freezing time,
> And shrivels with the cold.
> And yet, however hard it seems
> to generously comply,
> The heart, fraternal, throbbing, deems
> it harder to deny.
>
> Few love the weary Winter time,
> When trees are gaunt and bare,
> And fields are grey with silver rime,
> And biting keen the air.
> Though all without is weird and waste,
> And shrill the tempest's din,
> With those well suited to our taste
> How bright is all within!
>
> But oh! the Spring, the early Spring,
> Is brimming full of mirth,
> When mating birds, on happy wing,
> Rain music on the earth;
> And Earth, responsive, spreadeth wide
> Her leafy robe of green,
> Till March is wreathed in flowery pride—
> A smiling virgin queen.
>
> Oh! that time is dearer made
> By Love's mysterious will,
> Which in the sun and in the shade
> Its impulse must fulfil;
> In wood, or wild, or rosy face,
> The law is broad and clear;
> Love lends its all-entrancing grace
> To spring-time of the year.
>
> Spring-time, my friend, with mystic words
> Has filled thy life with joy,

Bound close thy heart with triple cords
That age can ne'er destroy.
For her, thy first—so fair, so good,
So innocent and sweet—
An angel! pure as model stood!
The copy how complete!

Oh! sacred season, ever blest,
When saints their offerings bring,
Thou to thy heart an offering prest
More fair than flowers of Spring.
A miracle!—long ere the yoke
Of winter passed away,
Thy Hawthorne into blossom broke,
Anticipating May.[5]

Una thought it a wonderful piece, as well she may, and Bennoch certainly seemed to have included many topical references in the poem, to the struggle for recovery from his firm's bankruptcy, the difficulties of winter contrasted with the blossoming of life in spring, the three Hawthorne children and Una in particular, and Nathaniel's own creation of a book at a time of natural regeneration. Una hurried to make a fair copy of it before it had to be returned to the author; but the Muse of Poesy had inspired not only Bennoch but some one else rather closer to home:

A Lay

Dear Una, beauteous and gay
E'en fairer than the lily white
That at the closing of the day
Shuts up its white cup for the night
I send you here a little lay
And hope that you will it receive
For if you do not Una gay
Know that I shall forever grieve.
But now I will my subject turn
And wish that which I ever wish
Not only on this festal morn
But all the days that surround this.
I wish then, to come out at once,
That you'll have many a glad return
Of that most blessed third of March
The day upon which you were born.
That you will never have a grief
To fill your gentle heart with woe
And dearest, if you'll give me lief
I'll say with truth I love thee so
O, so much more than I can tell.
Una, dearest, I must bid farewell.

Ever yours, dearest of the dear
And, if you ever wish to come
To see me know that I'm here
At Bath St Number 21.[6]

Which poem did she prefer? Who can tell? How long had Julian sweated over his composition? Did he have some assistance from Nathaniel or Sophia? What does it matter; it was a great performance! But whatever else the family did to make it a happy day for Una it appears that Nathaniel was already troubled about some apparent shortcomings of the denouement of the romance (apparent to others, that is). Apart from his qualms about how the book would be received by the public, there had been nothing to suggest that he was unhappy with its structure, plot, or characters; there *is* a suggestion in one of Sophia's letters that *she* was unhappy with it, but as she was the only other person apart from the author who had read the manuscript prior to publication, and would presumably have raised any queries at that stage (but which, if she had done so, were apparently not considered by Nathaniel to be worthy enough to warrant changing such an important part of the book as its denouement), it must have been Chorley's review in *The Athenæum*, at least, that made him think that there was, in fact, something unsatisfactory about the last few pages and the manner in which he had brought the story to its close (or rather, it was suggested, *not* brought it to a close). There would have been no question as to his not having been prepared to value Chorley's opinion, as his favorable reviews in the English newspapers had been of great perspicacity and of importance over the years in establishing his name before the English public. "Perhaps nobody will think it [the American copyright] worth stealing" he had said to Fields; and to Bennoch, "Nevertheless, I wish my friends would not read it; as for my enemies, I do not trouble myself."[7] Statements such as those would suggest that he did not write with the idea of maintaining his popularity (if any, in his own estimation) by creating works that would be acceptable to the reading public and certainly would not create stories and characters that were not acceptable to himself. And yet, the first review that he read persuaded him that something was wrong, and sufficiently wrong to warrant immediate action. Perhaps it was his pride that had been hurt but it may be imagined (uncharitably) that he was concerned with the likely adverse effect on the sales of the book in America (the level of sales in England would not radically affect him materially). He decided on an extraordinary course of action (perhaps after talking with Sophia about it, as Sophia's wrath had been raised by Chorley's review, not so much about the suggestion that the ending was unsatisfactory but more about certain of the characters' behavioral patterns); fairly extraordinary, insofar as he was not amending details of fact but was being forced to have second thoughts as to his capabilities in pre-senting (or ending) a work of fiction.

21 Bath-street, Leamington
March 4th 1860

Dear Bennoch
Your poem has had great success here; and, unlike my Romance, it goes on grow-ing better and better to the very end. Only that you voluntarily promise to pay the debt originally contracted, we should accept these verses in full of all demands; but as you still hold yourself responsible for the ode, we will not be such simpletons as to let you off easier.

As for the Romance, I am glad you can find in your conscience to praise it so much as you do. If it ever comes to a second edition, I have an idea of adding a few explanatory pages, in the shape of a conversation between the author and Hilda or Kenyon, by means of which some further details may be elicited.[8]

Dr. Sutherland tells us that the air of Richmond would be good for Mrs. Haw-thorne;[9] and this would bring us within a convenient distance of London. Do you know anything about Richmond?—or do any of your friends know?—or could you put us into communication with anybody who can tell us what is the best part of the town, and on what terms convenient lodgings can be procured?—and precisely the when, where, and how, and all about it? If the Doctor had given his opinion before I came to London, I think I should have run down to Richmond to make personal inquiries.

Mrs. Hawthorne continues to make progress, and I think, in the course of a week, she might be fully able to bear the journey. We have but about three months more to spend in England; so that we are loth to waste any more time hereabouts than can be helped.

With all our affectionate regards,

Your friend
Nath[l] Hawthorne

P.S. I enclose a note from Una to Mrs. Bennoch. She has copied your poem, and will send it tomorrow.[10]

The following day, Sophia rattled off a criticism to Chorley of *his* criticism of her husband's book, accompanied by a note from Nathaniel on the back of it that rather ingratiatingly attempted to laugh off Sophia's strong opinions:

My dear Mr. Chorley,
Why do you run with your fine lance directly into the face of Hilda? You were so fierce and wrathful at being shut out from the mysteries (for which we are all disappointed), that you struck in your spurs and plunged with your visor down. For indeed and in truth Hilda is not Phoebe, no more than a wild rose is a calla lily. They are alike only in purity and innocence; and I am sure you will see this whenever you read the romance a second time. I am very much grieved that Mr. Chorley should seem not to be nicely discriminating; for what are we to do in that case? The artistic, pensive, reserved, contemplative, delicately appreciative, Hilda can in no wise be related to the enchanting little housewife, whose energy, radi-ance, and eglantine sweetness fill her daily homely duties with joy, animation, and fragrance. Tell me, then, is it not so? I utterly protest against being supposed

partial because I am Mrs. Hawthorne. But it is so very naughty of you to demolish this new growth in such a hurry, that I cannot help a disclaimer; and I am so sure of your friendliness and largeness, that I am not in the least afraid. You took all the fright out of me by that exquisite, gem-like, aesthetic dinner and tea that you gave us at the fairest of houses last summer.[11] It was prettier and more _mignonne_ thing than I thought could happen in London; so safe, and so quiet, and so very satisfactory, with the light of thought playing all about. I have a deal of fight left in me still about Kenyon, and the "of course" union of Kenyon and Hilda; but I will not say more, except that Mr. Hawthorne had no idea that they were destined for each other. Mr. Hawthorne is driven by his Muse, but does not drive her; and I have known him to be in inextricable doubt in the midst of a book or sketch as to its probable issue, waiting upon the Muse for the rounding in of the sphere which every work of true art is. I am surprised to find that Mr. Hawthorne was so absorbed in _Italy_ that he had no idea that the story, as such, was interesting!— and therefore is somewhat absolved from having _ruthlessly_ "excited our interest to voracity."

We are much troubled that you have been suffering this winter. We also have had a great deal of illness, and I am only just lifting my head after seven weeks of serious struggle with acute bronchitis.

I dare say you are laughing at my explosion of muskets, but I feel more comfortable now I have discharged a little of my opposition.

With sincere regards, I am, dear Mr. Chorley, yours,

Sophia Hawthorne.

Leamington, March 5th 1860
21 Bath st.[12]

On the back of the letter, Nathaniel wrote:

Dear Mr. Chorley,
You see how fortunate I am in having a critic close at hand, whose favorable verdict consoles me for any lack of appreciation in other quarters. Really, I think you were wrong in assaulting the individuality of my poor Hilda; if her portrait bears any resemblance to that of Phoebe, it must be the fault of my mannerism as a painter.

But I thank you for the kind spirit of your notice; and if you had found ten times as much fault, you are amply entitled to do so by the quantity of generous praise heretofore bestowed.

Sincerely Yours,
Nathl Hawthorne.

21 Bath-street, Leamington.[13]

The following day, Nathaniel made the penultimate entry in his journal that related to this sojourn in Leamington, after taking the well-worn path to Lillington:

March 6th Tuesday There is a row of cottages near Lillington that have a homely picturesqueness; they are built of brick, and thatched, and stand contiguous and attached, with some breaks between. In front, there is a hedge of intermixed box and holly, and the gardens and entrance paths of each cottage are marked out by the same kind of hedge; and there are probably other similar designs. There are bee-hives before some of the cottages, and in one of the little gardens there is the likeness of a towered and turreted castle, made of oyster shells. The inhabitants seem to have a rude sense of beauty, and a care for the adornment of their exteriors such as I did not see in Italy. One or two old men were creeping about with shovels, beginning, I suppose, their garden work.[14]

Sophia didn't have long to wait for Chorley's reply, as by return mail there arrived a long defense of his opinions:

13 Eaton Place West
Tuesday March 6/60

Dear Mrs. Hawthorne,
I cannot but affectionately thank you, both for your remembrance of me, & your patience with my note.—If I do not return on my own critical fancies about "the Romance" (& pray, recollect, I am the last who would assume that critics wear a mail celestial & as such can do no wrong)—it may be from knowledge that those who have lived with a work while it is growing—& those who greet it, when it is born, complete into life,—cannot see with the same eyes. I don't think, if we three sate together, & could talk the whole dream out (a matter, by the way, hardly possible) we should have so much difference as you fancy—So much did I enjoy, & so deeply was I stirred by the book that (let alone past associations & predilictions,) I neither read, nor wrote (meant to write, that is) in a cavilling spirit; but that which simply & clearly seemed to present itself in regard to a book which had possessed me (for better for worse) in no common degree—by one on whom (I think is known) I set no common store.—If I have seemed to yourselves, hasty or superficial or flippant—all I can say is, such was not my meaning.—Surely the best things can bear the closest looking at.—whether as regards beauty or blemish.—
I repeat,—that, while I thank you affectionately for the trouble you have taken to expostulate with my frowardness (if so it be)—I am just as much concerned, if what was printed gave any pain.—But, when I look again, (I have been interrupted twenty times since I began this)—did I not say that Hilda was "cousin"—that is, family likeness, not identity—though it means, what I meant, the same sort of light of purity & grace, & redemption let into a maze, through somewhat the same sort of chink.—I totally resist any idea of mannerism, dear friend Hawthorne,—on your part—and as to the story growing on you, as you grow into it: well, I dare say that has happened ere this;—the best creations have come by chance: & if Hawthorne did not mean to excite an interest when he wanted merely to make a Roman idyl [sic], why did we go into those Catacombs?—
Might I say, (like Molière's old woman) how earnestly I desire that for a second edition, a few more openings of the door, should be added to the story towards its close?
You have been so kind in bearing with me,—in coming to me when in London,—& in remembering the nothing I could do here to make you welcome, as I fancied you might like best to be welcomed,—that I venture to send you this letter out of my heart,—& if there be nonsense in it, or what may seem spectacled critical pedantry,—I must trust to your good nature, to allow for them.
Won't you come to town again? & won't you eat another cosy dinner at my table?—& pray, dear friend Hawthorne, don't be so long again:—& pray, once &

for all, as of old, recollect that you have no more faithful nor real literary friend (perhaps, too, in other ways, might I show it)

Than yours, as always
Henry F. Chorley.

P.S. This is a sort of <u>salad</u> note, written both to "<u>He</u>" & "<u>She</u>", (as they said in old duetts [*sic*])—once again, excuse every incoherence. I am still very ill—& have all the day been interrupted.[15]

Maybe it was in the mail that same day that there arrived an invitation to dine from Dr. Mackay, for whom Nathaniel had supplied letters of introduction when he had made a visit to America two years previously; as Mackay had returned to England in June 1859 the invitation can only have been prompted as a result of Nathaniel's current literary value. He was sent one of the usual Hawthorne brush-offs:

Leamington, March 7th '60

My dear Dr. Mackay,

I thank you for your kind invitation to dinner for next week, and should particularly like to accept it, for the sake of meeting yourself and your expected guests. I scarcely feel myself a stranger to Lord Dufferin; for I remember a very kind and hospitable invitation I received from him, soon after my arrival in England; and Mrs. Norton I have long known through her works.[16] But I do not find it profitable to leave home just now; my wife being much out of health and myself in constant request as a paterfamilias, and engaged, moreover, in preparations for our departure homeward. But, before quitting England, and when all my affairs are wound up, I mean to spend some weeks in London or its vicinity; and then, perhaps, you may kindly renew your invitation.[17]

Most sincerely yours
Nath[l] Hawthorne[18]

The preparations were indeed being brought nearer to fruition, as the same day Nathaniel wrote to Wilding with definite (but, as usual, various) instructions for the departure.[19]

21 Bath-street, Leamington
March 7th 1860

My dear Sir,

I must again put you to trouble about our passages to Boston; and, <u>this</u> <u>time</u>, we are really going.

We wish to sail in the course of the month of June. The dates of the steamers for Boston, in that month, are the 2nd, the 16th, and the 30th—unless I have erred in my calculation. It is most probable that we shall like to sail on the 16th; but I should be glad to have the option of going either on the 2nd or 30th, as may best suit us. Will you engage rooms for us at one of those dates, with liberty of transfer to either of the other two? My wife and two daughters (the youngest eight years old) might, I suppose, occupy one room, Julian and myself would take another. We shall likewise want a good second-class berth for Fanny Wrigley, who has been a long time with us, and is rather a friend than a servant.

Before our departure, we intend spending a month or two either in London or Bath, or both; and we have three boxes, which we wish to send from this place to Liverpool, to await our arrival there. Would the Consul (as an act of grace to his predecessor) allow this luggage to be received and kept for us at the Consulate? Or, if this be inconvenient, could you find storage for them elsewhere?

I hope you and your family are in good health. We are all pretty well, except Mrs. Hawthorne, who has been confined to her chamber during some weeks, and is now slowly recovering.

I promise myself great pleasure in again seeing you in Liverpool. With kind regards to Mrs. Wilding,
Very truly yours,
Nath¹ Hawthorne.

P.S. I forgot to say that Mr. and Mrs. Fields of Boston (who are now in Italy) will probably return in the same steamer with us; and I should be glad if you could likewise secure a room for them.[20]

And to round off the day, Nathaniel wrote to Smith, Elder advising them of his intention to make an extraordinary addition to subsequent editions of the romance:

Leamington, March 7th '60

Gentlemen,
I don't think I have anything further to say by way of Preface; but I find that everybody complains that the mysteries of the Romance are not sufficiently cleared up; and I think of writing a few explanatory pages, in the shape of a conversation between the author, Kenyon, and Hilda. The proper place for this would be the close of the last Volume.[21]

On reading the printed book I notice two or three unimportant errors of the press, but remember only the two following. Page 9th, vol 2nd, line 7th from top, before "foot" insert "her"; same volume, page 30th, 4th line from bottom, for "literary", read "literally".[22]
truly yours,
Nath¹ Hawthorne.[23]

It could be wondered what the publishers thought of this rather unusual request to placate (theoretically) disenchanted readers, but they would have been relieved to note that at least the changes that were required would not mean any drastic reconstruction of the type that had been set up.

That day was publication day in America, where the book came out in two volumes, priced at $1.50, far cheaper than the English edition, and retaining Nathaniel's preferred title of *The Marble Faun*. The Boston daily papers had been running extracts from the book ever since the *Evening Transcript*'s "review" of 1 March and the *Boston Daily Advertiser* of 7 March covered the actual publication with a short piece of criticism:

Mr. Hawthorne like many another writer, has been greatly the gainer by his literary silence of seven or eight years,—he does not remember the exact period when he last addressed the public, but we believe it was just before a Presidential election. His present book is far more healthy and cheerful in tone than those which he had previously given to the world. He writes with his old power of fascination, but still it seems as thought his mind had recovered from its long rest something which it lacked before. Mr. Hawthorne can never, without losing his individual character, cease to deal in that which is wild and weird, but there is less of the actually "uncanny" in this book than he generally gives us. The reference to beings and influences beyond the limits of actual or visible existence, do not now point to dark or malignant agencies, but to the joyous and even attractive beings, with which the classic imagination once peopled the groves and fountains of Italy.

There is much that is sad in this romance, indeed its tone is in every part subdued, so that the reader never fails to be conscious of the pressure of the calamity and wrong upon which the story turns, but still it has no such deep and constant gloom as tinges some of Mr. Hawthorne's former productions. The skies are the sunny skies of Italy still, the groves and fountains are those where fauns and nymphs once sported, the classic ruins are softened and brightened by the fond maternal care of nature,—there is a beautiful and delightful external world to turn to, and there are also characters, whose steady goodness obtain the reward which is assigned them by the reader's sympathy. In short, although the tale teaches the sad lesson, that through sin and evil lies the way to a fuller development of some of man's high qualities, its tone is not more sad than befits the disclosure of a truth, of which the immediate aspect is so dark, but the future promise so bright.

We can readily believe Mr. Hawthorne's explanation that his book was written in Italy. For a sketch of Italy, as the Romans and the Italians of today have both known it, in those respects in which nature, the temperament and imagination of the people and their history have seemed to combine in forming its individual character, this book is superior to any book of travels, because it impresses the reader's mind with the author's view, without obvious effort and by enlisting the sympathy. The reader can even begin to understand the existence of that responsive chord which Horace struck by some of his odes, as one now reads of the scene in the grounds of the Villa Borghese, where the modern faun and nymph had an hour's wild delight, or of the Arcadian dance in those sylvan retreats. The sight of Italy, a keen appreciation of the thousand associations which history and literature have afforded to add a new charm when nature had already done so much, the genial influences of her soft climate and captivating scenery, and a close observation of the pursuits of art for which Italy is now the centre, seem to have breathed a new spirit into Mr. Hawthorne, which mingles with exquisite harmony with that which he draws from the original bent of his genius, and which has perhaps been cherished by the somewhat sombre tradition of New England.

So, plaudits from the *Daily Advertiser* and no reference to any dissatisfaction with the denouement; nor was there in the *Boston Daily Evening Transcript*'s much shorter notice that appeared in the evening of the same day:

HAWTHORNE'S GENIUS. What the scientific use of lenses—the telescope and microscope—does for us in relation to the external universe, the psychological writer achieves in regard to our own nature. He reveals its wonder and beauty, unfolds its complex laws, and makes us suddenly aware of the mysteries within and around individual life. In the guise of attractive fiction and sometimes of the most airy sketches, Hawthorne thus deals with his reader. His appeal is to consciousness, and he must therefore be met in a sympathetic relation; he shadows forth, hints, makes signs, whispers, muses aloud, gives the key-note of melody, puts us on a track; in a word, addresses us as nature does—that is, unostentatiously, and with a significance not to be realized, without recurrent silence and gentle feeling,—a sequestration from bustle and material care and somewhat of the meditative insight and intent sensibility in which his themes are conceived and wrought out.

That same evening, the *Boston Evening Transcript* carried a short notice that, in contrast to another review of a later date which called the book "repulsive" in parts, found there was in the book that which could be called both "chaste" and "suggestive":

HAWTHORNE'S NEW ROMANCE. Eight years of reticence have enlarged the scope if they have not intensified the power of Hawthorne's genius. It is his peculiar distinction felicitously to unite, in his literary production, the fruit of careful observation with that of reflection and sympathy. His residence in Italy laid open to his appreciative mind the associations of Art and filled his imagination with the impressions of Antiquity. These he has reproduced in "The Marble Faun." Crystallized in his pure and terse diction are the sentiments and experiences which make a visit to Rome such a poetical and memorable episode in modern life, especially to the natives of a new country, like our own. In his choice of this scene and subject he has been eminently true to himself—looking into his life as well as heart to write; and to the Romance of New England history and character adding that of Italian travel, wherein lettered genius of all times and countries instinctively expatiates—from the Gallic vivacity of a De Stael to the English scholarship of a Bulwer, and from the reminiscent patriotism of D'Azeglio to the northern fancy of Andersen the Dane. Welcome as this Romance on Monte Beni will be to all readers of taste and sensibility, to all lovers of art and epicureans in style, it will be most keenly relished by that now large class of the author's countrymen who have sojourned in Italy, and from amid the material prosperity and mechanical life of home, will luxuriate over its chaste and suggestive pages, in the revival of their most cherished memories of European travel.

The following day, the *New York Daily Tribune* carried an almost full-page spread on the new romance, occupying nearly six columns and including several very lengthy extracts from the book:

HAWTHORNE'S NEW ROMANCE
The scenery and local coloring of this strange and unnatural story are derived from the impressions of the writer during a long sojourn in Italy; but the characters with which he has peopled his canvas are the genuine products of his somber imagination, and in weird and repulsive feature, bear a strong family likeness to many of his previous creations. In constructing the plot, he has limited himself to a narrow range; the chief personages of the tale being only four in number; and the incidents, though surpassing the terrible pictures of Mrs. Radcliffe in gloom and terror, depend for their effect on their singularly curious elaboration, rather than their variety. The cheerful skies and sunny plains of Italy, where the scene is placed, present a strong contrast to the lurid atmosphere of the romance, and instead of softening its dismal tone, only heighten the effect, by presenting a

momentary, but delusive relief. With whatever admiration the reader may regard the genius of Mr. Hawthorne, he will not easily forgive him for throwing the subtle fascinations of his pen around such a horrible experience as forms the key note of the story. He will shrink from the stifling air of the charnel-house with which he is oppressed. The smell of blood which pervades the narrative becomes not only unwholesome, but sickening. The flavor of mortality which creeps over the senses amid scenes of exquisite beauty, almost stops the breath, and we ask in vain of the good apothecary for "an ounce of civet to sweeten the imagination."

The story takes its name from a strange tradition of the middle ages, which traces the origin of the house of Beni, to the pre-historic times of Italy, when deities and demigods appeared familiarly on earth, mingling with its inhabitants as friend with friend, when nymphs and satyrs, and the whole train of classic fable openly frequented the primeval woods. The progenitor of the noble family, though a monstrous being, partook largely of the gentlest human qualities. A sylvan creature, native among the woods, had loved a mortal maiden, and perhaps by the natural courtesies of love, or possibly by a ruder wooing, had won her to his haunts. In due time, he gained her womanly affections, and from their bridal union sprang a vigorous progeny that took its place unquestioned among human families. Still for a long time, it showed the trace of its wild paternity. Though a pleasant and kindly race of men, it was capable of savage fierceness, and was never quite subjected to the trammels of social law. They were strong, active, genial, cheerful as the sunshine, passionate as the tornado. They were filled with perpetual joy by an unsought harmony with nature. In the lapse of centuries, the FAUN's wild blood became attempered with constant intermixtures from the more ordinary streams of human life. It lost many of its original qualities, and served, for the most part, only to bestow an unconquerable vigor, which kept the family from extinction. Nature, however, from time to time peeped out in its original features. Ever and anon a descendant of the Monte Benis appeared bearing all the characteristics of the original race. It was even said that the blood of the Faun was sometimes betrayed in the ears, covered with a delicate fur, and shaped like a pointed leaf. An effective allusion is made to this circumstance soon after the introduction of the Faun to the story. . .

The lady, whom is here presented to our acquaintance under the name of Miriam, plays the more important part in the murky tragedy. There was a mystery about her position, which, though it did not necessarily imply anything wrong, would have compromised her reception in society, anywhere but in Rome. The truth was, that nobody knew anything about Miriam, either for good or evil. She had made her appearance without introduction, had taken a studio, put her card on the door, and showed considerable talent as a painter in oils. Her manners evinced great apparent freedom; it seemed easy to become acquainted with her, and not difficult to develop a casual acquaintance into intimacy; but by some strange quality, she kept people at a distance, without so much as letting them know that they were excluded from her inner circle. "She resembled one of those images of light, which conjurors evoke and cause to shine before us, in apparent tangibility, only an arm's length beyond our grasp; we make a step in advance, expecting to seize the illusion, but find it still precisely so far out of our reach. Finally, society began to recognize the impossibility of getting nearer to Miriam, and gruffly acquiesced." The young Italian, whose resemblance to the Faun of Praxiteles was the constant subject of remark, had, on a casual visit to Rome, been attracted by the rare beauty of Miriam; he had sought her, followed her, and insisted, with simple perseverance, on being admitted to her acquaintance; a boon which had been granted to his affectionate simplicity, when a more artful character

would have failed to obtain it. This young man, though quite destitute of intellectual brilliancy, had many agreeable characteristics, which won him the kindly and
half-contemptuous regard of Miriam, to whom his devotion was without bounds.

Not long after the opening of the narrative, the evil genius of Miriam, the human
specter who constantly haunts her with the remembrance of some mysterious
crime in her past history, is brought upon the scene, in the form of a "dusky,
death-scented apparition," calling forth a terrible dread in Miriam, and in Donatello exciting a hatred resembling the instinctive unreasoning antipathy of one
of the lower animals. Without further explanation, except to premise that Hilda
and Kenyon are artists residing at Rome, and the most intimate companions of
Miriam, we will introduce our readers abruptly to a scene from which the ghastly
interest of the subsequent narrative takes its origin. . .

A fresh glare of horror flashes on the scene, in the next chapter, though the
fearful mystery remains without solution. . .

Here we will draw the veil over the tragic spectacle, and leave our readers to
take the full "sup of horrors" at their discretion. We assure them that the story,
though redolent of crime and blood, possesses a seductive enticement, which few
will be inclined to resist. It abounds in sweet and gentle episodes, illustrative of
Italian life, vivid descriptions of some of the most celebrated works of art, and
profound discussions of æsthetic principles. The bright and delicate humor, which
Mr. Hawthorne insinuates, with such wonderful effect, into his dark cynicism,
preserves a lively human interest even in his most spectral conceptions. In the
delineation of Hilda, we have an exquisite specimen of a form of character, which,
though always rare, may be regarded, according to the intention of the author, as
the loveliest type of American womanhood. The style of the work, like everything
which Mr. Hawthorne writes, presents an inimitable union of gracefulness and
vigor, and exercises such a powerful charm over the reader as almost to atone for
the saturnine spirit and grim features of the narrative.

Another satisfactory review, and again no reference to anything incomplete in the manner in which the romance closes.

At some time around this period, Nathaniel received a letter from Richard
Monckton Milnes thanking him for the gift of a copy of the book; possibly
it had been the copy that had been handed to Bennoch "for a friend of mine"
on 28 February:

My Dear Sir,—I would not return you my thanks for the gift of your book till I
could return thanks for the delight of reading it. I enjoyed it as a true Anglo-
Roman; it took me back twenty years, and gave me a true sentimental journey
round all my old haunts and impressions. Your moral is bold and most true,—

> "Man cannot stand,—he must advance or fall,
> And sometimes, falling, makes most way of all!"[24]

Have you any real "Tales of Horrors" in your mind, as the solution of your enigma?
Where are you? Shall we meet?

Yours very truly,
Richd Monckton Milnes.[25]

J. T. Fields, Hawthorne, and W. D. Ticknor. Courtesy, Peabody & Essex Museum, Salem, Mass. Essex Institute Collection.

Once again, Nathaniel had a double dose of information from his American publishers as letters from both Ticknor and Fields[26] were received, but it appears that he didn't reply to the one from Fields:

Leamington, March 9th '60

Dear Ticknor,
Barings advise me of £100 remitted by you not long ago; and as there had been a previous £100, and as Smith & Elder have paid over the £600, I am fully provided with funds till I see you again.

I am sorry you have been so much hurried about the book. It came out in London at the time appointed, and seems to have gone off pretty well for Smith & Elder wrote me, some days ago, that their edition was nearly exhausted, and that they were about printing another. As everybody complains that the mysteries of the story are not sufficiently accounted for, I intend to add a few pages to the concluding chapter, in order to make things a little clearer.[27] The additional matter, when written, shall be sent to you in manuscript.

I think there would have been no danger, in the legal point of view, in changing the title of the Romance; and I therefore hope that you will have called it "The Marble Faun." But, after all, it is of no essential consequence.

I thank you for the number of the Atlantic, which seems to me a good one; also for the newspapers.[28] The only American papers that I have seen, for nearly a year, are those which you have sent me; but I shall see enough of them in a few months more.

I have a letter from Fields this morning, dated at Rome on 2nd of this month. He purposes leaving Rome in a few days, and will probably be here in April, at farthest. I have engaged passages for him and my own family at one of three dates—June 2nd, 16th, or 30th. Most probably, we shall sail on 16th; but if he chooses to come at an earlier date, it will be in his power. For my part, I absolutely long to be at home, and if an earlier voyage would be comfortable, I should certainly prefer it. I shall enjoy nothing, till I have touched my own native soil again.

Mrs. Hawthorne is quite comfortable now, in point of health; except that she feels the rawness of the English atmosphere very sensibly. All the rest of the family are well.

I went up to London, the other day, and found Bennoch in good trim. He says that the past year has been very favourable to him in his business relations; and I hope we shall yet see him as prosperous as formerly.

We shall soon remove from Leamington, but are in doubt whether to establish ourselves for a month or two at Bath, or in the neighborhood of London. Spring, in any part of England, is the worst portion of the year.
Your friend,
Nath[l] Hawthorne.[29]

It was round about this time, possibly on 10 March, that a letter came from Bright; he was so enthusiastic about the romance that he had written before actually having finished reading it, but was also making sure that Nathaniel remembered his promise about the final resting place of the manuscript:

. . . I'm in the middle of 'Monte Beni' (why did Smith and Elder transform it into 'Transformation'?—they are rather given to playing these pranks with author's titles), and I am delighted with it. I am glad that sulky 'Athenæum' was so civil; for they are equally powerful and unprincipled, and a bad word there would have done harm. I think your descriptions of scenery and places most admirable; and as for statues and pictures, I think they never were so described before,—you seem to enter into their (or their artists') very soul, and lay it bare before us. As I've not read more than a volume yet, I can say nothing about the plot, except that it interests and excites me. Donatello I hardly quite like and understand as yet; a being half man, half child, half animal, puzzles me; to me there seems a something a little—just a little—<u>wanting</u>, and that gives me an uncomfortable feeling of half-development, half idiocy, which is of course unpleasant. But as I know him better, I may like him more. Harriet says you have stolen the description of Miriam from <u>her</u> Jewess—as she calls the extract you gave her—and intends to accuse you of plagiarism if not of theft.[30] In Hilda it seems to me you had a thought of Una. My acquaintance with Kenyon is as yet too slight. You have not, I trust, forgotten about the precious manuscript which is to be the gem, the Koh-i-noor, of my autographs. . . .[31]

21 Bath-street
Leamington, March 10th '60.

Dear Mr. Bright,
I thank you very much for your letter, and am glad you like the Romance so far, and so well. I shall really be gratified if you will review it.[32] Very likely you are right about Donatello; for though the idea in my mind was an agreeable and beautiful one, it was not easy so to present it to the reader.

Smith & Elder certainly do take strange liberties with the titles of books. I wanted to call it "The Marble faun"; but they insisted upon "Transformation," which will lead the reader to anticipate a sort of pantomime. They wrote me, some days ago, that the edition was nearly all sold, and that they are going to print another; to which I mean to append a few pages, in the shape of a conversation between Kenyon, Hilda, and the author, throwing some further light on matters which seem to have been left too much in the dark. For my own part, however, I should prefer the book as it now stands.[33] It so happened, that, at the very time you were writing, Una was making up a parcel of the manuscript, to send to you. There is a further portion now in the hands of Smith & Elder, which I will procure when I go to London;[34] that is, if you do not consider this immense mass more than enough. I begin to be restless (and so do we all) with the anticipation of our approaching departure, and, almost for the first time, I long to be at home. Nothing more can be done or enjoyed, till we have breathed our native air again. I do not even care for London now; though I mean to spend a few weeks there before long taking a final leave; not that I mean to think it a last leave-taking, either. In three or four years, or less, my longings will no doubt be transferred from that side of the water to this; and perhaps I shall write another book, and come over to get it published.

We are rather at a loss for a suitable place to stay at during the interval between this and the middle of June, when we mean to sail. Liverpool is to be avoided, on Mrs. Hawthorne's account, till the last moment; and I am afraid there is no air in England fit for her to breathe. We have some idea of going to Bath, but more probably we may establish ourselves for a month or two in the neighborhood of London. But, as I said before, we shall enjoy little or nothing, wherever we may be. Our roots are pulled up, and we cannot really live till we stick them into the ground again. There will be pleasure, indeed, in greeting you at Liverpool (the most disagreeable city in England, nevertheless) but a sharp pain, soon afterwards, in bidding you farewell. The sooner it is over, the better. What an uneasy kind of world we live in!

With this very original remark, I remain

Most sincerely your friend
Nath¹ Hawthorne[35]

Nathaniel's constant remarks about the delicacy of Sophia's health in the face of the unsympathetic atmospheric conditions to be found not only in Leamington but, apparently, all over England, cannot be denigrated too much as the very local conditions of the air in Bath Street (normally being at the mercy of the trains passing over the bridge at the junction with High Street, anyway) were taking an extra pounding at this time from an unwanted source of pollution from further up the Parade:

THE PUMP ROOM CHIMNEY.—Dear Mr. Editor,—I wish you would use your powerful pen to get removed from Bath-street, that intolerable nuisance, the Royal Pump Room chimney. When the wind blows from the north, we are smothered with a nasty foul black smoke, which is not only a nuisance to passers by, but a positive injury to the shop-keepers. The smoke appears to come through the roof, and not up the chimney, which is not half high enough. What is the inspector about?—

Yours truly, A BATH STREET TRADESMAN.[36]

In the same edition of the paper there appeared an account of the Report of the Local Board of Health, concerning the meeting held on 6 March at which the superintendent of police advised (among other matters) that

I beg to report that large quantities of black smoke have been seen to issue from the following chimneys, upon several occasions lately, and I beg that the usual notice may be served upon the owners to construct the furnaces so as to consume the smoke arising therefrom, 10th and 11th Vic, cap 34:—Mr. Ratcliff, foundry, Clemens-street; Messrs Robinson, Gas Works; Mr. Wincot, Pump Rooms.[37]

After writing to Bright (assuming that he could see through the haze) Nathaniel's interest may have been aroused by another review that appeared that day in *The Literary Gazette*:

NEW NOVELS
A work from the pen which produced that marvellous book "The Scarlet Letter," can never fail to be cordially welcomed by the public on both sides of the Atlantic; and we accordingly took up the three volumes now before us with no common feeling of gratification. That Mr. Hawthorne cannot write anything that is not full of talent has become patent, but we are reluctantly compelled to confess that we like him far less upon Italian ground than on his own. Rome has so thoroughly enthralled him by her spells, that the body of the book is æsthetic—the word has

lately become so hacknied that we almost shrink from using it, but in this case we have no alternative—to a degree which is positively wearisome; while the plot, if plot it can be called, is simply romance run mad. We had already been deluged with descriptions of St. Peter's, the Vatican, and the monuments of the Eternal City; while as regards the Carnival, Hans Christian Andersen has so thoroughly made it his own, that every subsequent attempt to depict it has been as *fade* and colourless as a washed-out picture. Still there are fine bits of writing, if not precisely artistic delineations, scattered throughout these volumes, which will be acceptable to such as are less familiar with the subjects of which they treat than ourselves. As regards the fiction, however, of this singular book, we must be permitted to express our unfeigned dislike. It is by no means complicated, four individuals comprising the whole of its actual *dramatis personæ*: and these four consisting of two pairs of lovers, the first being a damsel *errante,* of whom nothing is known, except her dark and marvellous beauty, and the fact that, totally unprotected, she has established her easel in Rome, and spends her life in its halls and galleries, and in flirting with a strange mysterious Italian sprite, a living realisation of the Faun of Praxiteles, who turns out to be the descendant of one of those sylvan deities who wooed and won a mortal wife. Of Miriam our author tells us . . .

Here is her personal portrait . . . That of Donatello, the Faun-man, we confess to be beyond even the author's or our own description. We have now to deal with the other two personages of the romance, who are both Americans. Hilda is described as a "slender, brown-haired New England girl", several years younger than her friend Miriam—for the two women have become friends, without knowing anything of each other's antecedents, and simply by meeting day after day in the art-galleries of Rome:—for Hilda also, having availed herself of her early orphanhood, although at peace with her remaining transatlantic relatives, has come with the same views and the same disregard of the proprieties of female life, to pursue her pictorial studies in the Eternal City; and of her we are told, or rather of her habits and residence . . .

This is pretty enough; but we have strangely misconceived the rearing of American young ladies, if the following dash of independence is to be accepted as one of their characteristic experiments . . .

The fourth actor in the love drama is a sculptor named Kenyon, the only natural and rational member of the party, with whom we can sympathise without effort: a painstaking, conscientious artist, full of good sense and good-feeling. Miriam is, as we have already hinted, surrounded by mystery, and that too, of a sombre and repellant cast; yet she can dally, like Nero, with a fatal mirth, and encase her hand in a perfumed glove like Catharine de Medicis. Here is a specimen of her hyena-sport with her only half-human lover . . .

And what came—what could come of such an unnatural coalition as that between an intellectual, self-sufficing, and imperviously-mysterious woman many years older than her semi-human adviser, and that demi-witted being? We asked ourselves the question as we turned over page after page,—let our author solve it. Miriam is persecuted by the perpetual attendance of a being as unfathomable as herself; a species of mortal shadow, darkening ever, not only the ground upon which he treads, but also the spirit which he has enthralled; and the jealousy of the tricksy sprite Donatello is so roused at last that he resolves to rid himself of the intruder. He conservates all his imaginary wrongs; he condenses all his hatreds; and, finally, he resolves to dispose of this unknown encroacher on what he considers as his exclusive privilege. The opportunity is not long wanting. The lovers, if such indeed they may be called, are leaning side by side on a low parapet, overlooking the City of the Seven Hills, and hanging upon a precipitous slope of the Tarpeian Rock; alone, and musing over the fearful fate of those who, in the time of the Roman rule, were hurled thence into eternity for crimes against the republic; when suddenly, "From a deep empty niche that had probably once contained a statue," emerges the dreaded form slowly approaching Miriam. In an instant he is seized by the furious Donatello; for an instant, he is held aloft, writhing above the deadly abyss; and then flung down relentlessly into its depths. But the deed has had another witness; Hilda returning to rejoin her friends, has witnessed the whole of the scene by which the pure moonlight has been polluted; and hurries wildly away with the dark secret on her soul. Return we to the chief actors in the scene; there is great power in the following sketch, but it is a power which the reader instinctively recoils as from an evil influence . . .

The true meaning of the mystery is but faintly shadowed out; but we appear to gather that the murdered man was a Jew of high birth and great wealth, to whom Miriam had been affianced in her girlhood by her family, in which a deadly crime had been committed, wherein she herself had been innocently considered to be implicated; but whose pursuit she had evaded by a flight to Rome, leaving him, however, with the power of fastening upon her the guilt of her father. Thenceforward the tricksy sprite developes into the repentant and intellectual man; loathing the very sight of the beautiful tempter by whom he had been betrayed into a deadly and irreparable sin; while the lady, on her side, degenerates into a lovesick and humble woman, living only in his presence. What ultimately becomes of this worthy couple, who dance a gay round immediately before their crime in the gardens of the Villa Borghese, and consequently figure at the Carnival, our author does not condescend to inform us; but Hilda, puritan-born as she is, after having found no fitter method of releasing herself from the corroding secret which preys upon her soul than that of divulging it in a Roman confessional, ultimately becomes the wife of Kenyon, and returns to her own more rational country. And a sort of snow-bride she must have proved according to our author's showing, who paints her not only with a "white bosom" and "white arms", but also a "white soul", a "white fancy", a "white life", and, in short, as a white being altogether.

By those who have never seen Rome, either actually or through the eyes of modern travellers, much may be learnt from Mr. Hawthorne's books; but as a work of fiction we can only denounce it as a vapid extravagance. We trust ere long to meet him again on his own natural soil; real as her mountains, broadthoughted as her prairies, fresh as her primeval forests. He is not at home among the hybrid mythology and the mouldering ruins of the antique world.

Did it matter to Nathaniel that his work had been dismissed as being merely a good travel book? Perhaps not, though he could have noted that no real complaint had been made in this instance about an unsatisfactory denouement. Next day, Sophia received another letter from Chorley, who was somewhat overwhelmed at the attention he was attracting:

Saturday morning. March. 10/60
13. Eaton Place West.

Dear Mrs. Hawthorne,
I assure you I feel the good nature to to be on <u>my side</u> of the treaty. It is not common for a critic to get any kind construction or to be credited with anything save a desire to show ingenuity no matter whether just or unjust.—Most deeply too, do I feel the honour of having a suggestion such as mine adopted,—[38] I thought

when my letter had gone that I had written in a strange, random humour and that had I got a "Mind your own business" sort of answer, it was no more than such unasked-for meddling might expect. I am glad with all my heart at what you tell me about the success of the tale. But we really will not wait so long for No. 5?

Today's train takes you my Italian story:—[39] I had every trouble in the world to find a publisher for it, having the gift of no-success in a very remarkable degree. The dedication tells its own story. It was begun in 1848:—& ended just before the Italian war broke out.—Some of my few readers (within a dozen) are aggrieved at my having only told part of the story of Italian patriotism.—I meant it merely as a picture of manners: & have seen too much of the class "refugee", not to have felt how they have as a class retarded not aided the cause of real freedom & high morals. I should have sent it before, but I always feel like Teresa Panza, when she sent acorns to the Duchess.[40]

You will come to town, & eat in my quiet corner before you go, I know:— Perhaps, I may call on you at Easter: as there is just a chance of my being at Birmingham. There is an old house, Compton Winyates, that I very much wish to see. Has Hawthorne seen it?[41]

Once more thank you affectionately,—these sort of passages are among the very few set-offs to the difficulties of a harsh life & an ungracious career. My seeing you face to face, was, I assure you, one of my best pleasures in 1859.

Ever yours faithfully,
Henry F. Chorley.[42]

It was probably on or about 13 March that Nathaniel received another letter from Bright:

My dear Mr. Hawthorne,—Thank you most heartily for your kind letter, and for the manuscript of "Transformation", which has this morning reached me. Please get the missing pages from Smith and Elder.[43] I am going to bind the book up in three gorgeous volumes; there always seems to me to be a peculiar colour about every story you write, and my binding will depend on what I think when I have finished the book. What binding do you think would be most appropriate? I must really try to be in London again in May, that I may meet you in that heavenly place,—that we may again dine together at the Club, and see strange, out-of-the-way nooks, and watch the carriages in the Park. Please let me know where you are to be found. If before going to London you are looking for a pleasant place to spend a month, why not Malvern? I do so want you to see it and love it as I do.

Ever most truly yours
H. A. Bright.[44]

The following day some mail came in from America and Sophia hurried to write to Mary with all the latest news:

March 14th 1860

My dear Mary,
We have now engaged our passage for the 16th of June and shall be in Concord, I trust, before the first of July. Mr. Hawthorne thinks I should not be comfortable at an earlier season, because it is so cold at sea. Even in July we had occasion

Mary Mann. Courtesy of the Massachusetts Historical Society, Boston, Mass.

for all the wraps we could muster in coming over. And I am so sensitive now. Elizabeth fears the icebergs; but we must risk them. We shall leave Leamington on the 21st March, but not for Malvern. It is too expensive to go there. It is the most expensive place in the Kingdom. We shall either go to Bath or to Richmond—both salubrious on the heights, and on the first of June we go to Mrs. Blodget's in Liverpool till our embarkation. Mr. Wilding (of the Consulate) has procured for us the best staterooms in the steam-packet, and after Fanny and Rosebud have suffered their seasicknesses of a day or two, we shall have a joyful time homeward after our long wandering to and fro on the earth. I received your letter of February 24th this morning, dear Mary.[45] How kind of you to take so much care upon yourself about the beloved Wayside.

We wish you to use your own discretion about the trimming and clearing of the buckthorne hedges and the arrangement of the Norway pines. We sent word to Mr. Bull to set the pines out on the bare hill between the barn and Mr. Alcot's, and we sent three thousand. These he allowed to lie and die in the barn by hundreds—Nat wrote to me—Mr. Hawthorne now leaves it to your taste to place them. I am astonished that the grapes have not been set out as Mr. Bull promised—though I may as well cease to be astonished at any of his omissions by this time. We shall be very glad if you will have planted for us the grapevines in your own way and place.

I am sorry you must give up your Baucis and Philemon[46] but you will still have your good Mary whom you intended to give to me. Mr. Hawthorne says he does not wish to engage Bulger for any stated time because he does not wish to keep a cow or to go into farming—he only wants to have a kitchen garden to supply our own table. He will not have animals, because he does not want the care of them or the expense of caretakers—and the least extension of agriculture would also be what he has no time to superintend, and not capital enough to bring through properly. Cannot Bulger prepare and plant our garden &c as a separate job without an engagement for months? Mr. Hawthorne leaves to your judgement the manuring of the potatoe field—the how much—In short Mr. Hawthorne says he trusts the whole matter to you entirely, except that he does not want to hire Mr. Bulger for eight months—And I do not want him to touch my darling wood, even to clear it out—For I want to stand myself beside the woodman who cuts therein—"That is my music," which Nat has kept for me—So you will not let Bulger go there, will you? You and I together can plan it out this year. Yes, you "shall be our farmer pro tem" as you say & with a thousand thanks from us.

No, dear Mary, my cough did not commence with that family bout of hooping. I began two weeks after arriving in England during a fortnight's rain—It was emphasised by our damp Rock Park House and garden—I think with you that the dry hot and the clear cold of my native land will restore me best of all things—I cough very hard now, and my throat is good for nothing for talking. I rejoice that Georgie profits by the colder climate. How I thank God that my house was open for you at that moment! and that it was pleasant to you to see pictures and furniture when you could not have borne to see your own with their associations. I have never yet told you that I bought for you in Rome the twenty dollar's worth of Photographs and stereoscopic views which you requested me to buy. They will reveal to you and your boys some of the riches of the old world in your new house.

There was a written paper about the lease by which if we remember aright, Mr. Bull was bound to take faithful care of the estate, plant hedges and fruit trees and for his pay he was to get what good and profit he could out of the lot opposite the house, saving the garden patch, which was for Nathaniel, and this for five years. What his bill can be against, we cannot fancy. I fear he is a man of more talk than practice. We supposed him so gentlemanly and upright and conscientious that I dare say the lease was not very exact in detail, as he used to talk a great deal about what he would do,[47] and we supposed his word was better than an oath. It is the very hardest thing in the world to believe that people do not act from conscience and principle and I never can get used to it, live as long as I may or travel as much as I will. It is a thing so natural and inevitable to take for granted—and still to take for granted after all the rebuffs and experiences that we may have.

I assure you, dear Mary, there are no reserves at all between my husband and me about my health or upon any other subject and I would on no account conceal from him any truth. But you do not know him very well, if you think he would shrink from any thing he should bear. Though the most delicately organized mortal mixture that I ever knew or heard of and through his imagination, the most susceptible of an almost infinite suffering, yet if you knew him as I do from twenty years intimacy, you would know that he has a strength, courage and endurance as divine and as unflinching, when needed, as Abdiel's.[48] It seems to us both, and has seemed from the beginning of our first meeting, as if an eternity stretched behind us as well as before us and that this mortal life is a mere interlude—a happiest interlude too, with our harvest of Immortals, to increase the bliss of coming Eternity.

We are not required, we mortals, thank God, "to drink of the cup" by anticipation, or life would be a wail, but as far as faith and hope go, I rejoice always. I pray and trust that you will enjoy the fruition of faith in time, dearest Mary, and an assurance of nearness and union—in time you must, I am sure—and then you may feel a little consolation. Today I wrote to Mr. Cox again[49] and pressed for letters because the weeks are going fast. I hope you have received my last letter enclosing his note.[50] He wanted a date, and I trust you have sent it to him before this. There are but twelve weeks more in England! It is strange about your dreams—Perhaps it is a benign providence that your thoughts rest from too intense fixedness on the one subject while you sleep. "God giveth his beloved sleep"[51] and it is to rest the mind. It may be that when you can think of other subjects more by day, you will then be rested by dreams of him at night. I grieve that you do not sleep long slumbers.[52]

While Sophia was writing this letter Nathaniel was completing, or making a fair copy of, the postscript to the romance:

POSTSCRIPT

There comes to the Author, from many readers of the foregoing pages, a demand for further elucidations respecting the mysteries of the story.

He reluctantly avails himself of the opportunity afforded by a new edition, to explain such incidents and passages as may have been left too much in the dark; reluctantly, he repeats, because the necessity makes him sensible that he can have succeeded but imperfectly, at best, in throwing about the Romance the kind of atmosphere essential to the effect at which he aimed. He designed the story and the characters to bear, of course, a certain relation to human nature and human life, but still to be so artfully and airily removed from our mundane sphere, that some laws and proprieties of their own should be implicitly and sensibly acknowledged.

The idea of the modern Faun, for example, loses all the poetry and beauty which the Author fancied in it, and becomes nothing better than a grotesque absurdity, if we bring it into actual light of day. He had hoped to mystify this anomalous creature between the Real and the Fantastic, in such a manner that the reader's sympathies might be excited to a certain pleasurable degree, without impelling him to ask how Cuvier would have classified poor Donatello, or to insist upon being told, in so many words, whether he had furry ears or no. As respects all who ask such questions, the book is, to that extent, a failure.

Nevertheless, the Author fortunately has it in his power to throw light upon several matters in which some of his readers appear to feel an interest. To confess the truth, he was himself troubled with a curiosity similar to that which he has just deprecated on the part of his readers, and once took occasion to cross-examine his friends, Hilda and the sculptor, and to pry into several dark recesses of the story, with which they had heretofore imperfectly acquainted him.

We three had climbed to the top of St. Peter's, and were looking down upon the Rome which we were soon to leave, but which (having already sinned sufficiently in that way) it is not my purpose further to describe. It occurred to me that, being so remote in the upper air, my friends might safely utter, here, the secrets which it would be perilous to even whisper on lower earth.

"Hilda," I began, "can you tell me the contents of the mysterious pacquet which Miriam entrusted to your charge, and which was addressed to 'Signor Luca Barboni, at the Palazzo Cenci'?"

"I never had any further knowledge of it," replied Hilda, "nor felt it right to let myself be curious upon the subject."

"As to its precise contents," interposed Kenyon, "it is impossible to speak. But Miriam, isolated as she seemed, had family connections in Rome, one of whom, there is reason to believe, occupied a position in the Papal Government. This Signor Luca Barboni was either the assumed name of the personage in question, or the medium of communication between that individual and Miriam. Now, under such a government as that of Rome, it is obvious that Miriam's privacy and isolated life could only be maintained through the connivance and support of some influential person, connected with the administration of affairs. Free and self-controlled as she appeared, her every movement was watched and investigated far more thoroughly by the priestly rulers than by her dearest friends. Miriam, if I mistake not, had a purpose to withdraw herself from this irksome scrutiny, and to seek real obscurity in another land; and the pacquet, to be delivered long after her departure, contained a reference to this design, besides certain family documents, which were to be imparted to her relative as from one dead and gone."

"Yes; it is as clear as a London fog," I remarked. "On this head no further elucidation can be desired. But when Hilda went quietly to deliver the pacquet, why did she so mysteriously vanish?"

"You must recollect," replied Kenyon, with a glance of friendly commiseration at my obtuseness, "that Miriam had utterly disappeared, leaving no trace by which her whereabouts could be known. In the meantime, the municipal authorities had become aware of the murder of the Capuchin; and, from many preceding circumstances, such as his strange persecution of Miriam, they must have been led to see an obvious connection between herself and that tragical event. Furthermore, there is reason to believe that Miriam was suspected of implication with some plot or political intrigue, of which there may have been tokens in the pacquet. And when Hilda appeared as the bearer of this missive, it was really quite a matter of course, under a despotic government, that she should be detained."

"Ah! quite a matter of course, as you say," answered I. "How excessively stupid in me not to have seen it sooner! But there are other riddles. On the night of the extinction of the lamp, you met Donatello in a penitent's garb, and afterwards saw and spoke to Miriam, in a coach, with a gem glowing on her bosom. What was the business of these two guilty ones in Rome? And who was Miriam's companion?"

"Who?" repeated Kenyon. "Why, her official relative, to be sure; and as to their business, Donatello's still gnawing remorse had brought him hitherward, in spite of Miriam's entreaties, and kept him lingering in the neighborhood of Rome, with the ultimate purpose of delivering himself up to justice. Hilda's disappearance, which took place the day before, was known to them through a secret channel, and had brought them into the city, where Miriam, as I surmise, began to make arrangements, even then, for that sad frolic of the Carnival."

"And where was Hilda, all that dreary time between?" inquired I.

"Where were you, Hilda?" asked Kenyon, smiling.

Hilda threw her eyes on all sides, and seeing that there was not even a bird of the air to fly away with the secret, not any human being nearer than the loiterers by the obelisk, in the piazza below, she told us about her mysterious abode.

"I was a prisoner in the Convent of the Sacré Cœur, in the Trinità de' Monti," said she; "but in such kindly custody of pious maidens, and watched over by such a dear old priest, that—had it not been for one or two disturbing recollections, and also because I am a daughter of the Puritans—I could willingly have dwelt there for forever. My entanglement with Miriam's misfortunes, and the good Abbaté's mistaken hope of a proselyte, seem to me sufficient clue to the whole mystery."

"The atmosphere is getting decidedly lucid," observed I, "but there are one or two things that still puzzle me. Could you tell me—what were Miriam's real name and rank, and precisely the nature of the trouble that led to all these direful consequences?"

"Is it possible that you need an answer to these questions?" exclaimed Kenyon, with an aspect of vast surprise. "Have you not even surmised Miriam's name? Think awhile, and you will assuredly remember it. If not, I congratulate you most sincerely; for it indicates that your feelings have never been harrowed by one of the most dreadful and mysterious events that have occurred within the present century."

"Well," resumed I, after an interval of deep consideration, "I have but few things more to ask. Where, at this moment, is Donatello?"

"In prison," said Kenyon, sadly.

"And why, then, is Miriam at large?" I asked.

"Call it cruelty, if you like—not mercy!" answered Kenyon. "But, after all, her crime lay merely in a glance; she did no murder."

"Only one question more," said I, with intense earnestness. "Did Donatello's ears resemble those of the Faun of Praxiteles?"

"I know, but may not tell," replied Kenyon, smiling mysteriously. "On that point, at all events, there shall be not one word of explanation."

LEAMINGTON
March 14th, 1860

THE END[53]

There was a swift interchange of manuscript and proof sheets, and on Friday Nathaniel was able to write to Smith, Elder:

Leamington, March 16th '60

Gentlemen,
I return the proof of the postscript.

I am loth to overtax your liberality; but it would much oblige me if you would send a copy of the new edition to Mr. John Miller, American Despatch Agent, 26, Henrietta-street, Covent Garden, directed to "Madame O'Sullivan, Care of Colonel Morgan, American Minister: Resident, Lisbon, Portugal." I should also be glad of a copy for myself, to be left at Mr F. Bennoch's 77, Wood-st, Cheapside.
Very Respectfully,
Nathl Hawthorne.[54]

It was probably after reading the proof sheets and having mailed them to Smith, Elder that Nathaniel and Julian took the opportunity of walking into Warwick, presumably for the last time; it was certainly the occasion of the last entry recorded in Nathaniel's journal before the family finally left Leamington.

Julian and I walked to Warwick, [this forenoon] and went into St. Mary's church to see the Beauchamp Chapel. It is a stately and very elaborate chapel, with a large window of ancient painted glass, as perfect as any I remember seeing in England, and more bright. The roof is finely carved in stone; and there are several tombs with marble figures lying upon them, knights in antique armor, and their dames. Queen Elizabeth's Earl of Leicester lies on one of these tombs, with his last wife, looking like the very type of old integrity and conjugal faith. I wonder, now that it is the fashion to reverse so many historical verdicts, why some historian does not make Leicester out to have been an excellent man. In the center of the chapel is the monument of its founder; a bronze figure of a knight in gilded armour, admirably executed, for the sculptors of those days really seem to have had great skill in their own style. On one side of the chapel were some worn steps ascending to a Confessional, where the priest used to sit, while the penitent, in the body of the church, poured his sins through a perforated auricle into this unseen receptacle. The sexton showed us, too, a very old chest which had been found in the burial vault, I believe, with some ancient armour and other matters stored away in it. Three or four helmets of rusty iron, one of them barred, the rest with visors, and all intolerably weighty, were ranged in a row. What heads those must have been that could bear such massiveness! On one of the helmets was a wooden crest (some bird or other) that, of itself, weighed several pounds. This chapel was the burial place of the former family of Earls Warwick, now long extinct. On the other side of the church is the vault of the present family (who are Grevilles; descendants of the Lord Brooke of Parliamentary times) which, the sexton said, is calculated to hold sixty (or, I believe, he said eighty) coffins, of which number only sixteen have been thus far contributed. It is a question whether the number will be made up while the Grevilles hold Warwick Castle. This latter chapel seems to be as ancient as that of the Beauchamps, but contains few monuments of interest. The chancel of the church, with these two chapels on either side of it, is ancient; the nave is more modern, the original structure having been burnt, I believe, and restored by Sir Christopher Wren. I have seen many more impressive churches. Not the least interesting thing was a small monumental brass, in the antique style, but recently engraved, and representing the last vicar of the parish, a man, according to the sexton's account, of antiquarian propensities, and most attached to this old church, which he was continually haunting in his lifetime and perhaps haunts now. This engraved figure of him had a very characteristic look.
Leaving the church, we strolled about the old town, and I drank a glass of ale

in the comfortable little back parlor of an inn in the market-place. There was a good fire in the grate and the walls were hung with homely pictures and prints, among them some political caricatures of Lord Eldon's time. Before coming home, we stopt on the opposite side of the street to look at the venerable arched entrance of Leicester's Hospital, but did not go in, for I have already visited it at least twice and probably have described it as often.[55]

On this occasion, it appears that Julian did not take the opportunity of visiting the museum, even while his father was quaffing his liquid lunch. The following day two further reviews were published, one in *The Saturday Review*, the other in *The Albion;* as the latter was an American publication, Nathaniel would not have been aware of it until later, of course. *The Review* saw the book as a qualified success:

Genius is, to some extent, its own defence. No one but a man of genius could have written this novel, and if Mr. Hawthorne has chosen to write it in a way that exposes it to criticism of the ordinary kind, the end of such criticism is only to establish that he might have written something different. The tale not only tantalizes us by keeping us in the dim region of events that are neither probable nor improbable, neither possible nor impossible, but it defeats our expectations by sketching out a plot which comes absolutely to nothing. A mystery is set before us to unriddle, and at the end the author turns round and asks us what is the good of solving it. That the impression of emptiness and unmeaningness thus produced is in itself a blemish to the work, no one can deny. Mr. Hawthorne really trades upon the honesty of other writers. We feel a sort of interest in the story, slightly and sketchily as it is told, because our experience of other novels leads us to assume that, when an author pretends to have a plot, he has one. A story-teller who ends by asking why he should clear anything up is not dealing quite fairly by us. But when we have said this, and begin to estimate the book by what it does rather than by what it does not contain, there is too much in it that is beautiful and original to permit us to dwell on the points it presents for adverse criticism. It is really an account of Rome and Central Italy, of the appearance which the great city and its neighbourhood wore in the eyes of an American visitor, and of the reflections to which the religion, the art, and the people of Italy gave rise in the breast of a man born under influences which placed him in the most direct opposition to all that marks the centre of Catholicism, and yet attracted to all that he saw around him in Rome by strong ties of personal sympathy. Of course, if he had chosen, Mr. Hawthorne might have written a tourist's sketch of Central Italy; but he is a novelist, and has a peculiar vein of thought running through his mind which evidently affects his whole manner of thinking, and which has yet so remote a connexion with reality that he could scarcely allow it to intervene in a plain representation of facts. His former works abundantly show that the notion of great crime, its complexity, its subtle influences on character, its remote consequences, and more particularly the strange admixture of high feeling and innocence with which it may occasionally be found united, exercise such a fascination over his mind that he cannot separate his reflections on real facts from the thread of moral difficulties that is woven through all the efforts of his imagination. Some sort of fiction is therefore necessary in order to place the reader in the position of the writer.

In *Transformation* he introduces two principal characters who, like the hero and heroine of the *Scarlet Letter,* are bound together by the bonds of a common crime, dark and mysterious, and yet so conceived that the indulgence both of the author and the reader is bespoken beforehand. The special point taken in this general region of guilt is the effect on the character of the criminals that their common guilt may be supposed to produce. The hero, Donatello, Count of Monte Beni, is first introduced as an Italian with the beauty, simplicity, and the playful wildness of a light-hearted youth who alternately charms and repels his friends by the strange approximation of his nature to that of a wild animal. Mr. Hawthorne does not refrain here from giving the loosest rein to his fancy. Not only is Donatello curiously like the Faun of Praxiteles, but a legend of his family is told describing how they, in the remotest days of history sprang from the union of a human being with a creature of the woods; and to the very last it is carefully hinted that his ears, which he kept carefully concealed, were really long and furry, like those of a faun. The lady for whom this unhappy animal conceives a passionate love belongs scarcely less to the region of pure fancy. She first presents herself as an artist; and it appears to be accepted as an axiom in every description of artist life that a man or woman who paints pictures or moulds clay is released from all the ties and burdens of life—that it is impertinent to inquire whence they came or how they live, or with whom, or on what. In some way never cleared up, this girl has been innocently concerned in a great crime. A lunatic monk is aware of her secret, and crosses her path with that unexpected frequency which fanciful novelists introduce in order to create the impression of a terrible doom. Donatello and she are on the edge of a precipice when the tormentor comes by, and the faun, anxious to oblige his mistress, seizes the wretch, and, on reading a sign of acquiescence in her face, drops his burden over the rock, and the persecutor lies a shattered mass at the foot. Horror seizes the guilty pair. The faun, wakened to remorse by his crime, becomes transformed. A deep, gloomy sensitiveness replaces his beastlike playfulness and ignorance, and his sin reveals to him the knowledge of good and evil. Miriam is also changed. She feels cut off from the world, and pours the whole flood of her passion on the half-savage adorer whom she had previously despised. With this pair is contrasted a New England maiden, Hilda, who is the type of high-souled innocence, purity, and virgin modesty. She also is an artist; and we are therefore supposed not to feel surprise at finding that she lives, without any one to protect her, at the top of a high tower in the centre of Rome, where she feeds a brood of milky doves, and keeps a lamp burning in honour of the Virgin. She is a witness of the murder, and the burden cast on her mind by the dreadful secret impels her to the confessional, this affording Mr. Hawthorne an opportunity of interweaving his reflections on the Catholic system. A lover is assigned her, both that his successful love may mitigate the blackness of the story, and also because, as he is a sculptor, Mr. Hawthorne has the pleasure of describing the real work of American sculptors at Rome under the fiction that they were the creations of this imaginary artist. Their property is duly restored to the authors in an explanatory and laudatory preface. However faulty the story may be as a story, it does undoubtedly produce the impression of mysterious horror that is so dear to Mr. Hawthorne; and it undoubtedly gives him an opportunity of describing Rome and rural Italy, discussing ancient and modern art, and noting down the reflections suggested to a meditative and romantic Puritan by the great embodiment and centre of Catholicism. We may add, that the style is singularly beautiful, the writing most careful, and the justness and felicity of the epithets used to convey the effect of scenery unusually great. The Americans may be proud that they have produced a writer who, in his own special walk of English, has few rivals or equals in the mother country, and they may perhaps allow this excellence to atone for the sincere contempt with which he evidently regards the large majority of his countrymen who show themselves on this side of the Atlantic.

We are not aware that there is any book which contains such excellent descriptions of Rome generally, and of some few of the more remarkable lions of the Papal City. It is not only that the drawing of the thing to be represented is as full and accurate as can reasonably be expected in a sketch in words, but the general impression conveyed is exactly that produced by the grandeur and mournfulness, the sublimity and the pettiness, of Rome. As we read the description, we feel that it could belong to no other place, not merely because the special things of the locality are noted, but far more because the peculiar atmosphere of Rome seems to pervade all the author says. The description of the rude Tuscan castle, the ancestral home of Donatello, is equally good in its way, and is something quite new. The simple pride, the legendary nobility, the homely pomp of the masters of a remote Italian valley, with their precious vineyard, the juice of which is not to be had for gold, but flows freely for the guest, their devoted servants, their utter absence of thought for the present or care for the future, are brought home to us with the skill of a genuine artist. Extracts cannot do justice to the descriptive excellence of the book, as the whole is in this instance very much greater and better than any single part can be. No one who wishes for an entertaining novel ought to open *Transformation;* but those who sometimes open a novel to gain, if possible, some new thoughts from it, will find that there is seldom anything in fiction so new—or, so far as description of external objects are concerned, anything so good—as the many passages in *Transformation* in which Mr. Hawthorne has depicted his favourite studies from Tuscany and Rome.

On art Mr. Hawthorne has much to say. First of all, he has to give a kind lift to the reputation of some American friends. More especially he is anxious to sound the praise of a statue of Cleopatra, by Mr. William W. Story. Mr. Hawthorne is a good judge, and we do not mean for a moment to dispute his judgement as to a statue we have not seen; but it does not strike us as so great a triumph of original genius as he appears to think it, that Mr. Story, wishing to give Cleopatra new characteristics, has represented the daughter of the Ptolemies as a Nubian of Upper Egypt with a negro lip. Mr. Hawthorne has thought long and deeply about art, and although his conclusions are not those accepted in the artist world, we are convinced that for many minds they are extremely true. Hilda is represented in the early part of the story as the most successful copyist in Rome, so wonderful and complete is her power of throwing herself into the work she copies. But after her acquaintance with Miriam's terrible secret, she roams in vain through picture-galleries, seeking rest. She cannot find anything in art to satisfy her, except one or two pictures of extraordinary merit, inspired by the highest feeling. All but these she regards as acres of wasted canvas. We are not to suppose that this is Mr. Hawthorne's general opinion about art, but he wishes to point out that the limits within which art touches on the great permanent feelings of humanity are fixed and narrow. He sees that mere artistic appreciation of art attains its ordinary maximum in the development of those faculties and qualities which make a good copyist. The old masters meant something and had something to embody in almost all the works of their art; and a student of their designs is an apt and a worthy student if he can make out what they meant. But it does not follow that what they meant was anything very far above the common level of human thought. In the great crises of life, art, therefore, is apt to fail as a consolation and a guide. A few pictures, however, form a class by themselves, the thoughts under the spell of which they were designed being so evidently pure and heavenly. This conveys the feeling with which most persons of some sensibility go through and quit the great picture-galleries of European capitals. At first the novelty stimulates the intellectual effort by which the spectator sets himself to decipher the meaning of a master. Then comes the "icy demon of weariness", and a painful sense of the contrast between the coldness and emptiness of art and the warmth and fulness of real life. Lastly, there remains an abiding recollection of a few pictures that come home to all that is best both in the most and the least instructed of visitors.

Mr. Hawthorne seems to have been greatly attracted by Catholicism. He was struck not only by the depth and greatness of the feelings that have shaped themselves in the architectural splendours and gorgeous ceremonials of Rome, but by the wonderful plasticity with which Catholicism adapts itself to every difficulty and sorrow, to men of every race and every age. Hilda, after wandering round St. Peter's, in her anguish stops at a confessional, and suddenly disburthens herself of her secret. Her relief and her happiness are so great that she will not allow her lover to sneer at the system that has given her a remedy in the sorest hour of her need. No one could fall more entirely than Mr. Hawthorne into the modern fashion of asking, not whether a religion is true, but whether it is suitable to a particular individual. Hilda is made to ask whether it is possible that the Virgin, to whom as a woman it would be so sweet to her to pray, is really deaf to the prayers of her worshippers? Nothing changes faster than the fashions of religious discussion. A few years ago, a Protestant would have thought that the whole matter was to be settled by inquiring whether the literal construction of the Bible pronounced the Virgin an object of adoration. Now, a Protestant novelist is full of the thought that it would be sweet to pray to her. As it happens, the same sensibility that attracts him to Catholicism also repels him from it, and when he ceases to reason he is as little able to make allowances where they are due as to discover faults where they exist. It is the priests and the Papal Government that seem to have scared Mr. Hawthorne from the Romish Church. They were such poor mean creatures, and the Papal Government produced so much misery, poverty, and dirt, that, as the clean citizen of a State accustomed to make its own way in the world vigorously and demonstratively, he would not mix himself up with what he so thoroughly despised. His Protestantism seems to have been greatly indebted to the theory in which he finally rested—that the papal system is dying out. That it had once been the greatest and the best expression witnessed on earth of religious thought accounted to him for all the fascination to which he made his imaginary Hilda temporarily succumb. That it was now expiring accounted to him for his personal abhorrence of the priests and the Government. In an age when feeling supersedes logic, and the highest qualification of a religion is that it is suitable, we must own it to be not wholly undesirable that the *prestige* of Rome should be so largely counterbalanced, and its traditional skill so largely baffled, by the eminently uninspiring and unattractive spectacle which its temporal Government presents.[56]

The review in *The Albion* was complimentary, though objecting to the subject matter; the doubtful quality of the latter had apparently not concerned the many purchasers of the book since its publication in America but if, in fact, that *had* been the reason for the large number of sales those numbers could only be further increased now that a suggestion had been made as to its possible depravity.

The author of "The Scarlet Letter" reappears before the public after a retirement of some years, which we trust has proved more satisfactory to him than it has been to his many admirers. In his new book, *The Marble Faun, or the Romance of Monte Beni,* (of which, although it was published only on Wednesday of last week, Messrs. Ticknor and Fields have already sold thousands), his peculiar powers are exhibited in their highest, though not their happiest action. As a revelation of thoughts and feelings which in actual life never find actual expression, and of which ordinary people under ordinary circumstances have only the capacity, Mr. Hawthorne's last Romance takes the same peculiar rank in imaginative literature which is occupied by his previous works. It is also eminently distinguished by that rare felicity of language which is the marked feature of his style. But as a tale it is gloomy, morbid, unsatisfactory, and even in some respects repulsive; yet it cannot be read without a deal of interest.

Its characters are only four—Miriam, Hilda, Kenyon, and Donatello. Hilda is a New England girl, a painter, and she is loved by Kenyon a sculptor, upon whose affections she mildly beams in a watery, moony, way. Miriam also professes to paint, but does little at her art. A mystery hangs over her. No one knows what she is, whence she came, or what is the object of her presence in Rome. But she is "beautiful exceedingly" in a large and sumptuous style of beauty, contrasting strongly with Hilda's pale and slender type. She is not only veiled by mystery, but oppressed with the shadow of some awful crime. in which, however, we are led to infer she was not an accomplice; and she is pursued by a witness of that crime, who knows her connections with it, and who holds his knowledge over her head in unceasing and pitiless menace. She is beloved by Donatello, who, though a Count, with a castle and domains, spends his time in the enjoyment of a kind of life which is more suited to a lively, good-natured, uneducated boy, than to a man. But the truth is that Donatello is not all man, but part Faun. His family is so ancient that it stretches back into the mythical period, and is supposed to have sprung from the fruit of the violation of a human maiden by a Faun. This, the distinguishing trait of the story, and from that which it takes its name, is the repulsive feature to which we have alluded. The contemplation of such a monster—though purely fanciful and mythical—as a hybrid between the human race and one inferior, is revolting to our instincts; and we wonder that Mr. Hawthorne could be guilty of making such a creature the central figure of his story. Be this as it may, Donatello has inherited the nature of his Faun ancestor, whose characteristic traits appear in the line of his descendants about once in a century. It is almost implied that they are accompanied in Donatello's case by the hairy, pointed ears which the poets attributed to the fauns; and even hinted that the tail, with which the sculptors decorated their faunic figures, may not be wanting. Miriam laughs at the passion of her light-hearted, simple-natured lover; until he in a moment of rage, and inflamed by her appealing look, slays her tormentor by throwing him down the Tarpeian rock. Then gratitude and the sympathy of a common guilt produces an instant revulsion in his favour; and she loves him with the whole of her large nature. Hilda is the accidental and unsuspected witness of the murder; and is weighed to the earth by her secret, until she, although not a Roman Catholic, confesses it to a priest in St Peter's. Then, for some unexpressed purpose connected with Miriam, and in some unexplained manner, Hilda vanishes. Kenyon sets out upon a mad and fruitless search for her; Miriam and Donatello are seen going about in a sort of happy sadness (the reader of the story will understand the paradox) disguised as *contadini*;—but why, passes all human understanding. But the carnival comes on; and in the midst of it Hilda reappears in a balcony, how, or why, again no mortal can conjecture. Miriam and Donatello vanish as Hilda did before them; Miriam's mystery is all unexplained; but her fate and his to whom she is for ever bound are not even hinted at; and the curtain falls upon the marriage of the New England pair, to which Hilda has given the sort of consent that a woman under pressure of circumstance might be brought to give to the commission of some crime little short of felony.

A more unsatisfactory story—if story we must call it—could not be told. Nor are the characters which figure in it suited to the demain of a healthy moral appetite. Of Donatello, we have spoken; and while we see the skill with which his most singular individuality is made out and sustained, even though the change which comes over him as a consequence of his guilt—also giving him a soul, as love gave one to Undine[57]—we cannot permit this admiration of the artist's powers to blind us to the revolting nature of the object which he has created—Hilda is a sort of woman whom some folk will worship for her angelic grace and purity. She lives in a shrine, is encircled by doves, and burns a lamp before the Virgin. She dresses in white, and seems diaphanous. Now this sort of woman may have her uses in stories, although she can have none out of them. But even there we cannot see why she could not be just as pure, and just as lovely, as she would be infinitely more loveable, if she had a well-rounded figure, a good appetite, liked beef and mutton, and loved her lover as much as he loved her—Kenyon is but a lay figure on which the author can display the many tinted tissues of his fancy—Miriam is both the redeeming and the dominant character in this *partie quarré*. Her nature is large, rich, human, womanly;—full of "all impulses of soul and sense." Her passions are strong, but her will is stronger; and with all her impulsiveness she is reticent and even restrained, except when she is deliberately confiding. Her self-devotion is unbounded; it carries us away upon its glorious flood of feeling; and we should find fault with Kenyon if he were alive enough to be guilty, and that not being the case, we must find fault with Mr. Hawthorne for stigmatizing her confession to the sculptor of her love of Donatello as unwomanly. It was a love of which (setting aside Donatello's supposed hybridity) she had no reason to be ashamed; and her confession of it, under the peculiar circumstances in which she was placed, had a touch of womanliness, far truer, tenderer, ay, and really purer than any manifestation that we see of Hilda's narrow, thin, and luke-warm nature. But Miriam's character is distorted. It is like a noble stream swollen, and turbid, overflowing its proper bounds, and diverted from its channel. This might be well, if we saw the reason for it, as under like circumstances we do in the "Scarlet Letter". But here we do not. Miriam's trouble, as the author calls it, exists only on account of the necessity under which Mr. Hawthorne seems to labour, of presenting his most important character, the character—which gives the tone to his composition,—in a morbid state of mind, and under the most depressing circumstances. It appears to be impossible for him to write except as a sort of exercise in psychological pathology.

Prominent among the striking passages in this book are certain brief apophthegms, maxims, or "sentences" as they were called of old, in which Mr. Hawthorne expresses with united terseness and elegance some of the results of his reflection upon the problems of human life, which he has studied with so keen an insight. Such are his saying that "a taste for pictorial art is often no more than a polish upon the hard enamel of an artificial character"; that "it is the wont of women, young and old, to confuse themselves between right feelings and very foolish inferences"; that "people often do the idlest acts of their lifetime in their heaviest and most anxious moments"; that "what man calls justice lies chiefly in outward formalities, and is without close application and fitness" to the merits of individual cares; and his question, apropos of the fact that Donatello's reflection upon his crime elevates him—a question to which we must not be understood as replying in the affirmative,—"is sin, then—which we deem such a dreadful blackness in the universe—is it, like sorrow, merely an element of human education, through which we struggle to a higher and purer state than we could otherwise have attained? Did Adam fall, that we might ultimately rise to a far loftier paradise than his?"

The book is filled with beautiful fancies, of which the following is a characteristic specimen: "It is possible, indeed, that even Donatello's grief and Kenyon's pale sunless affection, lent a charm to Monte Beni, which it would not have retained amid a more redundant joyousness. The sculptor strayed amid its vineyards and orchards, its dells and tangled shrubberies, with somewhat the sensations of an adventurer who should find his way to the sight of ancient Eden, and behold its loveliness through the transparency of that gloom which has been brooding over those haunts of innocence ever since the fall. Adam saw it in a brighter sunshine, but never knew the shadow of pensive beauty which Eden won from his expulsion."

Mr. Hawthorne often shows that he is not a mere psychologist, and that he apprehends the spirit of his time even if he is not imbued with it. He says: "It is the iron rule in our day to require an object and a purpose in life. It makes us all parts of a complicated scheme of progress, which can only result in our arrival at a colder and drearier region than we were born in. It insists upon everybody's adding somewhat—a mite, perhaps, but earned by incessant effort—to an accumulated pile of usefulness, of which the only use will be, to burden our posterity with even heavier thoughts and more inordinate labour than our own. No life now wanders like an unfettered stream; there is a mill-wheel for the tiniest rivulet to turn. We go all wrong by too strenuous a resolution to go all right."

Again he shows his knowledge of healthful, normal human nature by reflections like the following: "It is a very miserable epoch, when the evil necessities of life, in our tortuous world, first get the better of us so far as to compel us to attempt throwing a cloud over our transparency. Simplicity increases in value the longer we can keep it, and the farther we carry it onward into life; the loss of a child's simplicity, in the inevitable lapse of years, causes but a natural sigh or two, because even his mother feared that he could not keep it always. But after a young man has brought it through his childhood, and has still worn it in his bosom, not as an early dew-drop, but as a diamond of pure white lustre—it is a pity to lose it, then. And thus, when Kenyon saw how much his friend had now to hide, and how well he hid it, he would have wept, although his tears would have been even idler than those which Donatello had just shed."

Finally we give our readers the following extract as eminently characteristic of the style in which this most interesting book is written . . .

Mr. Hawthorne's style is so clear and impressive, and generally so pure, that we are surprised to detect him in the not unfrequent use of those meaningless, extravagant phrases which are common on the lips of uncultivated Americans. "Terrible" is as favourite an epithet with him as "perfect" is with Tennyson. Thus he says of the statue of a nymph, "she looked terribly forlorn," and of the painters of our day, that "there is such a terrible lack of variety in their subjects." This reminds us that we heard a bright-looking girl, on her way home from a Ward school, say to her companion, "oh, our house is awful pretty." We also regret to see such an exaggerated use of a very awkward, though common, neologism as appears in the following sentence:" He drew away the cloth that had served to keep the moisture of the clay model from *being exhaled* !"—from exhaling, Mr. Hawthorne. There is no possible defence in this case of the other form.

Mr. Hawthorne makes his romance the occasion of giving to the world the impressions which his mind received from Italy; and especially from Rome, her people, her ruins and her art. This part of his work will be read with unalloyed pleasure, though not always with assent.

Prior to the Hawthornes' departure for Bath on 22 March[58] there are no further letters, diary, or journal entries that can throw any light on the manner in which the remainder of this last week in the town was passed. Nor is there anything to show why the family removed to Bath rather than to Richmond, Blackheath or, for that matter Devon, though despite Bath being an expensive place, it was presumably more for the benefit of Sophia's health that it was chosen rather than the environs of London, even though Nathaniel had indicated to Ticknor a few days previously that he had ample funds at the present time. Possibly Bennoch had not been able to suggest anyone to whom he could recommend the Hawthornes in Richmond or, more to the point, he may have advised Nathaniel that the likelihood of the expenses in that little town would be such that they would outweigh the convenience of a short stay for a month or so in the area, close to London. It is likely that one more of Mary's letters (at least one, dated 3 March)[59] was received while the family was still in Leamington but Sophia did not reply to it until after they were settled in Bath.

Overall, there is something basically unsatisfactory about the liaison between the Hawthornes and Leamington Spa, something incomplete, as though they had not really troubled to get to terms with the town and the district to discover all that it had to offer them. The family resided in the town for a total of 259 days. While the first visit lasted only three weeks, and during that and the second visit Nathaniel was away for lengthy periods, it appears that much of the time was spent closeted in the three houses in which they lodged. Excuses could be made that the weather was quite often pretty dismal (from an American's point of view) and that to continually seek amusement and instruction by traveling around the area in carriages and on trains would have cost more than they were prepared to spend, though despite his assertions that economy was of some importance, Nathaniel never really pulled the purse strings tight. And, it could reasonably have been objected, Leamington was a sufficiently modern town not to have within its boundaries anything of great historical value worth exploring (apart from its parish church and there is nothing to prove that the Hawthornes ever went inside it). And, it could have been further objected, they *did* see most of the local sites and areas of interest in Warwick, Kenilworth, Stratford, and Coventry.

But still there is the feeling that much, indeed most, of the time they remained holed up in their lodgings, not making any real effort to impress themselves on their surroundings. There is no evidence at all that any native of the town was spoken to (apart from shop assistants, landladies, and mill-owners) in an effort to establish friendly relations. Although both Nathaniel and Una wrote of looking at the lists of visitors that were published in the local newspapers each week, nobody is mentioned as having been worthy of notice (and many of them were Americans) and certainly not worth talking to (even Bostonians, of whom there were a number). It is certainly true that there was no artistic colony in the town with which they may have felt comfortable (there must have been *some* intellectuals though!). Given the opportunity, as when they were in Italy, their social life could flourish.

Ill health could have been offered as an excuse for nonfraternization, if any excuse was needed. Sophia was often ill and prostrated for long periods in her bed, particularly during the 1859–60 residence, and of the other members of the family each had his or her bad days. In the circumstances, the presence of a continually sick member of the family could have had a dispiriting effect on the activities of the rest of them (indeed, Nathaniel called the atmosphere gloomy in such circumstances), but there is ample evidence to show that most members of the family had their fair share of high spirits; even Nathaniel could become quite excited at times. But he certainly appeared to be the guiding influence and the instigator of most of the activities that the family indulged in outside the four walls of the home, wherever that happened to be. When he was away in Liverpool during the 1855 and 1857 residences the family apparently did little but await his return.

There is no record of Nathaniel having gone even once to any public entertainment while in Leamington; Sophia did go to see General Tom Thumb with the children. Una and Julian went to lectures at the Public Hall on a few occasions but apart from these instances, and despite living a few doors away from the Royal Music Hall in Bath Street during their last period of residence, the family appears not to have taken advantage of any of the numerous entertainments (all very proper and of suitable intellectual content) that the town offered at most times of the year. Sophia, who wrote of her appreciation of the power of music, apparently never attended any of the numerous concerts that took place (some of them a few yards down the road, in Bath Street). The town *did* have much more to it than just grand, modern architecture and noble trees. There is no record, either, of any of the family having made use of the several libraries in the town (the Public Library during their last residence was situated on the corner of Bath Street and Church Walk, less than a hundred yards from No. 21) though their reading habits seemed not to suffer as a result; perhaps they always bought what books and periodicals they read. All in all, the impression remains that the Hawthornes' and Leamington's relations with each other did not make the liaison an exciting one and it raises some doubt as to the reasons for returning to the town on two further occasions after the first visit of 1855. It was stated at the time that Manchester (in 1857) and Redcar (in 1859) were left behind due to their deleterious effect on Sophia's health and that they came to Leamington on both occasions for the benefits to be derived from its milder, cleaner atmosphere. This is all very well but eventually it was found to be a fallacy. Having returned to the benefits of Leamington, it remains very doubtful, taking all the circumstances into account, whether the family derived any real enjoyment from their immediate environment.

Apart from the particular circumstances that had prompted the Hawthornes to come to Leamington in 1855, 1857, and 1859 (and despite the few regrets with which they finally left it in 1860), the reasons for a visitor's appreciation of the attractions of the town and its environments cannot be put better than in the words of a contemporaneous correspondent in the columns of *The Leamington Advertiser,* words that could well have been included for the town's benefit in any of the guidebooks of the time. It only confirms, however, that the Hawthornes never really sampled all that was on offer:

A MONTH IN LEAMINGTON
(To the editor of the Leamington Advertiser)

Sir,—Permit me, through your excellent journal, to give the impressions which a month's residence in your town has made upon me. I hope I shall not be considered intrusive in thus briefly stating some of the thoughts which occupy my mind on leaving. It is not the first time I have been in Leamington, but it is the first visit of any long continuance affording leisure and opportunity for a thorough inspection of the town and neighbourhood, and truly I am surprised with its extent and beauty. I have been struck with its wide and spacious streets—the air of respectability which pervades it in every part—the number and extent of villa residences (indeed it might be called a city of villas)—and the charming rusticity which crowns the whole in its Parade, with its noble trees and rookery—its river—Jephson Gardens—beautiful bridge—and avenue of trees which line all the roads leading from the town. I cannot but mention the quietness and perfect order which prevails—the cleanliness and absence of everything offensive to the most fastidious taste, or the most delicate mind. The public authorities of the town deserve the gratitude and praise of every one, whether resident or visitor, and set an example to every town in the kingdom, especially when it is considered how lightly taxed the inhabitants are for these benefits. I might just enlarge on the advantages possessed in the splendid and well-furnished shops there are, so important to the comforts and convenience of the inhabitants and visitors. I have seen no town better supplied in this important matter than Leamington, and where everything purchasable is so reasonable. I have been deeply impressed with the religious privileges the town possesses; the large number of Churches and Chapels; the ability and excellence of the ministers; their piety and earnestness; and what can be more pleasing to strangers than to see the kind attention and the cordial welcome which is given to them in their attendance on public worship. I have been very much pleased with your Free Public Library—your Young Men's Christian Association—and the literary and intellectual advantages your town possesses in its many libraries and reading rooms, with the public lectures, the concerts and other entertainments calculated to interest, instruct, and amuse. I fear I am trespassing on your space, but I cannot refrain from alluding to the delightful neighbourhood with which you are surrounded—it may truly be said to be the garden of England. There is nothing I have enjoyed so much as the walks and excursions to the numerous places of interest within a short distance from your town; Warwick, with its historical associations—its venerable and princely Castle—its well endowed Hospital—and its Beauchamp Chapel in the Church of St. Mary; Kenilworth and its ruins; Stratford with its Shakespearean relics; Coventry with its antiquity and quaintness; Rugby and its celebrated school; Birmingham with its manufactures—these are all within a morning's visit; but the great charm to me has been the walks to the villages of Offchurch, Radford, Lillington, Cubbington, Whitnash, Tachbrook, Milverton, and to Guy's Cliff, Blacklow Hill, Stoneleigh Abbey, Chesford Bridge, &c., &c. I do assure you, Sir, the pleasure I have derived from these walking excursions is indescribable—so many interesting places—so many lovely spots, that it would fill the whole of your paper fully to describe them. I have adopted and can recommend to others your humourous Leamington peripatetics, or "use your limbs and have them," mirthfully inscribed to Dr. Jephson, and testify to their benefit. I have most imperfectly given some of my impressions during a month's visit to your town, and regret I cannot pourtray their reality in words sufficiently powerful, so as to convey to your readers the great pleasure and benefit I have derived.—I am, Sir, yours truly,

A Visitor.

April 10, 1860.

13

"This English trash"

Now that they had departed, no doubt with the usual fluster and worry about crushing all their belongings into trunks and carpetbags, backward glances were not part of the order of the day and Leamington was left with little, if any, regret. The only problem was how to pass the remaining months before boarding the steamer on 16 June for the return to America. Lodgings in Bath were found with little difficulty at No. 13 Charles Street, and apart from a two-week period during which Nathaniel went socializing in London and Cambridge, they all spent the time as best they could, walking, reading, and writing letters. Both Sophia and Fanny were taken ill again but soon recovered. Several more reviews were published, both in England and America, and Ticknor sent Nathaniel some of the notices that had appeared in the American press. The *New York Times* reviewed *The Marble Faun* on 24 March, the *North American Review* and the *Atlantic Monthly* did so in their April issues and *The Boston Courier* on 5 April, while in England there were reviews of *Transformation* in *The Examiner* (by Bright) on 31 March, in *The Westminster Review* and the *Art Journal* on 1 April, the *Birmingham Journal* and *The Times* on 7 April, and the *Dublin University Magazine* in its June issue. In a letter dated 26 April to Fields, who was now in England and making plans to accompany the Hawthornes back to America, Nathaniel wrote,

. . . The book has done better than I thought it would; for you will have discovered by this time, that it is an audacious attempt to impose a tissue of absurdities upon the public by the mere art of style and narrative. I hardly hoped that it would go down with John Bull; but then it is always my best point of writing, to undertake such a task, and I really put what strength I have into many parts of this book. The English critics (with two or three unimportant exceptions) have been sufficiently favourable, and the review in The Times awarded the highest praise of all. At home, too, the notices have been very kind, so far as they have come under my eye. Lowell has a good one in the Atlantic Monthly; and Hillard an excellent one in the [Boston] Courier; and yesterday I received a sheet of the May number of the Atlantic containing a keen and profound article by Whipple, in which he goes over all my works, and recognizes that element of unpopularity, which (as nobody knows better than myself) pervades them all. I agree with almost all he says; except that I am conscious of not deserving nearly so much praise. When I get

The Wayside, Concord. Courtesy of the Concord Free Public Library, Concord, Mass.

home, I will try to write a more genial book; but the devil himself always seems to get into my inkstand, and I can only exorcise him by pensfull at a time.[1]

On Saturday, 16 June, they all boarded the steamer *Europa* in the company of the Fields and the Beecher Stowes. The children were hugely excited to be on the way home at last, as was Sophia, but it can be questioned as to whether Nathaniel was wholly glad to be returning to America. For a man who proclaimed his disinterest in politics and whose political views (such as they were) would not afford him much popularity with his fellow Americans, the gathering war clouds formed an ominous umbrella under which to seek shelter. He was all for burying his head in the sands but the approaching years of the American Civil War was not a period of American history during which it was considered politic to state that one "stood on the fence." However much the turmoil was regretted, it was necessary to appear to be wholly for one side or the other. The war saddened Nathaniel and he never really came to terms with it or its causes. Despite his protestations to Ticknor and others that after the last few years of his growing to be an Anglophile he was now ready and willing to nurture his American roots once more, and that he would be returning to America to continue his writing career, to extend his house, to watch over the fruition of his children's growing maturity, he might well have not been prepared to acknowledge to anyone (not even to Sophia) that, other things being equal, he would rather have remained in England.[2]

When he *was* back in America, however, it wasn't long before Nathaniel's memories of the Old Country were forcibly rekindled by James Lowell, editor of the *Atlantic Monthly;* very soon he was being asked to provide articles for the magazine that would draw on his experiences while in England. No sooner had he had time to digest the review of *The Marble Faun* in the June issue of *Harper's New Monthly Magazine* and the long article on all his important works (including *Transformation*) that appeared in the June issue of the *Universal Review* (presumably he was sent a copy from England), than he was rereading his notebooks and preparing an article on Burns that appeared in the October issue of the magazine.[3] After that there was a lull due mainly to the difficulties of working at home while extensions to the Wayside were being carried out and because Nathaniel was struggling with the beginnings of more than one new romance, none of which, in the event, was completed. With the appointment of Fields as the new editor of the *Atlantic Monthly* in June 1861, he was given greater encouragement to prepare further articles based on his consular and English experiences (he also needed the money!). October saw the publication of an article on Oxford, and January 1862 one on Old Boston, followed in July by a rather controversial article on the American scene, "Chiefly about War-Matters." But then in July he produced an article on Leamington that so enthused Fields that he wrote on 24 July that "I don't think even your pen ever did a better thing in its way. It is truly a bit of England broken off from one of the best spots by a most skillful master-hand. Do break off some more pieces and hand them to me for exhibition in the atlantic Crystal Palace, for you will make it one by sending such rare specimens.—What a delectable <u>Book</u> you are building up out of these capital papers. Let us, Author and Publisher, be thinking of a sleek volume, for pretty soon we shall have made one. <u>We!</u>"[4] The article appeared in the October 1862 edition of the *Atlantic Monthly:*

LEAMINGTON SPA

My dear Editor,—

You can hardly have expected to hear from me again, (unless by invitation to the field of honor,) after those cruel and terrible notes upon my harmless article in the July number. How could you find it in your heart (a soft one, as I have hitherto supposed) to treat an old friend and liege contributor in that unheard-of way? Not that I should care a fig for any amount of vituperation, if you had only let my article come before the public as I wrote it, instead of suppressing precisely the passages with which I had taken most pains, and which I flattered myself were most cleverly done. The interview with the President, for example: it would have been a treasure to the future historian; and I hold you responsible to posterity for thrusting it into the fire. However, I cannot lose so good an opportunity of showing the world the placability and sweetness that adorn my character, and therefore send you another article, in which, I trust, you will find nothing to strike out,— unless, peradventure, you think that I may disturb the tranquillity of nations by

my plan of annexing Great Britain, or my attempted adumbration of a fat En-
glish dowager!
Truly, yours,
A Peaceable Man.[5]

In the course of several visits and stays of considerable length we acquired a
homelike feeling towards Leamington, and came back thither again and again,
chiefly because we had been there before. Wandering and wayside people, such
as we had long since become, retain a few of the instincts that belong to a more
settled way of life, and often prefer familiar and commonplace objects (for the
very reason that they are so) to the dreary strangeness of scenes that might be
thought much better worth the seeing. There is a small nest of a place in Leamington—at No. 16, [sic][6] Lansdowne Circus—upon which, to this day, my reminiscences are apt to settle as one of the coziest nooks in England, or in the world;
not that it had any special charm of its own, but only that we stayed long enough
to know it well, and even to grow a little tired of it. In my opinion, the very
tediousness of home and friends makes a part of what we love them for; if it be
not mixed in sufficiently with the other elements of life, there may be mad enjoyment, but no happiness.

The modest abode to which I have alluded forms one of a circular range of
pretty, moderate-sized, two-story houses, all built on nearly the same plan, and
each provided with its little grass-plot, its flowers, its tufts of box trimmed into
globes and other fantastic shapes, and its verdant hedges shutting the house in
from the common drive and dividing it from its equally cozy neighbors. Coming
out of the door, and taking a turn round the circle of sister-dwellings, it is difficult
to find your way back by any distinguishing individuality of your own habitation.
In the centre of the Circus is a space fenced in with iron railing, a small play-
place and sylvan retreat for the children of the precinct, permeated by brief paths
through the fresh English grass, and shadowed by various shrubbery; amid, which,
if you like, you may fancy yourself in a deep seclusion, though probably the mark
of eye-shot from the windows of all the surrounding houses. But, in truth, with
regard to the rest of the town and the world at large, an abode here is a genuine
seclusion; for the ordinary stream of life does not run through this little, quiet
pool, and few or none of the inhabitants seem to be troubled with any business
or outside activities. I used to set them down as half-pay officers, dowagers of
narrow income, elderly maiden ladies, and other people of respectability, but small
account, such as hang on the world's skirts rather than actually belong to it. The
quiet of the place was seldom disturbed except by the grocer and butcher, who
came to receive orders, or the cabs, hackney-coaches, and Bath-chairs, in which
the ladies took an infrequent airing, or the livery-steed which the retired captain
sometimes bestrode for a morning ride, or by the red-coated postman who went
his rounds twice a day to deliver letters, and again in the evening, ringing a handbell, to take letters for the mail. In merely mentioning these slight interruptions
of its sluggish stillness, I seem to myself to disturb too much the atmosphere of
quiet that brooded over the spot; whereas its impression upon me was, that the
world had never found the way thither, or had forgotten it, and that the fortunate
inhabitants were the only ones who possessed the spell-word of admittance. Nothing could have suited me better, at the time; for I had been holding a position of
public servitude, which imposed upon me (among a great many lighter duties) the
ponderous necessity of being universally civil and sociable.

Nevertheless, if a man were seeking the bustle of society, he might find it more
readily in Leamington than in most other English towns. It is a permanent

watering-place, a sort of institution to which I do not know any close parallel in American life: for such places as Saratoga bloom only for the summer season, and offer a thousand dissimilitudes even then; while Leamington seems to be always in flower, and serves as a home to the homeless all the year round. Its original nucleus, the plausible excuse for the town's coming into prosperous existence, lies in the fiction of a chalybeate well, which, indeed, is so far a reality that out of its magical depths have gushed streets, groves, gardens, mansions, shops, and churches, and spread themselves along the banks of the little river Leam. This miracle accomplished, the beneficent fountain has retired beneath a pump-room, and appears to have given up all pretension to the remedial virtues formerly attributed to it. I know not whether its waters are ever tasted nowadays; but not the less does Leamington—in pleasant Warwickshire, at the very midmost point of England, in a good hunting neighborhood, and surrounded by country-seats and castles—continue to be a resort of transient visitors, and the more permanent abode of a class of genteel, unoccupied, well-to-do, but not very wealthy people, such as are hardly known among ourselves. Persons who have no country-houses, and whose fortunes are inadequate to a London expenditure, find here, I suppose, a sort of town and country life in one.

In its present aspect, the town is of no great age. In contrast with the antiquity of many places in its neighborhood, it has a bright, new face, and seems almost to smile even amid the sombreness of an English autumn. Nevertheless, it is hundreds upon hundreds of years old, if we reckon up that sleepy lapse of time during which it existed as a small village of thatched houses, clustered round a priory; and it would still have been precisely such a rural village, but for a certain Dr. Jephson, who lived within the memory of man,[7] and who found out the magic well, and foresaw what fairy wealth might be made to flow from it. A public garden has been laid out along the margin of the Leam, and called the Jephson Garden, in honor of him who created the prosperity of his native spot. A little way within the garden-gate there is a circular temple of Grecian architecture, beneath the dome of which stands a marble statue of the good Doctor, very well executed, and representing him with a face of fussy activity, and benevolence: just the kind of man, if luck favored him, to build up the fortunes of those about him, or, quite probably, to blight his whole neighborhood by some disastrous speculation.

The Jephson Garden is very beautiful, like most other English pleasure-grounds; for, aided by their moist climate and not too fervid sun, the landscape-gardeners excel in converting flat or tame surfaces into attractive scenery, chiefly through the skilful arrangement of trees and shrubbery. An Englishman aims at this effect even in the little patches under the windows of a suburban villa, and achieves it on a larger scale in a tract of many acres. The Garden is shadowed with trees of a fine growth, standing alone, or in dusky groves and dense entanglements, pervaded by woodland paths; and emerging from these pleasant glooms, we come upon a breadth of sunshine, where the green sward—so vividly green that it has a kind of lustre in it—is spotted with beds of gemlike flowers. Rustic chairs and benches are scattered about, some of them ponderously fashioned out of the stumps of obtruncated trees, and others more artfully made with intertwining branches, or perhaps an imitation of such frail handiwork in iron. In a central part of the Garden is an archery-ground, where laughing maidens practise at the butts, generally missing their ostensible mark, but, by the mere grace of their action, sending an unseen shaft into some young man's heart. There is space, moreover, within these precincts, for an artificial lake, with a little green island in the midst of it; both lake and island being the haunt of swans, whose aspect and movement in the water are most beautiful and stately,—most infirm, disjointed, and decrepit, when, unadvisedly, they see fit to emerge, and try to walk upon dry land. In the latter case, they look like a breed of uncommonly ill-contrived geese; and I record the matter here for the sake of the moral,—that we should never pass judgement on the merits of any person or thing, unless we behold it in the sphere and circumstances to which it is specially adapted. In still another part of the Garden, there is a labyrinthine maze, formed of an intricacy of hedge-bordered walks, involving himself in which, a man might wander for hours inextricably within a circuit of only a few yards,—a sad emblem, it seemed to me, of the mental and moral perplexities in which we sometimes go astray, petty in scope, yet large enough to entangle a lifetime, and bewilder us with a weary movement, but no genuine progress.

The Leam, after drowsing across the principal street of the town beneath a handsome bridge, skirts along the margin of the Garden without any perceptible flow. Heretofore I had fancied the Concord the laziest river in the world, but now assign that amiable distinction to the little English stream. Its water is by no means transparent, but has a greenish, goose-puddly hue, which, however, accords well with the other coloring and characteristics of the scene, and is disagreeable neither to sight nor smell. Certainly, this river is a perfect feature of that gentle picturesqueness in which England is so rich, sleeping, as it does, beneath a margin of willows that droop into its bosom, and other trees, of deeper verdure than our own country can boast, inclining lovingly over it. On the Garden-side it is bordered by a shadowy, secluded grove with winding paths among its boskiness, affording many a peep at the river's imperceptible lapse and tranquil gleam; and on the opposite shore stands the priory-church, with its churchyard full of shrubbery and tombstones.

The business-portion of the town clusters about the banks of the Leam, and is naturally densest around the well to which the modern settlement owes its existence. Here are the commercial inns, the post-office, the furniture-dealers, the ironmongers, and all the heavy and homely establishments that connect themselves even with the airiest modes of human life; while upward from the river, by a long and gentle ascent, rises the principal street, which is very bright and cheerful in its physiognomy, and adorned with shop-fronts almost as splendid as those of London, though on a diminutive scale. There are likewise side-streets and cross-streets, many of which are bordered with the beautiful Warwickshire elm, a most unusual kind of adornment for an English town; and spacious avenues, wide enough to afford room for stately groves, with foot-paths running beneath the lofty shade, and rooks cawing and chattering so high in the tree-tops that their voices get musical before reaching the earth. The houses are mostly built in blocks and ranges, in which every separate tenement is a repetition of its fellow, though the architecture of the different ranges is sufficiently various. Some of them are almost palatial in size and sumptuousness of arrangement. Then, on the outskirts of the town, there are detached villas, inclosed within that separate domain of high stone fence and embowered shrubbery which an Englishman so loves to build and plant around his abode, presenting to the public only an iron gate, with a gravelled carriage-drive winding away towards the half-hidden mansion. Whether in street or suburb, Leamington may fairly be called beautiful, and, at some points, magnificent; but by-and-by you become doubtfully suspicious of a somewhat unreal finery: it is pretentious, though not glaringly so; it has been built, with malice aforethought, as a place of gentility and enjoyment. Moreover, splendid as the houses look, and comfortable as they often are, there is a nameless something about them, betokening that they have not grown out of human hearts, but are the creations of a skilfully applied human intellect: no man has reared any one of them, whether stately or humble, to be his life-long residence, wherein to bring up his children, who are to inherit it as a home. They are nicely contrived lodging-houses, one and all,—the best as well as the shabbiest of them,—and therefore inevitably lack some nameless property that a home should have. This was the case with our own little snuggery in Lansdowne Circus, as with all the rest: it had not grown out of anybody's individual need, but was built to let or sell, and was therefore like a ready-made garment,—a tolerable fit, but only tolerable.

All these blocks, ranges, and detached villas are adorned with the finest and most aristocratic names that I have found anywhere in England, except, perhaps, in Bath, which is the great metropolis of that second-class gentility with which watering-places are chiefly populated. Lansdowne Crescent, Lansdowne Circus, Lansdowne Terrace, Regent Street, Warwick Street, Clarendon Street, the Upper and Lower Parade: such are a few of the designations. Parade, indeed, is a well-chosen name for the principal street, along which the population of the idle town draws itself out for daily review and display. I only wish that my descriptive powers would enable me to throw off a picture of the scene at a sunny noontide, individualizing each character with a touch: the great people alighting from their carriages at the principal shop-doors; the elderly ladies and infirm Indian officers drawn along in Bath-chairs; the comely, rather than pretty, English girls, with their deep, healthy bloom, which an American taste is apt to deem fitter for a milkmaid than for a lady; the moustached gentlemen with frogged surtouts and a military air; the nursemaids and chubby children, but no chubbier than our own, and scampering on slenderer legs; the sturdy figure of John Bull in all varieties and of all ages, but ever with a stamp of authenticity somewhere about him.

To say the truth, I have been holding the pen over my paper, purposing to write a descriptive paragraph or two about the throng on the principal Parade of Leamington, so arranging it as to present a sketch of the British out-of-door aspect on a morning walk of gentility; but I find no personages quite sufficiently distinct and individual in my memory to supply the materials of such a panorama. Oddly enough, the only figure that comes fairly forth to my mind's eye is that of a dowager, one of hundreds whom I used to marvel at, all over England, but who have scarcely a representative among our own ladies of autumnal life, so thin, careworn, and frail, as age usually makes the latter. I have heard a good deal of the tenacity with which English ladies retain their personal beauty to a late period of life; but (not to suggest that an American eye needs use and cultivation before it can quite appreciate the charm of English beauty at any age) it strikes me that an English lady of fifty is apt to become a creature less refined and delicate, so far as her physique goes, than anything that we Western people class under the name of woman. She has an awful ponderosity of frame, not pulpy, like the looser development of our few fat women, but massive with solid beef and streaky tallow; so that (though struggling manfully against the idea) you inevitably think of her as made up of steaks and sirloins. When she walks, her advance is elephantine. When she sits down, it is on a great round space of her Maker's footstool, where she looks as if nothing could ever move her. She imposes awe and respect by the muchness of her personality, to such a degree that you probably credit her with far greater moral and intellectual force than she can fairly claim. Her visage is usually grim and stern, not always positively forbidding, yet calmly terrible, not merely by its breadth and weight of feature, but because it seems to express so much well-founded self-reliance, such acquaintance with the world, its toils, troubles, and dangers, and such sturdy capacity for trampling down a foe. Without anything positively salient, or actively offensive, or, indeed, unjustly formidable to her neighbors, she has the effect of a seventy-four gun-ship in time of peace;

for, while you assure yourself that there is no real danger, you cannot help thinking how tremendous would be her onset, if pugnaciously inclined, and how futile the effort to inflict any counter-injury. She certainly looks tenfold—nay, a hundred-fold—better able to take care of herself than our slender-framed and haggard womankind; but I have not found reason to suppose that the English dowager of fifty has actually greater courage, fortitude, and strength of character than our women of similar age, or even a tougher physical endurance than they. Morally, she is strong, I suspect, only in society, and in the common routine of social affairs, and would be found powerless and timid in any exceptional strait that might call for energy outside of the conventionalities amid which she has grown up.

You can meet this figure in the street, and live, and even smile at the recollection. But conceive of her in a ball-room, with the bare, brawny arms that she invariably displays there, and all the other corresponding development, such as is beautiful in the maiden blossom, but a spectacle to howl at in such an overblown cabbage-rose as this.

Yet, somewhere in this enormous bulk there must be hidden the modest, slender, violet-nature of a girl, whom an alien mass of earthliness has unkindly overgrown; for an English maiden in her teens, though very seldom so pretty as our own damsels, possesses, to say the truth, a certain charm of half-blossom, and delicately folded leaves, and tender womanhood shielded by maidenly reserves, with which, somehow or other, our American girls often fail to adorn themselves during an appreciable moment. It is a pity that English violets should grow into such an outrageously developed peony as I have attempted to describe. I wonder whether a middle-aged husband ought to be considered as legally married to all the accretions that have overgrown the slenderness of his bride, since he led her to the altar, and which make her so much more than he ever bargained for! Is it not a sounder view of the case, that the matrimonial bond cannot be held to include the three-fourths of the wife that had no existence when the ceremony was performed? And as a matter of conscience and good morals, ought not an English married pair to insist upon the celebration of a Silver Wedding at the end of twenty-five years, in order to legalize and mutually appropriate that corporeal growth of which both parties have individually come into possession since they were pronounced one flesh?[8]

The chief enjoyment of my several visits to Leamington lay in rural walks about the neighborhood, and in jaunts to places of note and interest, which are particularly abundant in that region. The high-roads are made pleasant to the traveller by a border of trees, and often afford him the hospitality of a way-side bench beneath a comfortable shade. But a fresher delight is to be found in the foot-paths, which go wandering away from stile to stile, along the hedges, and across broad fields, and through wooded parks, leading you to little hamlets of thatched cottages, ancient, solitary farm-houses, picturesque old mills, streamlets, pools, and all those quiet, secret, unexpected, yet strangely familiar features of English scenery that Tennyson shows us in his idylls and eclogues. These bypaths admit the wayfarer into the very heart of rural life, and yet do not burden him with a sense of intrusiveness. He has a right to go whithersoever they lead him; for, with all their shaded privacy, they are as much the property of the public as the dusty high-road itself, and even by an older tenure. Their antiquity probably exceeds that of the Roman ways; the footsteps of the aboriginal Britons first wore away the grass, and the natural flow of intercourse between village and village has kept the track bare ever since. An American farmer would plough across any such path, and obliterate it with his hills of potatoes and Indian corn; but here it is protected by law, and still more by the sacredness that invariably springs up, in this soil, along the well-defined foot-prints of centuries. Old associations are sure to be fragrant herbs in English nostrils: we pull them up as weeds.

I remember such a path, the access to which is from Lover's Grove, a range of tall oaks and elms on a high hill-top, whence there is a view of Warwick Castle, and a wide extent of landscape, beautiful, though bedimmed with English mist. This particular foot-path, however, is not a remarkably good specimen of its kind, since it leads into no hollows and seclusions, and soon terminates in a high-road. It connects Leamington by a short cut with the small neighboring village of Lillington, a place which impresses an American observer with its many points of contrast to the rural aspects of his own country. The village consists chiefly of one row of contiguous dwellings, separated only by party-walls, but ill-matched among themselves, being of different heights and apparently of different ages, though all are of an antiquity which we should call venerable. Some of the windows are leaden-framed lattices, opening on hinges. These houses are mostly built of gray stone; but others, in the same range, are of brick, and one or two are in a very old fashion,—Elizabethan, or still older,—having a ponderous frame-work of oak, painted black, and filled in with plastered stone or bricks. Judging by the patches of repair, the oak seems to be the more durable part of the structure. Some of the roofs are covered with earthen tiles; others (more decayed and poverty-stricken) with thatch, out of which sprouts a luxurious vegetation of grass, house-leeks, and yellow flowers. What especially strikes an American is the lack of that insulated space, the intervening gardens, grass-plots, broad-spreading shade-trees, which occur between our own village-houses. These English dwellings have no such separate surroundings; they all grow together, like the cells of a honey-comb.

Beyond the first row of houses, and hidden from it by a turn of the road, there was another row (or block, as we should call it) of some small, old cottages, stuck one against another, with their thatched roofs forming a single contiguity. These, I presume, were the habitations of the poorest order of rustic laborers; and the narrow precincts of each cottage, as well as the close neighborhood of the whole, gave the impression of a stifled, unhealthy atmosphere among the occupants. It seemed impossible that there should be a cleanly reserve, a proper self-respect among individuals, or a wholesome unfamiliarity between families, where human life was crowded and massed into such intimate communities as these. Neverthe-less, not to look beyond the outside, I never saw a prettier rural scene than was presented by this range of contiguous huts; for in the front of the whole row was a luxuriant and well-trimmed hawthorn hedge, and belonging to each cottage was a little square of garden-ground, separated from its neighbors by a line of the same venerable fence. The gardens were chock-full, not of esculent vegetables, but of flowers, familiar ones, but very bright-colored, and shrubs of box, some of which were trimmed into artistic shapes; and I remember, before one door, a representa-tion of Warwick Castle, made of oyster-shells. The cottagers evidently loved the little nests in which they dwelt, and did their best to make them beautiful, and succeeded more than tolerably well,—so kindly did Nature help their humble efforts with its verdure, flowers, moss, lichens, and the green things that grew out of the thatch. Through some of the open door-ways we saw plump children rolling about on the stone floors, and their mothers, by no means very pretty, but as happy-looking as mothers generally are; and while we gazed at these domestic matters, an old woman rushed wildly out of one of the gates, upholding a shovel, on which she clanged and clattered with a key. At first we fancied that she intended an onslaught against ourselves, but soon discovered that a more dangerous enemy was abroad; for the old lady's bees had swarmed, and the air was full of them, whizzing by our heads like bullets.

Not far from these two rows of houses and cottages, a green lane, overshadowed with trees, turned aside from the main road, and tended towards a square, gray tower, the battlements of which were just high enough to be visible above the foliage. Wending our way thitherward, we found the very picture and ideal of a country-church and church-yard. The tower seemed to be of Norman architecture, low, massive, and crowned with battlements. The body of the church was of very modest dimensions, and the eaves so low that I could touch them with my walking-stick. We looked into the windows, and beheld the dim and quiet interior, a narrow space, but venerable with the consecration of many centuries, and keeping its sanctity as entire and inviolate as that of a vast cathedral. The nave was divided from the side aisles of the church by pointed arches resting on very sturdy pillars: it was good to see how solemnly they held themselves to their age-long task of supporting that lowly roof. There was a small organ, suited in size to the vaulted hollow, which it weekly filled with religious sound. On the opposite wall of the church, between two windows, was a mural tablet of white marble, with an inscription in black letters,—the only such memorial that I could discern, although many dead people doubtless lay beneath the floor, and had paved it with their ancient tomb-stones, as is customary in old English churches. There were no modern painted windows, flaring with raw colors, nor other gorgeous adornments, such as the present taste for mediæval restoration often patches upon the decorous simplicity of the gray village-church. It is probably the worshipping-place of no more distinguished a congregation than the farmers and peasantry who inhabit the houses and cottages which I have just described. Had the lord of the manor been one of the parishioners, there would have been an eminent pew near the chancel, walled high about, curtained, and softly cushioned, warmed by a fireplace of its own, and distinguished by hereditary tablets and escutcheons on the inclosed stone pillar.

A well-trodden path led across the church-yard, and the gate being on the latch, we entered, and walked round among the graves and monuments. The latter were chiefly head-stones, none of which were very old, so far as was discoverable by the dates; some, indeed, in so ancient a cemetery, were disagreeably new, with inscriptions glittering like sunshine, in gold letters. The ground must have been dug over and over again, innumerable times, until the soil is made up of what was once human clay, out of which have sprung successive crops of gravestones, that flourish their allotted time, and disappear, like the weeds and flowers in their briefer period. The English climate is very unfavorable to the endurance of memorials in the open air. Twenty years of it suffice to give as much antiquity of aspect, whether to tombstone or edifice, as a hundred years of our own drier atmosphere,—so soon do the drizzly rains and constant moisture corrode the surface of marble or free-stone. Sculptured edges lose their sharpness in a year or two; yellow lichens overspread a beloved name, and obliterate it while it is yet fresh upon some survivor's heart. Time gnaws an English gravestone with wonderful appetite; and when the inscription is quite illegible, the sexton takes the useless slab away, and perhaps makes a hearthstone of it, and digs up the unripe bones which it ineffectually tried to memorialize, and gives the bed to another sleeper. In the Charter-Street burial-ground at Salem, and in the old graveyard on the hill at Ipswich, I have seen more ancient gravestones, with legible inscriptions on them, than in any English church-yard.

And yet this same ungenial climate, hostile as it generally is to the long remembrance of departed people, has sometimes a lovely way of dealing with the records on certain monuments that lie horizontally in the open air. The rain falls into the deep incisions of the letters, and has scarcely time to be dried away before another shower sprinkles the flat stone again, and replenishes those little reservoirs. The unseen, mysterious seeds of mosses find their way into the lettered furrows, and are made to germinate by the continual moisture and watery sunshine of the English sky; and by-and-by, in a year, or two years, or many years, behold the complete inscription—HERE LIETH THE BODY, and all the rest of the tender falsehood—beautifully embossed in raised letters of living green, a bas-relief of velvet moss on the marble slab! It becomes more legible, under the skyey influences, after the world has forgotten the deceased, than when it was fresh from the stone-cutter's hands. It outlives the grief of friends. I first saw an example of this in Bebbington church-yard, in Cheshire, and thought that Nature must needs have had a special tenderness for the person (no noted man, however, in the world's history) so long ago laid beneath that stone, since she took such wonderful pains to "keep his memory green." Perhaps the proverbial phrase just quoted may have had its origin in the natural phenomenon here described.

While we rested ourselves on a horizontal monument, which was elevated just high enough to be a convenient seat, I observed that one of the gravestones lay very close to the church,—so close that the droppings of the eaves would fall upon it. It seemed as if the inmate of that grave had desired to creep under the church-wall. On closer inspection, we found an almost illegible epitaph on the stone, and with difficulty made out this forlorn verse:—

> "Poorly lived,
> And poorly died,
> Poorly buried,
> And no one cried."

It would be hard to compress the story of a cold and luckless life, death, and burial into fewer words, or more impressive ones; at least, we found them impressive, perhaps because we had to re-create the inscription by scraping away the lichens from the faintly traced letters. The grave was on the shady and damp side of the church, endwise towards it, the head-stone being within about three feet of the foundation-wall; so that, unless the poor man was a dwarf, he must have been doubled up to fit him into his final resting-place. No wonder that his epitaph murmured against so poor a burial as this! His name, as well as I could make it out, was Treeo,—John Treeo, I think,—and he died in 1810, at the age of seventy-four. The gravestone is so overgrown with grass and weeds, so covered with unsightly lichens, and so crumbly with time and foul weather, that it is questionable whether anybody will ever be at the trouble of deciphering it again. But there is a quaint and sad kind of enjoyment in defeating (to such slight degree as my pen may do it) the probabilities of oblivion for poor John Treeo, and asking a little sympathy for him, half a century after his death, and making him better and more widely known, at least, than any other slumberer in Lillington church-yard: he having been, as appearances go, the outcast of them all.

You find similar old churches and villages in all the neighboring country, at the distance of every two or three miles;[9] and I describe them, not as being rare, but because they are so common and characteristic. The village of Whitnash, within twenty minutes' walk of Leamington, looks as secluded, as rural, and as little disturbed by the fashions of to-day, as if Doctor Jephson had never developed all those Parades and Crescents out of his magic well. I used to wonder whether the inhabitants had ever yet heard of railways, or, at their slow rate of progress, had even reached the epoch of stage-coaches. As you approach the village, while it is

Whitnash church and, to the right, the hollow elm, which was finally felled in 1960. Photograph from the 1860s. Courtesy of the Warwickshire County Record Office, Warwick.

yet unseen, you observe a tall, overshadowing canopy of elm-tree tops, beneath which you almost hesitate to follow the public road, on account of the remoteness that seems to exist between the precincts of this old-world community and the thronged modern street out of which you have so recently emerged. Venturing onward, however, you soon find yourself in the heart of Whitnash, and see an irregular ring of ancient rustic dwellings surrounding the village-green, on one side of which stands the church, with its square Norman tower and battlements, while close adjoining is the vicarage, made picturesque by peaks and gables. At first glimpse, none of the houses appear to be less than two or three centuries old, and they are of the ancient, wooden-framed fashion, with thatched roofs, which give them the air of birds' nests, thereby assimilating them closely to the simplicity of Nature.

The church-tower is mossy and much gnawed by time; it has narrow holes up and down its front and sides, and an arched window over the low portal, set with small panes of glass, cracked, dim, and irregular, through which a bygone age is peeping out into the daylight. Some of these old, grotesque faces, called gargoyles, are seen on the projections of the architecture. The church-yard is very small, and is encompassed by a gray stone fence that looks as ancient as the church itself. In front of the tower, on the village-green, is a yew-tree of incalculable age, with a vast circumference of trunk, but a very scanty head of foliage; though its boughs still keep some of the vitality which perhaps was in its early prime when the Saxon invaders founded Whitnash. A thousand years is no extraordinary antiquity in the lifetime of a yew. We were pleasantly startled, however, by discovering an exuberance of more youthful life than we had thought possible in so old a tree; for the faces of two children laughed at us out of an opening in the trunk, which had become hollow with long decay. On one side of the yew stood a framework of worm-eaten timber, the use and meaning of which puzzled me exceedingly, till I made it out to be the village-stocks; a public institution that, in its day, had doubtless hampered many of pair of shank-bones, now crumbling in the adjacent church-yard. It is not to be supposed, however, that this old-fashioned mode of punishment is still in vogue among the good people of Whitnash. The vicar of the parish has antiquarian propensities, and had probably dragged the stocks out of some dusty hiding-place, and set them up on their former site as a curiosity.

I disquiet myself in vain with the effort to hit upon some characteristic feature, or assemblage of features, that shall convey to the reader the influence of hoar antiquity lingering into the present daylight, as I so often felt it in these old English scenes. It is only an American who can feel it; and even he begins to find himself growing insensible to its effect, after a long residence in England. But while you are still new in the old country, it thrills you with strange emotion to think that this little church of Whitnash, humble as it seems, stood for ages under the Catholic faith, and has not materially changed since Wycliffe's days, and that it looked as gray as now in Bloody Mary's time, and that Cromwell's troopers broke off the stone noses of those same gargoyles that are now grinning in your face. So, too, with the immemorial yew-tree; you see its great roots grasping hold of the earth like gigantic claws, clinging so sturdily that no effort of time can wrench them away; and there being life in the old tree, you feel all the more as if a contemporary witness were telling you of the things that have been. It has lived among men, and been a familiar object to them, and seen them brought to be christened and married and buried in the neighboring church and church-yard, through so many centuries, that it knows all about our race, so far as fifty generations of the Whitnash people can supply such knowledge. And, after all, what a weary life it must have been for the old tree! Tedious beyond imagination! Such, I think, is the final impression on the mind of an American visitor, when his delight at finding something permanent begins to yield to his Western love of change, and he becomes sensible of the heavy air of a spot where the forefathers and foremothers have grown up together, intermarried, and died, through a long succession of lives, without any intermixture of new elements, till family features and character are all run in the same inevitable mould. Life is there fossilized in its greenest leaf. The man who died yesterday or ever so long ago walks the village-street today, and chooses the same wife that he married a hundred years since, and must be buried again to-morrow under the same kindred dust that has already covered him half a score of times. The stone threshold of his cottage is worn away with his hob-nailed foot-steps, scuffling over it from the reign of the first Plantagenet to that of Victoria. Better than this is the lot of our restless countrymen, whose modern instinct bids them tend always towards "fresh woods and pastures new." Rather than such monotony of sluggish ages, loitering on a village-green, toiling in hereditary fields, listening to the parson's drone lengthening through centuries in the gray Norman church, let us welcome whatever change may come,—change of place, social customs, political institutions, modes of worship,—trusting, that, if all present things shall vanish, they will but make room for better systems, and for a higher type of man to clothe his life in them, and to fling them off in turn.

Nevertheless, while an American willingly accepts growth and change as the law of his own national and private existence, he has a singular tenderness for the stone-incrusted institutions of the mother-country. The reason may be (though I should prefer a more generous explanation) that he recognizes the tendency of these hardened forms to stiffen her joints and fetter her ankles, in the race and rivalry of improvement. I hated to see so much as a twig of ivy wrenched away from an old wall in England. Yet change is at work, even in such a village as Whitnash. At a subsequent visit, looking more critically at the irregular circle of dwellings that surround the yew-tree and confront the church, I perceived that some of the houses must have been built within no long time, although the thatch, the quaint gables, and the old oaken frame-work of the others diffused an air of antiquity over the whole assemblage. The church itself was undergoing repair and restoration, which is but another word for change. Masons were making patch-work on the front of the tower, and were sawing a slab of stone and piling up bricks to strengthen the side-wall, or possibly to enlarge the ancient edifice by an additional aisle. Moreover, they had dug an immense pit in the church-yard, long and broad, and fifteen feet deep, two-thirds of which profundity were discolored by human decay and mixed up with crumbly bones. What this excavation was intended for I could nowise imagine, unless it were the very pit in which Longfel-low bids the "Dead Past bury its Dead," and Whitnash, of all places in the world, were going to avail itself of our poet's suggestion. If so, it must needs be confessed that many picturesque and delightful things would be thrown into the hole, and covered out of sight forever.

The article which I am writing has taken its own course, and occupied itself almost wholly with country churches; whereas I had purposed to attempt a de-scription of some of the many old towns—Warwick, Coventry, Kenilworth, Stratford-on-Avon—which lie within an easy scope of Leamington. And still an-other church presents itself to my remembrance. It is that of Hatton, on which I stumbled in the course of a forenoon's ramble, and paused a little while to look at it for the sake of old Doctor Parr, who was once its vicar. Hatton, so far as I could discover, has no public-house, no shop, no contiguity of roofs, (as in most English villages, however small) but is merely an ancient neighborhood of farm-houses; spacious, and standing wide apart, each within its own precincts, and offering a most comfortable aspect of orchards, harvest-fields, barns, stacks, and all manner of rural plenty. It seemed to be a community of old settlers, among whom everything had been going on prosperously since an epoch beyond the memory of man; and they kept a certain privacy among themselves, and dwelt on a cross-road at the entrance of which was a barred gate, hospitably open, but still impressing me with a sense of scarcely warrantable intrusion. After all, in some shady nook of those gentle Warwickshire slopes there may have been a denser and more populous settlement, styled Hatton, which I never reached.

Emerging from the by-road, and entering upon one that crossed it at right angles and led to Warwick, I espied the church of Doctor Parr. Like the others which I have described, it had a low stone tower, square, and battlemented at its summit: for all these little churches seem to have been built on the same model, and nearly at the same measurement, and have even a greater family-likeness than the cathedrals. As I approached, the bell of the tower (a remarkably deep-toned bell, considering how small it was) flung its voice abroad, and told me that it was noon. The church stands among its graves, a little removed from the wayside, quite apart from any collection of houses, and with no signs of a vicarage; it is a good deal shadowed by trees, and not wholly destitute of ivy. The body of the edifice, unfortunately, (and it is an outrage which the English churchwardens are fond of perpetrating,) has been newly covered with a yellowish plaster or wash, so as quite to destroy the aspect of antiquity, except upon the tower, which wears the dark gray of many centuries. The chancel-window is painted with a representation of Christ upon the Cross, and all the other windows are full of painted or stained glass, but none of it ancient, nor (if it be fair to judge from without what ought to be seen within) possessing any of the tender glory that should be the inheritance of this branch of Art, revived from mediæval times. I stepped over the graves, and peeped in at two or three of the windows, and saw the snug interior of the church glimmering through the many-colored panes, like a show of commonplace objects under the fantastic influence of a dream: for the floor was covered with modern pews, very like what we may see in a New-England meeting-house, though, I think, a little more favorable than those would be to the quiet slumbers of the Hatton farmers and their families. Those who slept under Doctor Parr's preaching now prolong their nap, I suppose, in the church-yard round about, and can scarcely have drawn much spiritual benefit from any truths that he contrived to tell them in their lifetime. It struck me as a rare example (even where examples are numerous) of a man utterly misplaced, that this enormous scholar, great in the classic tongues, and inevitably converting his own simplest vernacular into a learned language, should have been set up in this homely pulpit, and ordained to preach salvation to a rustic audience, to whom it is difficult to imagine how he could ever have spoken one available word.

Almost always, in visiting such scenes as I have been attempting to describe, I had a singular sense of having been there before. The ivy-grown churches (even that of Bebbington, the first that I beheld) were quite as familiar to me, when fresh from home, as the old wooden meeting-house in Salem, which used, on wintry Sabbaths, to be the frozen purgatory of my childhood. This was a bewildering, yet very delightful emotion, fluttering about me like a faint summer-wind, and filling my imagination with a thousand half-remembrances, which looked as vivid as sunshine, at a side-glance, but faded quite away whenever I attempted to grasp and define them. Of course, the explanation of the mystery was, that history, poetry, and fiction, books of travel, and the talk of tourists, had given me pretty accurate preconceptions of the common objects of English scenery, and these, being long ago vivified by a youthful fancy, had insensibly taken their places among the images of things actually seen. Yet the illusion was often so powerful, that I almost doubted whether such airy remembrances might not be a sort of innate idea, the print of a recollection in some ancestral mind, transmitted, with fainter and fainter impress through several descents, to my own. I felt, indeed, like the stalwart progenitor in person, returning to the hereditary haunts after more than two hundred years, and finding the church, the hall, the farm-house, the cottage, hardly changed during his long absence,—the same shady by-paths and hedge-lanes, the same veiled sky, and green lustre of the lawns and fields,— while his own affinities for these things, a little obscured by disuse, were reviving at every step.

An American is not very apt to love the English people, as a whole, on whatever length of acquaintance. I fancy that they would value our regard, and even recipro- cate it in their ungracious way, if we could give it to them in spite of all rebuffs; but they are beset by a curious and invariable infelicity, which compels them, as it were, to keep up what they seem to consider a wholesome bitterness of feeling between themselves and all other nationalities, especially that of America. They will never confess it; nevertheless, it is as essential a tonic to them as their bitter ale. Therefore—and possibly, too, from a similar narrowness in his own charac- ter—an American seldom feels quite as if he were at home among the English people. If he do so, he has ceased to be an American. But it requires no long residence to make him love their island, and appreciate it as thoroughly as they themselves do. For my part, I used to wish that we could annex it, transferring their thirty millions of inhabitants to some convenient wilderness in the great West, and putting half or a quarter as many of ourselves into their places. The change would be beneficial to both parties. We, in our dry atmosphere, are getting too nervous, haggard, dyspeptic, extenuated, unsubstantial, theoretic, and need to be made grosser. John Bull, on the other hand, has grown bulbous, long-bodied, short-legged, heavy-witted, material, and, in a word, too intensely English. In a few more centuries he will be the earthliest creature that ever the earth saw. Heretofore Providence has obviated such a result by timely intermixtures of alien races with the old English stock; so that each successive conquest of England has proved a victory, by the revivification and improvement of its native manhood. Cannot America and England hit upon some scheme to secure even greater advantages to both nations?

By the time that the article on Leamington had been published Nathaniel had already prepared most of another one, this time on Warwick, and eventually was able to send it to Fields on 5 October. He was finding it a bit of a struggle to maintain the enthusiasm (but not the quality) for producing the pieces as ". . . I always feel a singular despondency and heaviness of heart in re-opening these old journals now"; and once they were out of his hands he could muster little interest in their fate;

I have bothered my brains in vain, and can think of no better title for the Article. It is really of no consequence. Name it anything you like, provided the title shall promise no more than is to be found in the paper. This is the merit of my title; it expresses just what the article is. But call it "Warwick"—which implies a fuller description than I give—or "An Old English Town"—or "Leycester's Hospital"—which does not cover everything, and yet suggests a detailed description of the Hospital and full account of it; which I do not pretend to—or "About Warwick"—which is unexceptionable, and better than the present title, as being shorter. In a word suit yourself. I wash my hands of it; though I think the title last suggested is the best, on the whole. [However,] I want $100 [for the article] awfully and immediately.[10]

Before the article on Warwick came to be published he had already prepared a third, concerning Stratford–upon–Avon. Fields had increased the payment for the articles to $100 each for anything of up to ten pages in length and an additional $10 per page in excess of ten pages. This was greatly appreciated by Nathaniel and was a boost to his efforts to milk his English journals for all that would be of interest to his American readers. But, ominously, he was experiencing some periods of illness at this time and Sophia became very worried about his health and general well-being: "I was quite alarmed . . . to find Mr. Hawthorne very ill. It was a Roman cold, with fever and utter restlessness. . . . I do not feel at all secure about his health. I wish he could have a change . . . a new direction to his thoughts and life currents."[11] However, Nathaniel ploughed on and December 1862 saw the publication of the next article.

ABOUT WARWICK

Between bright, new Leamington, the growth of the present century, and rusty Warwick, founded by King Cymbeline in the twilight ages, a thousand years before the mediæval darkness, there are two roads, either of which may be measured by a sober-paced pedestrian in less than half an hour.

One of these avenues flows out of the midst of the smart parades and crescents of the former town,—along by hedges and beneath the shadow of great elms, past stuccoed Elizabethan villas and wayside ale-houses, and through a hamlet of modern aspect,—and runs straight into the principal thoroughfare of Warwick. The battlemented turrets of the castle, embowered half-way up in foliage, and the tall, slender tower of St. Mary's Church, rising from among clustered roofs, have been visible almost from the commencement of the walk. Near the entrance of the town stands St. John's School-House, a picturesque old edifice of stone, with four peaked gables in a row, alternately plain and ornamented, and wide, project-ing windows, and a spacious and venerable porch, all overgrown with moss and ivy, and shut in from the world by a high stone fence, not less mossy than the gabled front. There is an iron gate, through the rusty open-work of which you see a grassy lawn, and almost expect to meet the shy, curious eyes of the little boys of past generations, peeping forth from their infantile antiquity into the strangeness of our present life. I find a peculiar charm in these long-established English schools, where the school-boy of to-day sits side by side, as it were, with his great-grandsire, on the same old benches, and often, I believe, thumbs a later, but unimproved edition of the same old grammar or arithmetic. The new-fangled no-tions of a Yankee school-committee would madden many a pedagogue, and shake down the roof of many a time-honored seat of learning, in the mother-country.

At this point, however, we will turn back, in order to follow up the other road from Leamington, which was the one that I loved best to take. It pursues a straight and level course, bordered by wide gravel-walks and overhung by the frequent elm, with here a cottage and there a villa, on one side a wooded plantation, and on the other a rich field of grass or grain, until, turning at right angles, it brings you to an arched bridge over the Avon. Its parapet is a balustrade carved out of freestone, into the soft substance of which a multitude of persons have engraved their names or initials, many of them now illegible, while others, more deeply cut, are illuminated with fresh green moss. These tokens indicate a famous spot; and casting our eyes along the smooth gleam and shadow of the quiet stream, through a vista of willows that droop on either side into the water, we behold the gray magnificence of Warwick Castle, uplifting itself among stately trees, and rearing its turrets high above their loftiest branches. We can scarcely think the scene real, so completely do those machicolated towers, the long line of battlements, the massive buttresses, the high-windowed walls, shape out our indistinct ideas of the antique time. It might rather seem as if the sleepy river (being Shakspeare's Avon, and often , no doubt, the mirror of his gorgeous visions) were dreaming now of a lordly residence that stood here many centuries ago; and this fantasy is strength-ened, when you observe that the image in the tranquil water has all the distinctness of the actual structure. Either might be the reflection of the other. Wherever Time had gnawed one of the stones, you see the mark of his tooth just as plainly in the sunken reflection. Each is so perfect, that the upper vision seems a castle in the air, and the lower one an old stronghold of feudalism, miraculously kept from decay in an enchanted river.

A ruinous and ivy-grown bridge, that projects from the bank a little on the hither side of the castle,[12] has the effect of making the scene appear more entirely apart from the every-day world, for it ends abruptly in the middle of the stream,—

so that, if a cavalcade of the knights and ladies of romance should issue from the old walls, they could never tread on earthly ground, any more than we, approaching from the side of modern realism, can overleap the gulf between our domain and theirs. Yet, if we seek to disenchant ourselves, it may readily be done. Crossing the bridge on which we stand, and passing a little farther on, we come to the entrance of the castle, abutting on the highway, and hospitably open at certain hours to all curious pilgrims who choose to disburse half a crown or so towards the support of the Earl's domestics. The sight of that long series of historic rooms, full of such splendors and rarities as a great English family necessarily gathers about itself, in its hereditary abode, and in the lapse of ages, is well worth the money, or ten times as much, if indeed the value of the spectacle could be reckoned in money's-worth. But after the attendant has hurried you from end to end of the edifice, repeating a guide-book by rote, and exorcising each successive hall of its poetic glamour and witchcraft by the mere tone in which he talks about it, you will make the doleful discovery that Warwick Castle has ceased to be a dream. It is better, methinks, to linger on the bridge, gazing at Cæsar's Tower and Guy's Tower in the dim English sunshine above, and in the placid Avon below, and still keep them as thoughts in your own mind, than climb to their summits, or touch even a stone of their actual substance. They will have all the more reality for you, as stalwart relics of immemorial time, if you are reverent enough to leave them in the intangible sanctity of a poetic vision.[13]

From the bridge over the Avon, the road passes in front of the castle-gate, and soon enters the principal street of Warwick, a little beyond St. John's School-House, already described. Chester itself, most antique of English towns, can hardly show quainter architectural shapes than many of the buildings that border this street. They are mostly of the timber-and-plaster kind, with bowed and decrepit ridge-poles, and a whole chronology of various patchwork in their walls; their low-browed door-ways open upon a sunken floor; their projecting stories peep, as it were, over one another's shoulders, and rise into a multiplicity of peaked gables; they have curious windows, breaking out irregularly all over the house, some even in the roof, set in their own little peaks, opening lattice-wise, and furnished with twenty small panes of lozenge-shaped glass. The architecture of these edifices (a visible oaken framework, showing the whole skeleton of the house,—as if a man's bones should be arranged on his outside, and his flesh seen through the interstices) is often imitated by modern builders, and with sufficiently picturesque effect. The objection is, that such houses, like all imitations of by-gone styles, have an air of affectation; they do not seem to be built in earnest; they are no better than playthings, or overgrown baby-houses, in which nobody should be expected to encounter the serious realities of either birth or death. Besides, originating nothing, we leave no fashions for another age to copy, when we ourselves shall have grown antique.

Old as it looks, all this portion of Warwick has overbrimmed, as it were, from the original settlement, being outside of the ancient wall. The street soon runs under an arched gateway, with a church or some other venerable structure above it, and admits us into the heart of the town. At one of my first visits, I witnessed a military display. A regiment of Warwickshire militia, probably commanded by the Earl, was going through its drill in the market-place; and on the collar of one of the officers was embroidered the Bear and Ragged Staff which has been the cognizance of the Warwick earldom from time immemorial. The soldiers were sturdy young men, with the simple, stolid, yet kindly, faces of English rustics, looking exceedingly well in a body, but slouching into a yeoman-like carriage and appearance, the moment they were dismissed from drill. Squads of them were distributed everywhere about the streets, and sentinels were posted at various points; and I saw a sergeant, with a great key in his hand, (big enough to have been the key of the castle's main entrance when the gate was thickest and heaviest,) apparently setting a guard. Thus, centuries after feudal times are past, we find warriors still gathering under the old castle-walls, and commanded by a feudal lord, just as in the days of the King-maker, who, no doubt, often mustered his retainers in the same market-place where I beheld this modern regiment.

The interior of the town wears a less old-fashioned aspect than the suburbs through which we approach it; and the High Street has shops with modern plate-glass, and buildings with stuccoed fronts, exhibiting as few projections to hang a thought or sentiment upon as if an architect of to-day had planned them. And, indeed, so far as their surface goes, they are perhaps new enough to stand unabashed in an American street; but behind these renovated faces, with their monotonous lack of expression, there is probably the substance of the same old town that wore a Gothic exterior in the Middle Ages. The street is an emblem of England itself. What seems new in it is chiefly a skilful and fortunate adaptation of what such a people as ourselves would destroy. The new things are based and supported on sturdy old things, and derive a massive strength from their deep and immemorial foundations, though with such limitations and impediments as only an Englishman could endure. But he likes to feel the weight of all the past upon his back; and, moreover, the antiquity that overburdens him has taken root in his being, and has grown to be rather a hump than a pack, so that there is no getting rid of it without tearing his whole structure to pieces. In my judgement, as he appears to be sufficiently comfortable under the mouldy accretion, he had better stumble on with it as long as he can. He presents a spectacle which is by no means without its charm for a disinterested and unincumbered observer.

When the old edifice, or the antiquated custom or institution, appears in its pristine form, without any attempt at intermarrying it with modern fashions, an American cannot but admire the picturesque effect produced by the sudden cropping up of an apparently dead-and-buried state of society into the actual present, of which he himself is a part. We need not go far in Warwick without encountering an instance of the kind. Proceeding westward through the town, we find ourselves confronted by a huge mass of natural rock, hewn into something like architectural shape, and penetrated by a vaulted passage, which may well have been one of King Cymbeline's original gateways; and on top of the rock, over the archway, sits a small, old church, communicating with an ancient edifice, or assemblage of edifices, that look down from a similar elevation on the side of the street. A range of trees half hides the latter establishment from the sun. It presents a curious and venerable specimen of the timber-and-plaster style of building, in which some of the finest houses in England are constructed; the front projects into porticos and vestibules, and rises into many gables, some in a row, and others crowning semi-detached portions of the structure; the windows mostly open on hinges, but show a delightful irregularity of shape and position; a multiplicity of chimneys break through the roof at their own will, or, at least, without any settled purpose of the architect. The whole affair looks very old,—so old, indeed, that the front bulges forth, as if the timber framework were a little weary, at last, of standing erect so long; but the state of repair is so perfect, and there is such an indescribable aspect of continuous vitality within the system of this aged house, that you feel confident that there may be safe shelter yet, and perhaps for centuries to come, under its time-honored roof. And on a bench, sluggishly enjoying the sunshine, and looking into the street of Warwick as from a life apart, a few old men are generally to be seen, wrapped in long cloaks, on which you may detect the glistening of a silver badge representing the Bear and Ragged Staff. These decorated worthies are some of the twelve brethren of Leicester's Hospital,—a community which subsists to-day under the identical modes that were established for it in the reign of Queen Elizabeth, and of course retains many features of a social life that has vanished almost everywhere else.

The edifice itself dates from a much older period than the charitable institution of which it is now the home. It was the seat of a religious fraternity far back in the Middle Ages, and continued so till Henry VIII. turned all the priesthood of England out-of-doors, and put the most unscrupulous of his favorites into their vacant abodes. In many instances, the old monks had chosen the sites of their domiciles so well, and built them on such a broad system of beauty and conven-ience, that their lay-occupants found it easy to convert them into stately and comfortable homes; and as such they still exist, with something of the antique reverence lingering about them. The structure now before us seems to have first been granted to Sir Nicholas Lestrange, who perhaps intended, like other men, to establish his household gods in the niches whence he had thrown down the images of saints, and to lay his hearth where an altar had stood. But there was probably a natural reluctance in those days (when Catholicism, so lately repudiat-ed, must needs have retained an influence over all but the most obdurate charac-ters) to bring one's hopes of domestic prosperity and a fortunate lineage into direct hostility with the awful claims of the ancient religion. At all events, there is still a superstitious idea, betwixt a fantasy and a belief, that the possession of former Church-property has drawn a curse along with it, not only among the posterity of those to whom it was originally granted, but wherever it has subse-quently been transferred, even if honestly bought and paid for. There are families, now inhabiting some of the beautiful old abbeys, who appear to indulge a species of pride in recording the strange deaths and ugly shapes of misfortune that have occurred among their predecessors, and may be supposed likely to dog their own pathway down the ages of futurity. Whether Sir Nicholas Lestrange, in the beef-eating days of Old Harry and Elizabeth, was a nervous man, and subject to appre-hensions of this kind, I cannot tell; but it is certain that he speedily rid himself of the spoils of the Church, and that, within twenty years afterwards, the edifice became the property of the famous Dudley, Earl of Leicester, brother of the Earl of Warwick. He devoted the ancient religious precinct to a charitable use, endowing it with an ample revenue, and making it the perpetual home of twelve, poor, honest, and war-broken soldiers, mostly his own retainers, and natives either of Warwick-shire or Gloucestershire. These veterans, or others wonderfully like them, still occupy their monkish dormitories and haunt the time-darkened corridors and galleries of the hospital, leading a life of old-fashioned comfort, wearing the old-fashioned cloaks, and burnishing the identical silver badges which the Earl of Leicester gave to the original twelve. He is said to have been a bad man in his day; but he has succeeded in prolonging one good deed into what was to him a distant future.

On the projecting story, over the arched entrance, there is the date, 1571, and several coats-of-arms, either the Earl's or those of his kindred, and immediately above the door-way a stone sculpture of the Bear and Ragged Staff.

Passing through the arch, we find ourselves in a quadrangle, or inclosed court, such as always formed the central part of a great family-residence in Queen Eliza-beth's time, and earlier. There can hardly be a more perfect specimen of such an establishment than Leicester's Hospital. The quadrangle is a sort of sky-roofed hall, to which there is convenient access from all parts of the house. The four inner fronts, with their high, steep roofs and sharp gables, look into it from antique windows, and through open corridors and galleries along the sides; and there seems to be a richer display of architectural devices and ornaments, quainter carvings in oak, and more fantastic shapes of the timber framework, than on the side towards the street. On the wall opposite the arched entrance are the following inscriptions, comprising such moral rules, I presume, as were deemed most essential for the daily observance of the community: "HONOR ALL MEN"—"FEAR GOD"—"HONOR THE KING"—"LOVE THE BROTHERHOOD"; and again, as if this latter injunction needed emphasis and repetition among a household of aged people soured with the hard fortune of their previous lives,—"BE KINDLY AFFECTIONED ONE TO ANOTHER." One sentence, over a door communicating with the Master's side of the house, is addressed to that dignitary,—"HE THAT RULETH OVER MEN MUST BE JUST." All these are charactered in black-letter, and form part of the elaborate ornamentation of the house. Everywhere—on the walls, over windows and doors, and at all points where there is room to place them—appear escutcheons of arms, cognizances, and crests, emblazoned in their proper colors, and illuminating the ancient quadrangle with their splendor. One of these devices is a large image of a porcupine on an heraldic wreath, being the crest of the Lords de Lisle. But especially is the cognizance of the Bear and Ragged Staff repeated over and over, and over and over again, in a great variety of attitudes, at full-length and half-length, in paint and in oaken sculpture, in bas-relief and rounded image. The founder of the hospital was certainly disposed to reckon his own beneficence as among the hereditary glories of his race; and had he lived and died a half-century earlier, he would have kept up an old Catholic custom by enjoining the twelve bedesmen to pray for the welfare of his soul.

At my first visit, some of the brethren were seated on the bench outside of the edifice, looking down into the street; but they did not vouchsafe me a word, and seemed so estranged from modern life, so enveloped in antique customs and old-fashioned cloaks, that to converse with them would have been like shouting across the gulf between our age and Queen Elizabeth's. So I passed into the quadrangle, and found it quite solitary, except that a plain and neat old woman happened to be crossing it, with an aspect of business and carefulness that bespoke her a woman of this world, and not merely a shadow of the past. Asking her if I could come in, she answered very readily and civilly that I might, and said that I was free to look about me, hinting a hope, however, that I would not open the private doors of the brotherhood, as some visitors were in the habit of doing. Under her guidance, I went into what was formerly the great hall of the establishment, where King James I. had once been feasted by an Earl of Warwick, as is commemorated by an inscription on the cobwebbed and dingy wall. It is a very spacious and barn-like apartment, with a brick floor, and a vaulted roof, the rafters of which are oaken beams, wonderfully carved, but hardly visible in the duskiness that broods aloft. The hall may have made a splendid appearance, when it was decorated with rich tapestry, and illuminated with chandeliers, cressets, and torches glistening upon silver dishes, while King James sat at supper among his brilliantly dressed nobles; but it has come to base uses in these latter days,—being improved, in Yankee phrase, as a brewery and wash-room, and as a cellar for the brethren's separate allotments of coal.

The old lady here left me to myself, and I returned into the quadrangle. It was very quiet, very handsome, in its own obsolete style, and must be an exceedingly comfortable place for the old people to lounge in, when the inclement winds render it inexpedient to walk abroad. There are shrubs against the wall, on one side; and on another is a cloistered walk, adorned with stags' heads and antlers, and running beneath a covered gallery, up to which ascends a balustraded staircase. In the portion of the edifice opposite the entrance-arch are the apartments of the Master; and looking into the window, (as the old woman, at no request of mine, had especially informed me that I might,) I saw a low, but vastly comfortable parlor, very handsomely furnished, and altogether a luxurious place. It had a fireplace with an immense arch, the antique breadth of which extended almost from wall to wall of the room, though now fitted up in such a way that the modern coal-grate looked very diminutive in the midst. Gazing into this pleasant interior, it seemed to me, that, among these venerable surroundings, availing himself of whatever was good in former things, and eking out their imperfection with the results of modern ingenuity, the Master might lead a not unenviable life. On the cloistered side of the quadrangle, where the dark oak panels made the inclosed space dusky, I beheld a curtained window reddened by a great blaze from within, and heard the bubbling and squeaking of something—doubtless very nice and succulent—that was being cooked at the kitchen-fire. I think, indeed, that a whiff or two of the savory fragrance reached my nostrils; at all events, the impression grew upon me that Leicester's Hospital is one of the jolliest old domiciles in England.

I was about to depart, when another old woman, very plainly dressed, but fat, comfortable, and with a cheerful twinkle in her eyes, came in through the arch, and looked curiously at me. This repeated apparition of the gentle sex (though by no means under its loveliest guise) had still an agreeable effect in modifying my ideas of an institution which I had supposed to be of a stern and monastic character. She asked whether I wished to see the hospital, and said that the porter, whose office it was to attend to visitors, was dead, and would be buried that very day, so that the whole establishment could not conveniently be shown me. She kindly invited me, however, to visit the apartment occupied by her husband and herself; so I followed her up the antique staircase, along the gallery, and into a small, oak-panelled parlor, where sat an old man in a long blue garment, who arose and saluted me with much courtesy. He seemed a very quiet person, and yet had a look of travel and adventure, and gray experience, such as I could have fancied in a palmer of ancient times, who might likewise have worn a similar costume. The little room was carpeted and neatly furnished; a portrait of its occupant was hanging on the wall; and on a table were two swords crossed,—one, probably, his own battle-weapon, and the other, which I drew half out of the scabbard, had an inscription on the blade, purporting that it had been taken from the field of Waterloo. My kind old hostess was anxious to exhibit all the particulars of their housekeeping, and led me into the bed-room, which was in the nicest order; and in a little intervening room was a washing and bathing apparatus,—a convenience (judging from the personal aspect and atmosphere of such parties) seldom to be met with in the humbler ranks of British life.

The old soldier and his wife both seemed glad of somebody to talk with; but the good woman availed herself of the privilege far more copiously than the veteran himself, insomuch that he felt it expedient to give her an occasional nudge with his elbow in her well-padded ribs. "Don't you be so talkative!" quoth he; and, indeed, he could scarcely find space for a word, and quite as little after his admonition as before. Her nimble tongue ran over the whole system of life in the hospital. The brethren, she said, had a yearly stipend, (the amount of which she did not mention,) and such decent lodgings as I saw, and some other advantages, free; and instead of being pestered with a great many rules, and made to dine together at a great table, they could manage their own little household-matters as they liked, buying their own dinners, and having them cooked in the general kitchen, and eating them snugly in their own apartments. "And," added she, rightly deeming this the crowning privilege, "with the Master's permission, they can have their wives to take care of them; and no harm comes of it; and what more can an old man desire?" It was evident enough that the good dame found herself in what she considered very rich clover, and, moreover, had plenty of small occupations to keep her from getting rusty and dull; but the veteran impressed me as deriving far less enjoyment from the monotonous ease, without fear of change or hope of improvement, that had followed upon thirty years of peril and vicissitude. I fancied, too, that, while pleased with the novelty of a stranger's visit, he was still a little shy of becoming a spectacle for the stranger's curiosity; for, if he chose to be morbid about the matter, the establishment was but an almshouse, in spite of its old-fashioned magnificence, and his fine blue cloak only a pauper's garment, with a silver badge on it that perhaps galled his shoulder. In truth, the badge and the peculiar garb, though quite in accordance with the manners of the Earl of Leicester's age, are repugnant to modern prejudices, and might fitly and humanely be abolished.

A year or two afterwards I paid another visit to the hospital, and found a new porter established in office, and already capable of talking like a guide-book about the history, antiquities, and present condition of the charity. He informed me that the twelve brethren are selected from among old soldiers of good character, whose private resources must not exceed an income of five pounds; thus excluding all commissioned officers, whose half-pay would of course be more than that amount. They receive from the hospital an annuity of eighty pounds each, besides their apartments, a garment of fine blue cloth, an annual abundance of ale, and a privilege at the kitchen-fire; so that, considering the class from which they are taken, they may well reckon themselves among the fortunate of the earth. Furthermore, they are invested with political rights, acquiring a vote for member of Parliament in virtue either of their income or brotherhood. On the other hand, as regards their personal freedom and conduct, they are subject to a supervision which the Master of the hospital might render extremely annoying, were he so inclined; but the military restraint under which they have spent the active portion of their lives makes it easier for them to endure the domestic discipline here imposed upon their age. The porter bore his testimony (whatever were its value) to their being as contented and happy as such a set of people could possibly be, and affirmed that they spent much time in burnishing their silver badges, and were as proud of them as a nobleman of his star. These badges, by-the-by, except one that was stolen and replaced in Queen Anne's time, are the very same that decorated the original twelve.

I have seldom met with a better guide than my friend the porter. He appeared to take a genuine interest in the peculiarities of the establishment and yet had an existence apart from them, so that he could the better estimate what those peculiarities were. To be sure, his knowledge and observations were confined to external things, but, so far, had a sufficiently extensive scope. He led me up the staircase and exhibited portions of the timber framework of the edifice that are reckoned to be eight or nine hundred years old, and are still neither worm-eaten nor decayed; and traced out what had been a great hall, in the days of the Catholic fraternity, though its area is now filled up with the apartments of the twelve brethren; and pointed to ornaments of sculptured oak, done in an ancient religious style of art, but hardly visible amid the vaulted dimness of the roof. Thence we went to the chapel—the Gothic church which I noted several pages back—surmounting the gateway that stretches half across the street. Here the brethren attend daily prayer, and have each a prayer-book of the finest paper, with a fair, large type for their old eyes. The interior of the chapel is very plain, with a picture of no merit for an altar-piece, and a single old pane of painted glass in the great eastern window, representing—no saint, nor angel, as is customary in such cases—but that great sinner, the Earl of Leicester. Nevertheless, among so many tangible proofs of his human sympathy, one comes to doubt whether the Earl could have been such a hardened reprobate, after all.

We ascended the tower of the chapel, and looked down between its battlements into the street, a hundred feet below us; while clambering half-way up were foxglove-flowers, weeds, small shrubs, and tufts of grass, that had rooted themselves into the roughness of the stone foundation. Far around us lay a rich and lovely English landscape, with many a church-spire and noble country-seat, and several objects of high historic interest. Edge Hill, where the Puritans defeated Charles I., is in sight on the edge of the horizon, and much nearer stands the house where Cromwell lodged on the night before the battle. Right under our eyes, and half-enveloping the town with its high-shouldering wall, so that all the closely compacted streets seemed but a precinct of the estate, was the Earl of Warwicks's delightful park, a wide extent of sunny lawns, interspersed with broad contiguities of forest-shade. Some of the cedars of Lebanon were there,—a growth of trees in which the Warwick family takes an hereditary pride. The two highest towers of the castle heave themselves up out of a mass of foliage, and look down in lordly manner upon the plebian roofs of the town, a part of which are slate-covered, (these are the modern houses) and a part are coated with old red tiles, denoting the more ancient edifices. A hundred and sixty or seventy years ago, a great fire destroyed a considerable portion of the town and doubtless annihilated many structures of a remote antiquity; at least, there was a possibility of very old houses in the long past of Warwick, which King Cymbeline is said to have founded in the year ONE of the Christian era!

And this historic fact or poetic fiction, whichever it may be, brings to mind a more indestructible reality than anything else that has occurred within the present field of our vision; though this includes the scene of Guy of Warwick's legendary exploits, and some of those of the Rounf Table, to say nothing of the Battle of Edge Hill. For perhaps it was in the landscape now under our eyes that Posthumus wandered with the King's daughter, the sweet, chaste, faithful, and courteous Imogen, the tenderest and womanliest woman that Shakspeare ever made immortal in the world. The silver Avon, which we see flowing so quietly by the gray castle, may have held their images in its bosom.

The day, though it began brightly, had long been overcast, and the clouds now spat down a few spiteful drops upon us, besides that the east-wind was very chill; so we descended the winding tower-stair, and went next into the garden, one side of which is shut in by almost the only remaining portion of the old city-wall. A part of the garden-ground is devoted to grass and shrubbery, and permeated by gravel-walks, in the centre of one of which is a beautiful stone vase of Egyptian sculpture, having formerly stood on the top of a Nilometer, or graduated pillar for measuring the rise and fall of the river Nile. On the pedestal is a Latin inscription by Dr. Parr, who (his vicarage of Hatton being so close at hand) was probably often the Master's guest, and smoked his interminable pipe among these garden-walks. Of the vegetable-garden, which lies adjacent, the lion's share is appropriated to the Master, and twelve small, separate patches to the individual brethren, who cultivate them at their own judgment and by their own labor; and their beans and cauliflowers have a better flavor, I doubt not, than if they had received them directly from the dead hand of the Earl of Leicester, like the rest of their food. In the farther part of the garden is an arbor for the old men's pleasure and convenience, and I should like well to sit down among them there, and find out

Lord Leycester Hospital, the rear gardens, with the Egyptian vase. Photograph from the 1850s. Taken from a negative in the possession of Mr. Joseph G. Rosa, Ruislip, Middlesex.

what is really the bitter and the sweet of such a sort of life.[14] As for the old gentlemen themselves, they put me queerly in mind of the Salem Custom-House, and the venerable personages whom I found so quietly at anchor there.

The Master's residence, forming one entire side of the quadrangle, fronts on the garden and wears an aspect at once stately and homely. It can hardly have undergone any perceptible change within three centuries; but the garden, into which its old windows look, has probably put off a great many eccentricities and quaintnesses, in the way of cunningly clipped shrubbery, since the gardener of Queen Elizabeth's reign threw down his rusty shears and took his departure. The present Master's name is Harris; he is a descendant of the founder's family, a gentleman of independent fortune, and a clergyman of the Established Church, as the regulations of the Hospital require him to be. I know not what are his official emoluments; but, according to all English precedent, an ancient charitable fund is certainly to be held directly for the behoof of those who administer it, and perhaps incidentally, in a moderate way, for the normal beneficiaries; and, in the case before us, the brethren being so comfortably provided for, the Master is likely to be at least as comfortable as all the twelve together. Yet I ought not, even in a distant land, to fling an idle gibe against a gentleman of whom I really know nothing, except that the people under his charge bear all possible tokens of being tended and cared for as sedulously as if each of them sat by a warm fireside of his own, with a daughter bustling round the hearth to make ready his porridge and his titbits. It is delightful to think of the good life which a suitable man, in the Master's position, has an opportunity to lead,—linked to time-honored customs, welded in with an ancient system, never dreaming of radical change, and bringing all the mellowness and richness of the past down into these railway-days, which do not compel him or his community to move a whit quicker than of yore. Everybody can appreciate the advantage of going ahead; it might be well, sometimes, to think whether there is not a word or two to be said in favor of standing still, or going to sleep.

From the garden we went into the kitchen, where the fire was burning hospitably, and diffused a general warmth far and wide, together with the fragrance of some old English roast-beef, which, I think, must at that moment have been done nearly to a turn. The kitchen is a lofty, spacious, and noble room, partitioned off round the fireplace by a sort of semicircular oaken screen, or, rather, an arrangement of heavy and high-backed settles, with an ever open entrance between them, on either side of which is the omnipresent image of the Bear and Ragged Staff, three feet high, and excellently carved in oak, now black with time and unctuous kitchen-smoke. The ponderous mantel-piece, likewise of carved oak, towers high towards the dusky ceiling, and extends its mighty breadth to take in a vast area of hearth, the arch of the fireplace being positively so immense that I could compare it to nothing but the city-gateway. Above its cavernous opening were crossed two ancient halberds, the weapons, possibly, of soldiers who had fought under Leicester in the Low Countries; and elsewhere on the walls were displayed several muskets, which some of the present inmates of the hospital may have levelled against the French. Another ornament of the mantel-piece was a square of silken needlework or embroidery, faded nearly white, but dimly representing that wearisome Bear and Ragged Staff, which we should hardly look twice at, only that it was wrought by the fair fingers of poor Amy Robsart, and beautifully framed in oak from Kenilworth Castle at the expense of a Mr. Conner, a countryman of our own. Certainly, no Englishman would be capable of this little bit of enthusiasm. Finally, the kitchen-firelight glistens on a splendid display of copper flagons, all of generous capacity, and one them as big as a half-barrel; the smaller vessels contain the customary allowance of ale, and the larger one is filled with that foaming liquor on four festive occasions of the year, and emptied amain by the jolly brotherhood. I should be glad to see them do it; but it would be an exploit fitter for Queen Elizabeth's age than these degenerate times.

The kitchen is the social hall of the twelve brethren. In the day-time, they bring their little messes to be cooked there, and eat them in their own parlors; but after a certain hour, the great hearth is cleared and swept, and the old men assemble round its blaze, each with his tankard and his pipe, and hold high converse through the evening. If the Master be a fit man for his office, methinks he will sometimes sit sociably down among them; for there is an elbow-chair by the fireside which it would not demean his dignity to fill, since it was occupied by King James at the great festival of nearly three centuries ago. A sip of the ale and a whiff of the tobacco-pipe would put him in friendly relations with his venerable household; and then we can fancy him instructing them by pithy apothegms and religious texts which were first uttered here by some Catholic priest and have impregnated the atmosphere ever since. If a joke goes round, it shall be of an elder coinage than Joe Miller's,[15] as old as Lord Bacon's collection, or as the jest-book that Master Slender asked for when he lacked small-talk for sweet Anne Page.[16] No news shall be spoken of, later than the drifting ashore, on the northern coast, of some stern-post or figure-head, a barnacled fragment of one of the great galleons of the Spanish Armada. What a tremor would pass through the antique group, if a damp newspaper should suddenly be spread to dry before the fire! They would feel as if either that printed sheet or they themselves must be an unreality. What a mysterious awe, if the shriek of the railway-train, as it reaches Warwick station, should ever so faintly invade their ears! Movement of any kind seems inconsistent with the stability of such an institution. Nevertheless, I trust that the ages will carry it along with them; because it is such a pleasant kind of dream for an American to find his way thither, and behold a piece of the sixteenth century set into our prosaic times, and then to depart, and think of its arched door-way as a spell-guarded entrance which will never be accessible or visible to him any more.

Not far from the market-place of Warwick stands the great church of St. Mary's: a vast edifice, indeed, and almost worthy to be a cathedral. People who pretend to skill in such matters say that it is in a poor style of architecture, though designed (or, at least, extensively restored) by Sir Christopher Wren; but I thought it very striking, with its wide, high, and elaborate windows, its tall tower, its immense length, and (for it was long before I outgrew this Americanism, the love of an old thing merely for the sake of its age) the tinge of gray antiquity over the whole. Once, while I stood gazing up at the tower, the clock struck twelve with a very deep intonation, and immediately some chimes began to play, and kept up their resounding music for five minutes, as measured by the hand upon the dial. It was a very delightful harmony, as airy as the notes of birds, and seemed a not unbecoming freak of half-sportive fancy in the huge, ancient, and solemn church; although I have seen an old-fashioned parlor-clock that did precisely the same thing, in its small way.

The great attraction of this edifice is the Beauchamp (or, as the English, who delight in vulgarizing their fine old Norman names, call it, the Beechum) Chapel, where the Earls of Warwick and their kindred have been buried, from four hundred years back till within a recent period. It is a stately and very elaborate chapel, with a large window of ancient painted glass, as perfectly preserved as any that I remember seeing in England, and remarkably vivid in its colors. Here are several monuments with marble figures recumbent upon them, representing the Earls in their knightly armor, and their dames in the ruffs and court-finery of their day, looking hardly stiffer in stone than they must needs have been in their starched linen and embroidery. The renowned Earl of Leicester of Queen Elizabeth's time, the benefactor of the hospital, reclines at full length on the tablet of one of these tombs, side by side with his Countess,—not Amy Robsart, but a lady who (unless I have confused the story with some other mouldy scandal) is said to avenged poor Amy's murder by poisoning the Earl himself. Be that as it may, both figures, and especially the Earl, look like the very types of ancient Honor and Conjugal Faith. In consideration of his long-enduring kindness to the twelve brethren, I cannot consent to believe him as wicked as he is usually depicted; and it seems a marvel, now that so many well-established verdicts have been reversed, why some enterprising writer does not make out Leicester to have been the pattern nobleman of his age.

In the centre of the chapel is the magnificent memorial of its founder, Richard Beauchamp, Earl of Warwick in the time of Henry VI. On a richly ornamental altar-tomb of gray marble lies the bronze figure of a knight in gilded armor, most admirably executed: for the sculptors of those days had wonderful skill in their own style, and could make so life-like an image of a warrior, in brass or marble, that, if a trumpet were sounded over his tomb, you would expect him to start up and handle his sword. The Earl whom we now speak, of, however, has slept soundly in spite of a more serious disturbance than any blast of a trumpet, unless it were the final one. Some centuries after his death, the floor of the chapel fell down and broke open the stone coffin in which he was buried; and among the fragments appeared the Earl of Warwick, with the color scarcely faded out of his cheeks, his eyes a little sunken, but in other respects looking as natural as if he had died yesterday. But exposure to the atmosphere appeared to begin and finish the long-delayed process of decay in a moment, causing him to vanish like a bubble; so that, almost before there had been time to wonder at him, there was nothing left of the stalwart Earl save his hair. This sole relic the ladies of Warwick made prize of, and braided it into rings and brooches for their own adornment; and thus, with a chapel and a ponderous tomb built on purpose to protect his remains, this great nobleman could not help being brought untimely to the light of day, nor even keep his love-locks on his skull after he had done so long with love. There seems to be a fatality that disturbs people in their sepulchres, when they have been over-careful to render them magnificent and impregnable,—as witness the builders of the Pyramids, and Hadrian, Augustus, and the Scipios, and most other personages whose mausoleums have been conspicuous enough to attract the violator; and as for dead men's hair, I have seen a lock of King Edward the Fourth's, of a reddish-brown color, which perhaps was once twisted round the delicate finger of Mistress Shore.

The direct lineage of the renowned characters that lie buried in this splendid chapel have long been extinct. The earldom is now held by the Grevilles, descendants of the Lord Brooke who was slain in the Parliamentary War; and they have recently (that is to say, within a century) built a burial-vault on the other side of the church, calculated (as the sexton assured me, with a nod as if he were pleased) to afford suitable and respectful accommodation to as many as fourscore coffins. Thank Heaven, the old man did not call them "CASKETS"!—a vile modern phrase, which compels a person of sense and good taste to shrink more disgustfully than ever before from the idea of being buried at all. But as regards those eighty coffins, only sixteen have as yet been contributed; and it may be a question with some minds, not merely whether the Grevilles will hold the earldom of Warwick until the full number shall be made up, but whether earldoms and all manner of lordships will not have faded out of England long before those many generations shall have passed from the castle to the vault. I hope not. A titled and landed aristocracy, if any-wise an evil and an incumbrance, is so only to the nation which is doomed to bear it on its shoulders; and an American, whose sole relation to it is to admire its picturesque effect upon society, ought to be the last man to quarrel with what affords him so much gratuitous enjoyment. Nevertheless, conservative as England is, and though I scarce ever found an Englishman who seemed really to desire change, there was continually a dull sound in my ears as if the old foundation of things were crumbling away. Some time or other,—by no irreverent effort of violence, but, rather, in spite of all pious efforts to uphold a heterogeneous pile of institutions that will have outlasted their vitality,—at some unexpected moment, there must come a terrible crash. The sole reason why I should desire it to happen in my day is, that I might be there to see! But the ruin of my own country is, perhaps, all that I am destined to witness; and that immense catastrophe (though I am strong in the faith that there is a national lifetime of a thousand years in us yet) would serve any man well enough as his final spectacle on earth.

If the visitor is inclined to carry away any little memorial of Warwick, he had better go to an Old Curiosity Shop in the High Street,[17] where there is a vast quantity of obsolete gewgaws, great and small, and many of them so pretty and ingenious that you wonder how they came to be thrown aside and forgotten. As regards its minor tastes, the world changes, but does not improve; it appears to me, indeed, that there have been epochs of far more exquisite fancy than the present one, in matters of personal ornament, and such delicate trifles as we put upon a drawing-room table, a mantel-piece, or a what-not. The shop in question is near the East gate, but is hardly to be found without careful search, being denoted only by the name of "REDFERN," painted not very conspicuously in the top-light of the door. Immediately on entering, we find ourselves among a confusion of old rubbish and valuables, ancient armor, historic portraits, ebony cabinets inlaid with pearl, tall, ghostly clocks, hideous old China, dim looking-glasses in frames of tarnished magnificence,—a thousand objects of strange aspect, and others that almost frighten you by their likeness in unlikeness to things now in use. It is impossible to give an idea of the variety of articles, so thickly strewn about that we can scarcely move without overthrowing some great curiosity with a crash, or sweeping away some small one hitched to our sleeves. Three stories of the entire house are crowded in like manner. The collection, even as we see it exposed to view, must have been got together at great cost; but the real treasures of the establishment lie in secret repositories, whence they are not likely to be drawn forth at an ordinary summons; though, if a gentleman with a competently long purse should call for them, I doubt not that the signet-ring of Joseph's friend Pharaoh, or the Duke of Alva's leading-staff, or the dagger that killed the Duke of Buckingham, or any other almost incredible thing, might make its appearance. Gold snuff-boxes, antique gems, jewelled goblets, Venetian wine-glasses, (which burst when poison is poured into them, and therefore must not be used for modern wine-drinking,) jasper-handled knives, painted Sèvres teacups,—in short, there are all sorts of things that a virtuoso ransacks the world to discover.

It would be easier to spend a hundred pounds in Mr. Redfern's shop than to keep it in one's pocket; but, for my part, I contented myself with buying a little old spoon of silver-gilt, and fantastically shaped, and got it at all the more reasonable rate because there happened to be no legend attached to it. I could supply any deficiency of that kind at much less expense than re-gilding the spoon!

The *Atlantic Monthly* of January 1863, under the title "Recollections of a Gifted Woman," carried on the series of articles, this latest being about Nathaniel's impressions of Stratford-upon-Avon. It read, in part:[18]

From Leamington to Stratford-on-Avon the distance is eight or nine miles, over a road that seemed to me most beautiful. Not that I can recall any memorable peculiarities; for the country, most of the way, is a succession of the gentlest swells and subsidences, affording wide and far glimpses of champaign-scenery here and there, and sinking almost to a dead level as we draw near Stratford. Any landscape in New England, even the tamest, has a more striking outline, and besides would have its blue eyes open in those lakelets that we encounter almost from mile to mile at home, but of which the Old Country is utterly destitute; or it would smile in our faces through the medium of those way-side brooks that vanish under a low stone arch on one side of the road, and sparkle out again on the other. Neither of these pretty features is often to be found in an English scene. The charm of the latter consists in the rich verdure of the fields, in the stately way-side trees and carefully kept plantations of wood, and in the old and high cultivation that has humanized the very sods by mingling so much of man's toil and care among them. To an American there is a kind of sanctity even in an English turnip-field, when he thinks how long that small square of ground has been known and recognized as a possession, transmitted from father to son, trodden often by memorable feet, and utterly redeemed from savagery by old acquaintanceship with civilized eyes. The wildest things in England are more than half tame. The trees, for instance, whether in hedge-row, park, or what they call forest, have nothing wild about them. They are never ragged; there is a certain decorous restraint in the freest outspread of their branches, though they spread wider than any self-nurturing trees; they are tall, vigorous, bulky, with a look of age-long life, and a promise of more years to come, all of which will bring them into closer kindred with the race of man. Somebody or other has known them from the sapling upward; and if they endure long enough, they grow to be traditionally observed and honored, and connected with the fortunes of old families, till, like Tennyson's Talking Oak, they babble with a thousand leafy tongues to ears that can more understand them.[19]

An American tree, however, if it could grow in fair competition with an English one of similar species, would probably be the more picturesque object of the two. The Warwickshire elm has not so beautiful a shape as those that overhang our village-street; and as for the redoubtable English oak, there is a certain John-Bullism in its figure, a compact rotundity of foliage, a lack of irregular and various outline, that make it look wonderfully like a gigantic cauliflower. Its leaf, too, is much smaller than that of most varieties of American oak; nor do I mean to doubt that the latter, with free leave to grow, reverent care and cultivation, and immunity from the axe, would live out its centuries as sturdily as its English brother, and prove far the nobler and more majestic specimen of a tree at the end of them. Still, however one's Yankee patriotism may struggle against the admission, it must be owned that the trees and other objects of an English landscape take hold of the observer by numberless minute tendrils, as it were, which, look closely as we choose, we never find in an American scene. The parasitic growth is so luxuriant, that the the trunk of the tree, so gray and dry in our climate, is better worth observing than the boughs and the foliage; a verdant mossiness coats it all over, so that it looks almost as green as the leaves; and often, moreover, the stately stem is clustered about, high upward, with creeping and twining shrubs, the ivy, and sometimes the mistletoe, close-clinging friends, nurtured by the moisture and never too fervid sunshine, and supporting themselves by the old tree's abundant strength. We call it a parasitical vegetation; but, if the phrase imply any reproach, it is unkind to bestow it on this beautiful affection and relationship which exist in England between one order of plants and another: the strong tree being always ready to give support to the trailing shrub, lift it to the sun, and feed it out of its own heart, if it crave such food; and the shrub, on its part, repaying its foster-father with an ample luxuriance of beauty, and adding Corinthian grace to the tree's lofty strength. No bitter winter nips these tender little sympathies, no hot sun burns the life out of them; and therefore they outlast the longevity of the oak, and, if the woodman permitted, would bury it in a green grave, when all is over.

Should there be nothing else along the road to look at, an English hedge might well suffice to occupy the eyes, and, to a depth beyond what he would suppose, the heart of an American. We often set out hedges in our own soil, but might as well set out figs or pine-apples and expect to gather fruit of them. Something grows, to be sure, which we choose to call a hedge; but it lacks the dense, luxuriant variety of vegetation that is accumulated into the English original, in which a botanist would find a thousand shrubs and gracious herbs that the hedge-maker never thought of planting there. Among them, growing wild, are many of the kindred blossoms of the very flowers which our pilgrim fathers brought from England, for the sake of their simple beauty and home-like associations, and which we have ever since been cultivating in gardens. There is not a softer trait to be found in the character of those stern men than that they should have been sensible of these flower-roots clinging among the fibres of their rugged hearts, and have felt the necessity of bringing them over sea and making them hereditary in the new land, instead of trusting to what rare beauty the wilderness might have in store for them.

Or, if the road-side has no hedge, the ugliest stone fence (such as, in America, would keep itself bare and unsympathizing till the end of time) is sure to be covered with the small handiwork of Nature; that careful mother lets nothing go naked there, and, if she cannot provide clothing, gives at least embroidery. No sooner is the fence built than she adopts and adorns it as a part of her original plan, treating the hard, uncomely construction as if it had all along been a favorite idea of her own. A little sprig of ivy may be seen creeping up the side of the low wall and clinging fast with its many feet to the rough surface; a tuft of grass roots itself between two of the stones, where a pinch or two of way-side dust has been moistened into nutritious soil for it; a small bunch of fern grows in another crevice; a deep, soft, verdant moss spreads itself along the top and over all the available inequalities of the fence; and where nothing else will grow, lichens stick tenaciously to the bare stones and variegate the monotonous gray with hues of yellow and red. Finally, a great deal of shrubbery clusters along the base of the stone wall, and takes away the hardness of its outline; and in due time, as the upshot of these apparently aimless or sportive touches, we recognize that the beneficent Creator of all things, working through His handmaiden whom we call Nature, has deigned to mingle a charm of divine gracefulness even with so earthy an institution as a boundary-fence. The clown who wrought at it little dreamed of what fellow-laborer he had.

The English should send us photographs of portions of the trunks of trees, the tangled and various products of a hedge, and a square foot of an old wall. They can hardly send anything else so characteristic. Their artists, especially of the later school, sometimes toil to depict such subjects, but are apt to stiffen the lithe tendrils in the process. The poets succeed better, with Tennyson at their head, and often produce ravishing effects by dint of a tender minuteness of touch, to which the genius of the soil and climate artfully impels them: for, as regards grandeur, there are loftier scenes in many countries than the best that England can show; but, for the picturesqueness of the smallest object that lies under its gentle gloom and sunshine, there is no scenery like it anywhere.

In the foregoing paragraphs I have strayed away to a long distance from the road to Stratford-on-Avon; for I remember no such stone fences as I have been speaking of in Warwickshire, nor elsewhere in England, except among the Lakes, or in Yorkshire, and the rough and hilly countries to the north of it. Hedges there were along my road, however, and broad, level fields, rustic hamlets, and cottages of ancient date,—from the roof of one of which the occupant was tearing away the thatch, and showing what an accumulation of dust, dirt, mouldiness, roots of weeds, families of mice, swallows' nests, and hordes of insects, had been deposited there since that old straw was new. Estimating its antiquity from these tokens, Shakspeare himself, in one of his morning rambles out of his native town, might have seen the thatch laid on; at all events, the cottage-walls were old enough to have known him as a guest. A few modern villas were also to be seen, and perhaps there were mansions of old gentility at no great distance, but hidden among the trees; for it is a point of English pride that such houses seldom allow themselves to be visible from the high-road. In short, I recollect nothing specially remarkable along the way, nor in the immediate approach to Stratford; and yet the picture of that June morning has a glory in my memory, owing chiefly, I believe, to the charm of the English summer-weather, the really good days of which are the most delightful that mortal man can ever hope to be favored with. Such a genial warmth! A little too warm, it might be, yet only to such a degree as to to assure an American (a certainty to which he seldom attains till attempered to the customary austerity of an English summer-day) that he was quite warm enough. And after all, there

was an unconquerable freshness in the atmosphere, which every little movement
of a breeze shook over me like a dash of the ocean-spray. Such days need bring
us no other happiness than their own light and temperature. No doubt, I could
not have enjoyed it so exquisitely, except that there must be still latent in us
Western wanderers (even after an absence of two centuries and more) an adaptation to the English climate which makes us sensible of a motherly kindness in its
scantiest sunshine, and overflows us with delight at its more lavish smiles.

The spire of Shakspeare's church—the Church of the Holy Trinity—begins to
show itself among the trees at a little distance from Stratford. Next we see the
shabby old dwellings, intermixed with mean-looking houses of modern date, and
the streets being quite level, you are struck and surprised by nothing so much as
the tameness of the general scene; as if Shakspeare's genius were vivid enough
to have wrought pictorial splendors in the town where he was born. Here and
there, however, a queer edifice meets your eye, endowed with the individuality
that belongs only to the domestic architecture of times gone by; the house seems
to have grown out of some odd quality in its inhabitant, as a sea-shell is moulded
from within by the character of its inmate; and having been built on a strange
fashion, generations ago, it has ever since been growing stranger and quainter, as
old humorists are apt to do. Here, too, (as so often impressed me in decayed
English towns) there appeared to be a greater abundance of aged people wearing
small-clothes and leaning on sticks than you could assemble on our side of the
water by sounding a trumpet and proclaiming a reward for the most venerable. I
tried to account for this phenomenon by several theories: as, for example, that
our new towns are unwholesome for age and kill it off unseasonably; or that our
old men have a subtile sense of fitness, and die of their own accord rather than
live in an unseemly contrast with youth and novelty: but the secret may be, after
all, that hair-dyes, false teeth, modern arts of dress, and other contrivances of a
skin-deep youthfulness, have not crept into these antiquated English towns, and
so people grow old without the weary necessity of seeming younger than they are.

After wandering through two or three streets, I found my way to Shakspeare's
birthplace, which is almost a smaller and humbler house than any description can
prepare the visitor to expect; so inevitably does an august inhabitant make his
abode palatial to our imaginations, receiving his guests, indeed, in a castle in the
air, until we unwisely insist on meeting him among the sordid lanes and alleys of
lower earth. The portion of the edifice with which Shakspeare had anything to do
is hardly large enough, in the basement, to contain the butcher's stall that one of
his descendants kept, and that still remains there, windowless, with the cleaver-
cuts in its hacked counter, which projects into the street under a little pent-house
roof, as if waiting for a new occupant. The upper half of the door was open, and,
on my rapping at it, a young person in black made her appearance and admitted
me: she was not a menial, but remarkably genteel (an American characteristic)
for an English girl, and was probably the daughter of the old gentlewoman who
takes care of the house. This lower room has a pavement of gray slabs of stone,
which may have been rudely squared when the house was new, but are now all
cracked, broken, and disarranged in a most unaccountable way. One does not see
how any ordinary usage, for whatever length of time, should have so smashed
these heavy stones; it is if an earthquake had burst up through the floor, which
afterwards had been imperfectly trodden down again. The room is whitewashed
and very clean, but woefully shabby and dingy, coarsely built, and such as the
most poetical imagination would find it difficult to idealize. In the rear of this
apartment is the kitchen, a still smaller room, of a similar rude aspect; it has a
great, rough fireplace, with space for a large family under the blackened opening

Shakespeare's birthplace. Photograph from 1857, after the house in Henley Street had been isolated from its neighbors. Reproduced by permission of the Shakespeare Birthplace Trust, Stratford-upon-Avon.

of the chimney, and an immense passage-way for the smoke, through which Shakspeare may have seen the blue sky by day and stars glimmering down at him by night. It is now a dreary spot where the long-extinguished embers used to be. A glowing fire, even if it covered only a quarter part of the hearth, might still do much towards making the old kitchen cheerful; but we get a depressing idea of the stifled, poor, sombre kind of life that could have been lived in such a dwelling, where this room seems to have been the gathering-place of the family, with no breadth or scope, no good retirement, but old and young huddling together cheek by jowl. What a hardy plant was Shakspeare's genius, how fatal its development, since it could not be blighted in such an atmosphere! It only brought human nature the closer to him, and put more unctuous earth about his roots.

Thence I was ushered up-stairs to the room in which Shakspeare is supposed to have been born; though, if you peep too curiously into the matter, you may find the shadow of an ugly doubt on this, as well as most other points of his mysterious life. It is the chamber over the butcher's shop, and is lighted by one broad window containing a great many small, irregular panes of glass. The floor is made of planks, very rudely hewn, and fitting together with little neatness; the naked beams and rafters, at the sides of the room and overhead, bear the original marks of the builder's broad-axe, with no evidence of an attempt to smooth off the job. Again we have to reconcile ourselves to the smallness of the space inclosed by these illustrious walls,—a circumstance more difficult to accept, as regards places that we have heard, read, thought, and dreamed much about, than any other disenchanting particular of a mistaken ideal. A few paces—perhaps seven or eight—take us from end to end of it. So low it is, that I could easily touch the ceiling, and might have done so without a tiptoe-stretch, had it been a good deal higher; and this humility of the chamber has tempted a vast multitude of people to write their names overhead in pencil. Every inch of the side-walls, even into the obscurest nooks and corners, is covered with a similar record; all the window-panes, moreover, are scrawled with diamond-signatures, among which is said to be that of Walter Scott; but so many persons have sought to immortalize them-selves in close vicinity to his name that I really could not trace him out. Methinks it is strange that people do not strive to forget their forlorn little identities, in such situations, instead of thrusting them forward into the dazzle of a great re-nown, where, if noticed, they cannot but be deemed impertinent.

This room, and the entire house, so far as I saw it, are whitewashed and exceed-ingly clean; nor is there the aged, musty smell with which old Chester first made me acquainted and which goes far to cure an American of his excessive predilec-tion for antique residences. An old lady, who took charge of me up-stairs, had the manners and aspect of a gentlewoman, and talked with somewhat formidable knowledge and appreciative intelligence about Shakspeare. Arranged on a table and in chairs were various prints, views of the house and scenes connected with Shakspeare's memory, together with editions of his works and local publications about his home and haunts, from the sale of which this respectable lady perhaps realizes a handsome profit. At any rate, I bought a good many of them, conceiving that it might be the civillest way of requiting her for her instructive conversation and the trouble she took in showing me the house. It cost me a pang (not a curmudgeonly, but a gentlemanly one) to offer a downright fee to the lady-like girl who had admitted me; but I swallowed my delicate scruples with some little difficulty, and she digested hers, so far as I could observe, with no difficulty at all. In fact, nobody need fear to hold out half a crown to any person with whom he has occasion to speak a word in England.

I should consider it unfair to quit Shakspeare's house without the frank acknowl-edgment that I was conscious of not the slightest emotion while viewing it, nor any quickening of the imagination. This has often happened to me in my visits to memorable places. Whatever pretty and apposite reflections I may have had upon the subject had either occurred to me before I ever saw Stratford, or have been elaborated since. It is pleasant, nevertheless, to think that I have seen the place; and I believe that I can form a more sensible and vivid idea of Shakspeare as a flesh-and-blood individual now that I have stood on the kitchen-hearth and in the birth-chamber; but I am not quite certain that this power of realization is altogether desirable in reference to a great poet. The Shakspeare whom I met there took various guises, but had not his laurel on. He was successively the roguish boy,—the youthful deer-stealer,—the comrade of players,—the too familiar friend of Davenant's mother,—the careful, thrifty, thriven man of property, who came back from London to lend money on bond, and occupy the best house in Stratford,—the mellow, red-nosed, autumnal boon-companion of John a'Combe, who (or else the Stratford gossips belied him) met his death by tumbling into a ditch on his way home from a drinking-bout, and left his second-best bed to his poor wife. I feel, as sensibly as the reader can, what horrible impiety it is to remember these things, be they true or false. In either case, they ought to vanish out of sight on the distant ocean-line of the past, leaving a pure, white memory, even as a sail, though perhaps darkened with many stains, looks snowy white on the horizon. But I draw a moral from these unworthy reminiscences and this embodiment of the poet, as suggested by some of the grimy actualities of his life. It is for the high interests of the world not to insist upon finding out that its greatest men are, in a certain lower sense, very much the same kind of men as the rest of us, and often a little worse; because a common mind cannot properly digest such a discovery, nor ever know the true proportions of the great Man's good and evil, nor how small a part of him it was that touched our muddy or dusty earth. Thence comes moral bewilderment, and even intellectual loss, in regard to what is best of him. When Shakspeare invoked a curse on the man who should stir his bones, he perhaps meant the larger share of it for him or them who should pry into his perishing earthliness, the defects or even the merits of the character that he wore in Stratford, when he had left mankind so much to muse upon that was imperishable and divine. Heaven keep me from incurring any part of the anathema in requital for the irreverent sentences above written!

From Shakspeare's house, the next step, of course, is to visit his burial-place. The appearance of the church is most venerable and beautiful, standing amid a great green shadow of lime-trees, above which rises the spire, while Gothic battlements and buttresses and vast arched windows are obscurely seen through the boughs. The Avon loiters past the church-yard, an exceedingly sluggish river, which might seem to have been considering which way it should flow ever since Shakspeare left off paddling in it and gathering the large forget-me-nots that grow among its flags and water-weeds.

An old man in small-clothes was waiting at the gate; and enquiring whether I wished to go in, he preceded me to the church-door, and rapped. I could have done it quite as effectually for myself; but, it seems, the old people of the neighborhood haunt about the church-yard, in spite of the frowns and remonstrances of the sexton, who grudges them the half-eleemosynary[20] sixpence which they sometimes get from visitors. I was admitted into the church by a respectable-looking and intelligent man in black, the parish-clerk, I suppose, and probably holding a richer incumbency than his vicar, if all the fees which he handles remain in his own pocket. He was already exhibiting the Shakspeare monuments to two or three visitors, and several other parties came in while I was there.

The poet and his family are in possession of what may be considered the very best burial-places that the church affords. They lie in a row, right across the breadth of the chancel, the foot of each gravestone being close to the elevated floor on which the altar stands. Nearest to the side-wall, beneath Shakspeare's bust, is a slab bearing a Latin inscription addressed to his wife, and covering her remains; then his own slab, with the old anathemizing stanza upon it; then that of Thomas Nash, who married his grand-daughter; then that of Dr. Hall, the husband of his daughter Susannah; and lastly, Susannah's own. Shakspeare's is the commonest-looking slab of all, being just such a flag-stone as Essex Street in Salem used to be paved with, when I was a boy. Moreover, unless my eyes or recollection deceive me, there is a crack across it, as if it had already undergone some such violence as the inscription deprecates. Unlike the other monuments of the family, it bears no name, nor am I acquainted with the grounds or authority on which it is absolutely determined to be Shakspeare's; although, being in a range with those of his wife and children, it might naturally be attributed to him. But, then, why does his wife, who died afterwards, take precedence of him and occupy the place next his bust? And where are the graves of another daughter and a son, who have a better right in the family-row than Thomas Nash, his grandson-in-law? Might not one or both of them have been laid under the nameless stone? But it is dangerous trifling with Shakspeare's dust; so I forbear to meddle further with the grave, (though the prohibitions make it tempting,) and shall let whatever bones be in it rest in peace. Yet I must needs add that the inscription on the bust seems to imply that Shakspeare's grave was directly underneath it.

The poet's bust is affixed to the northern wall of the church, the base of it being about a man's height, or rather more, above the floor of the chancel. The features of this piece of sculpture are entirely unlike any portrait of Shakspeare that I have ever seen, and compel me to take down the beautiful, lofty-browed, and noble picture of him which has hitherto hung in my mental portrait-gallery. The bust cannot be said to represent a beautiful face or an eminently noble head; but it clutches firmly hold of one's sense of reality and insists upon your accepting it, if not as Shakspeare the poet, yet as the wealthy burgher of Stratford, the friend of John a'Combe, who lies yonder in the corner. I know not what the phrenologists say to the bust. The forehead is but moderately developed, and retreats somewhat, the upper part of the skull rising pyramidically; the eyes are prominent almost beyond the penthouse of the brow; the upper lip is so long that it must have been almost a deformity, unless the sculptor artistically exaggerated its length, in consideration, that, on the pedestal, it must be foreshortened by being looked at from below. On the whole, Shakspeare must have had a singular rather than a prepossessing face; and it is wonderful how, with this bust before its eyes, the world has persisted in maintaining an erroneous notion of his appearance, allowing painters and sculptors to foist their idealized nonsense on us all, instead of the genuine man. For my part, the Shakspeare of my mind's eye is henceforth to be a personage of a ruddy English complexion, with a reasonably capacious brow, intelligent and quickly observant eyes, a nose curved slightly outwards, a long, queer, upper-lip, with the mouth a little unclosed beneath it, and cheeks considerably developed in the lower part and beneath the chin. But when Shakspeare was himself, (for nine-tenths of the time, according to all appearances, he was but the burgher of Stratford,) he doubtless shone through this dull mask and transfigured it into a face of an angel.

Fifteen or twenty feet behind the row of Shakspeare gravestones is the great east-window of the church, now brilliant with stained glass of recent manufacture. On one side of this window, under a sculptured arch of marble, lies a full-length marble figure of John a'Combe, clad in what I take to be a robe of municipal dignity, and holding its hands devoutly clasped. It is a sturdy English figure, with coarse features, a type of ordinary man whom we smile to see immortalized in the sculpturesque material of poets and heroes; but the prayerful attitude encourages us to believe that the old userer may not, after all, have had that grim reception in the other world which Shakspeare's squib foreboded for him. By-the-by, till I grew somewhat familiar with Warwickshire pronunciation, I never understood that the point of all those ill-natured lines was a pun. "'Oho!' quoth the Devil, ' 't is my John a'Combe!'"—that is, "my John has come!"[21]

Close to the poet's bust is a nameless, oblong, cubic tomb, supposed to be that of a clerical dignitary of the fourteenth century. The church has other mural monuments and altar-tombs, one or two of the latter upholding the recumbent figures of knights in armor and their dames, very eminent and worshipful in their day, no doubt,, but doomed to appear forever intrusive and impertinent within the precincts which Shakspeare has made his own. His renown is tyrannous, and suffers nothing else to be recognized within the scope of its material presence, unless illuminated by some side-ray from himself. The clerk informed me that interments no longer take place in any part of the church. And it is better so; for methinks a person of delicate individuality, curious about his burial-place, and desirous of six feet of earth for himself alone, could never endure to lie buried near Shakspeare, but would rise up at midnight and grope his way out of the church-door, rather than sleep in the shadow of so stupendous a memory. . .

This has been too sad a story [i.e., Nathaniel's recollections of a gifted woman, the story of Delia Bacon as he remembered it]. To lighten the recollection of it, I will think of my stroll homeward past Charlecote Park, where I beheld the most stately elms, in clumps, and in groves, scattered all about in the sunniest, shadiest, sleepiest fashion; so that I could not but believe in a lengthened, loitering, drowsy enjoyment which these trees must have in their existence. Diffused over slow-paces centuries, it need not be keen nor bubble into thrills and ecstasies, like the momentary delights of short-lived human beings. They were civilized trees, known to man and befriended by him for ages past. There is an indescribable difference—as I believe I have endeavoured to express—between the tamed, but by no means effete (on the contrary, the richer and more luxuriant) Nature of England, and the rude, shaggy, barbarous Nature which offers us its racier companionship in America. No less a change has been wrought among the wildest creatures that inhabit what the English call their forests. By-and-by, among those refined and venerable trees, I saw a large herd of deer, mostly reclining, but some standing in picturesque groups, while the stags threw their large antlers aloft, as if they had been taught to make themselves tributary to the scenic effect. Some were running fleetly about, vanishing from light into shadow and glancing forth again, with here and there a little fawn careering at its mother's heels. These deer are almost in the same relation in the wild, natural state of their kind that the trees of an English park hold to the rugged growth of an American forest. They have held a certain intercourse with man for immemorial years; and, most probably, the stag that Shakspeare killed was one of the progenitors of this very herd, and may himself have been a partly civilized and humanized deer, though in a less degree than these remote posterity. They are a little wilder than sheep, but they do not snuff the air at the approach of human beings, nor evince much alarm at their pretty close proximity; although, if you continue to advance, they toss their heads and take to their heels in a kind of mimic terror, or something akin to female skittishness, with a dim remembrance or tradition, as it were, of their having come of a wild stock. They have so long been fed and protected by man, that they must have lost many of their native instincts, and, I suppose, could not live comfortably through even an English winter without human help. One is sensible of a gentle scorn at them for such dependency, but feels none the less kindly disposed towards the half-domesticated race; and it may have been his observation of these tamer characteristics in the Charlecote herd that suggested to Shakspeare the tender and pitiful description of a wounded stag, in "As You Like It."

At a distance of some hundreds of yards from Charlecote Hall, and almost hidden by the trees between it and the road-side, is an old brick archway and porter's lodge. In connection with this entrance there appears to have been a wall and an ancient moat, the latter of which is still visible, a shallow, grassy scoop along the base of an embankment of the lawn. About fifty yards within the gateway stands the house, forming three sides of a square, with three gables in a row on the front and on each of the two wings; and there are several towers and turrets at the angles, together with projecting windows, antique balconies, and other quaint ornaments suitable to the half-Gothic taste in which the edifice was built. Over the gate-way is the Lucy coat-of-arms, emblazoned in its proper colors. The mansion dates from the early days of Elizabeth, and probably looked very much the same as now when Shakspeare was brought before Sir Thomas Lucy for outrages among his deer. The impression is not that of gray antiquity, but of stable and time-honored gentility, still as vital as ever.

It is a most delightful place. All about the house and domain there is a perfection of comfort and domestic taste, an amplitude of convenience, which could have been brought about only by the slow ingenuity and labor of many successive generations, intent upon adding all possible improvement to the home where years gone by and years to come give a sort of permanence to the intangible present. An American is sometimes tempted to fancy that only by this long process can real homes be produced. One man's lifetime is not enough for the accomplishment of such a work of Art and Nature, almost the greatest merely temporary one that is confided to him; too little, at any rate,—yet perhaps too long, when he is discouraged by the idea that he must make his house warm and delightful for a miscellaneous race of successors, of whom the one thing certain is, that his own grandchildren will not be among them. Such repinings as are here suggested, however, come only from the fact, that, bred in English habits of thought, as most of us are, we have not yet modified our instincts to the necessities of our new forms of life. A lodging in a wigwam or under a tent has really as many advantages, when we come to know them, as a home beneath the roof-tree of Charlecote Hall. But, alas! our philosophers have not yet taught us to see what is best, nor have our poets sung us what is beautifullest, in the kind of life that we must lead; and therefore we still read the old English wisdom, and harp upon the ancient strings. And thence it happens, that, when we look at a time-honored hall, it seems more possible for men who inherit such a home, than for ourselves, to lead noble and graceful lives, quietly doing good and lovely things as their daily work, and achieving deeds of simple greatness when circumstances require them. I sometimes apprehend that our institutions may perish before we shall have discovered the most precious of the possibilities which they involve.

The increase in the rate of pay for the articles restored Nathaniel's flagging interest in the project and in January 1863 he was promising Fields further pieces, relating to his experiences in London, and was also agreeing that it would be possible and sensible to collect all the articles (those already written and others that were yet to be placed) into a "volume of, say, 325 pages." An article entitled "Up the Thames" appeared in the February edition and by May he had sent Fields another one, to be called "Consular Experiences," but suggested that it should be kept back for inclusion in what was now envisaged as the new book with the title of *Our Old Home: a Series of English Sketches.* Two further articles appeared in the July and August editions of the magazine, "Outside Glimpses of English Poverty" and "Civic Banquets," and by now Nathaniel was reading page proofs of the forthcoming book at the same time as writing articles for the magazine. He also prepared a new and expanded version of the article that had appeared in *The Keepsake* back in 1857, now to be called "Lichfield and Uttoxeter" but it was not published in the *Atlantic Monthly.*

Nathaniel was aware of, and prepared for, the likely displeasure that some parts of the new book would bring him. In referring to the proposed opening chapter, "Consular Experiences," he wrote to Fields that it "has some of the features that attract the curiosity of the foolish public, being made up of personal narrative and gossip, with a few pungencies of personal satire, which will not be the less effective because the reader can scarcely find out who was the individual meant. I am not without hope of drawing down upon myself a good deal of critical severity on this score, and would gladly incur more of it if I could do so without seriously deserving censure. . . . It seems to me quite essential to have some novelty in the collected volume, and, if possible, something that may excite a little discussion and remark." As it happened, the excitement occurred for several reasons, some of which he foresaw: "If you can get anything for the sheets in England, do it by all means—even if it were only five pounds. I don't see why anybody should give more, or so much, for a book that a dozen pirates will be ready to seize upon, if it prove to have any sellable value. However, it will not take in England, being calculated (by the objects which it describes, and the sentiments it expresses) for the American market only."[22]

Once again, his health was beginning to trouble him, suffering some attacks of dysentery in the summer, possibly in part brought on by his worries about money (which were somewhat soothed by Fields having obtained £150 from Smith, Elder for the copyright of the forthcoming book), the country's uncertain political future, and the difficulties that were arising from his intention to dedicate the new book to his old friend and ex-president, General Pierce, whose popularity and political reputation had waned dramatically after speeches that he had made from 1861 onward that were seen as attempts to overthrow the government and to distance the Democratic party from Lincoln's policies that he said were such that would result in true Americans losing their essential freedom. Nathaniel felt emphatically that he was right in dedicating the book to a friend, for the sake of their association over the years (not least because it had been Pierce who had got him the job of consul at Liverpool), never mind that friend's current political position. He wrote to Elizabeth Peabody that

I do not think that the Dedication to Gen[l] Pierce can have the momentous political consequences which you apprehend. I determined upon it long since, as a proper memorial of our life-long intimacy, and as especially suitable in the case of this book, which could not have been in existence without him. I expressly say that I dedicate the book to the friend, and decline any present colloquy with the statesman, to whom I address merely a few lines expressing my confidence in his loyalty and unalterable devotion to the Union. . . . Every body else has outgrown the old faith in the Union, or got outside of it in one way or another; but Pierce retains it in all the simplicity with which he inherited it from his father. . . . It has been the principle and is the explanation (and the apology, if any is needed) of his whole public life, and if you look generously at him, you cannot but see that it would ruin a noble character (though one of limited scope) for him to admit any ideas that were not entertained by the fathers of the constitution and the republic. . . . The Dedication can hurt nobody but my book and myself. I know that it will do that, but am content to take the consequences. . . . The best thing, as far as I can see, would be to effect a separation of the Union, giving us the West bank of the Mississipi, and a boundary line affording as much Southern soil as we can hope to digest into freedom in another century. Such a settlement looks impossible . . . and so does every other imaginable settlement, except through the medium of the peace Democrats. . . . You cannot possibly conceive . . . how little the North really cares for the negro-question, and how eagerly it would grasp at peace if recommended by a delusive show of victory. Free soil was never in so great a danger as now. . . . My views about Dis-union, for example, though long crudely entertained, are not such as I should choose to put forth at present: and I am very often sensible of an affectionate regard for the dead old Union, which leads me to say a kind thing or two about it, though I had as lief see my grandfather's ghost as have it revive.[23]

Fields was apprehensive as to the wisdom of dedicating the book to an unpopular political figure such as Pierce: "It is the opinion of wiser men than I am in the 'trade' that the Dedn & Letter to F.P. will ruin the sale of yr. book. I tell you this, in season that you may act upon it if you elect to do so. A large dealer told me he shd. not order any copies, much as his customers admired yr. writings, and a very knowing literary friend of yours says it will be, in these days, the most damaging move you could possibly make. So, this is what I feared. Now you must decide whether you will risk the sale of 'Our Old Home' by putting a friend's name to it. . . . Rough days we live in."[24] But Nathaniel was not prepared to alter his plans, much:

> . . . I have delayed my reply . . . in order to ponder deeply on your advice . . . I find that it would be a piece of poltroonery in me to withdraw either the dedication or the dedicatory letter. My long and intimate personal relations with Pierce render the dedication altogether proper, especially as regards this book, which would have had no existence without his kindness; and if he is so exceedingly unpopular that his name is enough to sink the volume, there is so much more the need that an old friend should stand by him. I cannot, merely on account of pecuniary profit or literary reputation, go back from what I have deliberately felt and thought it right to do; and if I were to tear out the dedication, I should never look at the volume again without remorse and shame. As for the literary public, it must accept my book precisely as I think fit to give it, or let it alone. Nevertheless . . . I have looked at the concluding paragraph, and have amended it in such a way that, while doing what I know to be justice to my friend, it contains not a word that ought to be objectionable to any set of readers.[25]

Proofreading continued throughout the rest of the summer, by which time Nathaniel was sufficiently sick of the whole business to tell Fields that ". . . I shall thank Heaven when I get all this English trash off my mind."[26] However, on 19 September the book was published simultaneously in England and America and, as anticipated by the author, it received a mixed reception, in some instances provoking angry critical responses.

Epilogue:
The End of the Affair: 1863–64

From the very first, the English and American critics adopted a marked difference in their attitude toward the book; on the whole, the Americans viewed *Our Old Home* as a product of America that reflected in many ways their own opinions of England and the English, their own experiences of the scenes and places that were described, and their own appreciation of a fellow American whose style, diction, and thoughts were natural products of American civilization and manners. After all, the book was not about America; they were safe in delighting in, and agreeing with, its humor as it was not, in its severest criticisms, leveled at things American. The English critics, on the other hand, while approving the style of the author, his reputation, and his general appreciation of the English scene, were quick to take offense at the continual critical attitude toward the English race, their manners, their appearance, their attitudes, their insularity, and the suggestion that England was struggling to maintain its position in the world and that shortly America would become more powerful due to the greater individuality and energy of its inhabitants, untainted as they were with the burden of a thousand years of history that was said to cloud the Englishman's vision and to restrict his movements in the race for supremacy in the future. What upset and puzzled so many of the English critics was the apparent ungraciousness of the sentiments regarding their country and people as expressed by an individual who was both intelligent *and* a visitor to the country, who might not have liked much of what he saw but who should have had the courtesy, in the circumstances, to have kept his uncalled-for (and American) opinions to himself!

The *Salem Register*[1] was able to be first off the mark with a review that ignored any kind of literary criticism and concentrated instead on the impropriety of Nathaniel's dedication of the book to the former president, Franklin Pierce: "This is more creditable to the strength and endurance of Hawthorne's college friendship than to his political sagacity and associations . . . the developments of the last few months have not added any thing to heighten the public estimation of him [Pierce] as a statesman and patriot, but on the contrary much to diminish it." The *Boston Post*[2] then spoke of Nathaniel's "style; it is natural, it is straight ahead and has none of the grimace and contortion of the eccentric genius" and of the "dignified and flowing sentences, now and then replete with a quiet humor that betokens a mind absolutely at ease in his labor." Later, the *Boston Transcript*[3] could not find much to complain of as the book was "subtly pervaded by those peculiarities of mental character which stamp them unmistakably with the impress of Hawthorne's mind and disposition," and although the *Boston Daily Advertiser*[4] referred to the dedication as "Mr. Hawthorne's intrusion of his hardly pardonable illusions respecting President Pierce and his administration [as being] a blemish upon the volume" it did not detract from the "beauties of the author's style [that] were never more distinctly marked than in reproducing those distant scenes, which seem half familiar and half a dream to all of us," and yet another Boston paper, the *Boston Evening Transcript,*[5] completed the chorus of praise for Massachusetts' own favorite, indigenous author: "One scarcely knows which most to applaud,—the chaste and charming style, the quiet, pure humor, or, the manly truthfulness of this classic New England writer."

The *New York Daily Tribune*[6] liked what it read, indeed quoted long extracts from the book, and saw little if anything at which to take offense and assumed that the English reader would relish the humor as much as the American, even wishing for something a bit stronger, and acknowledged that Nathaniel had as many hard things to say about Americans as the English:

> The miscellaneous papers which comprise a large portion of this volume, treat of a variety of topics connected with English manners, character, scenery, and customs. Most of them are singularly agreeable reading, full of pointed remark, sallies of malicious veracity, sly hints at personal and national follies, acute comments on society and life as seen by American eyes, and spiced with a vein of lively satire in which the author evidently takes no less wicked delight than he imparts to his least implacable readers. . . . Mr. Hawthorne's humor is the more effective from the strong basis of reality on which it rests, and from the quiet, often demure, tone in which it is presented.

The Albion,[7] however, was not sure that this was the kind of thing that Nathaniel ought to be doing: "The book may not be a great achievement. It certainly has not the genius of 'The Scarlet Letter'" and while "he does, indeed, sometimes wound the self-love of an English reader . . . his pen is much less severe than those of many English satirists of our national character and manners, while it nowhere drips the gall of American Anglophobia. He is, moreover, profoundly appreciative of all that is honorable and august in the history and the civilization of England."

Two more reviews in American papers could find little, if anything, wrong with the book. The *American Publisher's Circular*[8] felt that its style was an example of all that was best in American literature: "We trust our younger writers . . . will make a study of this book and of the other volumes of Hawthorne. Such a study will correct their vitiated tastes, and bring them back to a better class of models. They will here find pleasant thoughts, refined sentiments, shrewd distinctions, picturesque descriptions, and accurate characterizations, all charmingly expressed in clear, homely, vigorous, and unadulterated English." Perhaps Nathaniel would have given a wry smile at being placed in the older generation of American writers; maybe he would have been equally encouraged by the review in the *North American Review* [9] but in this instance he could just as well have flung up his arms and, if he was given to imprecations, muttered "God help us!"

> The two properties of the work which seem to us the most striking are its humor and its kindliness. The humor is unforced, we think generally unconscious. Things present themselves grotesquely to Mr. Hawthorne. He takes hold of them by some other than the usual handle, and offers to our view just the parts and aspects of them which it is conventionally fit to keep out of sight. It is a humor always delicate, frequently even serious, and never more manifest than when the writer is most in earnest. His kindliness, too, if not unconscious, is expressed unintentionally. There is, indeed, no little pretence of an opposite sort, an affectation (shall we call it?) of roughness and unsociableness; but it is very feebly maintained,—the ill-fitted mask keeps dropping from the face, in which we see the tokens of a tenderness of human fellow-feeling, such as it is equally impossible to counterfeit and disguise.

Harper's Weekly[10] liked Nathaniel's "pure, sinewy, racy, idiomatic style" but was more concerned with his politics in that time of political turmoil in the States: "That the great English authors should cant and misrepresent our war is intelligible upon the assumption of their ignorance; but that one of the most gifted and fascinating of American writers should fail to see, or care for, the very point of our contest is monstrous." However, in a long article the *New York Times*[11] found the book to be

> remarkable. . . . We like to read a book as we like to wear a coat, after its new gloss is worn off. . . . We know very little of the written criticism on this book, and we have heard none of the conversational criticisms on it. . . . This book of Hawthorne's is not a book of travels, nor yet a book of sentiment: it is a book of thoughts and pictures; oftentimes, too, a book of feelings. But in every part it illustrates our view of the tendency of Hawthorne's genius, to turn the actual into the ideal, and not to make the ideal seem like the actual. . . . The author has a special instinct for discovering traces of humanity at once sad and singular; he wanders through the by-ways of life, and carefully he notes the marks which pilgrims may have left upon their paths, of suffering or of sin. . . . His special excellence as a describer is, that he not only presents the object, whether of art or nature, distinctly and clearly in the mind, but along with the picture, infuses the feeling which it inspired. He loves nature in all its changes and phrases, and he has lovingly observed them. His sympathy with art is profound; and his descriptions, particularly of spiritual architecture, stir all that is spiritual in humanity, and have the soul in them of the highest and most fervent religious eloquence and poetry. . . . it may be safely said that this volume has all the finest characteristics of Hawthorne's genius, as it had been already known, and some qualities which it had hardly been suspected to possess. Readers will hope that the present volume does not exhaust all the author's 'Notes of Travel,' but that sufficient for another like it still remains behind.

These reviews in the American papers did not reflect the opinions that were expressed in the English newspapers, many of which took Nathaniel to task for his apparent antipathy to England and the English. Positive howls of rage were transposed to the printed page, berating this American for his sly (and sometimes not so sly) digs at the British character and way of life, contrasting them, to their detriment, with their modern (in all aspects of the word) and admirable American counterparts. Most reviewers, as was the case with that of *The Reader*,[12] were prepared to admit that

> Perhaps there is no American from whom a book about England would be expected with more affectionate interest and with higher anticipations of pleasure than from Nathaniel Hawthorne. He is a favourite with us all, [and] the present is a beautiful book, and worthy of Hawthorne. . . . It appears . . . that . . . he used to reside a good deal in Leamington and a large portion of the book is taken up with excursions in the neighbourhood of Leamington—more particularly to Warwick and Stratford-on-Avon. We follow him, also, to Oxford . . . to Lichfield . . . to Lincoln and Boston [but] while the reader is going through the varied richness of the book . . . he will have been conscious from the first, unless he is unusually good-humoured, or more deficient in patriotism than Englishmen generally are, of the perpetual presence of an irritating and disturbing element. This is Mr. Hawthorne's anti-English feeling. . . . From the beginning of the book to the end there is a succession, at intervals of only a few pages, of passages of the most acrid Americanism, conveying opinions respecting the English character which we should hardly have expected from Mr. Hawthorne, did we not know that somehow every American man, woman, and child has of late conceived a detestation of our nation so deep, so bitter, so intense, as to be comparable only to the feeling of the French, while yet revenge for Waterloo was the paramount desire of their Celtic souls.

Much the same thing was expressed by Chorley in *The Athenæum*;[13] indeed, in referring obliquely to the early recognition in England of Nathaniel's talents, a recognition stimulated by his own efforts on behalf of the little-known author, he seemed almost to take the whole thing as a personal insult: "A more charming, more unpleasant book has never been written concerning England than this. Mr. Hawthorne commands a style of poetical beauty such as belongs to few of his contemporaries. . . . There are passages in these English recollections excelling anything which he has until now written. 'What, then,' readers may ask, 'ails the book?' Its surprising bad temper. . . . We could go on for pages in a strain like this, were it edifying further to show how low a point of thought and consistency a man of genius, honour and liberality may be brought by listening to the suggestion of a morbid and perverse irritability." After quoting the Leamington dowager passage Chorley continued, "For such a passage . . . from the hand that wrote the 'Twice-told Tales' there is only one solution to be given. The aching discomfort which every travelled American, having an atom of generosity in his composition, must feel on regarding the lamentable spectacles to-day exhibited in the Disunited Union, may be well accepted as excuse for any amount of grudge, or bile, of exaggerating obliquity of vision with which one even so gifted and genial as Mr. Hawthorne now looks back across the Atlantic to his Old Home."

The Illustrated London News,[14] on the whole, liked the humor but also disliked the manner in which, apparently, the book had been written:

> To show how extremely bilious Mr. Hawthorne must have been when he penned his sketches, it is unnecessary to do more than append the following quotation:— "I desire, above all things, to be courteous; but, since the plain truth must be told, the soil and climate of England produce feminine beauty as rarely (!!!) as they do delicate fruit; and, though admirable specimens of both are to be met with, they are the hothouse ameliorations of refined society, and apt, moreover, to relapse into the coarseness of the original stock. The men are men-like, but the women are not beautiful, though the female Bull be well enough adapted to the male." Mr. Hawthorne should really have his eyes examined by a good oculist; something must have happened to them since he wrote 'Transformation,' when he seemed to be a judge of the beautiful.

The Spectator[15] found the sarcasm and humor directed at England and the English acceptable enough but would have welcomed something a little more penetrating from an author whose genius was considered to be self-evident:

> Even in this book, full of graceful sentiment and delicate fancy as it is, crowded with sentences the mere harmonious cadence of which makes them a pleasure almost apart from their meaning, and whose meaning has the fanciful kind of beauty which we see in the tinted clouds of sunset—even in the midst of Mr. Hawthorne's subtle and airy criticisms on English scenes, we waken up with a sensation of more vivid pleasures when he condescends to some of the many fair but pungent sarcasms on English manners with which he strews his half-dreamy and half-vigilant comments. . . . For our own parts, instead of being inclined to take offence at his sparing use of sarcasm, we could have enjoyed a good deal more of its pleasant stimulus, being quite aware not only that many of his caustic touches are deserved, but that even when they are least so, they are but set-offs against English *prestige,* which the sensitive patriotism of the American obliges him to put down and make much of, in order to satisfy himself that his own branch of the English stock has surpassed the parent stem in life and beauty. . . . In the very title of his book, and throughout its substance, he seems to divide the imaginative claims to a historic past somewhat unfairly between the two nations, leaving us all the weariness and stupidity of a burden of centuries and claiming for his own countrymen all the refining influences of national memory, without any of the disagreeable dead-weight of national responsibility. . . . Indeed, we doubt whether, in fact, 'the burden of the past,' as Mr. Hawthorne calls it, is near so keenly felt by those for whom the past still partially lives in the present, as by those whose *institutions* ignore, while their hearts and habits acknowledge it. With us the past, no doubt, partly obsolete, is, so far as it is alive at all, a part of the actual life of to-day, and, therefore, no more a burden to the imagination than any other part of our living organization. The burden is felt only when the past has impressed a *tendency* which the present is compelled to resist. . . . The passage, already famous, on the English dowager . . . is full of point and humour. . . . Yet the American critic is not insensible to the brighter side of English beauty.

In view of the topicality that *Our Old Home* could offer to those readers who resided in the areas of the country that Nathaniel had visited and included in the book, it would have seemed natural that reviews should have appeared in many local publications. Leamington itself, however, though in the thick of the fray regarding the outrage concerning Nathaniel's comments on the English dowager as seen in Leamington Spa, saw fit not to express any opinion on the matter. *The Royal Leamington Spa Courier* uttered not a word on the subject and all *The Leamington Advertiser* [16] could find to say was that the book had been made available to the public through Beck's Circulating Library. No doubt it came as something of a shock to those who read the book that the well-known author and his family had, in fact, been in their midst not so many years previously. However, somewhat further afield, *The Birmingham Journal*[17] recognized the interest that the book held for the Midlands as a whole:

> "Our Old Home" . . . is not as some have supposed, a novel or romance, but only a description of various scenes and incidents in England, witnessed by the author during his residence among us . . . in which many of our own immediate localities are described. . . . The volumes are clear, minute, and pleasant in description . . . full of much interesting matter and well worth reading, however we may differ from their views. . . . Some portions of Mr. Hawthorne's book are, however, unfair, vulgar, coarse. Many of his remarks on our English men, and even our English women, are in extreme bad taste, even if they were literally true. Some of the phrases applied to the description of our English matrons as compared with their attenuated sisters over the sea are such sins against literary good taste, not to say more, that they will seriously damage what is in the main, an admirable and interesting book.

"There are few things more welcome to an Englishman than a good description, by a foreigner, of England and the English"; wrote the critic in *The Saturday Review*,[18] "and, if the author is an American, he has the advantage of being near enough to understand and sympathize with us, and yet of being sufficiently a stranger to give point and originality to his criticisms." The book was thought to be admirable, and it was regretted somewhat that the criticisms had not been more deeply barbed; possibly the critic exhibited that characteristic that had troubled Nathaniel on more than one occasion, the Englishman's condescending sangfroid in the face of criticism (especially from foreigners).

> All these places [Liverpool, Leamington, Stratford, Oxford, the Scotch border, Greenwich, and many of the outlying parts of London] he paints with his usual gracefulness of style, and with that subdued humour, that oddness and yet soundness of imagination, and that relish at once for the beautiful and the grotesque, which characterize the novels that have made his name famous. Mr. Hawthorne seems to apprehend that some Englishmen may think that he has criticized them too freely and spoken his mind too frankly. He need not have any fear of the sort. In England we like to hear judicious criticisms of ourselves, and are entertained

and delighted when any shafts of wit come unexpectedly home to us. We have had plenty of foreigners to praise us up to the skies, and plenty to abuse us and call us every bad name under heaven; but strangers who can appreciate us, and can see the comic side of respectability, and can detect the weak points of our social system without exaggerating their importance or refusing to see how intimately they are associated with our past history, are very rare, and would be welcome even if they had not the taste, the grace, and the good-feeling of Mr. Hawthorne. . . . Of the English with whom he came into contact, his general impression was, that they were beefy, ungainly, heavy people, without much imagination or power, but with honesty and sense, and a willingness to be kind. . . . He does not seem to have greatly admired Englishwomen . . . in general they seemed to him ungraceful and dowdy. . . . 'All English people,' he says, 'are influenced in a far greater degree than ourselves by this simple and honest tendency, in case of disagreement, to batter one another's persons; and whoever has seen a crowd of English ladies (for instance, at the door of the Sistine Chapel in Holy Week) will be satisfied that their belligerent propensities are kept in abeyance only by a merciless rigour on the part of society. It requires a vast deal of refinement to spiritualize their large physical endowments'. . . . The picture is true, or very nearly true, and its liveliness and nicety of observation will be relished by Englishmen quite as much as they could be by Americans.

As requested by the author, Bright wrote a review in *The Examiner*.[19] He respected Nathaniel's talents and liked the book but was nonplussed by the apparent acrimony that it contained toward England and the English people. As was the case with Chorley in *The Athenæum*, he felt that it was something of an insult for a "guest" of the country to repay hospitality with so much rancor:

It was a strange streak of fortune which threw Mr. Hawthorne on our shores as American Consul at Liverpool. . . . What possible connection could there be between the "Scarlet Letter" and consular certificates? . . . Well, the experiment answered better than might have been expected. . . . These sketches of English life and scenery are by a master's hand; they are somewhat fragmentary indeed, and there is something of caprice in the choice of subject and of treatment. But, with all their wilfulness, they are full of grace and beauty, of a tender pathos, and of subtle humour. . . . He does not describe things as they are, but rather as they appear to him; and he takes no pains to disguise the fact that he saw things as an American with strong prejudices, and as a retiring man with dreamy tendencies was sure to see them. And then again, he does not always dwell upon the more important or striking scenes. . . . He declines to linger among the ruins of Kenilworth, while he spends a long morning with some old pensioners at Warwick. He has no word for Cambridge, which he visited, but he tells us of Uttoxeter and Lillington, and other places, which, perhaps, no stranger ever troubled to see before. . . . But we will at once turn to the one part in this book (in other respects so charming) which somewhat surprises us in our English self-complacency. Whatever Mr. Hawthorne may like in England, he certainly does not like us Englishmen. With us he is neither struck nor pleased. Englishmen, and Englishwomen more especially, seem to be his positive aversion . . . nothing can be more cynical and contemptuous than the expressions he uses of us as a race. . . . But we do not see why it was necessary to express these unpleasant opinions so unpleasantly. . . . The only way we can find of explaining Mr. Hawthorne's temper towards England is to suppose that he is jealous of us. He loves England so much, that he cannot endure those who possess her as their country. He contrasts his own love for what is old and venerable with our apparent indifference.

He admitted, however, "as we live in the sunshine of the substantial comforts and privileges that we enjoy, we can readily pardon a sharp word or two from the stranger across the seas . . . we in England are too well content to be sensitive; . . . let us turn again to the many beauties that lie thickly scattered through his book." The opinions of the bemused but gentle Bright were not likely to be mirrored by those held within the very heart of John Bull country and a Pavlovian reaction was duly recorded by *Punch* magazine:[20]

NATHANIEL HAWTHORNE, author of the *Scarlet Letter* and the *House with the Seven Gables* (you see we at once attempt to create a prejudice in your favour) you are a 'cute' man of business besides being a pleasing writer. We have often credited you with literary merit, and your style, dear boy, puts to shame a good many of our own writers who ought to write better than they do. But now let us have the new pleasure of congratulating you on showing that you are as smart a man, as much up to snuff, if you will pardon the colloquialism, as any Yankee publisher who ever cheated a British author. You have written a book about England, and into this book you have put all the caricatures and libels upon English folk, which you collected while enjoying our hospitality. Your book is thoroughly saturated with what seems ill-nature and spite. You then wait until the relations between America and England are unpleasant, until the Yankee public desires nothing better than good abuse of the Britisher, and then like a wise man, you cast your disagreeable book into the market. Now we like adroitness, even when displayed at our own expense, and we hope that the book will sell largely in America, and put no end of dollars to your account. There was once a person of your Christian name, who was said to be without guile. Most American pedigrees are dubious, but we think you would have a little extra trouble to prove your descent from NATHANIEL of Israel. In a word, you are a Smart Man, and we can hardly say anything more likely to raise you in the esteem of those for whom you have been composing. Come, there is none of the 'insular narrowness,' on which you complement us all, in this liberal tribute to your deserts. You see that in spite of what you say, 'these people' (the English) do not all 'think so loftily of themselves and so contemptuously of everybody else that it requires more generosity than you possess to keep always in perfectly good humour with them.' You will have no difficulty in keeping in perfectly good humour with us.

We are pleased with you, too, on another point. You stick at nothing, and we like earnestness. Not content with smashing up our male population in the most everlasting manner, you make the most savage onslaught upon our women. This will be doubly pleasant to your delicate-minded and chivalrous countrymen. And we are the more inclined to give you credit here, because you do not write of ladies whom you have seen at a distance, or in their carriages, or from the point of view of a shy and awkward man who sculks away at the rustle of a crinoline, and hides himself among the ineligibles at the ball-room door. Everybody knows that you have had ample opportunity of cultivating ladies' society, and have availed yourself of that opportunity to the utmost. Everybody in the world knows that the gifted American Consul at Liverpool is an idoliser of the ladies, and is one of the most ready, fluent, accomplished talkers of lady-talk that ever fascinated a sofa-full of smiling beauties. His gay and airy entrance into a drawing-room, his pleasant assurance and graceful courtesy, his evident revel in the refined atmosphere of perfume and *persiflage,* are proverbial, and therefore he is thoroughly acquainted with the nature and habits of English women. Consequently his tribute has a value which would not appertain to the criticisms of a sheepish person, either so inspired with a sense of his own infinite superiority, or so operated on by plebeian *mauvaise honte,* that he edges away from a lady, flounders and talks nonsense when compelled to answer her, and escapes with a red face, like a clumsy hobbadehoy, the moment a pause allows him to do so. No, no, this is the testimony of the lady-killer, the sparkling yet tender Liverpool Lovelace, NA-THANIEL HAWTHORNE, to the merits of our English women.

'English women seemed to me all homely alike. They seemed to be country lasses, of sturdy and wholesome aspect, with coarse-grained, cabbage-rosy cheeks, and, I am willing to suppose, a stout texture of moral principle, such as would bear a good deal of rough usage without suffering much detriment. But how unlike the trim little damsels of my native land! I desire above all things to be courteous.'

Courteous. Of course. How can the drawing-room idol be anything but courteous? He simply sketches our young ladies truthfully. Indeed he says so:—

'Since the plain truth must be told, the soil and climate of England produce feminine beauty as rarely as they do delicate fruit, and though admirable specimens of both are to be met with, they are the hot-house ameliorations of refined society, and apt, moreover, to relapse into the coarseness of the original stock. The men are man-like, but the women are not beautiful, though the female Bull be well enough adapted to the male.'

'The female Bull.' Cow would have been neater, and more entertaining, perhaps, to Broadway; but one would not mend after a master.

But our matrons. We, rather, in our weakness, piqued ourselves upon our matrons, with what we've thought their handsome faces, ready smiles, cheerful kindness, and tongues that talk freely because the hearts are innocent. Thanks to our Lovelace-Adonis, we now know that we must abandon this superstition. Here is his sketch of the English married lady of middle age:—

'She has an awful ponderosity of frame, not pulpy, like the looser development of our few fat women, but massive with solid beef and streaky tallow; so that (though struggling manfully against the idea) you inevitably think of her as made up of steaks and sirloins. When she walks, her advance is elephantine. When she sits down, it is on a great round space of her Maker's footstool, where she looks as if nothing could ever move her. She imposes awe and respect by the muchness of her personality, to such a degree that you probably credit her with greater moral and intellectual force than she can fairly claim. Her visage is usually grim and stern, seldom positively forbidding, yet calmly terrible.'

Calmly terrible. Is not this a momentary weakness, NATHANIEL? Can any created woman be terrible to you? Away, eater of hearts. You don't fear any matron. You show it in your next passage:—

'You may meet this figure in the street, and live, and even smile at the recollection. But conceive of her in a ball-room, with the bare brawny arms that she invariably displays there, and all the other corresponding development, such as is beautiful in the maiden blossom, but a spectacle to howl at in such an overblown cabbage-rose as this.'

Well painted, NATHANIEL, with a touch worthy of RUBENS, who was we think, your great uncle, or was it MILTON, or THERSITES, or somebody else, who, in accordance with American habit, was claimed as your ancestor. Never mind, you are strong enough in your own works to bear being supposed a descendant from a gorilla, were heraldry unkind. *Mr. Punch* makes you his best compliments on your smartness, and on the gracious elegance of your descriptions of those with whom you are known to have been so intimate, and he hopes that you will soon give the world a sequel to *Transformation,* in the form of an autobiography. For he is very partial to essays on the natural history of half-civilised animals.

Whether Nathaniel had seen all the reviews that appeared in England so far, up until November 1863 (presumably he read all the American ones) cannot be ascertained. Possibly Smith, Elder had felt it a duty to their author to send him the various reviews and he certainly received some of them through the good offices of his friends in England, much to his exasperation and anger. However, the reviews continued to appear on both sides of the Atlantic as there was no apparent slackening of interest in the book, as was evident from the volume of sales. Fields assured Nathaniel that it was selling "bravely" in America and asked him how his next book was progressing, and could he make some suitable announcement in the *Atlantic Monthly* in the New Year as to its probable publication? He also suggested that as he could "safely count on a handsome sum out of that book" he should "make another series. You cannot do better." But Nathaniel, despite trawling through his journals and diaries for good copy, was experiencing great difficulty in compiling more than a chapter or two and, in any case, couldn't think of a suitable title; besides, as he told Fields, he didn't feel well enough to get on with the writing, and he was depressed by the constant outflow of money for one thing and another (but Ticknor forwarded funds, of course, as soon as he heard of the need).

Two more reviews appeared in England, displaying the attitudes taken by most of the English critics, one being of the opinion that the whole thing was a disappointment, particularly as the book was by an author of Nathaniel's class, and taking offense at the unpleasant, unfamiliar, and uncharacteristically coarse tone of some of the writing, the other being of the view that there was nothing particularly in the book at which offense could be taken and that *more* severe criticism of the subject matter would have been welcome. The critic in *Blackwood's Magazine*[21] acknowledged that he was not one of Nathaniel's greatest admirers and in his article took five pages to explain why the book, in theory, could have been something extraordinary in the way of travel books and a further nineteen pages as to why the book (and the author) were both peculiarly disappointing:

What a deal of delicate machinery has been put in requisition to produce this book! A man of fine scholarly mind has been trained by time and thought and practice into a good novelist and a most excellent writer, whose finer fancies are never marred in expression for want of fittest language. He then spends several leisurely years among us, with an infinity of opportunity for studying us, and dreaming and poring over what he saw, till it should be sublimated in the subtle

Una, Julian, and Rose Hawthorne. Photograph ca. 1861. Reproduced by courtesy of Ms. Barbara L. Bacheler, Pittsburgh, Pa.

essences of the brain, and come to light idealised. Such are the elaborate means—
and, so far as the picture produced of the 'Old Home' goes, with what result? All
these complicated essences have been put in motion to tell us that people who
show public places in England expect money for their trouble, and that Englishmen
cannot exist without that diet of beef and beer which renders them the earthiest
of the earthy. Truly a remarkable sketch of a great people, and showing an insight
into their characteristics worthy of a profound philosopher. But there is still a
great deal of allowance to be made for the fact, that the work he had in hand, and
which may have been very dear to him, was marred by distracting influences,
which he was wroth at, and resented, perhaps, without due discrimination. There
are occupations in which no biped likes to be disturbed, and hatching is one of
them. Tread with ever so innocent intention near the sacred precincts where the
maternal fowl broods on the nest, and be she Dorking or Shanghae, bantam or
gallina, she will, as she flaps and scrambles from the nursery behind the orchard
fence, proclaim her injuries, and denounce you as a wrong-doer to the whole
neighbourhood. Mr. Hawthorne, who is, as we suppose, not rapid in elaborating
his conceptions, had, after a few years' residence in England, germinated an egg
which, could he have sat quietly upon it for a few years longer, would doubtless
have produced a charming chick. But lo! long before it could see the light, a great
turmoil arose in the West, and footsteps and voices were heard around, moving
to investigate and discuss the matter, and growing loud and shrill, and even angry;
till, scared by the increasing clamour, Nathaniel hurries from the nest, screaming
to the heavens a protest against the vile disturbers of the incubation, and leaving
them to comfort themselves as best they may with a view of the empty shell of
his addled romance.

Perhaps neither Smith, Elder nor any private correspondent forwarded a
copy of that particular review to Nathaniel! But by this time, it can be
considered that the liaison between Leamington Spa and the Hawthornes
had finally run its course and that memories of the spa and of the rest of
England were put aside and buried under the more tangible frustrations,
difficulties, and disappointments that increasingly came to dominate Nathaniel and the family's lives. Writing to Fields on 8 November that he had
"received several private letters and printed notices of Our Old Home, from
England," he said that "It is laughable to see the innocent wonder with
which they regard my criticisms, accounting for them by jaundice, insanity,
jealousy, hatred, on my part, and never admitting the least suspicion that
there may be a particle of truth in them. The monstrosity of their self-
conceit is such that anything short of unlimited admiration impresses them
as malicious caricature. But they do me great injustice in supposing that I
hate them. I would as soon hate my own people."[22]

The reviews continued to appear, the American ones applauding Nathaniel's maintenance of the genius of his style and not seeing anything amiss in
his opinions of the English scene and the English ones continuing to take
umbrage over his apparent Anglophobia. By this time, however, he had
ceased to take any notice of any of them and never referred to them again.
He became increasingly distressed over the state of the political situation
in America and the circumstances with regard to the Civil War that contin-

ued to rage, about his inability to continue with, let alone complete, the new book that Fields was waiting him to finish, about his finances, about death and illness in the families of some of his friends, and about his own growing incapacity to combat ill health.

The Times[23] in London now devoted half a page to *Our Old Home,* adopting a more relaxed attitude to the criticisms that Nathaniel had made about England and many things English, creating some unintentionally comic effects by its stately but somewhat pathetic attempts to assure its readers that they need not take the contents of the book much to heart as, basically, despite the writer being a genius in some respects, he was, after all, only a Yankee genius:

Mr. Hawthorne, is, after Washington Irving, the best prose writer that America has produced, and somewhat in Irving's manner he now favours us with a description of scenes in England, the old home of his fathers. All such works are interesting even if they are ill written. . . . Mr. Hawthorne's descriptions of England are particularly interesting, because he can write well, and he stayed among us for years. . . . As we glide over these easy pages we feel ourselves in the company of a gentle, kindly, pure-minded character, who, however hard he might try to smite us, cannot hurt us much, and might as well be pelting us with sugarplums and smothering us in roses. . . . Mr. Hawthorne's book is quite different from what—judging by the preface, and some of the opinions that have been passed on it, we were led to expect. We expected, from the preface, to find in it sharp writing, hard hitting, and good round abuse of old England . . . his blows fall on us like eider-down. . . . There is not a day in which we do not say of ourselves things infinitely harder than anything which Mr. Hawthorne has ventured to utter in his placid whispers. . . . And were Mr. Hawthorne, instead of being a mild, shy, and feminine person, a coarse, ill-grained Yankee, with all the bluster of Cape Cod in him, and brimming with hate for England, we should really pardon him . . . that he is willing to show bitterness of feeling to this country, not because he feels it, but because 'it happens to be tolerably well expressed'. . . . We believe that Mr. Hawthorne has a kindly feeling towards us notwithstanding his rather passionate objurgation of our stupidity in not making more of his countrymen, and some other attempts at recrimination. But why does he not allow the reverse of this? Why will he not allow that we may have the kindest feeling towards him and his, although we take the liberty of pointing out faults? The burden of this worthy gentleman's book is precisely that of an unhappy, jealous woman. . . . It is not pleasant to be told that we are boorish, and brutish, and selfish, but we can estimate these phrases at their proper worth when they are followed by expressions of real kindness towards us and lamentations over the deficiency of our love for the Americans. They long for our esteem and affection, and they lose heart and temper because they do not get all they want. . . . In these reflections we have dwelt chiefly on Mr. Hawthorne's opinions on men and women, and the relations between the two countries. We have not thought it necessary to spend time on his descriptions of our scenery nor to follow his footsteps from Liverpool to Leamington, and thence to Stratford. . . . The book is a readable one, but it will scarcely raise, perhaps it may lower, Mr. Hawthorne's reputation in English eyes. . . . We appreciate his powers highly, but among these are not to be reckoned the power of accurate statement and of sustained thought. . . . If it were worth while, we could easily show the laziness of Mr. Hawthorne as a thinker. . . . Even when he himself expresses a doubt as to the accuracy of his observation, he frankly declines the trouble of getting at the truth. If the fact which he relates is not true, why then it ought to be true, and that is enough. We do not pursue this enquiry, however, because to justify our criticism would require a very lengthy enumeration of trifles, and amid heaps of petty details we should seem to forget that Mr. Hawthorne has counter-balancing merits—a graceful style, an eye for the picturesque, and some true and subtle feeling.

By the New Year of 1864, memories of England were a thing of the past and the months passed as an accompaniment to the gradual diminution of Nathaniel's earthly powers, until his death on 19 May. Before that, however, three further reviews were published in England, varying in their opinions as to the worth of *Our Old Home* but acknowledging the genius of the author and, finally, unwittingly forecasting (in view of his untimely, premature death) the demise of the relationship between Nathaniel and the Old Country, though it was suggested that the relationship would be ended by the fact that the author would hardly dare to show his face again in England after publishing such opinions of its inhabitants. *The Westminster Review*[24] suggested that

To those who have the good sense to welcome rather than tolerate the expression of a national feeling that is not their own, these volumes will be the source of the greatest pleasure. The world has long since made up its mind on the remarkable ability of the author, and his account of the Old Home of the Americans displays, in some place or other, all his well-known merits, together with this new one— that they make us better acquainted with Mr. Hawthorne himself, an advantage that few will fail to avail themselves of, and fewer still will be the competent judges to whom better acquaintance will not also bring a better liking.

The Quarterly Review,[25] however, found much to complain of:

Mr. Hawthorne . . . only believes in one John Bull—the popular embodiment of beef and beer. . . . He also thinks us a one-eyed people, and the secret of our success is to be found in our way of shutting the other, so as to give the most distinct and decided view. . . . Mr. Hawthorne is almost as much oppressed in mind with what he elegantly terms the 'female Bull' as he is with the male. . . . In his experience of English character, and climate, and home, and its men and women, we find no warrant . . . for the bitterness of Mr. Hawthorne's book. Yet, from one end to the other, it is steeped in vinegar and gall. Something of this may come from the great national calamity; the 'Star, Wormwood' has fallen into the stream of American life, and turned it into blood for them, and bitterness for us. . . . We have no wish to see the ruin of Mr. Hawthorne's country, and trust that it may yet be averted. . . . We have not the least consolation for those who would not mind marching to ruin with their own country, if upheld by the proud thought that England also was doomed to a speedy fall. There is not the least sign of such a consummation, devoutly as it may be wished. . . .

And finally, *The Christian Remembrancer,*[26] while presuming the sincerity of Nathaniel's opinions assumed that the book was a kind of farewell, in that he could hardly show his face again in a country with which he had so uncompromisingly (in parts) expressed his disenchantment. . . . Taking our view of Mr. Hawthorne's impressions, we can scarcely call ourselves dissatisfied. There are no doubt many unpleasant things to digest as we can; and he often talks of the English people with a positive alienation. But the more these passages evince an eradicable prejudice, the more the admission of our good points extracted from his candour gain in value; and there are besides many warm voluntary testimonies to English hospitality, English integrity, English friendship, and English feeling, which engage—indeed, compel—our kindly feeling towards our author. Yet we suspect he does not mean to tread again on British ground; this book is farewell. He dare not again face the ladies; and knowing it to be human nature—man's as well as woman's—to retain satire and vituperation longer in the memory than the more ordinary language of civility and compliment, he might doubt his general reception on a second visit. But the work is, as every genuine record of impressions on important subjects and vast scenes of action must be, a useful and suggestive book. It tells us something even of ourselves, as reflected in a mind trained under influences opposite in many respects to our own, and it is a valuable lesson in habits of American thought, as expressed with much versatility and many graces of style by one of New England's model men.

And so the liaison was ended or, rather, had foundered. Whatever the reasons had been for Nathaniel having included in *Our Old Home* sentiments that antagonized many English people (or reviewers, at least), sentiments that were in one form or another, to a greater or lesser degree, to be found in his original journal entries, but that were then particularized and emphasized for the American market in the selection process that resulted in the articles for the *Atlantic Monthly* and the subsequent book, the memories of Leamington and of the Old Country were drowned in the rising waves of personal loss, disillusion, and ill health that marked the remaining months of his life. In December 1863, Jane Pierce, Franklin's wife, had died. In April 1864, Ticknor died in a Philadelphia hotel room, watched over by Nathaniel and finally, in May, during a trip to New Hampshire with Pierce, Nathaniel died peacefully in his sleep; peacefully, though in some quarters and "in family legend" it is held that "Nathaniel came to his untimely death [at the relatively early age of sixty] . . . because he could not overcome the torment aroused in him by Una's illness."[27]

The return to America in 1860 had not proved to be the happiest of homecomings and the few years since then had not brought contentment or lasting happiness to the family or any real artistic achievement on Nathaniel's part. Nor did the succeeding years result in a permanent alleviation of the consequences of his death for the rest of the family. Dwindling financial resources forced Sophia to produce versions of her husband's notebooks in the *Atlantic Monthly,* and in book form, but due to a mistaken suspicion on her part of Fields's arrangements concerning her royalties she lost his trust and friendship. She accompanied Julian to Dresden in Germany for the purposes of furthering his education and then went back to England, where she died in 1871. After Nathaniel's death, Una began to display increasingly difficult personality problems that could be related to the effects of the Roman illness, the loss of her father, and to an unsatisfactory relationship with Sophia. She was left with little purpose to her existence and suffered greatly from the emotional effects of a broken engagement with an army chaplain. She went to Germany with Sophia and Julian and then with Sophia to England, where she suffered a further emotional blow through her love for an American, George Lathrop, being rejected in favor of his eventual marriage to Rose. After returning to America she became engaged again, but her fiancé died of tuberculosis, and following a return to England, where she remained for some time in a convent, she died in 1871, aged thirty-three, being buried beside her mother in Kensal Green cemetery in London. Rose received little real educational benefit or emotional stability following the return to America in 1860, and after living in Germany and England with the rest of the family, she married George Lathrop. But the marriage was not a happy one. In 1895 she entered a Catholic order and achieved some sort of personal fulfillment through the care of terminally ill patients; she died in 1926, in New York. Julian led a very checkered life after his education at Harvard and in Dresden. He married while living in Germany and returned to America, leaving Sophia, Una, and Rose to fend for themselves. He and his wife had several children but, as with Rose, the marriage was not a happy one and in 1925, almost immediately after his wife's death, he married his companion of the previous quarter century. Throughout his long life (he died in 1934), Julian found it well-nigh impossible to create a persona of his own, always being known, rather, as "Hawthorne's son."

All four of them—Sophia, Una, Rose, and Julian—wrote books that were connected in one way or another with Nathaniel, despite his injunctions against the publication of biographical material. Even though his popularity declined all four of them decided, for various reasons, to cash in upon his literary fame though they were genuinely concerned with his reputation and with the presentation to the public eye of his personal attraction and the benefits of their somewhat unorthodox family life. Julian, in particular, wrote often of his memories of Nathaniel and also wrote novels of his own but they never achieved a fraction of the lasting fame and distinction commanded by his father.

Not much went right for the family after they had left England, no real and lasting personal happiness. As suggested, it could be that the return to Concord in 1860 was a mistake although there were many circumstances that combined to cast a golden haze over the prospect of a regeneration of their American roots and made it desirable and necessary to leave behind the apparent disappointments, and positive dangers, that they had experienced as a result of of their existence both in England and on the Continent. Although the family was divided in the degree of enthusiasm with which it viewed the prospect of having left behind such places as Liverpool, Leamington Spa, London, and Rome in favor of a return to grassroots, it was perhaps a personally accurate statement of his true feelings (feelings that were not shared by his family at the time) that Nathaniel confided to Harriet Beecher Stowe on board the *Europa* as it left England and steamed its way across the Atlantic to America: "I wish we might never get there."

Notes and References

Abbreviations

BERG	The Henry W. and Albert A. Berg Collection, The New York Public Library, Astor, Lenox and Tilden Foundations
BEINECKE	The Beinecke Rare Book and Manuscript Library of Yale University, New Haven, Conn.
CE	*The Centenary Edition of the Works of Nathaniel Hawthorne.* General eds. Thomas Goodson, William Charvat, Roy Harvey Pearce, and Claude M. Simpson. Columbus: Ohio State University Press, 1962 onward
DB	*Dearly Beloved: The Hawthornes and the Making of the Middle-Class Family.* T. Walter Herbert. Berkeley. University of California Press. 1993
EN	*The English Notebooks of Nathaniel Hawthorne*: (ed.) Randall Stewart. New York: Russell and Russell, 1941
HC	*Hawthorne and His Circle.* Julian Hawthorne. New York: Harper, 1903
LA	*The Leamington Advertiser*
MHS	The Massachusetts Historical Society, Boston, Mass.
NHEE	*Nathaniel Hawthorne: The English Experience.* Raymona A. Hull. Pittsburgh: University of Pittsburgh Press, 1980
NHW	*Nathaniel Hawthorne and His Wife.* Julian Hawthorne. Boston: Osgood, 1884
PE	Peabody Essex Museum, Salem, Mass.
PM	The Pierpont Morgan Library, New York
RLSC	*The Royal Leamington Spa Courier*
STP	*Shapes that Pass.* Julian Hawthorne. Boston: Houghton Mifflin, 1928

Prologue: Life before Leamington

1. DB
2. Official Correspondence Inwards: National Archives, Washington, D.C.
3. As is suggested in a letter of Sophia's, commenced on 11 July, to her sister, Mary. In NHEE it states that a guidebook had been purchased. If it had been a well-known one, such as *Black's Picturesque Tourist and Road and Railway Guide Book through England and Wales,* the description of Leamington read as follows:

> Two miles from Warwick is Leamington, or Leamington Priors, one of the most fashionable spas in the kingdom. It is pleasantly situated on the Leam, which is crossed by a handsome bridge. The waters are used, both internally and for the purpose of

bathing, and are found very efficacious in many chronic disorders, in diseases of the skin, and visceral obstructions. The principal buildings are the new pump-room and baths, which are supposed to be the most elegant in Europe; the assembly-rooms, concert and ball-rooms, the reading-rooms and library, the billiard-room, the Regent Hotel, the museum and picture gallery, the theatre, &c. The Ranelagh and Priory Gardens form delightful promenades. Leamington possesses also two churches, an Episcopal chapel, a meeting-house, a Roman Catholic chapel, an institution for the gratuitous supply of baths to the poor, national schools, several libraries, &c. The rides and walks in the vicinity are interesting and attractive; and very delightful excursions may be made to Warwick Castle, Kenilworth, Stratford, &c. Pop. 1851, 15,692.

Chapter 1: Leamington, that "handsome" town: June 1855

1. The journey took them through Chester, Wrexham, Ruabon, Oswestry, Shrewsbury, Wolverhampton, and Warwick. Bradshaw's *Threepenny Guide to all the Railways*, June 1855.

2. *Prince Henry*:   Why, Percy I killed myself, and saw thee dead.

    Falstaff: Did'st thou? Lord, Lord, how this world is given to
                      lying! I grant you I was down, and out of breath,
                      and so was he, but we rose both at an instant, and
                      fought a long hour by Shrewsbury clock.

I Henry IV act 5, scene 5

3. Farquhar: *Recruiting Officer*: "To all Friends round the Wrekin": Congreve: *Way of the World*, etc.

4. EN.

5. In NHEE it states that the weather had improved by the time the Hawthornes had reached Leamington, that "the sun had come out and the air seemed fresh and warm," basing this assertion on Sophia's journal fragment of two pages, one of them dated 23 June. At one point in my research, it appeared that the latter two pages might be connected with the fragment of Sophia's journal further on in this chapter but this proved to be incorrect. The two pages referred to (to be found in BERG) are annotated as being in an "unknown hand" but that appears to be Sophia's. They are actually a copy (or rough draft?) of part of Nathaniel's journal entry dated 22 and 23 June 1855 (EN) and thus refer to weather conditions of a different day to that of the family's arrival in Leamington.

6. LA: 21 June 1855.

7. RLSC: 23 June 1855.

8. PM: (MA.588): There is some mystery concerning this short and incomplete journal entry by Sophia. It is written on a loose sheet, the sheet having come from a notebook that "Hawthorne started using . . . in 1853. Sophia made some jottings in 1855 and then Hawthorne took it up again in 1858. The two pages containing the rest of Sophia's entry for 22 June 1855 were probably sliced out of the Morgan MS (before it came to this library) and made their way in the Berg Collection." This particular notebook must have been lost on occasions, as during the years between 1853 and 1858 Nathaniel made many entries in his journals, filling a number of separate notebooks, yet this one appears to have survived, uncompleted, over a period of five years.

9. The second daughter of Robert Manning, one of Nathaniel's uncles.

10. The location of this letter, if it is extant, is unknown to me.

11. The elder daughter of Sophia's brother, Nathaniel Peabody; the location of this letter, if it is extant, is unknown to me.

12. The Steeles are an unknown quantity.

13. PE: Hawthorne-Manning Collection: MSS.69.

14. For example, Fanny was entrusted with finding lodgings on the occasion of the Hawthornes' second visit to Leamington (Nathaniel's journal entry of 10 September 1857), while in March 1860, after leaving Leamington for Bath, Sophia, Fanny, and Rose joined forces in the hunt for suitable lodgings.

15. EN.

16. Information supplied by Mr. Bill Gibbons, Leamington Spa.

17. EN.

18. RLSC: 23 June 1855.

19. EN.

20. RLSC: 23 June 1855.

21. One of Nathaniel's quarterly accounts, rendered to the State Department for reimbursement of his consular expenses.

22. A new law had been passed on 20 April in Massachusetts, requiring liquor to be manufactured only under license and permitting the sale of such liquor only by authorized agents.

23. CE: vol. 17, 357–58.

24. PE: Hawthorne Family Papers: MSS.68.

25. EN.

26. Ibid.

27. RLSC: 30 June 1855.

28. The elm had a reputation of being a thousand years old. It lasted for another 105 years after the Hawthornes saw it, finally being bulldozed down by a council contractor as one stage of the "streamlining plans for the Green." So a centuries-old, historical, living thing (with who knows how many more years of life in it), which was the focus of local pride and Whitnash's community spirit, was sacrificed for the pathetic, wooden, four-seater bench that took its place. RLSC: 15 January 1960 and Jean Field's *Beneath the Great Elms: an Illustrated History of Whitnash* Studley, Warwickshire: Brewin Books, 1993.

29. EN.

30. After reconstruction, the new chancel was opened at Ascensiontide, 1856.

31. From this description, it is clear that they had walked along the Emscote Road from Leamington to Warwick, on which one can still get the middle-distance view of St. Mary's church tower, particularly from the bridge over the Warwick and Napton canal. The school is now St. John's Museum.

32. Having passed the school, they must now be in Smith Street.

33. They had now reached the East Gate, at the top of Smith Street. The "arched gate way" is still a public thoroughfare, though pedestrianized, the traffic going to one side of the gateway, down Smith Street. The "church" on top of the gateway is now part of King's High School for Girls.

34. The soldiers had gone up Jury Street, into Church Street.

35. EN.

36. Ibid.

37. Compare this with his feelings after visiting Sir Walter Scott's house at Abbotsford in May 1856: "there is no simple and great impression left by Abbotsford; and I felt angry and dissatisfied with myself for not feeling something which I did not and could not feel. But it is just like going to a museum, if you look into particulars; and one learns from it, too, that Scott could not have been a really wise man, nor an earnest one, nor one that grasped the truth of life;—he did but play, and the play grew very sad towards its close. In a certain way, however, I understand his romances the better for having seen his house; and his house the better, for having

read his romances. They throw light on one another." One wonders what Nathaniel would have thought of the present, immensely popular, highly sanitized birthplace at Stratford.

38. Did Nathaniel surreptitiously give the forty-seven-year-old Sophia a leg up onto the tomb, with the children on guard?

39. In Nathaniel's journal entry, the phaeton dropped them off at the Red Lion inn (although he calls it a hotel) but according to Sophia's Accounts Book, they had lunch at the Red Horse hotel, just across the road from the Red Lion.

40.   *First Lord*: Indeed my Lord,
         The melancholy Jacques grieves at that;
         And, in that kind, swears you do more usurp
         Than doth your brother that hath banish'd you.
         To-day my Lord of Amiens and myself
         Did steal behind him as he lay along
         Under an oak whose antique root peeps out
         Upon the brook that brawls along this wood;
         To the which place a poor sequester'd stag
         That from the hunter's aim had ta'en a hurt,
         Did come to languish; and indeed, my lord,
         The wretched animal heav'd forth such groans
         That their discharge did stretch his leathern coat
         Almost to bursting, and the big round tears
         Cours'd one another down his innocent nose
         In piteous chase.

                                         As You Like It, act 2, scene 1

41. Refer to S. Schoenbaum's *William Shakespeare; A Documentary Life*: New York: Oxford University Press: 1975 for the facts, as far as they are known, regarding the deer-stealing saga (he is dubious as to its having taken place) and to Eric Sams's *The Real Shakespeare.* New Haven: Yale University Press, 1995, for a different opinion.

42. EN.

43. RLSC: 30 June 1855.

44. Nathaniel *had* met him, at a party that Longfellow had held in June 1853 prior to the Hawthornes' departure for England.

45. BERG: Nathaniel was also acquainted with Ralph Waldo Emerson, the American transcendentalist author, poet, lecturer, and philosopher; the two men had a somewhat guarded and cynical respect for each other's work. Henry Arthur Bright, a businessman, literary critic, author, and Unitarian, lived in Liverpool and became one of the few Englishmen for whom Nathaniel had some real regard.

46. CE: vol. 17, 359.

47. What a drag those last few hours must have been! They had boarded by mistake the 4:45 P.M. train at Coventry and arrived at Brandon (the next station down the line in the wrong direction—toward London) at 4:55 P.M.; back to Coventry on the 5:48 P.M., arriving at 6:01 P.M.; after cooling their heels in Coventry and waiting for the 7:40 P.M. train to Leamington, they had arrived there at 8:15 P.M. *Bradshaw's Railway Guide,* June 1855.

48. EN.

49. Ibid.

Chapter 2. "Perfectly clean" Leamington: July 1855

1. CE: vol. 17, p. 361.

2. Benjamin Moran's *Journal* (vol. 1): 31 August 1857.

3. BERG.

4. Ibid.

5. By Monday, 2 July, Nathaniel had already extended his absence from the consulate beyond the ten days allowed by the rules governing a consul's permitted leave of absence (in excess of which, in theory, he was to remain unpaid for the duration), but in view of his leisurely movements during Monday and Tuesday he was apparently not too concerned about that. The new bill relating to United States consuls was to take effect on 1 July but was later delayed until the following 1 January 1856. In NHW there is a paragraph: "Just before that event [a visit by the family to the Lake District], however, the law had been passed by Congress, reducing the emoluments of the consulate by a serious amount. Wilding had written to Hawthorne, under the date of 29 June, that it would be put in force on Monday. 'What war-vessels,' he adds, 'are now in, must of course come under the old law. Under the Attorney-General's construction, I think the Consul—here at all events—may manage to make their expenses.'" The location of this letter from Wilding, indeed any of the letters that Wilding sent to Nathaniel while he was in Leamington during this or any other year, if they are extant, is unknown to me.

6. EN.

7. Henry Sacheverell, a political preacher, was impeached for inflammatory sermons delivered at Derby and St. Paul's in 1709 and was sentenced by the Lords in 1710 to a suspension from preaching for the next three years. Thus, although Boswell included the story in his *Life,* it seems unlikely that Johnson could actually have been present at a Sacheverell sermon in any case, during his early childhood;

> Yet there is a traditional story of the infant Hercules of toryism, so curiously characteristick, that I shall not withold it. It was communicated to me in a letter from Miss Mary Adye, of Lichfield. 'When Dr. Sacheverell was at Lichfield, Johnson was not quite three years old. My grandfather Hammond observed him at the cathedral perched upon his father's shoulders, listening and gaping at the much celebrated preacher. Mr Hammond asked Mr Johnson how he could possibly think of bringing an infant to church, and in the midst of so great a crowd. He answered, because it was impossible to keep him at home; for, young as he was, he believed he had caught the publick spirit and zeal for Sacheverell, and would have staid for ever in the church, satisfied with beholding him.' Boswell's *The Life of Samuel Johnson.*

8. "In short, he is a remarkable instance of what has often been observed, that the boy is the man in miniature: and that the distinguishing characteristicks of each individual are the same, through the whole course of life. His favourites used to receive very liberal assistance from him; and such was the submission and deference with which he was treated, such the desire to obtain his regard, that three of the boys, of whom Mr. Hector was sometimes one, used to come in the morning as his humble attendants, and carry him to school. One in the middle stooped, while he sat upon his back, and one on each side supported him: and thus he was borne triumphant. . . ." Boswell's *The Life of Samuel Johnson.*

9. "But there has been another story of his infant precocity generally circulated, and generally believed, the truth of which I am to refute upon his own authority. It is told, that, when a child of three years old, he chanced to tread upon a duckling, the eleventh of a brood, and killed it; upon which, it is said, he dictated to his mother the following couplet:

> Here lies good master duck,
> Whom Samuel Johnson trod on
> If it had liv'd, it had been *good* luck,
> For then we'd had an *odd one*."
>
> Boswell's *The Life of Samuel Johnson*

10. Richard Cockle Lucas, 1800–1883, a very successful (if minor) sculptor, medallionist, etcher, and author.

11. The house *is* there (in Dam Street) complete with an inscription over the door, so Nathaniel could not have searched too hard. But it is not the original house that was standing at the time of the Civil War.

12. A friend of Johnson's, one-time registrar of the Ecclesiastical Court of Lichfield, of whom Johnson said he could not name "a man of equal knowledge."

13. It was the spring of 1718 in Istanbul, where his parents had come on an embassy from London. The boy's mother was Lady Mary Wortley Montague and she had volunteered him as a guinea-pig in an experimental inoculation against small-pox. The embassy physician described the technique of the "old Greek woman, who had practised in this way for many years," selected by Lady Mary to perform the operation, "so awkwardly by the shaking of her hand." She "put the child to so much torture with her blunt and rusty needle that I pitied his cries." Yet the experiment was a merciful success and when London was threatened with an epidemic in 1721, Lady Mary repeated it on her daughter, converting society to the practice in consequence. Previous efforts by savants to introduce vaccination had been "regarded as virtuoso amusements"; now, however, Lady Mary fulfilled an ambition she had conceived as a patriotic duty, on seeing an inoculation performed at Adrianople, "to bring this useful invention into England". (Felipe Fernandez-Armesto. *Millennium*. New York: Bantam Press, 1995.)

14. A British officer to whom Benedict Arnold, the American traitor, delivered the plan for the betrayal of West Point during the American Revolution and who was executed as a spy in 1780.

15. "To Mr. Henry White, a young clergyman, with whom he now formed an intimacy, so as to talk to him with great freedom, he mentioned that he could not in general accuse himself of having been an undutiful son. 'Once, indeed, (said he) I was disobedient; I refused to attend my father to Uttoxeter market. Pride was the source of that refusal, and the remembrance of it was painful. A few years ago, I desired to atone for this fault; I went to Uttoxeter in very bad weather, and stood for a considerable time bareheaded in the rain, on the spot where my father's stall used to stand. In contrition I stood, and I hope the penance was expiatory.'" Boswell's *The Life of Samuel Johnson*.

16. There appeared in the 1857 edition of *The Keepsake* Nathaniel's short account of this visit to Uttoxeter, retaining in it the somewhat unsympathetic portrayal of the town and its inhabitants and his disappointment at not having found a suitable monument to Johnson's penance. The article was reprinted in the local (Uttoxeter) *Era* newspaper and it created some ill-feeling among the town's citizens. It was not until 1877, however, that a copy was made of that side of the Johnson memorial in Lichfield that related to the penance in Uttoxeter and placed on the small building enclosing the conduit and weighing machine in Uttoxeter marketplace (which is now used as a newspaper kiosk). It was, and still is, a matter of some dispute, locally, as to where the penance was supposed to have taken place; Francis Redfern's *History and Antiquities of the Town and Neighbourhood of Uttoxeter* (1865) placed it at the east end of the marketplace (relying on oral evidence by a local, aged inhabitant) but (during 1994) the various bars of the Old Talbot pub (at the west end of the marketplace) were being refurbished with a motif that suggested the penance had taken place outside the pub's doors, on the site of the former conduit.

17. Nathaniel had been plucking names out of the air when referring to the Cross Keys, Mitre, and Bull's Head, as there were no pubs with those names in Uttoxeter at that time. The Nag's Head was pulled down in 1878 and rebuilt as The Vine, which, in turn, was demolished in 1891; the site is presently occupied by the Derbyshire Building Society offices.

18. EN.

19. There could be some confusion experienced when attempting to clarify the particular days and dates of events during the first half of the week commencing Monday, 2 July. The entry dated "Wednesday July 4th 1855" in EN relates the events of Monday and Tuesday, 2 and 3 July. The last few lines of the entry read: "N.B. The boy above-mentioned said he resided in Uttoxeter. I mentioned my pilgrimage to Mr. Bright to-day; and neither had he any recollection of this incident in Johnson's life, nor seemed ever to have heard the name of Uttoxeter." But Bright did not, presumably, know of Nathaniel's presence in Liverpool until, at least, Thursday, 5 July after his receipt of Nathaniel's letter of that day (but that he *could* have received the same day and *immediately* rushed over to see the lonely consul). So the "N.B." at the end of the Wednesday, 4 July 1855 entry must have been added at least one or two days after 4 July. The next entry in Nathaniel's journal, "July 6th Friday," also contains a slight confusion, insofar as it starts "The day after my arrival, the door of the Consulate opened. . . ." I have taken this to mean the day after his first day back at the office, that is, Thursday, 5 July.

20. So far, Dr. Washington Evans remains a mysterious, unknown figure.

21. EN.

22. Bright's home.

23. The home of the Heywoods (particularly *Mrs.* Heywood) where, after an initial refusal on his part, Nathaniel was entertained on several occasions.

24. CE: vol. 17, 363.

25. A book by Charles Reade, another of Ticknor and Fields's authors.

26. CE: vol. 17, 364–65.

27. There was one of the queerest cases of a foolish American that I ever heard of, yesterday, in the person of a man who came to my office for assistance. . . . Some years ago, this man had two children, whom he named after Victoria and Prince Albert; and he sent the Queen daguerreotype-portraits of the children, his wife and himself. The gift was acknowledged by the Queen, in a letter from her equerry. . . . ; and on the strength of this letter, the poor devil has come over to present himself to her Majesty hoping, no doubt, for some great advantage from her friendship. During the voyage, he became acquainted with a German, who borrowed almost all his money under false pretences, and has lived upon him until the remainder is spent—and has now disappeared, leaving him penniless. In this condition, he presents himself at the Consulate. There certainly is something in Royalty, and the institutions connected therewith, that turns the Republican brain. EN: 7 June 1855.

28. EN.

29. BERG.

30. The Civil Reference Branch of the National Archives, Washington, D.C., has confirmed that there are no copies of letters on the Liverpool Consul Registers of Correspondence Outwards and Inward, of this period, between Liverpool and Leamington.

31. The location of this letter, if it is extant, is unknown to me.

32. Probably the elderly Miss Rawlins Pickman of Salem, a friend of Mary's for many years.

33. Their brother, Nathaniel Peabody.

34. Presumably Nathaniel's daughter, Sophia's niece. Perhaps Ellen wrote of her love for George Phineas How, of Concord, whom she was to marry four years later.

35. Probably Catharine Kelly, Mary's "perfect treasure" in the house.

36. Rebecca Pennell, Horace Mann's niece, the daughter of his sister, Mrs. Rebecca Mann Pennell. She had married the Reverend Austin Scannell Dean the preceding 16 July. Rebecca was a teacher at Antioch College, of which Horace Mann was president. The two of them did not always see eye to eye on curriculum matters, and the fact that the Reverend Dean's part in the raising of funds for the new college

was viewed with some suspicion by those concerned with proper accounting proce-
dures did nothing toward healing any hurt feelings in the family. The honeymoon
was spent on a trip to Europe.

37. For some reason, Nathaniel had not seen the need to include this little episode in his own description of the visit to Coventry. Perhaps he had forgotten about
it when writing the entry or, maybe, he had been so embarrassed by the outburst
that he had not thought it necessary to record it!

38. For a nine-year-old boy it is quite a formidable list of reading matter, one
result of the children's education having been undertaken by their parents; she could
have added other authors, such as Scott, Macaulay, Swift, and De Quincey, with
whose works the children were familiar. Both Nathaniel and Sophia were keen on
reading aloud to them in the evenings from such enlightening sources.

39. Their sister, Elizabeth Peabody.

40. Possibly a reference to Mary's occasional habit (and not hers alone) of completing letters by writing the last lines of them across (vertically) what had already
been written on the first few pages, thus saving space and cutting down on the
number of sheets of paper, but also thereby creating great difficulties in the deciphering of various words (both for her contemporaries and future generations).

41. The bark of the North American Red Elm, *Ulmus fulva,* was used medicinally
(apparently one chewed it!).

42. It is interesting that Sophia persists in referring to "Shakspere" rather than
Shakespear, Shakespeer, Shake-spear, or Shakespeare. Her spelling of the Bard's
name has come to be associated (in some quarters) with the controversy concerning
the identity of the real author of Shakespeare's plays, a controversy that began well
before 1855. It sounds as though Sophia *had* had some doubts on the subject but
that the book had convinced her of the error of her ways. It is almost impossible to
determine which book ("written some time ago") she had been reading; perhaps
Robert Bell Wheeler's *History and Antiquities of Stratford-upon-Avon* (1806), or his
Guide to Stratford-upon-Avon (1814), or (most unlikely) Nathan Drake's *Shakespeare
and His Times* (1817), all seventeen hundred pages and two volumes of it (!); or
Augustine Skottowe's *Life of Shakespeare* (1824), another two-volume work; or
Charles Knight's *William Shakespeare: A Biography* (1843); or, more likely, James
Halliwell's *Life of Shakespeare* (1848). It is to be hoped that Sophia did not read
any of John Payne Collier's works on the subject, as they incorporated opinions
based on facts that were related to his own forgeries of historical documents. There
are, moreover, several other possibilities; refer to S. Schoenbaum's huge and vastly
entertaining *Shakespeare's Lives:* New York: Oxford University Press, 1970 and
Warren Hope and Kim Holston's *The Shakespeare Controversy:* Jefferson, North
Carolina: McFarland & Co., 1992.

43.   The ousel-cock so black of hue,
        With orange-tawny bill,
        The throstle with his note so true,
        The wren with little quill.
        A Midsummer Night's Dream, act 2, scene 1

44.   When daisies pied and violets blue
        And lady-smocks all silvery-white
        And cuckoo-buds of yellow hue
        Do paint the meadows with delight.
        Love's Labours Lost, act 5, scene 2

45.   Hark, Hark! the lark at heaven's gate sings
        And Phoebus 'gins arise,

His steeds to water at those springs,
On chaliced flowers that lies.
Cymbeline, act 2, scene 3

46. Full many a glorious morning have I seen
Flatter the mountain-tops with sovereign eye,
Kissing with golden face the meadows green,
Gilding with pale streams with heavenly alchemy.
Sonnets, 33

47. See, see, King Richard doth himself appear
As doth the blushing discontented sun
From out the fiery portal of the east,
When he perceives the envious clouds are bent
To dim his glory and to stain the track
Of his bright passage to the occident.
King Richard II, act 3, scene 3

48. Perhaps it is a little unfair to point out that Nathaniel's own description of his feelings at this particular point in their journey does not suggest that they were quite so sublime as Sophia would have us believe.

49. Francis George Shaw and Sarah Blake Shaw (née Sturgis); Sarah, in particular, was an old friend of Sophia's.

50. This must have been Mary Stanley, detailed in the 1851 census as "Head of the family" (i.e., a widow), living at 22 Henley Street and being the "Exhibitor of the House in which Shakespear [!] was born."

51. BERG.This is where the letter ends, though quite obviously not finished, but the rest appears not to have been recovered.

52. This is the second time that it had happened within a month; see Una's letter to her cousin Richard of 18 June/1 July.

53. A medicine/tincture prepared from the Mountain Tobacco plant, and others, which would have been used by Sophia as a homeopathic prescription for curing almost anything: see Boericke's *Homoeopathic Materia Medica.*

54. This is the first time that the owner's name at No. 13 Lansdowne Crescent is mentioned. Mrs. Price was not in residence when the 1851 census was taken and her name does not appear in the *Warwickshire Directories* of 1850 and 1854 but she does figure in the 1860 edition, as a lodging-house keeper.

55. BERG.

Chapter 3. An Intermission (1)

1. United States Statutes at Large: X.623.

2. CE: vol. 20, 101.

3. BERG.

4. LA: no one is listed as being in occupation in the edition of 3 September but Miss York's name does appear in the 10 September edition (a Thursday) so it is possible that she got there *just* before Fanny did.

5. Mrs. Maloney's name, together with her occupation of "lodging-house

keeper" at No. 10 Lansdowne Circus, appears in the *Warwickshire Directories* of 1850, 1854, and 1860.

Chapter 4. "Genteel" Leamington: September 1857

1. EN.
2. It is of interest, however, that when Nathaniel wrote to Bennoch on the following 26 October to arrange lodgings elsewhere, he described the Lansdowne Circus accommodation as "five bedrooms, a parlor and dining-room" and said that in a pinch they might all "possibly exist with four bedrooms, but scarcely be comfortable," when he was referring to their party of four adults and three children.
3. The location of this letter, if it is extant, is unknown to me.
4. The Corner was that part of the Ticknor and Fields premises in Boston that had been partitioned off, which came to be used as a kind of literary/social club, where Nathaniel could often be found (usually in the background, usually silent).
5. CE: vol. 18, 95–96.
6. EN: 2 September 1853. A year previously, in a letter of 14 April 1852, he had commented on the depressing fact that in the first ten years of his married life, he and the family had already occupied seven different homes. Alas, the years 1857–60 were to be merely a continuation of their nomadic way of life, and even when they returned to America and the Wayside in 1860 it so turned out that there were to be only four more years left for him in which to settle down, and still he did not find real peace and contentment.
7. The location of this letter, if it is extant, is unknown to me.
8. Presumably James Freeman Clarke, brother of Sophia's old friend, Sarah.
9. The location of these letters, if they are extant, is unknown to me.
10. The location of Sophia's letter, if it is extant, is unknown to me.
11. BERG. On the back of the final page of this letter is a note in Elizabeth Peabody's handwriting: "Dear Mary Mann—Mary Long will send this to you—Then you can return it to Nat's family to read who may then return it to me as I value every scrap—you see there is a sheet abstracted—" The last two paragraphs of Sophia's letter (commencing "The reason why. . . .") are on a sheet that is filed separately in BERG as being part of an incomplete (and supposedly different) letter to Elizabeth Peabody. As these two paragraphs fill exactly two sides of one sheet of paper, they form a natural progression (both physically and from the point of view of the contents) of the letter that Sophia started on 9 September, carrying on from the eighth side (that ends ". . . very sweet and satisfactory."). It seems reasonable to assume that this separate sheet is the one referred to by Elizabeth Peabody as the "abstracted" sheet, so I have included it here.
12. It is interesting to speculate as to how much cooperation there was between husband and wife when writing their separate journals and letters, and from which of them originated certain phrases and details that are common to both. This entry by Nathaniel in his journal, for instance, was written on the day following the actual events, that is, Friday, 11 September. He includes this idea of any flat piece of ground being cultivated and improved by the English by the organized propagation of trees, flowers, and shrubbery; the same idea had already been included in Sophia's letter to Elizabeth, written two days previously, on 9 September. Other examples could be quoted and it could cause some speculation as to where Nathaniel (whose descriptive capabilities are well-known to all, as his journals have been published in full) may have gotten a certain proportion of his ideas. Sophia's letters and journals have not been published in full, to my knowledge, and so the copyright of a number of her

husband's ideas and phrases may, in fact, belong to her. Nathaniel was always ready to acknowledge his wife's talents as a writer, though he was also never in favor of her efforts being dignified by an appearance in print.

13. Not strictly true; it was Messrs. Satchwell and Abbotts who started it all, at the end of the eighteenth century.

14. Hopelessly wrong; Dr. Jephson died in 1878, fourteen years after Nathaniel!

15. EN.

16. Just what Nathaniel saw when looking at the church of St. Mary Magdelene on 10 September 1857 is not entirely clear. The original Norman church was rebuilt in ca. 1350, only the doorway in the chapel and the south wall, with one and a half arches of the chancel remaining from the original church. This, in turn, was rebuilt in "the middle of the last [nineteenth] century," incorporating the oldest remnants of the Norman church. The fifteenth-century tower was retained. The north side of the arcade in the nave was built in 1847, as was the north aisle. The south side of the arcade in the nave and the south aisle were built in 1858. The chancel, still retaining the oldest remnants of the earliest church, was rebuilt in 1884. Quite what was the "stained window (of recent date)" that he saw is rather difficult to pinpoint. In theory, the church should have presented an aspect rather akin to a builder's yard, according to the facts as shown in William Cooper's *The History of Lillington: Shipston-on-Stour: King's Stone Press, 1940, from which these details are taken.

17. Nathaniel and Julian's walk to Cubbington can be followed just as easily today, though there is a choice of two routes. Coming out of Lansdowne Circus, a left turn leads into Upper Holly Walk that in turn leads into the made-up footpath up Newbold Hill. With the distant view of Warwick Castle on the left, the road should be followed right along Black Lane and round, in its narrower continuation, almost into Redhouse Farm. The public footpath, to the left, should now be followed across the fields, and then through the Glebe Farm buildings to the village of Cubbington. The footpath ends on the Offchurch Road but a short walk up it, to the left, leads to Queen Street which, in turn, leads to the village and its "narrow, crooked and ugly street." The second route is similar at first but at the end of Black Lane, instead of following the (now narrower) road around to the right to Redhouse Farm, a narrow path (straight ahead) should be followed that crosses the fields in a more direct way to Cubbington, skirting Hill Farm but arriving on the Offchurch Road opposite the opening of Queen Street. Of the two routes, it appears more likely that Nathaniel and Julian took the first. It is not a short walk!

18. EN.

19. BERG.

20. BEINECKE (transcript): from a letter written over the period 8–15 September 1857.

21. On most occasions, it is never apparent what Rose did, or was allowed to do, when left behind on these trips, as she usually was. Of course, she would have been in Fanny's charge but we are never told what the two of them got up to; although on this particular day it appears from the Accounts Book that there was shopping to be done and certain items of clothing to be both bought and collected from the menders.

22. The Castle Inn, now called The Queen and Castle.

23. Nathaniel made an anatomical error here. The *Warwickshire Directories* of the period do not list any Kings Head in Kenilworth but there was, and still is in the main street of the town, a Kings Arms Hotel but the name of it now is, somewhat confusingly, Café Drummonds Bar.

24. EN.

25. As the National Heritage advertising hoardings (in 1995) in the locality of the castle succinctly put it, "It's a mile to get round it, but you'll never get over it."

26. According to the timetable, the journey was scheduled to take twenty minutes, arrival at 11:05 A.M.

27. At this point Sophia finished her eighteenth page and had to put the sketch at the head of the nineteenth.

28. Sophia is referring to their visit to Glasgow and its cathedral on the previous 30 June. The "Kist of Whistles" was the organ, kist being a northern/Norse word for chest.

29. Julian must have made an early visit to the hairdresser that morning, perhaps to Price's at 17 Upper Parade.

30. There were so many engravings of Kenilworth Castle that it is well-nigh impossible to decide which were those that Sophia bought, even by relating them to photographs of the period, as the latter were just as numerous. Neither is the print shop identifiable, as the *Directories* of the period do not list one and opinion is that no shop would have sold prints alone.

31. Presumably William Augustus Stearns, 1805–76, an American Congregational preacher and teacher.

32. The reader will have to consult (or even read!) Sir Walter Scott's *Kenilworth* to be able to appreciate all of Sophia's references to the various characters and events and their association with Kenilworth Castle.

33. Sophia is referring to their visit to Oxford and to the surrounding district in September 1856.

34. A force or natural power formerly held by some to reside in certain individuals and things to underlie hypnotism and magnetism and some other phenomena. *(Webster's Third New International Dictionary.)*

35. BERG.

36. They must have gone down either Vine Yard Street (now called Castle Lane) or Castle Street, both of which contained stables, but it was more likely the latter as The Gold Cup and The Coach and Horses public houses were there.

37. EN.

38. CE: vol. 18, 97–98.

39. EN.

40. BEINECKE (transcript): from the letter written over the period 8–15 September 1857.

41. The location of this letter, if it is extant, is unknown to me. Horatio Bridge, another old college friend of Nathaniel's, was the chief of the Bureau of Provisions and Clothing for the United States Navy (later Paymaster General) and was Nathaniel's main link with the Washington political scene while he was in England.

42. *The Washington Union*, 28 August 1857.

43. See chapter 5.

44. CE: vol. 18, 100–101. For some reason, Nathaniel refrained from telling Bridge the real reason for his return to the consulate, namely Wilding's illness.

45. Mayor of Stratford-upon-Avon.

46. Leonard Bacon, D.D., minister of the Congregational First Church of New Haven, Connecticut; Delia's elder brother.

47. The Flower family was one of the most influential in Stratford, owning the brewery that produced the ale that Nathaniel had sampled during his visit to the town in 1855, but that he had not cared for.

48. MS.Yc.2599. The Folger Shakespeare Library, Washington, D.C.

49. CE: vol. 18, 102.

50. Ibid, 99.

51. A novel by Mme de Stael.

52. BEINECKE (transcript): from a letter written over the period 16–23 September 1857.

53. CE: vol. 18, 104.

54. BEINECKE (transcript): from the letter written over the period 16–23 September 1857. The location of Sophia's letter, if it is extant, is unknown to me.

55. CE: vol. 18, 105.

56. LA, 24 September 1857.

57. The letter is not specifically dated, but in view of the information contained in its second sentence it must have been written during the week commencing Sunday, 20 September 1857.

58. The location of this letter, if it is extant, is unknown to me.

59. Presumably referring to Mackinaw Island, Michigan, where the Mann family had gone for a holiday.

60. The date 29 September was a Tuesday!

61. Dred Scott had maintained that his escape from slave territory to "free" territory meant that he was therefore a free man, despite having been taken back to slave territory. The Supreme Court under Chief Justice Taney ruled that a Negro was not a United States citizen and could not take his case to the courts.

62. Mary Motley, wife of the American author and diplomat John Motley; later, they were in Rome during the winter of 1858–59, seeing the Hawthornes frequently: Ada taught their daughter Elizabeth at that time. The location of this letter from Mrs. Motley, if it is extant, is unknown to me.

63. BERG.

64. BEINECKE: (transcript): from the letter written over the period 16–23 September 1857.

65. Evert Augustus Duyckinck, 1816–78, an American editor and critic.

66. Dr. Charles Mackay was the editor of the *Illustrated London News.* Nathaniel had met him on several occasions in London during 1856, one of them being at a dinner at the Reform Club; possibly his enthusiasm in writing letters of recommendation on Mackay's behalf was due to the fact that he had found him to be "a shrewd, sensible man, with a certain slight acerbity of thought" (a man after his own heart?). He would have been amused, if he had cared enough or been alive, not only to read Mackay's version of the dinner party in the latter's *Forty Years' Recollections:* (London: Chapman and Hall, 1877) but also to see that in the book Mackay omitted to mention Nathaniel's letters of introduction (he *did* mention Thackeray's) and that, apparently, he did not visit Duyckinck, Emerson, or Pierce.

67. CE: vol. 18, 106.

68. Ibid, 107.

69. Ibid, 108.

70. 26 September 1857. *The Journal of Benjamin Moran,* vol. 1, eds. Sarah Ann Wallace and Frances Elna Guillespie (Chicago: University of Chicago Press, 1948).

71. The *Atlantic* had docked at Liverpool on 23 September. The location of the letter, if it is extant, is unknown to me.

72. CE: vol. 18, 111.

73. Ibid, vol. 20, 180. This letter in CE is provisionally dated 26 September and that appears to be as good a date as any under the circumstances. But exception must be taken to the footnote (2) to the letter in which it is stated that "NH left Liverpool on September 24, intending to meet his family and accompany them to Paris." Nathaniel left Leamington to return to Liverpool on 15 September, due to his having received a telegraph from the consulate. There is no record of his having returned to Leamington until 14 October. He wrote letters from Liverpool on 17,

18, 21, 24, 25, and 26 September. Quite who "another person" was who was being instructed in the consulate's accounting methods is not made plain. It couldn't have been Pearce, since Nathaniel reported him at a later date as being prostrated by the confusion arising from Wilding's absence. Presumably, he either hired another clerk to do the job or the "other person" was himself. Nathaniel's subsequent submissions of accounts to the Department of State, bringing them up-to-date to the time he officially left the consulate, were made on 20 November and on 4, 10, and 24 December.

74. BEINECKE (transcript): from a letter written over the period 26–28 September 1857.

75. LA: 1 October 1857.

76. The transcript of the letter is annotated to the effect that it was written in "1855. Probably first week in July Leamington?" It cannot have been written at that time (18 June-9 July 1855) as Nathaniel, though absent in Liverpool part of the time, was not absent on a Sunday. Indeed, the only (fairly) confident reason for stating that this letter was written in Leamington is that Una *does* refer to the likelihood of Nathaniel's departure (i.e., leaving his job as consul) from the consulate "next month" (October), which, in fact, he did in October 1857. The other points in favor of dating the letter at some time (a Monday) in September 1857 from Leamington all contain difficulties. The weather conditions cannot be confirmed by reference to the local newspapers; the purchase of the particular items consumed at the Sunday dinner cannot be confirmed by reference to the Accounts Book; Sophia's respirator accompanied her all over the country and there are several references to it in journals and letters on other occasions; likewise with her "oil," although a purchase of "oil" was made in Leamington during this 1857 period; and Julian had been wanting an aquarium since 1856! However, I feel that the letter *could* be dated, with *some* confidence, as Monday, 28 September 1857 not only because of the departure from the consulate "next month" but also because Nathaniel *was* away from Leamington on Sunday, 27 September (he *was* also away on 20 September but in this letter Una makes no mention of their having visited Warwick on the previous Saturday) *and* he was away on the Sundays 4 and 11 October, but if this letter had been written on either Monday, 5 or 12 October, Una makes no mention of having seen the Tom Thumb show (or of Ada being with them). Another point that could be raised in opposition to dating the letter within this period in Leamington is whether or not the style of it is such as would have been written by an intelligent, fairly sophisticated girl of thirteen (even disregarding its jocular, teasing tone). The transcript is from the Louise Bennet Macpherson Deming Collection (Cage 215) of letters (typescript copies) of Sophia Peabody Hawthorne and others in the Washington State University Libraries, Pullman, Washington, to whom I am indebted for this reproduction.

Chapter 5. Leamington, that "cheerfullest of English Towns": October 1857

1. The location of this letter, if it is extant, is unknown to me.
2. The location of Ada's letter, if it is extant, is unknown to me.
3. GENERAL TOM THUMB.—This distinguished pupil of the celebrated P. T. Barnum, the Yankee showman, is about to pay this town a visit on Thursday, Friday and Saturday, the 1st, 2nd, and 3rd of October (next week). In order that our readers may have some idea as to the character of the exhibition they are invited, by advertisement in another column, to visit, we give the following extracts:—"Various reports having been circulated respecting this singular specimen of humanity, tending to throw doubt on his sex, age, and general developement, we were requested in conjunction with

Professor Fergusson, to institute an examination of 'the General', with the view of settling the question. This was accordingly made last week, and the results were satisfactory on the following points:—The General is very symmetrical, and his hands and feet are perfect models of proportion. The developement of his teeth (which are remarkably good) is such as to lead to the belief that his stated age (nineteen) is the correct one. The incisors in the upper jaw have come out irregularly, two in particular projecting from the palate beyond the others, so as to form a double row. Hence it is stated by his attendants that he has 'two sets' of teeth. The head is not large in proportion to the body, and the 'intellectual' and 'moral' developement preponderate over the 'animal'. His features are regular; his eyes are remarkably large, fine, and intelligent. The muscles of his arms and legs are large and firm, the results probably of his constant gymnastic exercises. The General has a slight tendency to *embonpoint*, owing to his sedentary habits, and, perhaps, to his free indulgence in the use of 'the weed', his cigars being one 'of his chief comforts'. His manners are those of a gentleman. In a line it may be said of him that he is 'an abridgement of most that is pleasant in man.'" The *Lancet*, 31 January 1857. Reproduced in LA, 24 September 1857.

4. The Halletts are unidentifiable.
5. From the Latin, *pessimo,* "to spoil completely"?
6. CE: vol. 18, 112–13.
7. One of the several gentlemen who were attracted to the apparently unattached Ada while she was at M. Fezandie's establishment. He was so persistent that Ada felt that it was going to be "necessary to tell him, or to intimate to him, that there was a Clay Badger in the world . . . although he [Mr. Lane] is certainly over forty, and has seven children."!
8. BEINECKE (transcript).
9. STP.
10. LA, 8 October 1857. Benjamin Moran, of the American Legation in London, also met Tom Thumb (whose real name was Charles Sherwood Stratton) and recorded on 26 July 1858 that

> . . . in came Gen'l Tom Thumb, and a showman by the name of West, for passports. This dwarf is 3 feet 1 inch high, and not 2 ft.7, as is publicly stated, he is not a parrot by any means, nor yet forbidding. He writes well and talks sensibly. Contrasted with such men as Drs. Patton and Porter [other visitors to the legation on that day] he is the merest conceivable pigmy, and the three men present a curious evidence of the freaks of nature in her creation of man. Whilst the Gen'l was here Dr. Collyer [an American showman who presented, in some people's eyes, somewhat tasteless *"tableaux vivants"* in New York], the famous introducer of Model Artists into the United States came in and the two began a conversation at once, probably from identity of calling. I gave the dwarf a passport and receiving his thanks dismissed both himself and guardian. *Journal of Benjamin Moran,* vol.1

11. RLSC, 3 October 1857.
12. As has been explained, accommodation at No. 10 Lansdowne Circus was not so lavish that the unexpected arrival of another adult (who presumably, in this case, would require her own room) would have caused no bother. There were now four adults and three children in the house (as well as, maybe, at least one live-in servant). It must be assumed that some sharing of rooms now took place, possibly Rose with Fanny or Rose with Una or, on a temporary basis until Nathaniel returned from Liverpool, one of the children with Sophia. But when he did, what happened then?
13. BEINECKE (transcript).
14. Heinrich Godefroy Ollendorff, some of whose works by 1857 (generally entitled "*A New Method of Learning to Read, Write and Speak a Language in Six Months, adapted to the . . . .*") had become very popular; the volume relating to

French was in its seventh edition by this time and those relating to German and Italian in their third editions.

15. HC.

16. BEINECKE (transcript).

17. The location of this letter, if it is extant, is unknown to me. It says great things for the postal service, however, that a letter delivered after 5:00 P.M. in Paris on a Friday was redelivered in Leamington Spa the following Monday morning.

18. Mr. Bennett and Miss Blaisdell are unidentifiable.

19. Another (unidentifiable) suitor!?

20. As she didn't arrive in London itself until 6:00 P.M. Ada would not have reached Euston Square station until a good deal later, by which time the last direct train to Leamington had left. Presumably she felt that it was better to get as near to her final destination that evening rather than stay the night in London. She caught the next train at 8:00 P.M., terminating at Rugby at 10:36. She would have been able to do no better by going to Paddington station, on the Great Western line, to reach Leamington via Oxford, according to Bradshaw's *Railway Guide.*

21. Presumably she caught the 11:06 from Rugby, arriving at Leamington at 1:40. Bradshaw's *Railway Guide.*

22. Dotheboys Hall, run by Wackford Squeers, is generally supposed to have been based on Bowes Academy in Bowes, Yorkshire, run by Mr. William Shaw. Refer to Peter Ackroyd's *Dickens,* (London: Sinclair-Stevenson, 1990).

23. Ada and Clay had promised each other that they would look to the heavens each night to search for the northern constellation Lyra, containing the star Vega which, during the summer months, is the fifth brightest star visible, thus joining their hearts and minds in this way.

24. BEINECKE (transcript).

25. Ada's adventures are like the very stuff of Victorian popular fiction or a Boon and Mills novel or *The Perils of Pauline* or, more sinisterly, since she appears unwittingly to have aroused the lust of every man that she met, more like those of a Terry Southern heroine. Since arriving in Paris (as she told Clay) she had been the focus of attention for Mr. Seabury (the first mate of the *Ariel*, on which she had crossed the Atlantic); M. Casson (an "interesting Frenchman"); Mr. Lane (an "exceedingly kind and pleasant Englishman," but who had seven children!); at M. Fezandie's establishment, a Dr. Lazarus who was "studying medicine in Paris"; Father James (!), who was "going to attempt my conversion"; and Mr. Jones, her "travelling companion from Paris to London."

26. Not an allusion that I have been able to trace.

27. BEINECKE (transcript).

28. *The Times* of 7 October 1857 reported: "Liverpool, Tuesday, The United States mail steamship Baltic, Comstock commander, arrived at midday, with advices from New York to the 20th ult. and 66 passengers, but no specie."

29. HC.

30. NHW. It is very tempting to quote in full the very long Despatch No. 90, which Nathaniel had sent to the Department of State on 17 June 1857, despite its considerable irrelevance to this book. Nathaniel was sincerely shocked by the conditions endured at sea by the seamen on American merchant vessels and the fact that many of those seamen were not Americans, having been pressed into service. As consul, he had had to arbitrate many times in cases of maltreatment (and sometimes murder) brought to his notice when such vessels docked at Liverpool after crossing the Atlantic. The masters of the vessels had supreme power over their crews and in many cases acted accordingly, to the seamen's misfortune. Nathaniel was greatly concerned about these injustices, and by the very low personal standards of

the individuals who manned and commanded the vessels; partly, at least, he saw it as an insult to the honor of the United States in the eyes of the world. Lord Napier had protested to the Department of State on the matter and the correspondence had been published in the English papers. Nathaniel had taken offense at part of the correspondence in which he assumed that he personally was being maligned in his capacity as the current United States consul at Liverpool. Despatch No. 90, to the Secretary of State, had set out at great length what he considered were his powers to combat the wrongs done (they were of very little use), what he had done to ameliorate the situation when cases of maltreatment were brought to his attention, and what he considered to be the remedy with regard to improving the standard of masters, officers, and men of the American merchant marine. He ended the Despatch, "I leave the matter with the Department. It is peculiarly unfortunate for me that my resignation is already in the hands of the President; for, going out of office under this stigma, I forsee that I shall be supposed to have committed official suicide, as the only mode of escaping some worse fate. Whether it is right that an honorable and conscientious discharge of duty should be rewarded by loss of character, I leave to the wisdom and justice of the Department to decide. I am, Sir, most respectfully, Your obedient servant, Nath. Hawthorne." (NHW) As has been shown, Nathaniel had toyed with the idea that on retirement from the consulate his first publication would be a book on the subject, bringing to the public's notice the shameful state of affairs in his country's merchant marine but the book was not written. It should be emphasized again that despite his own disparaging remarks about his worth as a consul and of the effects of his powers, he cannot be considered other than having been a conscientious official who discharged his duties to the best of his abilities.

    31. BEINECKE (transcript).

    32. CE: vol. 18, 115–16.

    33. BEINECKE (transcript).

    34. Emma Guild Fisher, possibly a childhood friend of Ada's as, apparently, Clay did not know her.

    35. Otis is unidentifiable.

    36. BEINECKE (transcript).

    37. This "another person" would now seem definitely to be another member of Nathaniel's staff (maybe hired for just this purpose) since it is unlikely that he would not tell Ticknor if it was he who was sorting out the accounts in Wilding's absence.

    38. More than one hundred fifty American banks had failed in the panic of the previous few months, due to the overexpansion of the American economy during the 1850s and due to the lack of international demand for American goods. The Bank of England had been unable to support British banks that had large investments in America. Nathaniel had withdrawn funds (both his and the American government's) from the Liverpool Borough Bank in time "owing to a rumor that reached" him. Letter to Ticknor 5 November 1857 (see chaper 6).

    39. Like other consuls, Nathaniel had little compunction about using the diplomatic bags to convey his and the family's mail and belongings to America and for the receipt of incoming personal goods and mail from America.

    40. The Republican movement in Italy was growing apace, supported by Louis Napoleon in France.

    41. CE: vol.18, 118–20.

    42. Ibid, 121. Herbert Fry had asked for permission to photograph Nathaniel for inclusion in his projected *National Gallery of Photographic Portraits*. It had been almost a year since the initial request had been made. The photograph was never taken.

    43. The location of this letter, if it is extant, is unknown to me.

44. That must have been on Saturday, 19 September.

45. BEINECKE (transcript).

46. None of these letters appears to have survived, except the one addressed to "Pessima," of 2 October.

47. Mary Richardson, a college roommate and friend of Ada's when they were both at Antioch.

48. BEINECKE (transcript).

49. Ibid.

50. For a reconstruction of Nathaniel's last day in office refer to Mr. Bill Ellis's *Hawthorne's Last Day at the Consulate: "To Think of Doing Good"* (Studies in the American Renaissance, 1991).

51. Mrs. Heywood (whose husband, John, was a banker in Liverpool) had overcome Nathaniel's initial shyness and reserve by virtue of her good looks; her deep knowledge of literature, local history, and the seamier of the Liverpool slums; and by her dinner parties in Liverpool and London (which he attended).

52. There is no record of Nathaniel returning to Liverpool after he left on 14 October (until 1860, when the family was leaving for America).

53. CE: vol. 18, 102.

54. Miss Wilmarth is unidentifiable. . . .

55. . . . as is Mr. Smith.

56. BEINECKE (transcript).

57. The location of this letter, if it is extant, is unknown to me.

58. Possibly "Beckie" was Rebecca Rice, who graduated from Antioch in 1860. The location of the letter, if it is extant, is unknown to me.

59. . . . and perhaps "Charlie" was either Charles F. Childs or Charles K. Robinson, both fellow graduates of Ada's in 1857.

60. BEINECKE (transcript).

61. Ibid.

62. Ibid.

63. The location of these letters, if they are extant, is unknown to me.

64. Presumably her sister; see pages 222–23.

65. Ada must have been referring to the disastrous accident at sea, concerning the American ship *Central America,* which was fully reported in the local newspapers; so how did she know about it, if she hadn't read *something?* "AMERICAN MAIL.—An American mail brings an account of a terrible shipwreck, that of the Central America, accompanied with the loss, it is believed, of four or five hundred passengers. The unfortunate vessel was in the New York Californian trade. The cause of the disaster was that the ship sprang a leak, by which the fires were extinguished and she was left at the mercy of the waves. The total loss is computed at more than two millions of dollars, a large portion of which is likely to be covered by insurance" (LA, 8 October 1857). RLSC on 10 October carried a much more detailed account of the accident, which differed in some essentials as to the cause of the accident and told of the likely loss of 426 of the 592 passengers.

66. BEINECKE (transcript).

67. CE: vol. 18, 123.

68. If Sophia did go to Coventry "about a month since" there was no mention made of the journey at the time nor was a note included in the Accounts Book as to the cost involved. When Nathaniel and Sophia made these trips together, such as to Kenilworth, Warwick, and Coventry, and subsequently made their separate descriptions in journals and letters, I had thought that it would be instructive to see them printed side by side in a double-column format but that would have been of no real value unless (a) they wrote of the same things in the same order, which they

didn't; (b) that they wrote at the same length, which they didn't; and (c) that the reader could take in two columns on a page at the same time, which most of us can't. The comparison between the two styles and content is, nevertheless, always fascinating.

69. Only 5s.6d. according to the Accounts Book.

70. EN.

71. "Two-pence" according to Nathaniel.

72. Well, that proves it, but it is still not apparent which day it had been.

73. ". . . six high windows of stained glass on each side" according to Nathaniel.

74. 3s.6d. worth, according to the Accounts Book.

75. Sepoys (native soldiers) in the employ of the East India Company had mutinied in various garrison towns in India against British rule earlier that year. Many British soldiers and civilians had been massacred. During September, Delhi had been recaptured from the sepoy forces and Lucknow was relieved in November. By July 1858 order had been restored but the India Act of the same year ended the administration of India by the East India Company and direct rule was assumed by the British Crown.

76. BERG.

77. NHW. In the chapter entitled "Eighteen Months before Rome" the anecdote is placed between an extract from Nathaniel's journal telling of his and Julian's visit to Warwick on 14 September 1857 and the paragraph that commences "Leaving Leamington on the 10 November. . . ." Julian had accompanied his father to Coventry on 29 June 1855 (Sophia was not with them and they had not, as far as is known, hired a cab). He did not accompany his parents on this latest visit; and the only other recorded visits by members of the family were by Sophia, Una, and Julian on an unknown date (but approximately 17 September 1857—see[72] above) and by Nathaniel and Una on 4 February 1860. Either this "mystery" visit to Coventry went completely unrecorded for some reason or else Julian's memory failed him and the town in question was simply not Coventry.

78. It appears from what Ada wrote in this and other letters that she had no official duties on Sundays.

79. As has already been noted, there were thirteen churches and chapels in the town; allowing for the unsuitability of the Anglican and Catholic denominations, it seems likely that there should have been at least one of the others that might have suited Ada's tastes, if she had been willing to try them.

80. LA, on 10 September, confirmed that Read's [sic] book had been added to the shelves of Beck's Circulating Library.

81. The former Rebecca Pennell, Horace Mann's niece, a member of the staff at Antioch College.

82. BEINECKE (transcript).

83. Ibid.

84. The location of this letter, if it is extant, is unknown to me.

85. Miss Allen is unidentifiable. . . .

86. . . . as is Horace

87. . . . and the Popes.

88. . . . and Henry, but it seems likely that he was related to the Popes.

89. Some of the ideas expressed by Ada as a result of seeing Lillington bear a strong resemblance to those expressed in Nathaniel's journal after his first visit there in 1855; perhaps, as they walked around the village and churchyard, he told the two girls of the emotions and ideas that had been aroused on that occasion. If the "slender, spiritual looking man" *was* the vicar, then it must have been the Reverend John Wise Jr. who, in 1857, was forty-eight-years old; like his father before him (the

Reverend John Wise Sr. who had been vicar from 1795 to 1830) he served the parish for many years, forty-one in his case.

90. BEINECKE (transcript).

91. "Fifty years ago" Dr. Jephson was nine years old! He began to practice in the town in 1823–24.

92. EN.

93. BEINECKE (transcript).

94. The location of this letter, if it is extant, is unknown to me.

95. Uncle Ayres is unidentifiable and the location of his letter, if it is extant, is unknown to me.

96. Joseph is also unidentifiable but presumably was connected with Antioch College at Yellow Springs and the location of his letter, if it is extant, is unknown to me.

97. The location of these letters, if they are extant, is unknown to me.

98. Whatever it was that "M. Fezandie wrote," it is not included in the transcript of Ada's letter.

99. BEINECKE (transcript).

100. Harris is unidentifiable. . . .

101. . . . as is Abby.

102. BEINECKE (transcript).

103. Ibid.

104. Ibid.

105. O days and hours, your work is this
    To hold me from my proper place,
    A little while from his embrace
    For fuller gain of after bliss;

    That out of distance might ensue
    Desire of nearness doubly sweet;
    And unto meeting when we meet,
    Delight a hundredfold accrue,

    For every grain of sand that runs,
    And every span of shade that steals,
    And every kiss of toothed wheels,
    And all the courses of the suns.
    Tennyson's *In Memoriam A.H.H.*, section 117.

106. BEINECKE (transcript).

107. CE: vol. 18, 124.

108. Samuel Parr, 1747–1825: educated at Harrow and Cambridge, ordained 1769, became a schoolmaster, and was presented with the curacy of Hatton in 1783. Thereafter, he became widely involved in matters of education, politics, and religion, writing voluminously but not always achieving publication.

109. Nathaniel would probably have just as much difficulty in finding Hatton church today as he did in 1857. There is still no real village, as such, Hatton (to the outsider) seeming to be an area rather than a place. The *Warwickshire Directory* of 1854 lists Hatton as having a population of 696, including the hamlets of Beausale and Shrewley, in an area of 3,010 acres. The church is about one mile from the station as the crow flies, but at least two miles by road; and judging by his description, he must have walked nearly four or five miles, perhaps almost reaching the adjacent hamlet of Shrewley, and back. The "one building that seemed new" must have been the school in Hatton Green, from where he followed the road around to the main

Warwick/Solihull Road, on which Hatton church still stands "quite beyond and out of the straggling village." If he had followed the road from the school across the Warwick Road, toward Haseley, he would shortly have come upon the tiny, beautiful, and (partly) very old church of St. Mary's.

110. This must have been the New Inn, the only one in the Hatton area then, where the present Waterman Inn stands.

111. There are sufficient entries in Nathaniel's journals on the subject of pubs and ale to warrant an opinion that he was by no means averse to an occasional pint of beer. As he suggested, an apprenticeship has to be served before many of the "local" varieties can be appreciated; when he was on his own, he often sought refreshment of this kind. He and Sophia had visited Oxford and the surrounding district in September 1856, and had been taken to dine at Merton College, the simple lunch "(the best the buttery could supply, out of term-time) consisting of bread and cheese, college-ale, and a certain liquor called Arch Deacon, in honor of the dignitary who first taught these erudite worthies how to brew it. It is a superior kind of ale, with a richer flavor, and of a mightier spirit. We ate and drank, and were much strengthened by the blood of the Arch Deacon" (EN).

112. It is still there, in the Holloway, off Market Square.

113. EN.

114. Ibid.

115. Ibid.

116. CE: vol. 18, 125.

117. The location of this letter, if it is extant, is unknown to me.

118. Presumably from Mary Richardson, but its location, if it is extant, is unknown to me.

119. Possibly the "Beckie" mentioned in her letter to Lucy, 13 October.

120. Maria Speer attended Antioch from 1856 to 1859.

121. And what is so rare as a day in June?
Then, if ever, came perfect days;
Then Heaven tries the earth if it be in tune,
And over it softly her warm ear lays.
J. R. Lowell, *The Vision of Sir Launfal,* part 2, Prelude.

122. It would appear from Ada's description that from Lansdowne Circus they walked right down Warwick St., continued on under the railway bridge, over the river Avon bridge, then over the Warwick and Napton canal bridge (from which they could see "the delightful view of the Castle and St. Mary's church"), turned right and passed by the (then) Emscote Mills and Guy's Cliffe Union Wharf, passed over the canal again, and turned right along the Warwick/Coventry road. Guy's Cliffe House was approximately three quarters of a mile further on. Today, that route is practically all a built-up area, except for the last few hundred yards to the house. The present-day walker, seeking an approximately similar "rural" walk to the same destination, has two alternatives, the first being shorter than the second but both of them are fairly lengthy. First, one could again walk right down Warwick Street, under the railway bridge but just before the Avon bridge turn back along the Rugby Road and take the second turning on the left, Old Milverton Road; this will lead the walker directly to the churchyard of St. James's church in Old Milverton, from which a path leads across fields to what was the mill that Ada and Una visited. The second route from Lansdowne Circus would be to turn right off Warwick Street before reaching the Parade, up Guy Street and then to continue straight up the Kenilworth Road until taking a left-hand turn down Old Milverton Lane, leading to Old Milverton, from where the same path can be taken across the fields to the former mill.

123. Guy's Cliffe house still stands (just!). Up until shortly before the Second

World War, it was occupied by the Percy family. They sold it after the war, the contents of the house being auctioned off on 3–5 April 1946. It was then allowed to fall apart and was subjected to the depredations of more than one "accidental" fire. The chapel continued to be used as a temple by the local Masons Society. It remains a forlorn, unoccupied, intended ruin. It is difficult to find any person or organization who acknowledges ownership of the property, which is not surprising when one considers the complete lack of concern exhibited over the years with regard to the slow lingering death of a house that contained and represented so much that is of historical value to the community at large.

124. The mill wheel is still in position, in what is now the Saxon Mill restaurant, on the Warwick/Coventry (A429) road.

125. Gaveston's Cross is now rather more inaccessible since the A46 road was constructed. However, continuing down the A429 road, from which runs the ruined driveway of the equally ruined Guy's Cliffe House, at the roundabout "under" the A46 the traveler should take the road to Leek Wootton and, almost immediately, turn left into North Woodloes. A footpath has then to be followed up the hill overlooking the A46 and eventually the Cross will be found in the copse on the summit. By choosing one's vantage point with care, a very good view can be gained over the surrounding countryside, with Guy's Cliffe House in the middle distance.

It is an unfortunate fact that when the monument was erected in 1821, at the instigation of Bertie Greathead of Guy's Cliffe House, Dr. Samuel Parr, who composed the inscription, got the date of Gaveston's death wrong. Gaveston was beheaded on 19 June 1312 (Julian Calendar). In changing that date in order to conform with the Gregorian Calendar (which took effect from 1752), Dr. Parr should have recorded the date as 27 June 1312. *Ripples from Warwickshire's Past.* Paul Bolitha. Wheaton: Warwickshire Books, 1991.

126. The location of this letter, if it is extant, is unknown to me.

127. BEINECKE (transcript).

128. Stratford's rail link with Leamington (via Hatton) was not opened until 11 October 1859 so, in the meantime, to get there from Leamington one used either one's personal transport, or hired a car/barouche/phaeton/cab/carriage, or traveled on the public stagecoach that still ran between the two towns, or went by shank's pony. It seems certain that the journey on this occasion was made in the "Star."

129. The inscriptions are illegible and the vase now lacks one handle (though that is in the hospital's possession). Cooke's *Guide to Warwick and Kenilworth Castles* (1847) states that "This curious and beautiful relic of Egyptian art formerly stood in the centre of the grand conservatory in the gardens of Warwick Castle from whence it was removed to make way for the celebrated Warwick Vase, and presented to the Hospital by the late Earl of Warwick, as appears from the inscription of the north side of the pedestal from the classic pen of Dr. Parr:

SITU
QUO HUNC HADR.AUG:
CRATER SUPERBIT
DEPORTATUM

The western side of the pedestal contains the following lines from the pen of the late Master—the Reverend J. Kendall—whose name is also inscribed on the south side, in Latin, having caused the vase to be placed there:

> In Oral times e'er yet the Prophet's pen
> God's laws inscribed, and taught his ways to men,
> The sculptured Vase and Memphian temples stood,

The Sphere's rich symbol of prolific flood:
Wise antients knew, when Crater rose to sight
Niles festive deluge had attained its height."

130. Samuel Rogers, 1763–1855, a banker, poet, socialite and art collector. The sale of his art collection and library in April 1856 produced a sum of £50,000.

131. EN. William Brown, 1784–1864, became a massively wealthy merchant (initially in the linen trade), banker and, later an M.P. He lived in Liverpool and in 1856 "contributed £100,000 to cover the entire cost of the building" of the Liverpool Free Public Library; refer to Aytoun Ellis's *Heir of Adventure: The Story of Brown, Shipley & Co.* London: Brown Shipley, 1960.

132. Since writing to Leonard Bacon on 17 September, Nathaniel had not been made aware of Delia Bacon's worsening circumstances. In fact, nothing could have been further from the truth that her brother had come in search of her.

133. Sophia was writing this journal entry on many sheets of locally bought writing paper, some of which had engravings of local scenes at their head.

134. A spring on Mount Parnassus, sacred to the Muses; the fount of Poesy.

135. More of Sophia's underlying uneasiness as to the identity of the man/men Shakespere/Shakespeare?

136. In November 1994 several Visitors Books, dating from the year 1853, were found at Lord Leycester's Hospital. The relevant book confirmed that Nathaniel had not signed it in 1855 (or had not been given the opportunity), perhaps because on that visit he did not report having been in "the outside half of the kitchen."

137. A novel (1843) by Edward George Earle Lytton Bulwer, first Baron Lytton (1803–73), set in the Wars of the Roses.

138. This mummy has been on "long-term loan" for some time now to the Birmingham Museums and Art Gallery but is not on display there. It was reexamined in 1973 and the body was pronounced definitely to be that of a man, a priest of the goddess Mut, named Pa-di-Mut, the son of Ankh-ef-en-Mut. Sophia's reference to it as a woman was probably due to the fact that on the inside of the outer wooden coffin is a large painting of the sky goddess, Nut, and she must have assumed that the picture was a representation of the occupant of the coffin.

139. The Warwickshire Natural History and Archæological Society was formed in 1836, and to house the growing number of exhibits the whole of the top floor of the Market Hall was taken over in 1840. In 1847 the museum was opened, on occasions, to the general public, free of charge. Declining membership of the society and the need to systematize the contents of the museum, together with the necessity for repairing the hall, led to the museum being taken over by Warwickshire County Council in the 1930s. During World War II the contents of the museum were removed for safekeeping; afterward, the Market Hall was repaired and renovated and the museum reopened in 1951. Lack of space resulted in parts of the collection being rehoused in the nearby St. John's House Museum.

140. Some idea of Sophia's enthusiasm for recording her experiences (mainly for the benefit of family members back home in America) can be gauged by the fact that this description of the visit to Warwick covered twenty-four pages of notepaper. On the following 11 November, she took another twenty-eight pages to describe just part of one day spent walking round the British Museum and other places in London!

141. They had visited Linlithgow during the previous July.

142. It is very interesting that Nathaniel sent Sophia home by herself in the omnibus; it was obviously threatening to rain at the time, so what was the point of taking a chance on getting soaked during his walk back to Leamington on a road with which he was already totally acquainted? Why did he refuse to visit St. Mary's and the castle during the afternoon (although, as he probably remembered, the castle

was open to the public on Saturdays only)? Was he just thinking of the doubtfulness of Sophia's stamina for prolonged walking and sightseeing? But he knew that when she was interested in a place she would walk for as far and as long as was necessary. They must have had a tiff!

143. BERG.

144. The windmill has gone and the hill is now called Black Hill, but it would appear that the "Windmill Inn" is likely to have occupied the site of what is currently called Windmill Hill Cottage, a modern building.

145. THE BIRTHPLACE.—The restoration of this interesting relic of Shakespeare has commenced. A formidable row of scaffold poles is erected in the front of the building; the windows and doors have disappeared from the modern brickwork of that portion known as "The Swan and Maidenhead", and the dismay of the multitude of perigrinating photographers, who have for the last six months been daily, nay, almost hourly, staring the poor old house out of countenance with the single eye of their mysterious machines, can be better conceived than described. In fact, such is the forlorn appearance of the building at this moment, that the disappointed operators shut up their magic lanterns in despair, and walk away, each with a sort of modified consolation, well expressed by the bard himself:

> It easeth some, though none is ever cured,
> To think their dolour others have endured.

The work of restoration is entrusted to Mr. Joseph Holtom, of this town, under the able superintendence of Mr. Gibbs, architect to the Birthplace Committee, and we have no hesitation in stating that the fullest confidence may be placed in his ability to carry out the wishes of the generous benefactor, Mr. John Shakespeare, and that all that the most careful supervision can do will be thoroughly accomplished. (RLSC, 3 October 1857).

Ada doesn't give any details of what stage the restoration was at at the time of her visit; it would appear from this newspaper report that the place should have been in a shambles, with scaffolding masking the exterior (frontage) of the building, but she made no mention of it. Possibly the work was already so far advanced that the scaffolding had been removed.

146. It is interesting that Ada *did* see Walter Scott's vandalism of the window but, two years previously, Nathaniel didn't, even though he tried. It is still to be seen, though with difficulty.

147. Stay passenger, why goest thou by so fast? / Read if thou canst, whom envious death hath plast, / With in this monument Shakspeare: with whome, / Quick nature dide; Whose name doth deck y tombe, / Far more then cost: sieh y he hath writ, / Leaves living art, but page, to serve his wit.

148. Mr. and Mrs. Barry.

149. BEINECKE (transcript).

150. The location of this letter, if it is extant, is unknown to me.

151. Possibly Una was using Gen. Joseph Bem's *Méthode mnémonique franco-polonaise. Manuel explicatif de la carte chronologique de l'histoire universelle, première partie . . .* (Paris, 1842) but it is even more likely that she was using Elizabeth's own version of it, *The Polish-American system of chronology, reproduced with some modifications, from General Bem's Franco-Polish method*, which Aunt Lizzie had published in 1850.

152. Priscilla Manning, the youngest daughter of Nathaniel's uncle, Richard Manning, married John Dike and lived in Salem.

153. Possibly Dr. Rutherford of 13 Clarendon Square, a homeopath.

154. Fanny's invaluable worth to Sophia is well illustrated in a fragment of one

of her letters (undated but that was certainly written sometime in 1856, possibly July). The recipient is unknown also, but it is assumed to be Elizabeth Peabody, which appears to be a little unlikely in the circumstances as it surely couldn't have taken two years before Sophia got round to telling her sister about Fanny for the first time. In the letter she said

> . . . I take a well-salted cold bath every morning, followed by friction & a teaspoonful of cod liver oil once a day. I cannot bear any more, & this is enough for me. The idea of Dr. Sibson is that I should be <u>self indulgent</u> & become fat and jolly. So that now he shows me it is my <u>duty</u> to be self indulgent, I can be so with a quiet conscience, & I shall soon be all right in body as I am happy in mind & heart. . . . I have had with me for two years an English woman of about thirty, who takes charge of Rosebud and sews a great deal & aids me in the toil of house-keeping—indeed takes it all when we are at lodgings. She is the most useful & convenient person in the world for me & is so simple as to worship me & for pure love would undergo any amount of labor or annoyance for my sake. She is a famous nurse too, having been well disciplined by an invalid step mother & she rubs me every day & pets me as if I were a little baby & is a mastiff at the door, if I wish to be quiet. She was never in any kind of service before—being the daughter of a once wealthy cloth-manufacturer, suddenly deprived of fortune by his own imprudent kindness. (BERG).

Bennoch had been involved in ensuring that Dr. Francis Sibson made an examination of Sophia while the family was staying at his house during July 1856. On 7 July, Nathaniel noted that ". . . when dinner was nearly over, Dr. Simpson [*sic*] came in. He is a physician eminent in diseases of the throat and lungs . . . and, after due examination, gave hopeful opinions respecting Sophia's case, and ordered some allo-pathic medicines—which she has great scruples of conscience and judgement about taking. But, for my part, I am inclined to put faith in what is tangible" (EN).

One can only wonder at the wisdom of continuing with the cold-water treatment but there can be no doubt of the benefits, both physical and moral, that Sophia gained from Fanny's character and work. Assuming that Sophia was the only one needing it at the time, the Accounts Book shows that another supply of cod-liver oil was bought for her on 23 October 1857.

155. A small community on the north side of Salem Bay.

156. The location of Una's journals, if they are extant, is unknown to me, more's the pity!

157. Mr. Samuel Ingram, a corn miller, is listed in the *Warwickshire Directories* as operating the mill on the Tachbrook Road all through the 1850s, very close to the Windmill Inn (which still stands, though much modified). The mill stood in what is now the inn's car park.

158. BERG.

159. CE: vol. 18, 126, but no text is given.

Chapter 6. "This goodly town of Leamington": November 1857

1. Redfern's Curiosity Shop in Jury Street has long since gone, having been closed down in 1868 following the death of Mr. Redfern, and the contents sold. The house in which it was situated still stands, however, at No. 29 Jury Street, at the East Gate end. The "toplight" of the front door contains what appears to be the original glass, in which the word Redfern can be made out, with some difficulty, as Nathaniel had found on their visit of the previous Thursday.

2. But which "old mansion"? According to C. S. Wharton's *Folklore of South Warwickshire* (1974), there were three such places that had the distinction of housing Cromwell on the eve of the battle; the manor at Bearley (a village to the northwest of Stratford, some ten miles from Warwick), the Bear Inn at Berkswell (a village to the east of Solihull, some fifteen miles north of Warwick), and Packwood House (some nine miles northwest of Warwick). Edge Hill is some twelve miles to the southeast of Warwick and can be seen from the tower of the chapel, but it is unlikely that any of these mansions would have been visible to the naked eye without the aid of perfect vision, the clearest of weather conditions, and the prior knowledge of their situation and aspect. The ascent to the top of the chapel is prohibited now, it is impossible to verify the accuracy of Ada's statement. If at all possible, they are more likely to be seen from the top of the nearby St. Mary's tower, which is both higher and taller than the chapel at the hospital.

3. Some discrepancies can be found in the circumstances noted in these letters of Una's to "Aunt Lizzie" (begun on 30 October, a Friday) and Ada's to Clay (begun on "Sunday morning," 1 November). Una mentioned having been to the mill at Guy's Cliffe, which was on 28 October, and to Stratford, which was on 29 October. She then completed the letter the day after it was begun, that is, on 31 October (although she dated it again as 30 October but acknowledged it to be "the last day of October"). She referred to the visit to the Tachbrook mill as having taken place "yesterday" (i.e., on Saturday) but Ada's letter to Clay told, first, of going to Warwick "yesterday" (on 31 October) and then of the Tachbrook visit as being on "the day before yester-day." It seems clear that the second part of Una's letter was not only misdated but that she had lost track of the order of events (which was, Guy's Cliffe on Wednesday, 28 October; Stratford on Thursday, 29 October; Tachbrook mill on Friday, 30 Octo-ber; and Warwick on Saturday, 31 October).

4. Lottie is unidentifiable, but possibly was another sister of Ada's.

5. BEINECKE (transcript).

6. The location of this letter, if it is extant, is unknown to me.

7. Mahala Jay (Mrs. Eli Jay), a fellow graduate of Ada's at Antioch in 1857.

8. BEINECKE (transcript).

9. The location of these letters, if they are extant, is unknown to me.

10. BEINECKE (transcript).

11. It probably came in the same delivery as Clay's did, on 2 November. The location of Ticknor's letter, if it is extant, is unknown to me. Among other news that he had to tell, he appears to have taken the opportunity of asking Nathaniel about the likelihood of a new book being in the offing now that he was free of the consulate; it had been four years since he had published anything new of Nathaniel's.

12. This reference to the Borough Bank in Liverpool is of great interest (it seems to me!). All of Nathaniel's letters that contain information regarding his finances and consular expenses (except for two) tell of his making deposits at the Liverpool branch of Baring Brothers (No. 1 India Buildings, Water Street); the relevant ledgers are held at the present headquarters of the bank in London. The Borough Bank was established in 1836 and closed on 27 October 1857, despite a guarantee from the Bank of Liverpool of £50,000 that was made in the hope of securing an advance of £1,000,000 to the Borough Bank from the Bank of England. What was this "large amount" that was held at the Borough Bank? Whose money was it? Did Mr. Wilding (who looked after the consulate and Nathaniel's finances) deposit "government" money in the Borough Bank and Nathaniel's savings in Barings? A good deal of time could be wasted in trying to clarify the state of Nathaniel's finances during the period 1853–60; he rarely appeared to have any real idea of how much he had in the bank (any bank!) and Ticknor rarely (if ever) appears to have made the effort of

informing his client/friend of the current state of his account. Whenever Nathaniel asked for more money or credit, he was sent it without query.

13. The Alcotts did not move onto "the piece of land" until 1858 but Nathaniel never had the chance of buying it in his lifetime as it was not on the market again until 1884.

14. This passage does not read easily, and *could* be understood to mean something slightly different *if* a slight misreading of the manuscript has occurred (!). Nathaniel's intentions as to the possibility of his writing something new take on a somewhat different aspect if the letter *does* read "As regards the announcement of a book, I am not quite ready for it yet. If I could be perfectly quiet for a few months, I have no doubt that something would result; but I shall have so much to see, while I remain in Europe, that I think I must confine myself to keeping a Journal, unless I return home next summer. However, I shall make a serious effort to produce something." In fact, it was to be more than two years before he had anything new published.

15. CE: vol. 18, 127–28.

16. BEINECKE (transcript).

17. Judge Mills had bought the land in Yellow Springs to be used for the building of Antioch College and had also given a large donation to the building costs fund.

18. Mr. Howells is unidentifiable.

19. It is interesting, and providential for Ada, that in addition to her intellectual accomplishments her personality was such that Nathaniel found her likable, and that she was not that sort of female who would put him "out of countenance with her wit and erudition." Ada's description of Nathaniel's character (and one has the feeling that she chose her words carefully) depicts him in some aspects of his character as not being too sympathetic a person. If she *was* accurate in her assessment, it underlines the fact that his was not the ideal personality for such a job as a consul; but that, in turn, means that he had done particularly well in some respects as he had been, on the whole, a hardworking and successful one. Alas, the Hawthornes' (particularly Sophia's) opinion of Ada's accomplishments were to suffer a sea change at a later date.

20. BEINECKE (transcript).

21. Ibid.

22. EN.

23. From Ada and Nathaniel's descriptions it seems very probable that the house in question was that called Home Farm, still standing on the main Whitnash Road from Leamington, just past the church. There are several other houses in the vicinity that would still be recognized by the Hawthornes.

24. This throws another shaft of light on Fanny's position within the family circle. At the beginning of this letter Ada says that they "shall have to ring for candles in a moment." Fanny is actually sitting with them at the time, so there must have been another person "below stairs" to perform such menial tasks as bringing candles into the room. So it appears that Fanny was a nurse to both Rose and Sophia, the purchaser of provisions and most likely other household goods (and therefore was trusted with the Hawthornes' cash), a housekeeper, and a friend and companion to them all. Two things she appears *not* to have been, however, is a cook and a maid. Yet, according to Ada's account, she did not eat with the family (as, it is to be assumed, Ada did, which was not always the case when one was a mere governess) and presumably after teatime in the evenings retired to "below stairs" (which, in this case, meant upstairs). Following from this supposition is the likelihood that there were two other persons in the house ("below stairs"), a cook and a maid; if so, they surely couldn't have both slept in the house? That would have meant a total of nine

people, if they did. Their daily presence is a probability, however, as it will be seen in a subsequent chapter concerning the Hawthornes in Leamington during 1859–60 that Sophia refers on one occasion to a servant being in the house whose presence is otherwise unsuspected. But then, it is supposed, such menials were not normally a topic of conversation or correspondence (unless they were causing trouble)!

25. That is an interesting observation! From November 1851 to May 1852, while Horace Mann and his family were in Washington due to his being a member of Congress, the Hawthornes had rented the Manns' home in West Newton. Nothing in Nathaniel's letters or journals gives a hint as to Ada being an acquaintance or a visitor at the time. Perhaps Ada had been one of several visitors as "Mary [Mann] had been holding a little dancing school at her house for her children and their neighbours. The mothers were determined to make Mrs. Hawthorne feel at home. Then there was the group of friends from the normal school who had been keeping up their French by meeting once a week at Mary's house to read and converse in what they sincerely hoped was a Parisian accent" (Louise H. Tharp, *The Peabody Sisters of Salem,* Boston: Little Brown, 1950) Ada would have been seventeen at that time.

26. BEINECKE (transcript).

27. LA, 22 October noted its having been added to the shelves of Beck's Circulating Library.

28. BEINECKE (transcript).

29. EN. When the family, plus Ada (but without Fanny), departed for Paris from London on 5 January 1858 they took with them twelve trunks and six carpetbags! When their essentially nomadic way of life over the past three years is considered (*and* the next three years to come) it seems to have been madness to keep on accumulating such a mountain of items to lug around with them (despite occasional dispatches of possessions, via the consulate, back to America). But, packing and unpacking apart, perhaps it couldn't be avoided.

Chapter 7. An Intermission (2)

1. The manuscript, *The Ancestral Footsteps,* is reproduced in CE, vol. 12.

2. CE: vol. 14, 178 (22 April 1858).

3. By referring to the diaries that Nathaniel kept during 1858 and 1859, it can be computed that he made withdrawals totaling £1070 from various banks while on the Continent. Reference to the statements of his account at Baring Brothers, London, show that a sum of £160 was debited to the account during the same period. He had the money to spend; perhaps that is why Ticknor apparently never wrote to him advising caution with regard to levels of expenditure (indeed, as Nathaniel reminded him on more than one occasion, he hardly wrote at all). And Nathaniel could have pointed out that nearly 50 percent of the Continental expenditure was recouped fairly quickly through the subsequent contract with Smith, Elder for the English edition of the romance. Presumably, at the same time, at least in America, he was still earning royalties on the sale of his other books.

4. DB.

5. "Mr. and Mrs. Field [*sic*], Boston, USA" stayed at the Regent Hotel during the week ending 6 August. Presumably they just missed meeting "Mr. and Mrs. Franklin Pierce and Miss Vandervout" who were at the Regent during the week ending 30 July. RLSC.

6. CE: vol. 14, 695.

7. Sophia had added a hurried note (3 October) to a letter written to Elizabeth

the day before, telling her that they were leaving Redcar on 5 October, but not disclosing their destination; and Una, writing to Aunt Lizzie on 4 October, told her that that was to be their last day in Redcar (BERG).

Chapter 8. "An unfashionable part of" Leamington: October 1859

1. CE: vol. 14, 695.
2. The location of this letter, if it is extant, is unknown to me.
3. Although Sophia was said to have been the only other person to have read the manuscript thus far, and despite Nathaniel's confirmation later in this letter that they had had no visitors while in Redcar (who, then, had been the mysterious "gentleman & lady, unknown" who had "called on me this evening, while I was out" that he had recorded in his diary on 20 August?), it is possible that it was common knowledge within English literary circles that he was hard at work on a new book. Since the family had returned from France he had met Bennoch, Fields, Chorley, General Pierce, Mrs. Heywood, Barry Cornwell, Leigh Hunt, and Thomas Hughes, all of whom, presumably (apart from Fields who was "in the know") would have asked him whether he was writing anything at the time and passed on to friends whatever information they had gleaned. Bright wrote to Nathaniel on 8 September, ". . . I saw Mrs. Gaskell the other day. She too is writing a novel, and the scene is to be somewhere near Redcar; so I think it is probable she may pay you a visit, and in that case the double magnet will draw me too. . . ." In a letter dated 20 September, to George Smith, Mrs. Gaskell wrote ". . . Do you know what Hawthorne's tale is about? I do . . . ." Presumably Bright had told her and they had remarked on the coincidence between the venue of her latest work-in-hand and the actual situation of the Hawthorne family. In a subsequent letter of early November (having lately been in Whitby) she gave details of the plot of Hawthorne's work to Emelyn Story in Rome and said that she had been in the vicinity of Redcar at the same time as the Hawthornes, but this would appear to be contradicted by the known movements of the two families during the summer and autumn of that year.
4. CE: vol. 18, 191–92.
5. Ibid, vol. 14, 695.
6. Franklin Pierce had been in Rome at the time of Una's serious illness and had been very solicitous for her and the family's welfare at the time. It is unknown whether Una's "last letter" to Aunt Lizzie had been written at that time or whether the Hawthornes had been in contact with Pierce after their return from the Continent, while Pierce and his wife were also in England.
7. PE: MSS.69.
8. CE: vol. 18, 195.
9. The location of this letter, if it is extant, is unknown to me.
10. The locations of these letters, if they are extant, are unknown to me. It is apparent that Bennoch had been able to contact Fields immediately, on receipt of Nathaniel's letter of 7 October, and that in his own letter to Nathaniel (which must have been dated 8 October) he advised of his intention to visit them all at Bath Street. There is no indication that he stayed the night with them, however.
11. CE: vol. 18, 196–97.
12. Ibid, vol. 14, 695.
13. PM: MA.1377.
14. The location of this letter, if it is extant, is unknown to me.
15. CE: vol. 14, 696.

16. PM: MA.1377.

17. CE: vol. 14, 696.

18. Benjamin Paul Akers (1825–61), an American sculptor who had worked in Boston, Florence, Washington, and Rome.

19. William Wetmore Story (1819–95), an American sculptor, considered the leader of the American artists living in Rome during 1858, had given up his legal training and profession in 1851 for the arts.

20. Randolph Rogers (1825–92), an American sculptor; the bronze doors were finally to be placed in the Capitol in Washington.

21. Harriet Goodhue Hosmer (1830–1908), an American sculptor, resident in Rome.

22. Perhaps now is as good a time as any for readers who are unfamiliar with *The Marble Faun* to read it?

23. The location of this letter, if it is extant, is unknown to me.

24. Ibid.

25. It is apparent that the "looking over" that took place on the 15 and 16 October had included an inspection and revision of the page-numbering of the manuscript, much of which was done by Sophia. (Refer to the Textual Introduction to *The Marble Faun* in CE: vol. 14, xiv-cxxxiii.)

26. It would seem reasonable to assume that in this letter Nathaniel would have intimated to Smith, Elder what his ideas were as to a title for the romance, but judging from his lack of any comment on the contents of their subsequent reply, it appears that he did not make any specific proposal with regard to the title until he sent them the remainder of the manuscript in November (and then it appears that he suggested the title that Fields had proposed).

27. The location of this letter, if it is extant, is unknown to me.

28. Ibid.

29. Ibid.

30. CE: vol. 14, 696–97.

31. The location of this letter, if it is extant, is unknown to me.

32. Presumably Mr. John Miller, the despatch agent of the American legation in London. Perhaps Nathaniel had communicated with him with regard to the eventual necessity of getting their belongings shipped back to America. The location of this letter, if it is extant, is unknown to me.

33. CE: vol. 14, 697.

34. One of Sophia's closest and oldest friends, going back to Concord days.

35. Like so many spinsters of her class and generation, Elizabeth had been teaching from an early age (in her case, not primarily for financial reasons) and subsequently her name became associated with the efforts to improve young children's education in America and the introduction of the kindergarten system. By 1859 she had already published a good deal of literature on these subjects but her primer, as such, was not to be published for some years. Perhaps, in the context of Rose's efforts to learn to read and write, Sophia was referring to Elizabeth's *First nursery reading book, intended to teach the alphabet, by means of English words, whose analysis shall give the true sounds that were originally, and even now are generally, attached to the characters in all languages,* published in 1849. Rose was six years old when Ada came on the scene as governess.

36. Presumably the wife of William Henry Channing, the Unitarian minister in Liverpool, who had baptized the children.

37. The check had been sent from Redcar as a wedding present to Ellen Peabody on her forthcoming marriage to George Phineas How.

38. Horace Mann had died on 2 August of "milk sickness," a usually fatal illness

at that time, caused by eating or drinking the milk products of cattle that had grazed on poisonous herbs.

39. Her brother's, not her husband's.

40. BERG.

41. Possibly, Nathaniel had found football just as incomprehensible as the cricket match (Liverpool vs. Derbyshire) that he had watched with Sophia in August 1854. Football at Rugby School was of a "local" variety. Following the subsequently world-famous action (in football circles) by William Webb Ellis, of picking up the ball and running toward the opponent's goal during a game at the school in 1823, the game was in the slow process of evolving into its modern form of rugby football. To clarify the new code, the *Laws of Football Played at Rugby School* had been written down for the first time in 1845. A typical game had been described in Thomas Hughes's *Tom Brown's Schooldays,* though the action of the book was set in the 1830s.

It is possible that the "George Hotel" was Nathaniel's name for the George Inn that stood (and still stands) a short distance from Bilton Hall (he often misnamed, in his journals, hotels and inns that he saw or visited) but it is more likely that they dined at the George Hotel in the center of the town, on the way back to the school and the railway station. Ada had stayed at the George Hotel in 1857 on her way from Paris to join the Hawthornes in Leamington.

42. The location of this letter, if it is extant, is unknown to me.

43. CE: vol. 14, 697–98. There seems to be no record of Bright having previously advised the Hawthornes of his intention to come to Leamington. From the tone of Nathaniel's diary entries it does not appear that Bright stayed with them but as the local newspapers do not detail him as having been in one of the town's hotels over the weekend it must be assumed that he *was* a guest at No. 21 Bath St. It has been suggested to me that it was "perhaps most likely" that Bright brought with him on this occasion the journals that Nathaniel had kept during the consular years 1853–57 and that he had entrusted to Bright's keeping in September 1857 (to be kept un-opened until 1900!). It is undeniable that the journals were returned to Nathaniel at some time as they formed the basis for his subsequent magazine articles in the *Atlantic Monthly* and for his book *Our Old Home.* The return of the journals *could* have been one of the reasons for Bright's visit at this time, but it seems unlikely. Nathaniel had made no reference to his desire for their return, he had not written to Bright asking for them (as far as is known), and he made no reference to their having been returned as a result of this visit. Also, in his letter to Fields of 17 November 1859, in referring to "my journal," Nathaniel stated that ". . . I have not got it here; . . . ." though in this context, as the letter from Fields is not recovered, it cannot be certain as to what the question was that Nathaniel was addressing, and "my journal" might have been (then) his English, French, or Italian journal(s).

Hopefully, over the weekend, the family had read the news item (RLSC, 22 October) reporting the recent victory in America by the All England Eleven over the U.S. cricket team (all twenty-two of them!). The England team contained two players from Leamington—Parr, and Wisden—the proprietors of the town's cricket ground that bore their name. It occupied part of what is now Victoria Park. The Cricketers' Arms pub is situated on what was the northeastern corner of the ground. (See Robert Brooke's *Cricket Grounds of Warwickshire.* West Bridgford, Nottingham: Association of Cricket Statisticians, 1989). Prior to playing the United States, the All England Eleven had beaten the Canadian Twenty-Two.

44. CE: vol. 14, 698.

45. Unfortunately, space precludes quoting the contents of the lectures; this one was reported in full in RLSC, 29 October 1857.

46. The location of the E. P. Peabody letter, if it is extant, is unknown to me.

47. CE: vol. 14, 698. The lecture was reported in full in RLSC, 29 October 1857.
48. MHS: part of a letter dated 5 October 1859.
49. The location of this letter, if it is extant, is unknown to me.
50. CE: vol. 14, 698. The lecture was reported in full in RLSC, 29 October 1859.
51. Nathaniel had noted in his diary that the letters came the day before.
52. An adaptation of Proverbs, chapter 14, verse 10.
53. BERG.
54. BERG. The "enclosed musings" are missing. The note is presumed to have been written in 1859, not unjustifiably so.
55. The location of this letter, if it is extant, is unknown to me. Again there is no reference as to what Mr. Miller was writing about although it must have had ex-consular/American connotations.
56. The location of this letter, if it is extant, is unknown to me.
57. CE: vol. 14, 698. Miss Annette Bracken was the companion of Isabella Blagden, an English novelist and poet. They had been living in Florence when the Hawthornes were there and had been very supportive of Una during her illness in Italy.
58. Presumably a slip of the memory, as Sophia had started her letter to Mary the day before, while Una and Fanny were at Mr. Mason Jones's third and last lecture, that concerning Wesley. Burke had been the subject of the second lecture on Wednesday, 26 October.
59. The location of this letter, if it is extant, is unknown to me.
60. After their marriage in 1842 the Hawthornes had rented the Old Manse in Concord, previously the property of Ezra Ripley, a Unitarian pastor in Concord for sixty-three years; obviously, the Ripley beds had harbored lives other than human ones.
61. BERG.
62. CE: vol. 14, 698–99.
63. It is slightly confusing that while Sophia's reference to "E." being well is obviously in response to Mary's news to that effect contained in her letter of 5 October, there is in the latter nothing regarding the "suspectable intruders" (vermin) at the Wayside that Sophia had been "amazed to hear about." Either that piece of news had been contained in an earlier letter or else Sophia had been correct in saying that she had received a "double letter this morning" (on 27 October) that is, letters on both 26 October (as noted by Nathaniel in his diary) *and* 27 October. If that is correct, the second letter is unrecovered.
64. BERG. Although the library has the letters headed 27 and 28 October filed separately, it appears from their layout that they are part of one letter (written over a three-day period, ending on 31 October) and I have included them here with that in mind.

Chapter 9. "Leamington is not so desirable a residence in winter": November 1859

1. RLSC, 29 October, had carried a long report on the total loss of the *Royal Charter* during a gale on 25 October, at Muffa Red Wharf Bay, near Bangor, with a loss of over 400 lives and about 500,000L in gold. Gales raged all round the English coasts for several days; on 5 November the *Courier* reported: "Up to the close of Lloyd's on Saturday afternoon intelligence was still coming in of casualties and losses during the late great storm. Its equal for violence and terrible consequence has not been experienced for the last twenty years; and the boisterous weather of Friday night led to some apprehension that there would be a renewal of the gale. By

a return made up to Friday evening of the result of the gale, we find the following:—
Vessels totally wrecked, 96; vessels stranded and other casualties, 530—total, 626.
Probable loss of life, including the Royal Charter, 600. . . ."

2. Julian is the only one to have suggested this, so far.

3. PM: MA.1377.

4. STP.

5. HC. Major Johnstone (Professor of Callisthenic and Riding Exercises), 13
Gloucester Street, had advertised his services in *The Leamington Advertiser* during
1855 but his name, in a professional capacity, did not reappear in the local newspapers
during 1857 or 1859–60. Although it is somewhat unlikely, it is possible that the
Hawthornes remembered the advertisement of 1855; much more likely is that the
major had a plaque on his front door advertising his name and services, and that as
Gloucester Street formed/forms a junction with Bath Street very near to the Hawthornes (on the opposite side of the road) at No. 21 they could have seen the plaque
on several occasions as they walked about the town.

6. As a complete red herring, it can be told here that at one glorious moment
during my research for this book I thought that I had been given a copy of a completely new document that apparently related to the Hawthornes' stay in Leamington
at this time. Mr. Bill Gibbons, the local historian of Leamington and district, brought
to my notice a page of manuscript that he had found in some old records, which at
first sight appeared to me to have been written by one of the Hawthornes. It was a
short poem, and read:

> On Leamington.
> As through thy streets I often pace
> And gaze upon the crowd
> I seldom see a smiling face
> The people are so proud.
>
> The ladies look so very white
> Parading up and down
> Their faces seldom beaming bright
> They carry such a frown.
>
> E. H. November 4th 1859.

It didn't take long for the excitement to evaporate when the initial E. was examined.

7. The location of the E. P. P. letter, if it is extant, is unknown to me.

8. The location of this letter, if it is extant, is unknown to me.

9. Ibid.

10. CE: vol. 14, 699–700.

11. MHS. Parts of a letter dated 17 October 1859.

12. NHW.

13. *George Eliot: a Life.* Rosemary Ashton. London: Hamish Hamilton, 1996.

14. CE: vol. 14, 700. Reported in RLSC, 12 November 1859.

15. The location of the E. P. Peabody letter, if it is extant, is unknown to me.

16. "Optics and Optical Illusions," reported in RLSC, 12 November 1859.

17. CE: vol. 14, 700.

18. MHS. Extracts from a letter dated 18 October 1859.

19. The location of this letter, if it is extant, is unknown to me. Several of the
letters that Nathaniel wrote to Smith, Elder in connection with the publication of
the romance came to be housed in the collection of Mrs. Reginald Smith who subsequently bequeathed them to John Murray (who had acquired Smith, Elder in 1917).
These letters are apparently no longer extant (or, at least, their whereabouts are

unknown) as they are not in the archives of John Murray or of the National Library of Scotland in Edinburgh that holds other Smith, Elder material.

20. CE: vol. 14, 700.

21. Ibid, 701.

22. RLSC, 12 November 1859.

23. The location of this letter, if it is extant, is unknown to me.

24. It is slightly suspicious that there is recorded here the receipt of yet another batch of letters from Elizabeth and Mary as there appears to be no letters extant whose dates would coincide with their receipt on 13 November.

25. The location of this letter, if it is extant, is unknown to me. It is obvious that, for some reason, Smith, Elder took immediate exception to the title that had been suggested; presumably Nathaniel then included in this reply all the various suggestions that he had made in his letter to Fields of 10 October and, possibly for good measure, added a few more.

26. CE: vol. 14, 701.

27. It is interesting that in all his walks to Lillington while the family was in Leamington during 1855, 1857, and now in 1859, during which it is likely that he always had a look at the church, Nathaniel only now appears to have noticed (and recorded) what was, and is, this well-documented gravestone. There is a great deal of confusion relating to it. Apparently he and Julian did not uncover all of the epitaph, as an article in the *Family Tree* magazine of May-June 1985, vol. 1, no. 4 states that the "original" first two lines of the epitaph read "Here lies the body of William Treen the meanest man that ever was seen." The story goes that a vicar in the early part of this century took offense at the un-Christianlike tone of these words and had them obliterated. The legible part of the epitaph now reads "In memory of William Treen who died 3rd Feb 1810 aged 77 years I poorly lived and poorly died poorly buried and no one cryed." In 1985 the vicar, the Reverend Don Philpot, was reported as saying that "Unfortunately it is weathering badly and is extremely difficult to read. It is just outside the vestry door and at some stage in the past it has been retouched, but the weather has again taken its toll and it won't be long before it is completely indecipherable."

28. According to William Cooper's *History of Lillington:* Shipston-on-Stour: King's Stone Press, 1940 a vestry forming an extension to the north aisle of the church had been built in 1857 and the south aisle had been completely rebuilt in 1858.

29. PM: MA.577–91.

30. CE: vol. 14, 701.

31. Ibid, vol. 18, 198.

32. The location of this letter, if it is extant, is unknown to me.

33. Ibid.

34. CE: vol. 14, 701–2.

35. So Julian *was* right (see his journal entry of 1 November).

36. How had he "foreseen" it? There had been no correspondence between him and Ticknor on the subject. Presumably he had read of the death of both Mr. Sampson and Mr. Philips of the publishers, Sampson & Philips (who published the *Atlantic Monthly*) and put two and two together. Ticknor had made a purely nominal offer for the magazine of $10,000, much against Fields's advice. To their mutual surprise, the offer was accepted as it was the only one made! Once it was theirs, however, Fields immediately took a real interest in the magazine and its contents.

37. See chapter 8, footnote 43.

38. CE: vol. 18, 200–201.

39. The location of this letter, if it is extant, is unknown to me.

40. CE.: vol. 14, 702.

41. NHW.
42. The location of this letter, if it is extant, is unknown to me.
43. CE: vol. 14, 702.
44. The location of this letter, if it is extant, is unknown to me.
45. Ibid.
46. CE: vol. 14, 702–3.
47. BERG.
48. CE: vol. 14, 703.
49. Ibid, vol. 18, 202.
50. Ibid, 203.
51. Nathaniel is referring to the period after they had left Leamington in November 1857 and before they crossed to France in January 1858, when the weather in London was very poor and when he became increasingly bored and frustrated.
52. Isaac D'Israeli (1766–1848), the father of Benjamin Disraeli, wrote several volumes of literary history, including *The Literary Character, Calamities of Authors* and, in 1814, *Quarrels of Authors*.
53. CE: vol. 18, 204.
54. The location of this letter, if it is extant, is unknown to me.
55. It would be interesting to know what "shopping" meant to Nathaniel. Certainly not food and household necessities.
56. CE: vol. 14, 703.

Chapter 10. "We have real winter weather in Leamington": December 1859

1. CE: vol. 18, 206–7.
2. The location of this letter, if it is extant, is unknown to me.
3. CE: vol. 14, 703–4.
4. Robert's illness has escaped my identification.
5. The Hoppins had not been mentioned in any of Nathaniel's letters or journals when they were all staying at No. 6 Golden Square, London, during the previous July, before leaving for the north of England and, ultimately, Redcar.
A Miss Caroline Plummer of Salem had died in 1854 and left a large sum to be appropriated "for the purchasing a piece of land in some central and convenient spot in the city of Salem, and erecting thereon a safe and elegant building, of brick or stone, to be employed for the purpose of depositing the books belonging to the said Corporation, with liberty also to have the rooms thereof used for meetings of any literary or scientific institution, or for the deposit of any works of art or natural productions." The Reverend James Mason Hoppin's Address, entitled *Hints to the Reform of Literature* (which he later had printed), given at the Dedication of the Plummer Hall on 6 October 1857, included references to the benefits of libraries in general and hoped that ". . . *this* library may not be without some instance of quickening power upon the youth of this city. A Niebuhr, or a Bowditch, or a Webster, or a Kane, or another Hawthorne, without the thorn, may be started from this quiet room on their diverse but glowing tracks." Evidently he was not too comfortable with Nathaniel's romantic but barbed literary characteristics.
In a letter from Bath to her cousin Richard (PE: Hawthorne-Manning Collection: MSS.69) written sometime in March/April/May 1860, Una wrote, ". . . Do you know where Mr. Hoppin is now? One day when we were in Leamington, Julian came home & assured us that he had seen him in the street, but Mr. Hoppin did not look at him, so he had not addressed him. I think he must have been mistaken, as we never saw

their names in the list of visitors,—but I know they did once think of going to Leamington. I wonder if Mr. Hoppin's allusion to Papa could mean that he hoped hereafter he would not be so satirical on Salem & its inhabitants as he has sometimes been in his writings? That seems the only solution of the mystery, but at all events it is a very clumsy affair in my opinion, and I suppose the poor man thought it a most delicate & felicitous reproof."

    6. PE: Hawthorne-Manning Collection: MSS.69.

    7. The location of this letter, if it is extant, is unknown to me.

    8. CE: vol. 14, 704.

    9. Ibid, vol. 14, xiv-cxxxiii, contains an immensely detailed commentary on all aspects of the production and printing of the English and American editions of the romance, including the evidence regarding Nathaniel's proficiency as a proofreader.

    10. Apparently, for the time being, the title on the proof sheets continued to be *The Romance of Monte Beni.*

    11. CE: vol. 18, 208.

    12. Ibid, vol. 14, 704.

    13. "A Lecture was announced to be delivered on Wednesday evening, at the Public Hall, by the Rev. J. H. Blake, of Sandhurst, the subject being 'Bunyan's Pilgrim's Progress,'" RLSC, 10 December 1859. There was no report on the contents of the lecture in the following week's edition.

    14. The location of this letter, if it is extant, is unknown to me. It appears that Smith, Elder had, once again, expressed their reservations about the title for the romance.

    15. The location of these letters, if they are extant, is unknown to me.

    16. CE: vol. 14, 704–5.

    17. The location of this letter, if it is extant, is unknown to me.

    18. Ibid.

    19. Ibid. As subsequent events were to prove it appears that the letter contained, at least, the information that Bennoch was coming to visit them in a few days time.

    20. CE: vol. 14, 705–6.

    21. MHS: extracts from a letter dated 10 November 1859.

    22. PE: Hawthorne-Manning Collection: MSS.69.

    23. CE: vol. 14, 706.

    24. THE WEATHER.—An idea of the intensity of the weather at the commencement of the week may be obtained from the fact that the frost burst pipes at Messrs. OLD-HAM'S WATERWORKS, which had stood the winters of forty previous years. We have met with no resident, 'however old,' who recollects ever before experiencing such severe weather in this country. The injury done to private individuals, by bursting of pipes, &c., is incalculable. The operations in our own office had to be suspended until the caloric of the fire had re-converted the frozen ink into a liquid! The lake in the Jephson Gardens was crowded with skaters and sliders, both ladies and gentlemen, on Saturday and the succeeding days, so long as the past-time could be pursued with safety. The rivers Leam and Avon, and also the canal, were much frequented for a like purpose. RLSC, 24 December 1859.

    25. CE: vol. 14, 706. Did Nathaniel and Julian come across the aftermath of the accident under the railway bridge, on their way up Clemens Street to Whitnash, or had the mess been cleaned up by then?

    BATH STREET RAILWAY BRIDGES AGAIN.—These bridges are rapidly proving that the fears entertained with respect to them are well founded. It is but too often that we are called upon to record accidents of which they are the exciting cause. We know not how the evil is to be remedied, but an evil it undoubtedly is, of great magnitude. Horses passing under them are alarmed by the rumbling noise of the trains overhead . . . a far more serious affair occurred on Saturday last. A woman of the name of HORTON, the wife of a huckster, of Moreton Morrell, was minding a small pony-cart. The pony, alarmed by the usual cause, took fright. The poor woman went to the horse's head; but, unhappily, was knocked down by one of the shafts. As some unfounded reports have obtained currency as to the extent of the injuries, we may observe that the following account may be relied upon, and taken as a corrective for any erroneous impression. It has been said that the wheel of the cart, containing a good many hundredweight, passed over the woman's head. As she is now in a fair way of recovery, that must be regarded as purely fiction . . . Mr. MARRIOTT, surgeon of this town, was immediately summoned . . . and found that she had received a severe contused lacerated wound over the left temple. For the first hour or so her life was in great danger . . . but by the skill of Mr. MARRIOTT . . . she is now progressing to complete recovery. RLSC, 24 December 1859.

26. Presumably containing an apology for his not having been able to visit them after all and possibly advising them that he would see them sometime after Christmas.

27. The location of these letters, if they are extant, is unknown to me.

28. A homeopathic physician, residing at No. 10 Euston Place, at the lower end of the Parade.

29. CE: vol. 14, 706.

30. Presumably a reference to the unrecovered letter mentioned in his diary entry, 12 December.

31. CE: vol. 18, 211–12.

32. Ibid, 209.

33. Ibid, vol. 14, 706–7.

34. NHW.

35. Ibid.

36. DB.

37. Rose Hawthorne Lathrop, *Memories of Hawthorne* (Cambridge: Riverside Press, 1897).

38. From the description of some of these presents it sounds as though there had been some secret Christmas shopping done, possibly at Redfern's Curiosity Shop in Warwick during Sophia's trip there on 24 November when she had been accompanied by Fanny. The descriptions also underline the perception of Rose's comments (in the preceding section) on the extravagance and luxury that her parents seemed unable or unwilling to forgo on occasions.

39. BERG: incomplete, undated, but judging from the rest of the contents it must have been written sometime soon after Twelfth Night, 1860. The letter continues (in part), ". . . and I was heavily depressed with the idea of dear Mary alone on this anniversary of sacred joy."

40. Those were the days, when you got mail on Christmas Day! The location of this letter, if it is extant, is unknown to me, but it must have contained a greeting for Christmas and a hope that they had received the gift of oysters.

41. Unrecovered.

42. The location of the letter from E. P. Peabody, if it is extant, is unknown to me.

43. CE: vol. 14, 707.

44. MHS: extracts from a letter dated 27–28 November 1859.

45. CE: vol. 14, 707.

46. CE: vol. 18, 213–14.

47. The location of this letter, if it is extant, is unknown to me.
48. CE: vol. 14, 707–8.

Chapter 11. "Dr. Sutherland says Leamington is a bad locality for me": January-February 1860

1. CE: vol. 18, 215.
2. It has to be presumed that in those days before the invention of domestic, mechanical means of writing a letter that it was naturally easier and more of a matter of course to be able to decipher a letter that had been written on, possibly, poor-quality paper with an inefficient pen. Despite the existence of innumerable documents and letters written in exquisitely clear copper plate writing, one wonders whether the handwriting of correspondents such as Emelyn Story or Bennoch (particularly Bennoch) gave as much trouble to the recipient as it does now.
3. The location of this letter, if it is extant, is unknown to me.
4. Ibid.
5. BERG.
6. MHS: extracts from a letter dated 10 January 1860.
7. If Una had gone to the dentist on the same day as Sophia, the previous 10 November, Nathaniel had made no mention of it in his diary entry for that day.
8. The location of this letter, if it is extant, is unknown to me.
9. A piece of news that must have been contained in the unrecovered letter from Horace.
10. It would appear that Mary had written a separate letter to Una (that is unrecovered) and also enclosed with hers the one from Horace.
11. BERG.
12. The location of this letter, if it is extant, is unknown to me.
13. Presumably in answer to Nathaniel's letter of 8 January, but its location, if it is extant, is unknown to me.
14. CE: vol. 18, 216–17.
15. Ibid, 218–19.
16. Ibid, 220.
17. This is rather pathetic, as he had already acknowledged to Smith, Elder that it must have been his own suggestion.
18. Edwin P. Whipple had been given the same opportunity in the case of Nathaniel's *The House of the Seven Gables* and *Blithedale Romance* and had subsequently written very favorable reviews of the books.
19. David Roberts, a lawyer and former mayor of Salem, was an old friend of Nathaniel's.
20. James Russell Lowell (1819–91), an author, teacher, man of letters, and at this time the editor of the *Atlantic Monthly*.
21. CE: vol. 18, 222–23.
22. Mary Anne Evans (1819–80) had already published, under the name of George Eliot, *Scenes of Clerical Life* (1857) and *Adam Bede* (1859), and *The Mill on the Floss* was to appear in 1860. The daughter of an estate manager, Robert Evans, her early intellectual precocity had been noticed and fostered by the ribbon manufacturer Charles Bray and his wife, Cara. Partly owing to their influence, she abandoned her father's Evangelical beliefs but retained a view that "religious belief [was] an imaginative necessity for man," though she did not attend any church. In 1854 she met G. H. Lewes and they lived together until his death in 1878; they did not marry, as he already had a wife.

23. PM: MA.591. In her letter to her cousin Richard from Bath (see chapter 10, footnote 5) Una told him ". . . One day Papa and I spent at Coventry, where a friend of ours took us to one of the great ribbon manufactories for which the place is celebrated, & we went over the beautiful church of St. Michael, & the old Council Hall, & saw the effigy of Peeping Tom looking out of the third story window of a house. The town is very dirty, but here and there you come upon some old 'bit' that makes it worth visiting. I believe there is to be a statue of Lady Godiva on horseback put up in the market place."

24. CE: vol. 18, 224.

25. The location of this letter, if it is extant, is unknown to me.

26. CE: vol. 18, 226–27.

27. The location of this letter, if it is extant, is unknown to me.

28. A number of instances can be found in Nathaniel's journals and letters, written while he was in England, in which he denigrates the British people and character for these very reasons, that they were beer-sodden, beef-bloated, and generally thick (both in girth and wit). Now he finds it a virtue that Trollope's writings are founded on these characteristics.

29. Nathaniel had sat fourteen times for Miss Lander in Rome during April-May 1858. On 17 May 1858 he noted in his diary, "Forenoon, drew £50 at the Bank, & deposited 100 scudi to pay for bust as the work progresses." (CE: vol. 14, 596). Whether the balance was paid (and what it amounted to) cannot be ascertained. However, in DB, Walter T. Herbert has a great deal to say about the Lander episode, suggesting that Nathaniel may have had sexual relations with the artist (as part of a midlife crisis), that the bust in its final form (of Nathaniel's head and shoulders, the latter being bare) offended by its suggestive appearance, and that it and Miss Lander's reputation of being somewhat lax in her moral behavior resulted in both Nathaniel and Sophia subsequently refusing to meet or speak with her (Nathaniel, it is suggested, due to guilt and Sophia due to jealousy).

30. CE: vol. 18, 229–31.

31. PM: MA.577–91.

32. The location of this letter, if it is extant, is unknown to me.

33. CE: vol. 18, 234.

34. Ibid, 232.

35. It is probable that the "diseased housemaid" went to the Warneford Hospital (since demolished), a few hundred yards from Bath Street. There are no individual patients records for 1860 available now, but perhaps she was one of the twenty patients treated at the hospital during 1860 for "diseases of the skin" by use of the baths (AGM Report 6 March 1860). There had also been an outbreak of smallpox in the area during late 1859-early 1860.

36. In the letter to her cousin Richard from Bath (see footnote 23), Una told him:

> . . . On looking in my diary I find that I have not written to you this year so I suppose you have not heard of Mamma's illness. In the beginning of January she had a severe attack of acute bronchitis, and for two months was very ill, even dangerously so for some of the time and it was only towards the end of March that we were able to leave Leamington. The winter there was very damp & disagreeable, though we had not much severe cold, & we were in a low situation to which we attributed Mamma's illness. . . . Mamma's illness prevented us from making any pleasant excursions of which there are so many around Leamington, & we scarcely went anywhere during the whole time. . . . Once or twice I walked to Warwick, that dear old town that is so inexhaustibly interesting, but I believe I told you about that in my last letter. I was not very well most of the time [we?] were in Leamington, or I should have taken some long walks. But unfortunately, since I was ill in Rome I have not been able to walk much, which is a great deprivation.

37. Her brother, not her husband.
38. The location of this letter, if it is extant, is not known to me.
39. The location of this letter/"book," if it is extant, is unknown to me.
40. BERG.
41. This copy may have been that sent to S. C. Hall, intended as a personal gift but that was taken to be a review copy. Or, it could have been the copy that was eventually sent to Richard Monckton Milnes.
42. CE: vol. 18, 235. In NHW, Julian wrote that

> On one of his trips to London, to arrange the details of the publication of his book, he [Nathaniel] called again on Leigh Hunt, accompanied by his wife and Una . . . and, Mrs. Hawthorne having accidentally left her cloak behind her, Hunt sent it back the next day, with this little note:—"Dear Mr. and Mrs. Hawthorne (for the "Scarlet Letter" and "The Indicator" will warrant me, I trust, in thus addressing you, to say nothing of gratitude for your visit),—Had there been any reason in time, weather, or any other contingency, for allowing me to expect the return of any one of you for the accompanying cloak, I would have kept it accordingly in that "look-out;" but as this is out of the question, I send it to you by parcels' delivery, trusting that it will at all events be in time before your departure. I guess it belongs to the young lady, the look of whose face upon the old man (with the others') I shall not easily forget. Your obliged visitor, Leigh Hunt.

Apart from the confusion as to whose cloak it was, the visit and the mishap cannot be connected with Leamington (which would appear to be the case according to Julian's memory) as Nathaniel published only one book while in England, and that occurred while he was in Leamington; but he made only one visit to his publishers and on this occasion was unaccompanied by any member of the family. The visit to Leigh Hunt must have been the one that Nathaniel, Sophia, and Una made on 4 October 1855 just prior to Sophia's departure for Lisbon. Nathaniel did not record the incident of the cloak but did recall Leigh Hunt kissing Una's hand on their departure, which would account for the look on her face (EN).
43. Elizabeth must either have had a very good memory or an efficient filing system. The missing charts would have to have been sent to Miss Browne sometime back in September-October 1857. The charts were to be used in connection with Elizabeth's version of Bem's system of chronology that the children studied as part of their lessons.
44. BERG. The major part of these two pages has already been quoted (in chapter 7) as it is the description of the distribution of the family's Christmas presents. These two pages are filed separately in the library's catalog though the sense and the physical layout of them appear to be a natural continuation of the letter that Sophia commenced writing on 27 February. Possibly a modern interpretation of "the turning tide" might take this passage about Una as a coded reference to the onset of menstruation (she *was* fifteen at the time)—rather in the manner of Queen Victoria's reference to her daughter's experience: "Early this year [in 1855, when the Princess Victoria was fifteen] she went through a critical time and did not suffer even the slightest indisposition." (Hannah Pakula, *An Uncommon Woman.* New York: Simon and Schuster, 1995)—but, there again, it may be Sophia's way of saying that her daughter's religious feelings had brought her a new maturity and peace. The pages do not end with any farewell or signature, nor do they give the impression that Sophia has finished the letter. It must, therefore, be considered as incomplete.
45. The location of this letter, if it is extant, is unknown to me.
46. Ibid.
47. Ibid.
48. Which suggests that there is an unrecovered letter of Una's to Aunt Mary of

around this date as there is no mention of the number of servants in the letter that she wrote, on Sophia's behalf, on 25 January.

49. The as yet unposted letter of 27 February.

50. Mr. J. Hordern, 13 Euston Place, possibly recommended to Sophia by Dr. Sutherland as they both had rooms (or lived) in Euston Place. The 1861 Census details the Horderns as living at 13 Euston Place—sons, John (12) and Edward (1), daughters, Margaret (10) and Agnes (8), together with a cook, housemaid, and nursemaid, but does not include the names of John (father) or a Mrs. Hordern! Confusingly, Slater's *Directory of Warwickshire* (1862) details John Hordern (dentist) as living (?) at 3 Spencer St., and Kelly's *Post Office Directory of Warwickshire* (1863) lists John Hordern, Esq., as being back at 13 Euston Place! Why does not Sophia mention Una's visit to the dentist as, *possibly,* they both went at the same time? Nathaniel ignored it as well. But then Sophia talks of "many days handling," whereas in Nathaniel's diary and Una's letter they refer to a single day's visit to the chair. Perhaps Sophia had had more than one appointment with Mr. Hordern.

51. BERG.

Chapter 12. "That weary old Leamington": March 1860

1. A novel by Hans Christian Andersen published in 1845.

2. It is considered to be a waste of space to include the sometimes excessively long quotations from the romance that were included in many of the reviews (especially those in the newspapers of the time) that are referred to here. It will be assumed (once again) that the reader of this book (if there is such a person) will be completely familiar by now with the plot and characters of *The Marble Faun/Transformation.*

3. Augustus Eugène Scribe (1791–1861), a French playwright and opera and comic-opera librettist. "For him, historic drama was a means of demystifying the past, of trivializing exalted figures and exalting banality, of having great Shades undress before a bourgeois tribunal." Fredrick Brown, *Zola: A Life,* (New York: Farrar, Strauss & Giroux, 1995).

4. *The Athenæum,* no. 1688, 3 March 1860.

5. Francis Bennoch, *Poems, Lyrics, Songs & Sonnets,* (London: Hardwicke and Bogue, 1877).

6. MS. Ulysses Sumner Milburn Collection of Hawthorniana, Canton, N.Y., St. Lawrence University.

7. In his letters of 11 and 23 February.

8. The location of Bennoch's letter, which had included Una's poem, if it is extant, is unknown to me. It does not appear to be completely clear from Nathaniel's remarks whether Bennoch had also expressed some misgivings about the ending of the romance.

9. Perhaps it is a little unfair to Dr. Sutherland's memory to point out that at first Sophia had been advised that she had done the right thing in coming to Leamington as it was "a very good place for a delicate person," but then she had been told that it would be better if she went back to America to regain her health (which was a pretty safe bet as they were going there anyway) and finally both Malvern and Richmond were pronounced to be more likely to be of benefit than Leamington.

10. CE: vol. 18, 236–37.

11. 4 July 1859.

12. CE: vol. 18, 238–39.

13. BERG, but no mention to Chorley of the intention to amend or add to the ending.

14. PM: MA.591.

15. Ibid, MA.3400.

16. Nathaniel had declined an invitation to meet Lord Dufferin (and his aunt Caroline Norton) on 8 November 1853, due to "circumstances." Mrs. Norton, a somewhat notorious lady whom Nathaniel described then as having "genius," was a popular author of poems and fiction, and a successful editor of literary annuals.

17. The meeting finally came about when Nathaniel dined with the noble lord and his aunt on the following 14 May.

18. CE: vol. 18, 241.

19. Nathaniel had previously issued Wilding with instructions regarding the passage home on 8 November 1858, 26 June 1859, (advising a delay in departure until 30 July), 30 June (canceling that and confirming a departure date of 13 August), and 6 July (canceling that last date).

20. CE: vol. 18, 243–44.

21. A letter of 9 March to Ticknor confirms that this letter to Smith, Elder was in answer to a recent one of theirs (which is unrecovered), in which it would appear that they confirmed that they were shortly to issue a second printing of the romance and asked Nathaniel whether he had any amendments or additions that needed to be made to the text. Nathaniel now says that "everybody" was complaining about the denouement. How did he become aware of this, closeted in "weary" Leamington? So far, he had read of Chorley's misgivings, been made aware of Bennoch's opinion, and might have known of any uneasiness on Sophia's part, but . . . "everybody"? No information is available as to what was Leamington Spa's opinion of the book. It seems likely that it was not on sale in the town for some time after publication. There was no review of it in the local newspapers in any of the columns devoted to "Literature, Art, Music, Drama"; however, the "new book" was added to the shelves of Beck's Circulating Library starting on 7 June. (RLSC).

22. It is characteristic of Nathaniel's personality that he read through the book looking for printing errors (a fairly natural thing to do in the circumstances) but could not be bothered to actually make a list of them.

23. CE: vol. 18, 242.

24. So far, an unattributable quotation.

25. NHW.

26. The location of these letters, if they are extant, is unknown to me.

27. It could be wondered whether either Ticknor or Fields would have encouraged Nathaniel to proceed with the idea of a postscript if the romance had been completed and published in America rather than while Nathaniel was in England, away from their influence. Probably they would have supported him in his opinion that the postscript was, in fact, "but a doubtful improvement of the book."

28. Which would have been of too early a date to have contained any reviews of the romance.

29. CE: vol. 18, 245–46.

30. This is a slightly mysterious comment. Presumably Harriet was Mrs. Harriet Beecher Stowe who was in Liverpool at the time with her family, at the end of a European tour. Bright must have met her then, but when did Nathaniel send her the "extract" from the romance? The Stowes sailed back to America on the *Europa* in June with the Hawthornes, so any little matters of plagiarism could have been sorted out on the voyage! "It was a beautiful voyage in every sense; and at that period a voyage was no little matter of six days, but a good fourteen days of sitting together on deck in pleasant summer weather, and having time enough and to spare. Hawthorne and his family also concluded to join the party. Mrs. Hawthorne, who was always the romancer in conversation, filled the evening hours by weaving magic

webs of her fancies, until we looked upon her as a second Scheherezade, and the day the head was to be cut off was the day we should come to shore. 'Oh,' said Hawthorne, 'I wish we might never get there.'" *Life and Letters of Harriet Beecher Stowe,* ed. Annie Fields, 1897.

31. NHW.

32. Which he did, in *The Examiner* on 31 March.

33. But no one was twisting his arm to alter it! And in a letter to Bennoch of 24 March he said of the new ending ". . . It explains most of the mysteries, but I really think it is but a doubtful improvement of the book. It was one of its essential excellencies that it left matters so enveloped in a fog." Quite so. So why *did* he do it?

34. This must have been the preface.

35. CE: vol. 18, 247–48.

36. RLSC, 10 March 1860.

37. Ibid.

38. This suggests that Sophia had replied to Chorley's letter of 6 March and had told him of Nathaniel's intention to add a postscript to the romance, although he may well have heard of such an intention through either Smith, Elder, or Bennoch. If Sophia did reply, the letter is unrecovered.

39. Presumably, this was Chorley's novel, *Roccabella: a Tale of a Woman's Life,* published in two volumes by James Blackwood, London, in 1859. Chorley had adopted the pseudonym of Paul Bell; according to the *Dictionary of National Biography* it was a "romance. . . ." and that all his works were "of great talent, but all are artificial, bearing the impress of literary aspiration rather than of literary vocation." Nathaniel acknowledged receipt of the book after the family had left Leamington.

40. Sancho Panza's wife in Cervantes's *Don Quixote;* the incident of the acorns is in part 2, beginning in chapter 1.

41. Compton Wynyates, "one of the most visually satisfying houses in England," situated eight miles west of Banbury and eleven miles southeast of Stratford-upon-Avon. There is no record of the Hawthornes having been to see it.

42. PM: MA.3400.

43. Nathaniel had told Bright, in his letter of 10 March, that a further "portion" of the manuscript was "now in the hands of Smith & Elder" and that he would collect it from them when he was next in London, and send it on to Bright. On 24 March he wrote to Smith, Elder, from Bath, and asked them to send the "portion" direct to Bright at his home address. Three days later he confirmed his actions to Bright ("If it does not come to hand, I will ask them about it when I go to London"). He wrote again to Bright on 4 April, from Bath, thanking him for his review of the romance (in *The Examiner*) but did not mention the missing "portion." Finally he wrote to Bright on 23 April from Bath (he had not been to London or contacted Smith, Elder in the meantime), saying "Here is this preface, which I somehow neglected to send with the former package of rubbish." Assuming that it was, in fact, the preface that had come to be known as the missing "portion" it is clear that it was not Smith, Elder's fault in not having sent it to Bright as Nathaniel had had it all the time. Bright had the manuscript bound in three volumes and eventually his daughter presented them to the British Museum (refer to letters in CE: vol. 18 and in the textual introduction to *The Marble Faun* in CE: vol. 4).

44. NHW.

45. The location of this letter, if it is extant, is unknown to me.

46. Presumably a reference to Mary's servants, Baucis and Philemon, being an aged couple in Jonathan Swift's poem of that name, which was based on a mythological tale in which Zeus thanked the aged pair for entertaining the gods by turning their cottage into a temple.

47. Nathaniel had written to Ticknor on 11 May 1855, "take a look at my place, and charge the expenses of the trip to me. First, read over the lease which I gave Mr. Bull . . . and then see whether he is complying with the terms of it, as respects the improvements to be made on the land in front of the house. It will be a great injury to me if he does not promptly fulfil the conditions as to setting out an orchard &c. . . ." and again, on 3 January 1856, "I am afraid Mr. Bull has been very unfaithful to the terms of the lease, as regards the improvement of the land and setting out fruit trees. . . . I wish I knew the truth, and yet I do not know how to ascertain it without quoting N. Peabody's testimony, and putting the matter directly to Mr. Bull—which would cause a quarrel between these two neighbours directly; for it is a very fiery-tempered bull, though outwardly of meek aspect," and again on 14 April 1858, "I intended that N. C. Peabody . . . should take the land at the beginning of the present month, after the expiration of Mr. Bull's lease, at the beginning of the present month . . . I enclose a note for Mr. Bull, which please to send." Nathaniel Peabody wrote to Ticknor on 21 September 1858, ". . . It was a great mistake, in my opinion, to have entrusted a man like Bull who has so many occupations beside that of personal ill health to attend to,—with the care of so large an estate for its improvement. It will be five years before it yields any thing of sufficient amount to pay for the outlay. Mr. Bull is an able agriculturist, but he has too much to do with his own affairs to give attention to Hawthorne's." Nathaniel wrote again to Ticknor on 4 March 1859, "My wife's brother is to leave the Wayside. . . . We have written to him, that, if he will engage some person to do the necessary work in the garden, we will arrange about the payment. . . . Tell him that I have asked you to pay whatever amount may be necessary for manure, labor, or other expenses. . . ." Bull's expenses confirm that he was still working at the Wayside long after the lease had expired, whatever his shortcomings (CE: vols. 17 and 18).

48. The faithful seraph who withstood Satan's urging of the saints to revolt, in Milton's *Paradise Lost*.

49. The location of this letter, if it extant, is unknown to me.

50. Sophia's letter of 29 February. Mary might *just* have received it in time.

51. Psalm 127, verse 2.

52. BERG. The letter would appear to be incomplete. It ends at the close of the eighth page, but does not give the impression that Sophia has finished; there is no signature.

53. The postscript was included in the second printing of *Transformation* that was issued soon after 16 March. Some corrections were made in this printing but the errors that Nathaniel had itemized in his letter of 7 March to Smith, Elder were not corrected. They were, however, in the third printing of the book, issued sometime between 14 and 21 April. According to Nathaniel's letter of 9 March, he was going to send the manuscript of the postscript to Ticknor for the American edition, "when written. . . ." Presumably he sent it on or immediately after 14 March; in a letter to Ticknor of 6 April he said that he had "transmitted [the postscript] several weeks ago." Whether he had sent Ticknor the original manuscript or a copy of it is not clear but in any event it appears subsequently to have been lost. It does not form part of the manuscript that came to be in Bright's possession or, thereafter, in the British Museum's archives. The forthcoming addition of the postscript to the American edition of *The Marble Faun* was not publicized by Ticknor and Fields and it appears that it was not included until at least the fourth edition in late March-early April or maybe not until a further reprinting in May-July (refer to the textual introduction to *The Marble Faun* in CE: vol. 4).

54. CE: vol. 18, 250.

55. PM: MA.591.

56. In NHW, Julian quoted this article from *The Review,* up until the paragraph ending ". . . on this side of the Atlantic." He then reproduced three sonnets by one William Bennett (entitled in the latter's book, *Poems by W. C. Bennett,* published by Routledge, 1862, "Written in Nathaniel Hawthorne's *Transformation*"). Nathaniel wrote to Bennett on 15 June, from Liverpool, the last letter he wrote before leaving for America, thanking him for "the beautiful sonnets with which you have honored me and my book." It seems possible that Bennett had forwarded a copy of the book (via Smith, Elder?), in which he had included the verses, while the Hawthornes were still in Leamington and Nathaniel, characteristically, had taken some two months to respond. This scenario seems the more likely as Julian (when including the poems in *his* book, in 1884) was quoting the verses as they were written in the book sent to his father (which was, presumably, still in his [Julian's] possession), unaware that when Bennett had published them in *his* book in 1862 he had revised them substantially, as there are thirty-three instances in which the verses in the latter publication differ from those in the former.

57. The water nymph who gained a soul through her love of, and marriage to, a human being in Fouqué's *Undine.*

58. Nathaniel to Bennoch on 24 March, from Bath, "Day before yesterday, we left that weary old Leamington" (CE: vol. 18, 251).

59. MHS.

Chapter 13. "This English trash"

1. CE: vol. 18, 271–72.

2. The evidence as to Fanny's whereabouts at this point is conflicting. Sophia's letters of 29 February, April 1860, and 27 May 1860 (BERG) suggest that Fanny was to go to America with the family. Mary Mann's letter of 10 July (BERG) and Raymona Hull, in NHEE, suggest that she did not go. On the other hand, Sophia's pocket diary entry of 16 May 1861 (BERG) stated that she had "packed Fanny's things" and Nathaniel's letter to Ticknor of 11 October 1861 (CE) advised him of "a certain trunk" that was ready for dispatch to England, to Wilding in Liverpool, that may have contained some of Fanny's belongings. There appears to be no corroboration of Fanny's travels, one way or the other, from the English side of the Atlantic.

Sophia's letter of April 1860 to Mary also contained a long diatribe on Ada's shortcomings as a governess, a sea change in opinion that can only be attributed to events that had taken place while they were all in Italy (see chapter 7).

Poor Ada's life ended in tragedy. After her marriage to Clay in 1859 she became Professor of Modern Languages at Antioch College, until 1861. Subsequently, a short period was spent in the Sanitary Commission, with Clay, and then she opened a girls' school in Cambridge, Massachusetts. Later, Clay became ill and, whether justifiably or not, both he and Ada feared for each other's sanity. Ada's conviction that Clay thought her mad led to her suicide by drowning, in 1874, at the age of thirty-nine. Clay lived until 1894.

3. Somehow or other, Nathaniel had had his English notebooks returned to him by Bright. As has been suggested, Bright did not return the journals to Nathaniel when he visited Leamington (and Rugby) on 21, 22, and 23 October 1859. Since then the journals *could* have been returned at any time, especially when the Hawthornes were in Liverpool for the few days prior to their leaving for America (indeed, this is the most likely time for them having been returned even though, in theory, Nathaniel had no reason at the time for wishing them to be returned to him); but no request for their return was made in writing. All that can be certain is that they *were*

returned and with a little less certainty it can be said that they must have been returned in time for Nathaniel to take them back with him to America (rather than asking for them at a later date).

4. Quoted in CE: vol. 18, 472 (MS, Henry E. Huntington Library, San Marino, California).

5. Nathaniel had been persuaded by Fields and Ticknor that several passages in the article called "Chiefly about War-Matters," published in July 1862, had required amending or deleting, particularly the familiar tone that Nathaniel used toward President Lincoln, whom he had interviewed, calling him Uncle Abe and using phrases that cast aspersions on his appearance. It was felt that the article, unless changed in parts, would not reflect too well on the American situation in the eyes of the magazine's mainly American readership. Nathaniel wrote a tongue-in-cheek letter to Fields after the article appeared in the July *Atlantic Monthly*. Fields retaliated by printing the letter in full at the head of the "Leamington Spa" article.

6. Nathaniel's error? A printer's error? A proofreading oversight? The correct number (10) duly appeared when the article appeared in book form.

7. At least Nathaniel is consistent; he never seems to have realized that Dr. Jephson was still alive.

8. This description of the English dowager did not feature in any of Nathaniel's journal entries while he was in Leamington. The basis for it was included in his journal on 24 September 1853 and on 26 September 1854. Quite why he decided to include it in the article for the *Atlantic Monthly* is a little difficult to understand as, while it displays his particular sense of humor, it is also somewhat uncharacteristically tasteless. He may well have decided that it would be attractive to the American taste and that it was unlikely that the magazine would be widely read in England. In any case, he would not have been unduly concerned about any ill feeling that the article may have brought upon him.

On the other hand, if Nathaniel had had a chance of reading Anthony Trollope's *North America,* vol. 1, published in 1862, he would have seen in chapter 14, devoted to Trollope's experiences in, and opinions of, the city of New York, a diatribe on the appearance and behavior of "a certain class" of American womanhood; "Their manners . . . are to me more odious than those of any other human beings that I ever met elsewhere." That might have reminded Nathaniel of Mrs. Francis Trollope's book (Anthony's mother), *Domestic Manners of the Americans* (1832), in which Americans in general received a real going-over. In which case, perhaps the Leamington "dowagers" passage was written as a kind of riposte!

Trollope, in turn, had a dig at Nathaniel with regard to the "beefiness" of English ladies of a certain age, in chapter 33 of his *Can You Forgive Her?* that he started to write in August 1863, publication commencing in monthly parts from January 1864. Thus he would have had ample opportunity of reading the Leamington article in both the *Atlantic Monthly* of October 1862 and *Our Old Home* (published in September 1863). In his novel, Trollope described Lady Monk, a society hostess: "Her figure was very good. She was tall and of fine proportion, though by no means verging to that state of body which our excellent American friend and critic Mr. Hawthorne has described as beefy and has declared to be the general condition of English ladies of Lady Monk's age. Lady Monk was not beefy." "Beefiness" had also featured in Nathaniel's *Scarlet Letter* (published in 1850, before he had had an opportunity of examining English ladies in person): in chapter 2 he described a group of "wives and maidens of old English birth . . . and the beef and ale of their native land . . . entered largely into their composition."

9. There are, in fact, over sixty churches and chapels within a ten-mile radius of the center of Leamington (Coventry being outside the area), all of which were

standing at the time of the Hawthornes' visits to the spa. Given such problems as illness in the family, the absence of Nathaniel on occasions, the inclement weather, and the expense involved in hiring transport, it is still somewhat surprising that the family, or at least Nathaniel and Sophia, did not inspect more of the local churches than the paltry few that they did (three of those that they *did* visit were in Coventry). Several of those that they did not visit had specific or unique architectural or historical interest and many of them had and still have great beauty and atmosphere (such as the closely circumscribed church of The Assumption of our Lady at Ashow on the banks of the Avon, and in contrast the church of St. Giles standing alone in the fields at Chesterton, to name but two).

10. CE: vol. 18, 494, 498.

11. BERG: letter to Annie Fields, 17 December 1862.

12. This was the original medieval bridge over the river, which brought traffic and pedestrians into the town from the Banbury road.

13. No doubt this is how Nathaniel preferred to think of the castle; it could be wondered if, for this reason, he deliberately refrained from inspecting its interior, for there is no record in his diaries or journals that he ever went inside the building.

14. In 1995, after much research, restoration, and renovation, the present Master's wife was able to present to the public the hospital's gardens in much the same format as had existed at the time of the Hawthornes' visit. During the renovations, a pineapple frame was discovered (based on a Roman heating system [hypocaust] that gave underfloor heating), as well as the foundations of the "beautiful little thatched summer-house" that Ada wrote of in her letter to Clay, on 1 November 1857. For the first time since early in this century, the gardens are now open to the public, six days each week, from Easter to September.

15. John Mottley compiled a book of facetiae in 1739, which (without authorization) he entitled "Joe Miller's Jest-book," from Joe Miller (1684–1738), a popular comedian of the day, who could neither read nor write. A "Joe Miller" is a stale joke, implying that it is stolen from Mottley's compilation. (Brewer's *Dictionary of Phrase and Fable*).

16. *Slender:*   O Heaven! this is Mistress Anne Page.

    Page: How now, Mistress Ford!

    Falstaff: Mistress Ford, by my troth, you are very
                  well met: by your leave, good Mistress. (*kissing her*)

    Page: Wife, bid these gentlemen welcome.
                  Come, we have a hot venison pastry to dinner:
                  come gentlemen, I hope we shall drink down all
                  unkindness.
                  (*Exeunt all but Shallow, Slender and Evans*)

    Slender: I had rather than forty shillings I had
                  my Book of Songs and Sonnets here.
                  (*Enter Simple*)
                  How now, Simple! Where have you been?
                              Merrie Wives of Windsor, act 1, scene 1

17. Nathaniel couldn't have read his original journal entry accurately at this point (or checked with Sophia) as he had said in it, quite correctly, that they had proceeded from the hospital *along* High Street toward the East Gate, and would have walked on into Jury Street, where Mr. Redfern's shop was situated.

18. The "Gifted Woman" was Delia Bacon, whose theories as to the true authorship of Shakespeare's plays were published in 1857, *The Philosophy of the Plays of*

Shakspere Unfolded, largely as a result of Nathaniel's financial assistance. Much of this very long article is devoted to his reminiscences of his actions on behalf of Delia, but being strictly irrelevant here, they have been omitted.

19. A poem published in 1842 that Tennyson composed as "an experiment meant to test the degree in which it was in [my] power as a poet to humanise external nature."

20. Eleemosynary—a rather splendid word, used by Nathaniel on more than one occasion in his writings, although according to EN he misspelled it in his original journal entry covering the Stratford visit of 27 June 1855. "Eleemosynary: . . . . 2.dependent on or supported by alms . . . . 1860. Hawthorne *Marb Faun* (1879) I.vi.62 Threw forth . . . . food, for the flock of eleemosynary doves." *Oxford English Dictionary.*

21. In Nicholas Rowe's *Some Account of the Life, etc., of Mr. William Shakespeare,* ed. Rowe, 1709, the story is told of a friendly conversation between Shakespeare and John Combe in which Shakespeare was asked to compose an epitaph for Combe and that it be done immediately as it may well be that Shakespeare could die before Combe. Shakespeare is said to have taken little time to provide the following verse which, apparently, did not best please Combe!

> Ten in the Hundred lies here engrav'd,
> 'Tis a Hundred to ten, his soul is not fav'd.
> If any Man ask, who lies in this Tomb?
> Oh! ho! quoth the Devil, 'tis my John-a-Combe!

22. CE: vol. 18, 560, 567–68.
23. Ibid, 589–92.
24. Henry E. Huntington Library, San Marino, Calif.
25. CE: vol. 18, 586–87.
26. Ibid, 598.

Epilogue. The End of the Affair: 1863–64

1. 24 September 1863.
2. 26 September 1863.
3. 28 September 1863.
4. 30 September 1863.
5. 2 October 1863.
6. 3 October 1863.
7. 10 October 1863.
8. 15 October 1863.
9. October 1863.
10. 21 November 1863.
11. 28 November 1863.
12. 26 September 1863.
13. 3 October 1863.
14. 3 October 1863.
15. 3 October 1863.
16. 1 October 1863.
17. 10 October 1863.
18. 10 October 1863.
19. 17 October 1863.
20. 17 October 1863.

21. November 1863.
22. CE: vol. 18, 610.
23. 9 November 1863.
24. January 1864.
25. January 1864.
26. January–April 1864.
27. DB.

Index